# The Travel Industry

Equator

N

# The Travel Industry

**THIRD EDITION**

Chuck Y. Gee

James C. Makens

Dexter J.L. Choy

VAN NOSTRAND REINHOLD
I(T)P® A Division of International Thomson Publishing Inc.

New York • Albany • Bonn • Boston • Detroit • London • Madrid • Melbourne •
Mexico City • Paris • San Francisco • Singapore • Tokyo • Toronto

Copyright © 1997 by Van Nostrand Reinhold

I(T)P® A division of International Thomson Publishing Inc.
The ITP logo is a registered trademark used herein under license

Printed in the United States of America

For more information, contact:

Van Nostrand Reinhold
115 Fifth Avenue
New York, NY 10003

International Thomson Publishing GmbH
Königswinterer Strasse 418
53227 Bonn
Germany

International Thomson Publishing Europe
Berkshire House 168-173
High Holborn
London WCIV 7AA
England

International Thomson Publishing Asia
221 Henderson Road #05-10
Henderson Building
Singapore 0315

Thomas Nelson Australia
102 Dodds Street
South Melbourne, 3205
Victoria, Australia

International Thomson Publishing Japan
Hirakawacho Kyowa Building, 3F
2-2-1 Hirakawacho
Chiyoda-ku, 102 Tokyo
Japan

Nelson Canada
1120 Birchmount Road
Scarborough, Ontario
Canada M1K 5G4

International Thomson Editores
Seneca 53
Col. Polanco
11560 Mexico D.F. Mexico

2  3  4  5  6  7  8  9  10  QEB-FF  01  00  99  98  97

Library of Congress Cataloging-in-Publication Data

Gee, Chuck Y.
    The travel industry / Chuck Y. Gee, James C. Makens, Dexter J.L. Cho.—3rd ed.
        p.   cm.
    Includes bibliographic references and index.
    ISBN 0-442-02297-2
    1. Tourist trade.   I. Makens, James C.   II. Choy, Dexter J.L.   III. Title.
G155.A1G35   1996
380.1'4591—dc20                                                    96-16166
                                                                   CIP

**http://www.vnr.com**

product discounts     free email newsletters     software demos     online resources

**email: info@vnr.com**

A service of I(T)P®

# Contents

# PART 3: *T*OURISM DEVELOPMENT

# PART 4: *S*ELLING TRAVEL

# PART 5: *T*RANSPORTATION SERVICES

# PART 6: *H*OSPITALITY AND RELATED SERVICES

# Foreword

On the threshold of the third millennium, the travel and tourism industry represents one of the best opportunities for the economic and cultural development of the peoples of our planet.

Indeed, no other industry has, on a global level, a similar capacity to generate employment, income, and wealth, and no other sector—save possibly that of information—can contribute in a similar way to the strengthening of cultural diversity and the cause of peace. Two hundred million jobs and almost six hundred million international tourists pay eloquent testimony to the importance of this industry, which is growing at a rate at least double that of the world economy as a whole.

But the *future is not what it appears to be* and the development of the industry will differ greatly from that of the past decades. The *Fordian age* of tourism (i.e., the age of non-differentiated products and massive consumption) has been lagging behind, and with it the rapid growth of demand that made it possible to supply almost any type of tourism product, ignoring considerations of quality or environmental and cultural impacts. In actual fact, some tourist resorts may have been the victims of their own success during that stage, having on occasions devoured their natural and cultural resources under the influence of a tourist influx that was too concentrated in time and space and travelers who were ill-prepared for *understanding* their surroundings.

The tourism industry finds itself at this moment in the midst of a paradigm shift. The old rules become more irrelevant by the day: from mass demand we have gone on to supersegmentation; from the rigidity of products and services to the need to adapt to heterogeneous and rapidly-changing demand; from profitability based on mass production to system economies and integrated values.

The new tourism management paradigm, which I have been calling the *New Age of Tourism* (NAT), has different rules: it is no longer a question of producing more at lower prices; global competition and supersegmentation demand new management strategies.

Among these strategies, it is interesting to underscore here the vital role of information and know-how in the NAT. Information understood as data useful for management decision-making in real time, and know-how in a broad sense that should encompass both the traditional technological area of R&D and the *humanology* of education, training, and conceptual innovations.

In this context, the book *The Travel Industry* has special relevance. Its authors, Professors Chuck Y. Gee, Dexter J.L. Choy, and James C. Makens are well known for their significant contributions to tourism research and education. Chuck Gee has a very wide experience in teaching tourism in his capacity as Dean of the School of Travel Industry Management at the University of Hawaii for the last 30 years and a well-established reputation as researcher and advisor, through his intensive activity as author of books and professional associations and his many years of professional attachment to the World Tourism Organization, governments throughout the world, and many other public institutions. Dexter Choy is a Professor at the School of Travel Industry Management, a well-known author of scholarly publications, with research ranging from airline pricing to tourism forecasting and planning in developing countries; he has lectured extensively in executive in executive seminars for many international audiences. James Makens has a twenty-five-year experience in the travel industry, working as a consultant to airlines, hotels, restaurant chains, tourism ministries, and heritage restorations; he has many publications on hospitality, travel agency management, and tourism marketing and is currently a faculty member in the Babcock Graduate School of Management at Wake Forest University. Professors Gee, Choy, and Makens, who with their first edition of 1984 and second edition of 1989 already achieved a benchmark, are now managing this, their third edition, to come closer still to the point of educating by asking the relevant questions and providing the appropriate information so that the reader may answer those questions for himself, and create an appropriate conceptual structure in the process.

*The Travel Industry* begins by offering a very necessary global vision of the sector in the NAT and clarifying basic concepts for understanding the structure and interrelations of the tourism industry. Farther on, the book penetrates into an area that I consider absolutely essential despite its absence in other works, i.e., the role of government and the non-private aspects of tourism. At a time when highly-developed countries appear to be questioning the expediency of public policies in the tourism area, it is vital to examine the evidence for and against tourism policy, regardless of general considerations about the size of government. What is really important is to define the contents of that tourism policy and then to consider who can implement it most efficiently.

Finally, *The Travel Industry* studies the most important tourism subsectors, and it does so with highly-topical information, projecting a live image of the current situation and of foreseeable developments in hospitality, transport of travelers, and the distribution of tourism products.

*The Travel Industry* is equally useful for the student and for professionals who work and think within the sector and who need a panoramic view of it, rich in information and thought-provoking know-how. A symbiosis of knowledge of the tourism industry and scientific treatment of it is seldom seen; *The Travel Industry* achieves this. If, as is often stated, the aim of education is to prepare us for constantly asking questions, there is no doubt that the work of Gee, Choy, and Makens is an excellent tool for tourism education, a tool that, in passing, also provides us with intelligent replies to many of those questions.

Dr. Eduardo Fayos-Solá
*Director, Education and Training*
*World Tourism Organization*
*Madrid*

# Preface

The travel industry has been hailed as one of the great growth enterprises of the 21st Century. According to futurist John Naisbitt, three industries will lead the global information-driven economy of the next century—telecommunications, information technology, travel and tourism. Recognizing the travel industry's enormous untapped economic potential, the first ever White House Conference on Travel and Tourism, attended by one of the coauthors, was convened in October, 1995, to bring together all sectors of the industry, including airlines, lodging, restaurants, attractions, tour operators, travel distribution, retailers, travel and entertainment card companies, tourism educators and hundreds of other players along with local and state government officials, congressional leaders, members of the cabinet, the Vice President and the President of the United States to develop a public policy position for this fragmented and perhaps least understood engine of the American economy.

Even within the walls of academe, travel and tourism as a field of study is not always well understood, for it is a field cutting across many disciplines. European universities tend to study tourism as a macro analysis of a developing industry, including applied tourism research and tourism policy analysis. American universities, on the other hand, are inclined to concentrate on micro analysis and the needs of organizations supplying visitor services. From a macro perspective, tourism may be considered from such aspects as environmental impact and the use of natural resources, culture and the arts, changing lifestyles and social values psychological motivations, political decisions or economic variables. From a micro perspective in the "industry" sense, travel and tourism can be narrowed to specific subjects as transportation management and logistics, hotel and restaurant management, travel and tour operation, destination planning and development, convention and business meetings, or recreation and leisure activities. In either approach is the overlay of functional business subjects in marketing, management, human resource development, finance and investments, law and regulations, technology and other areas applied to the tourism field.

In short, the phenomenon of travel and tourism can be studied from different angles, depending on the educational or training objectives to be achieved. In the first edition of this book, our objectives were to introduce concepts about travel as an interlinked industry composed of many sectors and to acquaint students to different industry practices within both public and private sectors. Our intention was for students to acquire a comprehensive understanding of a very large and complex industry from both a macro and micro perspective, including research, development and trends, marketing and management aspects. These objectives still hold true for this third edition as it did for the second edition, which was prompted by changes brought by deregulation, new technological developments, increased worldwide competition, shifting travel patterns, social and economic instabilities and international politics. In our third edition, we continue to focus on the dynamism of the national and the global travel industry, and to chronicle the changes that have occurred since 1989. Since then, many more nations have opened to the world of tourism as political systems restructured with the end of the cold war. Airlines are moving towards greater efficiencies and consolidation after a decade and a half of deregulation, offering a staggering array of fares that change from hour to hour with the aid of yield management systems. Travel agencies fret for their very existence with the capping of commissions and the introduction of ticketless travel, forcing this sector to consider a different role and to pursue different relationships within the travel distribution system. The accommodations sector, like others, has moved towards greater market segmentation to offer a dazzling choice of lodging niches to fit every pocketbook level. And technology is changing the face of everything from the way industry operates to the way people access travel information or book reservations. Through all of these changes, the industry has continued to grow and to retain its position as the world's largest economic activity, estimated at $3.4 trillion in terms of output in 1995.

*The Travel Industry* is designed as a introductory textbook for students interested in travel distribution, tourism development, hospitality management and other leisure business-related fields. Each chapter in the text covers a distinct topic that serves as one of the building blocks in the architecture of the industry.

In each chapter, we provide a list of learning objectives and key terms at the beginning, and a short summary and discussion questions at the end. Additionally, we have now included suggested exercises that students may do individually or collectively to further their understanding of the topic. In some instances, these exercises may be a short case study or a practical exercise to assess tourism practices in the community.

Throughout the text, students will be exposed to ideas that may suggest possible career options within the worldwide travel and tourism industry. The industry, as students will discover as they delve into the subject, is an exciting world offering unlimited opportunities—but it is also one that will demand greater knowledge, total commitment and the highest degree of professionalism from those who would seek to enter its portals in tomorrow's incredibly competitive environment.

# Acknowledgments

The third edition of *The Travel Industry* contains even more extensive revisions than did the second edition. While many of these revisions simply reflect the fact that much more information is available than ever before about the dynamic travel industry, other revisions were born from the excellent suggestions of the various reviewers of the initial draft chapters and the executives at Van Nostrand Reinhold who supported us in the editorial and production processes of this third edition.

In particular, we would like to thank Mimi Melek, acquisitions editor for hospitality and tourism; Maxine Effenson Chuck, editorial specialist at B. Czar Productions; and Joan Petrokofsky, project development editor, for their continuous flow of helpful suggestions and diligent oversight to assure the progress of the work.

We also want to give special thanks to the following individuals: first and foremost, to Winifred Miura, secretary to the Dean of the University of Hawaii School of Travel Industry Management, for her countless hours of entering changes and help with research verification, much of which was done as contributed time; to Lucille Choy for her many hours of technical assistance; and to Susan Paulachak and Tami Hashimoto for their help in word processing.

Finally, the authors owe thanks to the individuals and organizations that have allowed us to reproduce their materials or contributed original materials and photographs used as illustrations. They have been individually credited in the appropriate chapters of the text.

# Overview of the Travel Industry

Part 1 introduces the concept of travel as an industry network and provides an overview of its historic and current development. It begins with definitions of travel and tourism, and identifies the types of businesses included in the travel industry. These basic definitions are important for understanding the scope of the travel industry, as well as for measuring the volume and flow of travel.

The importance of the travel industry to world economics has raised many questions about the shifting role of services versus production-based industries within the economy. Factors influencing growth in both domestic and international travel are discussed, as are the motivations for travel. The need for the application of marketing research, which is a critical element underlying tourism development and promotion, is emphasized.

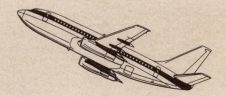

# Chapter 1

# The Travel Industry Network

## LEARNING OBJECTIVES

- To appreciate the scope and types of businesses within the travel industry.
- To understand the linking concept and components of the industry.
- To understand the evolution and use of the term "tourist."
- To understand internationally-accepted definitions of tourism and classification of travelers.
- To be able to define and use the following terms:

| | |
|---|---|
| Development organization | Outbound tourism |
| Direct provider | Support services |
| Domestic tourism | Tourism |
| Excursionist | Tourist |
| Inbound tourism | Travel industry |
| Linking concept | Visitor |

## THE TRAVEL INDUSTRY—DOES IT REALLY EXIST?

It is often debated whether there truly exists a **travel industry** in the sense of a distinct group of enterprises such as the steel, automobile, or electronics industries. Part of the problem is that the term *industry* itself is more commonly identified with manufacturing and production-based enterprises—a point of no small consideration to public policymakers in determining import/export quotas, tariffs, employment, national economic importance, and the like. The other part of the problem is that the travel industry is not one industry but, in reality, a collection of businesses—all selling travel-related services. The general public is likely to be more familiar with each component of the travel industry, that is, the airline industry, the hotel industry, the restaurant industry, or the entertainment business. The individual industries also do not necessarily act together as an integrated group and very often have conflicting views among themselves. In addition, there are businesses involved that serve both travelers and residents with respect to eating, shopping, recreation, and entertainment.

An early definition of the travel industry simply called it "that part of the national economy which caters to the traveler who is visiting places outside the locality where he/she resides or works." *(1)* Travel was not looked upon as an industry, but as a collection of businesses whose only common link was providing services to travelers.

The fact that there exists a travel industry is becoming increasingly less academic and more real as common denominators are identified and links among travel-related businesses are established through communications and practice.

## PRIVATE AND PUBLIC SECTORS

Although the early definition is not entirely obsolete, it tends to reflect the simpler conditions that preceded the modern tourism movement beginning in the 1950s and to focus on only the private sector of the economy. The travel industry today involves both the private and public (that is, the government) sectors of the economy in the development and production of products and services for travelers. In many countries, the production of travel services, in fact, is both regulated and operated by the government. Governments today also have invested heavily in developing the travel industry as a source of economic growth for their areas. In recent times, travel and tourism have been included in regional trade pact negotiations as well. Consequently, the role of government must be explicitly recognized in any definition of the industry. We will discuss the public sector role in tourism in Part 2.

## DEFINING THE TRAVEL INDUSTRY

For our purposes throughout this text, the travel industry will be defined as "the composite of organizations, both public and private, that are involved in the development, production, and marketing of products and services to serve the needs of travelers." Such a broad definition of the travel industry raises the question of which agencies, organizations, or businesses should be included in the industry, and how they should be categorized. It also points up the difficulty of dealing with more fluid, heterogeneous groups. Oftentimes we perceive things to be homogeneous at first glance when they are actually heterogeneous upon closer scrutiny. For example, the retail industry may be simplistically defined as businesses that sell directly to consumers. In reality, the types of businesses that comprise the retail industry will vary widely by types—clothing, food, drug, gasoline—and by volume, size, and customers. The only common link is that these businesses provide direct services to consumers.

# TYPES OF BUSINESSES IN THE TRAVEL INDUSTRY

Similar to the retail industry, there is variation among the diverse organizations and businesses that comprise the travel industry. Nevertheless, all are involved directly or indirectly in providing travel services to consumers. An examination of the U.S. Standard Industrial Classification System (SIC) reveals that more than 35 different major industrial components serve the traveler and, in some cases, the nontraveler (see Table 1.1).

| TABLE 1.1 Travel and Tourism-Related Industrial Components | |
|---|---|
| **SIC Code** | **Industrial Component** |
| 4011 | Railroad |
| 4111 | Local and suburban transit, including airport transportation and local bus operations |
| 4119 | Local passenger transportation not otherwise classified, including sightseeing buses and limousine rental |
| 4121 | Taxicabs |
| 4131 | Intercity and rural highway passenger transportation |
| 4142 | Passenger transportation charter service, except local |
| 4173 | Bus terminal and service facilities |
| 4431 | Great Lakes-St. Lawrence Seaway transportation |
| 4459 | Sightseeing boats, water taxis, swamp buggy rides, and excursion boats |
| 4481 | Deep-sea transportation of passengers, except by ferry |
| 4489 | Water transportation of passengers |
| 4493 | Marinas, not elsewhere classified |
| 4511 | Air transportation, certified carriers |
| 4512 | Air transportation, scheduled |
| 4521 | Air transportation, noncertified carriers, including sightseeing plane service |
| 4581 | Services related to air transportation |

*Continued*

**TABLE 1.1** *(CONTINUED)*
**Travel and Tourism-Related Industrial Components**

| SIC Code | Industrial Component |
|---|---|
| 4724 | Travel agencies |
| 4725 | Tour operators |
| 4729 | Arrangement of passenger transportation not elsewhere classified |
| 5541 | Gasoline service stations |
| 5561 | Recreation vehicle dealers |
| 5812 | Eating and drinking places—primarily eating establishment—may or may not serve alcoholic beverages |
| 5813 | Eating and drinking places—primarily drinking establishment—may or may not serve food |
| 5946 | Camera and photographic supply stores |
| 5947 | Gift, novelty, and souvenir shops |
| 6052 | Foreign exchange establishments |
| 7011 | Hotels, motels, and tourist courts |
| 7032 | Sporting and recreational camps |
| 7033 | Trailer parks and camp sites |
| 7514 | Passenger car rental without drivers |
| 7922 | Theatrical producers |
| 7929 | Bands, orchestras, and other entertainment groups |
| 7948 | Racing, including track operations |
| 7993 | Coin-operated amusement devices |
| 7996 | Amusement parks |
| 7999 | Amusement and recreation services not classified elsewhere |
| 8412 | Museums and art galleries |
| 8422 | Botanical and zoological gardens |
| 8941 | Professional sports clubs |

*Source:* U.S. Department of Commerce Standard Industrial Classification System

With but few exceptions, the vast majority of enterprises classified under "travel and tourism-related industrial components" are small businesses according to federal government definitions. However, these businesses in the aggregate comprise the third largest retail industry after automotive dealers and food stores in the U.S., and the largest industry on a worldwide basis in 1994.

Approximately one-half of this textbook is devoted to familiarizing students with the operations of businesses in the travel industry. The role of the travel agent and recent

changes in agency operations are discussed in Chapter 9. Water, land, and air transportation operations are covered in Chapters 10 through 12. Hospitality and related services
such as accommodations, restaurants, entertainment, and retail stores are examined in the
last four chapters of the text.

Knowing the various businesses that comprise the travel industry is very useful in
helping students to understand the service-based nature of travel and tourism enterprises
and the alternative career paths that exist within the industry. Travel is one of the largest
and fastest-growing industries worldwide, and career opportunities have multiplied in
conjunction with the growth in travel. Hundreds of job titles and occupations are identified to this industry under the national standard industrial classification codes.

## Linking Concept

The **linking concept** illustrated in Figure 1.1 is a useful way to perceive the extent of the
travel industry. The concept delineates three categories of businesses and organizations
and how they are linked to each other and to the traveler. In accordance with the linking
concept, these businesses and organizations can be thought of as components of the travel
industry and are categorized as **direct providers**, **support services**, or **developmental
organizations**.

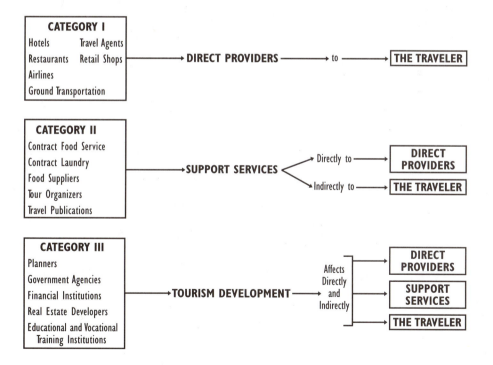

**Figure 1.1**  The linking concept.

The first category, **direct providers**, includes businesses typically associated with travel, such as airlines, hotels, ground transportation, travel agencies, restaurants, and retail shops. These businesses provide services, activities, and products that are consumed and/or purchased by the travelers. They tend to reflect those sectors of the industry that are visible to the travelers. But, like an iceberg, they represent only the visible tip.

Below the surface lies a large variety of businesses lending support to direct providers. This second category, **support services**, includes specialized services, such as tour organizers, travel and trade publications, hotel management firms, and travel research firms. It also includes basic supplies and services, such as contract laundry and contract food service. Businesses providing specialized services, such as those listed above, depend on the travel market for almost all of their business. Businesses supplying the basics to direct providers are not solely dependent on them for their existence, although in an area where travel and tourism are the mainstay of the economy, the bulk of the business for providers of basic supplies and services may come directly from travelers, as in the case of resort areas.

The third category under the linking concept, **developmental organizations**, is distinct from the first two in that it includes planners, government agencies, financial institutions, real estate developers, and educational and vocational training institutions. These organizations deal with tourism development, which tends to be more complex and broader in scope than production of everyday travel services. The development process for a major resort area may take as long as 15 to 20 years to complete. It will involve sensitive issues regarding the environment, people, and culture of an area (which will be discussed in Part 3 of the text). Skilled individuals in such professions as consultancy, finance, real estate, architecture, engineering, environmental science, and so on are typically employed by developmental organizations to work on tourism projects. The decisions and resulting outcomes of tourism development are more long term in nature than the first two categories, which focus more on operations.

In practice, a single corporation may provide direct travel services, secondary support services, and developmental activities. Distinguishing between these categories is useful, because some corporations may have different divisions focused on different target markets and goals, whereas other companies have combined with other businesses to provide comprehensive services in all three categories. The formation of Allegis in 1987, formerly UAL, Inc., is an example of a corporation that tried to provide across-the-board services for travelers through such well-known subsidiary companies as United Airlines, Westin Hotels Corporation, Hertz, and Hilton International. The concept of having a one-umbrella, multiservice travel organization was ahead of its time and failed for various reasons, not least among which was the fact that Allegis as a whole provided less value for stockholders than did the separate companies in their own right. Allegis eventually sold its Hertz, Westin, and Hilton International subsidiaries and changed its name back to United Airlines, Inc. In other cases, mature corporations may be "holding companies" that control the assets of diverse operations. For example, International Telephone and Telegraph (ITT) is essentially a telecommunications company that also owns a hotel management company. Under existing conditions, almost any company, even those not engaged in the travel industry, can sell travel as a direct provider.

Costa del Sol on the Southern Coast of Spain.
Courtesy of the Costa del Sol/Malaga Tourist Board.

The development of a hotel illustrates the interrelationships among the three categories of the linking concept: direct providers, support services, and developmental organizations.

• The hotel would be the direct provider of services to travelers.

• Support services for the operations of the hotel would include local suppliers of basic products and professional companies providing marketing and/or management assistance. The types of supplies, staffing, and other resources would be determined by the standards which the hotel was designed to meet.

• Developmental organizations would include government agencies which usually have approval power over whether a hotel will be built and consulting companies which conduct feasibility studies as well as impact studies.

Consequently, all three categories eventually interrelate through meeting travelers' needs, though they are separate in terms of providing services directly or indirectly to travelers.

Before examining the different types of travelers, it is important to note that most of the businesses and organizations within the travel industry have one important characteristic in common: they provide services. The travel industry is basically a service industry whose products are largely intangibles; for travelers, the output of the travel industry is the production of an experience. It has often been noted by suppliers of tourism that the industry is ultimately in the business of "selling dreams."

## TRAVEL AND TOURISM

Travel is a multidimensional phenomenon that, on the one hand, evokes images of adventure, romance, mystery, and exotic places, and, on the other, involves sobering realities such as business, health, and personal emergencies. Since the 1970s, the term **tourism** has been commonly used to describe the field of travel and reflected to some extent the increasing growth in pleasure travelers, who usually were called **tourists**. However, tourism actually comprises only one segment of the travel market, a fact that was recognized in one of the earliest modern writings in the field, *The Travel Trade*, by Likorish and Kershaw. *(1)* Because tourism means different things to different people, and the world has not yet adopted a universal definition, the term is an inadequate synonym for travel, and its use as such results in inconsistent data when the total travel market is examined. The results of a recent study have shown that states and city organizations still have not accepted a standard definition for travel and tourism. *(2)*

Confusion over definitions also exists when the field of travel is varyingly referred to as the *travel industry*, *tourism industry*, and more recently, *visitor industry*. You will see and hear all of these terms. For general use, perhaps one is as good as another. One may wonder, then, why so much attention is given to these definitions. The concern is twofold: first, research on travel and tourism requires a standard definition to establish parameters of the industry; and second, without standard definitions, there would be no agreement on the measurement of tourism as an economic activity or its impact on the local, state, national, or world economy.

## TOWARD A COMMON DEFINITION OF TRAVEL AND TOURISM

It is crucial that the same criteria be used as qualifiers in comparable studies if valid data are to be obtained. For example, if an organization such as a Chamber of Commerce were to undertake research to determine numbers of travelers staying in local hotels, and the Chamber used a definition of traveler that meant both business and nonbusiness (pleasure) travelers, and the hotels undertook similar research using a definition of traveler that meant only *tourist*, the results of the two studies would not be comparable.

One should understand that the pursuit of common definitions is not merely an academic exercise. As we will see in Chapter 3, the role of marketing research is critical for decision-making at all levels of the travel or tourism industry, and the closer researchers can come to using common definitions, the more meaningful the data will be for market analysis, forecasting, and other purposes. Similarly, it is important in studying travel and tourism to understand what the authors mean when they use certain terms.

In recent years, it has become common, in the United States at least, to adopt a broad concept of travel—one that encompasses tourism but recognizes it as only one of the kinds of travel that comprise the total travel market. For the sake of clarity, this text has also adopted this broad definition of travel.

Most people can agree with *Webster's New Collegiate Dictionary* on the general definition of travel as "the act of going from one place to another." For the purpose of this book, we exclude two types of travel: (1) travel within a person's home community and associated with daily routines and (2) travel as part of a permanent change in residence. Also excluded in the first case is travel such as commuting to and from work, even though it may involve going from one community to another.

Attempts have been made in the past to achieve a standard definition of tourism and tourists among countries throughout the world. The term tourist is actually something of a misnomer, for tourism, as it is officially defined, denotes many different types of travelers.

## Rome Conference Definitions

Definitions of tourists have been proposed as early as 1937. In 1963, a United Nations Conference on International Travel and Tourism, recommended a definition that encompassed "any person visiting a country other than that in which he has his usual place of residence, for any reason other than following an occupation remunerated from within the country visited." *(3, 4)*

Such an individual was defined as a **visitor**. The term visitor covered two distinct classes of traveler:

1. **Tourists**: Temporary visitors staying at least 24 hours in the country visited and the purpose of whose journey can be classified as:

   a. leisure (i.e., recreation, holiday, health, study, religion, or sport);

   b. business;

   c. family;

   d. mission; or

   e. meeting.

2. **Excursionists**: Temporary visitors staying less than 24 hours in the destination visited and not making an overnight stay (including travelers on cruises). *(4)*

Most countries of the world—at least, at the national level—accepted the above definitions. In 1991, a conference was held which proposed new international definitions and standards for travel and tourism.

## Ottawa Conference

Over 250 participants from more than 90 countries attended the International Conference on Travel and Tourism Statistics held in Ottawa, Canada, during June, 1991. *(5)* This was the first worldwide conference to deal with travel and tourism statistics since the Rome Conference. It reemphasized the need for an integrated system of definitions, concepts, and classifications for tourism that are universally applicable. Consensus among researchers and practitioners on the scope of tourism and its pervasiveness is necessary to build credibility among key policy decision makers when competing for government funds or investments.

The conference recommended a new definition of tourism: "tourism comprises the activities of persons traveling to and staying in places outside their usual environment for not more than one consecutive year for leisure, business and other purposes." *(5)* By introducing the concept of usual environment, this definition excludes everyday activities such as commuting and shopping, or a change in residence (see Figure 1.2) which is consistent with the approach of this book.

In regard to the classification of travelers, distinctions were made between visitors versus other travelers and tourists versus same-day visitors. Figure 1.3 delineates the classification of travelers, and Appendix 1A gives detailed definitions recommended by the conference.

The conference also went further than the Rome Conference in defining different forms of tourism within national boundaries and between countries. The forms of tourism (Figure 1.4) are important in recognizing the scope of the industry. In their quest for foreign exchange, countries tend to focus on **inbound tourism** which brings in foreign exchange and often ignore **domestic tourism** and **outbound tourism.** Inbound tourism refers to non-residents traveling to and within a given country. Domestic tourism refers

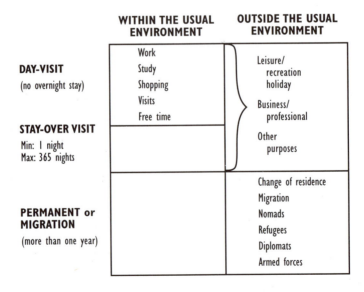

**Figure 1.2**  Tourism and population mobility.

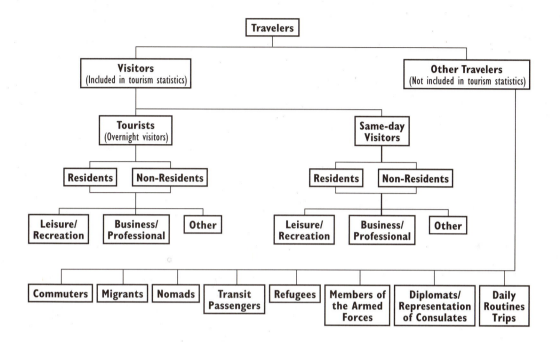

**Figure 1.3** Classification of travelers.

| Units Destination | | Tourism Units | | Forms of Tourism |
|---|---|---|---|---|
| | | Residents | Non-Residents | |
| Travelling | Within the Country | (1) | (3) | Internal (1) + (3) |
| | Abroad | (2) | | |
| Forms of Tourism | | | National (1) + (2) | International (3) + (2) |

In relation to a given country, the following forms of tourism can be distinguished:

**(1) Domestic tourism**—involving residents of the given country travelling only within this country;

**(2) Outbound tourism**—involving residents travelling in another country;

**(3) Inbound tourism**—involving non-residents travelling in the given country.

**Figure 1.4** Forms of tourism.

to travel by residents within their respective countries. Outbound tourism refers to travel by residents of a given country to another country. Recognizing the three forms of tourism (domestic, outbound, and inbound) provides a more complete picture of the industry than one measured by international statistics.

Confusion over the use of the term "tourist" may be expected given the variations discussed above. Within a domestic context, additional criteria may be necessary since international boundaries are no longer relevant for demarcation purposes. Readers who are interested in pursuing this topic further can gain additional insights from Appendix 1B.

## INTERDISCIPLINARY APPROACHES TO TRAVEL

The explosive growth of travel in modern times has generated a high level of interest from government, commerce, host communities, and social scientists. The obvious reasons for this interest are the economic benefits in terms of income and employment generated by travel to and within countries. Over the last two decades, however, governments and host communities have become increasingly concerned about the possible negative side effects of having hordes of travelers encroaching on their lifestyle and culture and competing for the use of natural resources. Anecdotal cases describing the impact of tourism upon the Amish culture in Pennsylvania, the Balinese culture in Indonesia, and the flora and fauna of the Galapalos Islands are examined in Chapter 7, which discusses various impacts of tourism on the economy, environment, and community. The total effects of mass travel on modern societies, and especially on developing areas, involve complex interrelationships with far-reaching implications—many of which are yet unknown.

As travel increases, businesses involved with the development and production of travel services have found their operations becoming increasingly complex. Advancements in technology have affected not only the internal operations of business, but also travel patterns with respect to increased access to new destinations, shorter time for long-distance travel, increased comfort, and a host of other factors. Equally, if not more important, the rapid social changes experienced in tourist destination countries have made business operations in those countries more complex with respect to meeting the needs of travelers.

Constant change and increased complexity in travel have created the need for efficient management of available capital and human and natural resources. This is equally applicable to government, private business, and individuals. The interactive nature of the economic, social, environmental, and often political impacts of the travel industry on its host community, whether rural township, city, state, or nation, has required new interdisciplinary approaches and analyses for studies of the travel industry.

## SUMMARY

The scope of the travel industry encompasses a variety of activities, organizations, and businesses. Historically, this has presented certain difficulties, particularly in terms of roles—public versus private relationships—and definitions. Given the complexity of the

Balinese dancer performs the barong—a mystical figure in Bali—for visitors.
Credit: Garuda Indonesia Airlines.

industry, determining which organizations and businesses are to be considered part of the travel industry is also somewhat arbitrary. The linking concept of travel serves mainly to represent how the various organizations and businesses are involved, either directly or indirectly, in developing and/or providing services for travelers. Subsequent chapters will discuss in greater detail the major components of the travel industry, from both the standpoint of how these components operate as a part of the larger infrastructure and travel marketing network and as industries (for example, hotels, airlines, and cruise lines) in their own right.

## DISCUSSION QUESTIONS

1. What is the definition of the travel industry used in this text?

2. Which industrial components are related to travel and tourism?

3. What is the linking concept? How do developmental organizations differ from direct providers and support services?

4. Why is it important to have standard definitions of tourism?

5. What are two types of travel that are excluded from the definition of the term "travel" as it is used in the concept of travel as an industry?

6. How has the definition of "tourists" evolved on an international basis?

7. What are the differences between inbound tourism, domestic tourism, and outbound tourism for a given country?

8. What are the differences between visitors versus other travelers? Who are included as tourists?

9. Why do studies of the travel industry require interdisciplinary approaches?

## Questions from the Appendices

10. How did the Ottawa Conference define "tourists?" "Residents"?

11. What are the four dimensions used for defining travelers?

12. What is the difference between a tourist and an excursionist?

# SUGGESTED STUDENT PROJECT

Have students research the definition of tourists used by the city and/or state where they live or are attending school. What are the criteria used by the city or state in defining tourists? How do these criteria compare to those discussed in this chapter?

# REFERENCES

1. Likorish, L.J., and A.G. Kershaw. *The Travel Trade*. London: Practical Press Ltd., 1958.

2. Hunt, J.D., and D. Layne. "The Evolution of Travel and Tourism Terminology and Definitions." *Journal of Travel Research*, (Spring 1991).

3. OECD Tourism Committee. *International Tourism and Tourism Policy in OECD Countries Report*. Paris: Organization for Economic Cooperation and Development, July 1973.

4. *Technical Handbook on the Collection and Presentation of Domestic and International Tourist Statistics, Introduction*. Madrid: World Tourism Organization, 1981.

5. Paci, E. "International Issues Forum: Common Measures of Tourism." Conference Proceedings, 23rd Annual Conference of the Travel and Tourism Research Association, June 14–17 1992.

# *A*PPENDIX 1A—OTTAWA CONFERENCE DEFINITIONS RECOMMENDED FOR THE MEASUREMENT OF TOURISM DEMAND

## International (Inbound and Outbound) Tourism

**Travelers**   Any person on a trip outside his/her own country of residence (irrespective of the purpose of travel and means of transport used, and even though s/he may be traveling on foot).

**Resident**   A person is considered to be a resident in a country if the person:

a. has lived for most of the past year (12 months) in that country, or

b. has lived in that country for a shorter period and intends to return within 12 months to live in that country.

**Visitor**   Any person who travels to a country other than that in which s/he has his/her usual residence but outside his/her usual environment for a period not exceeding twelve months and whose main purpose of visit is other than the exercise of an activity remunerated from within the country visited.

**Tourist (overnight visitor)**   A visitor who stays at least one night in a collective or private accommodation in the country visited.

**Same-day Visitor**   A visitor who does not spend the night in a collective or private accommodation in the country visited.

## Domestic Tourism

**Travelers**   Any person on a trip within his/her own country of residence (irrespective of the purpose of travel and means of transport used, and even though s/he may be traveling on foot).

**Resident**   A person is considered to be a resident in a place if the person:

a. has lived for most of the past year (12 months) in that place, or

b. has lived in that place for a shorter period and intends to return within 12 months to live in that place.

**Visitor**   Any person residing in a country, who travels to a place within the country outside his/her usual environment for a period not exceeding twelve months and whose main purpose of visit is other than the exercise of an activity remunerated from within the place visited.

**Tourist (overnight visitor)**   A visitor who stays at least one night in a collective or private accommodation in the place visited.

**Same-day Visitor**   A visitor who does not spend the night in a collective or private accommodation in the place visited.

This definition includes:

a. **Cruise passengers** who arrive in a country on a cruise ship and return to the ship each night to sleep on board even though the ship remains in port for several days. Also included in this group are, by extension, owners or passengers of yachts and passengers on a group tour accommodated in a train;

b. **Crew members** who do not spend the night in the country of destination; this group also includes crews of warships on a courtesy visit to a port in the country of destination, and who spend the night on board ship and not at the destination.

*Source*
World Tourism Organization.

# *A*PPENDIX 1B—DIMENSIONS OF TRAVEL

Four basic dimensions are included in the criteria used for defining travelers in relation to the travel industry: distance, length of stay at the destination, residence of the traveler, and purpose of travel.

Frequently, a fifth dimension—mode of transport—is included as well. From an economic perspective, mode of transport can be a useful qualifier in analyzing tourism statistics. The diagram in Figure 1B.1 shows these travel dimensions.

## Distance

Excluding commuting to and from work and changes in residence, what must be considered under the first dimension of travel—distance—is the difference between **local travel** (traveling within a person's home community) and **nonlocal travel** (traveling away from home). This distinction tends to pose a problem on shorter trips and on those where artificial boundaries exist. For example, many people who work in Washington, D.C., live in the surrounding states of Virginia and Maryland. Their commuting to work during the workweek is excluded by our definition of travel; but, on weekends they may return to the District of Columbia for pleasure and recreational activities. Similar situations also occur between countries in Europe and between the United States and Canada.

A measure that has been used to distinguish travel away from home is the distance traveled on a trip. The U.S. Travel Data Center, for example, defines a trip as "each time a person goes to a place at least 100 miles away from home and returns." *(2)* Travelers, on this basis, are defined as individuals who travel at least 100 miles in one direction from home. This definition may be applicable for measuring travel by the residents of a country. It, however, does not meet the purpose of measuring international travelers coming into a country regardless of the trip distance. The same may be said of interstate, intercity, and interprovincial travel, depending upon separations in governmental and taxation jurisdictions.

## Length of Stay at Destination

The second basic dimension of travel used as a criteria for defining travelers is the length of stay at a destination. Definitions of tourists and visitors tend to use the criteria of an

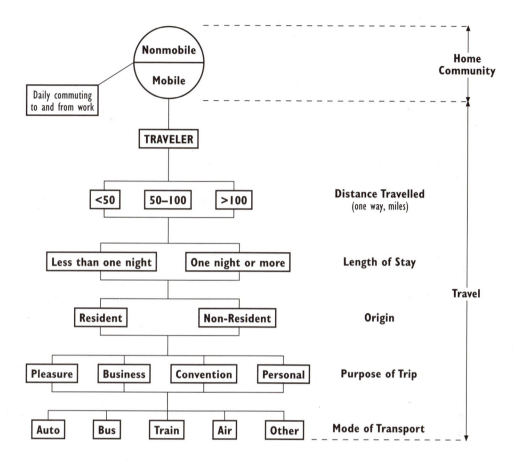

**Figure 1B.1**   Diagrammatic representation of travel dimensions.

*Source:*   National Tourism Policy Study.

overnight stay to distinguish between travelers who are in transit and those actually visiting a destination. This can pose problems, since one-day trips for sightseeing, recreation, shopping, and/or entertainment provide substantial business to historic sites, theme parks, cities, and other attractions. One attempt to resolve this problem is by using the term **excursionist** or **same-day visitor** to refer to a temporary visitor not making an overnight stay.

## Residence of the Traveler

The third basic dimension of travel—the residence or origin of the traveler—is important to businesses that are interested in better identifying the market for their services. For research or business purposes, it is frequently more important to know where people live than to know their nationality or place of citizenship.

## Purpose of Travel

The fourth basic dimension—purpose of travel—has been used to identify different types of travel. The U.S. Travel Data Center finds that the main purpose for trips can be broken down into the following seven categories:

1. visiting friends and relatives;

2. conventions, seminars, and meetings;

3. business;

4. outdoor recreation—hunting, fishing, boating, and camping;

5. entertainment—sightseeing, theater, and sports;

6. personal, family—medical, funeral, and wedding;

7. other.

If tourism is taken to mean travel for pleasure and recreation, then business travel and personal travel may be excluded. However, such distinction may be somewhat simplistic because travelers often combine business travel with pleasure or personal travel. Indeed, it is often difficult to separate the primary motivation for a trip from secondary but equally strong motivations; for example, a convention held in a city where one has close friends or relatives or where a major event is also taking place.

From this discussion, it is obvious that there have been long debates concerning definitions for the term tourism. The criteria selected to distinguish one kind of traveler from another often depends on the particular situation and the researcher's focus of interest. The variations in definitions of tourism emphasize the difficulty in comparing data on tourism.

### Sources

*National Tourism Policy Study, Final Report.* Washington, D.C.: U.S. Government Printing Office, 1978.

*National Travel Survey.* Washington, D.C.: U.S. Travel Data Center, 1984.

# Chapter 2

# The Development of Travel

## LEARNING OBJECTIVES

- To understand the basic prerequisites for growth in travel worldwide.
- To obtain an overview of the early development of travel and tourism.
- To know the size and importance of worldwide travel.
- To understand the significance of domestic travel.
- To appreciate the scope and importance of travel within and to the United States.
- To define and use the following terms:

| | |
|---|---|
| BITS | Social tourism |
| Cultural interpretation | Spas |
| Cultural tourism | Trade fairs |
| Grand tour | Travel gap |
| Health tourism | VFR |
| Package tour | World Tourism Organization (WTO) |

# CONDITIONS FOSTERING THE GROWTH OF TRAVEL

Religion, health, commerce, adventure, quest for fortune, and politics all served as reasons for travel long before the beginning of Christianity and continue to do so today. Precedents for recreational and pleasure travel go back to ancient peoples—the Greeks, Phoenicians, Chinese, and Egyptians—whose privileged classes all understood the enjoyment of leisure travel and had servants and guards to see to the rigors of the road. The era of the Roman Empire from 27 B.C. to 395 A.D. was relatively peaceful, and upper-class merchants and middlemen prospered through extensive trade and commerce within the empire and with other countries. The Romans had a universal coinage that was accepted throughout the empire, and they had an efficient network of roads. Wealthy Romans had a significant amount of leisure time for pursuing recreational and pleasure activities and for traveling.

The situation of the Roman Empire exemplifies the general conditions that apply to modern times in fostering the growth of travel, namely, peace and political stability, economic prosperity, accepted medium of exchange (currency), efficient transportation system, and leisure time. All of these conditions facilitate travel. During periods where political stability or other necessary conditions are missing, travel tends to be limited to reasons other than recreation or pleasure.

For example, the Middle Ages (which lasted from 400 A.D. to 1400) was a period in which travel was hindered by feudal wars, political instability, lack of extensive trade and commerce, inefficient transportation, and scarce leisure time. Travel was also dangerous and burdensome. The Middle Ages was more representative of the origin of the word travel, that is, *travail*, meaning to labor or toil. It was not until the Industrial Revolution in the early 19th century (first in Britain, then 50 years later in the U.S.) that travel began to slowly transform from a "class to mass" phenomenon. *(1)*

The Industrial Revolution brought about not only technological changes, but also substantial social changes that encouraged modest leisure travel, thanks to rise of a growing middle class in urban centers where factories and jobs were located. Working and living conditions in the crowded, poorly-maintained cities, however, were bleak; and large numbers of people began to look forward to leaving the city and traveling to the countryside or seashore for their holidays.

As a modern mass phenomenon, however, travel has a relatively short history which is closely linked with the development of mass transport systems—railroads, passenger steamships, private automobiles, and modern jet aircraft. Different forms of lodging establishments also emerged in tandem with transportation systems, beginning with stage coach or post houses and inns and followed by hotels, motels, summer and winter resorts, skyports, and so on. These developmental factors in travel will be discussed in later sections.

Although technological changes, economic prosperity, and other conditions play an indispensable role in the travel industry, social and lifestyle changes are probably the most important factors influencing people's travel behavior. In economically advanced societies, travel for tourism and other leisure purposes is often viewed as a quality of life entitlement made possible by a number of factors, including workplace productivity gains, paid holidays, annual vacations, and fewer hours in the work week (brought about by organized labor demands and progressive social legislation). Higher educational attainment and modern mass communications have also stimulated an increased consumption of tourism by the members of these societies. Indeed, the correlation between educational attainment and the desire to travel is a close one. Ironically, while the workplace has freed up time for leisure pursuits, changes in the modern family structure and dual-income households have created intense time shortages, conflicting schedules, and pressures which affect travel patterns and behavior.

Business travel, on the other hand, differs from leisure travel and is influenced by economic factors. The trend in commerce and trade since World War II has been moving rapidly toward globalism. Today, major companies tend to be transnational or multinational in scope, requiring their executives to do business almost anywhere in the world. Although advances in telecommunications partially offset the need for business travel, many commercial transactions still require on-site visits and face-to-face meetings. Interestingly, advances in telecommunications assisted by earth satellites such as teleconferencing also create new opportunities for some sectors of the travel industry.

# EARLY DEVELOPMENT OF TRAVEL AND TOURISM

Travel for religious, health, and business purposes has existed throughout history. This section describes the early development of travel and the origins of different types of travel, such as cultural tourism. The concept of social tourism is also introduced as subsidized travel to achieve social goals and purposes.

## Religious Travel

Whether motivated by religious conviction or curiosity about their own or another faith, people will travel great distances to visit the Holy Land, Lourdes, the Vatican, Oberammergau and its Passion Play, Angkor Wat, Mecca, the Ganges in Bengal, or hundreds of other significant attractions associated with religion and religious beliefs. Religious travel is not new; it has precedent in the pilgrimages of the Middle Ages, which Jusserand (2) describes as "incessant." One of the earliest example of the **package tour** was created during the Middle Ages to serve pilgrims traveling from Venice to the Holy Land. The tour package included the cost of passage, food and wine, hostel accommodations, and not least, bribe money to secure baggage and personal possessions from seizure along the way.

Pilgrimages had almost as many purposes as there were pilgrims. Some pilgrimages were made to fulfill a vow, others to expiate sins or to plead for divine favors. Confessors frequently ordered a pilgrimage as penance and sometimes required the traveler to pay homage or to travel barefoot or in a hair shirt. By no means were pilgrimages or religious travel confined to the Western World. The Venetian Marco Polo encountered pilgrims in the thirteenth century during a visit to the Island of Seilan (Ceylon, now Sri Lanka).

Along with Rome and Jerusalem, St. James of Galicia was the leading destination of English pilgrims in the fourteenth century. Frequently, pilgrims traveling to these shrines encountered great hardship and difficulty. Beginning in 1388, English pilgrims were required, by order of King Richard II, to obtain and carry permits, the forerunner of the modern passport. Eleven years later, the number of ports from which pilgrims were permitted to depart for overseas destinations was limited, by order of Richard, to two—Dover or Plymouth—unless special license was obtained from the King. *(2)* Pilgrims' motivation for traveling was not just for religious reasons. While some pilgrims were devout, others just traveled for the love of travel.

## Travel for Health

Developments in the field of medicine and notions about cures have influenced travel for centuries, giving rise to the concept of **health tourism**. As long ago as Roman times, the Emperor Caracalla traveled to the mineral springs at Baden-Baden to cure his rheumatism. The discovery of Florida by Ponce de Leon in 1513 was an aftermath to his original intent to find the legendary Fountain of Youth.

Mineral springs were still an attraction in 1839, when Americans first began touring the Continent. At the German spa in Wiesbaden, dinner was served at 1 p.m., normally an elaborate affair with roasts and Rhine wine. Concerts were given in the afternoon, causing the gardens of the Kursaal to overfill with people, hundreds sitting at their small tables smoking, sipping coffee, wine, and seltzer-water, eating ices while enjoying the music. In the evening there was lavish banqueting, musicales, dancing, and gambling. *(3)*

Natural clay mineral water bath is featured at an American health spa.
Courtesy of Glen Ivy Hot Springs Spa.

Different springs were believed to hold the cure for different maladies. The iodized sulfur springs of Bad Wiessee were recommended for treatment of rheumatism, heart, and circulation disorders. Bad Neuenahr was a spa for diabetics. The resort of Bad Ems treated rhinopharyngeal afflictions; Bad Wildungen, problems of the kidneys and gall bladder.

**Spas**—after Spa, Belgium—continue to attract tourists today, partially because there is still faith in the curative powers of mineral water and partially because international conference facilities have been built on the sites of mineral springs at Baden-Baden, Bad Godesberg, and Wiesbaden.

Health-related travel is not limited to trips to thermal springs. "Reducing ranches" attract middle-aged women with weight problems. Romania, with its controversial "restorative" Gerovital, beckons the geriatric set. Businessmen with frazzled nerves journey to the seashore or the mountains to escape the pressure of work and demanding schedules. Americans suffering from bursitis and other ills travel to the Orient to undergo acupuncture. As populations age in postindustrial societies, health-related travel becomes increasingly popular.

## Travel and Commerce

For centuries, commerce has given impetus to travel. Men have traveled throughout recorded history to buy and sell goods, to attend trade fairs and expositions, and to search for gold or other resources. **Trade fairs**, the precursor of the modern exposition, were important commercial attractions even during the Middle Ages and constituted another reason for international travel. English product fairs were especially notable—and numerous.

The largest and best known of the English fairs were held at Winchester, Abingdon, Smithfield, Stourbridge, and Wexhill. However, even in medieval England, the importance of tourists and traders to the host community was well recognized and competition between villages for the privilege of operating a fair was formidable. The Rolls of Parliament of the day refer constantly to petitions which beseeched the king to grant a fair to a certain nobleman or to a certain town or sometimes to suppress a neighboring town's fair to avert competition. When fairs were held, they were stringently regulated to produce the greatest possible attendance and maximum income.

Expositions were still important attractions for tourists in mid-nineteenth century England. The Great Exhibition of 1851 at Crystal Palace drew more tourists to London than ever before. Travelers came not only from the United Kingdom and from the Continent, but from the United States. Exhibit goods also came from the United States and promptly became "the object of 'persistent and unsparing disparagement' in the British press...ploughs and reaping machines, agricultural products, model railways, dental instruments...little...which might disabuse Europeans of their firm conviction that the U.S. represented a wholly materialistic society, with no appreciation of the finer things of life." *(3)*

Product fairs, trade shows, and markets are still attractions today to pleasure travelers as well as business people. Some examples of trade markets that also serve as attractions include what Dutch tour operators bill as "the world's largest flower auction" at Aalsmeer and the Cheese Carriers Guild Market at Alkmaar. Guidebooks to Paris tout the Marche aux Fleurs, across the street from Sainte-Chapelle, the open-air bookstalls along the quays of the Left Bank and Les Halles, once the "central market," but now relocated in the southern outskirts of the city.

In London, the tourist trail leads to the Billingsgate Fish Market, Covent Garden—made famous by the musical play, *My Fair Lady*—and Leadenhall Market, on the site of the old Roman forum. These markets attract international travelers who are interested in seeing the sights of the city, but one should not forget the importance of markets for commerce. There is an axiom in the travel business that "tourism follows trade as trade follows the flag." This axiom would seem to be as true today as it was in medieval England.

## Tourism, History, and the Arts

History and the arts have also molded the course of tourism. For decades, tourists have been attracted to destinations of historic and cultural significance. **Cultural tourism**, as we know it, had its origin in the **grand tour**—an extended tour of the Continent commonly taken by youth of the British aristocracy as a part of their education during the seventeenth, eighteenth, and much of the nineteenth centuries. *(4)*

The basic purpose of the grand tour was to learn. Normally, it lasted about three years and often, the young person was accompanied by an entourage of tutors and servants and carried letters of introduction to members of the European aristocracy. In many cases, the tour would begin modestly with a stay in a French provincial town, preferably where the English were few so that the student would be forced to speak French. Strasbourg, Dijon, and Lyon were favored because they afforded convenient places for short tours to Germany and Switzerland. The typical grand tour also included a number of Italian destinations: Turin, Milan, Rome, and Naples—to see the ruins and attend the opera—and Venice for its carnival.

Expensive or not, the grand tour attracted an increasing number of participants—from both the middle and the upper classes. Gradually, under middle class values, aristocratic standards of education began to give way, and enjoyment was the focus of travel abroad rather than education. *(5)* The "class" tour gradually became the "mass" tour.

For many around the world, travel is still seen as important for completing one's liberal education as it was during the era of the grand tour. Despite the advantages of modern information technology, history does not truly come alive until one sees it in the flesh and begins to develop a sense of appreciation for the cultural achievements of mankind over the centuries. Countries, especially those identified as part of the ancient or "old world"—Egypt, China, India, Greece, Italy, among others—understand the gravity of their role as guardians of the great cultural monuments, relics, and sites of their past civilizations and work actively to promote them as visitor attractions, even as they cope with the problems of continual erosion and high cost of preservation.

To give greater substance to the educational value of historic monuments, relics, and sites, the art of **cultural interpretation** has been supported by tourism ministries in numerous countries. Cultural interpretation is an educational activity which attempts to combine factual information with relevant experiences and presentations designed to pique the interest of specific audiences. Through cultural interpretation, history comes to life as

The Parthenon—a celebrated Doric temple of Athena built on the Acropolis at Athens in the 5th century, B.C.—is one of the great historic attractions of Greece. Credit: Greek National Tourist Organization.

the story of the building of the Great Pyramids at Giza or of the Great Wall of China is told. The displays and treasures of numerous museums around the world are also made more meaningful to visitors by licensed tour guides trained in cultural interpretation. A tour, for example, of the living museums of the Hermitage in St. Petersburg or Versailles is as captivating as it is educational when interpreters tell the story of the monarchs responsible for the building of these palaces and the artisans who designed their contents—framed against the backdrop of the political and social events of the times. Thus, where the young aristocrats of earlier centuries had their tutors to teach the lessons of the places they visited on the grand tour, so the mass travelers of today can learn history, art, and architecture from lessons offered by qualified guides.

## Transportation and Package Tours

In addition to changes in the purpose for foreign travel, other forces of change were also at work. New modes of transportation, such as the development of the steam locomotive, representing a form of mass transportation, were affecting the grand tour and international tourism. In 1830, the first railroad in Europe, between Liverpool and Manchester, was built. At about the same time, track was laid in France, linking Paris and Versailles, and in Germany, joining Nuremberg and Furth. (3)

The mid-1800s, between 1830 and 1860, saw the advent of trans-Atlantic steamships—floating hotels—which brought Europe within two weeks of the United States. Screw-propelled luxury liners were introduced in the 1860s, reducing crossing time still further. By 1889, the *City of Paris*, a twin-propelled steel-hulled liner, had cut travel time between the old Continent and the new to six days. *(3, 6)*

By the end of the 19th century, American tourists began to discover Europe. Soon, they also discovered Thomas Cook, the forerunner of today's travel agent and the package tour which combined transportation, accommodations, sightseeing, plus other activities on a preplanned itinerary. Traveling on a package tour meant that American travelers were going to the same places, seeing the same sights, and crowding the same resorts. It opened up Europe to thousands of newcomers by making travel convenient and less expensive. On the eve of World War I, all-inclusive tours of Europe were being offered, ranging in price from $178 to $400 for five weeks, to $1,000 for an eight country, all-summer luxury tour. *(3)*

The emergence of air travel further revolutionized tourism, reducing travel time between Europe and North America from five days to one. The introduction of the passenger jet in 1958 created the "global village," further cutting transit time between Europe and North America from 24 hours to eight. Today's jet airplanes travel faster than the first passenger jets—a trip that once took about three weeks to cross the Atlantic Ocean by ship can now be accomplished in less than six hours.

The first jet service by any U.S. airline began on October 26, 1958, when this Pan American World Airways Boeing 707 left New York for Paris.
Courtesy of Pan American World Airways, Inc.

The sixties brought what has sometimes been called the *democratization* of foreign travel. The middle class traveled abroad in great numbers. By the beginning of the decade, Americans were spending close to $700 million on foreign travel, and a new word entered the national vocabulary—***travel gap***. *(3)* U.S. residents were spending more on travel abroad than foreign nationals in tours to the United States. This gap in spending led to the promotion of the United States as a tourist destination. Citizens of the "Old Continent," the Far East, the Pacific, Central and South America were beseeched to "See a New World. Visit the U.S.A.!"

## Social Tourism

The term **social tourism** has various meanings, depending on the objectives associated with its movement. In a general sense, it means a subsidized system of travel through government, employer, or labor union intervention to achieve social goals and purposes.

During the late 1930s, many countries of Europe passed legislation for workers to receive their full pay on holidays when they did not work. It was recognized that the right to legal holiday could only be meaningful if the ordinary worker were able to afford the means to travel for recreation and rest. To that end, a number of voluntary associations in the field of social tourism set to work obtaining reduced fares and creating a network of holiday centers for vacationers of modest means.

In 1963, the **International Bureau of Social Tourism (BITS)** was founded in Brussels to encourage the development of social tourism on an international scale. With its present membership of over 100 associations worldwide, BITS has devoted its energies to promoting tourism to achieve social objectives by studying such issues as youth and senior citizen travel, staggering of holidays, camping and caravanning, building and financing moderate-cost tourist facilities, and preservation of the local culture and environment.

Because most of the businesses involved in tourism in the United States are private enterprises, the federal role in tourism is not usually recognized. However, there are more than 100 different major programs of the federal government involved in the provision of recreation, tourism, travel, and environmental conservation with activities ranging from the dedication of close to one billion acres of public lands for recreation to the operation of historic sites, national parks, and forests where vacationers may go.

# INTERNATIONAL TRAVEL

From a worldwide perspective, the travel industry is enormous. Estimates of international travel compiled by the **World Tourism Organization (WTO)** Secretariat show that there were approximately 500 million international travelers who spent $316 billion in 1993. *(7)* These figures may be somewhat conservative, given the lack of a universal system of gathering statistics and accounting for all forms of traveler spending.

## Total Expenditures

How large is the total world market for travel in terms of expenditures, domestic and foreign? One estimate indicates that worldwide spending for domestic and foreign travel combined was over $2.0 trillion in 1993. *(8)* Based on this estimate, the travel industry is the world's largest industry, accounting for 12% of the world's gross national product. Tourism expenditures exceed the gross national product of all countries except for the United States. The growth of world tourism has not advanced without problems. The Persian Gulf War in the Middle East had a negative impact upon 1991 world tourist arrivals. Prolonged recessions and economic restructuring in Europe, Japan, and the United States have resulted in slower growth for many destinations. Political instability and open hostilities erupting in the former Soviet Union, the former Yugoslavia, and elsewhere are impediments to tourism development.

Spain plays host to over 55 million visitors each year. This number exceeds the entire population of Spain. A tourist market this large could be viewed as an invasion despite the economic benefits that international tourism receipts bring to the people of Spain. This has been recognized by officials in Spain as reflected by Dr. Pablo Cela of the Ministry of Commerce and Tourism, who said of the dramatic growth of tourism in his country, "We cannot feel proud of this achievement. We have now reached a peak and must reflect; we cannot go on growing like this." *(9)* There are many other destinations today besides Spain where the number of annual visitors exceeds the resident population—Hawaii, Switzerland, and Bermuda being examples.

While popular destinations struggle with the problem of how to accommodate ever-increasing numbers of visitors, other countries are grappling with the question of how to attract more. Australia, South America, and Africa receive only a fraction of the world's travelers even though their land mass is enormous and offers untapped opportunities for tourism. Other nations with excellent potential for travel industry development, such as Eastern Europe, China, Malaysia, South Korea and Vietnam, are actively engaged in development and promotion.

As the world travel industry grows, it will undoubtedly face problems and downturns created by such factors as recessions and regional conflicts. It is useful, therefore, to view the industry in terms of both short- and long-term concerns. In the long-term, the future for worldwide tourism growth looks excellent. Recent projections indicate that total worldwide spending on tourism should exceed $4 trillion by the year 2000, reflecting an annual average growth rate of 5%. Total world airline passenger revenues are projected to reach $343 billion in 2000 and worldwide accommodations revenue are expected to reach $301 billion. *(8)*

## Receipts and Arrivals

In spite of the Gulf War and slower economic growth of industrialized countries during the early part of the 1990s, international travel continued to increase rapidly over the last decade. Based on WTO data, worldwide receipts from travel increased over threefold, from approximately $100 billion in 1983 to $316 billion in 1993. International arrivals increased by 71% over the same period, from 293 million to 500 million arrivals.

Following a historic pattern, Europe receives the lion's share of all arrivals and receipts. As shown in Table 2.1, Europe accounts for 60% of all international arrivals and about 52% of international travel expenditures. The Americas account for 21% of arrivals but 28% of receipts. Although Asian and Pacific regions realize only 13% of worldwide

| TABLE 2.1 International Travel Flow in 1992 | | |
|---|---|---|
| **Region** | **Arrivals (%)** | **Receipts (%)** |
| Africa | 3.6 | 2.0 |
| Americas | 21.0 | 28.1 |
| Asia and Pacific | 13.5 | 16.0 |
| Europe | 60.3 | 52.1 |
| Middle East | 1.6 | 1.8 |

*Source:* World Tourism Organization *(8)*

arrivals, these regions experienced a faster rate of growth, averaging 6 to 8% annually during the last decade than did other regions.

The world's top spenders on international travel in rank order are: the United States, West Germany, Japan, United Kingdom, Italy, France, Canada, the Netherlands, Austria, and Belgium. *(8)* A substantial proportion of international travel occurs between the United States and western Europe. Europe generates about half of all overseas travelers to the United States. Travel between European countries—intracontinental travel—historically has been very popular, which partly explains Europe's large share of the worldwide travel market.

# TRAVEL WITHIN THE UNITED STATES

While international travel may sound more interesting, exciting, or glamourous, most travel actually occurs within one's own country. Estimates on worldwide travel, both domestic and international, suggest that 91% of total world receipts for tourism is expended for domestic travel. In the United States, an estimated $323.3 billion or 85% of the $380.9 billion tourism and travel receipts for 1993 was generated from domestic travel. *(8)* The U.S. is somewhat unique among nations in the sheer size of its domestic market. The dominance of the domestic market in the United States has not changed significantly up to present times. Given the higher costs usually associated with international travel, it should not be surprising that domestic travel generates greater volume and flow. People may desire to travel to faraway places, but most are limited in terms of what they can afford. This will be seen more clearly in the discussion that follows. An examination of domestic travel in the United States, its size and scope, will provide insight on the importance of domestic travel in general.

## American Travelers *(10)*

For the past four decades, the United States has been considered one of the largest travel markets in the world. The most recent statistics from the U.S. Travel Data Center show that Americans generated 648 million trips and 1.06 billion person-trips during 1993. The

**Mt. Rushmore National Monument in the Black Hills of South Dakota is one of the best known visitor attractions in the U.S.**
Courtesy of the South Dakota Department of Tourism.

definition of traveler used here is a person who takes a trip at least 100 miles away from home and back. A "person-trip" is one person traveling on a trip. Excluded from these statistics are trips taken by transportation crew members, students between home and school, military personnel while on active duty, and commuters. The average trip involved two persons traveling 830 miles and staying away from home for 5.2 nights. The overwhelming majority of person-trips—92%—taken by Americans involves domestic travel within the contiguous United States.

Since 1972, travel surveys have shown that the purpose for taking trips has remained relatively consistent. Most trips taken by Americans are for nonbusiness reasons, principally **for visiting friends and relatives (VFR)**, outdoor recreation, sightseeing, and entertainment. From this perspective, 70% of all travel by Americans in 1995 (see Table 2.2) involved pleasure travel and 51% of pleasure travel involved visiting friends and relatives.

As shown in Table 2.3, 79% of all trips taken in 1995 were by automobile or trucks owned by individuals. This is not surprising, because the automobile is the major means of transportation in the United States. Business travelers, as opposed to pleasure travelers, are more likely than others to use air transportation. Given the economic value of

| TABLE 2.2 Main Purpose for Trips | | | | |
|---|---|---|---|---|
| **Main Purpose for Trips** | **1972** | **1977** | **1984** | **1993** |
| Visiting friends or relatives | 38 | 37 | 34 | 32 |
| Business or conventions | 20 | 20 | 22 | 26 |
| Other pleasure trips | 25 | 26 | 32 | 38 |
| All other trip purposes | 16 | 18 | 12 | 4 |
| Total | 100 | 100 | 100 | 100 |

*Note:* Given as percentage of total person trips.
*Source:* U.S. Department of Commerce for 1972 and 1977. U.S. Travel Data Center/Travel Industry Association of America *(10)* for 1984, 1993, and 1995.

| TABLE 2.3 Means of Transportation, 1995 | | | |
|---|---|---|---|
| | **TRIP PURPOSE** | | |
| **Transportation Mode** | **All Trips** | **Pleasure** | **Business/Convention** |
| Auto/truck/RV/rental car | 79 | 84 | 67 |
| Airplane | 18 | 13 | 31 |
| Bus | 1 | 1 | 1 |
| Train | 1 | 1 | — |
| All other | 1 | 1 | 1 |
| Total | 100 | 100 | 100 |

*Note:* Given as percentage based on person-trips.
*Source:* U.S. Travel Data Center/Travel Industry Association of America. *(10)*

time, the speed of air travel over other modes of travel often outweighs its higher costs. The average trip distance for business travel is almost 600 miles one way, less than one hour by air, but which would take 12 hours by car. As a general pattern, the majority of all trips—70%—are under 500 miles one way.

## Foreign Travel to the United States

In 1993 foreign arrivals to the United States totaled 45.7 million people, representing approximately 9% of the total international travel arrivals worldwide. *(11)* Because of the growing importance of international trade in travel, market research was conducted in five overseas countries which demonstrated substantial potential for vacation travel to the United States. The purpose of the research was to determine foreign interest in specific vacation activities in the United States. Table 2.4 summarizes the major inter-

## TABLE 2.4
## Travelers' Interest in Specific Vacation Activities in the United States

| Activity | PERCENTAGE WITH INDICATED INTEREST | | | | |
|---|---|---|---|---|---|
| | West Germany | United Kingdom | France | Australia | Japan |
| Meet pleasant and interesting people | 69 | 74 | 69 | 61 | 22 |
| Visit scenic place | 67 | 76 | 76 | 68 | 49 |
| Beach vacation | 63 | 53 | 41 | 30 | 48 |
| Enjoying good food | 52 | 74 | 52 | 47 | 37 |
| Shopping | 41 | 51 | 41 | 44 | 44 |
| Visit historic places | 45 | 51 | 58 | 52 | 21 |
| Visit museums and art galleries | 31 | 30 | 57 | 33 | 27 |
| Gambling | 25 | 9 | 14 | 14 | 20 |
| Theater/nightlife | n/a | n/a | n/a | 44 | 38 |

*Note:* Survey Respondents were requested to indicate what types of vacation activities they would be interested in participating in the United States.

*Source:* Adapted from a 1984 Gallup Survey of Potential Vacation Travelers to the United States, USTTA. *(12)*

ests of visitors from the five countries—West Germany, United Kingdom, France, Australia, and Japan. The top two interests for the West Germans, British, French, and Australians were the same—meeting pleasant and interesting people and visiting scenic places. For the Japanese, however, the top two interests were visiting scenic places and beach vacations.

The two countries generating the largest volume of travel to the United States are Canada and Mexico. Approximately 17.5 million Canadians and 9.2 million Mexicans traveled to the United States during 1993. Canada alone accounts for 38% of all foreign travelers to the United States. *(11)*

The proximity of Canada and Mexico to the United States with automobile access across the borders is an obvious reason for the large amount of travel from these two countries. Travel to the United States is also less expensive for Canadian and Mexican residents when compared to overseas travel.

With respect to overseas travel, Japan is the country that generates the largest number of travelers to the United States, followed by the United Kingdom and West Germany. As shown in Table 2.5, five out of the top ten countries generate 59% of all foreign travelers to the United States. The top ten countries together account for 65% of all foreign travelers to the United States. Foreign travelers spent $74.6 billion in the United States during 1993.

**TABLE 2.5**
**Top Ten Countries Generating Visitors to the United States In 1993**

| Rank | Country | Number of Arrivals | Percentage of Total |
|------|---------|--------------------|--------------------|
| 1 | Canada | 17,520,000 | 38.4 |
| 2 | Mexico | 9,250,000 | 20.3 |
| 3 | Japan | 3,301,000 | 7.2 |
| 4 | United Kingdom | 3,075,000 | 6.7 |
| 5 | West Germany | 1,962,000 | 4.3 |
| 6 | France | 821,000 | 1.8 |
| 7 | Italy | 590,000 | 1.3 |
| 8 | Brazil | 576,000 | 1.3 |
| 9 | Australia | 502,000 | 1.1 |
| 10 | Venezuela | 453,000 | 1.0 |

Source: United States Travel and Tourism Administration. (12)

# SUMMARY

Travel as an activity dates back to the earliest of civilizations, though the motivation to travel has taken many different forms over the centuries. These reasons range from health, education, and religion to commerce, culture, and recreation. Many important factors have converged to influence the volume and direction of long-haul discretionary travel, including perceived political stability and safety of a destination, economic prosperity, comparative currency value, availability of leisure time, and efficient transportation. The transportation improvements of the past half-century, for example, have been a decisive factor in the development of mass tourism on a domestic and international level.

The travel industry today is enormous both in terms of number of travelers and travel expenditures, the latter of which has caused many governments to actively seek tourism development as a means of economic growth. Countries, and specific regions or destinations within countries, receive and generate varying amounts of tourism traffic depending on such factors as location, economic conditions, and types of attractions.

People also travel for many different reasons, including business, visiting friends and relatives, and vacation. In terms of vacation or leisure travel, motivations for selecting a particular destination also vary. The important motivational aspects of travel will be further discussed in Chapter 3. Grasping the underlying factors that affect travel volumes and flows is an important element in gaining an understanding of the international travel market and the development of private sector industries specific to tourism.

# $\mathcal{D}$ISCUSSION QUESTIONS

1. What factors fostered the growth of travel?

2. How did the earlier forms of travel transform into modern tourism?

3. What were the major factors which brought about "mass" tourism?

4. Why are product fairs, trade shows, and markets important to tourism?

5. What issues relate to the objectives of social tourism?

6. How large is the international travel market in terms of arrivals and expenditures?

7. Which regions of the world receive the largest proportion of international travel arrivals and receipts? Which region is experiencing the fastest growth in international arrivals?

8. How large is domestic travel in the United States?

9. What are the main purposes for domestic travel by Americans?

10. What are the main characteristics of domestic trips taken by Americans?

11. Which countries generate the most travel to the United States?

12. What are some of the vacation activities which international travelers are interested in doing during their visit to the United States?

## Suggested Student Exercise

1. Look for tours in the travel sections of Sunday newspapers, both local newspapers and those of large cities such as New York and San Francisco. Are there tours which are based on history, culture and/or the arts such as traveling on the Silk Road or visiting the Taj Mahal? What are other popular types of travel being advertised?

# $\mathcal{R}$EFERENCES

1. Likorish, L. J., and A. G. Kershaw. *The Travel Trade*. London: Practical Press Ltd., 1958.

2. Jusserand, J. J. *English Wayfaring Life in the Middle Ages*. London: Ernest Benn Ltd., 1950.

3. Dulles, F. R. *Americans Abroad, Two Centuries of European Travel*. Ann Arbor, Mich.: University of Michigan Press, 1964.

4. Levy, A. *The Culture Vultures, or Whatever Became of the Emperor's New Clothes?* New York: G. P. Putnam's Sons, 1968.

5. Plumb, J. H. "The Grand Tour" *Horizon* II, No. 2 (November 1959).

6. Villiers, A. *Men, Ships and the Sea*. Washington, D.C.: National Geographic Society, 1973.

7. *Compendium of Tourism Statistics, 1988–1992*. Madrid: World Tourism Organization, 1994.

8. *Travel Industry World Yearbook—The Big Picture*, 1993–94. New York: Child and Waters, Inc., 1993.

9. *International Tourism Quarterly*, No. 1. London: The Economist Intelligence Unit Ltd., 1979.

10. National Travel Survey. Washington, D.C.: U.S. Travel Data Center/Travel Industry Association of America, 1996.

11. International Travel to and from the United States. Washington, D.C.: United States Travel and Tourism Administration, February 1994.

12. Adapted from a 1984 Gallup Survey of Potential Vacation Travelers to the United States. Washington D.C.: United States Travel and Tourism Administration, 1984.

# Chapter 3

# Travel Trends and Motivations

## LEARNING OBJECTIVES

- To understand factors influencing recent growth in pleasure travel.
- To be aware of factors motivating people to travel.
- To understand the need for segmenting markets within the travel industry.
- To appreciate the role of marketing research in the travel industry.
- To define and use the following terms:

| | |
|---|---|
| Business traveler | Market segments |
| Demographic | Nonbusiness traveler |
| DIT | PRIZM |
| FIT | Psychographics |
| Frequent traveler programs | Target markets |
| GIT | Tour Package |
| Incentive Travel | Traveler profile |
| IT | VALS |
| Intercept Survey | |

# FACTORS INFLUENCING GROWTH IN PLEASURE TRAVEL

*C*hapters 1 and 2 covered growth and development of travel from both conceptual and factual viewpoints. While facts and figures are needed for developing an understanding of the size and importance of travel, equally important is knowledge of the factors that influence travel and tourism. What makes the industry grow at the rates we have been seeing? While Chapter 1 introduced some of the factors that have influenced travel growth in general, we will now explore this topic further by examining factors influencing recent growth in discretionary travel. At the same time, we will be looking at what motivates people to travel for pleasure.

Although pleasure travel has always been considered a discretionary item in consumers' budgets (after basic necessities are provided for), the purchase of travel for vacation and leisure is not considered exceptional for many families in countries with developed economies. Today, the tourism statistics of many developing countries also show healthy growth in pleasure travel. The economies of developing countries have been underestimated in the past. The most recent estimate by the International Monetary Fund suggests that developing nations account for 34% of world spending and a larger share of travel spending than previously thought. *(1)* For example, domestic travel in China now exceeds 400 million tourists with expenditures of $15 billion. International travel by Chinese citizens was restricted to official and business travel until recently. In 1993, Chinese citizens took 3.7 million international trips which reflected a 28% increase over 1992. Thus, as travel has become more of a social norm on a global scale, especially for the educated, higher-income segments of the population, it increasingly has been viewed as an integral part of living—an important aspect of the quality-of-life factor.

The factors that influence growth in pleasure travel are:

- Changes in lifestyle
- Dual household income
- Travel promotion and tourism awareness
- Demographic changes
- Expanded travel industry

The above list is not meant to be exhaustive. Changes, such as the adoption of year-round scheduling for elementary and secondary school levels, are occurring constantly and it would not be possible to discuss all factors.

## Changes in Lifestyle

Changes in lifestyle have resulted in different attitudes concerning pleasure travel. A recent nationwide survey in the United States asked Americans what they meant by "the good life." Travel took first place, as 60% responded that travel indicated "the good life." Home ownership came in second place. Similar surveys in Europe showed the same results except that Europeans enjoy longer vacations than Americans. Previous generations of Americans would have been appalled to think that anyone could possibly prefer vacation travel to the security of home ownership.

The length and choice of vacations have also been affected by changing lifestyles. A number of recent studies seem to confirm that Americans increasingly prefer shorter, more frequent vacations to the standard two-week vacation of past decades. These travelers are also more likely to stay in a hotel or motel than earlier travelers, who often stayed with friends and relatives. Marriott Corporation's research, for instance, revealed that 50% of those surveyed traveled over a weekend and stayed in a hotel or motel at least once. *(2)* Furthermore, a survey by the U.S. Travel Data Center indicates that weekend trips comprised 54% of all trips taken by Americans in 1993, and 49% of the trips involved the use of hotels or motels. *(3)* Such shorter, more frequent trips throughout the year has been beneficial to the industry, in general, because demand fills airplane seats and hotel rooms on weekends and other times of the year when business is normally slow.

In the past, the "model nuclear family" of four going on a holiday trip for two weeks might be limited to economy travel accommodations. Today's pleasure travelers, on the other hand, want both value and quality in vacation and accommodation options. A four-day ski weekend package to Aspen or Quebec City may be available in an exclusive lodge or relatively less expensive condominium. With a limited number of days for a vacation,

Backpack excursions through Europe are among the most popular forms of youth travel.
Credit: Hostelling International—American Youth Hostels, Inc.

travelers are willing to pay more to stay in an exclusive lodge to make the most of their short stay and enjoy "the good life."

Throughout the industrialized world, consumers are opting for later marriages and smaller families or are choosing to remain single, all of which allows for more income to be spent on individual pursuits such as travel. Some people even delay their college education and/or careers to spend a year traveling throughout the world.

In short, given a strong desire to travel, people today will do so even though their incomes may be limited. Expenditures on alternative purchases may be delayed, minimized, or even sacrificed to make travel possible. In Japan, for instance, the typical Japanese household has spent as much as 25% of its income for travel since the mid-1980s.

## Dual Household Incomes

The American household has experienced two particularly dramatic changes since 1970: (1) a large increase of households in which both spouses work, and (2) unmarried couples living together with both individuals working. This trend toward dual "breadwinners" within a household means that total household income is higher. On the other hand, dual "breadwinners" often present households with difficulties in planning release time from work. The likely result is an increase in separate vacations and vacations of shorter duration.

## Travel Promotion and Tourism Awareness

Commercial promotions have a powerful effect in influencing discretionary travel and tourism. In 1993, Americans were bombarded with nearly $1 billion worth of travel advertising by air carriers, cruise ships, states, and foreign countries. (4) (See Table 3.1) This figure does not include the millions of dollars in expenditures for media that could not be measured, such as brochures distributed by ski resorts or travel informational seminars sponsored by individual destinations.

As travel to an area has increased, state and local authorities have established budgets for travel advertising and promotion. Many countries and states have enacted hotel room taxes, where the proceeds are used for advertising their destinations. Communities that previously spent nothing for tourism promotion suddenly have budgets of $500,000 or more. The increased promotion by destinations, travel companies, and others has resulted in heightened travel awareness and desire.

## Demographic Changes

The maturity of the "baby boomers" has created a consumer group which is an important travel market with aspirations and lifestyle characteristics different from previous generations. For those catering to pleasure travelers, the over-50 age market is also a very important consumer group.

The over-50 market will grow in numbers and importance in the United States, Canada, Western Europe, Australia, New Zealand, Japan, and other industrialized nations. In the United States, about 30% of these consumers travel. Moreover, they stay longer and travel farther than younger segments, making this market the single most

### TABLE 3.1
### Advertising Expenditures by Major Travel Categories—1993 (in $1000)

**Airlines**

| | |
|---|---|
| U.S. flag carriers | 465,807 |
| Foreign flag carriers | <u>91,534</u> |
| Total | 557,341 |
| **Cruise Ships** | 171,115 |

**Domestic Destinations**

| | |
|---|---|
| U.S. states | 76,969 |
| Other | <u>89,000</u> |
| Total | 165,969 |

**Foreign Destinations**

| | |
|---|---|
| Countries | 73,621 |
| Canadian provinces | 11,571 |
| Other | <u>4,199</u> |
| Total | 89,391 |
| **Grand Total** | 983,816 |

*Source:*  Ogilvy and Mather. *(4)*

important U.S. traveler abroad. The United States can also expect to see an increase in mature pleasure travelers from abroad, as this market segment swells in size.

By the year 2030, persons 65 and older are expected to number 65 million and represent 21% of the U.S. population. With better health care and longer life expectancy, the opportunities for an expanded travel market seem certain for this older group.

## Expanded Travel Industry

It can be argued that an expanded travel industry with more hotel rooms, larger airlines, larger cruise ships, and millions of persons directly employed is the direct result of increased travel demand. On the other hand, a larger industry also means more promotion and advertising which, in turn, stimulates the desire to travel.

In recent years, the expansion of tourist facilities has temporarily outpaced demand as reflected by a surplus of hotel rooms, cruise ship berths, and airline seats. Many companies within these sectors have responded with increased promotion, better products, lower prices, and a higher degree of professionalism to increase the demand for their products. At the national, municipal, and regional levels, governments have become aware of the importance of tourism, and many have created new public or quasi-public positions for tourism executives and planners. The past growth of the travel industry has resulted in new destinations being developed, better products, and lower prices—all of which are conducive to further growth.

Visitors to New York City enjoy a spring flower and garden show at
Rockefeller Center.
Credit: Rockefeller Center Management Corporation, N.Y.C.

# FACTORS MOTIVATING TRAVEL

Travel motivations have their roots in psychological and sociological factors that are difficult to analyze, especially on a mass scale. Yet, to market travel services and destinations effectively, travel sellers and suppliers must understand the motivating factors that lead to travel decisions.

A significant amount of travel is motivated by specific objectives involving business, education, health, religion, politics, and personal emergencies. The motivation for these specific types of travel usually can be more readily pinpointed than the motivation for pleasure travel.

Pleasure travel encompasses a wide range of human emotions and motivations that modern science still has difficulty measuring. One of the pioneering efforts in behavioral theory was Abraham Maslow's explanation of motivation based on a hierarchy of human needs. His model proposes five levels of needs, ranging from physiological ones, such as food, shelter, and clothing at the lowest order, to self-fulfillment needs at the highest level. *(5)* The theory is that so long as human needs remain unsatisfied, they monopolize a person's consciousness and have the power to motivate behavior until the need becomes satisfied. Interestingly, when primary needs are satisfied, it does not produce contentment, but rather a new series of wants will be triggered. At this point, secondary needs gain the power to motivate and impel behavior. People, in short, do not stop wanting. As basic needs are met, people begin to want in succession, safety, love, esteem and recognition, and self-fulfillment. The desire to travel may be stimulated by different motivators at different levels. People with strong safety and security needs, for instance, will presumably seek out safe and familiar destinations. On the other hand, people with a need for self-fulfillment may seek an adventure in some unfamiliar place or go backpacking in the mountains to have an experience of self-discovery. The problem for tourism planners, however, is that a single motivator can result in many different forms of behavioral expression, making it difficult to predict how potential travellers might respond to particular tourism promotions and market campaigns.

## Psychological Motivators

Certain primal motivators play a role in the pursuit of pleasure through travel: power, ego enhancement, and love. Visitors demanding services and attention feel a sense of power over the people catering to their whims. The sense of power also may reinforce their egos and self-image. The search for love and romance through travel has been popularized through movies and novels, as well as real life experiences of famous people. Psychological factors that motivate people to participate in pleasure travel include:

- Cultural experience
- Leisure/escape
- Personal values
- Social contact
- Social trends

Other factors could be added to the list, but the intent here is to explore some of the key psychological motivations for undertaking pleasure travel.

### Cultural Experience

Humanistic reasons such as cross-cultural exchanges, experiencing how other people live, and fostering international understanding may be a form of pleasure travel, which satisfies curiosity about other cultures, lifestyles, and places. Studies among U.S. travelers abroad typically demonstrate that seeking a new cultural experience is a prime reason for international pleasure travel. With respect to the two largest travel markets closest to the United States—Canada and Mexico—Americans tend to view Canadian culture as having little distinction from their own but regard Mexico as a completely different cultural experience.

### Leisure/Escape

As a leisure activity, travel may fulfill an individual's needs for catharsis, independence, understanding, affiliation, and getting along with others. *(6)* Leisure travel is also becom-

Tourists to Hong Kong experience how the boat people live by taking an excursion through Aberdeen Harbour.
Courtesy of Hong Kong Tourist Association.

ing a means of maintaining a healthy balance between work and relaxation or of escaping routine cares, especially with the accelerated pace of modern life. Escape for some people leads them to taking adventure tours or pursuing recreational interests; for others, escape means rest and relaxation.

## Personal Values

The concept of personal values is known to be an important travel motivator. Travelers during the Greek and Roman eras traveled to satisfy personal values, such as a quest for spiritual enlightenment. Personal values are still important motivators for traveling today.

"Personal values appear particularly useful in describing those individuals who visit a specific travel attraction versus those who do not visit the attraction. This comparison allows identification of a value comparison profile." This conclusion was reached by researchers who studied the relationship between personal values and travel decisions of South Carolina visitors and nonvisitors. *(7)*

Travelers to Lourdes, Mecca, and other holy sites do so to satisfy deep personal values. Other personal values such as patriotism and wholesomeness might be fulfilled by visiting Cape Canaveral and Disney World.

## Social Contact

Studies show that the populations of unmarried individuals and senior citizens are large and growing but remain virtually untapped markets. For instance, a study done by J.C. Penney points out that 77 million singles reside in the United States today. This figure includes anyone over 15 years of age and not now married. The study also found that 38% of American adults, 18 years or older, are single. Another report estimates that singles account for more than 15% of total vacation expenditures. *(8)*

Some tour operators are taking notice of these figures and are catering to these markets by grouping individuals together with similar interests. For widows, empty-nesters, singles, and many others, travel may provide a means for simply being with other people. Human beings are social animals and typically need contact and communication with others. They enjoy the feeling of companionship when traveling alone and not worrying about with whom to eat or with whom to sightsee. People in similar circumstances very often can reminisce, commiserate, or simply enjoy each other's company.

## Social Trends

Travel for many people represents fashion. Travel to "in places" can provide a means of mingling with the jetset and trendsetters. It also can serve as an informal means of being part of a social group. Keeping up with the Joneses, one-upmanship, and following the social trends are all motivating factors.

Countless other factors also motivate people to travel. Although the research is limited, we know that people will react differently and seek different avenues of pleasure according to their own psychological, social, physical, and cultural dispositions. Changes in their physical and social environment also will influence their motivations for "getting away from it all."

It is important to recognize that motivations to travel, whatever they may be, are essential elements in understanding the growth in travel and tourism. Very often, this simple fact is overlooked by planners, developers, and operators. Even with the time and money to travel, a large proportion of the population still chooses not to do so. Conversely, a small proportion of the population travels frequently and accounts for a substantial portion of the trips taken.

# MARKET SEGMENTATION

Successful members of the travel industry recognize that it is impossible to be all things to all people. One of the biggest mistakes any member of the industry can make is to view the travel market as homogeneous and to try to satisfy all travelers with a "one size fits all" product or service. The travel market is composed of many sub-markets known as **market segments**, that is, groups of consumers with similar characteristics. The process of segmenting markets assumes that the group of consumers identified as a market segment has similar purchasing habits.

It is common practice in the travel industry to begin the process of market segmentation by separating travelers from nontravelers, visitors from nonvisitors, and users of certain travel services from nonusers. The list of characteristics used to describe travel market segments are referred to as a **traveler profile**. Strategic marketing in the travel industry begins by studying the characteristics of the various market segments. Once the characteristics are known, certain segments can be selected as targets and appropriate strategies designed to reach them. These selected segments are referred to as **target markets**.

A profile of a target market, for instance, business travelers, allows management to plan specific strategies to effectively penetrate the selected market segment. It is important to use characteristics that will provide a meaningful description (profile) of the target markets. Capturing a large enough share of target markets to ensure economic return is a basic goal of suppliers of products and services. This applies to all suppliers, whether they are transportation carriers, hotels, restaurants, tour operators, retailers, or travel destinations.

Thousands of market segments exist within the travel industry, and there is no standard classification system for all of them. Instead, segments are classified according to characteristics that are meaningful to a particular organization or business within the industry. For instance, a hotel is likely to classify market segments differently than would an airline, a restaurant, or a tourist promotion board.

# *S*EGMENTING TRAVEL MARKETS

Several methods are commonly used in the travel industry to segment travel markets. Some organizations might segment travel markets by travel habits and preferences, group versus individual travelers, purpose of travel, demographics, and psychographics.

## Segmentation by Travel Habits and Preferences

Knowledge of travel habits and consumer preferences is vital information for marketers and other planners. Such information may include data on the mode of transportation used, the originating source of travel arrangements and bookings, the method of payment, the class of service purchased, and the season of the year a person travels, among other factors. Different organizations within the industry segment the market according to their own market information requirements. National or state tourism organizations for example, may segment on the basis of type of trips taken and activities which tourists are interested in doing at a destination. (see Figure 3.1 and Table 3.2). Airlines, on the other hand, may segment customers into those receiving first-class and business class service versus coach and economy class service; motels may segment guests as individual versus group; resorts may segment guests as off-season versus prime season guests; and restaurants may segment customers by meal periods (breakfast, lunch, dinner) or by locals versus tourists, and so forth.

Since travel preferences and habits are not the same for all market segments, it is interesting to compare the similarities and differences among various groups. In some cases, seemingly unlike segments may exhibit similar travel preferences and habits. For example, young career persons without children sometimes have surprisingly similar travel preferences and habits to those of older, well-established persons with substantially

## Type of Trip Taken

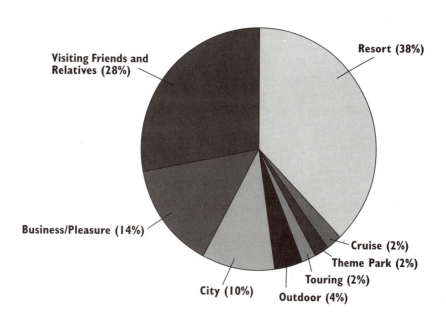

**Figure 3.1** German travel market.

*Source:* United States Travel and Tourism Administration, *Highlights Report,* August 1987.

| TABLE 3.2 |
| :---: |
| **German Travel Market—Top Ten Activities (Rank Order)** |
| 1. Dining out in restaurants |
| 2. Sampling local foods |
| 3. Sightseeing in cities |
| 4. Taking pictures/filming |
| 5. Contacting the local inhabitants |
| 6. Shopping |
| 7. Visiting scenic landmarks |
| 8. Visiting the seaside |
| 9. Swimming |
| 10. Touring the countryside |
| *Source:* United States Travel and Tourism Administration, *Highlights Reports,* August 1987. |

higher incomes. The combined income of a couple in their late twenties who both work may allow them to pursue a lifestyle similar to older, wealthy persons and to visit exotic destination resorts or dine in exclusive restaurants. On the other hand, a young career person who is supporting a family most likely cannot afford these luxuries.

## Segmentation by Group versus Individual Travelers

Travelers are frequently divided into two segments, each of which is important to the travel industry. The first segment consists of independent travelers, who usually are referred to as **FIT** or **DIT** travelers. The acronym FIT at one time referred to **foreign independent travelers**, but today it is also used to refer to domestic travelers traveling independently. DIT may be applied to either a **domestic independent traveler** or **domestic independent tour**, prepaid and unescorted. These travelers may purchase tours, but their main distinction is that they travel on their own and not as part of a group.

The second segment consists of group travelers, referred to as **GIT** travelers. Originally used to designate a group-based airfare offered by scheduled air carriers, it now commonly means **group inclusive tour**, which is a tour package that commonly includes transportation, lodging, airport transfers, and frequently sightseeing and entertainment as well.

A major disadvantage in traveling on a group package basis is that the itinerary is fixed, and all members of the group must travel together in going from one destination to another. In Europe, it is common to refer to GITs as simply **inclusive tour (IT)** travelers. It is probably less confusing in the U.S. to refer to the two market segments simply as group or independent travelers.

The travel preferences and habits of the group and independent market segments are different. Members of the industry, such as tour bus operators, ground operators, tour wholesalers, hotels, airlines, and others, can be immediately affected by a percentage change in the number of group versus independent travelers. However, it has only been with the advent of mass tourism that this factor has gained importance. Citing one of the few such studies comparing group to independent visitors, group travelers to Hawaii on the average spent more per day in total and for specific items such as sightseeing and entertainment than did independent travelers (see Table 3.3).

Within the group and independent categories, each may be further segmented. The independent segment consists of many types of individuals, ranging from the adventurous backpacker, who may spend very little on travel services, to the wealthy jet-setter, who may spend $500 or more per night on a suite alone. The group segment may be broken down into convention travel, special interest groups (such as study tours), and incentive travel, among others.

## Segmentation by Purpose of Travel

One of the most widely-used means of segmenting markets in the travel industry is classifying consumers by purpose of travel. In segmenting travel markets, it is important to distinguish between **business** and **nonbusiness**, that is, nonpleasure and pleasure travel-

**TABLE 3.3**
**Group Versus Independent Visitors to Hawaii**
**Average Expenditure per Day per Visitor, 1993**

| Specific Items | Group Visitors | Independent Visitors |
| --- | --- | --- |
| Lodging | $55.98 | $41.74 |
| Food and Beverage | | |
| Restaurant | 20.36 | 17.99 |
| Nightclub | 2.19 | 1.65 |
| Dinner shows | 4.17 | 2.70 |
| Dinner/lunch cruise | 2.09 | 0.94 |
| Groceries | 3.77 | 3.45 |
| Total food/beverage | $32.58 | $26.73 |
| Transportation | | |
| Ground transportation | 0.52 | 0.58 |
| Rental vehicles | 5.88 | 6.70 |
| Gasoline/parking | 2.14 | 1.68 |
| Interisland travel | 3.57 | 3.19 |
| Sightseeing tours | 3.15 | 2.60 |
| Total transportation | $15.26 | $14.75 |
| Souvenirs | 4.47 | 3.96 |
| Clothing/jewelry/fashions | 20.99 | 13.46 |
| Entertainment | 9.95 | 6.69 |
| Other | 10.97 | 7.38 |
| Total | $150.20 | $114.71 |

*Source:* 1993 Visitor Expenditure Survey, Hawaii Visitors Bureau.

ers. Although there is no uniform system for grouping these travelers, they may be further subclassified as follows:

| **Business Travelers** | **NonBusiness Travelers** |
| --- | --- |
| Government | Vacationers |
| Self-employed | Visiting friends and relatives |
| Private company | Family emergency |
| Nonprofit organization | Accompanying members of family on business |
| Other | Other |

Convention travelers and incentive travelers are often classified as business travelers, but they may also be independently grouped. **Incentive travel** is company-sponsored pleasure travel with all expenses paid and awarded to qualified employees as a bonus. As the name implies, incentive travel is earned by individuals as a reward for meeting or exceeding specific job performance criteria; it may also be used as a motivational tool to promote business—for instance, a car company might use incentive travel to reward its top distributors.

Regardless of the categories and subdivisions adopted, it seems to be universally accepted that business travelers are different from nonbusiness travelers and should be segmented accordingly. Experience and research has shown that the business traveler often has different needs and different spending patterns from the nonbusiness traveler. In general, the demand for travel services by the business traveler is inelastic to price changes, whereas the nonbusiness traveler's demand for travel services is elastic to changes in prices. This means that the price of travel services is less apt to be of concern to the business traveler than to the nonbusiness traveler, even during periods of economic downturn. The business traveler will likely continue to fly rather than drive or take a bus even if airline prices increase.

Managers of downtown hotels believe that the business traveler is more concerned with convenience of location than with price. Of course, not all business travelers exhibit similar travel habits and preferences. There are times when business will be combined with pleasure on trips—for instance, convention meetings at resorts. The corporate executive on an unlimited expense account is likely to behave quite differently from a government employee on a per diem allowance or a struggling entrepreneur who must watch every penny.

Just as habits and preferences exhibited by different types of business travelers vary, the same is true with the nonbusiness traveler. For example, one traveler may visit a destination on a holiday and stay in a commercial lodging establishment, whereas another will visit friends and relatives and stay in their homes. Those in the industry responsible for developing marketing strategies to reach particular market segments must be aware of these variations. The traveler who stays in a commercial establishment, thereby creating employment, is obviously more significant to the travel industry and the host community than one who stays with friends and relatives. However, travelers who stay with friends and relatives may spend more on entertainment and shopping, which benefits those businesses.

A recent study conducted by Tourism Canada in researching the U.S. market showed that in a 12-month period, a total of 130.6 million Americans took a total of 468 million personal pleasure trips, representing 1.94 billion person-nights. The typical U.S. resident takes 3.6 pleasure trips a year lasting 4 days on average.

The Canadian study divides the U.S. tourist market into eight distinct vacation type segments (see Figure 3.2):

1. A visit to friends and relatives (VFR), where the primary purpose is to visit and spend time with friends or relatives.

2. A close-to-home leisure trip, where facilities related to a beach, lake, seashore, or park can be enjoyed.

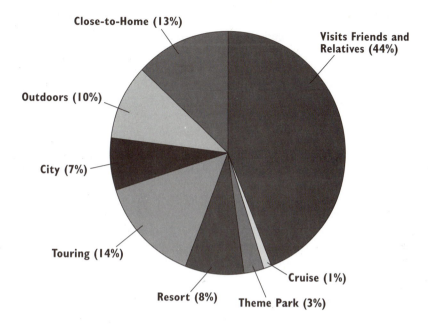

**Figure 3.2**  Structure of U.S. pleasure travel market (based on total trip nights).
*Source:*  Tourism Canada.

3. A touring trip by car, bus, or train through areas of scenic beauty and places of cultural or general interest.

4. A city trip for shopping, entertainment, dining, attending plays or concerts, visiting museums, or just strolling around and enjoying the city.

5. An outdoors trip in a natural area to enjoy activities such as camping, hunting, fishing, hiking, or rafting.

6. A visit to a resort or resort area where a wide variety of activities such as beaches, skiing, golf, and tennis are available.

7. A cruise to enjoy all the onboard activities, dining, and planned stops at points of interest along the way.

8. A trip to a theme park, exhibition, or special event such as the Super Bowl, World's Fair, or Olympic Games. *(9)*

## Segmentation by Demographics

Profile descriptions of market segments are only partially complete when they describe consumer preferences and habits, group versus individual travelers, and purpose of trip. As discussed earlier, **demographic** characteristics of the market segment need to be described.

Demographic variables describe the physical, geographic, and personal characteristics of consumers. These may include age, income, sex, marital status, military service, size of family, ethnic origin, religion, residence, place of birth, education, as well as others. Selecting demographic variables should not be done haphazardly in view of the potentially high costs of collecting such information.

The type of demographic factors selected to provide a profile of a market segment should, whenever possible, correspond to known demographic statistics about that population. There are many sources, such as the U.S. census and previous market studies, for data about populations. Assume that those sources had data about people in the following age brackets: under 25, 25–35, 36–47, 48–57, 58 and over. It would make sense for airlines, hotels, national tourism offices, or other members of the travel industry to use the same groupings on their own market research results.

An airline, for instance, might use these age groupings and discover that 30% of its passengers were in the 36–47 age bracket. For comparison, the airline might look at census information and see that only 20% of the population fell into this bracket. This would tell the airline which age segments of the population it was or was not attracting in proportion to the total population. If the airline had elected to use an age bracket of 34-48, it would not be possible to make such a comparison.

## Segmentation by Psychographics

The term **psychographics** refers to the lifestyle characteristics of consumers. The use of psychographics to identify the profile of travelers is newer and less frequently used than demographics. Psychographic research attempts to measure people's activities, interests, opinions, and basic characteristics, such as their stage in life and their income, education, and residence to discover behavior patterns that can be used in marketing. With more knowledge and understanding of consumers, it is assumed that one can communicate and market more effectively. *(10)*

A standardized list of lifestyle characteristics appropriate for identifying segments of the travel market does not exist. Past attempts to identify characteristics usually described segments according to such lifestyle traits as political activism, political leaning (conservative versus liberal), participation in fine arts, recreational interest, and religious activism.

Recognizing the motivational differences of individuals, SRI International, a research firm located in Menlo Park, California, developed a system for categorizing consumers according to their values and lifestyles rather than just demographics. The system, referred to as **VALS (values and lifestyles)**, isolates and identifies different types of consumers. Each type of consumer is sufficiently distinctive in behavior and emotional makeup that it constitutes a market segment. *(11)* The Pennsylvania Bureau of Travel Development used VALS as a tourism marketing research tool to help measure the effectiveness of its advertising campaign, "You've Got a Friend in Pennsylvania." *(12)* This tool enabled the Pennsylvania Bureau to compare the psychographic profile of travelers against their attitudes and perceptions concerning Pennsylvania.

A market segmentation technique, developed by the Claritas Company, referred to as **PRIZM**, has also proven useful in segmenting consumers. This research approach identifies consumers by census block groups, census tracts, postal carrier routes, and zip codes. *(13)* PRIZM classifies consumers by 12 social groups and 40 lifestyle clusters,

# Pennsylvania's Use of VALS

The VALS system divides Americans into nine lifestyles or types:

1. Survivors—the most disadvantage group

2. Sustainers—struggling at the edge of poverty

3. Belongers—middle-class, conservative and conforming

4. Emulators—trying to "make it big," status-conscious

5. Achievers—successful, self-reliant and wealthy

6. I-Am-Me—typically young, fierce individualism

7. Experimental—most inner directed; educated, artistic

8. Societally conscious—mission or cause-oriented

9. Integrated—self assured, self-actualizing

Through a survey of visitors, the Pennsylvania Bureau of Travel Development discovered that three VALS groups accounted for most of the visitors to Pennsylvania. Achievers accounted for 37% of visitors, belongers accounted for 36% and the societally conscious, 18%. Based on research by SRI International, the media habits of achievers indicate that they read newspapers and magazines and do not watch much television. Belongers tend to watch television, and the societally conscious reads mainly the business section of newspapers and major news magazines. Consequently, advertising to each segment should use different media.

The ratings of Pennsylvania as a destination was also analyzed for the three VALS group. The results substantiated the "You've Got a Friend in Pennsylvania" advertising campaign as an effective theme for Pennsylvania. "Friendly people" ranked among the top ten criteria for selecting a destination; and the achievers, belongers, and societally conscious gave Pennsylvania high ratings in regard to "friendly people."

Source: *Journal of Travel Research*, Vol. 24, No. 4, Spring 1986. *The Journal of Travel Research* is published by the Business Research Division, University of Colorado and the Travel and Tourism Research Association.

providing marketers with psychographic and demographic information concerning consumers within zip code geographic zones. (See Table 3.4)

There is a well-known axiom that "birds of a feather flock together." Although brand preferences and purchasing habits of consumers may vary throughout the United States, there is surprising commonality in consumption habits within a given neighborhood or

## TABLE 3.4
## The PRIZM Social Groups and Lifestyle Changes

| Group Codes | Group Titles | Lifestyle Clusters |
|---|---|---|
| S1 | Educated, affluent executives and professionals in elite metro suburbs | Blue blood estates<br>money and brains<br>Furs and station wagons |
| S2 | Pre- and post-child families and singles in upscale, white-collar suburbs | Pools and patios<br>Two more rungs<br>Young influentials |
| S3 | Upper-middle, child-raising families in outlying, owner-occupied suburbs | Young suburbia<br>Blue-chip blues |
| U1 | Educated, white-collar singles and ethnics in upscale, urban areas | Urban Gold Coast<br>Bohemian mix<br>Black enterprise<br>New beginnings |
| T1 | Educated, young, mobile families in exurban satellites and boom towns | God's country<br>New homesteaders<br>Towns and gowns |
| S4 | Middle-class, post-child families in aging suburbs and retirement areas | Levittown, U.S.A.<br>Gray Power<br>Rank and file |
| T2 | Middle-class, child-raising, blue-collar families in remote suburbs and towns | Blue-collar nursery<br>Middle America<br>Coalburb and Corntown |
| U2 | Middle-class immigrants and minorities in dense urban row and hi-rise areas | New melting pot<br>Old Yankee rows<br>Emergent minorities<br>Single City blues |
| R1 | Rural towns and villages amidst farms and ranches across agrarian mid-america | Shotguns and pickups<br>Agri-business<br>Grain Belt |
| T3 | Mixed gentry and blue-collar labor in lo-mid rustic, mill and factory towns | Golden ponds<br>Mines and mills<br>Norma Rae-Ville<br>Smalltown downtown |
| R2 | Mixed Whites, Blacks, Spanish and Indians in poor rural towns and farms | Back-country folks<br>Sharecroppers<br>Tobacco roads<br>Hard scrabble |
| U3 | Mixed Blacks, Spanish and immigrants in aging, urban row and hi-rise areas | Heavy industry<br>Downtown Dixie-style<br>Hispanic mix<br>Public assistance |

district of any community. Consumers in high-income neighborhoods—for instance, Highland Park in Dallas, Texas, or Shaffer Heights in Cleveland, Ohio—may share many lifestyle and consumption behavioral similarities even though they live in different states. But residents of these areas will normally share little in common with individuals who may live in a different neighborhood only blocks away.

It is important to have a system for identifying particular consumer groups throughout the United States. This allows pinpointed—or targeted—marketing by travel suppliers and destinations. Because of the complexity of psychographics, there still is confusion as to which variables should be included in a study and how to use the results. One of the major airlines in the United States used psychographic variables to identify market segments and discovered that people who drove sports cars also held a good opinion of that airline. This information could have been used in a number of creative ways—for instance, in marketing the airline to the sports car enthusiast segment of the market. Although uncertainty exists in determining the best way to use them, psychographics do provide a valuable tool in defining the profile of market segments.

Properly identifying the segment of the market appropriate to the seller—whatever his or her product or service may be—is the key to success in the industry. Segmentation is one of the most important marketing tools available in helping management satisfy travelers by matching products and services with their needs.

## Segmentation by Frequency of Travel

Frequent travelers are key customers and usually comprise the most important market segment for any firm in the travel industry. Airlines, hotels, and automobile rental firms have initiated **frequent traveler programs** that allow companies to identify key customers, frequency of use, travel preferences, addresses, phone numbers, credit card usage, and other vital marketing data.

The American Hotel and Motel Association and the Proctor and Gamble Company conducted a study of frequent travelers. The results pointed out that when selecting a hotel, the frequent traveler was most concerned with the basics: location, service, cleanliness, and value for rates rather than frills. Frequent travelers were younger as a group than the general population and were relatively affluent. Men represented the majority, accounting for 77% of room nights occupied (the number of rooms multiplied by the nights stayed). *(14)*

An individual chain or hotel property might find that their frequent travelers did not exactly meet these findings. Many companies must carve out a particular market niche and appeal to a slightly different customer than the average frequent traveler; therefore, it is critical for each company to identify the demographic and psychographic profile of its frequent traveler and to compare these data with information about the customers for the entire industry.

# MARKETING RESEARCH

Today, the need for information about various market segments is very important. Managers make decisions that will commit their firms to vast operational or capital expenditures, affecting the future of the enterprise. Intelligent decisions concerning the consumer cannot be made unless up-to-date information on market segments is available and management understands how to use it.

The role of marketing research in the travel industry is to provide information for management to use in planning, finance, operations, as well as marketing. Maximum use of marketing research is possible only if the firm has an ongoing program to identify current changes and trends in the market. Additional research may be needed to determine why certain changes have occurred and to enable a firm to adjust its strategies and operations to account for market changes.

A hotel chain, for instance, might find that it has been attracting a decreasing percentage of the business-traveler market segment each year. If it could identify why this is happening, it could either take action to attract more business travelers or look to other market segments for new customers.

## Gathering Information

An important aspect of marketing research in the travel industry is to profile past and current customers served by an organization. Members of the transportation sector such as airlines, motorcoach buses, and cruise ships obtain this information typically through on-board surveys of passengers.

Hotels and motels obtain their information from questionnaires given or mailed to guests and through analysis of guest histories. Some hotels place a computer terminal in the lobby where guests can use it to provide information regarding their satisfaction with the hotel as well as profile information. *(14)* Destinations such as the American Pacific Islands (Hawaii, Guam, Northern Marianas, American Samoa), Australia, Japan, and other countries whose travelers enter the area by air, receive information from passenger questionnaires that are distributed on inbound airline flights. **Intercept surveys** requiring personal interviews of travelers are also performed at airports, train or bus terminals, popular tourist sites, or other places where there will be a large representational gathering of visitors.

Information gathering is more difficult for such destinations as Canada or Mexico, which may be entered by land or air. In these cases, it is common to conduct surveys to obtain visitor profiles at border crossings, at high traffic areas in visitor destinations, in hotels, or at airports.

Many members of the travel industry—airlines in particular—employ a full-time staff of marketing research professionals to gather information about present and past visitors and about new market segments. Outside marketing research companies and consultants also may be hired to conduct special marketing research programs. In addition to a profile description, managers within the travel industry need marketing data concerning changing preferences of travelers, buying behavior, trip planning behavior, and customer satisfaction.

Knowledge of the travel market becomes especially critical when one is developing a new product, service, or destination. Relevant information is critical for determining who the potential customers are; which services, activities, and so forth are important to travelers; why they select a certain product or destination; and how to communicate and market the product and/or services to potential consumers. This type of information can only be gained through systematic and organized marketing research.

## Free Research

Members of the travel industry are fortunate to have an abundance of free or low-cost research available to them. Travel destinations at national, state, city, and regional levels annually spend millions of dollars for research. Valuable information about visitor trends and preferences is generally available from destinations throughout the world. There are few other industries where competitors willingly provide information about their customers.

Private corporations such as American Express and Pannell Kerr Forster, banks, airlines, auto rental firms, and hotel chains occasionally conduct studies that are made available to members of the industry. Travel associations, universities, institutes, and foundations also conduct research and publish the results.

Travel industry firms can take advantage of this wealth of data by developing in-house libraries. Many executives within the industry make it a practice to subscribe to journals, trade magazines, and other services that allow them to keep abreast of the latest research in the field.

# SUMMARY

Chapters 1 and 2 provided an overview of the travel industry and explained the interrelationship of component industry sectors within travel and tourism, tourism's historic development, and its current economic and demographic statistics measuring the size and flow of world and U.S. travel activities. Central to the entire issue of tourism development and the movement of people, however, is the question of what motivates people to travel, whether for satisfying economic, political, educational, religious, recreational, health, social, or personal needs.

In recent years, discretionary pleasure travel has become an increasingly important component of modern life, further stimulated by large sums of promotional dollars spent by individual tourist destinations and travel-related enterprises. As the travel market grows, it is important to recognize its increasing segmentation. Many different methods exist to segment the market based on demographic and psychographic characteristics and travel habits, and as new identifiable market segments emerge.

The travel market is a dynamic one. Changing lifestyle and demographic characteristics continue to affect travel flows, the development of new travel products, and the way business is conducted within the industry. Tourism-related research to identify trends and travel motivations and analyze markets has consequently become of paramount importance. Increasingly sophisticated research methods have been developed in recent years to measure travel and tourism; and the use of such research has become a necessity for both private enterprise and government jurisdictions.

# DISCUSSION QUESTIONS

1. What are the major factors that have influenced recent growth in pleasure travel?

2. Which motivations for travel appear to be more important relative to the others?

3. How is Maslow's theory used to explain travel motivation and behavior?

4. What is market segmentation? Why is it important to the travel industry?

5. What is the key assumption underlying the process of segmenting markets?

6. What are the main methods used to segment the total travel market?

7. What are different types of business travelers?

8. What do demographic variables describe about consumers? What are examples of demographic variables used to segment markets?

9. What do psychographics describe about consumers?

10. What is the importance of marketing research to the travel industry?

11. How do organizations collect information on their markets?

## SUGGESTED STUDENT EXERCISES

1. Choose a popular visitor attraction in your area; it may be a state or national park, historic site, local museum, aquarium, zoo or any other place likely to keep track of visitors. Find out how the attraction researches its market and profiles its visitors. Does the attraction make use of its demographic data for promoting tourism and building attendance? Suggest ways in which the data might be segmented for analysis and creatively applied to enhance existing marketing efforts.

2. Gather the available tourism data and statistics in your state. What type of information does your state collect? If there is both demographic and psychographic data, are the two correlated? Where do the visitors to your state come from? What motivates them to visit your state? Given your analysis, what themes or slogans would you recommend to your state tourism bureau for promoting inbound tourism? You may wish to look up the slogans/themes used by other states.

3. Check one of the local businesses that is involved with travel—hotel, tour operator, transport company, etc. How does this company collect psychographic information about its customers? Recommend ways in which the information might be used to improve operations or guest satisfaction.

## ℛEFERENCES

1. Waters, S.R. *Travel Industry World Yearbook 1994–95*, New York: Child & Waters Inc. 1995.

2. "Are Drastic Changes in Vacation Plans Ahead?" *Motel/Hotel Insider* 17, No. 25 (March 3, 1986).

3. *1993 Travel Market Report.* Washington D.C.: U.S. Travel Data Center, June 1994.

4. "Trends in Travel and Tourism Expenditures in U.S. Measured Media, 1989–1993." Ogilvy and Mather, 1994.

5. Maslow, A. H. *Motivation and Personality*. New York: Harper and Row, 1954.

6. Tinsley, H. E. A., and R. A. Kass. "Leisure Activities and Need Satisfaction: A Replication and Extension." *Journal of Leisure Research* 10, No. 3 (1978).

7. Pitts, R. E., and A. G. Woodside. "Personal Values and Travel Decisions." *The Journal of Travel Research* XXV, No. 1 (Summer 1986).

8. Clancy, R. "Desperately Seeking Singles." *Travel Weekly's Guide to Group Travel* (March 30, 1986).

9. *The U.S. Travel Market Study: Canadian Potential Highlight Report.* Tourism Canada, January 1986.

10. Stewart, C. D. and R. J. Calantone. "Psychographic Segmentation of Tourists." *Journal of Travel Research* 16, No. 3 (Winter 1978).

11. Howard, N. "A New Way to View Consumers." *Dun's Review* 118, No. 2 (August 1981).

12. Shik, D. "VALS as a Tool of Tourism Research: The Pennsylvania Experience." *Journal of Travel Research* XXIV, No. 4 (Spring 1986).

13. PRIZM, Claritas, the Target Marketing Company, 201 N. Union Street, Alexandria, VA 22314.

14. "Measurement of Consumer Satisfaction: An Innovation." *Journal of Marketing* (July 1978).

# Part 2

# Government Role and Public Policy

# Chapter 4

# Diplomatic and Consular Framework

## LEARNING OBJECTIVES

- To understand how diplomatic relations are established between countries and their effect on international tourism.

- To understand the basis for international agreements on commerce, navigation, visa issuance, and air transport services.

- To understand how internal government regulations control the movement of foreign tourists.

- To define and use the following terms:

| | |
|---|---|
| Accord of Mutual Understanding and Cooperation in Sports | Consular convention |
| | Convention |
| Advance import deposit-like requirements | Credit item |
| | Customs |
| Air Transport Services Agreements | Debit item |
| | De facto recognition |
| Balance of payment | De jure recognition |
| Bermuda Agreements I and II | Diplomatic recognition |
| Bermuda Principles | Entry requirements |
| Bilateral Agreements | Exit restrictions |
| Commercial Agreement | Foreign exchange earnings |

General Agreement on Tariff and Trade (GATT)

General Agreement on Trade in Services (GATS)

Helsinki Accord

Import duty-like measures

Import license-like requirements

Import quota-like restrictions

Memorandum of Understanding

No Objection Certificate (NOC)

Nonscheduled air service

Procompetition

Protective tariffs

Re-entry permit

Sailing permit

Tourism Agreement

Trade barriers

Trade deficit barriers

Trade in services

Treaty of amity

Transparency

Travel Allowances

Visa

Visa Agreement

Visa waiver program

# $\mathcal{I}$NTERNATIONAL AGREEMENTS

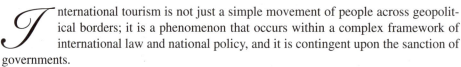

nternational tourism is not just a simple movement of people across geopolitical borders; it is a phenomenon that occurs within a complex framework of international law and national policy, and it is contingent upon the sanction of governments.

Before international tourism can occur, governments must take certain fundamental actions, such as,

1. extending diplomatic recognition and establishing reciprocal relations;

2. negotiating agreements on commerce, navigation, consular rights, visa issuance, and air transport services;

3. exchanging consular and ambassadorial officials;

4. establishing facilities and procedures for issuing passports and visas.

## Diplomatic Recognition

**Diplomatic recognition** is an acknowledgment by one government that it recognizes the legality and/or existence of another. Recognition may be of two types: **de facto** or *de jure*.

De facto recognition carries a lesser status than de jure recognition. De facto recognition might be extended, for example, after a revolution in which the legally constituted government has been overthrown and a new ruling clique has taken over. In such a case, recognition means only that the recognizing government acknowledges that the clique is, in fact, governing the country regardless of the means by which it came to power. De jure recognition implies that the recognizing government acknowledges that the party in power is the lawful government and has legal franchise.

In the absence of reciprocal diplomatic recognition, treaties governing the reciprocal issuance of visas, the mutual protection of travelers, and the exchange of navigation and/or air service rights are not negotiated. Under such circumstances, normal, *bilateral* (two-way) tourism cannot develop. As a rule, a government will refuse entry to residents of any nation it does not recognize or with whom it has severed diplomatic relations. At the same time, it restricts travel by its own citizens to the unrecognized nation.

The U.S. State Department, for example, generally refuses to validate U.S. passports for travel to any country (1) with which the United States is at war; (2) where armed hostilities are in progress; or (3) where travel may harm national interest and would seriously impair the conduct of U.S. foreign affairs.

The case of Cuba illustrates the importance of diplomatic recognition to the tourism development process and why it is essential to have normalized relationships with key source countries. (See the sidebar, *The Case of Cuba*, on the next page)

## Commercial Agreements/Tourism Agreements

Normally, one of the first steps in establishing relations between nations is negotiating a treaty on trade and commerce, sometimes referred to as a **treaty of amity**, commerce, and navigation. Such a treaty is, in some respects, similar to a marriage contract—it enumerates the rights and privileges parties promise to accord each other. Chief among these privileges are the mutual protection and security of travelers.

Since 1978, the U.S. government, through the Travel and Tourism Administration (formerly known as the U.S. Travel Service) within the U.S. Department of Commerce and the U.S. Department of State, has executed bilateral **tourism agreements**, which are an extension of a **commercial agreement**, with eight countries—Argentina, Egypt, Hungary, Mexico, Morocco, the Philippines, Poland, and the former Yugoslavia. With respect to the latter country, the agreement would no longer be valid as Yugoslavia disintegrated in 1991 and no longer exists as one nation, but as six separate states whose political status are as yet unresolved. In addition, the U.S. has a **Memorandum of Understanding** with three countries—China, Israel, and Canada. A Memorandum of Understanding is a preliminary agreement or simplistically, an agreement to agree, and which may later develop into a full-fledged agreement with formal terms. These tourism agreements are a form of cooperative agreement to promote tourism jointly through an exchange of statistical information, vocational training, marketing activities, border facilitation and documentation, sales representation, cultural exchange programs, and other important arrangements between the two parties. Although the substance of a tourism agreement is the promotion of commerce and trade, from a U.S. perspective these bilateral tourism agreements perhaps serve a greater national objective in promoting international understanding, friendly relations, and goodwill than they do trade.

## Accord of Mutual Understanding and Cooperation in Sports

Accords and understandings may be used to further a nation's bilateral or multilateral interest in particular areas. Whether they are internationally binding or simply act as a set

# The Case of Cuba

Prior to the takeover of Cuba by Fidel Castro in 1959, the nation was considered to be the most successful tourist destination in the Caribbean region. According to the Caribbean Tourism Organization, Cuba attracted some 350,000 visitors annually at the time, or about 30% of the total arrivals to the entire region. 90% of the island's visitors came from a single source market—the United States.

As relationships between the U.S. and Cuba continued to worsen with the growing influence of the USSR over the Island, President John F. Kennedy, among other sanctions, declared a U.S. travel embargo on Cuba in 1962. The embargo, which still remains in force, was an effective measure to cut off the flow of dollars from American tourists who flocked to Cuba for its sunny climate, inviting beaches, and once high stake casinos, spectacular entertainment, and glittering nightlife. Immediately after the embargo, tourism to the Island plunged, then gradually returned to the pre-crisis level and stagnated until 1991 when an increasing number of Latin Americans and Western Europeans "rediscovered" Cuba as a cheap holiday destination. Embargo notwithstanding, in recent years the media has reported the occasional sighting of American tourists who slip into Cuba through the "back door" of third country tour operators. Because of the strict enforcement of prohibitions, U.S. citizens wishing to travel to Cuba must first obtain clearance through the Office of Foreign Assets Control in the Treasury Department.

The U.S. travel embargo, in tandem with Cuba's need to pursue tourism as part of the nation's urgent economic development, has resulted in opportunities for non-U.S. hotel companies. As international visitor arrivals to Cuba from Western Europe, Canada, and Latin America have increased dramatically since 1990 to reach 546,000 and generated some $500 million in foreign exchange in 1993, the tourism industry is becoming the top recipient of foreign direct investments. Hoteliers from Europe and Latin America are actively establishing joint ventures with Cuban partners, mainly the quasi-governmental tourism companies Cubanacan, Intur and Gaviota.

| | 1990 | 1991 | 1992 | 1993 |
|---|---|---|---|---|
| **International Inbound Tourism** | | | | |
| Visitors | 340 | 424 | 461 | 546 |
| Tourists (overnight visitors) | 327 | 418 | 455 | 544 |

*Continued*

| | | 1990 | 1991 | 1992 | 1993 |
|---|---|---|---|---|---|
| **International Inbound Tourism** | | | | | |
| Same-day visitors | | 13 | 6 | 6 | 2 |
| Cruise passengers | | 7 | | | |
| **Arrivals by Region** | | | | | |
| Africa | | 2 | 2 | 3 | 2 |
| Americas | | 164 | 207 | 226 | 288 |
| Europe | | 169 | 197 | 218 | 246 |
| East Asia and the Pacific | | 2 | 2 | 2 | 2 |
| **Arrivals by Purpose of Visit** | | | | | |
| Leisure, recreation, and holidays | | 266 | 337 | 399 | 498 |
| Business and professional | | 4 | 5 | 5 | 6 |
| Other | | 57 | 76 | 51 | 40 |
| **Accommodation** | | | | | |
| Number of rooms | H&S | 19 945 | 22 196 | 23 221 | 26 358 |
| Number of bed-places | H&S | 40 526 | 44 419 | 47 139 | 53 394 |
| Occupancy rate | Percent | 75.40 | 69.80 | 60.40 | 57.90 |

Not wishing to be frozen out of the investment opportunities, such U.S. companies as Days Inn with vested interest in Latin America are urging to have the embargo lifted. Although there are over 26,000 rooms, as of 1993, not many of these are suited for upper scale tourism and more properties are needed at the mid-scale level to attract value-minded tourists. Cuban resorts, as the whole, tend to be basic, uninspiring structures with few amenities and limited service. The country requires massive new investments to rebuild its deteriorated tourism infrastructure and to develop additional recreation, dining, entertainment, and shopping facilities for visitors. Even with the new investments, Cuba's success will ultimately depend on its ability to renegotiate the U.S. market—and that will require normalization of relations with the United States as the first step.

Source:  Berman, Scott D., The Challenge Cuban Tourism, *The Cornell H.R.A. Quarterly*, Vol. 35, No. 3, June 1994, p. 10–15.
Compendium of Tourism Statistics 1989–1993, World Tourism Organization, 5th Edition, 1995, Madrid.

The 1980 Olympic Games in Moscow was the event that sparked international debate about the use of international sports competition for political purposes. Credit: AP/Wide World Photos.

of guiding principles for each party to observe will depend upon their exact language and mutual intent. Nonetheless, even when an accord or understanding does not have the force of international law behind it, there are usually moral or political persuasions that require the signatory parties to act in good faith.

For example, boycotting of the Moscow Olympic Games by the United States in 1980 to express the U.S. concern over the USSR-Afghanistan situation, and the subsequent boycott by the Eastern bloc nations of the 1984 Los Angeles Games to retaliate for the 1980 American boycott, signaled the imminent need to bring together nations of the world to agree upon the rules for future Olympic Games. The debate which followed these boycotts led to the conclusions that it was morally reprehensible to use the Olympic Games—whose aim is to promote world peace and harmony through the ideals of international sports competition—as a weapon of retribution and political payback. From this crisis, the "**Accord of Mutual Understanding and Cooperation in Sports**" was drawn to strengthen and foster cooperation among countries around the world in sports events—particularly, the Olympics. *(1)* The United States and the former USSR, among others, are signatories to the accord. Although the USSR no longer exists, each former Eastern Bloc country has followed the spirit of that accord into the 1996 Olympic Games.

## Consular Rights and Responsibilities

Relations between nations are conducted by commissioned personnel who represent their respective governments and whose duties are determined by mutual agreement. Often, as was the case in Franco-American relations, the first office to be established in a reciprocating country is a consulate to represent the commercial interests of citizens of the appointing country and to exchange consular officers. These officers carry out a wide range of functions that are essential to the development and growth of two-way tourism. For example, American consular personnel are responsible for

- protecting Americans abroad;
- providing services for distressed Americans abroad;
- promoting American interests abroad;
- reporting accidents involving U.S. civil aircraft abroad;
- reporting maritime disasters involving vessels of the United States;
- providing documentation of nonimmigrants (e.g., tourists) who wish to visit the United States on a temporary basis

Foreign consular personnel assigned to this country perform substantially similar functions to Americans abroad who are assigned to consular duty. Their rights and responsibilities are defined in **consular conventions**, arrived at by mutual agreement of the affected nations.

## Visa Agreements

Despite the much-heralded arrival of the global village, international travel between countries tends to be treated by governments as a privilege, not a right, and is subject to governmental control. Although controls vary, depending on the government and diplomatic precedent, most nations require some form of entry permit such as a border crossing card or **visa**, that is, an endorsement on a passport or document used in lieu of a passport by a consular official, indicating that the bearer may proceed. Some nations also require an exit permit, a document entitling the holder to leave the country. A few governments insist on a **re-entry permit** for alien residents returning from trips outside the country.

Visa requirements and visa fees are established in bilateral administrative conventions. There are four general reasons that visas are required: (1) to discourage illegal permanent residence, (2) to prevent the entry of undesirable aliens, such as individuals with criminal records, (3) to reciprocate in kind and, (4) to raise revenue. *(2)* These **visa agreements** are negotiated by nations and tend to vary widely in their applicability. For example, U.S. nonimmigrant visa requirements do *not* apply to

1. Canadians and aliens having a common nationality with Canadians;
2. Citizens of Commonwealth countries or Ireland who are residents of Canada or Bermuda;
3. Landed immigrants of Canada entering the United States from Canada or Mexico;

4. Nationals of the Bahamas and British subjects who are residents of the Bahamas, who are "precleared" in Nassau;

5. British subjects who are residents of, and arriving from, the Cayman Islands or the Turks and Caicos Islands, and who present a current certificate from the Clerk of Court of the islands attesting that they have no criminal record,

6. British, French, and Netherlands nationals who reside in Jamaica, Trinidad and Tobago, Barbados, Grenada, or nationals of those countries, who are bound for Puerto Rico or the U.S. Virgin Islands;

7. Citizens of Mexico holding a valid U.S. border crossing identification card;

8. Natives and residents of the Commonwealth of the Northern Marianas, Republic of the Marshall Islands, Federated States of Micronesia, and the Republic of Palau (known formerly as Trust Territory of the Pacific Islands) who proceed in direct and continuous transit from these countries to the U.S. *(3)*

U.S. visa policy is largely an extension of U.S. immigration policy; all applicants for a nonimmigrant visa, including would-be tourists, are presumed to be immigrants until they establish, to the satisfaction of the consular officer, that they are entitled to nonimmigrant status. On the whole, the U.S. is more restrictive in issuing temporary visas to foreigners than Western Europe, Canada, Mexico, or Japan. Aliens who wish to visit the United States as tourists must first prove that they (1) will leave the United States at the end of the temporary stay; (2) have permission to enter some foreign country at the expiration of their stay; and (3) have adequate financial arrangements to permit them to carry out the purpose of their visit.

In borderline cases, the consular officer is authorized to require an applicant to post bond with the U.S. Attorney General "in sufficient sum to insure that upon the conclusion of his temporary visit…the alien will depart from the United States." *(3)*

In addition, the applicant may be asked to submit supporting documents, such as a brief from an attorney or police certificate, and/or undergo a medical examination by a medical officer of the U.S. Public Health Service or a contract physician, if "the consular officer has reason to believe…the alien is medically ineligible (for) a visa." *(3)* Some applicants are subject to a fingerprinting requirement if there is reason to run a crosscheck on the individual for identity verification or background check.

The result, if not the object, of these procedures is to discourage the following foreign nationals from visiting the United States: prostitutes or persons who have engaged in prostitution; paupers, professional beggars, or vagrants; narcotics addicts or traffickers, spies and saboteurs; anarchists or persons who advocate or teach opposition to all organized government; suspected terrorists; communists or persons who have personally advocated the establishment in the United States of a totalitarian dictatorship; persons afflicted with contagious diseases, such as tuberculosis; individuals who might become charges of the public; persons convicted of a crime involving moral turpitude; and aliens whose primary purpose in coming to the United States is to engage in an immoral sexual act. *(3)*

Under federal regulations, such persons are ineligible to receive a U.S. visitor visa. Foreign travel agents who process U.S. visa applications for their clients complain that restrictions of this kind are cumbersome. Not surprisingly, international incidents of great notoriety have sometimes developed over visa procedures, as was the case when the U.S. state department refused to issue visas to individuals infected with the human immunodeficiency virus, setting off a boycott of the Sixth International AIDS Conference held in San Francisco in 1990 by health experts from many participating nations.

In rare instances, it might be as difficult for a nonimmigrant alien to get out of a country as it is to get in. U.S. federal visa regulations, for instance, prohibit the departure of any alien whose exit is deemed prejudicial to the nation's interest, such as one who: has technical or scientific training and knowledge that might be utilized by an enemy or potential enemy of the United States; has knowledge of plans for the national defense and is *believed likely* to disclose it to unauthorized persons; wants to leave the United States to engage in activities designed to obstruct or counteract the effectiveness of the national defense; is a fugitive from justice; is needed in connection with any investigation or proceeding of an official agency; wants to leave the United States to organize or participate in an overthrow attempt against the United States, wage war against the United States or its allies, or similar hostile activities. *(3)*

Few international travelers are exempt from some form of governmental control. Even American Alaskan Eskimos, who had been visiting their Russian relatives in Chukotsk every summer for years, were, at one point in diplomatic history, subjected to **entry requirements** after the Russians discovered their annual arrival. The United States today has visa agreements in force with more than 140 countries.

Many nations, on the other hand, have unilaterally eliminated visa requirements for travelers from certain countries; this has helped to boost tourism traffic from these countries. At the behest of USTTA and members of Congress intent in promoting inbound tourism to the U.S., the State Department agreed to a trial **visa waiver program** in 1988 initially for residents of the United Kingdom and Japan. Under the visa waiver program, tourists from exempted nations can travel to the U.S. for a period of 90 days or less for business or pleasure without having to obtain a tourist visa if they have valid passports. Since 1993, the program has been expanded to include 22 countries, and in 1994, the U.S. Congress passed a two-year extension of the visa waiver program. *(3)* More than 30 million travelers have used this program since it began in 1988. *(4)*

# $\mathscr{A}$ IR TRANSPORT SERVICES AGREEMENTS

Scheduled air transport services between nations are governed by bilateral accords known as **air transport services agreements**. Today, the United States has such agreements with more than 60 countries. Many are based on the so-called **Bermuda Principles**—the agreement that the United States signed with the United Kingdom at Bermuda on February 11, 1946. Commonly, Bermuda-type agreements place no restrictions or limitations on schedule frequency. Virtually all such agreements call upon the parties to

> foster and encourage the widest possible distribution of the benefits of air travel for the general good of mankind at the cheapest rates consistent with sound economic principles, and to stimulate international air travel as a means

of promoting friendly understanding and goodwill among peoples and ensuring as well the many indirect benefits of this…form of transportation to the common welfare of both countries. *(5)*

The first accord signed in 1946 is now known as the **Bermuda Agreement I**. Three decades later, Britain informed the United States that it was terminating the Bermuda Agreement because it did not have any capacity or flight frequency restrictions. In order to ensure the continuance of commercial air transportation with Britain, the United States agreed to new restrictions on capacity and multiple-carrier designations, resulting in the **Bermuda II Agreement**.

During the late 1970s, the United States began to negotiate a new, **procompetitive** type of air transport services agreement with foreign countries. This type of agreement was intended to make air travel accessible to a broader spectrum of the population by fostering low air fares through price competition. Procompetitive agreements have three distinguishing features:

1. multiple designation of carrier;

2. no unilateral limits on flight frequency; and

3. fares determined by the marketplace.

In the early 1970s, the United States had negotiated memoranda of understanding with foreign countries on **nonscheduled air services**. Nonscheduled air services refer to air services offered by some airlines at irregular times with less frequency and often at lower fares than the service provided by scheduled carriers. By the mid-1970s, the U.S. government had concluded nonscheduled air services agreements with four countries and had negotiated understandings on specific types of charters with six.

In recent years, air transport services agreements concluded by the United States have covered both scheduled and nonscheduled service. Following the Airline Deregulation Act of 1978, which deregulated domestic air transportation, Congress passed the International Air Transportation Competition Act of 1979. The International Air Transportation Act established ten goals to increase competition in international aviation. Subsequent **bilateral agreements** have been more liberal in eliminating restrictions on competition.

## GOVERNMENT FINANCIAL AND TRADE POLICIES

The international movement of tourists is affected not only by diplomatic consular relations between nations; it is also influenced by the financial and trade policies—and balance of payments position—of governments. International tourism is either an export or an import. As discussed in Chapter 2 with regard to the issue of travel gaps, tourism services purchased abroad by U.S. residents result in an outflow of exchange from the United States to the countries where the services are obtained. The amount spent for these services is, therefore, treated as a **debit item** (which represents a charge against the U.S.) in the U.S. International Transaction Tables and, for national accounting purposes, is entered as an import expenditure. (See Table 4.1—U.S. International

## TABLE 4.1

### U.S. International Transactions
[Millions of dollars]

| Line | (Credits +; debits −)¹ | 1994 | Not seasonally adjusted 1994 II | III | IV | 1995 I | IIr | IIIp | Seasonally adjusted 1994 II | III | IV | 1995 I | IIr | IIIp |
|---|---|---|---|---|---|---|---|---|---|---|---|---|---|---|
| 1 | Exports of goods, services, and income | 838,820 | 205,268 | 213,818 | 223,698 | 231,408 | 241,066 | 240,836 | 204,161 | 214,305 | 223,180 | 232,443 | 240,070 | 242,213 |
| 2 | Merchandise, adjusted, excluding military² | 502,485 | 124,802 | 123,900 | 135,183 | 138,448 | 144,800 | 140,882 | 122,730 | 127,384 | 133,926 | 138,061 | 142,850 | 145,315 |
| 3 | Services³ | 198,716 | 47,832 | 54,397 | 50,045 | 49,716 | 50,440 | 55,775 | 49,093 | 50,890 | 50,947 | 51,128 | 51,749 | 52,279 |
| 4 | Transfers under U.S. military agency sales contracts⁴ | 12,418 | 3,085 | 3,619 | 3,023 | 2,997 | 3,047 | 3,241 | 3,085 | 3,619 | 3,023 | 2,997 | 3,047 | 3,241 |
| 5 | Travel | 60,406 | 14,872 | 18,226 | 14,179 | 13,558 | 14,948 | 17,743 | 14,999 | 15,297 | 15,368 | 15,220 | 15,049 | 14,790 |
| 6 | Passenger fares | 17,477 | 4,213 | 5,301 | 4,019 | 4,196 | 4,395 | 5,356 | 4,349 | 4,467 | 4,409 | 4,520 | 4,533 | 4,519 |
| 7 | Other transportation | 26,078 | 6,324 | 6,689 | 7,073 | 6,803 | 7,091 | 7,186 | 6,357 | 6,601 | 7,017 | 6,924 | 7,124 | 7,097 |
| 8 | Royalties and license fees⁵ | 22,436 | 5,348 | 5,671 | 6,368 | 6,368 | 6,377 | 6,417 | 5,458 | 5,840 | 5,793 | 6,297 | 6,510 | 6,599 |
| 9 | Other private services⁵ | 59,022 | 13,843 | 14,665 | 15,126 | 16,025 | 14,447 | 15,647 | 14,698 | 14,839 | 15,079 | 14,982 | 15,351 | 15,848 |
| 10 | U.S. Government miscellaneous services | 880 | 147 | 227 | 258 | 188 | 135 | 185 | 147 | 227 | 258 | 188 | 135 | 185 |
| 11 | Income receipts on U.S. assets abroad | 137,619 | 32,634 | 35,521 | 38,470 | 43,244 | 45,826 | 43,979 | 32,338 | 36,031 | 38,307 | 43,254 | 45,471 | 44,619 |
| 12 | Direct investment receipts | 67,702 | 16,065 | 17,528 | 18,857 | 21,332 | 23,174 | 21,303 | 15,569 | 18,145 | 18,734 | 21,402 | 22,527 | 22,058 |
| 13 | Other private receipts | 65,835 | 15,774 | 16,937 | 18,515 | 20,603 | 21,527 | 21,640 | 15,774 | 16,937 | 18,515 | 20,603 | 21,527 | 21,640 |
| 14 | U.S. Government receipts | 4,082 | 795 | 1,056 | 1,098 | 1,309 | 1,125 | 1,036 | 995 | 949 | 1,058 | 1,249 | 1,417 | 921 |
| 15 | Imports of goods, services, and income | −954,304 | −233,276 | −250,664 | −257,743 | −255,492 | −275,733 | −278,805 | −233,389 | −245,645 | −255,218 | −263,844 | −276,117 | −273,885 |
| 16 | Merchandise, adjusted, excluding military² | −668,584 | −162,950 | −173,835 | −181,655 | −177,592 | −190,029 | −190,369 | −164,224 | −172,011 | −177,414 | −183,111 | −191,652 | −188,748 |
| 17 | Services³ | −138,829 | −35,463 | −37,960 | −33,587 | −32,847 | −37,391 | −39,367 | −34,522 | −35,070 | −34,926 | −35,518 | −36,380 | −36,365 |
| 18 | Direct defense expenditures | −10,270 | −2,709 | −2,619 | −2,344 | −2,455 | −2,460 | −2,505 | −2,709 | −2,495 | −2,344 | −2,455 | −2,460 | −2,505 |
| 19 | Travel | −43,562 | −11,835 | −13,272 | −9,598 | −9,068 | −12,594 | −13,538 | −10,826 | −10,929 | −11,072 | −11,062 | −11,527 | −11,106 |
| 20 | Passenger fares | −12,696 | −3,365 | −3,742 | −2,902 | −2,892 | −3,542 | −3,806 | −3,218 | −3,289 | −3,176 | −3,234 | −3,380 | −3,339 |
| 21 | Other transportation | −28,373 | −6,972 | −7,526 | −7,278 | −7,206 | −7,382 | −7,658 | −7,014 | −7,355 | −7,299 | −7,318 | −7,419 | −7,481 |
| 22 | Royalties and license fees⁵ | −5,666 | −1,240 | −1,406 | −1,494 | −1,483 | −1,551 | −1,642 | −1,283 | −1,384 | −1,429 | −1,532 | −1,611 | −1,612 |
| 23 | Other private services⁵ | −35,605 | −8,672 | −8,814 | −9,343 | −9,005 | −9,231 | −9,568 | −8,802 | −8,913 | −8,977 | −9,179 | −9,352 | −9,672 |
| 24 | U.S. Government miscellaneous services | −2,657 | −670 | −705 | −629 | −738 | −631 | −650 | −670 | −705 | −629 | −738 | −631 | −650 |
| 25 | Income payments on foreign assets in the United States | −146,891 | −34,862 | −38,869 | −42,500 | −45,053 | −48,313 | −49,069 | −34,623 | −38,564 | −42,878 | −45,215 | −48,795 | −48,772 |
| 26 | Direct investment payments | −22,621 | −4,839 | −7,306 | −6,937 | −6,938 | −8,023 | −8,611 | −4,600 | −7,001 | −7,315 | −7,100 | −7,795 | −8,314 |
| 27 | Other private payments | −77,251 | −18,802 | −19,729 | −22,404 | −23,876 | −25,229 | −24,558 | −18,802 | −19,729 | −22,404 | −23,876 | −25,229 | −24,558 |
| 28 | U.S. Government payments | −47,019 | −11,221 | −11,834 | −13,159 | −14,239 | −15,061 | −15,900 | −11,221 | −11,834 | −13,159 | −14,239 | −15,061 | −15,900 |
| 29 | Unilateral transfers, net | −35,761 | −8,143 | −8,538 | −11,786 | −7,703 | −6,722 | −7,697 | −8,778 | −8,374 | −11,239 | −7,624 | −7,220 | −7,810 |
| 30 | U.S. Government grants⁴ | −15,814 | −3,703 | −3,488 | −6,245 | −2,867 | −2,284 | −2,834 | −3,703 | −3,488 | −6,245 | −2,867 | −2,284 | −2,834 |
| 31 | U.S. Government pensions and other transfers | −4,247 | −669 | −1,176 | −1,632 | −633 | −726 | −824 | −1,063 | −1,064 | −1,063 | −782 | −989 | −987 |
| 32 | Private remittances and other transfers⁶ | −15,700 | −3,771 | −3,874 | −3,909 | −4,203 | −3,712 | −4,039 | −4,012 | −3,822 | −3,931 | −3,975 | −3,947 | −3,989 |
| 33 | U.S. assets abroad, net (increase/capital outflow (−)) | −125,851 | −7,543 | −29,389 | −51,182 | −76,240 | −102,102 | −44,088 | −5,973 | −27,940 | −55,156 | −75,343 | −100,242 | −42,852 |
| 34 | U.S. official reserve assets, net⁷ | 5,346 | 3,537 | −165 | 2,033 | −5,318 | −2,722 | −1,893 | 3,537 | −165 | 2,033 | −5,318 | −2,722 | −1,893 |
| 35 | Gold | | | | | | | | | | | | | |
| 36 | Special drawing rights | −441 | −108 | −111 | −121 | −867 | −156 | 362 | −108 | −111 | −121 | −867 | −156 | 362 |
| 37 | Reserve position in the International Monetary Fund | 494 | 251 | 273 | −27 | −526 | −786 | −991 | 251 | 273 | −27 | −526 | −786 | −991 |
| 38 | Foreign currencies | 5,293 | 3,394 | −327 | 2,181 | −3,925 | −1,780 | −1,264 | 3,394 | −327 | 2,181 | −3,925 | −1,780 | −1,264 |
| 39 | U.S. Government assets, other than official reserve assets, net | −322 | 491 | −283 | −931 | −152 | −180 | 136 | 491 | −283 | −931 | −152 | −180 | 136 |
| 40 | U.S. credits and other long-term assets | −5,182 | −983 | −1,205 | −2,247 | −1,578 | −813 | −1,178 | −983 | −1,205 | −2,247 | −1,578 | −813 | −1,178 |
| 41 | Repayments on U.S. credits and other long-term assets⁸ | 5,044 | 1,642 | 1,343 | 948 | 1,043 | 647 | 1,563 | 1,642 | 1,343 | 948 | 1,043 | 647 | 1,563 |
| 42 | U.S. foreign currency holdings and U.S. short-term assets, net | −184 | −168 | −421 | 368 | 383 | −14 | −249 | −168 | −421 | 368 | 383 | −14 | −249 |
| 43 | U.S. private assets, net | −130,875 | −11,571 | −28,941 | −52,284 | −70,770 | −99,200 | −42,331 | −10,001 | −27,492 | −56,258 | −69,873 | −97,340 | −41,095 |
| 44 | Direct investment | −49,370 | −9,320 | −11,504 | −7,946 | −23,401 | −18,988 | −22,931 | −7,750 | −10,055 | −11,920 | −22,504 | −17,128 | −21,695 |
| 45 | Foreign securities | −49,799 | −7,128 | −10,976 | −15,238 | −6,567 | −21,731 | −34,251 | −7,128 | −10,976 | −15,238 | −6,567 | −21,731 | −34,251 |
| 46 | U.S. claims on unaffiliated foreigners reported by U.S. nonbanking concerns | −32,621 | −10,230 | −6,051 | −12,449 | −11,518 | −18,499 | n.a. | −10,230 | −6,051 | −12,449 | −11,518 | −18,499 | n.a. |
| 47 | U.S. claims reported by U.S. banks, not included elsewhere | 915 | 15,107 | 1,590 | −16,651 | −29,284 | −39,982 | 14,851 | 15,107 | 1,590 | −16,651 | −29,284 | −39,982 | 14,851 |
| 48 | Foreign assets in the United States, net (increase/capital inflow (+)) | 291,365 | 46,848 | 80,214 | 84,076 | 94,683 | 124,643 | 106,198 | 46,528 | 79,736 | 84,715 | 94,841 | 124,331 | 105,664 |
| 49 | Foreign official assets in the United States, net | 39,409 | 9,162 | 19,691 | −421 | 22,308 | 37,836 | 39,479 | 9,162 | 19,691 | −421 | 22,308 | 37,836 | 39,479 |
| 50 | U.S. Government securities | 36,748 | 8,279 | 18,699 | 8,698 | 11,257 | 26,495 | 21,115 | 8,279 | 18,699 | 8,698 | 11,257 | 26,495 | 21,115 |
| 51 | U.S. Treasury securities⁹ | 30,723 | 5,919 | 16,477 | 7,470 | 10,131 | 25,169 | 20,597 | 5,919 | 16,477 | 7,470 | 10,131 | 25,169 | 20,597 |
| 52 | Other¹⁰ | 6,025 | 2,360 | 2,222 | 1,228 | 1,126 | 1,326 | 518 | 2,360 | 2,222 | 1,228 | 1,126 | 1,326 | 518 |
| 53 | Other U.S. Government liabilities¹¹ | 2,211 | 174 | 494 | 692 | −154 | 506 | 194 | 174 | 494 | 692 | −154 | 506 | 194 |
| 54 | U.S. liabilities reported by U.S. banks, not included elsewhere | 2,923 | 1,674 | 1,298 | −9,856 | 10,940 | 7,886 | 18,398 | 1,674 | 1,298 | −9,856 | 10,940 | 7,886 | 18,398 |
| 55 | Other foreign official assets¹² | −2,473 | −965 | −800 | 45 | 265 | 2,949 | −228 | −965 | −800 | 45 | 265 | 2,949 | −228 |
| 56 | Other foreign assets in the United States, net | 251,956 | 37,686 | 60,523 | 84,497 | 72,375 | 86,807 | 66,719 | 37,364 | 60,045 | 85,136 | 72,533 | 86,495 | 66,185 |
| 57 | Direct investment | 49,448 | 6,268 | 20,196 | 18,939 | 17,067 | 13,177 | 19,875 | 5,946 | 19,718 | 19,578 | 17,225 | 12,865 | 19,341 |
| 58 | U.S. Treasury securities | 33,811 | −7,317 | 5,428 | 25,929 | 29,910 | 30,315 | 36,778 | −7,317 | 5,428 | 25,929 | 29,910 | 30,315 | 36,778 |
| 59 | U.S. securities other than U.S. Treasury securities | 58,625 | 12,551 | 14,762 | 10,195 | 15,816 | 20,549 | 30,024 | 12,551 | 14,762 | 10,195 | 15,816 | 20,549 | 30,024 |
| 60 | U.S. liabilities to unaffiliated foreigners reported by U.S. nonbanking concerns | −4,324 | −2,047 | 487 | −5,242 | 10,113 | 10,527 | n.a. | −2,047 | 487 | −5,242 | 10,113 | 10,527 | n.a. |
| 61 | U.S. liabilities reported by U.S. banks, not included elsewhere | 114,396 | 28,231 | 19,650 | 34,676 | −531 | 12,239 | −19,958 | 28,231 | 19,650 | 34,676 | −531 | 12,239 | −19,958 |
| 62 | Allocations of special drawing rights | | | | | | | | | | | | | |
| 63 | Statistical discrepancy (sum of above items with sign reversed) | −14,269 | −3,154 | −5,441 | 12,936 | 13,344 | 18,847 | −16,244 | −2,567 | −12,082 | 13,718 | 19,527 | 19,178 | −23,330 |
| 63a | Of which seasonal adjustment discrepancy | | | | | | | | 587 | −6,641 | 782 | 6,183 | 331 | −7,086 |
| | Memoranda: | | | | | | | | | | | | | |
| 64 | Balance on merchandise trade (lines 2 and 16) | −166,099 | −38,148 | −49,935 | −46,472 | −39,144 | −45,229 | −49,487 | −41,494 | −44,627 | −43,488 | −45,050 | −48,802 | −43,433 |
| 65 | Balance on services (lines 3 and 17) | 59,887 | 12,368 | 16,437 | 16,458 | 16,869 | 13,049 | 16,408 | 14,571 | 15,820 | 16,021 | 15,610 | 15,369 | 15,914 |
| 66 | Balance on goods and services (lines 64 and 65) | −106,212 | −25,780 | −33,498 | −30,014 | −22,275 | −32,180 | −33,079 | −26,923 | −28,807 | −27,467 | −29,440 | −33,433 | −27,519 |
| 67 | Balance on investment income (lines 11 and 25) | −9,272 | −2,228 | −3,348 | −4,030 | −1,808 | −2,487 | −5,090 | −2,285 | −2,533 | −4,571 | −1,961 | −2,614 | −4,153 |
| 68 | Balance on goods, services, and income (lines 1 and 15 or lines 66 and 67)¹³ | −115,484 | −28,008 | −36,846 | −34,044 | −24,084 | −34,666 | −38,169 | −29,208 | −31,340 | −32,038 | −31,401 | −36,047 | −31,672 |
| 69 | Unilateral transfers (line 29) | −35,761 | −8,143 | −8,538 | −11,786 | −7,703 | −6,722 | −7,697 | −8,778 | −8,374 | −11,239 | −7,624 | −7,220 | −7,810 |
| 70 | Balance on current account (lines 1, 15, and 29 or lines 68 and 69)¹³ | −151,245 | −36,151 | −45,384 | −45,830 | −31,787 | −41,388 | −45,866 | −37,986 | −39,714 | −43,277 | −39,025 | −43,267 | −39,482 |

Source: U.S. Department of Commerce, *Survey of Current Business*, Table 1, November/December 1995.

Transactions, lines 19–24, which shows the travel and transportation expenditures of U.S. residents to other countries in 1993/1994.) *(6)* Conversely, tourism services purchased in the United States by residents of foreign countries result in an influx of exchange into the United States from other nations. The amount spent for these services is consequently treated as a **credit item** (which represents income to the U.S.) in the U.S. International Transaction Tables, and for national accounting purposes, is entered as export income. (See lines 5–7, U.S. International Transactions in Table 4.1 for travel and transportation expenditures of visitors from other countries to the U.S. in 1993/94.) In 1993, the U.S. earned a trade surplus of $17 billion in its travel account plus $3.8 billion in transportation. *(6)*

Countries that are experiencing a **trade deficit** (more imports than exports) or a flight of capital (capital outflow in excess of capital inflow) cannot survive on borrowing forever. Sooner or later, they must adopt measures to improve their **balance of payments**.

Before tourism developed into an industry where internationally important traded items were common, most balance of payments measures were based on the following:

- import duties, that is, **protective tariffs** imposed on the price of foreign merchandise imported from abroad to make foreign produced goods more expensive, thereby protecting domestic manufacturers from foreign competitors;

- import quotas, that is, restrictions on the quantity of specific types of foreign merchandise allowed into the country;

- advance import deposits, that is, a requirement obligating the purchaser to place a prescribed amount of money, equal to the price of or to a percentage of the price of the item to be imported, into a non-interest-bearing bank account in advance of receipt of the item for a mandatory time period; and

- import licenses, that is, a requirement obligating the purchaser to obtain central bank approval before ordering merchandise manufactured, produced, or processed abroad.

When services began to emerge as a factor in world trade, finance ministers began to adopt protective measures previously applied to trade-in-goods and apply them to **trade-in-services** such as finance and banking, engineering, consulting, insurance, transportation, tourism, and other services. However, because most traded services cannot be shipped internationally and physically do not enter into the customs territory of the importing country, the measures had to be carefully tailored. *(7)*

Today, an ingenious array of quantitative and nonquantitative restrictions—many of which are not immediately apparent to travelers or to travel suppliers—on the importation of tourism services has been put into place by the world's finance ministries. Regulations or practices designed to restrict importation of trade in services may include: (1) **import duty-like measures**; (2) **import quota-like restrictions**; (3) **advance import deposit-like requirements**; and (4) **import license-like requirements**. All of these measures, which are viewed as **trade barriers** to the development of an open global economic system, distort a free market system by limiting consumer choice, discouraging foreign travel, and encouraging the substitution of domestic travel services for foreign tourism services.

## Import Duty-like Measures

Duties are taxes imposed on imported goods to protect home industries and to raise revenue for government. A duty-like measure is not an import tax per se, but it acts like one by making the consumption of foreign services more expensive and thereby discourage people engaging in activities that will incur spending abroad. Import duty-like measures, as applied to tourism, can take many forms. The most common are

- a surtax (collected by banks or currency dealers) on foreign currency that residents of a country purchase before departure from home to pay travel-related expenses incurred abroad;

- a surtax (collected by travel agents or airlines) on the price of foreign air transportation or on the price of tour packages purchased by residents of a country and featuring one or more foreign destinations;

- a steep airport departure tax (for example, $100 or more);

- an excessive passport processing fee (for example, $100 or more or one that greatly exceeds the actual cost to the government of processing the passport application).

Often governments, faced with serious balance of payments problems, may impose several different types of import duty-like measures in order to deter the purchase of foreign travel services.

## Import Quota-like Restrictions

Import quotas are designed to limit the quantity of foreign goods flowing into a country as a protective measure. In the case of tourism, a quota-like restriction is intended to limit the amount of currency that may leave the country for the purchase of foreign services. The most common forms of import quota-like restriction perhaps are

- a limit on the amount of foreign exchange residents of a country may purchase from the central bank or authorized dealers before departure to pay for travel-related services procured abroad;

- a limit on the amount of national currency residents of a country may take out of the country and convert into foreign currency abroad to pay for travel-related services procured abroad.

More than 100 countries had such restrictions in place in 1986. These restrictions—sometimes referred to as **travel allowances**—ranged from lows of zero and $55 per traveler per year to $10,000 per person per trip. In one case, the travel allowance for residents bound for other countries within the same currency area was unlimited, whereas that for residents bound for countries outside that area was $750.

In other cases, exchange for foreign travel was allowed only for visits to countries whose political/economic system or predominant religion was similar to that of the traveler's country of origin. In still other cases, the amount of the allowance depended upon the purpose of travel. For example, a larger allowance was permitted for business travel than for tourism, even though the universally accepted definition of the term *tourist* includes business travelers. Laws and regulations that prescribe a more generous travel

Customs inspection, although an impediment to travel, is a necessary function in most countries.
Courtesy of David Kizer.

allowance for the business traveler unfairly discriminate against suppliers of travel-related services who cater exclusively or primarily to individuals who travel for study, health-related reasons, or recreation and leisure.

Two other common forms of import quota-like restrictions are

• prohibition or limits on residents' use of credit cards while abroad;

• extremely limited personal **customs** allowances.

Customs are taxes that a government may levy on specific types or quantities of goods purchased in a foreign country and brought home by returning residents. Custom laws and regulations affecting travelers are normally imposed for trade-related and revenue generation reasons. A country may be strict or liberal in its duty-free customs allowance, depending upon its international trade policies. The country with an excessively strict allowance is in effect penalizing other countries with generous allowances, and is behaving in a protectionist manner.

One country, for example, allows its returning residents to import free-of-duty only the baggage and personal effects they took with them when they went abroad. Another permits returning residents to claim a personal customs exemption only once a year.

A returning U.S. resident who has been out of the country for 48 hours or more and has not claimed a personal customs exemption within the previous 30 days may import, duty-free, up to $400 worth of personal and household goods acquired abroad. Returning residents who do not meet the 48-hour or 30-day time requirements may import free-of-duty up to $25 worth of personal and household goods purchased abroad. *(8)*

U.S. residents returning directly or indirectly from Guam, American Samoa, or the U.S. Virgin Islands may bring in up to $1200 worth of personal and household goods acquired abroad duty-free, providing those returning from Guam and American Samoa stayed there at least 48 hours. Those returning from the U.S. Virgin Islands are not subject to the 48-hour requirement.

## Advance Import Deposit-like Requirements

Governments use advance import deposit-like requirements to discourage purchases of foreign tourism services less frequently than they resort to duty-like measures or travel allowance restrictions. Typically, the way an advance import deposit-like requirement works is to require the would-be traveler to deposit in a non-interest-bearing bank account for a specified period, such as one year, a sum of money equal to a fixed percentage (up to 100%) of the amount of foreign currency he or she purchases before departure to pay for travel services to be obtained abroad. However, such requirements are imposed from time to time, especially in South America.

## Import License-like Requirements

A license is permission granted by government regulatory agencies as a lawful requirement before a person may engage in certain businesses, occupations, or activities. In tourism, a license-like requirement may be imposed by government to prequalify certain individuals before they leave the country. These include exit visa requirements and similar permit-type prerequisites to foreign travel, such as: *(9)*

• A sailing permit.

The United States requires residents having *resident alien* status to obtain a sailing permit from the U.S. Treasury at least 30 days before departure, attesting that they are not delinquent in the payment of any income tax liability.

• A military release or authorization.

Under certain conditions, for instance, in times of national emergency or war, the government may require that travelers of military age have either fulfilled their military obligation or have the approval of military authorities to travel abroad.

## The Need for Internationally Agreed Rules for Trade in Services

Measures such as travel allowance restrictions, travel allowance surcharges, and departure taxes exist, partly because there are no internationally agreed-upon rules for trade in services. Since the conclusion of the **General Agreement on Tariffs and Trade (GATT)** in 1947, virtually all international efforts to reduce barriers to trade have been focused on reducing and removing impediments to trade in goods among countries.

The United States has been at the forefront of efforts to bring barriers to trade in services to the international bargaining table. Some countries have joined the United States in urging the GATT machinery to examine services trade issues. However, there has been powerful resistance to the idea of making barriers to trade in services, including barriers to trade in tourism, subject to international negotiation.

Member countries of the Organization for Economic Cooperation and Development (OECD) are also taking steps to eliminate impediments to travel and to the travel-related businesses in the 24-nation area, which covers Western Europe, Scandinavia, the United States, Canada, Japan, Australia, and New Zealand.

In 1985, the OECD Tourism Committee approved an Instrument on International Tourism Policy, which reaffirmed the importance of tourism to international understanding and goodwill and its contribution to the economic prosperity and international earnings of OECD member states. In recognition of these benefits, member countries agreed to set up procedures to identify travel impediments and to take cooperative steps to eliminate them. *(10)*

## General Agreement on Trade in Services (GATS)

On April 15, 1994, 125 participants representing different governments concluded the eighth round of multilateral trade negotiations with the signing of the Uruguay Round Agreements in Marrekech, Morocco. Under the agreement, provisions on travel and tourism were considered and a subsidiary of the GATT agreement referred to as the **General Agreement on Trade in Services (GATS)** was drafted for continuing debate and eventual adoption if agreement can be reached. *(11)* GATS outlines rules that govern tourism and other service-related enterprises. The goal of GATS is to liberalize international trade policies. This requires ensuring free trade by eliminating monetary barriers, such as license fees. It also eliminates non-monetary barriers, such as import quotas, and is beneficial to all the countries involved. *(12)*

The principles mentioned in the GATS include issues such as

- market access: markets will be accessible and open to competition among member countries

- national treatment: countries will accord competitors from other member countries the same treatment as they do their own domestic service-related businesses

- commercial presence: countries will encourage investments by their own nationals to establish service-related enterprises in other member countries so as to have commercial presence for promoting international trade

- **transparency**: the published laws and regulations of member countries are "transparent" or clear to all and nothing is to be hidden that would obstruct transnational competition.

These principles ensure open market access and a level playing field for tourism service providers wishing to do business in the member countries of the GATT/GATS.

If and when agreement on the application of these four principles is reached, it will represent a "first" in the annals of international tourism *and* international trade.

# $\mathcal{T}$HE IMPACT OF BARRIERS TO TRADE IN TOURISM SERVICES

The economic impact of governmental financial and trade policies on international trade in tourism and on the tourism industry has never been measured. Nevertheless, there are compelling reasons to suspect that such policies may affect the tourist industry more negatively than they do other commercial activities and other industries.

The sale of tourism services internationally is unlike trade in goods, wherein the merchandise is sold and shipped to the foreign market. It is also unlike trade in other services, such as insurance, banking, or consulting, wherein the provider exports the service by making it available in the foreign market. A hotelier cannot float his or her hotel to a foreign country and sell accommodations to that country's residents or visitors—his or her "product" is stationary. Even an airline, which does own portable working assets, is rarely permitted to sell available seat-miles between points within a foreign country; it can "export" transportation only to those foreign nationals who are leaving or returning to (and are, therefore, outside of) their own country. In short, tourism services can be exported only if a resident of one country visits another country and, either enroute or at the destination, procures the services of that country's airlines or consumes its tourism products.

Financial and trade policies that prevent or deter a national tourism market from traveling abroad, therefore, severely limit the *export ability* of foreign tourism enterprises. Goods exporters would be affected in a comparable manner only if governments prevented the importation of foreign-made goods altogether or imposed such restrictive quotas that meaningful trade could not occur.

Another reason why government financial and trade policies may affect tourism more negatively than other industries is that tourism services, unlike goods and many other services, are highly perishable. They cannot be stored in inventory for future sale if not sold when offered. A hotel room-night, if unused, perishes at checkout time the next day. Unused available seat-miles expire once an airplane takes off. If trade barriers prevent or deter a market from being created at the time that the service is offered, the value of the service expires, contributing nothing to cover the cost of the provider's investment. Unused services, however, by virtue of being offered, add to the investor's fixed overhead and sunk costs.

## The Impact of Barrier-free Travel

Nowhere are the benefits of free trade in international tourism more obvious than in the Asia-Pacific area, where arrivals and receipts are growing more rapidly than in any other region of the world. Over the past decade, visitor arrivals in the region have risen nearly 250% from 29 million in 1985 to over 72 million arrivals in 1994. *(13)* Since 1985, the average annual tourist growth rate for Asia-Pacific, according to the World Tourism Organization, has been 10.7% as compared to 5.8% for the world as a whole. The average annual growth rate in receipts for the Asia Pacific region has been at 21.4% compared to 15.7% for the world as a whole. Roughly two-thirds of the Asia-Pacific's visitor arrivals originate within the region itself.

In making a case for the benefits of free trade, it cannot be a coincidence that of the region's nearly 20 constituent countries, four countries—Singapore, Malaysia, and Japan, and the Special Administrative Region (SAR) of Hong Kong—impose *no* travel allowance restrictions. Two others, South Korea and Australia, permit relatively generous travel allowances.

# Trade Barriers and International Dairy Queen

When Minneapolis-based International Dairy Queen went to set up shop in Korea, the government provided the company with a list of products that could be imported to supply the operation. But when the operations were set to go and International Dairy Queen tried to import toppings for its sundaes, the company found it wasn't allowed to import anything with preservatives. So the manufacturer had to scramble to create an importable product for the scheduled grand opening.

In China, six months after International Dairy Queen launched a successful unit in Beijing, the government notified the company that the department-store building in which it and other stores were housed would be torn down to accommodate road expansion. "That sets you back," says Ed Watson, executive vice president of operations for International Dairy Queen. "There were no explanations, no discussion, and no government compensation. Our partner lost $2 million on that site."

Problems with local governments represent just a few of the difficulties that can arise in doing business abroad. Other serious differences and problems may occur, such as customs, business etiquette and ethics, graft, and fluctuating exchange rates.

*Source:* An excerpt from Restaurants USA, November 1995, used with the permission of the National Restaurant Association.

Dairy Queen in Seoul, Korea.
Credit: International Dairy Queen, Inc.

# INTERNAL GOVERNMENT REGULATIONS

Nations sometimes restrict the freedom of movement and itineraries of inbound foreign tourists for political, security, or other reasons, even if the two states are not at war and do recognize each other diplomatically. As mentioned earlier, U.S. visitor visas are denied to aliens who are believed to engage in activities that are prejudicial to the interest of the United States or harmful to its security, as in the case of known terrorists.

Because some adult citizens of Communist countries are Party members, they can be granted a U.S. visitor visa only by exception. Successful applicants must obtain a "Waiver of Grounds of Inadmissibility," a document that may be granted at the discretion of the U.S. Attorney General if temporary admission of the prospective visitor is recommended by a consular officer and is believed to be in the national interest. *(14)*

In practice, communists whose admission to the United States would serve educational, cultural, scientific, or humanitarian objectives, such as artists, writers, actors, and scientists, tend to find it easier to obtain the necessary waiver than those with other occupations.

The means to which governments resort to regulating the activities of tourists can be as ignominious as they are ingenious. Under U.S. regulations, for example, polygamists are *not* ineligible for a visitor visa, but prostitutes and former prostitutes are. Moreover, visa eligibility standards can be written to favor certain nationalities or genders.

## Admission Restrictions

Special admission restrictions may be imposed by countries to regulate tourism or its effects. Iran refuses both admission and transit to "women not wearing Islamic head cover, scarf, long sleeves, or stockings." Libyan law denies entry to "women married to nationals of Arab League countries traveling without their husband, unless holding a **No Objection Certificate (NOC)** issued by the Libyan Immigration Department *and* is met upon arrival by the resident relative who applied for the NOC" or "unless traveling to join their husband *and* met upon arrival by their husband. The passenger must hold a telegram specifying that the husband is waiting at the airport of the destination and must submit a marriage certificate if traveling in a 'single' status." Syria refuses admission to "all female nationals of Afghanistan, Bangladesh, the Philippines, Sri Lanka, and Thailand, even if holding a visa, unless they have written approval from the head of immigration at Damascus."

With respect to denial on the basis of appearance, Singapore reserves the right to deny entry to visitors with long untidy hair and dressed in an offensive manner. Costa Rica bans "gypsies of any country and visitors (wearing)…long and unkempt hair, beards, and indecent clothing." The Dominican Republic refuses entry to nationals of "any country in case they are members of the religious group 'Hare Krishna,'" and "persons with long hair, beard, mustache, or highly informal clothing and those *under suspicion* may be subject to a body search…"

Where behavior is the basis for denial, Saudi Arabia denies admission to travelers "arriving in an apparent intoxicated state, women exposing legs or arms, or wearing too thin or too tight clothes, men wearing shorts exposing legs, and men and women displaying affection in public in any manner or mixing in supermarkets or market places…Wives traveling unaccompanied, joining their husband, must be met at the airport by sponsor or husband if their final destination is in the Eastern Province (Al Hasa)."

## Exit Restrictions

Some governments establish **exit restrictions** to curb outbound travel to other countries and to serve political-economic objectives. By demanding that its nationals obtain permission to leave the country, an authoritarian government can:

- ensure that they are not exposed to democratic self-rule or alternative economic systems;
- muzzle opposition leaders whose views might embarrass the regime if communicated to the free press in other countries;
- demonstrate its displeasure with and disapproval of the policies of other governments;
- protest what it believes to be discriminatory admission restrictions imposed on its citizens by another government or governments;
- limit the amount of exchange flowing out of the country and into the tourist industry of an "unfriendly" nation.

## Import Restrictions

In some cases, international politics or religious considerations determine what types of goods and how much a government will permit a traveler to bring home. For example, Libya prohibits, among other things, "goods of Israeli origin and certain makes of records and tapes (RCA), Coca Cola (and) other articles produced by companies which trade with Israel." Equatorial Guinea bans "Spanish newspapers for passengers and crew." The Maldive Islands does not allow passengers to bring in "alcoholic beverages, pork, opium, ganja, cocaine, pornographic materials, goods of Israeli origin or idols of worship." Residents of, or visitors to, Sudan may not bring in "goods from Israel." Turkey prohibits "more than one set of playing cards."

The purposes behind other customs prohibitions and restrictions are less apparent. For instance, Fiji permits the importation of dogs and cats from New Zealand and certain Australian states, provided "the animals are shipped in a 'nose and pawproof' container." Nigeria imposes a "penalty of heavy fine or imprisonment of at least six months" on passengers attempting to bring "champagne or sparkling wine" into the country.

The crux of the matter with respect to travel restrictions is that tourism has a significance far greater than whatever therapeutic, educational, or cultural value it may offer the individual tourist, or whatever profit it may bring to the travel seller. It has consequences for governments. In the case of totalitarian nations, it affects their ability to manage public opinion and control dissent.

A government's decision to admit foreign tourists is a political action. To allow in travelers from other countries is to showcase the nation, its institution, its economic system, and its standard of living and to invite comparison—one reason, perhaps, why even developing countries have spent millions of scarce, hard-earned dollars to spruce up their countries prior to a major convention that attracts thousands of visitors. Inbound tourism builds an image of the country abroad, exposing the visiting foreign tourist to the good and the bad. At the same time, it exposes host country nationals to the visitor who, in addition to being a witness to the local lifestyle, can be a source of information—or impressions—about his or her own country and culture and, provided there is no language barrier, a potential protagonist for his or her nation's policies.

President Dwight D. Eisenhower recognized the political ramification of tourism when he issued his personal message to American citizens who traveled abroad during the late 1950s:

> Year after year, increasing numbers of our citizens travel to foreign countries. In most of these lands there exists a reservoir of goodwill for the United States and knowledge of what we stand for. In some areas, our country and its aspirations are less well understood.

> As you travel abroad, the respect you show for foreign laws and customs, your courteous regard for other ways of life, and your speech and manner help to mold the reputation of our *country*. Thus, you represent us all in bringing assurance to the people you meet that the United States is a friendly nation and one dedicated to the search for world peace and to the promotion of the well-being and security of the community of nations. *(15)*

Tourism has political implications for the governments of the Third World as well as for those of East and West. In the words of the French magazine, *Economia*, "not only do tourists impose their lifestyle and beliefs, but, to a certain extent, they create a political dependence—you don't stage a revolution in front of paying guests!" There are exceptions, of course; tourists are sometimes the political targets of dissidents who seek attention from the world press. But these contentions, as a rule, contain an element of truth.

Tourists take with them their own peculiar tastes and standards of living, to which the host country must cater if it expects repeat business. The need to accommodate these special requirements often results, at least in less developed areas, in a further need for imported capital, imported technology, or even imported management skills. Some host countries, as a consequence, find themselves offering investment incentives to prospective foreign investors or searching for foreign financial participation in local projects such as hotels, casinos, country clubs, or other resorts designed to serve the inbound visitor. Once built, these foreign-financed facilities become indispensable as economic assets. They provide jobs, generate tax revenues, and result in **foreign exchange earnings**.

This fact has political as well as economic significance. The government of a country whose economy depends on inbound tourists and/or imported capital must maintain internal stability and order—or try to—for it cannot afford to alienate its absentee investors or the tourists who constitute its major source of export revenue and job opportunities.

In any other export industry, the product is manufactured or otherwise processed and leaves the country. In international tourism, the export product remains stationary, and the buyer, the tourist, comes to the seller. If the product has been blown up by terrorists, if there is civil war, religious or racial unrest, or danger of a surprise terrorist attack or military takeover, the tourists do not come; they go elsewhere.

In a very real sense, one nation's tourist investments in and/or its tourist traffic to another country constitute a subtle form of political influence. That influence may be inadvertent, or even unrecognized, on the part of the traffic-generating country, but it is there nonetheless. One noted authority, Jean-Maurice Thurot, of the Tourism Studies

Center, Universite d' Aix-en-Provence, has likened tourism (with apologies to von Clausewitz) to "a simple continuation of politics by other means."

Thurot wrote in *Economia*:

> In a system where the techniques of military confrontation become more and more burdensome, *touristic subversion*...is an interesting alternative. These days, a successful political influence can be accomplished not by military bases but by tourists' investments. Or by both at once, as the Americans have done, establishing hotels that *protect* the bases...In this regard, the successful American touristic development of Puerto Rico, compared to the failure of American military operations in Cuba, symbolizes the efficiency of *touristic subversion* as opposed to classic military strategy. *(16)*

## The Helsinki Accord

Because international tourism is often promoted as the "peace industry" since tourism cannot survive where there is hostility or conflict, many governments will at least pay lip service to facilitating it.

In 1975, at the European Conference on security and Cooperation in Helsinki, Finland, 35 nations, including the United States, were signatories to the **Helsinki Accord**. The accord, among other things, established principles "in favor of simplification and a harmonization of administrative formalities in the field of international transport, in particular at frontiers" and expressed the member nations' intention to encourage increased tourism on both an individual and group basis by

- dealing in a positive spirit with questions connected with the allocation of financial means for tourist travel abroad, as well as with those connected with the formalities required for such travel;

- facilitating the activities of foreign travel agencies and passenger transport companies in the promotion of international tourism;

- encouraging tourism outside of the peak season;

- gradually simplifying and administering flexible procedures for exit and entry;

- easing regulations concerning movement of citizens from the other participating states in their territory, with due regard to security requirements;

- considering, as necessary, means for improvement of arrangements to provide consular assistance; and

- facilitating the convening of meetings as well as travel by delegations, groups, and individuals. *(17)*

In the accord, the member states acknowledged the significant contribution of international tourism to the development of mutual understanding among people. They further acknowledged that more opportunities for tourism would be essential for the development of cooperation among nations. Although the Helsinki Accord was drafted more than two decades ago, the principles embodied in this document still serve today as world guidelines for dealing with tourism issues.

## WTO Facilitation Efforts

In December 1986, the Executive Council of the World Tourism Organization transmitted to member-governments for comment a "Draft **Convention** to Facilitate Travel and Tourist Stays Through Passport, Visa and Health and Exchange Control Measures." Prepared by, and under the aegis of the Organization's Facilitation Committee, the convention was designed to facilitate travel between contracting states. If and when this agreement is formally adopted, the member-governments of the WTO would be obligated to undertake to facilitate travel and tourist stays in accordance with the Standards and Recommended Practices contained in the following three Annexes:

- Annex I contains Standards and Recommended Practices on Passport and Visa Formalities and Facilities;

- Annex II, Recommended Practices on Health Formalities and Facilities and Facilitation of Travel and Tourist Stays for the Disabled; and

- Annex III, Recommended Practices on Currency Formalities and Facilities and Taxes, Fees, Duties and Related Charges Applicable to Travel and Tourist Stays. *(18)*

The draft convention, or agreement, was adopted by the Organization's General Assembly at its 7th Session in September 1987, and the subject remains one of continuing discussion.

## The Developmental Role of Governments

Governments promote and control international tourism. In fact, tourism has the distinction of being one of the few industries that governments of all persuasions and intergovernmental bodies have sought to develop. In their book, *The Golden Hordes*, Louis Turner, a research specialist in multinational corporations and his coauthor, writer John Ash, sum up the situation well: "In most industries...competition is normally just between companies; in tourism...(it is)...between nations." *(19)*

# SUMMARY

Governmental control over the flow of international travel is often underestimated or unrecognized by the general public. Before citizens of one nation may cross the borders of another nation, there must first be established diplomatic agreements which permit travel between the two countries. Moreover, the various types of government agreements can serve to either encourage or hamper the flow of travelers. Internal government regulations such as those relating to import, exit, and admission restrictions generally pose as barriers to the development of tourism, while bilateral agreements on tourism cooperation can encourage tourism. Because tourism dollars are viewed either as an import or an export, trade issues are frequently at the heart of a government's policy toward travel and tourism development.

It is important to understand that tourism has a significance reaching far above its educational, cultural, or environmental implications. Not only does it affect a country's finances and balance of trade, but, for certain authoritarian societies, exposure to people of other countries may have political ramifications as well. Efforts have been made by numerous international and regional tourism organizations to facilitate travel among countries; and there has been agreement in principle that the simplification of travel is a desired goal. Notwithstanding these intentions, travel barriers imposed by governments continue to be a major obstacle in the development of international travel.

# DISCUSSION QUESTIONS

1. What are the fundamental actions that governments must take for international tourism to occur?

2. What are the two types of diplomatic recognition? How do they differ from each other?

3. What are typical responsibilities of consular personnel?

4. What are the main features of procompetitive air transport agreements?

5. Why do governments restrict the movement of foreign tourists? What types of internal government regulations exist to restrict travel of foreign tourists?

6. Why might governments wish to restrict the outbound travel of its own nationals? What types of regulations or policies would a government impose to restrict the departure of nationals from visiting other countries?

7. Explain the general issue of tourism trade barriers and how these barriers may affect a nation's or the global economy.

8. What were some of the underlying principles of the Helsinki Accord and why did so many nations support this accord?

9. Why are limits imposed on the amount of a product being brought from one country to another?

10. What is the Bermuda Agreement? Is it still in effect?

11. Describe what a trade deficit is in terms of exports and imports.

12. Name four import duty-like measures.

# SUGGESTED STUDENT PROJECTS

Research the travel and tourism policies of two different countries—one that you think has more liberal policies and one you suspect has more restrictive policies.

1. Compare the two countries' travel requirements in the following:

   a. Passport processing fees and conditions for issuance

   b. Visa application—difficulty and cost of application

   c. Entry and exit requirements, if any

   d. Travel allowances for departing residents

    e. Currency restrictions, if any, applied to foreign visitors or to departing residents

    f. Surcharge, if any, on foreign air transportation

    g. Surcharge, if any, on tour packages purchased by residents

    h. Departure taxes

    i. Duty-free exemptions on customs for returning residents

    j. Duty-free (tax rebates) for purchases made by visitors

    k. Travel impediments, such as excessive hotel and other taxes

2. Compare the tourism statistics of the two countries. Which one is more successful? Analyze and explain. (In some cases, you may find the answers surprising.)

# $\mathcal{R}$EFERENCES

1. USTTA, *World Tourism at the Millennium*. U.S. Department of Commerce. April 1993. pg. 34, 42.

2. World Travel and Tourism Review 1993, Vol. 3, CAB International, p. 91.

3. Title 22—Foreign Relations, Code of Federal Regulations, Office of the *Federal Register*. National Archives and Records Service, General Services Administration, Washington, D.C.: Government Printing Office, 1994.

4. Pina, Michael. *Travel Weekly*, October 17, 1994.

5. Bevans, C.I. *Treaties and Other International Agreements of the United States of America, 1776–1949*, Vol. 7. Washington, D.C.: Government Printing Office, 1980.

6. U.S. Department of Commerce. Bureau of Economic Analysis. "Table 1—U.S. International Transactions." Survey of Current Business, Vol. 74, No. 12, (Washington, D.C.: December 1994).

7. International Monetary Fund. "Main Developments in Restrictive Practices, Current Invisibles." *Exchange Arrangements and Exchange Restrictions, Annual Report 1985*. (Washington, D.C.:1985).

8. U.S. Customs Service. Department of the Treasury. *Know Before You Go. No. 512, Customs Hints for Returning Residents*. Washington, D.C.: 1994.

9. Linaras, P. "U.S.A." *TIM, Travel Information Manual* (Schiphol Airport, The Netherlands: May 1985)

10. "Travel & Tourism: OECD Countries Move to Eliminate Travel Obstacles." *Business America* (April 15, 1985).

11. Handszuh, Henry K. "Trade in Tourism Services under the Uruguay Round." *Tourism Management*. Sept. 1992: pg. 263.

12. USTTA. *World Tourism at the Millennium*. U.S. Department of Commerce. April 1993, pg. 35.

13. PATA Annual Statistical Report 1994, Pacific Asia Travel Association, San Francisco, California, 1995.

14. Treaties and International Agreement Series, TIAS 9903. Office of the Legal Advisor, Office of Treaty Affairs, Washington, D.C.: Department of State, 1980.

15. Randall, C.B. *International Travel*. Report to the President of the United States. Washington, D.C.: Government Printing Office. April 17, 1958.

16. Thurot, J.M. "Tourism: Political Weapon." *Economia* (May 1975).

17. U.S. Department of State, Conference on Security and Cooperation in Europe: Final Act. Bulletin 73, no. 1888, September 1, 1975.

18. Facilitation Committee, World Tourism Organization. *Report on the Subsidiary Organs of the Council, (a) Facilitation Committee, Appendix, Draft Convention to Facilitate Travel and Tourist Stays Through Passport, Visa and Health and Exchange Control Measures*. 29th Session, WTO Executive Council, Provisional Agenda Item 10(a). Madrid: November 12, 1986.

19. Turner, L., and J. Ash. *The Golden Hordes, International Tourism and the Pleasure Periphery*. London: Constable and Company Ltd., 1975.

# Chapter 5

# National Tourism Administration and Public Policy

## LEARNING OBJECTIVES

- To gain an insight into the evolving role of national tourism administration.

- To appreciate the shaping of national tourism goals and public policy.

- To understand forms of public policy and the policy-making process.

- To have a perspective of the functions of national tourism offices.

- To be familiar with the organizational structure of national tourism offices.

- To have an overview of the functions of international tourism organizations.

- To define and use the following terms:

| | |
|---|---|
| Amicus curiae brief | Canadian Tourism Commission (CTC) |
| Asia Pacific Economic Cooperation (APEC) | Gross Domestic Product (GDP) |
| Australian National Tourism Organization | Japan National Tourist Organization (JNTO) |

National Tourism Policy Act

North American Free Trade Agreement (NAFTA)

National Tourism Administration (NTA)

National Tourism Organization (NTO)

Organization of American States (OAS)

Organization for Economic Cooperation and Development (OECD)

Privatization

Public Private Partnership

Public policy

Tourism policies

Tourism Policy and Export Promotion Act

Travel Industry Association of America (TIA)

U.S.-Japan Tourism Exchange Promotion Program

# ROLE OF THE NATIONAL TOURISM ADMINISTRATION

*A* **national tourism administration (NTA)**, also known as a **national tourism organization (NTO)**, is the central governmental body charged with the responsibility of carrying out public policies addressed to the travel and tourism interests of a nation. For the sake of uniformity, the term NTA will be used throughout this chapter; however, the student should be aware the term NTO may be more commonly used in his/her part of the world. It is difficult to fully explain the role of an NTA/NTO in other than general terms since no single model exists as a common standard globally, and there are numerous factors which determine and shape the structure, status, role, and specific functions of the NTA/NTO office of any given country. These factors include, but are not limited to, the following:

- The macro-economic policy of a country.

- The type of economy, whether mainly free enterprise or mainly centrally planned.

- The framework of public administration and assignment of responsibility for different aspects of travel and tourism

- The various institutions—public, private, and voluntary—that are involved in tourism development, promotion, distribution, operation, or education

- Compelling national interests and government priority assigned to the pursuit of travel and tourism goals

In the U.S., for instance, tourism is considered as being largely a private sector activity, thus the federal role in tourism has never been a clear mandate of any particular administration. In general, however, there is consensus among the member states belonging to the World Tourism Organization that the central role of the NTA should be *to ensure that the country will benefit to the maximum extent possible from the economic and social contributions of tourism.* These contributions are defined in such economic terms as the growth in **gross domestic product (GDP)**—which is income produced within a nation—tourism employment or regional development, or in such social terms as the protection of cultural heritage, promotion of cultural and social values or preservation of the natural environment for the enjoyment of generations.

To fulfill its role, the NTA seldom, if ever, has all of the power and authority it requires to implement the goals and policies identified to tourism. Instead, its role must often be one of persuasion, compromise, and coordination with other agencies within government administration and/or with the private sector if anything is to be accomplished. It is perhaps the ambiguity of the entire situation that makes the NTA an endlessly interesting subject for study and debate.

## Tourism Goals, Objectives, and Policies

The objective of **tourism policies** are not always understood nor accepted by the industry most affected by it. The travel industry often sees itself as being over-regulated and under-supported by government. It is *not* the job of government, for instance, to promote or foster the growth in tourism for its own sake, but rather for the benefits that will accrue to the people from such growth. The goal in tourism may indeed be expressed as one of fostering growth, but the policy which follows this goal will be more broadly stated and have deeper implications. Ultimately, the objective of government policy is to improve the lives of citizens and advance the progress of the nation.

Goals and objectives in tourism may encompass both domestic and international concerns. Although they are not the same, they may at times overlap. The goal of generating revenues from tourism, for example, may have application to either domestic or international tourism. The difference is that in domestic tourism, the revenues from tourism represents a redistribution of national income, whereas the revenue from international tourism represents export income that will contribute to the balance of trade of a country within the international community.

Among the more typical tourism goals and objectives adopted by NTAs for policy resolution are the following:

### Domestic Goals and Objectives

- national cohesion and a sense of national identity;
- public understanding of national institutions and of the political responsibilities of citizens;
- public health and well-being;
- balanced economic growth/redistribution of national income;
- public respect for the environment;
- preservation of regional and minority traditions;
- protection of the right of the individual to leisure time for recreation and tourism activities as a quality of life issue.

International Goals and Objectives

- increased export earnings;

- economic development through foreign investments in tourism enterprises and jobs creation;

- increased national income and more tax revenue;

- expanded infrastructure to serve foreign visitors and community needs;

- closer ties with citizens living abroad as expatriates;

- favorable foreign public opinion and greater understanding of the nation's social and cultural accomplishments and contributions to the world community;

- preservation of the nation's cultural heritage;

- strengthened diplomatic ties with other nations;

- promoting international understanding and contributing to peace.

Table 5.1 provides a synopsis of national tourism policies of selected countries. Despite the clear-cut goals, NTAs as a whole tend to occupy one of the most ambiguous positions in government. Because tourism, at least mass tourism, is a relatively recent phenomenon, most NTAs are late arrivals, comparatively speaking, on the governmental scene and are less powerful—and less accepted—than the traditional departments in government that deal with the affairs of state, health and welfare, labor, education, justice, defense, and so on.

**TABLE 5.1**
**National Tourism Policy of Selected Countries**

| Country | Existence of National Tourism Policy | Sources/Form of Tourism Policy | Key Tourism/Policy Goals/Objectives |
|---|---|---|---|
| Australia | Yes | Legislative mandate for Department of Tourism | Optimize tourism contribution to national income, employment growth and balance of payments; provide for sustainable tourism development; enhance access to quality tourism experience; and support tourism promotion, research and statistical information |
| Austria | No | Internal tourism agency policy | Maximize visitor traffic through marketing strategies such as image building and active promotion of attractions |
| Canada | Yes (federal policy; no national policy) | Legislative mandate for Dept. of Industry, Science and Technology | Sustain a vibrant and profitable Canadian tourism industry |

*Continued*

| | TABLE 5.1 *(CONTINUED)* | | |
|---|---|---|---|
| **National Tourism Policy of Selected Countries** | | | |
| **Country** | **Existence of National Tourism Policy** | **Sources/Form of Tourism Policy** | **Key Tourism/Policy Goals/Objectives** |
| France | Yes | Legislative mandates for tourism/ tourism-related agencies Economic/social development plans | Expand overall tourism demand; stimulate development of employment and income in rural areas; support tourism opportunities for medium- and low-income segments of the population |
| Hong Kong | No | Internal tourism agency policy | Maximize international visitor traffic |
| Ireland | Yes | Independent legislative mandate | Maximize benefits from promotion/development of tourism by optimizing income from tourism as well as tourism's contribution to the balance of payments, quality of life, enhancement and protection of cultural heritage, and conservation of physical resources |
| Japan | Yes | Independent legislative mandate | Support growth of domestic and international tourism; contribute to international tourism; combine to international friendship, development of the economy, and reduction in regional economy, and reduction in regional economic and social differences |
| Mexico | Yes | Independent legislative mandate | Promote tourism; protect tourism activities; and create, conserve, protect, and develop tourism resources |
| Spain | Yes | Legislative mandates for tourism/ tourism-related agencies Economic/social development plans | Support growth in international visitor traffic; promote growth in urban recreational facilities; maximize employment and income from tourism; reduce regional disparities in income |
| Sweden | Yes | Legislative mandates for tourism/ tourism related agencies | Government support to planning and evaluation of tourism promotional activities abroad but leaving operational activities to private sector |
| United Kingdom | Yes | Independent legislative mandate | Encourage visitor traffic to and within Great Britain; encourage provision and improvement of tourism amenities; maximize tourism's contribution to employment and income |
| United States | Yes | Legislative mandates for U.S. Travel and Tourism Administration | Promote travel to and within the U.S.; encourage economic growth and stability; improve international competitiveness; and expand foreign exchange earnings |

*Source:*  Compiled from tourism studies listed in endnotes 4, 10, and OECD Tourism Policy and International Tourism.

The policies and actions of other agencies, moreover, are often diametrically opposed to those of the NTA. For example, a finance ministry may advocate higher interest rates at the very time the NTA is encouraging investment in new tourist class hotels. Or, a civil aviation authority may approve a hike in international air fares just as the NTA releases its overseas advertising campaign. Or immigration officials may impose a stringent person by person entry check to stem terrorism just as the NTA introduces a "Come Visit the Friendly People" campaign in neighboring countries. Such counterproductive wheel spinning is not necessarily due to any deliberate decision to thwart tourism; rather, it is understood that a country will always give higher priority to matters of safety, health and welfare, internal security, immigration control, and similar national concerns than it will give to tourism promotion or tourism facilitation.

## The Bureaucracy Problem

Even in nations with planned, highly-controlled economies and authoritarian political systems, government is rarely the monolithic, highly-calibrated, precision machine it is often believed to be. It is an assortment of departments, commissions, administrations, agencies, and bureaus—or their equivalent—each with a different goal and mission.

In democracies, with their tendency toward decentralized control and separation of powers, the governing apparatus is even more labyrinthine. There are not only different *levels* of government, but different *branches*; and within a single branch, there may be agencies or sub-committees that represent diverse constituencies with conflicting interests and sometimes irreconcilable differences. Bureaucrats are organized into homogeneous units with narrowly defined objectives, highly specialized tasks, and reasonably cohesive "clientele" groups.

In such an environment, communication between bureaus is often an ideal to be attained; and efficient management borders on the impossible. Policies and programs tend to be framed in semi-isolation by autonomous groups of functionaries who do not always consider the possible impact of their decisions on the mission or work of other agencies. Because state intervention in immigration and travel (the requiring of entrance and exit permits and customs inspection of travelers) preceded governmental entry into tourism promotion, those agencies whose missions include the investigation or inspection of inbound tourists tend to regard their work as having precedence over that of the national tourism office. In their view, tourism is a nuisance that aggravates security problems, complicates the collection of customs duties, and increases the likelihood of entry by illegal or undesirable aliens.

The proper role and place of national tourism offices in the administrative hierarchy vary widely from country to country, and are heatedly debated by public administrators. There is virtually no agreement as to (1) whether the NTA should be autonomous or located within a ministerial department; (2) the appropriate ministerial department for housing the NTA—assuming it is agreed that the office should be lodged in a department; (3) the functions and responsibilities that should be assigned to the NTA; (4) the governmental character or status of the NTA (at least six of the world's national tourist organizations are nongovernmental and some dozen or more, semigovernmental), and more recently (5) the question of whether there should be an NTA at all or, alternatively, to privatize the NTA. This latter issue will be discussed in another section.

# 𝒯OURISM ADMINISTRATION AND THE PUBLIC POLICY FORMULATION

The process of **public policy** formulation is complicated. In the United States, public policy at the federal level is developed by each of the three branches of government, both jointly and separately. A policy, once declared as such, may take various forms including:

1. *regulations* or orders issued by an agency of the executive branch, such as the Department of Transportation, or by a quasi-independent regulatory agency;

2. *legislation* proposed by (a) an agency of the executive branch and transmitted to the Congress by "executive communication;" (b) a member of committee of the Congress, or (c) constituents or interest groups exercising the First Amendment right of petition;

3. *decisions* or decrees handed down by courts of the judicial branch in civil and criminal cases;

4. *treaties* or other international agreements negotiated by the executive branch (e.g., the Department of State) with foreign countries and ratified by the Senate.

Regardless of the crucible in which it is formed, public policy is subject to a variety of influences and inputs at every juncture of the shaping process. The regulated present their views to their regulators by submitting petitions, motions, briefs, or exhibits relevant to proposed rule-makings, rate-settings, or route awards or by presenting oral arguments at public hearings. Affected interest groups may influence policy decisions by giving testimony on pending legislation at hearings. They may also lobby individual legislators and provide volunteer information to committee staff preparing the reports representing either majority or minority views on a specific bill. In court cases that may determine policy, an interest group who is not party to a suit may submit a "friend of the court brief" (**amicus curiae brief**) to give information to the court on some matter of law which is in doubt or to urge a particular resolution on behalf of public interest.

Corporations, associations, unions, and other groups whose rights or interests are likely to be affected by proposed treaties or agreements advise U.S. negotiators prior to or during the negotiation process. These groups may also testify at open hearings on the signed agreement, lobby key senators, and make their opinions known at the White House. In addition, groups with an interest in legislative or administrative action often attempt to influence public policy by still another avenue—by molding public opinion and mobilizing public support via cogently conceived, carefully conducted publicity campaigns.

It has been estimated that the United States harbors thousands of individual interest groups. The 1995 *Encyclopedia of Associations* (Vol. 1 and 2) lists over 22,000 national and over 80,000 regional, state, and local professional and business groups that share common interests and hold regular meetings. Not all of these groups are politically active, but many have at least participated in ad hoc lobbies in order to affect some phase of the political process.

Public administrators, such as department and agency heads, also attempt to influence legislative action. Federal agencies propose legislative programs, which are packages of draft legislation that they believe will advance their objectives. The purposes of these programs include helping to shape the administration's position on legislation proposed by members of Congress, other agencies, citizens, or interest groups; presenting testimony at public hearings; and providing advice to the President on the desirability of enrolled enactments.

Public policy formulation, in short, is a process of conflict and compromise, a matter of mediating between competing groups with "private interests" and defining the "public interest" or the "national interest." (See Figure 5.1) Public agencies, such as national tourist offices, make and impact on this process only if they make their priorities and imperatives known at the right time to the right people. Herein lies the problem. As a rule, national tourism offices have tended to see their most important function as marketing rather than policy-making. Consequently, they have not always obtained the cooperation, or been able to influence the actions of other agencies whose support is essential. Even in countries that have attempted to give the NTA a greater policy voice, other interests have been more vocal or more powerful.

Efforts to strengthen the political muscle of the U.S. Travel Service (USTS)—the forerunner to the **U.S. Travel and Tourism Administration (USTTA)**—experienced slow progress in early years. In 1971, former Director C. Langhorne Washburn was elevated by law to the status of assistant secretary of commerce for tourism in an attempt to place

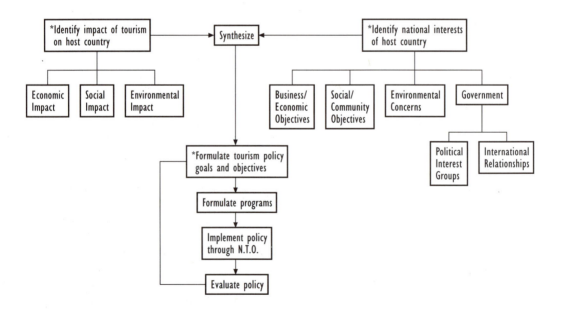

*Input from the general public and the industry may be solicited or invited at each decision point.

**Figure 5.1**   Tourism policy formulation.

the organization on par with other national tourist organizations in foreign countries. But the elevation bestowed no additional or expressed policy-making powers and, in Washington, D.C., where emperors, sheiks, and other potentates are commonplace, there was little lasting impact. In 1975, the agency barely escaped being abolished after the President's Office of Management and Budget (OMB) proposed that it be terminated. OMB's reasoning was that the USTS was not essential for balance of payments purposes or to the foreign policy objectives of the United States. *(1)* The U.S. Travel and Tourism Administration (USTTA), which replaced the USTS in 1981, was in constant threat of abolishment under successive White House administrations. Ironically, at the first ever White House Conference on Travel and Tourism held in October, 1995, USTTA Under Secretary Greg Farmer announced that USTTA would cease to exist as of August 1996 even as President Clinton declared his support for the travel industry at the conference. This is simply one more example of the uncertain status of the world's national tourism organizations.

## Tourism Administrations and the National Interest

Capitalist governments intervene in the private sector to protect or to pursue perceived national interests, such as national security, domestic order, access to vital natural resources, economic stability, full employment, and public health. A crisis in any of these areas of national interest inevitably alters the rank and priority not only of the affected interest, but of all other interests. A shortage of fuel can make it more imperative to conserve energy than to stimulate industries that consume it. An air quality alert can raise public health to a higher level of priority than industrial development and full employment. Civil rioting or terroristic threats can, if only temporarily, cause domestic order to take precedence over civil liberties.

In rank order of national priorities, tourism is especially vulnerable. Its negative impact on important national interest, such as environmental quality, fuel conservation, and wildlife preservation, is all too visible, while its positive impact on equally important national interests, such as national security, domestic order, economic stability, full employment, and public health, is strictly invisible and, for the large part, undocumentable.

The ambiguous status of the world's NTAs is partly a reflection of the amorphous nature of the travel industry itself—an industry that is highly fragmented, comprising more than 30 subindustries (see Chapter 1), each with its own trade association. Consequently, the travel industry does not always speak with one voice or exert the leverage necessary to move the cumbersome gears of government. In 1981, the U.S. travel industry, spearheaded by the **Travel Industry Association of America** (TIA), was instrumental in moving the National Tourism Policy Act through the 97th Congress. But such unanimity and singleness of purpose are not the rule—an important fact when one considers that departments and agencies of government tend to be organized on the basis of constituency. In other words, the Department of Agriculture represents the farmer; the Department of Labor, the worker; the Department of Education, the educator; the Department of Housing and Affairs, the real estate and housing industries; and so on.

## Typical Tourism Office Functions

For all of the ambiguity of their position at the federal level and their lack of hierarchal and structural uniformity, most national tourism offices do engage in certain common functions.

The WTO separates these functions under five major headings: *(2)*

1. General Administration of Travel and Tourism

2. Planning and Investment
   - Physical planning at national level
   - Economic planning
   - Planning social aims
   - Tourism area development
   - Financing of tourism infrastructure
   - Financing of tourism accommodations

3. Research and Statistics
   - Collecting tourism and travel statistics
   - Research on tourism
   - Tourism marketing surveys

4. Vocational Training
   - Administrative and planning activities
   - Establishing and/or operating training schools
   - Organizing training courses and study cycles
   - Producing handbooks for training schools

5. Promotion
   - Advertising
   - Public relations
   - Promotional material
   - Fairs and exhibits
   - Familiarization tours
   - Organization of seminars
   - Establishing and operating tourism information offices

Figure 5.2 illustrates the general functions and activities involved in tourism, which concern the role and responsibilities of the NTA under the various headings of product development and planning, marketing, manpower development, and coordination and control of the tourist industry. These are quite similar to the WTO categorization above.

# *N*ATIONAL TOURISM ADMINISTRATION FORMS AND STRUCTURES

In recent years, the rationale for government involvement in tourism has been increasingly questioned. This comes in response to current political and economic developments,

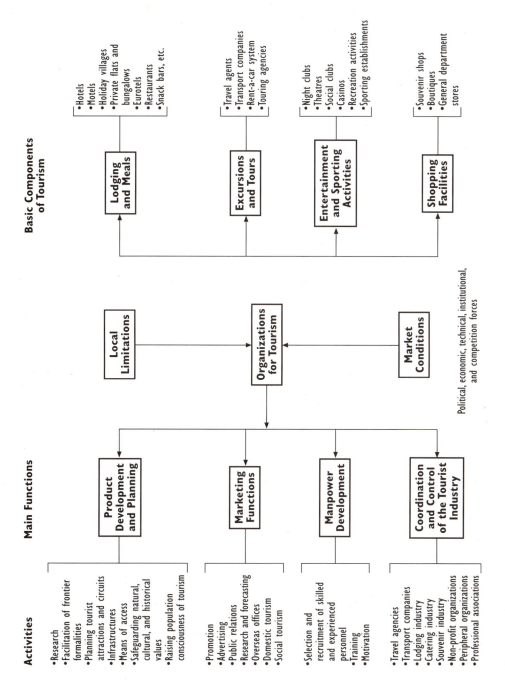

**Activities**

**Main Functions**

**Basic Components of Tourism**

**Product Development and Planning**
- Research
- Facilitation of frontier formalities
- Planning tourist attractions and circuits
- Infrastructures
- Means of access
- Safeguarding natural, cultural, and historical values
- Raising population consciousness of tourism

**Marketing Functions**
- Promotion
- Advertising
- Public relations
- Research and forecasting
- Overseas offices
- Domestic tourism
- Social tourism

**Manpower Development**
- Selection and recruitment of skilled and experienced personnel
- Training
- Motivation

**Coordination and Control of the Tourist Industry**
- Travel agencies
- Transport companies
- Lodging industry
- Catering industry
- Souvenir industry
- Non-profit organizations
- Peripheral organizations
- Professional associations

**Local Limitations**

**Organizations for Tourism**

**Market Conditions**

Political, economic, technical, institutional, and competition forces

**Lodging and Meals**
- Hotels
- Motels
- Holiday villages
- Private flats and bungalows
- Eurotels
- Restaurants
- Snack bars, etc.

**Excursions and Tours**
- Travel agents
- Transport companies
- Rent-a-car system
- Touring agencies

**Entertainment and Sporting Activities**
- Night clubs
- Theatres
- Social clubs
- Casinos
- Recreation activities
- Sporting establishments

**Shopping Facilities**
- Souvenir shops
- Boutiques
- General department stores

**Figure 5.2** Typical NTA functions.

*Source:* Managerial Aspects of Tourism, 1976.

notably the liberalization of political systems, which have encouraged closer public scrutiny of fiscal budgets. Traditional public sector activities now face accountability issues, forcing many governments to adopt administrative reforms geared towards reduction in the size and burden of government—and **privatization**, which is the shifting of certain nonproductive government functions to the private sector.

The sporadic and limited phenomenon of privatization in the 1960s has become widespread and frequent through the 1980s and into the 1990s. National tourism administrations have not been immune to this privatization trend. As a bureaucratic extension of government, the NTA has stimulated arguments in many countries against its continuance as a public entity. In an industry predominantly driven by private businesses, the argument remains as to whether there is justification in using public funds to support tourism development, a cause whose tangible benefits appear to accrue only to those business interests. Privatization would presumably shift the burden of funding tourism promotional activities back to the private sector.

Alternatively, there is the **public-private partnership model** which considers private administration with government participation and shared contribution for tourism promotion activities. Examples of NTA structures where both the public and private interests work cooperatively include the United Kingdom, Australia, Switzerland, and recently, Canada.

In the United States, the USTTA will be phased out as the 104th Congress seeks ways to downsize government and proposes a public-private partnership, which would eliminate the need for the USTTA in its present form.

## Most Common Forms of NTAs

There are three basic forms of national tourist office or administration: (1) state tourism secretariats (independent or within larger ministries); (2) government agencies or bureaus within larger departments; and (3) quasi-public tourism authorities or corporations.

In addition, there may be a coordinating body within government to bring all of the affected departments to review and consider tourism policy decisions. The head of the tourism secretariat or agency is often the chair of the interagency coordinating body. In some cases, the coordinating bodies have been set up by specific legislation, in other cases, by executive order. More commonly, the councils meet at regularly specified times, with a general mandate to advise the government on tourism policy, resolve conflict among agencies, and ensure that the national tourism interest is considered when national policy is formulated. (*3*) Table 5.2 provides comparative information in terms of form, budget and size of various national tourist organizations.

## Models of Common Forms of NTAs

Most national tourist offices are organized internally along functional lines into divisions and branches. In the following sections, current examples of NTAs are presented to illustrate the three more common forms and structures of NTAs for comparative analysis. These include (1) the **Australian National Tourism Organization** as a state tourism secretariat model, (2) the **Japan National Tourism Organization** as a model of a tourism agency within the Ministry of Transport, and (3) the **Canadian Tourism Commission** as

TABLE 5.2
**Comparison of Various National Tourism Administrations**

| Country | Name of Principal NTO | Form of Principal NTO | NTO Budget* (U.S.$) and Staff |
|---|---|---|---|
| Australia | Australian Tourist Commission | Quasi-public, government funded enterprise | 64.9 million; 266 staff |
| Austria | Austrian National Tourist Office | Private association with government funding | 43.9 million; 271 staff |
| France | Maison De La France | Quasi-public, government funded enterprise | 69.0 million; 270 staff |
| Spain | Spanish Tourist Authority | Government department | 74.6 million; 595 staff |
| Thailand | Tourism Authority of Thailand | Government department | 49.5 million; 811 staff |
| United Kingdom | British Tourist Authority | Quasi-public, government funded enterprise | 67.4 millon; 400 staff |
| United States | U.S. Travel and Tourism Administration | Government department | 17.5 million; 94 staff |

*Source:* Compiled from tourism studies listed in endnotes 4, 10, and OECD Tourism Policy and International Tourism.
*1992 estimates.

a model of a quasi-public tourism organization. The United States Travel and Tourism Administration will be discussed separately.

## Australian National Tourism Organization

Reorganized in late 1991, three agencies (see Figure 5.3) share responsibility for Australia's tourism development: (1) the Department of Tourism (DOT), under the jurisdiction of the minister for tourism; (2) the Bureau of Tourism Research (BTR), a nonstatutory body, which is part of the Department of Tourism; and (3) the Australian Tourist Commission (ATC), a statutory authority which reports directly to the minister for tourism. Together, they constitute Australia's federal government's tourism portfolio.

The Department of Tourism is headed by an executive director who advises the minister of tourism on policy issues relating to tourism in Australia. The DOT works with industry, other federal government agencies, and state, territory, and local governments to maximize the contributions of tourism to Australia, which include the following charges:

- encourage the development of tourism in Australia;
- identify opportunities in tourism;
- reduce barriers to industry development; and
- provide information to aid industry decision making.

The DOT is broadly divided into two functional programs: tourism and corporate support. Under its tourism program, the DOT is responsible for developing and implement-

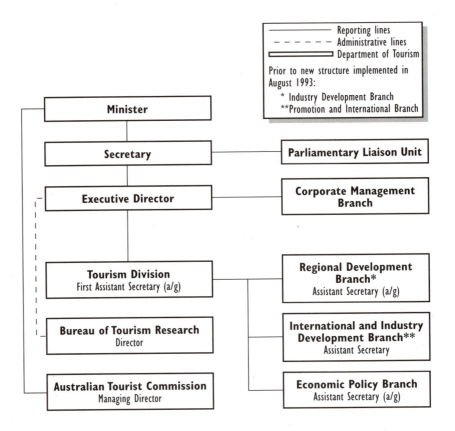

**Figure 5.3** Australian National Tourism Organization structure.

*Source:* Australia Department of Tourism, *Annual Report 1993–94.*

ing government tourism policy, administering funding programs, and organizing Australia's participation in international expositions. These responsibilities are carried out within three branches: (1) Regional Development Branch, (2) International and Industry Development Branch and (3) Economic Policy Branch. The Regional Development Branch is responsible for undertaking activities that support the development of a competitive, ecologically sustainable tourism industry, drawing on Australia's regional and cultural diversity and heritage. The International and Industry Development Branch works to enhance the international competitiveness of Australia's tourism industry and to strengthen international relations in the tourism area. The Economic Policy Branch is responsible for developing an environment in which tourism can most benefit the economy. Under DOT's corporate support program, the department monitors the efficiency and effectiveness of its internal operations. It also provides strategic direction and monitors the department's performance.

Within the overall tourism portfolio, the BTR is responsible for providing relevant tourism statistics and research analyses on tourism to aid industry and government decision-making. Finally, the ATC is responsible for marketing and promoting Australian tourism internationally. It maintains a head office in Sydney and nine overseas offices. *(4)*

## Japan National Tourist Organization

In Japan, four agencies (see Figure 5.4) share responsibility for the development of tourism: (1) the Department of Tourism, a function of the Transport Policy Bureau, Ministry of Transport; (2) the non-profit, government-subsidized Japan National Tourist Organization (JNTO), which promotes tourism to Japan; (3) the Liaison Conference in Tourism; and (4) the Council for Tourism Policy.

The Department of Tourism is in charge of administrative functions relating to the development, improvement, and coordination of the tourist industry in Japan. It has three divisions: a Planning Division, a Travel Promotion Division, and a Regional Development Division. Among the responsibilities assigned to the Planning Division are overall coordination and planning of tourism administration, supervision of JNTO, improvement of reception services for foreign visitors, financial affairs and a taxation system relating to the

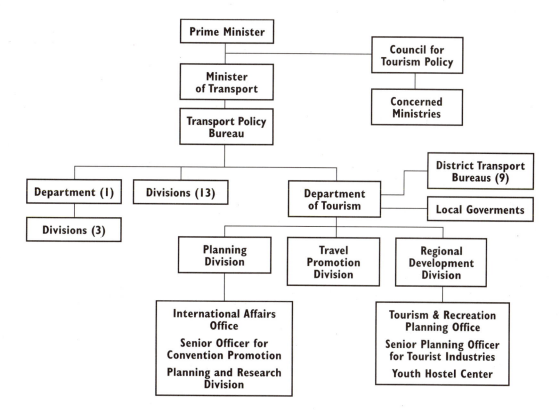

**Figure 5.4**   Tourism administration in Japan.

*Source:*   Japan National Tourist Organization (JNTO) "Tourism in Japan 1995/96."

Visitors leaving the main gate at the Nijo Castle in Kyoto, the fabled historic city once the capital of Japan.
Credit: Japan Airlines.

tourist industry, research and study on tourism, subsidies to the tourism industry, and handling of general affairs for the Council for Tourism Policy. An international affairs office is located within the Planning Division with the purpose of improving international relations. A senior officer position was established in 1987 to promote conventions in Japan. The Travel Promotion Division is responsible for the supervision of the travel agency business, travel agents association, and the guide interpreter business. Some of the Regional Development Division's assigned responsibilities include registration and supervision of hotels, improvement of tourist souvenirs, planning development of tourist facilities, and promotion of campaigns to improve tourist courtesy.

The Japan National Tourist Organization (JNTO) has an administrative council of 30 members, which oversees its operations. JNTO maintains 6 departments in the head-office and 14 overseas offices in key cities around the world to conduct promotional efforts under the direction of the head office. The 6 departments at headquarters are General Affairs, Finance, Overseas Promotion, Tourism Exchange, International Marketing, and Promotion and Support (the latter 2 are under the Japan Convention Bureau).

The Tourist Exchange Department is responsible for improving reception service for tourists to Japan. Additionally, it conducts the national examination for guide-interpreters; and administers three tourist information centers in Tokyo, Kyoto, and the Narita International Airport, providing overseas visitors with traveling information in Japan.

Central administrative affairs regarding such issues as national parks, the travel agency business, and the guide business are partially entrusted to the 47 prefectural (district) governments. Within these local autonomous bodies, specific sections have been charged with responsibility for promoting tourism, improving tourist facilities, developing plans for regional tourism development, and protecting tourism resources.

Additionally, the Ministry of Transport has district bureaus in the nation's key cities to administer regional transportation. Each bureau has a division in charge of local tourist administration under the control of the Ministry. *(5)*

In order to coordinate and promote closer ties among the related administrative agencies, thereby encouraging an integrated and effective tourism administration, the Inter-Ministerial Liaison Conference on Tourism has been established as a standing committee. The conference is chaired by the director-general of the prime minister's office and consists of 21 members of the related ministries and agencies. The Council for Tourism Policy was established so that views and opinions of private and academic circles would be reflected in the tourism administration. The council, which is composed of 27 educated and experienced civilians, investigates and deliberates on important tourism issues.

## Canadian Tourism Commission

In early 1995, the Canadian government announced the establishment of the Canadian Tourism Commission (CTC), a special agency that focuses on forging a new business-government partnership to promote the growth of Canada's tourism industry. The CTC organization is divided into two sections: (1) decision-making board; and (2) public service staff (see Figure 5.5). The decision-making board consists of 26 members, including the chairperson, the president, the deputy minister of Industry Canada, up to 16 private sector members, and 7 provincial/territorial government members, representing all regions and diverse tourism interests. The decision-making board is vested with the authority to plan, direct, manage and implement programs to generate and promote tourism in Canada. It will develop and deliver: (1) national promotional programs in Canada, the U.S. and abroad; (2) business services including industry assessment, program development and policy analysis; (3) a technology plan; (4) a research program; and, (5) information services. The board will be assisted in its functions by eight advisory committees. The public service staff, drawn from the former Tourism Canada—predecessor of the CTC—is led by a president, who is a member of, and directly accountable to, the decision-making board.

The CTC's core programs and services can be divided into two broad areas: marketing and industry competitiveness. The marketing programs include:

- development and maintenance of data on markets of opportunity;
- advertising;
- public relations;

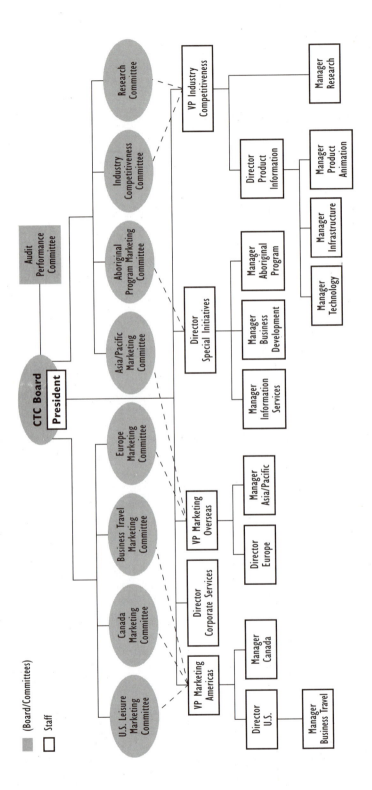

**Figure 5.5** Canadian Tourism Commission organization chart.

*Source:* Canadian Tourist Commission, 1995.

- promotional projects;
- media relations;
- travel trade development; and
- cooperative as well as buy-in initiatives.

The industry competitiveness programs include:

- industry assessments on the structure and performance of the tourism industry and its sub-sectors. These activities include bench marking and quality performance measurements tools;

- program development services, such as how-to manuals, seminars, consultations and advice;

- study and interpretation of developments in the domestic and international arenas and provision of that analysis to industry decision-makers; and

- development and maintenance of data on industry activity, industry revenues, capacity and tourist consumption of specific products and services.

Funding for the CTC's promotional activities will come partly from Canada's federal government and partly from provincial and local governments and the private sector. The CTC is forbidden from undertaking lobbying activities, applying for additional federal government grants to fund programs, or engaging in capital development programs. *(6)*

## The U.S. Travel and Tourism Administration: Early History to Present Times

The evolution of the present U.S. Travel and Tourism Administration (USTTA) has come by the way of a long, difficult, and at times, intriguing, history in the Congress and the executive branch. The legislature never truly concurred about the need to establish a federal agency to promote international tourism to the United States. Nor was there a full understanding of what functions such an agency might have if it were created.

The idea of a national tourism office for the United States was not seriously considered until 1931. It was the brainchild of Charles Hatfield, secretary and general manager of the St. Louis Convention, Publicity, and Tourist Bureau; vice-president of the International Travel Development Association; and a founder, in 1930, of the International Travel Federation. A seasoned travel veteran, Hatfield helped sell the Louisiana Purchase Exposition and the Panama-Pacific Exposition. He was also an author of the "Know America" slogan in 1915 used to promote travel from the continent to the U.S., and proposed that the U.S. Congress appropriate $1 million to stimulate travel. *(7)* Sixteen years passed, however, before legislation was introduced into Congress to create a federal instrument to promote tourism.

Throughout the 1930s, several bills were introduced in the Senate and the House regarding the establishing of a national tourist office; but it was not until 1940 that both the Senate and the House approved H.R. 6884, which directed the Secretary of the Interior through the National Park Service, "to encourage, promote, and develop travel within the United States, its territories and possessions, providing such activities do not

The 1915 World's Fair and Panama-Pacific Exposition in San Francisco.
Credit: New York Public Library Picture Collection.

compete with the activities of private agencies; and to administer all existing travel promotion functions of the Department of the Interior through such services." (8)

The fledgling bureau survived only a year. With the advent of World War II, domestic gasoline rationing and the cessation of normal passenger traffic across the Atlantic, tourism travel promotion became impractical. Funding for the Park Service's travel program was not renewed.

International travel, as a subject of foreign economic policy, was further studied during the 1950s under the Eisenhower administration. An Office of International Travel was created within the Commerce Department of Foreign Commerce in 1958 to serve "as the government spokesman for the travel industry, and provide…liaison…between the industry and the…U.S. Government agencies whose functions affect the industry's operations." The office operated no branches abroad. Rather, it disseminated travel information about the United States through U.S. diplomatic and consular posts and the U.S. Information Agency.

The debate on tourism legislation continued during the 1960s. In 1961, no fewer than 15 bills that would have created a national tourist office in some form were dropped into the legislative hopper. In a special message to the Congress on February 6, 1961,

President Kennedy recommended a "major new program" of foreign travel promotion and welcomed the introduction of legislation.

The International Travel Act of 1961, was signed into law on June 29, 1961. From this legislation, the U.S. Travel Service was born. The mission of the new service was multiple and included:

1. promotion of travel to the United States;

2. encouragement of host arrangements and facilities;

3. coordination of travel facilitation activities of U.S. agencies, and the simplification and reduction of barriers to travel;

4. collection and publication of tourism statistics and technical information.

In 1970, the International Travel Act was amended, giving new powers to the U.S. Travel Service. The director was elevated to the rank of Assistant Secretary of Commerce for Tourism, a position on a par with the post of assistant minister in other governments. The amendment also created a National Tourism Resources Review Commission.

The chief tasks of the new commission were to determine: (1) the domestic travel needs of Americans and foreign visitors, (2) the resources available to meet those needs, and (3) the policies and programs that would ensure that domestic travel needs were adequately met. The commission was also to recommend a program of federal assistance to help states promote domestic travel and whether a separate agency would be established or whether an existing entity should be designated to consolidate and coordinate tourism research, planning, and development activities in the U.S. government. Three years later, the commission released its recommendations. Perhaps the most significant was: "the number one need (in tourism) is effective leadership at the federal level." *(9)*

In 1974, observing that there were a very large number of government policies and activities with impacts on travel, tourism, and associated recreational activities which were fragmented and often duplicative and conflicting, the Senate Committee on Commerce, Science, and Transportation commissioned the National Tourism Policy Study. The study concluded the following *(10):*

• a national tourism policy should be enacted;

• an interagency council should be created to coordinate federal programs impacting on tourism;

• an independent U.S. Travel and Recreation Agency should be created from the Heritage Conservation and Recreation Service and

• the U.S. Travel Service to carry out the National Tourism Policy or, alternately, that a U.S. Travel Bureau should be created within the Department of Commerce for the same purpose.

In public testimony, the Carter administration accepted, in principle, the recommendation for a national tourism policy, but opposed creation of either a U.S. Travel and Recreation Agency or a U.S. Travel Bureau.

In 1981, there was a new development: Congress enacted the **National Tourism Policy Act** and, on October 16, President Reagan signed it into law. The act accomplished exactly what its title implies; it established, for the first time, a national tourism policy. The underlying premises were:

- the tourism and recreation industries are important to the United States;

- tourism and recreation will become ever more important aspects of our daily lives;

- the existing federal government involvement in tourism needs to be better coordinated.

Title II of the measure replaced the U.S. Travel Service with a new U.S. Travel and Tourism Administration, headed by an Under Secretary for Travel and Tourism reporting directly to the Secretary of Commerce. The principal functions of USTTA were to help develop U.S. tourism as a stimulus to economic growth and stability; to improve international competitiveness; and to expand foreign exchange earnings. Other responsibilities assigned to the agency included coordinating and negotiating international tourism policy, conducting statistical and market research, and directing a dynamic program of tourism development.

Title III created a Travel and Tourism Advisory Board composed of representatives of the travel industry, organized labor, the academic community, and the public interest sector. Title III also established a national Tourism Policy Council to coordinate federal policies, issues, and programs that affect tourism, recreation, and heritage resources.

The next more significant legislation dealing with the federal role in tourism occurred in 1992 when Congress passed the **Tourism Policy and Export Promotion Act**. This act was passed to help provide U.S. tourism interests with better access to international markets by creating the International Tourism Trade Development Financial Assistance Program. Other salient issues of the act include:

- increasing the awareness of tourism as an important export market by improving survey methods;

- providing research on international markets to the U.S. tourism industry;

- establishing the Rural Tourism Development Foundation to increase travel and tourism by foreign visitors to rural America; and

- coordinating tourism trade policies and legislative initiatives and reduced restrictive barriers to the growth of U.S. tourism services.

## White House Conference on Travel and Tourism

In October, 1995, the first ever White House Conference on Travel and Tourism was convened. The purpose of this historic conference was to focus national attention on the tourism industry's significant impact on the economy and employment, America's competitiveness in tourism, the role of the states and the private sector, and to discuss challenges facing the industry and their solutions. Perhaps the most important issue presented at the conference was the proposal to establish a new public-private partnership organization by early 1996 to replace USTTA after 1996. To provide the new organization with leadership at a high level, the Vice President of the United States has been suggested as chair. (See the sidebar *National Tourism Strategy*) Although this matter has not yet been enacted, it clearly signifies that the last chapter on travel and tourism administration in the U.S. is not yet written.

President Bill Clinton addresses the delegates attending the first White House Conference on Travel and Tourism in October, 1995.
Courtesy of the Travel Industry Association of America.

# CHANGING STRUCTURES AND LOCUS OF NTAs

In spite of the many difficulties they face, national tourism offices continue to proliferate. The World Tourism Organization estimated that there were more than 200 official tourism bodies in 1992/93. These tourism organizations, with governmental, semi-governmental, and private status, belong to the 185 members of the United Nations and various territories worldwide. Moreover, there are 134 NTAs who are members of WTO as of 1995. Of this, 130 are sovereign states with full membership and 4 are territories with associate membership. The most recent survey, conducted among some 80 countries by the WTO Secretariat in 1992/93 to study the changing patterns of NTA structures and locus, reveal the following:

- A limited number of countries (about 25) have established a full-fledged ministry or similar government bodies, whose sole responsibility is tourism;

- In countries without a dedicated ministry, tourism is most frequently relegated to ministerial bodies dealing with essentially economic matters. The next most common pattern is to link tourism with other sectors dealing with culture, environment and transport;

# National Tourism Strategy

## Proposal to Form a Public/Private Partnership to Implement the National Tourism Strategy

There is universal consensus that the United States needs a national tourism strategy. This strategy should be shaped, implemented, and equitably financed by a number of public/private partnerships. To realize the industry's agreed upon approach, a public/private partnership organization will be needed at the national level to guide implementation of the national tourism strategy. This new entity will provide national tourism policy direction to federal entities and coordinate the elements of the national strategy to be implemented by various industry organizations at the national, regional, state, and local levels. In addition, this entity will oversee the Visit USA international promotion program.

Given these goals in an environment where government is decreasing its role, it becomes clear that a single USTTA and an assortment of largely disconnected organizations is not the best way to organize for maximum tourism benefit. Instead, a broader approach is needed—an approach that provides vision and high-level leadership to set priorities; an approach that is more inclusive, designed specifically to build bridges between public and private groups and between city, state, and regional organizations; and finally, an approach better able to support and coordinate the delivery of critical data, technical assistance, and resources to industry-wide programs and organizations best able to impact international market share and regional opportunities.

The structural framework required to implement the national tourism strategy will require a partnership among the following: (1) the direction-setting, national tourism policy coordinating body (the new national public/private partnership organization), (2) a restructured Tourism Policy Council made up of federal entities key to the success of a national tourism strategy, (3) a national tourism office (Visit USA, Inc.) to compete against 140 governments in the global tourism marketplace and (4) numerous travel and tourism industry organizations accepting leadership responsibility for financing and implementing program elements of the national tourism strategy.

## Recommended Actions:

- By July 1996, the President should create a public/private partnership organization to advise the Administration on national tourism economic and trade policy issues, approve the White House Conference on Travel and Tourism Strategic Plan, develop assessment criteria for overall travel and tourism program performance, approve Visit USA, Inc. marketing plans and provide policy guidance to the Tourism Policy Council and private sector partner organizations.

• By July 1996, the President should, with the advice of the travel and tourism industry, appoint the initial board of directors of the public/private partnership organization. The board should be composed of high-level leaders/CEOs from both the public and private sectors representing the diversity of the industry. The organization should be chaired by the Vice President of the United States. (See Figure 5.6)

*Source:*  Working Document: Proposed National Tourism Strategy, White House Conference on Travel and Tourism, October 30–31, 1995, Washington D.C. Excerpts pp 34–37.

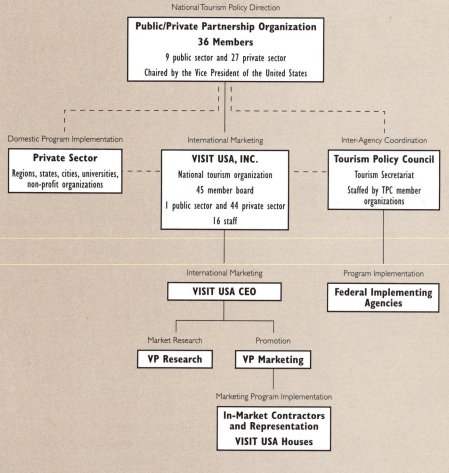

**Figure 5.6**  National tourism strategy structural framework.

- On a regional basis, the trends over the past decade show:
  - East Asia, the Pacific and South Asia regions where an increasing number of states have established central ministerial bodies for tourism with administrative responsibility at the highest level.
  - Africa as the only region where tourism is most directly linked with environment issues (i.e., natural resources, wildlife, national parks, etc.).
  - The Americas and Europe as the regions where tourism is most strongly affiliated with the economic branches of government (trade and industry).
  - The Middle-East, Africa, East Asia and the Pacific, and Europe, as regions where a large number of states recognize the inter-related role of culture and tourism.
  - South Asia, East Asia and the Pacific, and Africa, as regions with numerous countries where the fundamental importance of the development of air transportation is reflected in the present administrative structures of tourism within the central government.

# $\mathscr{P}$OLICY BODIES AT THE INTERNATIONAL LEVEL (11)

Numerous international and intergovernmental bodies are involved with worldwide tourism policies. The United States has been involved in mainly three: the **Organization of American States (OAS) Tourism Development Program**, the **Organization for Economic Cooperation and Development (OECD) Tourism Committee**, and the World Tourism Organization (WTO).

The Tourism Development Program of the OAS was formed in 1970 to assist tourism authorities of the member states in developing, promoting, and regulating their respective tourism sectors. It was recently integrated with the International Trade and Export Development Program to form the International Trade and Tourism Program. An important activity of the OAS tourism program is to provide expertise in the field of tourism training. The program provides training in a wide range of topics at its three regional Inter-America Tourism Training Centers located in Argentina, Barbados, and Mexico.

The OECD has a Tourism Committee concerned with tourism policy and international tourism trends in the member nations. The Tourism Committee prepares a comprehensive yearly publication entitled *Tourism Policy and International Tourism in OECD Member Countries,* which contains policy developments and tourism information. Most recently, the Tourism Committee has devoted considerable attention to lowering international barriers to trade in tourism.

The only worldwide tourism policy body is the WTO, the successor to the former IUOTO (International Union of Tourism Organizations), which was based in Geneva. The WTO, inaugurated in 1975 and headquartered in Madrid, provides a world clearinghouse for the collection, analysis, and dissemination of tourism statistics and information. It offers technical services on tourism development to national tourism administrations and organizations, and provides a forum to debate important tourism issues and policies. Additionally, the organization is expected to set up a mechanism for the amicable settlement of tourism enterprise disputes at the international level.

Recently, the U.S. has became involved with two new regional institutions: **NAFTA (North American Free Trade Agreement)** and **APEC (Asia Pacific Economic Cooperation)**. NAFTA and APEC are economic-related institutions created to facilitate growth of regional trade and investments among member countries. NAFTA, which involves Canada, Mexico, and the United States, establishes a free trade area by eliminating barriers to trade and facilitating cross-border movement of goods and services between the three countries. NAFTA also provides the framework for trilateral cooperation to protect intellectual property rights and to promote fair trade in goods and services, including tourism. APEC, inaugurated in 1989, is a regional consultative body which presently includes 18 countries. APEC is committed to promoting and liberalizing trade and investment in the Asia-Pacific region as well as to provide a forum for consultation on economic cooperation among member countries at different stages of economic development. Among the standing committees of APEC are ones addressed to tourism, transportation, and telecommunications.

## U.S.-Japan Tourism Exchange Promotion Program

The United States and Japan enjoy a bilateral relationship that extends beyond trade. This relationship has been described as a three-legged stool resting on security, politics, and economics. Nonetheless, as security and political tensions in the region continue to lessen, it is the economic leg that seems to dominate as fairness in trade issues are aired in the public media.

Until recent years, tourism was not viewed as an activity of significant consequence in trade negotiations. However, as the gap of trade in manufactured goods continued to widen between Japan and the U.S., trade in services—especially tourism—helped to reduce this U.S. deficit. In 1993, Japan held a $54.2 billion trade surplus with the U.S. Inbound travel expenditures from Japan to the U.S. reduced that deficit by $11 billion as more than 3.5 million Japanese visited the U.S., spending more than $14.4 billion as compared to the $3.4 billion Americans spent while visiting Japan.

To further redress trade imbalances, the United States and Japan have agreed to work independently and cooperatively on a tourism exchange promotion program. The term "exchange program" means, in principle, that each country will encourage its nationals to visit the other country. The objective of the program is to double the number of visitors between the U.S. and Japan—from 4 to 8 million by the year 2000. While the U.S. has a clear advantage in tourism trade balance over Japan at present, Japan's new tourism policy is to promote "two-way tourism" in anticipation of its own internal economic structural problems and the growing importance of trade in services.

# SUMMARY

National tourism organizations have been established in numerous countries for the purpose of serving national goals and implementing public policy with respect to tourism. Although the size, structure, functions, and responsibilities of NTAs vary widely from one country to the next, NTAs typically deal with the marketing, research, planning, and investment aspects of tourism and increasingly with tourism employment and training.

For most NTAs, significantly less effort has been expended trying to influence or help develop public policy affecting tourism.

In recent years, many governments have changed the funding structure of their NTAs in response to downsizing many public sector activities. There is a distinct trend towards forging cooperation with private sector interests to promote tourism growth.

The role of NTAs will continue to evolve in response to market competition and changing public policy. Many NTAs will face an increasing emphasis on performance measures and privatization. Tourism organizations at the international level will continue to be instrumental in developing international policies relating to tourism and assisting individual nations in their respective tourism development efforts.

# $\mathscr{D}$ISCUSSION QUESTIONS

1. What are some of the key goals and policies of national tourism administrations? How do they differ among countries?

2. What problems are encountered by NTAs in formulating policies and achieving their stated goals?

3. How are NTAs affected by political and economic development in the 1990s?

4. What are the five areas that NTAs are typically involved in?

5. How could you describe the contrasting organizational model or structure of the Canadian, Australian, Spanish, Japanese or American NTAs?

6. What are the key elements of the U.S. National Tourism Policy Act?

7. What impact would international bodies such as WTO/OMT, OECD, NAFTA or APEC have on national tourism interests?

8. What effect would privatization have on NTAs? Why might this be a reasonable step for some countries to take?

9. What is the Encyclopedia of Associations?

10. What is the role of the National Tourism Policy Council in the U.S.?

# SUGGESTED STUDENT PROJECTS

1. Many states have their own state tourism offices which may mirror the policies and functions of an NTA at the state level. In addition, city governments may also have a local convention and visitors bureau whose responsibility it is to promote conventions, market tourism, conduct research, and related tourism functions. Arrange to visit your state tourism office or city convention and visitors bureau and interview the state tourism director or the director of the city conventions and visitors bureau. Ask how these offices relate to the NTA functions and activities. Are they similar or quite dissimilar? Are state/local promotional efforts complementary to national efforts or are they competitive? In what ways could state, local, and national tourism activities come together to benefit the nation as a whole while optimizing state and local goals?

2. USTTA will be phased out after 1996. A public-private partnership is being proposed. Is the public-private model the best form? What other forms or models might you consider? How does the form of an organization affect its functions? What are the policy implications for the national tourism interests when a government NTA is replaced by a partnership between public and private sectors? Explain your answers.

# *R*EFERENCES

1. Thurot, J.M. "Tourism: Political weapon." *Economia* (May 1975).

2. *Budgets of National Tourism Administration 1983–84–85*. Madrid: World Tourism Organization, 1986.

3. *Tourism Assessment of Eight Foreign Government Tourism Programs*. Report for U.S. House of Representatives Subcommittee on Transportation and Commerce. Washington, D.C.: Arthur D. Little, Inc., January 1978.

4. Australia Department of Tourism. *Annual Report 1993–94*.

5. *Tourism in Japan 1995/96*. Japan National Tourist Organization (JNTO) and Ministry of Transport.

6. The Canadian Tourism Commission Charter 1995.

7. U.S. Congress. Senate. Committee on Commerce. Hearings on S.33, a Bill to Encourage Travel to and Within the United States by Citizens of Foreign Countries, and for Other Purposes. 75th Congr., 1st sess., 1935.

8. U.S. Congress. Proceedings and Debates of the 76th Congress, first Session. July 31, 1939.

9. National Tourism Resources Review Commission, *Destination U.S.A. Vol. 1* (Summary Report). Washington, D.C.: Government Printing Office, June 1973.

10. U.S. Congress. Senate. Committee on Commerce, Science and Transportation. *National Tourism Policy Study Final Report*. 95th Congress, 2nd sess., 1978.

11. Edgell, D.L. "United States International Tourism Policy." *Annals of Tourism Research* (1983).

## Supplemental Reading

*Tourism Policy and International Tourism in OECD Member Countries*, Paris: Organization for Economic Cooperation and Development, Annual publication.

U.S. Department of Commerce. Travel Service. *Tourism: State Structure, Organization and Support*. Washington, D.C.: Government Printing Office, 1979.

*Budgets of National Tourism Administrations,* Madrid: World Tourism Organization, Biennial publication.

# Part 3

# Tourism Development

# Chapter 6

# Destination Planning and Development

## LEARNING OBJECTIVES

- To understand the need for and importance of tourism planning and policy.
- To be familiar with the major elements involved in planning a destination.
- To understand the different types of destination attractions.
- To understand the product life cycle theory as it applies to the stages of destination development.
- To understand the four major stages of the development and growth of a destination: inception, growth, maturity, and decline.
- To define and use the following terms:

| | |
|---|---|
| Allocentric | Infrastructure |
| Carrying capacity | Inventory of tourism assets |
| Comprehensive master plan | Midcentric |
| Core attraction | Psychocentric |
| Cottage industry | Social carrying capacity |
| Destination | Superstructure |
| Destination development | Supporting attraction |
| Destination lifecycle theory | Tourism planning |
| Feasibility study | Trend analysis |

# TOURISM PLANNING AND DEVELOPMENT

In the past **tourism planning**—if it was considered at all—was generally seen as a private sector concern, which required little government participation or intervention, especially in countries with market-based economies. A common misconception was that tourism planning meant no more than encouraging new hotels to open in an area, promoting airline flights, easing border crossings, mounting a promotional campaign, and then counting the revenue from tourist activities. Tourist destinations, however, have learned from experience over the last three decades that this perception is naive, and at best a haphazard method of planning and developing tourism.

As a major industry for many developing countries and regions throughout the world, tourism has a pervasive effect on the economy, social structure, and environment of an area. Developing communities, which might look to tourism as a means for economic growth, are in precarious positions because of their limited resources and cultural constraints. As we will see in Chapter 7, the development of tourism in such circumstances can upset the delicate balance among economic, social, and environmental forces. For this reason, many governments are viewing tourism from a broader perspective in terms of its full impact on their countries, regions, or local communities, and are playing an increasingly larger role in tourism planning and development. In addition to concerns about the potentially disruptive impact of tourism on residents and the possible destruction of natural resources, governments are concerned about the huge costs of infrastructure and public services that they must usually provide. As shown in Figure 6.1, there are many other facets and problems of the travel industry that must be addressed in tourism planning.

**Destination development**, as a topic, has been widely discussed—at times heatedly debated—at various forums sponsored by the World Tourism Organization, the Pacific Asia Travel Association, and other tourism federations. The concern with the subject stems from a general awareness that the adverse impacts of development are sometimes irreversible. Destination countries, host communities, land owners, institutional lenders, resort investors, and many others have a vested stake in the long term sustainability and success of a destination. Developed correctly, the destination will be environmentally supportable and economically sound, providing ample opportunities for the host community. Developed badly, the market life of the destination may be short-lived, with losses for everyone involved, especially for the community whose land and environment are indelibly blighted.

The term "destination development" may be applied broadly or narrowly, since destination can mean an entire country, a region, a resort enclave, or a single resort project. When the NTA refers to destination development, the administration is considering either developments that will help the country compete successfully against other countries as a destination of choice in the tourism marketplace or a specific development that would bring economic benefits to a region. For instance, the French government's interest and substantial investment in Euro-Disneyland, since renamed Paris Disneyland, were motivated by the need to create jobs and economic opportunities in a disadvantaged region of the country.

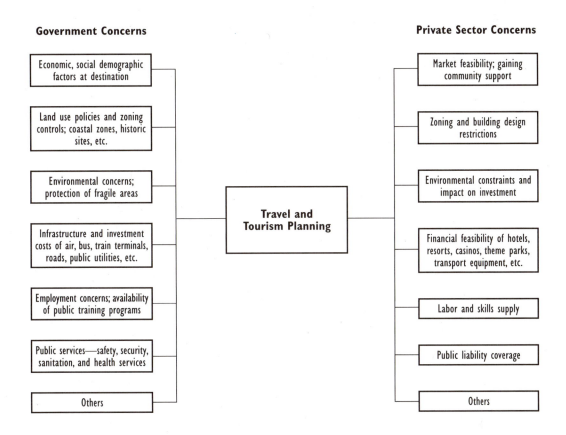

**Government Concerns**

- Economic, social demographic factors at destination
- Land use policies and zoning controls; coastal zones, historic sites, etc.
- Environmental concerns; protection of fragile areas
- Infrastructure and investment costs of air, bus, train terminals, roads, public utilities, etc.
- Employment concerns; availability of public training programs
- Public services—safety, security, sanitation, and health services
- Others

**Travel and Tourism Planning**

**Private Sector Concerns**

- Market feasibility; gaining community support
- Zoning and building design restrictions
- Environmental constraints and impact on investment
- Financial feasibility of hotels, resorts, casinos, theme parks, transport equipment, etc.
- Labor and skills supply
- Public liability coverage
- Others

**Figure 6.1** Some facets of tourism planning.

## The Example of Kyongju as a Planned Resort Development

As discussed in Chapter 5, the role of national tourism organizations in the past typically was limited to promotional and marketing activities. This has gradually changed to give NTAs broader responsibility in the process of tourism planning, especially in countries that are developing planned resort destinations. South Korea provides a noteworthy case for discussion. During the early 80s, the South Korean government planned and developed the Bomun Lake area in Kyongju—located approximately 5 hours from Seoul by bus or train— as a resort destination. Kyongju had once served as the ancient capital of the Shilla Dynasty (57 B.C. to 935 A.D.) and remained an important cultural and religious center of the nation. Through its NTA, the Korea National Tourism Corporation, the government decided to develop this area as a tourist destination in cooperation with domestic and foreign private investors. A man-made lake was created and hotels encompassing some 3,000 rooms were built on the lakeshore. A hotel school to train resort workers was also built in the complex as well as a convention center, an 18-hole golf course, a shopping center, a gaming center, a children's park, fishing sites, and other attractions. (See Figures 6.2 and 6.3) To promote

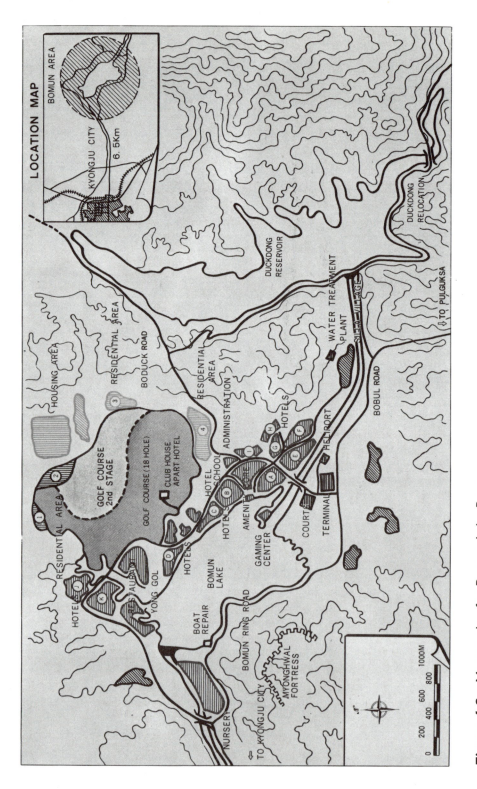

**Figure 6.2** Master plan for Bomun Lake Resort.

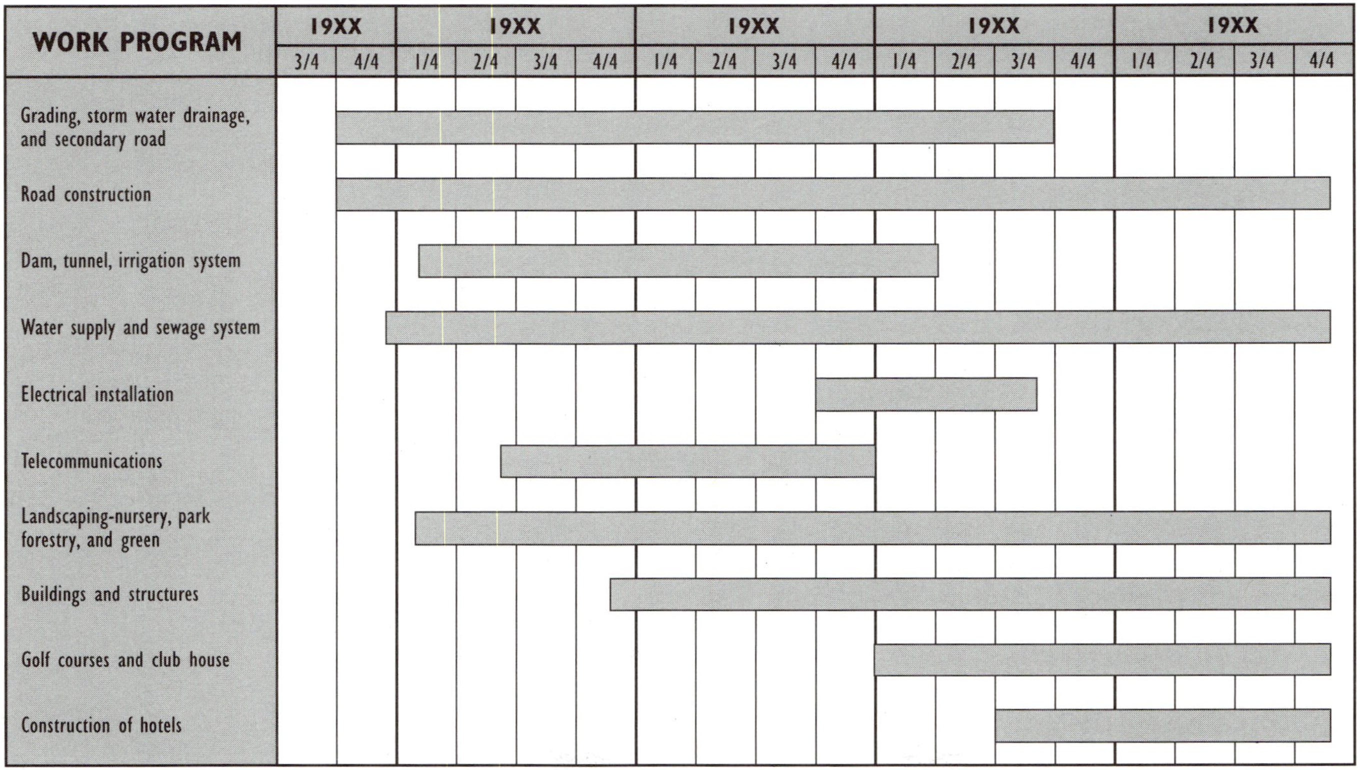

**Figure 6.3** Program for construction—Bomun Lake Resort.

| WORK PROGRAM | 19XX | | 19XX | | | | 19XX | | | | 19XX | | | | 19XX | | | |
|---|---|---|---|---|---|---|---|---|---|---|---|---|---|---|---|---|---|---|
| | 3/4 | 4/4 | 1/4 | 2/4 | 3/4 | 4/4 | 1/4 | 2/4 | 3/4 | 4/4 | 1/4 | 2/4 | 3/4 | 4/4 | 1/4 | 2/4 | 3/4 | 4/4 |
| Grading, storm water drainage, and secondary road | | | | | | | | | | | | | | | | | | |
| Road construction | | | | | | | | | | | | | | | | | | |
| Dam, tunnel, irrigation system | | | | | | | | | | | | | | | | | | |
| Water supply and sewage system | | | | | | | | | | | | | | | | | | |
| Electrical installation | | | | | | | | | | | | | | | | | | |
| Telecommunications | | | | | | | | | | | | | | | | | | |
| Landscaping-nursery, park forestry, and green | | | | | | | | | | | | | | | | | | |
| Buildings and structures | | | | | | | | | | | | | | | | | | |
| Golf courses and club house | | | | | | | | | | | | | | | | | | |
| Construction of hotels | | | | | | | | | | | | | | | | | | |

Source:   KNTC-Kyongju Tourism Agency.

the development of Kyongju as a tourist destination area, the government provided capital to conduct archeological investigations of ancient burial mounds in the vicinity to develop a park there. Temples and a museum were renovated and improved. The government also improved the railroad and highway system serving this area.

The Kyongju example is analogous to resort developments in many parts of the world—Cancun in Mexico, Phuket in Thailand, Nusa Dua in Indonesia, or Roussillon-Lanquedoc on the Mediterranean in France, to name a few—where government has participated or taken the lead in tourism planning, development, training, marketing, and promotion. Ideally, however, tourism planning should be a shared function between the various levels of government and the host communities, with adequate input and advice from the private sector.

## Tourism Policy Planning

Besides investing in planning for tourism development, it is also necessary to provide direction for the extent and quality of future tourism growth in an area through the establishment of sound policies. An example of progressive tourism policy planning on the state level is one adopted by Hawaii. Under the enabling legislation of the State Policy Planning Act of 1975—which set into motion a combination of public discussions, workshops, public opinion surveys and technical studies—the Hawaii State Plan was developed and enacted into law in 1978. Hundreds of citizens and government officials were involved in vetting the plan and then in drafting more detailed State Functional Plans in 12 separate subject areas. *(1)* These 12 plans covered such major concerns of state as energy, transportation, water resources, historic preservation, recreation, health, conservation lands, education, housing, higher education, agriculture, and not least, tourism. A State Tourism Functional Plan (STFP) was developed under the oversight of the Department of Planning and Economic Development (later reorganized as the Department of Business, Economic Development and Tourism) and an advisory body appointed by the Governor. In 1984, the first statewide tourism functional plan was approved as official state policy under Sec. 226-8 *(2)* (see the sidebar *Hawaii State Plan*).

Since the adoption of the first STFP, the plan has been periodically revised and updated. The most recent version, approved in 1991, addresses a number of special concerns facing the tourism industry in Hawaii, including

1. Growth
   - Past, current and future trends
   - Positive and negative impacts on the community
   - Defining and determining an optimum rate of growth

2. Physical development
   - Product quality and diversity
   - Land use planning
   - Adequacy of infrastructure
   - Visitor use of public services

# Hawaii State Plan

## SEC. 226-8 Objective and Policies for the Economy—Visitor Industry

(a) Planning for the State's economy with regard to the visitor industry shall be directed towards the achievement of the objective of a visitor industry that constitutes a major component of steady growth for Hawaii's economy.

(b) To achieve the visitor industry objective, it shall be the policy of this State to:

(1) Support and assist in the promotion of Hawaii's visitor attractions and facilities.

(2) Ensure that visitor industry activities are in keeping with the social, economic, and physical needs and aspirations of Hawaii's people.

(3) Improve the quality of existing visitor destination areas.

(4) Encourage cooperation between the public and private sectors in developing and maintaining well-designed, adequately serviced visitor industry and related developments which are sensitive to neighboring communities and activities.

(5) Develop the industry in a manner that will continue to provide new job opportunities and steady employment for Hawaii's people.

(6) Provide opportunities for Hawaii's people to obtain job training and education that will allow for upward mobility within the visitor industry.

(7) Foster a recognition of the contribution of the visitor industry to Hawaii's economy and the need to perpetuate the aloha spirit.

(8) Foster an understanding by visitors of the aloha spirit and of the unique and sensitive character of Hawaii's cultures and values.

3. Environmental resources and cultural heritage
   • Competition between visitors and residents for limited outdoor recreational resources
   • Preservation, protection, and interpretation of historic and cultural resources
   • Maintenance of a clean environment

4. Community, visitor, and industry relations
   - Resident attitudes toward the visitor industry
   - Visitor understanding and respect for the community
   - Visitor well-being and safety
   - Industry support of the community

5. Employment and career development
   - Labor supply
   - Training and education for new sources of labor
   - Opportunities and education for upward mobility

6. Marketing
   - Increasing competition
   - Market diversification
   - Market research
   - Balanced growth

The foregoing represents only a brief outline of the contents of the STFP; the plan itself offers numerous practical recommendations for policies and program actions, including a timetable for program implementation, budget requirements, and key players to be involved.

Many communities have established a centralized body responsible for the planning and development of tourism. Community level tourism organizations generally work closely with state level organizations. Figure 6.4 shows how a tourism council in one community divided its specific functions among numerous committees and subcommittees.

## Global Tourism Planning

Beyond the examples of national and state involvement in the development of tourism policy is policy planning on a global basis. In 1980, the World Tourism Organization held its first conference after 17 years of inactivity. The purpose of this conference was to consider issues affecting both the public and private sectors involved in the development of tourism. *(3)* One of the goals of the conference was to gain consensus on the issues by all WTO member countries and to develop guidelines for future policy directions to foster balanced growth of tourism worldwide. Among the numerous topics debated were the following key issues: (1) better management of tourism supply, (2) technological cooperation; (3) human resources, (4) freedom of movement, and (5) border facilitation. These five issues, plus the field of tourism statistics, have since been adopted as the standing program of work for the WTO.

Since 1980, the WTO General Assembly has met biannually to consider numerous other global tourism policy matters touching on the rights of visitors and host countries, the preservation of archaeological treasures and cultural heritage as a responsibility of nations, training and technology transfer, domestic versus international tourism, youth tourism, social tourism, tourism impacts, and other universal concerns. An important premise of the WTO is that tourism works as a vital force for world peace, providing a socio-economic platform for building international understanding and community interdependence.

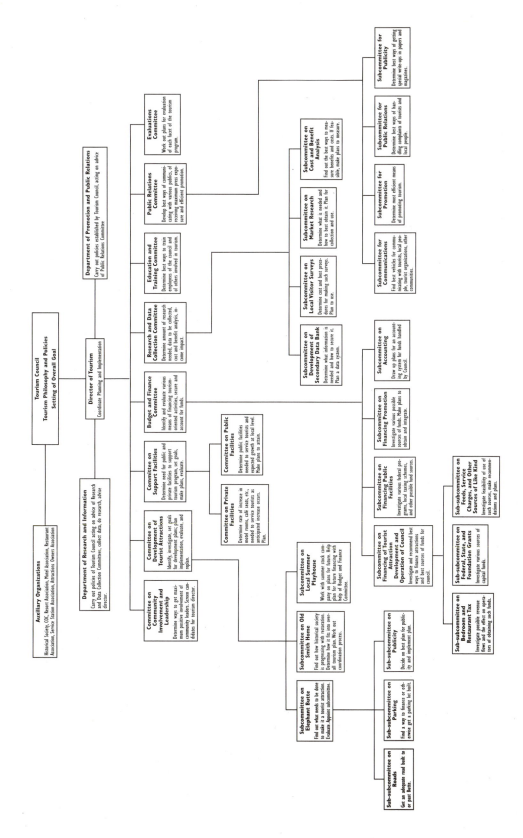

**Figure 6.4** Tourism Council organization chart.

# *D*ESTINATION DEVELOPMENT

The planning, developing, and marketing of a destination requires the close cooperation of government officials, developers, architects, financial analysts, and investors. It also may involve economists, sociologists, archeologists, and other professionals as consultants. Entire textbooks have been devoted to this topic because of its complexity and technical aspects. This chapter is meant to provide only an overview of the major elements that are usually involved in the planning, developing, and marketing of a destination. Before we discuss the elements, let us first examine the definition of destination.

As defined by the travel industry, **destinations** are specific places chosen by travelers for temporary stays. They are not simply transit or stopover points that travelers must pass through to reach their ultimate destination. People will select a given destination to visit, based on their preferences and purpose for travel, whether it be to vacation, do business, visit friends, or sightsee. Areas as large as a continent or as small as a village may be considered destinations in the minds of travelers.

Destinations may be broadly classified into two types. One is the self-contained resort destination which has been developed with tourism as its specific economic focus, providing all of the accommodations, services and amenities required by vacationing visitors within the resort community. The other type is a destination which also draws visitors, but where tourism is only a part of its total economy. Disney World is an example of a self-contained resort, complete with recreational activities, entertainment, attractions, hotels, restaurants, and shopping amenities. Many people consider Disney World itself as the destination, not the city of Orlando, where it is located, or even the state of Florida. Other destinations, however, were not developed to attract visitors. Some of the cultural attractions of Europe, for example, are the remains of civilizations of past eras. The Tower of London and the Roman Coliseum were built for functional purposes during their times, although they have immeasurable value as visitor attractions for their respective countries. These types of attractions cannot be replicated and their value lies in people's interests in the culture, history, art, and architecture of different times and places.

Capital cities of the world, such as Rome, Paris, London, and Washington D.C., attract thousands of visitors annually. Many tourists are attracted to capital cities because they tend to be the most developed in a country and usually contain some of the finest cultural resources typifying the history and development of a country. Others may wish to visit the capital cities because they serve as the seat of government and power. In any case, the services and facilities in an area must be sufficient to meet the needs of visitors. Adequate food, lodging, and transportation facilities; auxiliary facilities such as recreational, entertainment, and shopping complexes; and support services for safety, security, sanitation, and health must already exist or be developed. Most importantly, a destination must have an appeal or attraction—whether psychological or tangible—to draw visitors.

## Attractions and Attributes of a Destination

The attractions and attributes of a destination are important with respect to sightseeing, recreation, sports, shopping, entertainment, and meetings/convention opportunities. In

The Piazza St. Pietro is a popular gathering place for tourists in Rome.
Courtesy of the Italian Government Travel Office.

Chapter 3, we discussed motivational factors that drive individual decisions to travel for pleasure. The quality of available attractions in a given destination will affect these travel decisions, especially discretionary holiday travel. Disney World, for example, is world class and has mass appeal. The local amusement park of a destination city is another matter altogether.

The same destination may offer different attributes to different people. Picture two unrelated individuals who board a plane for Rome, remain there for a week, then return at the same time. For statistical purposes, both are considered tourists with similar lengths of stay. One is visiting Rome for a week of *la dolce vita*. This person stays in a five-star hotel, goes sightseeing, and attempts to experience as much of the delights of Rome as possible in a week. The second traveler may have no specific interest in getting to know Rome or to enjoy its pleasures, but instead spends the entire week at a convent, meditating, praying, and resting from the cares of everyday life. In the case of the first visitor, the purpose of the trip was to enjoy Rome. The second traveler, on the other hand, went to Rome to visit a religious order located there, not the host city itself. The purchasing patterns of the two travelers were as different as their reasons for going to Italy.

There are many destinations that have multiple attractions, which can appeal to a broad segment of the market. One way of categorizing destination attributes and attractions is based on the following:

1. *natural resources*, such as climate, beaches, and mountains;

2. *cultural resources*, such as historical sites, museums, theaters, and the people themselves;

3. *convention and conference facilities*—these represent major public investments to attract business visitors to resort or city destinations;

4. *recreational facilities*, such as theme parks, ski slopes, and marinas;

5. *events* such as Mardi Gras in New Orleans or Carnival in Rio, Olympic Games, marathons, international expositions, music festivals, etc.;

6. *specific activities*, such as gambling in Las Vegas or Monaco, shopping in Hong Kong, or theatre in New York;

7. *psychological appeal* of romance, adventure, and remoteness.

Numerous studies have been conducted over the years by different Travel Trade Associations, NTAs, and tourism scholars to measure the attributes deemed to be important by travelers in choosing a holiday destination. With but little variation among studies, the list of the most important attributes are as follows:

• Weather

• Scenic beauty

• Hospitable attitudes of the local people

• Suitable accommodations

• Interesting culture and way of life

• Reasonable prices

• Safety and security

• Favorable currency exchange

These attributes may rank higher or lower on the preference scale in motivating different market segments to choose one destination over another. For instance, Germans—the most traveled citizens among Europeans—are strongly motivated by climate and nature in choosing holiday destinations. Pleasure trips, especially those featuring beach, swimming and sun, are their vacation of choice; 30–37% of Germans choose these types of experiences and seek destinations that offer them. *(4)*

The five top destination features that are most important to Japanese travelers—the single largest outbound market from the Asia-Pacific region—were identified by the Japan Travel Bureau Foundation for the 1990s as follows: (1) resort, (2) safety, (3) scenic beauty, (4) a city's charm and (5) culture. The first three features far outweigh the other two. *(5)*

Tourism, as a product, has been defined as "an amalgam of three main components: the attractions of the destination, the facilities at the destination, and the accessibility of it." *(6)* The planning and development of a destination are involved, to a large degree, in the physical resource or product components of tourism. Of equal importance are analyses of potential visitors, costs of development, pricing policies, competitive destinations, and other financial aspects to determine the feasibility of development. As discussed earlier, environmental, cultural, and social aspects have recently emerged as key dimensions in developing a destination.

## Elements Included in Destination Planning (7)

There are numerous elements that are important in the planning and development of a tourist destination. They deal with such pertinent issues as the long term market viability of the destination, investment costs and benefits, human and capital resource requirements, adequacy of existing infrastructure and expansion needs, and the potential consequences of development. The list includes

- Environment for tourism
  — Location and proximity to markets
  — Natural environment
  — Historical influences
  — Government support
  — Local community support
- Market analysis
- Assessment of available resources and required resources
  — Historic sites
  — Scenic areas and green zones
  — Visitor attractions
  — Recreational activities
  — Indigenous culture
  — Arts and handicrafts
  — Manpower and skills supply
  — Infrastructure and superstructure
  — Transportation access by land, sea, air
  — Transportation systems
  — Support services
  — Duty-free shopping
  — Visitor accommodations
  — Marketing and promotion
  — Economic and financial analysis
  — Investment requirements
  — Environmental impact
  — Social impact

Other elements, such as state and county planning and zoning regulations, financing packages for destinations and resorts, and construction timetables are often covered in a

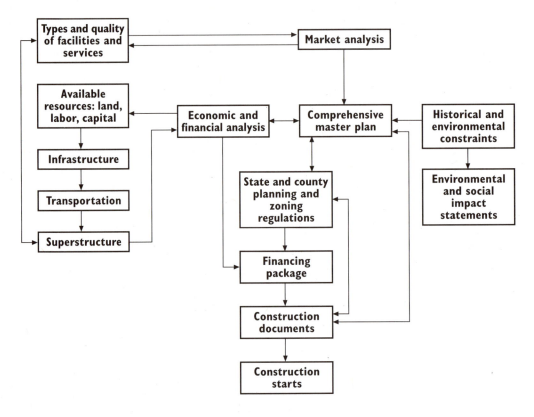

**Figure 6.5**   Elements involved in developing a destination.

comprehensive master plan (see Figure 6.5). It is beyond the scope of our discussion to cover each element in view of the fact that they do vary from place to place. Nonetheless, students should be aware that all of the elements shown in Figure 6.5 are important in the destination planning process.

   The following is a brief discussion of some of the major elements:

## Market Analysis

Market analysis requires the careful study of past and present trends, traveler profiles, traveler preferences and habits, market positioning, and destination image. Not only is it important to know past and current market trends, but it is also important to anticipate future trends as well—say, 2, 5, or 10 years ahead—for planning, budgeting, and marketing purposes. In marketing, this process is referred to as **trend analysis**. Trend analysis is useful not only for developing strategies that are responsive to the needs of different market segments and for promoting an optimal visitor mix, but also for planning future capital improvements required by the destination as tourism grows.

## Assessment of Available Resources

Determining what the community already has or can develop is a critical step in deciding the type of developments that should be pursued. Tourism planners would describe this step as taking stock or making an **inventory of tourism assets** within the community. The inventory should list and evaluate all actual and potential attractions. What is an attraction? It is anything which will draw visitors. Attractions may be classified on the inventory as a **core attraction** or a **supporting attraction**. Core attractions represent the basic assets or attributes of the community. They form the main theme of the destination. They may be natural or man-made, historic or cultural, recreational or spectator events. Supporting attractions represent the facilities and services that serve the needs of visitors—lodging, food service, local transportation, shopping, foreign currency exchange, and so on.

The Taj Mahal—one of the great architectural wonders of the world was built by the Mogul emperor Shah Jahan in the 17th century as a mausoleum for his beloved second wife, Mumtaz Mahal.
Credit: Air India Library.

## Core Attractions

The success of a destination depends not only on its power to attract visitors, but also on its ability to hold them. This means that the destination must have sufficient attractions that are appealing to a wide market. In many instances, the core attractions are natural ones. The mass appeal of the Grand Canyon, Niagara Falls, the Great Barrier Reef of Australia or African wildlife requires no elaboration. In other instances, the core attractions will be man-made. Some are monumental like the Taj Mahal in Agra, the Great Wall of China, the pyramids of Egypt; others are cultural such as the French Quarters of New Orleans or the arts and architecture of Dresden (see sidebar); still others offer entertainment, as in Las Vegas or Atlantic City. Destination planning, however, must consider not only existing attractions, but also the need to develop new ones over time as markets mature and new market segments must be cultivated. Attractions such as ski areas, parks, lakes and marinas, scenic highways, or historic restorations are major investments which require years of advance planning and deliberation on means of financing.

## Culture

Appropriate development of a destination area encourages the incorporation of that area's cultural heritage into tourism. Archeological sites, native crafts, native foods, ceremonies, rituals, customs, music, dance, and the traditional architecture should be considered in tourism planning to enable a new destination to conform to and support native culture, and not to diminish or depreciate it.

## Human Resources

It is often easier to deal with the physical planning aspects of tourism than it is to develop a skilled high-performance workforce. Tourism, being labor intensive, requires a sizable workforce. For each direct job created in tourism, two indirect jobs may occur. Direct jobs are those established by primary tourism service providers such as hotels, restaurants, attractions, tour operators, transport carriers, etc. Indirect jobs are generated by secondary suppliers to the travel industry, for example, entertainers or consultants to the hospitality industry. It is estimated that 70–75% of tourism-related jobs require only basic, entry-level or mid-entry skills and a good hospitality service attitude. The other 25–30% are high skill jobs that will require professional training or technical training, often including a working knowledge of foreign languages.

For tourism to succeed, a destination must consider establishing education and training resources, if none exists, to provide a constant stream of qualified employees to the industry. The responsibility for education and training of the tourism workforce should be a shared one between the public and the private sectors. Governments, as a rule, have responsibility only for general education; but to the extent that government may be concerned with the employability of its citizens, it may also provide vocational and professional development programs through publicly funded hotel and tourism schools. The private sector, on the other hand, is ultimately responsible for technical training to meet each employer's specific requirements and for developing professional standards at the industry level.

# Rebirth of Dresden

## Rebirth of Dresden Renews Tourism Appeal

Once known as "Florence on the Elbe" for its awesome combination of historic architecture and art treasures, Dresden, located in the Saxony region of eastern Germany, was destroyed by Allied bombing in 1945 during World War II. Reconstruction began during the days of Communist rule under former Soviet occupation, but with the reunification of Germany, new resources and investments have come to spur a redevelopment and nascent revival of this historic city.

The rebirth of Dresden is evidenced by the progressive renovation of historic buildings, the opening of new hotels and restaurants, luring visitors by the thousands to its famed museums, cathedrals, gardens, palaces, and concert halls. Local newspapers lead with such headlines as "Castle Renovations Almost Complete" or "Famed Building Shines Again." The most visible symbol of the renaissance is the 18th century Church of Our Lady, which had occupied the center of the skyline until it was reduced to a bare shell by the bombing. With help from sponsors around the world, including a group of British pilots who took part in the air raids, the church is being rebuilt stone by stone. Although the work will not be finished until well into the 21st century, the building site is already an attraction for visitors.

With the blooming of tourism, ten new hotels have opened or are scheduled to open in 1995, bringing the city's total to over 60 hotels with some 9,000 beds. Visitor arrivals have climbed steadily from 464,896 in 1992 and 528,078 in 1993 to 662,742 in 1994, averaging a nearly 20% growth rate over the two-year period.

Adapted from article by Steven Kinzer, "Correspondent's Report," *New York Times,* July 16, 1995.

## Infrastructure and Superstructure

The term **infrastructure** refers to "all forms of construction on and below ground required by an inhabited area in intensive communication with the outside world and as a basis for intensive human activity within." *(8)* Infrastructure includes roads, transportation terminals, electric lines, sewage systems, water systems, power supply, and other related services. The infrastructure precedes the **superstructure**, which includes all of the facilities built to serve visitors—hotels, resorts, restaurants, entertainment centers, recreational amenities, casinos, shops, and so on. The superstructure cannot exist without a well-planned and constructed infrastructure. The lack of an adequate infrastructure often restricts the development and growth of destinations. A community, for instance, may have interesting natural scenic areas, but these scenic areas are meaningless for tourism if there are no roads or transport systems to get visitors there or if the existing infrastructure is so poorly developed that it makes visitor access all but impossible.

Hotel investors and other suppliers of services for travelers generally cannot afford to develop the infrastructure. This is normally a public responsibility, or at least one that is partly borne by government in resort areas. Developing countries may qualify for assistance from such international agencies as a regional bank or the World Bank or through direct loans from industrial countries for developing infrastructure. Indeed, loans for infrastructural development is often a priority of regional banks and the World Bank, since infrastructure is as fundamental to general economic development opportunities as it is for tourism.

## Transportation

Transportation is a crucial consideration when planning for development. The movement of passengers and goods involves a study of present and future transportation needs including air, highway, rail, and water. This information can assist the government in many ways, such as planning expansion of air routes, assessing traffic patterns between terminals and destinations, and measuring the impact of congestion at major visitor attractions, historic sites, parks, and beaches.

## Support Services

A modern tourist destination requires a considerable amount of support services—some for safety and security requirements, such as police protection, fire protection, sanitation, health care; and others as conveniences for visitors, including currency exchange, babysitting, laundry, postal, packing and mailing, repairs, and so forth. It is important to consider how these services can be provided without disrupting services to residents.

## Supporting Attractions

A master plan for tourism can help government decision-makers in the development of supporting attractions—visitor accommodations, convention facilities, etc.—according to a timetable and community priorities. Tied with the master plan are such essential issues as zoning designation, density allowance, and design control of hotels and resorts, especially in the case of conservation or historic districts. In resort communities, the development of supporting attractions may at times involve decisions requiring land swap or land conversion from one use to another. And decisions on capital investments for infrastructure must be considered in concurrence with support attractions planning.

# Marketing

Upon the completion of the inventory of destination assets and attributes which represent the tourism "products" that the community has to offer, the next step is to develop a marketing strategy. As no destination can be all things to all people, an important aspect of the marketing strategy will be to match the community's tourism products with the right markets.

Markets may be defined in a number of ways. In Chapter 3, we discussed market segments according to demographic or psychographic characteristics. However, the major effort must be given over to locating a few specific markets having potential for the destination and to pass over others offering less promising returns. Seldom are budgetary resources so plentiful as to allow a shotgun approach to market development. This being the case, it will be necessary (1) to identify target markets, (2) determine the motivational factors that will stimulate these markets, (3) develop a marketing plan with clear promotional goals, (4) develop an advertising campaign with a well-focused theme aimed at the target markets, (5) determine a media and public relations strategy, (6) determine a budget to implement the marketing plan and not least, (7) develop a system to evaluate the effectiveness of the marketing plan and the returns on marketing investments.

## Economic and Financial Analysis

Economic and financial analysis involves a careful analysis of economic and financial requirements of capital projects in tourism, including the cost of capital, cash flow, rate of amortization and returns on investment. This information along with pertinent marketing and other data will form the substance of a **feasibility study** which allows decision-makers to determine whether or not to proceed with a tourism project on the basis of its potential for profitability and long term viability in the marketplace.

## Environment

Destinations should be planned to take advantage of natural settings and natural resources without destroying them. The ultimate goal of tourism planning should be to protect the natural beauty of an area and to avoid exploitation since natural resources are not inexhaustible. There is also the matter of ecological balance to consider. Every area has a natural ecosystem that will be altered in some way when pristine or agricultural land is converted to commercial use for tourism purposes. The concept of **carrying capacity** is an important one in addressing tourism development within the limitations of environmental constraints. The carrying capacity of an area defines its biophysical limits and ability to accommodate given numbers of visitors with least destruction to the natural environment and the ecosystem. Carrying capacity in economic theory may also be defined as a tradeoff in use of resources whereby the production or value of one resource (natural environment) may be applied to maintain the productivity of another (tourism).

## Social Impact

Developers of a destination often overlook the effect that tourism growth will have on the resident population. Officials in some developing nations believe that too much contact between the resident population and visitors can lead to internal unrest. This is one of the reasons many countries plan and develop resort areas away from population centers. Dispersing visitors away from population centers is also a means of avoiding congestion and of distributing the benefits of tourism over a wider area. Similar to the concept of environmental carrying capacity, tourism behaviorists believe that destinations have finite **social carrying capacities** as well. The social carrying capacity is defined as the ability of a given place—a beach for instance—to accommodate a given number of users, beyond which a place is no longer pleasant nor provides an enjoyable experience for anyone, ultimately resulting in a loss of market.

## Comprehensive Master Plan

The end products of the above analyses are a series of plans and projections, providing guidelines for decision makers in assessing the probable outcomes of alternative actions. From a physical resource perspective, a **comprehensive master plan** of the area is commissioned to identify planned attractions, visitor facilities, required infrastructure, traffic flow through the area, and other physical aspects. Manpower studies are usually furnished as a part of the feasibility study to address labor, employment and training, and community planning questions. Separate statements on environmental, cultural, and social aspects also may be required by local or national governments.

By using complex programming techniques, quantitative computer models have been developed as a approach to destination planning. One such model served as a basis for the Tourism Master Plan of Israel with a focus on detailed supply and demand variables. *(9)* The proposed Israeli model was to provide answers to four aspects of planning:

1. What are the feasible and optimal numbers and categories of tourists that the economy is able and willing to serve?

2. Which types and what scope of touristic services and activities are necessary?

3. Which activities and services can be most profitably developed in each locality?

4. What would be the feasible and optimal seasonal distribution of the various activities during a year?

The main purpose of the model was to maximize the country's total net income in foreign exchange from tourism. It did not deal with other aspects, such as environmental, social, and cultural considerations; these aspects, in any case, tend to be more difficult, if not impossible, to quantify. This should invite caution in relying exclusively on a quantitative model with respect to destination development. The intrinsic value of such resources as open space, an inspiring view, clean air, and pristine scenery is difficult to convert into monetary value, yet are undeniably important to the productivity of the destination.

# $\mathcal{F}$ACTORS AFFECTING A DESTINATION'S SUSTAINABILITY

Thus far, we have looked at the planning of a destination pertaining to policy decisions, market needs, destination attributes, resource requirements and feasibility. Once a destination begins to grow, different patterns of behavior, attitudes, and fulfillment will recur at various stages. Before we discuss the stages of growth through which a destination evolves, let us first look at some factors contributing to the success or decline in popularity of a destination.

To paraphrase Karl Marx: tourism contains the seeds of its destruction. When a destination becomes too popular, heavily trafficked, and no effort is made to maintain quality, the destination gradually loses its appeal and deteriorates when competition from newer and better destinations appears. There are histories describing how once popular resort destinations fell out of favor and eventually disappeared when upscale visitors left, to be replaced by middle-income and eventually budget visitors who overwhelmed the community with their numbers, noise, and behavior. *(10)* At that point, community support wanes even as economic crisis sets in. Advances in technology, particularly in construction and air transportation, may enable the rapid development of new resort destinations, but unless attention is also paid to the "software" aspects of the visitor experience, the success of the destination may well be short-lived.

## Travelers Personalities and Propensities

One theory on the rise and fall of destinations relates the popularity of a destination to the inherent personalities of travelers. *(11)* The originator of this theory, Stanley Plog, hypothesized that travelers may be classified according to personality type, ranging from **psychocentrics** to **allocentrics** at either extreme of the personality scale.

Individuals with psychocentric personalities have a strong need for consistency and the familiar or the tried-and-true in their lives. When traveling, they prefer to visit "safe" destinations. For the most part, this would seem to exclude any foreign destination. Psychocentrics are typified as people who are suspicious of anything not known. They are not likely to experiment with unbranded accommodations, food, or entertainment in travel. They seek experiences that are not likely to cause personal stress or which will bring them into contact with unusual situations.

At the other extreme, persons with allocentric personalities have a strong need for variety and new life experiences. When traveling, these people seek destinations that offer an opportunity to see and participate in totally different cultures and environments. Many prefer to stay in local accommodations, rather than in branded hotels. They try new foods and seek self-fulfilling learning experiences and adventures that psychocentrics would shun.

Varying personality types fall between the psychocentric and the allocentric, and it is in these midranges that the majority of tourists are found. This group, the **midcentrics**, can be characterized as a group with personality types that are attracted to certain popular destinations—for example, Waikiki Beach on Oahu in Hawaii. Waikiki's appeal to visitors from different countries or areas—the U.S. mainland, Japan, Australia, New Zealand, Canada, and Europe—may be explained by the fact that the core attractions of a tropical island with good climate and the overlay of an exotic Hawaiian culture in combination with such midcentric supporting attractions as name brand hotels, multilingual services, franchised fast foods and popular ethnic restaurants are user-friendly to either first time or repeat visitors from anywhere. While visitors to Waikiki may come from different cultures, as a whole, they have in common certain psychographic characteristics and consumer preferences that favor Waikiki as a destination of choice. Put another way, the characteristics of a destination predisposes the type of customers that will be attracted. Obviously there are differences among the visitors to Hawaii, but the differences between a Japanese, an Australian, a Norwegian, and a New Yorker visiting Waikiki may be much less than the differences between them and their fellow countrymen who vacation in Paraguay or Zambia.

The mass market for travel does not lie with personality groups at either extreme. It resides with the midcentric personality. Midcentrics are not particularly adventurous, yet they are not afraid to try new experiences as long as these are neither bizarre nor too challenging. The most popular destinations in the world today have built sizeable travel industries around the midcentric personality groups. Figure 6.6 illustrates this point.

Personality typology aside, a destination may fail to attract visitors altogether if it is deemed unsafe. Revolution, crime, hostile attitude of the resident population, infectious disease, and in recent times—terrorism—are primary reasons that destinations lose visitors. The tourist market may shift from boom to bust within a short period, as has happened in parts of the world where violence against tourists or a revolution took place. See the sidebar *Atomic Tests.*

The attraction of particular destinations may also change for given personality groups. For instance, Mexico, at one time appealed primarily to allocentrics and had little allure for midcentrics who had heard unfavorable stories of unsanitary conditions, unsafe water, polluted air, crime against visitors, language miscommunications, service shortfalls, and

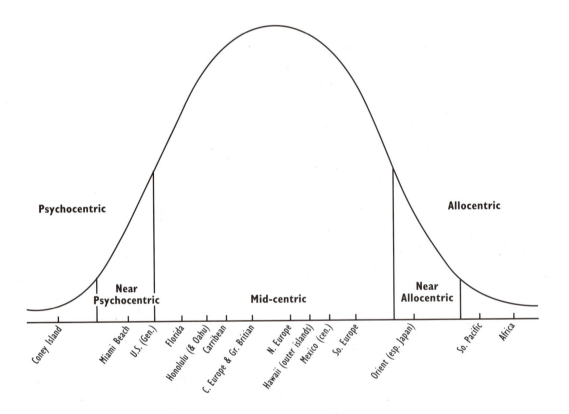

**Figure 6.6** Plog's theory on the rise and fall of destinations.

*Source:* "Why Destination Areas Rise and Fall in Popularity." *(11)*

## *A*tomic Tests

### Atomic Tests and Rioting Scare Off Tahiti Tourists

The resumption of French nuclear tests in the South Pacific and the rioting it sparked last month on the French-administered island of Tahiti have frightened away thousands of foreign travelers from French Polynesia.

The rioting began on Sept. 6, the day after France conducted the first of a planned series of nuclear tests at Mururoa Atoll, about 750 miles southeast of Tahiti, the largest of the islands of French Polynesia.

Major hotels throughout French Polynesia, which includes the resort islands of Moorea and Bora Bora, say they have been flooded with cancellations from travelers who fear the violence could resume if France continues with the nuclear tests, which it has vowed to do. A local hotel association said that a week after the rioting, its members had already recorded more than 26,000 cancellations.

The damage to the tourist industry is expected to be especially serious on Tahiti, which many experienced travelers have avoided for years, describing it as a spoiled paradise. The islands of Moorea, Bora Bora, and Huahine were reported quiet even as Tahiti was torn by rioting.

Before France's announcement in June that it planned to resume nuclear testing, tourism officials here had projected this year as a record year for visitors to French Polynesia. Tourisme Tahiti had initially expected 200,000 foreign travelers in 1995. But the projection has since been reduced to only 170,000.

Shenon, Philip, "Atomic Tests and Rioting Scare Off Tahiti Tourists," *New York Times,*
September, 1995.

other discouraging allegations. The nation gradually improved its infrastructure and invested heavily in new resort areas, visitor accommodations and services. At the same time, it stepped up its promotional efforts and advertising. With these improvements in combination with a falling peso, tourism began to boom by the 1990s.

As destinations begin to appeal to the midcentric tourism market, inevitable changes occur. Midcentrics represent the mass market, yet they cannot be attracted without certain changes of supporting attractions. The destination must become less "foreign" and more familiar to attract midcentrics and psychocentrics. Holiday Inns are safe, but who knows anything about the Hotel Daiichi? When changes are made to accommodate one group of traveler's needs, they inevitably become less appealing to other groups. When a destination starts appealing to midcentrics, this causes allocentrics to leave for places less traveled. Part of the color and personality that had enticed allocentrics may become too mainstream when a destination begins to cater more to the mass market.

As the globalization of travel and business accelerates, a destination's uniqueness may lessen with the introduction of branded goods and franchised services that travelers will also find at home. It remains an urgent challenge and responsibility for policymakers and tourism developers to try to sustain the cultural sanctity and unique character of their destinations even as they accommodate marketplace changes that accompany tourism growth.

## STAGES OF DESTINATION DEVELOPMENT

The **destination life cycle theory** is yet another way of characterizing the stages of destination development (see Figure 6.7). In marketing, it is theorized that destinations, like products, have a finite life, passing through four stages of development from inception to growth to maturity, finally declining when there is no longer any demand for the market. Applying the life cycle theory to tourism development, the stages may be identified as *(12)*

I. inception—discovery,

II. growth—local response and initiative,

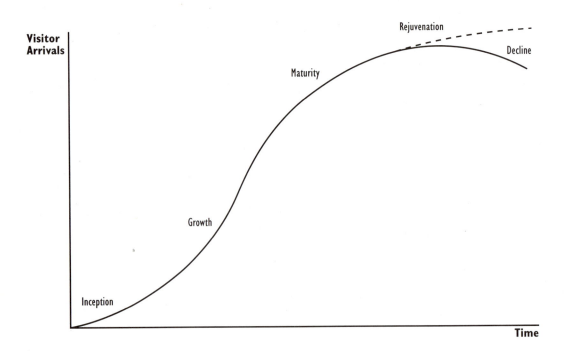

**Figure 6.7**    Hypothetical evolution of a tourist area.

III. maturity—institutionalization,

IV. decline—saturation and alienation.

Recognizing these four stages enables policy makers to possibly avoid problems associated with mass development and to ensure the continued success of a destination.

## Stage I Scenario. Inception—Discovery

During this stage of destination development, a few adventurous tourists find their way to an area. These are allocentric personality types. The travel style exhibited by allocentrics in the Discovery Stage is leisurely, exploratory, multipurpose, and multidestinational. *(13)* Among these early visitors are a few who decide to stay and become residents.

Members of the expatriate group become a factor in the evolutionary process of the region. They may establish guest homes, restaurants, souvenir shops, and tour services. These enterprises often prosper, because they offer services that are comparatively more sanitary, modern, and reliable than those offered by the native population. The availability of services that are acceptable, if modest, encourages a greater number of allocentrics to visit the destination.

During Stage I, tourists are generally welcomed by the host residents, and their visits are viewed in a positive manner. *(12)* There is a great deal of interpersonal contact between residents and visitors. The nature of the tourist is to accept the resident population for what it is and to adjust to the local environment and the people. There is usually little necessity for the resident to adjust to the visitor except in the case of a few individuals who, by their appearance or conduct, encounter resident disapproval. "Hippies" in the 1960s, for instance, were sometimes viewed as lazy, drug-addicted, unclean people who were not welcome, even in backwater areas.

## Stage II Scenario. Growth—Local Response and Initiative

The number of tourists increases in stage II. The destination has begun to develop in reputation largely by word of mouth. Although tourism is growing, the ownership and control of facilities and services remain largely in the hands of residents. As yet, nothing is standardized with respect to accommodations or services. Tourism development continues to be spontaneous and uncoordinated, rather than planned. A tourist association may be formed with local resident expertise. The tourist continues to adapt to the local culture, although there are signs that the tourist industry is also beginning to adapt to the needs of the tourist. Motorboats may replace canoes and other manually-propelled watercraft; taxis are more regularly available at popular visitor sites. Increased attention may be paid to sanitation and guest comfort even if the change is nothing more than installing screened doors and windows.

The increased interaction between tourists and residents causes residents to reassess their life goals and the means to attain them. This may result in a desire for better education to prepare for career opportunities, a trend toward egalitarianism, an increased awareness of the outside world, and perhaps a shift away from traditional vocations and lifestyles.

Toward the end of this stage, contact between tourists and residents becomes more impersonal and formal. Tourism continues to grow, but local tourist services and local resources—administrative, economic, and professional skills—are no longer able to keep up with the volume of tourists. *(12)*

In many cases, the entrepreneurial talents that permitted the growth of the initial tourist-oriented hotels, restaurants, and other services are no longer valuable in organizing and managing the types of facilities needed. A few of the original entrepreneurs are able to adjust; in many cases they become prominent figures in the tourist industry; but others will leave or if they stay, will not be significant players. The economy is now ready for the next plateau in development.

## Stage III Scenario. Maturity—Institutionalization

Stage III, Maturity, is characterized by a large number of tourists and formalization of services, itineraries, and roles. The community begins to sense a loss of local decision-making power and control over the tourism industry.

Many of the hotels, airlines, and other services are now affiliated with international corporations exercising decisions from offices located in other states or in other countries. Thus, the community population becomes economically dependent on organizations or individuals who do not live in the area, but who exert ownership or control over business, creating a feeling that outsiders have taken over.

As maturity leads to institutionalization, procedures and facilities become standardized. This leads to greater efficiency but may also provoke feelings of community resentment against the loss of indigenous culture, symbolized by the appearance of franchised structures and services everywhere. On the other hand, the material quality of life improves for the local population as residents are exposed to new ideas and have more disposable income. A revival of native crafts may occur since these items are desired by travelers. The increased production of native crafts to meet the tourists' demand generates revenues and helps create a **cottage industry** comprised of small craft businesses operated from the home or local art studios.

The resident population is forced to accept changes in work patterns. Employers will no longer accept casual work habits or sloppy dress; more formal attire and professional behavior is required. This creates stress within a population that previously had little concept of time or other customs labeled as *good work habits* in an industrialized society.

The availability of jobs creates population growth in the area, intensifying social pressures. What may once have been a quiet rural community suddenly finds itself in an urban or semiurban environment. With growing urbanization and the addition of newcomers to the community, the character of the community gradually changes and there is a decline in neighborly goodwill and helpfulness. Conflicts between generations and between sexes may arise. Unskilled women can generally find employment as chambermaids, but unskilled adult men may have difficulties. Younger people of both sexes find fairly abundant employment opportunities if they have some basic education and show a willingness to adopt new work habits. However, changes in household employment and income patterns may weaken the traditional system of authority within the family.

Consumption patterns of individuals in the community symbolizes and intensify local social stratification. Those at the top in income levels and positions can emulate the consumption behavior of visitors. They may purchase all of the goods and services originally developed to serve high-end tourists. These individuals may be envied or resented as they are observed by other residents who participate only as workers. Depending on the community, social changes seeded by tourism may be more favorable than unfavorable. But in worse case scenarios, tourism may introduce more crime, suicides, and prostitution in the community; and AIDS or new forms of venereal disease and influenza may also surface.

## Stage IV Scenario. Decline—Saturation and Alienation

At this final stage, the destination has become saturated and residents are disenchanted because tourism has not produced all of the promised benefits. For visitors, the factors that were responsible for the destination's earlier success—the enthusiastic welcome, the open hospitality and receptivity of the residents, the appeal of the community, the clean and uncongested environment, and the lack of gross commercialization—have disappeared and travelers respond by seeking other unspoiled destinations.

It is not inevitable for a destination to pass through all of these stages. Some never grow beyond Stage I. It is also possible for a destination to move directly from Stage I to Stage III, as was the case with Fiji and Guam; neither of these destinations ever truly experienced a Stage II growth pattern of local response and initiative as visitor traffic was generated quickly once government policymakers decided to promote tourism *(12)* An area can move directly into Stage III without passing through either of the previous stages. The destination resort area of Cancun in Mexico is an example. Before a resort was constructed, Cancun experienced very little, if any, tourism. Even in the decline stage, measures can be taken to rejuvenate a destination. The introduction of gambling in Atlantic City (with not altogether satisfactory results) and the repositioning of Miami as a **gateway city** to and from Latin America provide examples of efforts taken to rejuvenate declining destinations.

# SUMMARY

With the advent of mass tourism, the need to engage in formal destination planning and to establish sound policies with respect to development has become more evident. Not only for the sake of residents who are captive hosts in the visitor destination or just for the preservation or conservation of natural resources, but proper planning also helps to ensure the sustainability of a destination. Closely tied to the success of any destination are the specific markets served by the community and the various types of traveller personalities that must be accommodated in developing supporting attractions. Destinations that have failed to plan for the orderly growth of tourism with special attention to community and visitor needs have frequently paid the price when problems of a social and environmental nature became overwhelming and once booming tourism traffic began to disappear.

Destination planning entails numerous processes and activities in the conscious planning, financing, developing, and marketing of a destination to attract visitors. It requires the cooperation and commitment of many parties, including government officials, community leaders, architects, engineers, investors, environmentalists, sociologists, economists, and other experts. It requires also an understanding of the concepts of environmental and social carrying capacities of tourist communities on the part of the decision-makers. The key to orderly development seems to lie in proper planning for controlled development, awareness and vigilance on the part of host communities and governments, and careful monitoring of actions. Above all, destination development requires education and the understanding of the rights and responsibilities of both hosts and visitors.

# *D*ISCUSSION QUESTIONS

1. Why is tourism policy and planning important?

2. What are the major types of destination attractions?

3. What elements would you consider in planning for a new destination?

4. Explain the carrying capacity concept and economic tradeoffs.

5. Explain the social carrying capacity concept and its importance to visitors and host communities.

6. How does the Plog theory apply to the planning, development or marketing of destinations? Do policymakers have any real control over who may be attracted to a destination?

7. Discuss the different personality types among tourists.

8. What type of destination would accommodate an allocentrist? Midcentrist? Psychocentrist?

9. How is destination life cycle theory applied in destination planning and development?

10. Is Stage IV, Decline—Saturation and Alienation, a necessary outcome of tourism growth? What policies would you develop to prevent entering this stage of tourism growth?

## SUGGESTED STUDENT EXERCISE

### Case Study of Karimun Island (14)

Foreign tourism to Karimun only started in the late 1980's when improved high-speed ferry services from Batam made overnight visits from Singapore possible. The place quickly developed a reputation in Singapore's mountain cycling fraternity as "dirt bike heaven."

In May 1995, an international ferry terminal opened in Tanjung Balai Karimun (TBK), thus allowing passengers from Singapore to reach the island in just an hour and a half, compared to three hours previously. Four ferry companies became locked in fierce competition to provide direct service between Singapore's World Trade Centre (WTC) and TBK. Eight return trips today operate daily, up from only one in 1993. And it is now viable to organize short one-day tours.

Basic Facilities

Karimun's business community, cash-rich but inexperienced in the requirements of modern tourism, is now facing the challenge of how to develop attractions which warrant the surging investment in basic facilities.

Karimun lies near the mouth of Sumatra's giant Siak River, the major cause of the silt-colored waters in this area. This limits Karimun's potential to develop beach resorts. Talks of a golf course and country club abound, although there is no sign of work having actually commenced. A recently opened fishing resort at Karimun's Pelawan Beach enables visitors to try their luck on the rich fishing grounds near Teluk Setumbul. (See Figure 6.8)

Singapore's Sembawang group is building a shipyard and oil tank terminal which will take advantage of Karimun's deepwater frontage onto the Malacca Strait. Three new hotels opened in the first quarter of this year, which doubled TBK's 1993 room capacity. Several more hotels are planned or under construction.

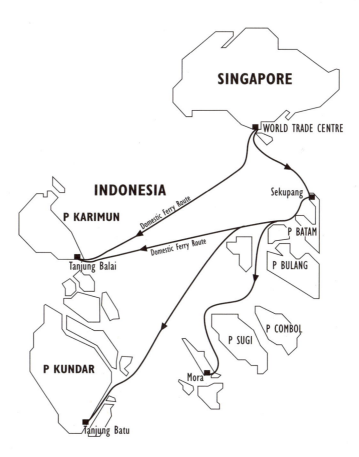

**Figure 6.8**  Map of Karimun Island.

### Tanjung Balai

So far, foreign tourism to Karimun has been confined to three main areas: budget-priced weekend seafood package deals aimed at Singapore's Chinese speaking market; family soft-adventure tours for educated Singaporeans and expatriates; and sex tourism for Singaporean males.

Tanjung Balai has become Singapore's major jumping-off point for outdoor soft adventure activities such as cycling, trekking, and sea-kayaking tours where guests explore the unspoiled islands which lie to Karimun's south. The town's ethnic mix is very similar to Singapore's. A mostly Chinese entrepot town, it has one of Southeast Asia's largest and prosperous distant-water fishing fleets.

Since a flourishing entrepot trade often involves smuggled goods, Karimun has Indonesia's second-largest customs post. Over 1,000 officers struggle to contain the huge illicit export and import trade, which occurs in the thousands of islands which make up the Riau archipelago. A crowded, scruffy town of 60,000, it is remarkably safe and crime-free in spite of being the center of such large-scale illicit activities.

Address the following in your analysis of the above case:

1. Describe the type of hotels/restaurants/attractions you would envision for this land. (Think in terms of size, price range, style, etc.) Also mention potential infrastructure needs.

2. Describe some of the potential positive and negative economic, social, cultural, and environmental impacts from the surge in arrivals. What measures could be taken to counter any negative impacts?

3. Describe a marketing campaign to a likely target market. Mention the various activities and attractions.

4. Present your arguments on why Karimun Island **should not** encourage tourism growth.

# $\mathcal{R}$EFERENCES

1. Hawaii State Plan Policy Council, Department of Planning and Economic Development, *The Hawaii State Plan Revised* (Honolulu: DPED 1986) pg. 5.

2. Hawaii State Plan Appendix: *Chapter 226, Hawaii Revised Statutes As Amended* (Honolulu, Department of Planning and Economic Development 1986), pg. 4.

3. *Declaration of Manila*, Manila: World Tourism Conference, September-October 1980.

4. Travel Industry Association of America, *Marketing the U.S. Travel Product: Selling to Germany*, (Washington, D.C.: TIA, 1993) pg. 14.

5. Travel Industry Association of America, *Marketing the U.S. Travel Product, Selling to Japan* (Washington D.C.,: TIA, 1993) pg. 62

6. Medlik, S., and V. T. C. Middleton. "The Tourism Product and Its Marketing Implications." *International Tourism Quarterly* No. 3, September 1973.

7. Helber, L. E. " How to Develop a New Destination Area." Paper presented at Pacific Area Travel Association Workshop, Kyongju, Korea, April 20, 1979.

8. Burkhart, A. J., and S. Medlik. "Infrastructure and Facilities." *Tourism*. London: Heinemann, 1974.

9. Bangur, J., and A. Arbel. " A Comprehensive Approach to the Planning of the Tourism Industry." *Journal of Travel Research* 14, No.2 (Fall 1975).

10. Likorish, L. J., and A. G. Kershaw. *The Travel Trade*. London: Practical Press Ltd., 1958.

11. Plog, S. " Why Destination Areas Rise and Fall in Popularity." Paper presented at meeting of Southern California Chapter of Travel Research Association, October 10, 1972.

12. Noronha, R. *Social and Cultural Dimensions of Tourism: A Review of the Literature in English*. Tourism Projects Dept., World Bank, May 18, 1977.

13. Nolan, Jr., S. D. " Variations in Travel Behavior and Cultural Impact." Paper presented at the 74th Annual Meeting of the American Anthropological Association, San Francisco, 1975.

14. Jones, Evan. Karimun Island Prepares for a Surge in Arrivals, *Asia Travel Trade*, September 1994.

# Chapter 7

# Impacts of Tourism

---

## LEARNING OBJECTIVES

- To understand the nature of economic impacts of tourism.
- To understand possible social and cultural impacts of tourism.
- To understand environmental impacts of tourism.
- To understand some of the possible negative side effects of tourism growth.
- To define and use the following terms:

| | |
|---|---|
| Community interpretation | Leakages |
| Cost-benefit analysis | Multiplier |
| Cultural impact | Secondary effects |
| Direct effects | Social impact |
| Environmental impact | Sociological cycle |
| Exports | Sustainable tourism |
| Human environment | Tourism Bill of Rights and Tourist Code |
| Imports | |

# IMPACTS OF TOURISM ON DESTINATIONS

We have seen that as tourism grows and the number of travelers increases, so does the potential for both positive and negative impacts. Chapter 6 discussed how proper planning and tourism policies can help alleviate some of the potentially adverse effects, particularly for communities considering tourism as a means of economic growth.

The advent of mass communication and education have had a significant role in the development of modern travel. Advancements in technology, innovations and changes in the travel market have affected all segments of the economy and simultaneously provoked new concerns in terms of social and environmental issues.

A great deal has been written about the various impacts that tourism can have on destinations, and these writings discuss both positive and negative aspects at length. Government policies, which were discussed in Chapter 5, often reflect expressed public concerns about tourism impacts not only on the economy, but on social development, culture, and the environment. Our intent in this chapter is to provide students with a fuller understanding of this all-important subject.

# ECONOMIC IMPACT

When travelers from outside the host community purchase goods and services within the community, tourism acts as an **export** industry by bringing in new revenues from external sources. Travelers' expenditures also increase the general level of economic activity in the host community in numerous ways, directly and indirectly, the two most visible being new jobs and income. Taxes collected by government will also increase with the higher level of economic activity. In the case of international travelers, a host nation will gain foreign exchange, which will help to improve that nation's balance of payments in import/export trade. As the number of visitors making purchases increases, demand for the products and services produced in a host community increases. If the community has sufficient resources to increase production to meet this higher level of demand, the full amount of visitor expenditures will remain in the community. If production is not increased locally, the community will have to import resources such as raw materials, capital, and labor. Figure 7.1 illustrates this situation.

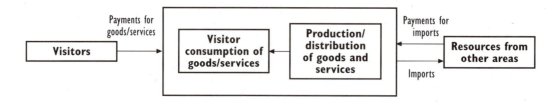

**Figure 7.1**   Tourism as an export industry.

Visitor expenditures in a community are considered exports, since the products and services are sold to people who come from outside the host community. Imports are **leakages** to an economy, in that monies leave an area to purchase these outside resources. Payments for imports must be subtracted from the expenditures generated by visitors in estimating the total economic impact upon the community.

Tourism's economic impact on a country, state, or community can be enormous in terms of revenues and employment, even when we consider only domestic revenues from tourism. The revenues from domestic tourism in the United States in 1994, for example, were estimated at $416 billion (based on trips 100 miles from home). These domestic expenditures generated some 6.2 million direct jobs and $56 billion in federal, state, and local taxes. *(1)*

To assess the full economic impact of visitor expenditures, one must account for both international and domestic tourism. Although international tourism in the United States currently represents only 9% of the total worldwide tourism market, the revenue from foreign travel to the United States has become an increasingly important factor in its international trade account. International visitors to the U.S. spent $75 billion in 1994, which created a $22 billion surplus as international visitors spent more money in the U.S. than Americans spent abroad. *(1)*

## Importance of Foreign Travelers to the United States

While domestic tourism mainly redistributes wealth within a nation, foreign tourism generates new funds. Prior to 1989, the United States consistently incurred deficits in the U.S. travel balance, as Americans spent more abroad than foreign travelers spent in the United States. Travel dollar accounts, however, have shown consecutive surpluses since 1989, as shown in Table 7.1. The estimated travel surplus for 1993 was approximately $22 billion. Tourism is now America's largest service export *(2)* and is one of the few trade accounts that shows a surplus, which helps to offset the U.S. trade deficit. Clearly,

| **TABLE 7.1** **U.S. International Travel Account 1989–1993** | | | | | |
|---|---|---|---|---|---|
| **Number of Travelers (thousands)** | **1989** | **1990** | **1991** | **1992** | **1993** |
| Foreign Arrivals | 36,564 | 39,539 | 42,986 | 44,647 | 45,650 |
| U.S. Departures | 41,138 | 44,623 | 41,566 | 43,895 | 45,490 |
| **Balance** | **−4,574** | **−5,084** | **1,420** | **752** | **160** |
| **Dollar Account (millions)** | **1989** | **1990** | **1991** | **1992** | **1993** |
| Receipts | $46,863 | $58,305 | $64,237 | $71,214 | $74,560 |
| Payments | $41,666 | $47,879 | $45,334 | $50,815 | $52,585 |
| **Balance** | **$5,197** | **$10,426** | **$18,903** | **$20,399** | **$21,975** |

*Source:* U.S. Travel and Tourism Administration. *(3)*

travel and tourism around the world has become a major player in helping countries to achieve or to offset favorable or unfavorable international trade balances.

## Direct and Secondary Effects

In order to measure the actual economic impact of tourism on a community, we should emphasize that a host community may not actually receive all travel expenditures. For example, payment for air transportation is usually made at the traveler's point of origin and does not accrue to the destination. Other examples include payments for imported food, beverages, and retail products. While travelers may consume or purchase these products during their stay, these payments leave the host community and represent a debit to the community's trade account as previously shown in Figure 7.1.

The amount of visitor expenditures that remains in a community provides a source of income for residents and businesses. Visitor expenditures received as income by businesses such as hotels, restaurants, car rentals, tour operators, and retail shops serving tourists have a **direct effect** on the economy of the host community. The term "direct" reflects the fact that the monies received by direct providers (recall the linking concept in Chapter 1) triggers the first round of spending by businesses providing visitor services to pay for salaries and wages, supplies, equipment, taxes, and so on.

Indirect or **secondary effects** come about as the monies received by support services and other local businesses, are used in turn to pay for supplies, wages of workers, and other items used in producing the products or direct services purchased by the visitors. The initial amount of visitor expenditures that remains in the host community generates income within the community typically exceeding the initial amount; that is, $1 of visitor expenditure can be ultimately worth $2 or more in total economic value. The flow of the visitor or tourist dollars in a local economy is diagrammed in Figure 7.2. (4)

To illustrate the foregoing, consider the example of a visitor who spends $1,000 at a tourist destination. He or she stays in an international-class hotel, dines in upscale restaurants, and buys several foreign-made items as souvenirs. Since the expenditures can encompass items such as imported supplies for the hotel, gourmet items and wines from abroad, and foreign-made souvenirs, it is possible that 50% of the expenditures directly leaves the community as payments for imports. The amount remaining in the community would be $500. Part of the remaining $500 would go directly to pay local personnel whose income is spent on products for personal use. The personal expenditures of these people, in turn, provide income for other businesses in the area such as grocery and clothing stores. Another part of the $500 would go to stockholders of hotels, restaurants, and airlines; the support companies that provide materials and services to these businesses; and other sectors of the economy. The people employed in other sectors also would spend their incomes on products for personal use, which would pump the money back into the local economy.

Through such successive rounds of spending, the initial $500 remaining in a community out of $1,000 spent by a visitor creates additional income for many sectors of the economy. By generating new jobs and, in many cases, new businesses, tourism can affect the distribution of income in a community. The redistribution of income may have both economic and social impacts, depending upon the pattern of ownership and availability of local resources.

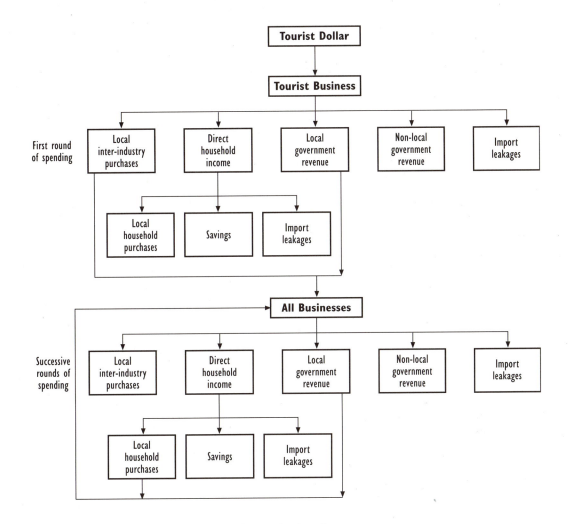

**Figure 7.2** Flow of the tourist dollar in the local economy.

*Source:* "The Economic Impact of Tourism on an Island Economy: A Case Study of Victoria, B.C."

## Tourism Multiplier

The term **multiplier**, which comes from macroeconomics, is used to describe the total effect, that is, both direct and secondary, of an external source of income introduced into an economy. The concept of the multiplier typically is used in the travel industry to encompass the direct and secondary effects of visitor expenditures on an economy.

It should be noted that there is no such thing as "the" multiplier; that is, no single, all-encompassing multiplier. Multipliers can be estimated for sales or output produced by businesses, employment, payroll, or other variables. As shown in Table 7.2, the output multiplier of foreign visitors to the United States is 2.37; employment, 2.28; and for payroll, 2.76.

| TABLE 7.2 | | | |
|---|---|---|---|
| **Economic Impact of Foreign Visitor Spending in the United States, 1994** | | | |
| | **Direct Impact** | **Multiplier** | **Total Impact** |
| *Output* | $51.8 billion | 2.37 | $137.8 billion |
| *Employment* | 947,900 | 2.28 | 2,160,500 |
| *Payroll* | $15.8 billion | 2.76 | $43.6 billion |

*Source:* U.S. Travel Data Center/Travel Industry Association of America, Tourism Industries/International Trade Administration. *(5)*

| TABLE 7.3 | |
|---|---|
| **Tourism Income Multipliers** | |
| **Country or Region** | **Tourism Income Multiplier** |
| Ireland | 1.776–1.906 |
| United Kingdom | 1.683–1.784 |
| Dominica | 1.195 |
| Antigua | 0.880 |
| Cayman Islands | 0.650 |

*Source:* From Archer. *(6)*

One also should be aware that the value of multipliers will not be the same for all countries or communities (see Table 7.3), depending on the availability of local resources in the respective areas. Island communities with limited resources, for instance, may lose 50% or more of their visitor expenditures as direct payments for imports of all kinds—construction materials, textiles, food, etc.—and therefore have lower multipliers. Note the low multipliers for Dominica, Antigua, and especially the Cayman Islands.

## Price Changes

The prices of products and services can change in response to changes in demand and/or supply conditions. For example, lower production costs can result in lower prices for the respective products and services. Higher prices can result from an increase in demand or increases in production costs. Visitor spending in a host community may result in higher prices because their purchases would increase the demand for goods and services. This leads to an inflationary situation, whereby residents would also have to pay more for goods and services which are in demand by both visitors and residents. Through the multiplier, prices of other goods and services may also increase as income in the community increases and people want more goods and services.

Rising land values caused by tourism development is also a major contributor to inflation. As prime land in scenic locations is acquired for resort, recreation, or attraction

# Santa Fe, New Mexico

In a 1992 reader's survey by *Conde Nast Traveler*, Sante Fe, New Mexico was named the Number One destination in the world, surpassing San Francisco, Vienna, Florence, and Rome. The weather during the summer is cool due to its altitude at 7,200 feet above sea level; in the winter the dry cold makes it an attractive base for skiing. The development of a colorful artists' colony boosted Sante Fe's popularity with sophisticated travelers. The town has numerous galleries of folk and modern art, luxury hotels, and gourmet restaurants specializing in Southwestern cuisine. Perhaps the greatest assets of Santa Fe, however, are its buildings of pueblo and territorial adobe-style architecture, especially surrounding The Plaza or town square.

The construction or renovations of buildings in the town must meet city codes requiring them to be built in low-rise adobe-style architecture. With limited land, the popularity of Sante Fe and low-rise construction have accelerated the value of land within the town. Well-heeled newcomers have bid up housing prices to the point where a small two bedroom adobe on a rutted dirt street could easily fetch a quarter million dollars. In recent years, some older residents have been forced to sell their land due to their inability to pay high property taxes. Younger residents cannot afford to purchase homes within the town due to high prices.

Thus, maintaining the architectural integrity of the town has inadvertently made it difficult for residents to afford living within the town limits. At the same time, the Pueblo-style architecture is one of the features which has made Sante Fe attractive to tourists.

*Epilogue 1995:* After soaring throughout the decade with an influx of newcomers, the real estate market has fallen as tourism and housing construction—two important economic mainstays of Santa Fe—are declining, each affecting the other. Some of the decline in tourism and real estate are cyclical, but the possibility remains that as Santa Fe grows from a town into a city, it is inevitably losing much of its only real commodity—its charm. The town, according to many residents, was becoming too expensive and overdue for property inflation correction.

development, land prices are bid up in surrounding areas for commercial or residential purposes. Improvements—infrastructural and building enhancements—increase property value and tax bases, which are ultimately reflected in prices passed on to consumers.

## Economic Instability

Pleasure travel, as a discretionary item, is subject to fluctuations in travel prices and income of travelers. Because of these fluctuations, a host community's growth may be unstable. Periods of rapid growth, static growth, and declines put an economy that is heavily dependent on tourism on shaky ground. Natural disasters such as the volcanic eruption in the Philippines, hurricanes in the Caribbean, and flooding through parts of the United States are unpredictable. These disasters have destroyed communities and discouraged travel to affected areas. Tourism is also sensitive to acts of terrorism, outbreaks of disease, and other unfavorable conditions which put the economy of a host community at risk.

# SOCIAL IMPACT (7)

The social implications of tourism development are complex and not altogether well understood, even to professionals in the tourism field. The most obvious social impacts are also economic ones. These relate to the creation of new jobs and the influx of new income to the area. Although such jobs are usually analyzed in terms of economic benefits, their social implications cannot be overlooked.

Although economic impacts can be quantified, many of the studies on social impacts measure perceived impacts. This is also true for studies on cultural and environmental impacts, since it is difficult and in some cases impossible to measure actual social, cultural, or environmental impacts. Examples of social impacts of earlier tourism developments are discussed in this section to illustrate their potential application to underdeveloped areas today. A sociological cycle of tourism development is presented as a possible framework for understanding the social phases that a tourist destination may experience.

## Employment and Migration

New opportunities for employment created by tourism are not only visible to residents; they also can attract new migrants to the host community. As a result, the question arises as to whether or not these newcomers actually fit into the community. One well-known case was the situation in Manila, the capital of the Philippines, when a rash of hotel construction during the mid-1970s resulted in a rapid population boom in the metropolis. Country dwellers and laborers hungry for work surged into the city seeking job opportunities, creating new social dilemmas and aggravating existing problems. A political solution requiring identity cards for people in the Metro-Manila area as a means of population control was attempted, but ultimately repealed when citizens objected and thousands demonstrated in the streets. A later example is provided by the People's Republic of China, where thousands of migrant workers were drawn from the rural areas to such already overcrowded cities as Shanghai, Beijing, Xian, and other places where new hotels and resorts were being built to meet visitor needs during the booming decade of the '80s.

To understand the social impacts of a growing population, it is necessary to examine such factors as the arrival of new migrants. The faster a community is required to assimilate new residents, the greater the stress on the present structure of the community. Another aspect to consider is the fact that tourism may create job dislocations in other sectors. This may prove to be detrimental to established industries, such as agriculture or fisheries in the area, when workers choose to work in tourism and abandon jobs in agriculture or other industries which are perceived as being less rewarding. These dislocations may disrupt a community's economy built on agriculture or other traditional industries.

Many of the jobs created by the travel industry do not require high-level skills. However, as the travel industry matures in specific destinations, the number of skilled and professional jobs generally increases. While lower-level positions may be easy to fill, positions that require specialized managerial and technical skills are often difficult to fill in communities with technical or professional skills shortages. As a result, the better-paid and higher-status jobs tend to be held by outsiders. In order for a community to fully benefit from tourism, decision makers must include measures to educate and train local residents for higher positions; to ignore this problem is to invite inevitable community resentment and subsequent government intervention.

## Traditional Role of Women

Women in the workforce are today a common phenomena of modern industrialized countries; but there are still many countries and communities in the world where women occupy traditional homemaking roles. As travelers seek new or less well-trodden destinations, tourism is being developed in some of the places where conventional family structures and social values remain unchanged. The conservative social structure of these communities which have opened to tourism may be disrupted when women enter the work force for the first time. The case of the Mauna Kea Beach Resort on the island of Hawaii illustrates what can happen when tourism is introduced into a traditional community. Frances Cottington, psychiatrist, and Mary H. Smith, sociologist, in separate studies examined the first-time employment of large numbers of women when the luxury-class Mauna Kea Beach Resort opened on the rural North Kohala coast of the Island of Hawaii in the late 1960s. At that time, the island's economy centered around rural plantations, mainly sugar and pineapple. Men were the sole breadwinners in these agricultural communities. The Mauna Kea Beach Resort was the North Kohala area's first entry into the tourist industry. The opening of tourism employment opportunities to plantation women, however, stirred unexpected conflicts and tensions in the rural lifestyle and family social order. Interestingly, each researcher reached opposite conclusions on whether the changes overall, had been harmful or beneficial to the community.

Cottington's conclusions (8) were essentially negative, citing the following:

- loss of self-respect among husbands of working women who, in some cases, began to earn more than their husbands or who became the sole family support as men were laid off by local sugar plantation closings;

- jealousy of some husbands whose wives had to dress up "glamorously" to serve hotel guests;

- increased divorce rates, crime, and juvenile delinquency;

- frustration and financial insolvency from rising expectations and subsequent overspending by workers exposed to high consumption patterns of hotel guests;

- increased anxiety and illness among females who were unaccustomed to and unprepared for the increased pressures and responsibilities of working for the first time.

Smith, in a paper written three years later, acknowledging the validity of Cottington's observations, tentatively concluded that the hotel's "culture shock" on the community was subsiding somewhat and that the benefits were beginning to outweigh the negative effects. *(9)* She cited these examples:

- increased family income visibly raised the standard of living in the community;
- new skills and salaries gave women workers a sense of increased self-worth and accomplishment;
- expanded social contacts with fellow employees and tourists produced an expanded awareness of the outside world among the women workers;
- family roles were changing for the better as husbands assumed more of the household and child-rearing chores;
- husbands were beginning to develop more respect for their wives as competent individuals able to hold good jobs;
- increased income and an expanded world view could result in more opportunity for higher education for the workers' children.

Consequently, although initial effects of tourism appeared to be negative, the longer term effects seem to be beneficial for the women and their families.

## Consumption Behavior

From a sociological perspective, tourist expenditures can have both a positive and negative effect on a community. When business is good, the additional revenues generated by visitors raise the general level of income in the community, which in turn raises the standard of living for residents. On the obverse side, when residents begin to emulate the lifestyles of outsiders, their own values and consumption behavior may change, shifting from conservative consumption patterns towards the instant gratification of wants and desires. Residents of rural communities quickly observe that their own locally produced consumer goods are often inferior to imported goods. As a result, residents begin to save less and borrow more in order to support altered consumption habits.

## Sociological Cycle

Analogous to the life cycle theory of a destination discussed in Chapter 6, it has been suggested that tourist destination development from a sociological perspective follows five basic phases: (1) discovery stage, (2) developmental stage, (3) conflict stage, (4) confrontation stage, and (5) decline stage.

The discovery stage is noted for its low volume of visitors, and hence, residents are not exposed to any of the effects of development. Residents welcome tourism development enthusiastically in the development stage, because of its visible contribution to the local economy. Benefits are perceived in terms of improved infrastructure and higher income levels generated directly by tourism or tourist-related jobs. However, development also encourages crime as visitors become visible prey for perpetrators and juvenile mischief makers.

Local resentment first appears in the conflict stage, which is reflected in hostile attitudes toward visitors. This hostility usually results from competition over resources—water, energy, land usage, recreational facilities, beach front property, and so on. For example, recreational facilities are oftentimes land intensive as in the case of golf courses, recreational parks, coastal beaches, and marinas. This can be perceived positively when acknowledged as a means of preserving open space and reducing overall development densities. However, problems arise when residents are excluded from such facilities or when a resort developed primarily for visitors cramps the traditional leisure activities of residents.

Problems are further accentuated in the confrontation stage, which results in organized opposition to new developments, land use rights, and fights over the use of scarce resources. In numerous countries, for example, there have been open confrontations between the agricultural and tourism sectors over the use of precious water during the development of new resort areas. The decline stage is usually signaled by hostile activities, such as forms of sabotage, rampant crime, lack of safety, and outflow of capital. The last three stages are attended by a progressive erosion of community goodwill; once goodwill and community support are gone, the consequences are difficult, if not impossible, to reverse.

It is essential that these social phases be understood in order to prevent, or at least deter the erosion; social planning is one of the viable means to do so effectively. Research on the social consequences of tourism on the community is the first step. The information generated by research should lead to an action plan to circumvent possible unfavorable social impacts and to reinforce tourism's positive contributions. Second, it is mandatory that the community be involved in the actual planning and development process. Residents should be made to feel that they have a stake in the success of the destination.

Social planning is necessary at all levels of development—for mature as well as new tourism destinations. Mature destinations are more susceptible to social deterioration when destinations become saturated, markets dissipate, and new investments are not forthcoming. Planning efforts at this point must be focused on halting the erosion process, although the measures taken may not always be successful.

Community resentment is manifested in many forms. In terms of the workforce, the industry may experience lower employee morale, reduced productivity, poor service, absenteeism, delays, or strikes. In more general terms, the industry loses community support for tourism projects and law-makers are less willing to provide resources for tourism promotion, or may even pass legislation detrimental to tourism growth. Any and all of these will have a visible impact on a destination's quality, reputation, and ultimately, on its profitability. A social plan, therefore, must be given as much weight as an economic or an environmental plan in tourism development.

# CULTURAL IMPACT

The impact of tourism development on culture is difficult to assess. Tourism development creates an economic demand for the trappings of local culture. The demand cultivated by tourism provides opportunities, good and bad, to preserve or exploit local art forms and customs. On the positive side, local artists, musicians, craftsmen, and individuals engaged in the performing arts are able to make a living in their crafts and vocations, thus helping to keep the arts alive and well in the community. This core of employed artists can spark a general renewal of interest by residents in their own cultural heritage.

On the negative side, selling or performing for pay on a regular basis of what was once done ceremonially or to perpetuate a tradition, can break down the cultural value and respect of local residents for their own art forms, religion, and traditions. These cultural displays, which once were ends in themselves, now become just a means of achieving a different end—earned cash income.

Some sociologists believe that tourism in its less benign form is nothing short of an invitation to a collision of cultures and values—an opening for a direct confrontation between peoples with vastly differing values and social patterns.

## Cultural Collision

When cultural collision occurs, several results are possible:

1. accommodation, or more accurately "toleration," in which both the visitor and the visited coexist in a live and let live fashion;

2. segregation in which the tourists and host population maintain a social distance or separation by means of either avoidance or containment of visitors within"golden ghettos" of luxury hotels, golf courses, shops and other amenities designed for tourists;

3. opposition in which the tourists are rejected by members of the host community (exhibited by surly behavior, discourtesy, etc.). Or, the host community is rejected by tourists who behave in a condescending manner toward residents or ridicule local customs, lifestyles, vocabulary, or speech;

4. diffusion in which either or both groups, the tourists and the host population, borrow or adapt cultural traits or elements of the other.

In earlier times, these processes were activated only through migration, colonization, religious proselytization, political occupation, or inter-regional trading. Today, with increasingly efficient modes of transportation and numerous package tours, tourism has stimulated contact between people of varying cultures as never before. Thus, tourism has become an agent of, as well as an impediment to, cultural change.

The experiences of some countries have been, at once, comic and tragic. According to one source, Uganda had tried unsuccessfully to persuade one of its tribes to wear clothes to protect the country's international image *(10)*, while Malaysian tour guides have outfitted Iban girls with white, Western-style brassieres to wear while dancing the heretofore topless Ajat Main for tourists. *(11)* Portugal, at one point, launched a series of television commercials to instruct its citizens to be polite to tourists and not to spit on the sidewalk.

National tourist offices in tropical island destinations point out another aspect of tourism-induced cultural collision: the natives "soon replace their picturesque costumes with cheap imitations of the metropolitan tourist's dress (T-shirts and jeans), while the tourists adorn themselves with expensive imitations of native costumes." *(12)*

Invasion by tourists can ruin the tranquil and unique way of life in areas such as Pennsylvania, where this Amish farmer is planting winter wheat.

On Bali, where the inhabitants feel that theirs is the superior culture, tourist dress is not imitated. However, a more sensitive subject than dress involves the Barong, a sacred figure represented by a bright, horse-like costume with a wooden, lion-like face that can be carved only from a tree growing in a cemetery. Before tourism was developed in Bali, the Barong danced in the temple on festival days or at a time of calamity. Two men, considered by the Balinese to be under the spell of the Barong, manipulate the costume from inside. Today, Barong dances are performed almost constantly—not for ceremony, but for tourists. During one such performance, according to a Washington Post report, one of the dancers fell into a trance, professed to be "possessed" by the Barong, which, he said was "tired of dancing for tourists." Another Barong, so the account reported, "has never refused to dance, but at times has been wont to change, knocking over tripods and cameras…when persistent photography threatens to disrupt the ceremony." *(13)*

Not all host communities, unfortunately, are protected by Barongs. In the case of Finland, for instance, international tourism has accelerated the extinction of the Lapp culture and interfered with local occupations, such as reindeer herding and berry picking. "Old village culture has completely disappeared—it is merely revived artificially with the aim of making money," says author P. J. Ropponen. *(14)*

In the United States, the invasion of Lancaster County, Pennsylvania by tourists has all but extinguished the unique and fragile way of life of the Amish and plastered the once-tranquil countryside with motels, gas stations, golf courses, drive-ins, frozen custard stands, souvenir shops, and an amusement park. An Amish farm bakery, once noted for its shoo-fly pie, is now selling canned, homemade pizza sauce. Tour bus visitors, all with the determination of amateur lens enthusiasts on a photo safari, subject horrified Amish children to "forced photography." The children have been raised to believe that a photograph is a graven image and equate being photographed with breaking the second of the Ten Commandments.

## Cultural Interpretation

Cultural or **community interpretation** is one means of mitigating the negative impacts of tourism upon a host region's culture. One of the main objectives of cultural interpretation is to assist visitors in developing a keener awareness, appreciation, and understanding of the area and culture of the people they are visiting. Before this can be achieved, it often is necessary to first educate residents about the area within which they live.

The general goal of community interpretation is to link people with sites, stories, and information about an area, as well as to link people with other people in a community and residents with visitors. Effective interpretation relates a site or subject matter to everyday life and presents information from unique viewpoints to stimulate thinking. *(15)* The environment can be used in terms of sounds, smells, taste, and touch to arouse visitors' curiosity and interest in learning.

Interpretation can be incorporated into the training of tour guides to ensure the authenticity and quality of information presented to visitors. The U.S. National Park Service, for example, has been a leader in training its staff to interpret and present the information on historic sites and national parks so that visitors can learn and better appreciate the areas. Unique cultural and community towns have been designed in Hawaii to explore historic Waikiki, the ghosts of downtown Honolulu, Chinatown, and other parts of the community. Both residents and visitors have gone on these walking tours accompanied by a guide trained in community interpretation.

The better informed visitors are about a place and its people, the more respect and sensitivity they will have toward them. Community interpretation also provides a more enriching experience for visitors and helps them to differentiate one destination from another. For residents, community interpretation enriches their understanding and also provides a means for preserving the cultural integrity of an area.

## International Tourist Code and Tourism Bill of Rights

A report *(16)* by the United Nations Economic Commission for Europe (ECE) in 1975 examined problems regarding tourism's impact on culture and questioned "whether the objective of greater mutual understanding is consistent with policies which make maximum flows of international tourism its overriding concern." The report concluded that in order to make tourism an effective means for the development of social and cultural contact in the ECE region (which includes the United States), great efforts need to be made in the field of education and information in both tourist-sending and tourist-receiving countries and recommended

> that the ECE and the World Tourism Organization (a) examine the possibility of establishing a code of conduct for tourist, both domestic and international, and ground rules for tourist project developments, particularly those of a multinational character; (b) promote public information programs, public participation, and pedagogical efforts, all designed to ameliorate public awareness of benefits to, and responsibilities of, tourists; (c) explore possibilities of reconciling tourism growth with environmental and social problems in specifically exposed

areas of common concern, such as the Alpine region, the Mediterranean basin, European coastlines, the Baltic Sea, the Danube River basin, and the Black Sea area; (d) convene symposia and expert group meetings to examine various issues related to comprehensive planning and development of tourism.

In 1985, during its Sixth General Assembly in Sofia, Bulgaria, the WTO adopted a *Tourism Bill of Rights and Tourist Code. (17)* Prior to the adoption of the *Tourism Bill of Rights and Tourist Code* by the World Tourism Organization, WTO and the United Nations Environment Programme (UNEP) had held an earlier joint workshop in 1983 on the Environmental Aspects of Tourism. *(18)* Among other conclusions reached by the Workshop participants, several statements touched on the social-cultural problems introduced by mass tourism:

- "When tourists enter the host country, they do not just bring their purchasing power…they also, and above all, bring a different type of society which profoundly transforms local social habits by removing and upsetting the basic and long-established values and patterns of behavior of the host population.

- Tourism is indeed, therefore, a 'total social event' which leads to structural changes in all sectors of society and which becomes generalized by progressively being extended to all regions of the globe.

- During the tourist season, the resident population not only has to accept the effects of overcrowding, which do not exist for the remainder of the year, but they must often completely modify their way of life (increased work rhythm, dual activity, etc.) and live in close contact with a different type of population, mainly urban who are there simply for leisure; however, this 'coexistence' is not always easy and often leads to social tension, xenophobia, particularly noticeable in very popular tourist areas or where the population, for psychological, cultural, or social reasons, is not ready to be submitted to 'the tourist invasion.'"

# *E*NVIRONMENTAL IMPACT (7)

The environmental impact of tourism development is a basic issue that must be considered whether we are discussing tourism in a developed or a developing country or community. In a developing community, tourism can be an answer to some of the prevalent life-threatening environmental problems, such as poor water supplies, inadequate sanitation and sewage facilities, deficient nutrition, bad housing conditions, sickness and disease, and vulnerability to natural disasters. In a developed community, on the other hand, these fundamental environmental problems for the most part already have been solved, but secondary environmental problems, such as congestion, waste disposal, pollution and other side effects of growth become mounting issues.

In addition to the natural environment, the human environment as it relates to people must also be considered. The objectives of sustainable tourism recognizes the importance of balancing economic goals within the constraints of both the natural and human environments, which will be discussed in the following sections.

Outdoor camping is a popular form of tourism, especially around scenic lakes. However, overuse of these natural sites for recreation and lack of control over waste disposal can harm the environment.
Credit: New York State Dept. of Economic Development.

## Natural Environment

In a developed community, particularly a rapidly growing one, the problems of urbanization—human and vehicular traffic, congestion, noise, exhaust fumes, air pollution, sewage, loss of green belts, and other detriments—can destroy the pleasant ambiance of the community for visitors and residents alike. One means of combatting environmental pollution is to control a community's rate of development. For example, when a new resort is to be built, its developer could make a conscious decision to set aside a portion of the land for conservation purposes. In the United States, some resort developers, owners, and management companies have strong environmental commitments, devoting a part of their investment capital for conservation and enhancement uses with the intent of preventing further loss of native species and promoting green policies.

Even as the impact of tourism is undergoing closer scrutiny, there is also growing awareness of the importance of the environment to tourism. In far too many communities, unfortunately, the awareness has come at the eleventh hour, when damage has already been done to both the environment and the tourism industry. In many coastal and lakeside areas around the world, pollution from resort communities, along with industrial waste of nearby factories and plants, have rendered waters so polluted and toxic that warning signs must be posted to alert tourists not to swim or fish from these waters. An example is the La Boca resort area in Bueno Aires, which is notorious for the foul waters which flow from the adjacent river carrying meat-plant waste, chemicals, and sewage; the odors are obnoxious—especially on days when the air is stifling and still—driving visitors to seek other more hospitable destinations. In Spain, the Ministry of Trade and Tourism along with the Ministry of Public Works, is undertaking strategic action to downsize tourism in the Costa del Sol and other resort areas because of alarming "symptoms of growing tourist dissatisfaction." According to the ministry, the areas of dissatisfaction include "the adequacy of infrastructure, noise pollution, hygienic conditions, beach congestion, etc." Programs to improve the situation and to prevent further loss of tourism quality will address orderly land use, renovation and modernization of the visitor plant, adequacy of infrastructure, and stopping environmental contamination and further environmental deterioration.

The Galapagos Islands is an example of a destination that is essential to science and to the tourist economy of Ecuador. These islands are an isolated archipelago 600 miles west of Ecuador in the Pacific with unique species of wildlife, both flora and fauna. Because of the importance of these islands for natural science study and the need to guard against the adverse effects of unrestrained human intrusion on wildlife, the Ecuador government devised a way to use controlled tourism as a means of raising funds to save the environment and to establish protected areas. Controlled tourism in this instance required a working definition of the carrying capacity of the Galapagos and limiting the number of visitors to a safe level in order to protect the wildlife and ecology of the islands. The first standard of visitor capacity limitation set at 25,000 annual arrivals was established according to the number of spaces and baths available on cruise ships, boats, and small hotels on the islands. *(19)*

## Human Environment

**Human environment** is the environment as it relates to people. It embraces factors that are physical, psychological, and ecological. Beauty, harmonic proportion, and naturalness are qualitative elements of these factors. Changes in the physical environment should be made with the objective of creating a destination that is pleasing to visitors, yet that blends into, or further enhances, the natural landscape. Developers attempt to accomplish this objective by promoting the use of organic materials, low-rise architecture, and landscaping design that complements the natural advantages of scenic sites and exceptional land features. Additional reinforcement can be provided by using indigenous building materials. Excellent examples are the Lobo Wildlife Lodge, owned by the Tanzanian government, and the Mara Serena Lodge in East Kenya. The former is nestled into and hewed out of a rock outcropping and the latter is blended into the grassy mesa of the Great Serengeti Plains. Almost seeming to have sprung naturally from their surroundings, these resorts offer luxury and comfort without detracting from the beauty that surrounds them.

Another means of enhancing or preserving the human environment is to maintain the historical and/or cultural integrity of an area. Tourism offers many opportunities for bringing people and their heritage together, thus building a bridge between past and present. An example of this is Colonial Williamsburg in Virginia. Tourist accommodations

The Mount Kenya Mountain Lodge is an example of how tourist facilities can be incorporated into the natural environment where visitors can view a spectacular parade of big game at the waterhole from their room balconies.
Courtesy of Kenya Tourist Office.

are often renovated religious retreats or hospitals. In other cases, they may be converted mansions or other types of buildings with local historic value. Many examples of this conversion exist in Europe, notable in the United Kingdom and Spain. On the resort grounds, it is not unusual to find a museum, which may house important collections of cultural value ranging from antique furniture to native folk art. An example of cultural preservation is the Will Rogers Shrine of the Sun at the Broadmoor Hotel in Colorado Springs, which preserves Americana by collecting and exhibiting valuable mementos of the life of a legendary midwestern humorist.

At present, the long-range environmental effects of tourism development are not yet well understood and vary greatly from one location to another, depending on a host of variables, including physical characteristics of the site, historical land use patterns, and the type of visitor facilities proposed. What is known, however, is that environmental effects must be considered in the planning process, since tourism development (as does any kind of land or industrial development) alters the landscape and the ecological bal-

Colonial Williamsburg provides demonstrations of a working reproduction of a fire engine first ordered for the city from London in 1754.

ance of living things. The environment, which is such an important part of an area's attraction, is fragile and too easily destroyed if responsible planning is neglected.

## Sustainable Tourism

As tourism has continued to grow, there has been increased concern over environmental problems resulting from tourism development. The issue of **sustainable tourism** development—that which is consistent with an area's present and future needs—has been discussed at various forums.

What exactly is "sustainable tourism?" Academic and industry analysts have yet to arrive at a common definition. Indeed, sustainable tourism is frequently confused with other terms, such as "alternative tourism," "responsible tourism," "ecotourism," "endemic tourism," "appropriate tourism," and the like. In an attempt to develop a common understanding of the term, the Bruntland report, entitled *Our Common Future*, loosely defined sustainable tourism as the "…meeting of the needs of present tourists and host regions while protecting and enhancing opportunity for the future." The concept of sustainable tourism calls for participating nations to envision the management of resources in such a way that the economic, social, and aesthetic needs can be fulfilled, while maintaining cultural integrity, essential biological processes, biological diversity, and life support systems. In sum, sustainable tourism is aimed at: (1) protecting and promoting the environment, (2) meeting basic human needs, (3) enhancing current and intergenerational equity, and (4) improving the economic standards and quality of living of host residents. *(20)*

# The Case of Lapa Rios

Lapa Rios is a resort of 20 private villas with a main lodge located on a 1,100 acre site within a virgin lowland rainforest in the remote Osa Peninsula of Costa Rica. All manners of exotic wildlife, including scarlet macaws and howler monkeys throng the forest.

The resort's developers and its architect were careful not to endanger the fragile ecosystem on the peninsula by developing a plan and environmental guiding principles for a modest resort that would be unobtrusive and complementary to the site and local culture. Small scale architecture, thatched rooflines, local motifs, and traditional forms make the resort a special place for both the host community and guests.

Since its opening in 1992, Lapa Rios has become well integrated with the rainforest's rebirth. The development is seen as an excellent example of responsible planning in fostering the ideals of ecotourism.

Lapa Rios is striving to be a model demonstration of responsible ecotourism by adhering to the following:

1. Utilizing tourism to acquire and protect endangered prime rain forest wilderness.

2. Educating and motivating guests into being actively aware of conservation and rain forest preservation.

3. Aiding and integrating with the local community for sustainable development.

Lapa Rios does the following in futhering its stated goals:

- No caged animals or clipped birds.

- No live trees were cut for the construction of the resort.

- Access to the 1000 acres wildlife refuge only with trained guides.

- Volunteer reforestation project involving our resort guests.

- Hiring only local people from the immediate community with an emphasis on training.

- Building a school for the local children in the area who previously received no education.

- Distribution of literature on local and global environmental topics.

- Organization of local chamber of tourism with emphasis on ecotourism.

- All structures made from natural time-tested materials.

- Architectural design by international ecotourism design consultant to ensure local compliance with overall natural site appearance.
- Local guide to inform guests of local customs and cross-cultural issues.
- On-site managed waste disposal and separation program.
- Solar heated water.
- No non-returnable containers. No off-site purchases permitted—to eliminate litter.
- Only 14 units for occupancy to eliminate overcrowding and wilderness deterioration.
- Initiation of forest products demonstration.

One of the first countries to address the issue directly was Canada. A National Round Table on the Environment and Economy was established to promote sustainable development. In 1991, the Tourism Industry Association of Canada (TIAC) agreed to work with the Round Table to produce a code of ethics for tourists, a code of ethics for the industry, as well as guidelines. *(21)*

The code of ethics for tourists included the following:

1. Enjoy our diverse natural and cultural heritage and help us to protect and preserve it.

2. Assist us in our conservation efforts through the efficient use of resources, including energy and water.

3. Experience the friendliness of our people and the welcoming spirit of our communities. Help us to preserve these attributes by respecting our traditions, customs, and local regulations.

4. Avoid activities which threaten wildlife or plant populations, or which may be potentially damaging to our natural environment.

5. Select tourism products and services which demonstrate social, cultural, and environmental sensitivity. *(21)*

Industry leaders feel that commitment to the codes and guidelines will enhance Canada's image as a destination and attract tourists who are seeking environmentally responsible tourist experiences.

Private companies, among them—Intercontinental Hotels, British Airways, Ramada International, Hilton International—also have developed environmental programs. Tourists are becoming more aware of selecting companies—airlines, hotels, and tour companies—which are environmentally sensitive, and in this way, encourage other companies to be supportive of the environment.

Leading travel and tourism associations, including The World Tourism Organization with its Blue Flag program, The World Travel and Tourism Council with its Green Globe program, and The Pacific Asia Travel Association with its Green Leaf program, are actively promoting environmental consciousness among destinations, travel trade suppliers, and tourism consumers, as a necessary step in the evolution of sustainable tourism.

# COSTS AND BENEFITS OF TOURISM DEVELOPMENT (7)

All actions that accompany or result from the decision-making process of tourism development have various alternative impacts on costs and benefits from economic, social, and environmental standpoints. It is important to keep in mind that tourism development is, above all other considerations, an economic process. Social and environmental issues become irrelevant if tourism does not prove to be economically viable.

To measure the economic and other impacts of tourism, a **cost-benefit analysis** may be undertaken by decision-makers to weigh the benefits from tourism. Factors taken into account for this analysis include revenue, foreign exchange, employment, household income, taxes, and other benefits against the costs of investments. Also considered are the use of various resources, including land, water, displaced labor, infrastructural support, social services, etc., needed for tourism development. For maturing destinations with saturated markets, depreciating assets and high marketing expenses, the costs may begin to equal or exceed benefits. In the case of newer destinations with growing market demand and modest investment requirements, there will be an opposite experience of greater benefits than costs. The cost-benefit concept is important for policy-makers and investors who consider making trade-off decisions when weighing the consequences of development alternatives. This section provides a listing of costs and discussion of benefits to consider when conducting a cost-benefit analysis.

## Capital Investment Costs

When considering the cost of tourism development, one must recognize the extensive investments required of both government and private capital to finance the preliminary planning and development stages. Further, it requires extensive capital investments in fixed assets and tends to offer a low rate of return on investment during the early years of operations.

Examples of capital investments for tourism structures include:

- infrastructure—airports and other types of transportation terminals, roads, and land improvements;
- transportation systems and equipment;
- accommodations—luxury, medium-quality, and budget;
- food and beverage establishments;
- cultural institutions—museums, theaters, and galleries;
- exhibition and convention centers;
- recreation and sporting facilities;

- retail shopping facilities;
- theme parks, amusement centers, gaming, and other attractions;
- historic preservations and restorations.

## Social and Cultural Costs

Other aspects of the cost of tourism development are the social and cultural costs. The list is long and includes the following, some of which have already been introduced in previous sections:

- additional demands on social services and supporting infrastructure;
- costs of creating new jobs;
- costs of creating and maintaining positive community relationships;
- psychological costs to the employees related to the disparity between their own lifestyle and that enjoyed by visitors;
- costs of possible friction between visitors and local residents over shared usage of valued local recreational facilities (for example, a ski mountain);
- opportunity costs to the community of spending limited public capital for support of infrastructure, rather than for other projects of potentially greater direct benefit;
- quality of life costs of increased stresses on employees' home lives and unanticipated lifestyle changes;
- cultural costs of alterations in locally espoused ceremonial or traditional values;
- loss of privacy in rural communities where tourism development occurs.

## Environmental Costs

Another aspect of costs is environmental costs. Here, again, the list is long and includes those previously discussed:

- increased levels of generalized congestion and pollution;
- alterations to the natural landscape and changes in the ecological balance of living things;
- costs of preventing localized congestion or pollution;
- costs of the loss of wilderness areas or inevitable degree of lessening the natural attraction;
- costs of creating conservation areas on resort lands;
- costs of undertaking enhancement projects, including unforeseen or undesirable side effects;
- costs of undertaking historical or cultural preservation.

Some costs related to the environment are applicable to tourism development in particular. Others are applicable to all forms of real estate or community development. Careful planning and analysis by government, industry, and the surrounding community can help to reduce or eliminate some of these costs, but the planning itself is an additional cost.

## Benefits

Just as we saw both positive and negative sides in our discussion of the impacts of tourism, costs and benefits must also be weighed one against the other. We have listed economic, social, cultural, and environmental costs. We will also look at the benefits in each of these categories.

On the benefit side, tourism development provides employment and revenue to support local business in the community. Sophisticated infrastructure systems required by tourism development often benefit the community by encouraging and serving economic development in other industrial sectors. The daily contact of residents with visitors may broaden educational and cultural horizons, improve feelings of self-worth, and promote upward mobility and acquisition of material advantages. New revenue generated by tourism also has a social benefit for the community in terms of improvements in the quality of life related to a higher level of income and improved standards of living.

The interest of visitors in local culture provides employment for artists, musicians, and other performing artists and often tends to revive the community's interest in its own cultural heritage. Philanthropic programs and educational and cultural interchanges sponsored by travel businesses also have a social benefit.

Environmentally, tourism development in underdeveloped regions with scarce raw material resources generally solves or ameliorates prevalent life-threatening environmental problems. In developed regions, recreational land set-asides preserve open space and reduce overall development densities. Because the natural attraction is so important to the long-term economic viability of a destination, tourism development often includes conservation of endangered species of flora and fauna, enhancement of the natural and human environments, and historical and cultural preservation projects—all of which have direct or indirect benefits to the surrounding community.

## ᔑUMMARY

As tourism grows, the impacts of the industry—positive and negative—become more pronounced; and the economic, social, cultural, and environmental impacts of tourism on its host community are profound once "critical mass" is reached. However, with proper planning, controlled development, and the use of appropriate guidelines, potentially negative impacts can be significantly reduced. It is critical that policymakers and planners understand the nature of all tourism impacts. Too frequently in the past, economic questions were the sole concern of planners and policymakers, whereas social, cultural, and environmental issues and problems were given only a superficial analysis because the latter are difficult to identify, measure, and quantify.

Today, as social, cultural, and environmental questions take on greater weight because of public concern, planners are seeking better tools to evaluate these impacts as well. The need for comprehensive cost and benefit information is key. The host community, in supporting tourism as an economic activity, must be able to look at tourism from a balanced perspective and, in planning for the future, objectively weigh known or anticipated gains against anticipated risks in seeking sustainability of tourism as a goal. Ultimately, the goal is one of satisfied hosts and visitors in an ecologically wholesome environment.

# DISCUSSION QUESTIONS

1. What are possible economic impacts of tourism upon an area? Are all of the possible impacts beneficial to residents of the area?

2. What are direct and secondary effects of tourist expenditures?

3. What is meant by the term tourism multiplier? How do imports affect the size of the tourism multiplier?

4. How does tourism development affect the social structure of a host area?

5. What are the phases of the sociological cycle of a destination?

6. What is cultural collision?

7. How does community interpretation mitigate the negative impacts of tourism upon a host region's culture?

8. How do environmental impacts differ for developed versus under developed areas?

9. Are there positive benefits of tourism development on the environment? What are some of these benefits?

10. How is the human environment affected by tourism development?

11. What is meant by the term, "sustainable tourism?"

12. What is cost-benefit analysis and how is it used in assessing tourism development? Who would or should be concerned with the cost-benefit issues of tourism? Why?

13. What are the major costs and benefits of tourism development?

# SUGGESTED STUDENT PROJECTS

Develop your own case study of a rural or a coastal community which has potential for tourism development. The community may be an existing or hypothetical one.

1. What kinds of possible problems should decision-makers identify from the outset of tourism development?

2. What plans are needed to avoid or minimize the problems you have identified?

3. How would you preserve and protect the cultural assets of the community and avert cultural collisions between residents and visitors?

4. How would you define the carrying capacity of the community for tourism development?

5. What types of environmental guidelines would you adopt to protect the natural environment?

6. What measure or policies would you impose to promote "sustainable tourism" goals?

7. Develop a tourism cost-benefit measurement for your community.

# ℛEFERENCES

1. Travel Industry Association of America, "Updates on Industry Trends and Information," March 1995.

2. *Travel Industry World Yearbook—The Big Picture*, 1993–94. New York: Child and Waters, Inc., 1993.

3. International Travel to and From the United States. Washington, D.C.: United States Travel and Tourism Administration, February 1994.

4. Liu, J. "The Economic Impact of Tourism on an Island Economy: A Case Study of Victoria, B.C.," Ph.D. diss., Simon Fraser University, Burnaby, B.C., 1979.

5. Impact of Travel on State Economics in 1994. Washington, D.C.:U.S. Travel Data Center, December 1995.

6. Archer, B. H., "Tourism Multipliers, The State of the Art." Bangor Occasional Papers in Economics, Bangor: University of Wales Press, 1977.

7. Gee, C. Y. *Resort Development and Management*. East Lansing, Mich.: American Hotel and Motel Association Educational Institute, 1988.

8. Cottington, F. "Socio-psychiatric Effects of Luxury Hotel Growth and Development on a Rural Population." Paper presented at American Psychiatric Association meeting, Honolulu, 1969.

9. Smith, M. H. "Socio-economic Transition in North Kohala." *Preliminary Research in Human Ecology*, R. W. Armstrong and H. T. Lewis (Honolulu: Science Research Institute, University of Hawaii, 1972).

10. Turner, L. "Tourism—The Most Subversive Industry." *Multinational Companies and the Third World*. New York: Hill and Wang, 1973.

11. Morgan, G. "Discovering the Sights of Borneo." *The Washington Post* (January 12, 1975).

12. Turner, L., and J. Ash. *The Golden Hordes, International Tourism and the Pleasure Periphery*. London: Constable and Company Ltd., 1975.

13. Greenway, H. D. S. "Time and Tourism and the Morning of the World, Gods and Tourists Don't Mix Well." *The Washington Post* (October 6, 1974).

14. Ropponen, P. J. "Tourists v. Reindeer." *Tourism International Policy*. London: Tourism International Press, 1976.

15. Klemm, R. "Community Interpretation—Not Just Another Tourist Trap." *Makai* 6, No. 11 (University of Hawaii: November 1984).

16. "Topic C: Social Implications, Proceedings of the Symposium on the Planning and Development of the Tourist Industry in the ECE Region." Dubrovnik, Yugoslavia: Economic Commission for Europe, November 5, 1975.

17. *Tourism Bill of Rights and Tourist Code* A/6/11(a), adopted by the Sixth General Assembly, September 17–26, 1985, Sofia, Bulgaria: World Tourism Organization.

18. "The Socio-cultural Impact of Tourism, Effects on Social Behavior and Values." *Proceedings of the WTO/UNEP Workshop on the Environmental Aspects of Tourism.* Madrid: World Tourism Organization, 1983.

19. Gee, C. Y. and E. Coe. *Strategic Tourism Market Plan for Ecuador.* A special report prepared for USAID/Quito, Private Sector Office, Bureau for Latin America and the Caribbean. Washington, D.C.: December 1986.

20. Gee, C. Y. "Sustainable Tourism Development: A Strategic Issue for the Asia-Pacific Region." *Presented before the Commission on Asia and the Pacific of the World Tourism Organization.* Kuala Lumpur: July 7, 1994.

21. D'Amore, L. J. "Promoting Sustainable Tourism—the Canadian Approach." *Tourism Management*, September 1992.

# Part 4

# Selling Travel

# Chapter 8

# Travel Sales Distribution Systems

## LEARNING OBJECTIVES

- To understand the basic sales distribution systems used within the travel industry to sell travel services.

- To understand the advantages/disadvantages of one distribution system versus another.

- To understand the basic types of sales organizations used by primary suppliers.

- To be aware of the changes that are occurring in the sales organizations of suppliers.

- To define and use the following terms:

| | |
|---|---|
| Automated sales systems | Dual-level sales organization |
| Certified Meeting Professionals | Escorted tours |
| City ticket office (CTO) | Familiarization trips (FAM trips) |
| Cooperative | Four-stage distribution system |
| Corporate accounts | Fulfillment marketing |
| Cross-selling | Ground operator |
| Custom tours | Inbound agents |
| Destination planners | Incentive firms/houses |
| Direct response | Independent tours |

Junket reps

Key account management

Land arrangements

Meeting and Planners International

Meeting/convention planners

Motivation-incentive travel company

Motorcoach brokers

Multilevel sales organization

National Tourism Officers (NTOs)

One-stage distribution system

Pareto's 80/20 Rule

Primary supplier

Product positioning

Professional Congress Organizer (PCO)

Receiving agents

Retail travel agents

Retailers

Sales distribution system

Satellite ticket offices

Seamless connectivity

Secondary supplier

Single-level sales organization

Specialty intermediaries

Supplier

Three-stage distribution system

Ticketless travel

Tie-in selling

Tour operator

Tour program

Travel agency

Travel agent

Travel clubs

Travel consolidators

Travel and entertainment card

Travel intermediaries

Travel nights

Two-stage distribution system

Wholesale travel agents

Wholesalers

# TYPES OF SALES DISTRIBUTION SYSTEMS

Like other basic industries, the travel industry has its own system of moving products and services from suppliers to ultimate consumers. To understand the economics of the travel industry, it is important to have a basic understanding of the structure and efficiencies of the industry's distribution system, including the intermediaries who comprise this system. The term **sales distribution system** refers to the method by which a travel industry supplier sells its products and/or services to customers. Within the sales distribution system, there are wide variations, combinations, and interactive relationships. Analysis of business practices in the travel industry show that there are four types of sales distribution systems, employed separately or simultaneously by

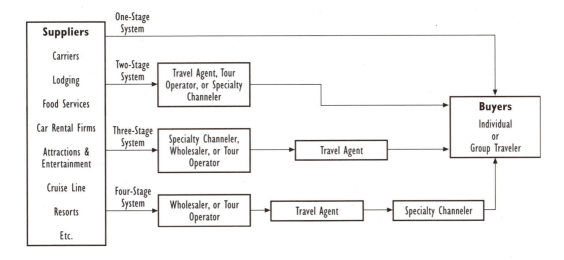

**Figure 8.1** Travel industry distribution systems.

suppliers in the travel industry. Figure 8.1 shows these systems as one-, two-, three-, or four-stage systems.

## Travel Intermediaries

Before discussing the advantages and disadvantages of the four basic sales distribution systems, it is useful to present the types of travel intermediaries involved in distributing travel services. A two-, three-, or four-stage distribution system encompasses **travel intermediaries**. There are three types: **travel agencies** (**wholesale** and **retail**), **tour operators**, and **specialty channelers**.

## Travel Agencies

A **travel agent** is a member of a travel agency who is qualified to sell travel services offered by the agency's principal suppliers, including airlines, cruise ships, railroads, bus companies, car rental firms, hotels, and sightseeing operators. He or she provides clients with information needed to make travel decisions and arranges reservations and bookings with suppliers on behalf of the clients. Generally speaking, there are two types of travel agents, wholesale and retail.

A **wholesale travel agent** or **wholesaler** specializes in organizing tour packages, which are marketed to the public through a network of **retail travel agents**. Wholesalers do not deal directly with the consumer unless they also operate at the retail level. Most large wholesalers, however, do have retail divisions. A wholesaler travel agent may or may not operate the tours it markets. In many cases, wholesalers contract with a tour operator or operators for all or only certain land arrangements.

Wholesaler travel agents may design tour packages marketed under the agency's name, or, as is sometimes the case, they may take land packages already assembled by a

**ground operator** and combine them with air or surface transportation to form new packages. The latter practice is especially common in the international tourism field. For example, rather than negotiating directly with such individual suppliers as a hotel, sightseeing operator, or attraction in New York, a German wholesaler who wishes to offer a New York City program may find it more convenient to contract with a New York ground operator for land arrangements and then add his/her own arrangements for international air transportation between the point of origin and destination.

As the name implies, retail travel agents or **retailers** sell travel services directly to the consumer. They typically represent airlines, cruise lines, motorcoach companies, railroads, hotels, car rental firms, or sometimes but not always, wholesale travel agencies. The distinction between wholesaler and retailer is sometimes fuzzy. Retail agents may design **custom tours** for individual clients by assembling, in prepaid, pre-arranged packages, the basic services requested by the prospective traveler. Occasionally, they may develop a package or packages that will be sold on a wholesale basis to other retailers. The dividing line is further blurred by the fact that some travel agencies operate both retail and wholesale divisions. In addition, individual retail agencies sometimes unite and form a **cooperative** that functions as a wholesaler. A cooperative is an association of independent retail agencies who join together for the express purpose of acquiring products that wholesalers normally offer but at a reduced cost. Members share in the profits generated by the activities of the cooperative.

## Travel Agency Income

The majority of income produced by a travel agency is derived from commission on sales paid by travel providers. Unlike retailers such as department stores, convenience stores, or supermarkets, travel agencies have historically not taken possession of the products (travel services) they sell. A few agencies may sell travel-related products and services such as luggage, insurance, and traveler's checks, but the bulk of revenue continues to come from commissions.

Travel agents serve as a vital intermediary in selling travel services. The airline and cruise line sectors are particularly dependent upon independent travel agents as 95% of all cruise sales and 90% of airline sales are made through travel agents. By contrast, only 25% of all hotel rooms are reserved through travel agents. *(1)*

Although transportation constitutes the bulk of agency sales, travel agents also book clients on a commission basis for auto rental firms, hotels, destination resorts, and other suppliers. Other sectors of the travel industry, including major events—for instance, a world's fair or the Olympic Games, historic restorations, motorcoach lines, theme parks, and others often court travel agents as travel intermediaries. On the other hand, smaller businesses which comprise the largest sector of the travel industry—restaurants, shops, local entertainment, amusement parlors, etc.—have found it too difficult and costly to work with the thousands of travel agents in North America.

There are many problems confronting the independent travel agent today, and some of these problems will continue into the next decade along with new opportunities to re-rationalize the role of travel agencies in the dynamic environment of the 21st century. Travel agencies are currently under intense pressure from suppliers, particularly airlines, to reduce commissions. They are also feeling the effects of discount airlines who promote direct sales to the passenger. Additionally, computer technology available to millions of PC users is certain to place greater pressure on travel agents as these users book travel directly, bypassing the use of a travel agent.

The Internet, which had 10 million users a few years ago, now reportedly has 30 million users and growing. Online users are considered demographically attractive—upscale and highly educated. Many travel suppliers are listing their products and services on the Internet for direct sales to online users. However, a number of large travel agencies have also made use of the Internet to list their services to online users as well.

Some industry leaders believe that travel agencies must become value-added businesses, with agents regarded as professionals offering their services for a fee—similar to professionals in other fields—in order for agencies to survive. American Express Travel Services, a division of American Express, not only books tickets for clients but also helps them to manage their travel and expense budgets, negotiates discounts with hotels, and compiles data on travel expenditures. In 1994, American Express received over $4 billion in fees rather than commissions. By the year 2000, American Express expects to have 100% fee-based revenue. *(2)*

Despite the revenue pressure felt by travel agencies, new players have entered the field. The American Automobile Association (AAA), for example, has announced plans to substantially improve its travel agency business, making it a revenue source that will equal its core motor club and emergency road service business. The strategy employed by AAA was to create strategic alliances with a limited number of travel suppliers, such as Hertz Corporation, Walt Disney, and selected cruise lines. The travel service established through these alliances would then be sold to AAA members. *(3)*

The travel agency industry has been dramatically affected by change in the travel industry. The full effects remain to unfold, but several trends appear certain:

1. Surviving travel agencies will become more efficient and more professional.

2. Travel agencies will face increased competition not only from other agencies, but also from corporate clients who use in-house agencies and from suppliers who may find ways to bypass travel agencies.

3. Many travel agencies will be forced to specialize in market niches.

4. Large travel agencies may find it profitable to purchase airline seats or other travel services for resale to clients instead of working on commissions.

5. Increased automation will help increase agency productivity.

6. The number of travel agents in North America is likely to continue to consolidate, and growth will occur only among the most progressive and efficient agencies. Much of the growth will come from increased yield per outlet rather than from horizonal expansion.

7. Income will increasingly be derived from value added services, not simply from commissions.

## Tour Operators

Tour operators are responsible for organizing and selling the services specified and advertised in a tour package. Some tour operators have their own buses, hotels, or other tour facilities; others will contract services with hotels, ground transportation, restaurants, attractions, car rental companies, or other tour operators to assemble all of the components required to comprise a marketable tour package.

In some cases, tour operators' offerings (packages) are developed for and marketed directly to the general public. Many operators also work with sponsors of alumni bodies, clubs, churches, and social organizations to create special tour packages for these groups. In some cases, the packages are designed to the specification of a wholesale travel agent who markets them under the agency's name through agency-owned retail agents and/or through an airline.

An operator typically offers a variety of packages in a single season, which collectively is termed as a **tour program**. Packages may cater to individuals or groups and may be **independent** (without escort) or **escorted** (with tour escort). A package may include services such as transportation to the destination or destinations, transfers, overnight accommodations, certain meals, sightseeing (including or excluding admissions), and car rental. Tour operators, however, are careful to offer options to the various components included in a package as buyers increasingly seek these options.

**Ground operators**, a form of tour wholesaler, normally provide services at the destination only and do not include transportation to or from the destination. Their services usually cover hotel transfers, overnight accommodations, sightseeing, and sometimes special arrangements, which are collectively referred to as **land arrangements**. Ground operators who specialize in services for incoming visitors, particularly tourists from foreign countries, are called **receiving agents** or **inbound agents**.

**Inbound agents** are critical to the success of many foreign travel destinations. The Australian and New Zealand inbound tour operator industry, for example, is becoming highly sophisticated and specialized. One company in North Sydney specializes in **motivation-incentive travel** from Japan, North America, and Europe. Companies seeking ways to increase productivity or sales performance of employees sometimes offer a free travel package as a reward for meeting or exceeding objectives. Client companies use **incentive houses** (**incentive firms**) to help them plan an internal promotional campaign to promote the travel reward, to select the appropriate travel package, and to take responsibility for travel details, thus ensuring a successful incentive program.

Foreign inbound tour operators often specialize by the FIT (independent traveler) or GIT (group inclusive tour) market. In many parts of the world, the FIT market has become highly segmented by interest areas, creating the need for increasingly specialized tour operators. A New Zealand company, for instance, specializes in sailboat charters and arranges ground transportation to match this market.

## Specialty Intermediaries

**Specialty intermediaries** include incentive firms (variably called incentive houses or **motivation-incentive travel companies**), meeting and convention planners, hotel representatives, interline representatives, association executives, corporate travel offices, travel consultants, motorcoach brokers, junket representatives, and others. These intermediaries, sometimes referred to as specialty channelers, have the power to influence how, where, and when the travel product will be distributed. Specialty channelers usually receive commission fees from clients. Corporate travel offices employ salaried professionals who contract for travel services with outside travel providers.

The importance of the specialty intermediary is increasing as the travel industry becomes more specialized. Specialty intermediaries include the following:

- *The incentive or motivation travel company*    The incentive company may either sell its professional services to design, promote, and execute an incentive travel program for a buyer or act as an intermediary for both buyers and suppliers. Incentive travel is a deluxe segment of the industry and one of the faster-growing specializations, as an increasing number of destinations, resorts, retailers, and others actively seek upscale incentive business.

- *Motorcoach brokers/tour operators*    The motorcoach tour industry is highly dependent upon independent tour operators (**motorcoach brokers**) who organize and sell different kinds of tours—shopping, historic, cultural events, reunions, outdoor sports, and so forth. Tour operators who carry a minimum of $1 million professional liability insurance and have at least two years of experience may become members of the National Tour Association (NTA), which is the largest tour operator association in North America, with over 600 professional tour companies. *(4)*

- *Meeting and convention planners*    **Meeting and convention planners** specialize in planning and organizing meetings principally for corporate clients and professional associations. Some of these meeting planners have credentials as **Professional Congress Organizers** (PCOs) or **Certified Meeting Professionals** (CMPs), holding membership in organizations such as **Meeting and Planners International**, a society that serves as a professional and educational resource for those who manage meetings.

- *Destination planners*    **Destination planners** generally work as independent support professionals to assist meeting and convention planners. They are able to organize support activities, such as city tours, limousine service or fleet bus service, and special events.

- *Junket representatives*    Casinos and casino hotels utilize the services of **junket reps** who organize groups of players to visit a specific casino/casino hotel. *(5)* Junket reps who are able to provide groups of premium players are particularly valuable to the casinos. As casino gambling spreads throughout North America, junket reps developed to organize player groups for casinos outside the traditional areas of Las Vegas, Reno, and Atlantic City. Today, gambling junkets are available at a low cost for players to visit casinos in many places, including Central City and Blackhawk, Colorado; the Gulf area of Mississippi; Elko, Nevada; Riverboat casinos and Indian reservation casinos.

- *National Tourism Officers (NTOs)*    **NTOs** are government or quasi-governmental tourism officers representing cities, states/provinces, or other jurisdictions. They are not normally considered specialty intermediaries, but they do perform some of the duties of a private sector intermediary. These individuals have the responsibility for marketing their communities or destinations. They work closely with the private sector in performing marketing research, organizing groups, planning travel packages, and promotion. Some offer toll-free telephone inquiry service, visitor information centers, and lodging reservation services.

## One-stage Distribution System

A **one-stage system** directs sales from primary suppliers to travel services to the traveler. An example is an airline selling tickets directly to customers through its own sales and reservations department.

A few travel suppliers—cruise lines in particular—avoid this system and depend almost entirely upon intermediaries. Airlines, on the other hand, use both the one-stage system and travel intermediaries. A one-stage system is expensive, as it requires a permanent sales and reservations system. Small travel suppliers, such as discount airlines, often find the cost prohibitive. Larger companies, such as major airlines and hotel chains, that can afford the cost of maintaining national and regional sales offices feel it is unwise to depend entirely on intermediaries. The cost-effectiveness of hiring a salaried sales force versus the use of commission intermediaries is the subject of continuing debate within the travel industry.

The one-stage system offers certain advantages for both seller and buyer, including:

- *Simplicity*   The one-stage system is direct and obviates the need for third party intervention. The buyer and seller can easily decide on reservations or changes between themselves. If a travel intermediary is involved, most decisions would require cross-check communications and multiple follow-ups.

- *Additional sales opportunities*   The ability to talk directly with the traveler provides the supplier with an opportunity to upgrade, sell additional services, and make advance reservations for a return trip or a future booking.

- *Flexibility*   Many travelers follow a travel itinerary with a fixed schedule of places they intend to visit. Travelers who do not have fixed itineraries value the ability to modify travel plans at the last minute.

- *Greater profitability to supplier*   The independent traveler who purchases directly from the supplier provides a greater per unit profit than clients who use intermediaries. This is especially true when the traveler pays the full fare in cash. Sales generated through travel agencies may provide larger total gross receipts for a supplier because of volume, but the net profit per customer or yield will be less after commissions are subtracted.

- *Personal control over the sale*   In some cases, the individual traveler may also be wary of travel agents because of nationally publicized stories about travelers who were stranded overseas when a travel agent unknowingly booked the trip through an unscrupulous tour operator. Such travelers are apt to feel more secure if they have personally made the reservations, handled each step of their travel agenda, and have confirmed reservations with tickets in hand.

- *Management of key accounts*   Travel industry companies generally recognize the validity of the **Pareto 80/20 rule**, which states that a majority of a company's business will result from a minority of its customers. Government officials, especially congressmen and senators, for instance, have a need to travel four to five times more frequently than the average business traveler. Business executives, in turn, fly far more frequently than the average discretionary traveler. The growth of frequent flyer programs by airlines, hotels, auto rental firms, and others is a reflection of key account management. Computers now allow companies to identify key customers and their patterns of usage. Specific marketing strategies can be directed to these important customers. **Key account management** is difficult or impossible unless a company has direct control of the sales process.

The one-stage marketing distribution system for the travel industry has always existed. But as direct selling costs escalate and the ability to achieve wider market distribution becomes more difficult given dynamic market changes, the one-stage system demonstrates obvious limitations. Moreover, the loss of goodwill from bypassing travel intermediaries is no small factor in the promotion and support of a supplier's products and services.

## Two-stage Distribution System

A **two-stage** system involves a single intermediary—a travel agent, for example—interacting with the supplier and the traveler. The advantages of two-stage distribution are as follows:

- *Professional assistance*   The buyer receives assistance from professionals who specialize in travel and can give personalized attention and advice, often saving the customer both time and money in the process.

- *Multiple options*   Unlike the one-stage system, a traveler can obtain information on a variety of products and services through a single intermediary. In the one-stage system, a traveler must call numerous suppliers before he or she knows all the available options. The situation is similar to that of the auto buyer who attends an auto showcase containing every model of every make of automobile available versus the auto buyer who has to visit individual dealers to get the same information.

- *Free or low-cost assistance*   Generally speaking, professional assistance is available to travelers in a two-stage system at no extra cost to the traveler. Some travel agents, however, have found it necessary to charge a nominal fee for services that were formerly offered for free. Fee for service is preferred by a number of large corporate and government clients who have instructed their travel agents that they must pass commission savings on to the client and charge a fee instead for services rendered.

- *Cumulative group power*   An intermediary generally has more leverage over suppliers than the individual traveler. Influence with suppliers is especially important during peak seasons. An intermediary who is responsible for hundreds of thousands of dollars worth of business for a particular hotel, airline, or cruise ship carries considerable clout. In some developing nations where the supply of airline seats is limited, a travel agent may have important political or business connections, which can mean the difference between securing a seat on the next available flight out of the country or waiting for a future seat opening.

- *Travel clubs*   **Travel clubs** serve as a member of a two-tier system, providing members with advantageous discount travel. Clubs and businesses selling discounted travel to consumers are increasingly popular. Some of these are last minute tour travels. The club is able to purchase tours at highly discounted rates when it becomes apparent these will not sell out. Members who can travel on a moment's notice may benefit from these travel bargains.

- *Travel consolidators*   **Travel consolidators** are private companies that acquire discounted unsold seats in volume and sell them directly to the public at bargain rates. Consolidators may also combine individual bookings from travel agencies to obtain supplier discounts and override commissions, passing on part of the commission overrides and discounts to the originating agencies.

- *Single-charge billing*   The process of paying for multiple travel services is simplified through an agent. The agent can charge the client for all services, including ground transportation, lodging, restaurant, and entertainment packages on a single billing.

- *Price or service advantages*   In some cases, the traveler can obtain lower prices for travel services by going through a travel agent. Travel agents are sometimes able to upgrade services for corporate account travelers or major buyers at no additional cost. This is especially true when agents book sizable group business for hotels or resorts.

- *Out-of-town assistance*   Some travel intermediaries have multiple branches, even extending into foreign countries. Others have out-of-town or overseas affiliates. A traveler who may experience difficulty while traveling can often find assistance through a branch or affiliate office.

- *Sales force without overhead*   The foremost advantage offered by travel intermediaries to suppliers is that they serve as a sales force with no overhead costs to the supplier. Elimination of overhead is especially helpful to small suppliers who cannot afford a nationwide or worldwide sales force.

- *Credit and billing assistance to suppliers*   Travel intermediaries can facilitate the credit and billing functions of suppliers, by running credit checks on clients, processing credit card billings, and submitting single payments to suppliers.

- *Off-season promotions*   Intermediaries often assist suppliers in creating new business by developing off-season travel packages.

## Three-stage Distribution System

A **three-stage system** involves two intermediaries, usually a retail travel agent and a wholesaler or tour operator. An airline or cruise line might supply a package of travel services, including lodging, transportation, and ground transfer. The package could be sold through a wholesaler who can offer it to hundreds of travel agencies who would, in turn, sell it to individual travellers. The system provides the traveler and the supplier with benefits similar to the two-stage system. The added benefits come from travel services being purchased in large quantities at discounted prices by wholesalers. With the three-stage system, the traveler is generally able to obtain lower-priced travel packages or packages that are tailored to the traveler's wishes.

## Four-stage Distribution System

A **four-stage system** follows the pattern of the three-stage distribution process, but there is an additional intermediary, generally a specialty channeler, who is involved in customizing a tour package. To illustrate the four-stage distribution system, take the case of a university group that is planning a period of study abroad in a foreign country. Such a group might first express its interest to the Study Abroad Office on its campus. The Study Abroad Office, as a specialty channeler of educational tours, determines the needs of the group, including its academic interest focus, and recommends preliminary itineraries, suitable accommodations, overseas contacts, and other arrangements. Following a consultation with the group, the Study Abroad Office may then channel the purchase of the tour through a retail travel agent who will make direct airline arrangements on a group fare basis and, at the same time, may contract with a tour operator in the specific foreign country to handle the remaining details of the study group's itinerary. The benefits of having this additional stage in making travel arrangements for the group are basically those of obtaining professional assistance in developing a program to satisfy the group's exact requirements and assistance in securing services from reliable suppliers.

# $\mathcal{T}$RAVEL SUPPLIERS AND THEIR SALES ORGANIZATIONS

The businesses that produce the services which are sold through the distribution channel are called **suppliers** in the travel industry. Suppliers obviously play an important role in distribution since they are involved in both a marketing and a selling function. Marketing is not the same as selling. Marketing focuses on the needs of the buyer, selling on the needs of the supplier. In marketing, the supplier must have or must try to provide what buyers want at different price, product, and service levels. The supplier must satisfy the customer by offering value for service delivered as well as securing the confidence of those who sell the service on the supplier's behalf. In selling, the supplier must decide how best to move his or her products and services through the distribution channel with least cost and maximum effectiveness to reach the right customers in the right numbers and profit volume.

## Types of Suppliers

Travel industry suppliers may be grouped into two classifications; they are either **primary** or **secondary** suppliers.

1. Primary suppliers of travel services are those who provide services directly to the traveler and are paid by the traveler or the intermediary buyer. Airlines, hotels, restaurants, theme parks, bus lines, and cruise ships are examples of primary suppliers.

   The size and complexity of the distribution system used by primary suppliers depends on a number of factors. For instance, a supplier may opt for a simpler distribution system when the total market potential for the supplier's products or services may be limited and the number of persons who have the time, interest, and discretionary income to purchase these services is relatively small or the location of potential customers is limited to a few geographical areas, or the business is highly seasonal. The supplier whose products and services are international in scope, on the other hand, may require a fairly broad and sophisticated sales distribution system to reach customers in different countries with different cultural buying patterns.

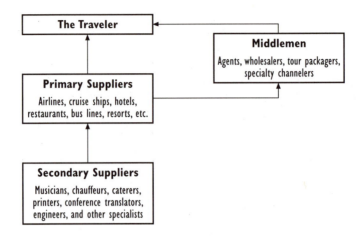

**Figure 8.2** The supplier sales system.

2. Secondary suppliers are those who provide services to the traveler through one of the primary suppliers. They are usually small niche players who offer specialized products or services. In some instance, they may deal directly with customers, as in the case of caterers. But for the most part, the services of secondary suppliers are contracted through a primary supplier as part of the primary suppliers' responsibility. The problem for customers who wish to contract directly is one of sourcing and knowing the quality or reliability of the supplier. Hotels, for example, are usually in a better position to arrange for the services of a reliable chauffeur or name entertainer when one is required by the customer. (See Figure 8.2)

## Levels of Sales Organizations

The sales organization of travel industry suppliers may be simple or complex, depending on the nature of the products or services to be sold and the scope and depth of the market. An international airline, for example, may have an elaborate hierarchy of sales branches, divisions, or regions under its sales manager. For a small independent business with a limited marketing budget, like a bed-and-breakfast lodge, the owner/manager will often act as a sales force of one. The more the complex the business, the more likely that a multitiered sales organization with a sizable salesforce will be required to penetrate a vast marketplace composed of different types and groupings of customers served by different channels in different geographic locations.

### Single-level Sales Organization

The sales organization of small primary suppliers is usually **single-leveled**, consisting of one or two persons. In many cases, the owner or manager himself/herself assumes all sales responsibilities. Fishing lodges, most restaurants, summer camps, houseboat rentals, travel trailer parks, and small sightseeing companies are typical examples.

Suppliers with a single-level sales organization depend heavily on advertisements in the travel sections of newspapers and specialized magazines, brochures in travel racks, free publicity, booths at travel shows, travel desks in hotels, and word-of-mouth advertising. These firms generally do not rely much on intermediaries.

## Dual-level Sales Organization

Medium-sized companies often have a **dual-level sales organization** with a sales manager plus a small tier of salespeople to serve **corporate** and **key accounts** or to work with intermediaries. Theme parks, large sightseeing tours, and many hotels and resorts are typical examples of firms that normally have a dual-level sales office. These firms rely heavily on intermediaries to generate the volumes needed to support the business. Often the primary function of the dual-level sales force is calling on wholesalers, travel agencies, and other travel-related companies.

## Multilevel Sales Organization

Major national and international airlines are the principal examples of companies employing **multilevel sales organizations** in the travel industry. Others include major car rental firms, national bus lines, and large hotel chains. A company with a large multilevel sales organization may have a national vice president of marketing and sales. The second level within the organization may be regional sales managers in charge of regional sales offices and national account managers in charge of key accounts. Regions are formed by groupings of states or provinces which may be further divided into sales territories.

For multinational companies, the sales department may also be divided into national and international divisions. An international sales department may be organized in different ways, but the following two approaches seem to be most common:

- *Corporate office directed*  Responsibility for all international sales may be placed under the oversight of an international sales department at the corporate headquarters. Companies that direct international sales from corporate headquarters believe that it promotes efficiency and provides maximum control, allowing the company to standardize sales policies and procedures.

- *Regional office directed*  Regional sales offices allow more autonomy within given geographic areas. Countries, singly or in combination, may be regarded as a region, and the person responsible for all the company's sales and marketing operations in each region may be given the title of regional vice president. There are various reasons for a regional approach. Generally, it permits more efficient grouping of sales functions in markets with similar characteristics or allows better oversight and quick response to dynamic market changes. A company may also feel that it is politically important to have a regional vice president in charge who can deal more effectively with local politicians, labor unions, other suppliers, or particular customers.

In reality, companies often have international sales organizations that combine corporate and regional office functions. The promotional mix employed by suppliers with multilevel sales organizations is typically extensive and costly, covering both worldwide advertising and sales promotion activities.

## Sales Methods of Primary Suppliers

The sales force of a primary supplier is responsible for calling on major sales accounts and travel intermediaries. As visiting all travel agencies in a given area might prove too expensive, such means as professional workshops and supplier-sponsored seminars are frequently employed.

Travel programs and "**travel night**" events, typically held in conjunction with trade association meetings, are staged for travel agents. Travel nights are promotional events sponsored by one or more travel suppliers who may provide cultural entertainment, refreshments, and information about a destination through videos, travel literature and knowledgeable sales people and speakers. Travel nights are normally programmed to feature a single vacation community or country, or to promote a special travel product.

Suppliers, particularly cruise lines and airlines, may have their salespeople help with these programs. If the travel night is hosted by a travel agency, films, brochures, and specialty advertising items may be provided by the supplier at no cost to the agency for use in selling the product.

In addition to its efforts to reach agents and wholesalers, the sales force of a travel supplier also makes direct calls to major corporations, government agencies, universities, and social organizations with large numbers of members who travel frequently. Some corporations have in-house travel departments where employees can make reservations for either business or pleasure travel. In the majority of cases, however, the reservations will be handled by secretaries.

Suppliers understand that secretaries can be vital links and, therefore, will work at maintaining special relations with them. Southwest Airlines, as a classic case, relied heavily on secretaries for sales when the company first entered the marketplace. The carrier had to compete with older and better established airlines. The company and its ad agency came up with a creative "Love" theme which was consistently promoted throughout Southwest's entire service system. Customers purchased their tickets from "love machines," not just ordinary ticketing machines at Southwest ticket counters; Southwest flights left from Love Air Field in Dallas; Southwest attendants wore love shorts and served passengers "love potions," not mere cocktails. The company used the theme "Someone Up There Loves You" in all its advertising. A special program was developed for secretaries of firms in its market area. Each secretary was given a glass jar filled with candy kisses. A large valentine with the name Southwest Airlines was stenciled on the jar. When the candy was consumed, many secretaries retained the jar for use as a pencil holder, keeping the company's name as a reminder on the desk.

## Cross Selling

The carrier and lodging sectors of the travel industry are in a unique position to use a variety of creative promotional techniques on their captive customers. Although there is always the risk of over-bombarding a passenger or guest with what might be regarded as crass commercialization, excellent opportunities for internal promotion exist and business can be captured by those with creative ideas. Many hotels have discovered that they can sell in-house restaurant services simply by asking guests during check-in whether

Sales outlets of major car rental companies provide direct service and convenience for customers.
Courtesy of Alamo Rent A Car, Inc.

they would like to make a dinner reservation. Likewise, the hotel telephone operator can help promote breakfast sales or laundry services along with wake-up calls. Even an automatic-dial wake-up call may be preprogrammed to sell such services. Use of an in-house TV channel to promote hotel services and the products of local advertisers has been adopted by many properties.

This process of selling referral products or services to a customer is known as **cross-selling**. Food supermarkets frequently do this by grouping together products with logical cross-sales appeal, for instance, placing shortcakes next to the strawberries. Travel suppliers may likewise increase revenues through suggestive cross-selling. A travel agency, for example, can sell insurance, travel books, or travel accessories along with the airline ticket.

## Direct Sales Channels

Transportation carriers, hotel chains, car rental companies. and other major suppliers requiring direct links to the customer may do so through direct mail, telemarketing, and/or their own sales outlets. While direct mail and telemarketing are direct techniques, they do not provide the means of servicing the needs of customers that an outlet would, and are considered only as supplemental market approaches by some suppliers.

Maintaining sales outlets is important for primary suppliers interested in selling directly to travelers. The outlets can be located anywhere there is potential customer traffic: in city sales offices; owned or leased counter space in airports, hotels, department stores, convention centers; satellite ticket offices; and automated systems. A sales space is sometimes shared by two or more suppliers to reduce costs.

The business mix produced through supplier-oriented sales outlets versus sales produced through intermediaries is an important consideration in managing the finances of a company. Company-owned sales outlets serve other important functions as well, including the following:

- *As a source of information for travelers*  Consumers are able to obtain information concerning accommodations, schedules, fares, discounts, and regulations.

- *As advertising media*  Sales outlets are often powerful image builders for the supplier. Given a choice, suppliers will almost always select premium locations with high pedestrian traffic so that company logos and display materials can make an impact on prospective customers.

- *As office locations of regional personnel*  Offices must be maintained for regional and area personnel regardless of the existence of a sales outlet. A sales outlet with sufficient space can be used for regional and area personnel as well as for local sales staff.

- *As a means of acquiring information on changing customer preferences*  Daily contact with travelers provides valuable information about shifts in consumer preferences. Companies can also do customer research—a survey for instance—at the outlets.

- *As test sales outlets for new ideas*  New ideas can be tested on a limited basis in specific markets through selected sales outlets before going national with new programs.

## Types of Sale Outlets

Sales outlets of travel suppliers may take various forms, from the familiar city ticket office in a downtown location, satellite ticket counters in department stores, to the newer automated systems accessed by an 800 toll-free number. These various types of sales outlets are discussed below.

### City Ticket Offices

The **City Ticket Offices (CTOs)** at one time served as the principal sales outlets for airlines, but this may no longer hold true in the U.S. as suburbs continue to attract population and cities remain static or decline. Some major U.S. cities are also losing major corporate headquarters to the secondary locations as companies seek to reduce overhead costs and save on taxes. Moreover, new technology provides people with alternative access to sales and service, making the location of a ticket sales outlet a moot issue. In places where cities continue to grow and remain established centers of commercial and social importance, the CTOs are vital sales outlets.

## Satellite Ticket Offices

Travel suppliers have established **satellite ticket offices** in a variety of locations. Satellite offices are established wherever convenience is an important consideration for large number of users. Satellite locations may include shopping malls, hotels, office buildings and cruise ships. Temporary satellite offices are sometimes established in ski resorts, at universities before vacation breaks, and at other establishments that have large numbers of potential travelers. In some cases, the satellite offices are managed by independent agents rather than salaried employees; this is particularly true of overseas satellite offices.

## Automated Sales Systems

Increasingly, suppliers have introduced **automated sales systems** that do not require face-to-face contact between a salesperson and the consumer. An example is the 800 number in the United States, which has proven to be an indispensable sales tool for many suppliers. A toll-free number permits both the traveler and the intermediary to call long distance free of charge for information and to make reservations. Airlines, such as small foreign carriers, often advertise an 800 number in the telephone directories of cities where they do not have sales outlets. Independently-owned hotels and motels are at a particular disadvantage without an 800 number.

Computer-to-computer sales have also been initiated in some large organizations. With increases in computer knowledge and access among the general public, this system offers great potential. **Seamless connectivity** is viewed by many as the next generation of reservations systems. Such a system would allow the traveler to access the reservation systems of travel suppliers from a PC and directly make reservations without the aid of a third party. While the advantages would seem obvious, there are also many questions concerning possible problems that may be created by such a system. For instance, will a seamless reservation system encourage overbooking and how will the security of credit card numbers be protected as confidential data is transmitted electronically on an imperfect information superhighway?

Another technological advance is vending machines which are tied directly to a computer reservation system. This form of automation is increasingly understood and accepted by the traveling public. Vending machines have been installed in major airports and in selected retail stores on an experimental basis. The traveler can insert his or her credit card in the machine, punch in the desired destination code or key button and receive a ticket.

A travel ticket vending machine could conceivably be shared by an airline, a hotel chain, a car rental firm, and a company selling traveler's checks. The consumer could insert a major bank or **travel and entertainment credit card**, select the desired travel services, and receive a reservation printout and travelers checks all from one machine that

# On-line Reservation Service

In October 1995, USAir announced the introduction of Priority Travel Works, the first on-line service in the U.S. airline industry. This service was offered to Priority Gold and Priority Gold Plus frequent flyer members. It allowed members to book flights, hotel rooms, and rental cars directly from their personal computers.

After installing a single-diskette program, members would be connected to the Apollo computer reservation system, from which they could view air fares, room rates, flight schedules, and airline cabin seating charts for 740 airlines, 24,000 hotels, and 37 car rental companies. Users could also see their frequent-flyer mileage balance and real-time gate and flight information. Members could then make reservations through their computers and have tickets mailed to their home or office.

Priority Travel Works was offered free to USAir and British Airways frequent fliers. Other airlines announced they would be introducing similar programs such as the United Connection package by United Airlines which was developed during a joint venture with Microsoft Corporation. The airlines admitted that a major purpose for the introduction of this new technology was to lower reservation costs, including the elimination of commissions paid to travel intermediaries.

interacts with other computers to ascertain space/seat availability, verify credit, and so on. Great potential for this concept exists within an integrated company offering diversified travel services, including air transportation, ground reception, automobile rentals, and hotel accommodations.

## Ticketless Travel

Airlines have tested the concept of **ticketless travel**. Each year, it is estimated that airlines issue some 500 million tickets. The cost in paper, printing, and labor amounts to as much as $15 to $30 per ticket. *(6)* To avoid such cost, passengers may be given a confirmation number instead of a ticket to reserve a seat. The method used by one airline is described as follows:

1. The customer reserves a flight through the airline, pays with a credit card, and receives a confirmation code.

2. If the individual booked sufficiently far in advance, the airline mails him/her an itinerary with flight number and confirmation code. If not made far enough in advance, the customer completes the transaction at the airport.

Airline ticket vending machine.

3. At the airport, the customer swaps the code for a boarding pass and seat assignment. If he or she has forgotten the code, the airline will request credit card and identification verification.

4. For customer needing expense account receipts, the airline suggests using either the itinerary or the boarding pass.

Despite certain advantages for both airlines and customers, ticketless travel has its detractors. There are travelers who are afraid that any shut-down in computers may mean the possible loss of their travel confirmation; other individuals simply feel more secure when they have a paid ticket in hand. Some corporate buyers, on the other hand, fear that ticketless travel will erode their ability to control travel costs when executives book arrangements directly. However, until such time as ticketless travel becomes a more widespread practice, the actual problems of this advanced system will not be known.

## Innovative Forms of Selling

Innovative forms of selling offer entrepreneurial opportunities for creative individuals who can devise strategies that offer cost savings, convenience, or increased value to the traveler and the supplier. A supermarket chain in The Netherlands, for instance, has experimented with selling package tours in tin cans placed on grocery shelves. Popular tours, such as a three-day trip to London or Paris, were packaged complete with tickets in the can; the cans were attractively presented and labeled with the appropriate national flag of the destination. Thus, shoppers had all the conveniences of buying a trip as easily as they might a tin of food off the shelf.

Another example of innovative marketing is **tie-in selling**. La Selva, a resort in the Amazon jungle area of Ecuador, created a special promotion and sales program to link or tie-in its travel products with those of a well-distributed U.S. retailer of trendy, fun, jungle-wear garments. Each seller reinforced and enhanced the product of the other to potential customers.

Destinations, too, have increasingly become aware of the possibilities of tie-in promotions with suppliers to sell both the destination and products associated with the destination. Alaska and Hawaii are examples of two states that from time to time apply tie-in techniques to promote their respective destinations in cooperative efforts with retailers. Virtually any merchandise distinctive to the destination will work as a tie-in—food, fashion, native flowers and plants, sporting equipment, books, and of course, local travel services.

Kona coffee grown on the island of Hawaii, for example, has experienced spectacular sales results as one of many tie-in products with Hawaiian tourism. Kona coffee, increasingly billed among the world's more rare and expensive coffee, lends an aura of mystique to Hawaii as a destination even as Hawaiian tourism popularizes the coffee. It is impossible to quantify the benefit to both parties from this tie-in, but few would dare argue that the relationship has no value.

## Travel Information Sources

The success of the travel industry relies heavily on a continuous flow of information. The entire industry depends on accurate and timely information. If the flow of information is interrupted or is inaccurate, the travel business would come to a standstill.

Information is disseminated in various ways: consumer advertising, trade publications, travel guides and brochures, newspaper features by travel writers, and public relations programs, to name a few. Suppliers are constantly faced with the problem of balancing the need to build an image against the need to provide information. Critics of travel advertising often complain that money is wasted by companies on image reinforcement when all the consumer wants is information on rates, schedules, and services offered. While it is true that seasoned travelers may only want specific information, the mass market relies heavily on branded products and services. A brand is ultimately only as credible as its image and reputation in the marketplace.

Image reinforcement is much more than a public relations gimmick. It is central to the concept of **product positioning**. Consumers have so many choices of products and services that few people, if any, can be expected to remember the names of all sellers for any product or service. Often, it is only the market leaders or leading brands that the average buyer will recall when polled. A traveler wishing to book a reservation for a car rental, for instance, might think only of Hertz, Avis, National, or Budget, although there are other good companies, such as Alamo, Dollar, or Thrifty Rent-A-Car, offering competitive services. A ski family thinking of a ski vacation, likewise, might have Aspen, Vail, Squaw Valley, or Sun Valley as top of mind destinations, whereas lesser known Steamboat Springs or Breckenridge could be equally good choices.

Major suppliers of all products and services know it is important to "position" their brand as a top of mind choice to potential customers. There are niche players, on the other hand, who serve niche customers in specific locations and do not expect to be known by the market at large. Many techniques are used to position a brand, including the use of a unique name—for example, Rent-a-Wreck or Motel 6; or employing a distinctive logo or symbol such as a kangaroo, which immediately calls to mind Australia and Qantas Airlines.

The variety of travel information sources include electronic means such as videotape for use in personal VCRs and closed-circuit TV channels within hotels that advertise restaurants, tours, and other travel-related services and products. The personal computer and cable TV offer great potential as a means of providing travel information to consumers

In spite of advances in electronic information delivery systems, printed communication will continue to remain important. Printed communication offers the advantages of: (1) longevity, (2) visual appeal, (3) low cost per reader, (4) detailed information, and (5) circulation as literature is passed from one reader to another.

The use of advertising to invite prospective travelers to write for additional information will involve the need for **fulfillment marketing**. The term fulfillment refers to the process of sending something requested by the consumer. Many new companies today advertise their products or services to consumers through mail, telemarketing, cable TV, or other media in which a **direct response** is solicited. A direct response could be one of asking the consumer to send a check to buy a product or to simply request additional information. The terms fulfillment marketing and direct response marketing are used interchangeably by the advertising trade.

As postage and labor costs continue to increase, the fulfillment aspect becomes more costly and requires innovative thinking. The Iowa State Tourism Office provides an example of creative thinking by its employment of prison inmates to fill 14 telemarketing positions which deal with the tourist telephone inquiries and mail-out brochures. *(7)* Few people were aware they were speaking to or corresponding with inmates until the matter was publicized, but the news was favorably received.

## Travel Writers

The fact that the general public enjoys reading about travel is evidenced by the expanding shelf space in bookstores given to travel literature and guidebooks and the abundance of magazines and newspaper sections devoted to travel and leisure. In recent years, the editorial direction of travel writing has been changing. At one time travel writing was characterized by colorful stories describing pageants, interesting places to see, and friendly natives. Today's traveler is more discriminating and might suspect that destinations and travel products are not always what they appear in alluring posters and travel brochures. These travelers are interested in factual information advising as much on things to avoid as about things to see and do. First-time travelers especially want to be forewarned about hotels with inferior accommodations and service, restaurants with dubious cuisine, and shops where price haggling is the rule. Travel stories need to present unfavorable as well as favorable aspects of destinations and supplier services.

An editorial decision to fairly present both sides of the story carries a price. Newspapers and magazines depend on paid advertising from national tourist boards and suppliers.

Consequently, there is always a chance that advertising will be canceled if an article portrays advertisers in a negative way. One newspaper, the *San Diego Tribune*, however, did not experience cancellations by advertisers when it decided to print truthful stories, telling readers about the downside experiences of the writer with the destination or with the travel supplier. Instead, the newspaper received positive response from readers and advertisers alike.

There are three general categories of travel writers; they include:

1. *Staff members of print media*   Professional journalists who are paid a salary and work for magazines, newspapers, or travel guidebook publishers.

2. *Freelance writers*   Professionals who take freelance assignments and sell their travel stories to magazines and newspapers. They may also write travel books, have them published, and receive royalties. Others may write syndicated columns or publish their own newsletter, which they sell by subscription.

3. *Entrepreneurs*   People of diverse and well-traveled backgrounds may serve as author, publisher, and salesperson. Their subjects are usually restricted to areas of special interest travel. Various entrepreneurs have developed successful businesses by publishing travel guides or travel newsletters which are distributed free of charge at tourist locations. Travel guide and tourist news publications usually carry short stories of interesting local places to see along with historical insights. These publications are supported by advertising revenue.

Travel writers frequently receive courtesy invitations from suppliers and government tourist boards to take **familiarization trips (fam trips)**. Fam trips are fully or partially paid trips offered to travel agents and travel writers to acquaint them with specific destinations or new travel products—for instance, the opening of a new hotel or the inaugural flight of a new air route. Some newspapers have policies against accepting these invitations, but most publishers are flexible. Publications that allow their writers to accept courtesy invitations may advise the host that the trip is being accepted with the understanding that the writer is free to cover the story objectively. Freelance writers may pay their own expenses so they can feel free to report their experiences without bias.

Most hotels, resorts, attractions and other large operators have a public relations officer on their staff or they will contract with an independent public relations firm. Sometimes they do both. Similarly, an NTA may have its own public relations department to handle stories or contracts with a public relations firm that works with travel writers to cover the destination. The NTA pays the firm on a per-writer-delivered basis, while the firm compensates writers on a retainer or fee-per-article basis.

An important task of a public relations office is to obtain the support of travel writers. A brief and favorable mention of a company's travel services or a destination's unique attractions and amenities is always welcome. The benefits of a feature story in a major travel publication are many, usually resulting in increased travel volume and tourist revenues.

 UMMARY

Travel sales distribution systems provide a framework for rationalizing the unique way in which travel products are channeled through the marketplace. There are several types of distribution systems, varying in complexity, with each system offering specific advantages for a given situation. At the most direct level is the one-stage distribution system, with the most complex being a four-stage system. Within the two-, three-, and four-stage distribution systems are intermediaries—travel and tour wholesalers, retailers, and specialty channelers—who perform specialized services in the marketing and sales of travel products. Their services, which benefit both suppliers and ultimate buyers, ultimately influence the efficiencies and economics of the travel industry as a whole.

On the supply end, numerous specialized sales and marketing functions are performed by primary suppliers, who use a variety of methods to create and facilitate product demand or to provide informational services to the traveling public.

# DISCUSSION QUESTIONS

1. What are the types of sales distribution systems used within the travel industry to sell travel services?

2. Why do members of the industry use different distribution systems?

3. What are some key differences between a retail and a wholesale travel agent?

4. What is the difference between a primary and secondary supplier of travel services?

5. How do the sales systems used by various suppliers differ from one another?

6. What are the primary objectives of ticketless travel? Does it have a future?

7. Discuss the sources of income for a travel agency. How these are changing?

8. What role do ground operators play in the travel industry?

9. Who purchases incentive or motivational travel?

10. Of what possible importance is cross-selling to travel suppliers?

11. Are city ticket offices of value in overseas markets? If so, why? If not, why not?

12. How can tie-in selling benefit members of the travel industry?

13. What is "positioning?" How is it used in the travel industry?

14. What is fulfillment marketing? How does it differ from direct response marketing?

15. How is travel information disseminated to the general public? How has travel writing changed in recent years?

# SUGGESTED STUDENT EXERCISE

## Short Case Discussion—The Incentive Travel Program at Duracell Batteries

Duracell International, Inc., uses a travel incentive program to keep its sales force fully charged. Apparently it is working, as net sales for Duracell grew from $1.3 billion in 1990 to over $2 billion in 1995. Duracell also enjoys 85% market penetration. "It's consistently successful. It's one of the few consumer product companies that has consistent double digit volume sales and earnings growth" said Carol Warner, analyst for Salomon Brothers.

Duracell has a sales incentive program called the President's Club. "We used to have some short-term contests from time-to-time but they were infrequent and weren't consistently applied across the country," said Jim Barone, Vice President of Field Sales. To earn a place in the President's Circle, salespeople are required to meet their quota at least two years in a row. Members of the President's Circle earn a gold ring and a chance to go on an annual group incentive trip with their spouse or friend. Destinations have included Hawaii, Bermuda, Italy, England, France, and Scotland.

One of the reasons the management of Duracell decided to offer trips was to bring spouses into the Duracell family. "Some people never get a chance to do these things in their life," said Barone, "so it becomes very special. It is a kind of payoff for all the hard work the employee does and all the time spent at night in planning and preparation. At least there would be something in it for the spouses if they could join us on one of the trips."

Duracell creates excitement by announcing the next destination at the national sales meeting and promoting it to both the sales people and their spouses throughout the year. "Nobody wants to miss out on that trip. They want to be there with people they've met from around the country," said Barone. Six time winner, Peter Armstrong said, "Now I have friendships with people all over the country and my spouse has friendships with their spouses."

"Our surveys consistently show that its one of the best incentive programs we run," said Barone. "People love it. They will kill themselves to make the numbers to go on this trip. It's one of the biggest motivating factors we've had." "I'm looking forward to going on the trip," said Armstrong, "but the real fun is when you get your name announced as a winner for the trip. Just to be recognized by your peers—people you work with, like, and trust—that's the greatest thing for me."

## Discussion Questions

1. Why do you think Duracell has experienced such success with its sales incentive programs using travel as the reward?

2. Wouldn't a cash bonus instead of travel be a better incentive since an employee could spend the money in any way he or she wishes?

3. Discuss the possible benefits to Duracell that derive when friendships are formed among Duracell salespeople and their spouses. What is the role of travel in helping to create these friendships?

*Source:* Cara Chang Mutert. "Incentives Bolster Duracell's Strong, Steady Growth," *Sales and Marketing Strategies and News*, September 1995, Volume 5, No. 6, pg. 1, 4, 7.

# $\mathcal{R}$EFERENCES

1. Schulz, Christopher. "Hotels and Travel Agents: The New Partnership," *The Cornell Hotel and Restaurant Administration Quarterly*, Vol 35, No. 2, April 1994, pg. 45–50.

2. O'Brian, Bridget. "Ticketless Plane Trips: New Technology Force Travel Agencies to Change Course," *The Wall Street Journal*, September 13, 1994, pg. B1.

3. Stone, John. "AAA: Travel Agency Business to Get More Attention," *Tour and Travel News*, November 8, 1993, pg. 10.

4. *See It, Feel It, Do It, Have It All*, The National Tour Association, Inc. 546, E. Main Street, Lexington, KY 40508, pg. 12.

5. Makens, James C., and John T. Bowen. "Junket Reps and Casino Marketing," *The Cornell Hotel and Restaurant Administration Quarterly*, Vol 35, No. 5, October 1994, pg. 63–69.

6. Dahl, Jonathan. "Airlines Try Using Ticketless Systems Giving Passengers New Gripes," *The Wall Street Journal*, November 30, 1994, pg. B6.

7. Coleman, Calmetta. "These Travel Advisers are Experts on Going Away for a Long Time," *The Wall Street Journal*, July 8, 1994, pg. B1.

# Chapter 9

# Travel Agencies and Other Intermediaries

---

## LEARNING OBJECTIVES

- To understand the scope of the travel agency industry in the United States and beyond.

- To understand the importance of major conferences and trade associations that influence the travel agency industry.

- To understand how travel agents and other intermediaries perform their functions and are compensated.

- To define and use the following terms:

| | |
|---|---|
| ARC | Commissioned intermediary |
| ARTA | Compensation mix |
| ASTA | Computerized Reservation System (CRS) |
| Automated Ticket Machines (ATM) | |
| Booking | Customer-Premises agencies |
| Block Booking | Destination Specialist |
| Certified Travel Counselor | Disclaimer |
| CLIA | Electronic Ticket Delivery Network (ETDN) |
| Conference | |

| | |
|---|---|
| Fulfillment incentive company | Override commissions |
| Full-service incentive company | Packages/Tour packages |
| Graduated rate schedule | Respondeat superior |
| IATA | Restricted-Access agencies |
| IATAN | Satellite Ticket Printer (STP) |
| Incentive department | SITE |
| ICTA | Teleticketing |
| Motorcoach broker | Ticket stock |
| National Tour Association (NTA) | Tour brokers |
| Official Airline Guide (OAG) | Travel insurance |
| Official Hotel and Resort Guide (OHRG) | USTOA |

# *T*HE RETAIL TRAVEL AGENT

*A* retail travel agent is a **commissioned intermediary** who is authorized by carriers, hotels and resorts, attractions, car rental companies, and other suppliers, including wholesalers, to sell on their behalf. As a commissioned intermediary, the travel agent does not own the services he or she sells to travelers. The agent is paid a commission by suppliers for sales of airline tickets, hotel rooms, and so on. The sales are referred to as **bookings**, meaning, for example, that a travel agent who had $1 million worth of bookings during a year would have sold that dollar value of travel services to clients. In 1993, U.S. travel agencies employed some 178,000 employees to sell $93.4 billion in bookings for travel suppliers. *(1)*

Travel agents represent all suppliers of travel services. They are free to make reservations with any supplier of travel services—with the exception of suppliers who do not pay commissions to travel agents, small suppliers who are not experienced or equipped to work with travel agencies, and a few suppliers who do not believe they need business generated by travel agents. Some travel agencies may limit the services they sell, in order to specialize in certain segments of the travel industry.

## Travel Agency Industry Structure

The travel agency industry in the United States consists of thousands of agencies, nearly half of which are members of co-ops or consortiums to help boost sales. *(2)* Despite intense competition, the total number of agency locations has continued to increase from 23,000 in 1983 to 32,446 in 1993. However, the majority of agencies have sales volume of $2 million or more annually. In 1993, travel agencies with bookings of $2 million or more accounted for 74% of the total agencies. This is a sharp contrast to the 1970s when

**TABLE 9.1**
**Changes in the U.S. Travel Agency Industry**

|  | 1970 | 1983 | 1993 |
|---|---|---|---|
| Number of Agencies | 6,700* | 23,059 | 32,446*** |
| Industry Sales Volume ($ billion) | 5 | 36 | 93 |
| Distribution of Industry by Sales Volume (%) |  |  |  |
| Under $1,000,000 | 71 | 9 | 7 |
| $1,000,000–$1,999,999 | 29** | 24 | 19 |
| $2,000,000–$4,999,999 |  | 43 | 28 |
| $5,000,000 and over |  | 24 | 46 |

*Estimated.
**Agencies $1,000,000 and over.
***Excludes satellite ticket printers.
Source:   1986 Travel Weekly Louis Harris Survey, *The Travel Industry World Yearbook—The Big Picture*,
          1984, 1994.

virtually all industry sales were made by agencies with sales volume below $2 million. (See Table 9.1) Over the last ten years, there also has been a dramatic growth in the largest agencies with over $5 million in sales, which now account for almost half of total industry sales volume.

The number of travel agencies within each state differs considerably. (See Figure 9.1) California, with 6,513 agencies, has the largest number of travel agency locations, and South Dakota has the lowest number at 58 agencies. The top six states with the largest number of travel agency locations, are California, New York, Florida, Texas, Illinois, and New Jersey. These six states account for almost half of all agency locations in the United States.

Other major changes in the industry include the growth of on-site agency branches to serve business clients, corporate travel departments of companies, and **satellite ticket printers** (STPs). These are automated ticket machines which can be placed in locations away from an agency's office. Beginning in 1986, STPs allowed agencies to establish remote ticket machines on the premises of business clients. There were 304 STP locations in 1986. The number of STP locations have increased dramatically, to 10,263 in 1993. *(2)*

The growth of STPs encouraged the development of independent STP networks, which permitted travel agencies to use a network for ticketing without having to build the network themselves. The next stage is the use of **electronic ticket delivery networks** (**ETDNs**), which will include STPs at airports, banks, office buildings, and shopping malls. 6% of agencies that handle business travel already make use of ETDNs. *(2)* ETDNs are targeted primarily at business travelers, but there is nothing to stop agencies from using them for leisure travelers as well.

## Agency Sales and Income

The income of a travel agency is derived from commissioned sales. While travel agencies earn their commissions from various suppliers and wholesalers, including cruise

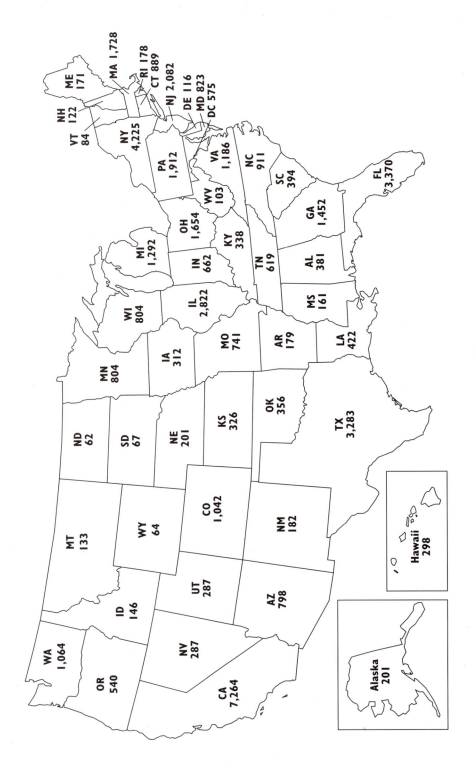

**Figure 9.1** Distribution of travel agencies as of December 1993. Includes satellite ticket printer locations.

*Source:* Airlines Reporting Corporation.

A satellite ticket printer (STP) extends the productivity of travel agencies to remote locations.
Courtesy of Unimark, Inc.

lines, tour operators, hotels, car rentals, trains, attractions, entertainment, etc., the primary source remains airline bookings. Commissions from airlines can vary, even among the various types of suppliers. A travel agency, for example, has historically received a higher percentage commission from a cruise line than from a domestic airline. The major source of revenues for travel agencies is from airline commissions, which today account for 60% of agency revenues. In 1994, major U.S. airlines established a cap on commissions which made it difficult for many agencies to generate sufficient revenues to cover their costs of ticketing.

## Override Commissions and Other Sales Incentives

Retail travel agents may also obtain **override commissions** from wholesalers and other suppliers, such as hotels. Overrides are a form of performance bonus. Wholesalers commonly offer a graduated rate schedule for overrides. This means that the percentage override offered to a travel agent increases as the number of bookings produced by the agent increases. It is also possible to receive retroactive overrides. In such cases, the wholesaler applies the higher override rate to earlier bookings by the travel agent and not just to the latest bookings. Assume that a wholesaler paid a basic commission of 10% on bookings but offered a **graduated rate schedule** up to 15%. The schedule offered agents a 1% override for $10,000 to $14,999 in sales; 2% for $15,000 to $24,999; 3% for $25,000 to $34,999; 4% for $35,000 to $44,999; and 5% for $45,000 and over. Under a retroactive override system, a travel agent who sold $45,000 worth of cumulative bookings with that wholesaler would receive a 15% commission on all the bookings.

Travel agents are able to keep themselves apprised of commissions offered by various suppliers by reading a monthly publication, *Exclusive Guide to Commission*, which is published by *The Travel Agent* magazine. Commission rate information on hotels can be found in the **Official Hotel and Resort Guide (OHRG)**.

Suppliers also offer other forms of incentives to travel agents to entice them to sell their services. For example, National Car Rental provided a quarterly bonus and supplier discounts to agents based on increased volume from the same quarter of the previous year. International air carriers may offer a bonus for selling a certain volume of ticket sales and they may offer an override in addition to regular commissions. Cruise lines offer a free room to travel agents for a certain number of cabins booked on the ship; for example, one free room for every 20 cabins booked.

## Cash Flow Management

Managers and owners of successful agencies must carefully watch all areas of the company's operations to generate a profit. Unlike many other businesses that may purchase on monthly credit, travel agencies must operate on a cash basis for the weekly payment of airline tickets which usually comprise the bulk of an agency's sales. To achieve financial success, an agency must generate sufficient sales volume to cover overhead costs and maintain at least minimum liquidity (cash on hand) to stay in business. This requires high productivity per employee, producing high-volume bookings and maintaining higher average profit margins on the bookings.

## Maximizing Profits

The goal of any business is to manage operations efficiently to maximize profits. There are four areas that can help travel agencies achieve that goal:

1. *Use of supplier's assistance*   Many suppliers offer toll-free numbers for obtaining information and for making reservations. Using these toll-free numbers can result in significant cost savings for an agency. Suppliers without toll-free numbers put themselves at a disadvantage in trying to obtain sales from travel agencies because the travel agencies will be more likely to use those suppliers who offer the toll-free ser-

vice. Suppliers also offer free promotional materials such as tour brochures and free professional assistance such as sales training with sales campaigns.

2. *Selling other travel services*   Travel agencies often sell travel insurance which travelers may purchase to insure against losses incurred while traveling. Insurance is also available to recover deposits and/or the costs of tours when a traveler is unable to travel due to sickness or an accident. Agencies may also sell travelers checks which are used in lieu of cash but are insured against loss or theft. Commission rates for travelers checks are usually not very high, but insurance sales have high commission rates.

3. *Managing revenues*   The term **compensation mix** is often used to describe the way in which all commissions, overrides, bonuses, and other volume incentives go together to produce revenues for the agency. Effective management of this mix requires the management of an agency to establish objectives and a strategy to produce a desired profit margin. This means management must develop a sales plan and not just wait for whatever business that might chance to come along.

   To appreciate the importance of managing the compensation mix, assume that two agencies had bookings of $1,000,000 each. Agency A did business as usual and realized total commissions of 11%. Agency B carefully managed its mix by promoting tours with higher commissions and working with wholesalers who paid high overrides on a retroactive basis, thus producing an average of 13% on its bookings. The difference of 2% on a million dollars is $20,000. In this case, both agencies had the same dollar amount of bookings, but one received $20,000 more in income than the other.

4. *Automation*   In the United States, approximately 96% of the agencies use a **computerized reservations system (CRS)**. Three out of ten agencies also have automated accounting systems. *(2)* As shown in Figure 9.2, over half of the operating costs for agencies relate to personnel expenses. Automation is generally seen as the key to increased personnel productivity in travel agencies.

## Regulations Governing Travel Agencies

Travel agents are subject to many restrictions and obligations, including regulations imposed by carriers and conferences. In addition, professional associations have been established to advance standards in the industry, and laws are strictly applied to protect consumers when they do business with travel agents. It should be noted that some state governments require travel agents to be licensed and to pass an examination by state licensing boards.

## Obligations and Responsibilities to Customers

In general, a travel agency can avoid liability problems by performing precisely the services contracted for with the client. The best-intentioned and most reliable agency can, nevertheless, encounter problems because of misunderstandings or unreasonable clients. Customers and consumer protection agencies have not hesitated to sue when services were not delivered as specified or implied.

Automation allows the travel agent and her client to view a travel product on CD-ROM.
Courtesy of Worldspan.

The travel agent may be held responsible for the following: (1) performing every task agreed to with the client; (2) performing every task in a manner consistent with industry-wide levels of performance; and (3) looking out for special known interests and require-ments of a client.

The degree of care needed for an 80-year-old person with disabilities is different from that needed for a healthy 28-year-old. Any agent who recommends an unescorted tour to a developing country with poor health facilities and frequent political disturbances for an 80-year-old person would be subjecting himself or herself to possible litigation if prob-lems arose on the trip. The key question would be whether or not the agent knew about the special needs of the client.

There is a considerable difference between giving professional advice to a client and simply making a booking at the client's request. In general, a travel agent cannot be held responsible for the following: weather; hotel operation, food or liquor; criminal or polit-ical activity at the destination; baggage; carriers' management practices, restaurants, and car rentals (for instance, overbooking); carrier operation; or how much a customer enjoys the destination. *(3)* Even though an agent cannot be responsible for social conditions—crime or riots, for instance—the agent does have a responsibility to inform the client about known adverse factors of the destinations he or she sells.

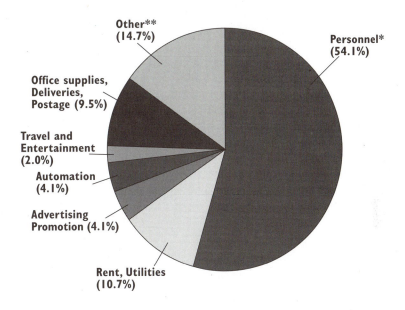

## Median Company Expenses

**Other\*\*** (14.7%)

**Personnel\*** (54.1%)

**Office supplies, Deliveries, Postage (9.5%)**

**Travel and Entertainment (2.0%)**

**Automation (4.1%)**

**Advertising Promotion (4.1%)**

**Rent, Utilities (10.7%)**

\* Salaries and other personnel costs, such as payroll costs and benefits.

\*\*Percentage, insurance, professional fees, depreciation, bad debts, rebating, etc.

**Figure 9.2** Agency operating costs.

*Source:* ASTA Agency Profitability Survey: 1991.

## Actions of Employees

A travel agency is responsible for the actions of its employees under a legal principle known as **respondeat superior**, which states that an employer is liable to third parties for the acts of its employees that are within the scope of the employer's authority. *(3)* A travel agency, thus, is potentially liable for mistakes or fraudulent acts committed by its employees when those acts relate to the operations of the travel agency. Consequently, it is important for an agency to provide employee training and to be aware of the services provided by employees to the agency's clients.

## Dealings with Other Travel Intermediaries

Retail travel agencies often sell travel services supplied by a wholesaler. The agency then receives a commission from the wholesaler, instead of from the supplier. Some wholesalers have gone bankrupt after the traveler purchased the travel services from the agents. In cases where travelers had already begun a trip, they have been left stranded without services.

In the *Bucholtz v. Sirotkin Travel* case, the court determined that the traveler purchased travel services—a packaged tour—through a travel agency and was unaware of the existence of another intermediary—the wholesaler. As a consequence, the agency was found to be liable for the travel services purchased by the traveler. *(4)* The ruling of this case indicates that a travel agency has a responsibility to check the integrity and reliability of wholesalers and to inform travelers of the involvement of other travel intermediaries, because the agency could be found liable for wholesalers' actions.

The danger of being sued by a client for problems created by an intermediary has forced travel agents and such suppliers as airlines to seek protection through insurance and the use of disclaimers. A **disclaimer** is a statement that is written into a contract explaining that the travel agent or supplier will not be liable for acts or errors of wholesalers and other third parties, such as tour guides and chauffeurs. For an agency to be fully protected, a disclaimer must be presented to the client both in writing and orally. Before doing this, however, travel agents and suppliers must carefully review all of the advertising and promotional materials they give to clients to make certain the wording in such material does not negate their disclaimers.

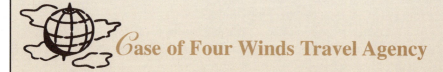

## Case of Four Winds Travel Agency

It is natural for a travel agency to want to convince clients that it is professional and its service is dependable; however, such claims may create problems should they prove untrue. For example, an agency called the Four Winds Travel Agency once stated the following in its advertising:

> Four Winds also guarantees that every tour will be escorted by a qualified professional tour director. Our directors are carefully selected and trained. Your Four Winds jet tour is an escorted tour. From the moment you leave until your journey ends, you are cared for by a carefully selected Four Winds Tour Escort. *(5)*

A client purchased a 47-day tour for a Four Winds tour to South America. During her visit to Brazil, she was being transported in a boat on the Amazon River near Manaus. The boat was not owned by Four Winds, and the guide was not a Four Winds employee. As the boat docked at Manaus, the client slipped and fell in the Amazon. Although it was an accident, she sued Four Winds for damages. The court agreed that the promotional literature had led her to believe Four Winds would be in charge of the tour and, therefore, could be held liable for the safety and care of its clients.

## Regulations by Carriers and Conferences

Although travel agents have a responsibility to all suppliers, their responsibility to the carriers is of particular importance. A travel agent can be fined or suspended for not assuming obligations imposed by the carriers.

Travel agents are regulated and given official appointments to serve as agents for carriers by what are known as **conferences**. The term conference as used here does not refer to a meeting; instead, it refers to a regulatory body that has the right to set standards for travel agencies. In most cases, a travel agency cannot sell tickets on carriers and receive commissions from them until it is appointed and receives accreditation by the respective conference.

There are three major conferences: (1) The Airline Reporting Corporation (ARC), (2) The International Airline Travel Agency Network (IATAN), composed of U.S. and foreign airlines with international routes; and (3) The Cruise Lines International Association (CLIA), composed of major cruise lines operating throughout the world.

Of these conferences, the two most influential ones regarding the manner in which a travel agency does business, are ARC and IATAN. Some of the key regulations imposed upon travel agents by ARC and IATAN are the following:

1. *Documentation Procedure*  Both conferences require detailed documentation concerning promotional methods, descriptions of the agency and its location, replies to questionnaires, financial data, and personal information.

2. *Bonding*  Travel agents are required to be bonded in the event of a default. The bond is calculated by a formula based on sales of standard **ticket stock**. Ticket stock refers to the supply of tickets an agency keeps on hand.

3. *Ticket Stock Procedures*  The ARC regulates travel agencies as to the amount of ticket stock they may keep on hand, where they may store it, and how it may be used. These precautions are necessary, because the stock of tickets is like having blank checks which can be issued for air travel before the airlines are paid.

4. *Change of Ownership Procedure*  Travel agencies cannot change ownership without the new owners meeting specific regulations to be appointed by the respective conferences.

## Airline Reporting Corporation

The stockholders of ARC are comprised of major U.S. airlines, but many additional airlines, including foreign airlines, participate in ARC. Travel agencies must meet ARC requirements in order to sell tickets and receive commissions from airlines participating in ARC. Within the United States, ARC appointment is very important to travel agencies since the majority of their revenues are from airline ticket sales.

ARC provisions reflect the fact that travel agencies no longer have exclusive rights to distribute airline tickets. Now an airline can appoint an agent to issue its own tickets even though the agent may not meet all ARC requirements. Customer-premises agencies (those located on the premises of customers) allowed the growth of on-site agencies to service business clients. As mentioned previously, STPs have been located on the premises of business clients to issue ARC travel documents.

## International Airlines Travel Agent Network

The **International Air Transport Association (IATA)** is comprised of scheduled international airlines. The Passenger Network Services Corporation is a subsidiary of IATA that does business under the name International Airlines Travel Agent Network. The IATAN is similar to ARC in appointing agencies for international airlines. Some U.S. travel agents believe it is important to be appointed by both ARC and IATAN. Other U.S. agents feel it is not necessary to have both appointments since they can issue tickets for most international airlines through ARC.

## Travel Agency Industry Standards

Three professional associations have been established to advance standards in the industry and to represent the industry: **The Institute of Certified Travel Agents (ICTA)**, **The American Society of Travel Agents (ASTA)**, and **The Association of Retail Travel Agents (ARTA)**. While these are not regulatory bodies, they do exert pressure to promote standards. These groups have a written set of codes and standards to serve as guidelines for travel agents. Both ASTA and ICTA also offer home study courses for travel agents. Those who successfully complete the ICTA courses can receive the **Certified Travel Counselor** (CTC) or the **Destination Specialist** (DS) professional designation.

## Future of Retail Travel Agencies

Over the course of the post-airline deregulation years, the demise of retail travel agencies has been periodically predicted as changes in the airline industry and advances in technology have occurred. Yet, the number of agencies have continued to increase in spite of increased competition, higher operating costs, and numerous bankruptcies. What has occurred and is still happening is an evolution in which travel agencies are adapting to meet changing conditions.

The travel agency role, as briefly discussed in Chapter 8, has been shifting from one of an order-taking mode to a highly professional "travel management" service. Even though customers today can book directly through the Internet or take advantage of ticketless travel, an agent's expertise on travel information will still be needed. Advances in technology will also offer agents with the opportunity to better serve clients by customizing travel to meet their exact needs. *(6)*

The travel agency business will also continue to be a source of numerous entrepreneurial opportunities, offering such options as operating an agency through a virtual office or a home workstation, specializing in niche markets, to establishing large megaagencies and travel superstores. The superstore concept promotes the idea of travel shopping as entertainment through the use of interactive systems and computer technology, including virtual reality. *(7)* Thus, travel agencies will continue to evolve and prosper in the future by providing value-added professional services for clients.

# $\mathcal{T}$HE WHOLESALER

As defined in Chapter 8, a wholesaler specializes in organizing tour packages which are marketed through retail travel agents. This section describes the activities of tour wholesalers, their method of operations and factors which may affect wholesalers' future operations. In addition, a specialized form of tour wholesalers for the motorcoach industry in the United States will be discussed at the end of this section.

## Wholesaler Industry Structure

In 1970, approximately 300 to 400 wholesalers existed in the United States. This number doubled by 1975, and by 1993 the number exceeded 2,000. The bulk of the wholesale business in the United States is relatively concentrated. The 50 largest wholesalers represent well over 50% of the industry revenue. Most wholesalers belong to ASTA. The largest wholesalers also are members of the U.S. Tour Operators Association (USTOA), a trade organization supporting the common interests of tour operators who have met certain qualifications. This organization helps to establish industry standards and serves as a lobbying force for wholesalers. USTOA requires each member to put up a $1 million bond to cover defaults. *(1)*

## Wholesaling Activities

The tour wholesaler in the travel industry is functionally similar to a wholesaler in any other industry. A common characteristic of most wholesalers is that they purchase and own the merchandise they sell to retailers; however, this is not true of tour wholesalers. A tour wholesaler does not necessarily buy the travel services which it arranges into tour packages. Instead, tour wholesalers use minimum deposits to secure future space from hotels, airlines, and other suppliers. Well-known firms such as Cartan, Maupintour, and Unitours are examples of tour wholesalers.

A tour wholesaler or wholesale travel agent does not work on a commission basis as do retail travel agents. A wholesaler secures large blocks of advance reservations, referred to as **block bookings**, on airlines and for ground services such as hotels, restaurants, entertainment, and sightseeing tours. In order to do this, a wholesaler usually must put down large deposits with suppliers. These deposits and other prepayments to suppliers can be lost by a wholesaler if he or she fails to generate sufficient volume to fill the large number of rooms or seats that were reserved for months and sometimes years in advance. Suppliers, however, are interested in selling to wholesalers, because it assures them of committed sales; consequently, wholesalers are able to contract for the space or services from suppliers at substantially reduced prices. Thus, a wholesaler assumes risk in reserving block bookings as opposed to a retail travel agent who sells on behalf of the wholesaler for a commission.

The wholesaler must decide what type of tour packages would appeal to travelers, and package the services for sale through retailers. The packaged tours are made attractive to potential travelers by prices lower than what the traveler would pay for the same services on an itemized or individually booked basis and by creative merchandising. Package tour merchandising does not simply list the hotels and airlines a traveler will use. In fact, these may or may not be mentioned. What is emphasized is the total package—a "Rome Getaway" or "Wonders of Ancient Egypt"—that will capture the attention of potential buyers seeking a specific travel experience.

## Method of Operation

Wholesalers sell their packages *through* retail travel agents, not *to* them. Retail travel agents receive a commission from wholesalers to sell their packages and, at times, an override based on volume. Wholesalers may also sell through incentive companies, which act as agents in selling packages to corporations and other organizations. These firms use the tours as motivational incentives for employees. In some cases, wholesalers, as tour operators, also sell tour packages directly to groups of tourists. Wholesalers also serve as retailers when they own travel agencies.

## Future of Wholesalers

As we have discussed previously, travel market conditions are constantly changing. Increased competition and new consumer concerns are a reality in this marketplace. Wholesalers could be affected by the following:

1. *Competitive packages by suppliers*   Suppliers have demonstrated a willingness to work with each other to create air, ground, and/or sea packages. These packages could be sold directly in greater numbers by suppliers in competition with wholesalers. Both U.S. and foreign airlines usually offer package tours by creating subsidiary tour companies to package and sell tours on routes served by the parent airline.

2. *Low individual prices from suppliers*   Discount fares and other low prices from suppliers could effectively discourage travelers from purchasing group tours put together by wholesalers. Also, more people are becoming seasoned travelers and prefer to travel independently rather than in group tours.

3. *Increased litigation aimed at wholesalers*   As consumers become increasingly experienced in travel, and understand their rights, they are quick to sue wholesalers and suppliers for real or alleged breach of duty to perform, or for breach of contract to provide what has been advertised, even when the failure may have been caused by circumstances beyond the wholesaler's control.

## Motorcoach Brokers

A motorcoach is often referred to as a bus, but a motorcoach is designed to provide greater comfort for distance travel than the typical mass transit buses used in cities. Motorcoaches, unlike city buses, usually have a restroom, reclining fully-padded seats, music, and air-conditioning. A specialized form of tour wholesaler exists in the United States for the motorcoach industry. These individuals are known as **motorcoach brokers**. They are licensed and bonded by the Federal Interstate Commerce Commission to offer packaged touring by motorcoach in the United States. Some motorcoach brokers also sell tours extending into Canada.

### Method of Operation

Motorcoach brokers are a unique concept developed during the 1930's under the Interstate Commerce Commission to promote interstate travel and tourism. The broker charters motorcoach transportation from such certified carriers as Greyhound Lines or Continental

Trailways and prepares the itinerary and any or all of the other components of the tour. Brokers also commonly operate travel agencies in which the tour packages are sold to clients. Motorcoach tours particularly appeal to groups who want tailor-made tours tied to special events—for example, an alumni group headed for a rival college football game in another state. However, most tours are prepackaged and open to any buyer.

Most tours sold by motorcoach brokers are referred to as all-expense, sightseeing, and pleasure tours. The cost of these tours includes transportation, hotel or motel accommodations, some or all meals, admission tickets to attractions or events, and required guides and escorts, tips, and baggage handling. The broker assumes complete responsibility for the trip or tour.

Motorcoach tours can represent an important part of the business for motels and hotels en route to and at destinations. It is important for management of these concerns to study the needs of the charter motorcoach customer and to make special efforts to have their hotels or motels included in tour packages sold by brokers.

Many motorcoach brokers belong to the **National Tour Association (NTA)**, a trade group dedicated to advancing the professional interest and business of motorcoach brokers and operators. The NTA holds an Annual Convention and Tour & Travel Exchange for its membership to discuss travel trends and new ideas in marketing and tour operations. Another function of this annual event is to bring together tour brokers and operators with potential buyers. During a full week of intensive buyer/seller appointments, more than 55,000 individual meetings are held to plan the coming year's tour programs.

# $\mathcal{T}$HE INCENTIVE COMPANY

Incentive companies, sometimes referred to as motivational houses, are professional companies that assist clients with designing, promoting, and executing programs to motivate employees or customers through the offer of company paid or subsidized travel.

Many firms have discovered that the promise of an all-expense paid trip to some exotic area can be a powerful motivational tool. This concept is not new. As early as 1906, the National Cash Register Company offered a travel incentive program to visit its Dayton headquarters.

The concept behind incentive travel is that it should be a self-liquidating promotion, meaning that the incentive program should result in sufficient extra profit to the company to pay for the trips. The definition of incentive travel used by the **Society of Incentive Travel Executives (SITE)** is a "modern management tool used to achieve extraordinary goals by awarding participants a travel prize upon attainment of their share of the uncommon goal." *(8)*

## Types of Incentive Companies

There are three types of incentive companies: **full-service companies**, **fulfillment companies**, and **incentive departments** within travel agencies.

1. A *full-service incentive company* specializes in incentive travel. It is able to offer a
   client assistance in developing and managing the incentive program within the client's

## *H*ow the Maritz Travel Company Develops an Incentive Travel Proposal

Maritz Travel Company creates, plans, and operates group and individual travel awards, business meetings, special events, and corporate travel management programs on a worldwide basis. The incentive travel business unit concentrates on designing group awards for many Fortune 400 companies. Sponsoring companies use the awards to motivate distribution chain performance in achieving (primarily) sales and cost containment goals.

In a typical selling situation, once a Maritz sales person receives permission to bid on a client's business, a travel program manager is called upon to coordinate the presentation development process which includes the next seven steps:

1. Qualify the client's specifications by defining variables such as group size, operation dates, participant demographics, budget, etc.

2. Develop a presentation strategy that weighs competitive factors, seasonal and budgetary restrictions and overall campaign limitations.

3. Create a short list of potential destinations that fit the client's specifications and targeted presentation strategy.

4. Involve geographically-assigned destination experts in the site and hotel selection process to take advantage of their up-to-date industry knowledge.

5. Develop and enhance an itinerary that reflects the client's specifications and differentiates the proposal from previous ones the client may have received from Maritz or a competitor. Remember, creating Incentive awards is a custom business involving innovation.

6. Block space with hotels, cruise lines and airlines and negotiate rates, terms and conditions prior to finalizing the proposal.

7. Present the proposal to the client's marketing or purchasing departments, either in a live "stand-up" format or as a "drop off."

### Example of a Maritz Incentive Program—Great Pursuits Work Their Magic in Maui

Great Pursuits programming is far more in-depth than any traditional travel experience. For instance, those who select culinary arts have an opportunity to work beside an accomplished sous chef, learning the art of presentation and helping to prepare one of their own meals. Golfers and tennis buffs enjoy playing with professionals, participating in swing analyses, skill drills, and fun competitions. Haute couture participants dabble in wearable arts, have a private runway luncheon and enjoy accompanying an expert on a shop-till-you-drop spree.

Late each afternoon, all participants are encouraged to enjoy high tea while tuning into their client's television channel in the client's signature lounge to see the "Replays of the Day," actual video clips of participant's Great Pursuits. (An edited video collection sent to each participant's home becomes a lasting memento of their travel award.)

And when the group assembles each evening, wonderful surprises are in store for them. For instance, one night guests think they're going on a routine dine-around to Maui's most popular restaurants. When they meet for cocktails in the foyer, they're surprised to be led into the ballroom where a cookoff competition between the island's top chefs is staged. Participants sample the best cuisine the best chefs have to offer, voting for their favorite specialties. A personalized recipe book, tastefully presented with a pillow note from Fleetwood, concludes another memorable evening. On another night, guests drive their rental cars on a rally to a pre-determined rendezvous. They are led to a promontory where they are welcomed to a sunset symphony and creatively catered alfresco bill of fare.

When it comes time to say farewell to Fleetwood and their holiday home, participants have a quiver full of memories and are committed to turning in next year's winning performance, if only to see how they outdo this year. And that's the magic of incentive group travel.

*Source:*  Al Geismar, Vice President, Product Communications, The Maritz Travel Company, February 26, 1996.

**Hawaiian entertainment and alfresco dining create excitement and fun for incentive program participants on the Island of Maui.**
Courtesy of Marriott Hotel, Maui, Hawaii.

company and in planning, organizing, and directing the travel. A full-service company assists the client in all stages of the travel incentive program, including the development of intracompany communications, sales pep rallies, and establishing quotas to qualify for an incentive trip. Such work can involve hundreds of hours of professional time plus travel expenses to visit different plants or sales offices. Compensation for the work of a full-service company is usually received on the basis of professional fees, expense reimbursement, and normal commissions on the sale of travel services such as transportation and hotel. Examples of full-service firms in the United States are E.F. MacDonald Travel Company, Maritz Travel Company, Top Value Enterprises, and S & H Motivation Inc.

2. A *fulfillment type of incentive company* is usually a smaller company that may have been started by a former executive of a full-service firm. A fulfillment company tends to specialize in selling the travel portion of the package; and it does not offer fee-paid professional assistance in planning the incentive program. Compensation comes from normal travel commissions.

3. Several travel agencies have established special *incentive travel departments*. These firms may or may not be able to offer a client professional assistance in the incentive planning portion. If they do, they will often charge on the same basis as a full-service firm.

## Users of Incentive Travel

The primary use of incentive travel by businesses is to motivate employees and other persons to attain company objectives. The typical goals of these incentives are to increase company sales volume, to boost morale and goodwill, and to introduce new products. Incentive travel has also been used as a prize to motivate employees to improve attendance, reduce accidents, and reduce costs. Incentive travel is generally provided for salespersons, distributors, and dealers. Ten of the top industry users of incentive travel are listed in Table 9.2.

The destination selected for an incentive program must be exciting and yet have a broad-based appeal. The choice of an appropriate site cannot be left solely to the personal likes or dislikes of a travel agent, sales manager, or incentive company executive. A large sales organization is likely to have people of varying ages, lifestyles, and personal interests with different travel preferences. The destination should, therefore, also be somewhat self-promoting and generally popular. Hawaii or Las Vegas, for example, usually needs little or no sales promotion since they are well-known destinations. A trip to Haiti or Bosnia, on the other hand, would require considerably more effort to sell. The destination offered in an incentive program must be changed from time to time in order to maintain the interest of those employees who have been winners. Some of the requisites of an incentive program are:

1. *Adequate budget* If insufficient money is allocated to promote the incentive program, there is a high probability that the results will be disappointing.

2. *Measurable and challenging objectives* Objectives should be established by the user to ensure above-normal performance, such as increased sales of a given percentage.

| TABLE 9.2 | |
|---|---|
| **Industry Users of Incentive Travel** | |
| **Type of Company** | **($Million)** |
| 1. Insurance | 215.0 |
| 2. Electronics, radio, and television | 152.0 |
| 3. Automotive parts and accessories | 147.2 |
| 4. Cars and trucks | 134.7 |
| 5. Farm equipment | 91.8 |
| 6. Heating and air-conditioning | 90.1 |
| 7. Office equipment | 71.6 |
| 8. Electrical appliances | 56.7 |
| 9. Building materials | 48.6 |
| 10. Toiletries and cosmetics | 46.3 |

Source: Travel and Tourism Analyst. (9)

Enough extra profit through higher sales or lowered costs should be generated to cover the cost of the incentive travel program. The objectives must be measurable and time specific; say, in the case of an appliance company, an increase of $10 million in sales of home air-conditioners by May 1.

3. *Assigned responsibility and accountability*   A specific person in the user's company must be given responsibility and accountability for the program. The travel incentive company should also assign a specific account executive to work with the designated person from the user's company.

4. *Quotas*   Establishing a sales quota system provides greater motivation than a program in which only the top *x* percent of the participants may take the trip. A program of quotas allows each participant to qualify, as long as the given quota is met.

5. *Short reward periods*   In general, programs with a shorter time span for achieving incentive goals are most effective, since people tend to forget, lose interest, or become distracted after a while. Most travel incentive programs seem to be 3 to 6 months long and very few are for more than 1 year.

6. *Professional communications and sales promotion of incentive plan*   For programs to be successful, they must be adequately promoted. This requires frequent communications, carefully timed and stimulating motivational techniques, and the support and enthusiasm of all members of the marketing and sales management group. Personal contact is important.

7. *Correct timing of the trip*   The trip should be scheduled during a time of year when there is no undue strain on the operations of the user's company. It should be timed to

take advantage of off-season rates but also be a time when participants want to travel. Because these requirements often conflict, flexibility and compromise are necessary.

8. *Desirable and/or unusual destinations*  The trip destination must match the interests of the participants. It is sometimes necessary to conduct a survey among participants before selecting a location to ensure a proper match.

# $\mathcal{T}$RAVEL AGENCIES WORLDWIDE

Worldwide, there were approximately 67,000 travel agencies which were accredited by IATA in 1992. *(1)* The agency locations in the United States comprised 47% or almost half of the worldwide total. U.S. travel service companies have also continued to expand globally. In 1993, American Express bought Nyman and Schultz, one of Europe's largest travel agencies; and it bought the majority shares of two Australian agencies in 1994. *(1)*

Besides American Express, major international travel service companies include Japan Travel Bureau, London-based Thomas Cook Group, and Wagon-Lits of France. The number of independent agencies in other countries has also grown in spite of setbacks due to the Gulf War in 1991 and recessions. A recent study estimated that there were approximately 34,175 travel agency outlets in the European Union (EU) as of 1993. *(10)* These agencies employed 200,000 people and generated $80 billion in sales.

Germany, with a domestic and international market of 53.6 million travelers, accounted for 26% of the total sales for the EU, followed by the United Kingdom with 19%, France with 15%, Spain with 13%, and Italy with 12%. Other EU countries accounted for the remaining portion of sales.

As compared to the United States, package tour holidays are still very popular in Europe. Depending on the specific country, revenues from package tours may account for anywhere from 30 to 75% of travel agencies' income in Europe *(10)*, whereas airline sales will account for more than 60% of agency income in the United States.

Travel agencies in Europe may operate both retail and wholesale departments similar to agencies in the United States. Well-known European tour operators include NUR (Neckerman) of Germany, Thomson Holidays of the United Kingdom, and Jet Tours of Air France and Kuoni. Most of these tour operators are transitional companies with subsidiaries or branches in other countries.

With the rapid growth of travel in the Asia-Pacific region, major travel companies have also emerged to serve inbound and outbound tourist traffic. As a subsidiary of the Swire Group, Swire Travel of Hong Kong is linked to one of the reputable "hongs" or established historic houses of foreign trade, to become a major source travel service provider in Hong Kong and the region. The opening of China has made China International Travel Service (CITS) and China Travel Service (CTS) two of the leading travel companies in the region. The recent development of outbound travel by Chinese citizens will extend their impact beyond Asia. Other well-known agencies in Asia include Jetours of Japan and Pacific Leisure, with offices throughout Asia.

International expansion for travel agencies has met increased competition from airlines as well as other travel suppliers. Global distribution systems and advances in electronic shopping for travel through the Internet pose additional challenges. Large travel companies, nevertheless, are finding it necessary to expand internationally to serve their clients better and to capitalize on opportunities on fast growth segments of the worldwide travel market.

# SUMMARY

Travel agents, wholesalers, and tour brokers are the most common intermediaries in the travel distribution system. A travel agent is a commissioned intermediary who sells on behalf of carriers, hotels, car rental companies, and other suppliers under their authorization. The size and structure of travel agencies, along with the way they are managed and regulated, have undergone significant changes since the 1980s due to advances in technology, strict liability interpretation by the court, the loss of exclusive rights to sell airline tickets, and dynamic market forces.

The travel agency business is becoming increasingly complex, as managers face tough new problems of competition from nontraditional sources and conditions imposed by suppliers, government, trade conferences, and trade associations. With the continual evolvement of travel sales distribution systems toward higher degrees of cost efficiency in responding to changing market demands and economic circumstances, the central question will be one of survival of the travel agency in its present form. However, we conclude that travel agencies will not only survive, but will flourish, albeit in a different role—no longer merely as agents of travel suppliers but as merchandisers, "customizers," and marketeers of travel and tourism in their own right to serve an increasingly diverse marketplace.

# DISCUSSION QUESTIONS

1. What are major characteristics of the travel agency industry in the United States?

2. What are some of the key requirements of ARC and IATA that agencies must meet to be appointed?

3. What are the important differences between the operations of a retail travel agency versus those of a tour wholesaler?

4. What responsibilities does a travel agent have toward clients?

5. Describe ways in which travel agencies can protect themselves against potential lawsuits.

6. How do ground operators and incentive companies relate to travel agencies and wholesalers?

7. Describe the role of a motorcoach broker.

8. What factors may affect the future of wholesalers? Why?

9. Name three different types of companies that deal with incentive programs. How do the companies differ?

10. What are the essential elements of a successful incentive program?

11. In what ways are travel agencies becoming more globalized?

12. How might the development of advanced information technology systems, such as Internet, affect the future of the agency business?

## SUGGESTED STUDENT EXERCISE

It has been suggested that today's travel agency must change to survive the future. The "order-taker" agency must begin to give way to one that offers services on a value-added basis, as well as actively merchandising and marketing travel. In the face of advancing technology, the use of retail agents and agencies for commercial travel management and point-to-point sales may diminish as customers are able to deal directly with suppliers.

1. Review some of the trends in travel and tourism—supplier structure, sales distribution, agency revenue, technology, and markets—that will have an impact on the travel agency business.

2. Develop a scenario for travel agencies of the future in the year 2015. What functions will these agencies serve in the marketplace? Who will they serve?

3. Describe the professional skills (knowledge of geography, marketing, communications, etc.) that will be needed for employment in the travel agency of the future. Will the term "travel agent" mean something different in the future than it does now?

# REFERENCES

1. Waters, S.R. *Travel Industry World Year Book: The Big Picture 1994–95*. New York: Child & Waters Inc., 1994.

2. Travel Weekly 1994 *U.S. Travel Agency Market Survey*. Conducted by Louis Harris and Associates. 1994.

3. Quinn, P. S., and S. A. Laver. *The Travel Agent, The Consumer, and the Law*. Washington, D.C.: Princess Hotels International, October 1977.

4. Anolik, A. *The Law and the Travel Industry*. San Francisco: Alchemy Books, 1977.

5. Dickson, T. A. "How to Disclaim Liability When Things Go Wrong." *The Travel Agent* (January 4, 1971).

6. Martin, D. "Staying in the Mix." *The Travel Agent* (November 6, 1995)

7. Fine, P. "Agency of the Future." *The Travel Agent* (November 6, 1995)

8. "How it all Began and Where it is Today—Incentive Travel from A to Z." *Meetings and Conventions*. (July 1981).

9. Bredemeier, J. "Incentive Travel in the USA." *Travel and Tourism Analyst*. The Economist Intelligence Unit, U.K. (September 1986).

10. Smith, C. and P. Jenner. "Travel Agents In Europe." *EIU Travel & Tourism Analyst*, No. 3, 1994.

Part **5**

# Transportation Services

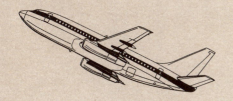

# Chapter 10

# Water Transportation

## LEARNING OBJECTIVES

- To understand the role of the water transportation industry in the travel industry.

- To appreciate the forces likely to affect the future of cruise ships.

- To define and use the following terms:

| | |
|---|---|
| Adventure cruises | Diversification |
| All-inclusive packages | Exotic cruises |
| Backward vertical integration | Ferry boats |
| Bareboat charters | Foreign flag carriers |
| Barge | Forward vertical integration |
| Big wheels | Horizontal integration |
| Canoes | Houseboats |
| Cargo liner/freighter | Jones Act |
| Charter yachts | Lowers |
| CLIA | Luxury cruises |
| Cross-substitutability of demand | Megaliners |
| Cruise directors | Mini-cruiser |
| Cruise ships | Paddle wheelers |
| Deluxe cruises | Passenger Services Act |
| Destination sampling | Passenger ships |

| | |
|---|---|
| Ports of call | Staterooms |
| Ports of embarkation | Submarines |
| Reposition | Ultra-yacht |
| Resort cruises | Vertical integration |
| Revenue management | Wilderness outfitters |
| River boats | Yield management |

# *S*IZE AND SCOPE OF THE CRUISE INDUSTRY

*O*ne of the fastest growing fleets in the world carries no guns, firearms, or torpedoes, yet the rate of its growth worldwide has rivaled that of navies committed to defense. The fleet we refer to is comprised of cruise ships, yachts, and boats. In recent years, the cruise industry has indeed been building new ships, visiting new ports, and drumming up an increasingly diverse group of customers.

In 1994, over 4.5 million people worldwide took a cruise and many more used other forms of water transportation for travel/recreation. The Caribbean attracted half of all cruise passengers followed by western Mexico, the Mediterranean, Alaska, the Panama Canal, and Europe. Remarkably, 95% of passengers surveyed indicated they enjoyed the cruise experience and would do it again. *(1)* **CLIA** (**The Cruise Line International Association**) has forecasted that by the year 2000, more than 8 million passengers will take a cruise each year.

**Passenger Ships** were forerunners of the present-day **cruise ships**. The primary purpose of a passenger ship was to transport people from one destination to another; and for many years it represented the mainstay of the passenger water transportation industry, primarily for transatlantic travel. The era of regularly scheduled passenger ships between major ports began with sailing vessels when the U.S. and Canada were young nations, and continued with diesel-driven ships until the late 1960s. High costs of operation and the beginning of mass travel by jet aircraft were primary reasons for the end of passenger ships.

Even when regularly scheduled passenger ships were no longer economically feasible, ocean travel did not phase out as numerous passenger ships were converted into cruise ships. Those that were too old or too large were junked for scrap, whereas others with historic value were converted into tourist facilities. *The Queen Mary*, a beautiful and large ship that had been the pride of the British passenger fleet, was permanently docked in Long Beach, California and transformed into a tourist attraction, restaurant, and hotel.

The United States and Canada dominate the international cruise market, followed by Europe. Estimates of the total dollar size of the cruise industry are difficult to derive, because income is earned from multiple sources, including sale of berths, gaming, bars, shops, and miscellaneous services.

A study by Price Waterhouse placed cruise line employment at 450,166 in 1992, and predicted growth of 134,712 additional jobs by 1996. The study also showed that the cruise industry had generated $14.5 billion in wages and $6.3 billion in tax revenues in 1992. *(2)* CLIA estimated the total size of the cruise market to be $50 billion in 1992.

The cruise line sector has become a major buyer and partner with other members of the travel industry. Carnival Cruise Lines alone, for example, has become one of the largest food buyers in the U.S. To feed its hungry passengers, the line buys over two million pounds of prime cuts each year from one Colorado beef supplier. The cruise and tour operation of Carnival created over $240 million in sales for Delta Airlines in 1994. Other cruise lines and other suppliers also enjoy profitable business relationships. *(3)*

North American cities serve as major ports for cruise ships. Some 36 cruise lines serve the North American market (see Table 10.1). In 1993, the number of embarkations was nearly 4.2 million, up 3% from 1992 (see Table 10.2). Miami, with 35% of the total embarkations in 1994, is clearly the dominant North American port. Cruise ships picking up passengers at American ports, regardless of the origin of the passengers, must put up a bond with the Federal Maritime Commission.

In recent years, there has been a trend toward shorter, more frequent vacations. U.S. Cruise lines have responded with 3–7 night cruises. At the same time, there is a greater

---

### TABLE 10.1
### Cruise Lines Serving North American Cruise Line Market in 1996

Including 1995 capacity additions, CLIA member lines represent 96.8% of North American cruise market and 83.7% of ships.

| SUMMARY | | | | |
|---|---|---|---|---|
| | **Lowers (operating)** | | **Ships (operating)** | |
| CLIA member lines | 101,384 | (96.8%%) | 103 | (83.7%) |
| Non-CLIA | 3,343 | (3.2%) | 20 | (16.3%) |
| TOTAL | 104,727 | 100.0% | 123 | 100.0% |

| **CLIA Member Lines** | **Lowers** | **Ships** | **Primary Non-CLIA** | **Lowers** | **Ships** |
|---|---|---|---|---|---|
| American Hawaii Cruises | 790 | 1 | American Canadian Cruise Line | 244 | 3 |
| Carnival Cruise Lines | 16,556 | 10 | American West Steamboat Co. | 163 | 1 |
| Celebrity Cruises | 8,510 | 5 | Classical Cruises | 140 | 1 |
| Commodore Cruise Line | 729 | 1 | Clipper Cruise Line | 240 | 2 |
| Costa Cruise Lines | 5,863 | 8 | Club Med | 772 | 2 |
| Crystal Cruises | 1,894 | 2 | Dolphin Heliss Cruises | 568 | 1 |
| Cunard Line, Ltd. | 5,344 | 8 | Renaissance Cruises | 856 | 8 |
| Delta Queen Steamboat Company | 1,024 | 3 | Star Clipper | 360 | 2 |
| Dolphin Cruise Line | 1,572 | 2 | TOTAL | 3,343 | 20 |

*Continued*

### TABLE 10.1 (CONTINUED)
### Cruise Lines Serving North American Cruise Line Market in 1996

| CLIA Member Lines | Lowers | Ships |
|---|---|---|
| Epirotiki Line | 1,898 | 3 |
| Holland America Line | 8,781 | 7 |
| Majesty Cruise Line | 1,056 | 1 |
| Norwegian Cruise Line | 7,014 | 5 |
| Oceanic Cruises | 120 | 1 |
| Orient Line | 845 | 1 |
| Premier Cruise Lines | 2,278 | 2 |
| Princess Cruises | 11,130 | 9 |
| Radisson Seven Seas | 714 | 3 |
| Regal Cruise Lines | 735 | 1 |
| Regency Cruises* | 4,247 | 6 |
| Royal Caribbean Cruise Line | 15,020 | 9 |
| Royal Cruise Line* | 2,776 | 4 |
| Seabourn Cruise Line | 408 | 2 |
| Seawind Cruises | 724 | 1 |
| Silversea Cruises | 592 | 2 |
| Sun Line Cruises | 1,320 | 3 |
| Windstar Cruises | 444 | 3 |
| World Explorer Cruises | 0 | 0 |
| TOTAL | 101,384 | 103 |

*As of the date of compiling this report, Regency Cruises was included as a result of bankruptcy proceedings and Royal Cruise Line included because of uncertainty regarding redeployment of assets.

Source: CLIA 5-Year Capacity Analysis.

assortment of extended length cruises, including round-the-world cruises priced at $20,000 or more and lasting several weeks.

Cruise lines have also found lucrative international markets in the United Kingdom, West Germany, and Australia. Sitmar Cruises has placed the *Fairstar* cruise ship in the South Pacific to serve the Australian and New Zealand markets. Russia also caters to this market. Russian ships sail from ports in Italy, the United Kingdom, and Holland. They reportedly offer low rates and good service.

## Pleasure Cruising

Cruise ships are used for pleasure sailing, rather than for point-to-point transportation. They may be divided into the categories of large vessels and small vessels. Large vessels

| TABLE 10.2 |
|---|
| **North American Port Embarkation 1993–1994** |

| | TOTAL EMBARKATIONS—1994 VS. 1993 | | |
|---|---|---|---|
| | **1993*** | **1994*** | **% Change 94 vs. 93** |
| Anchorage | 3,500E | 3,500E | — |
| Boston | 2,182 | 30,258 | +1287 |
| Galveston | 3,551 | 5,803 | +63 |
| Honolulu | 70,000E | 70,000E | — |
| Los Angeles | 425,127 | 393,702 | (7) |
| Miami | 1,578,565 | 1,483,540 | (6) |
| Montreal | 5,278 | 2,984 | (43) |
| New Orleans | 60,097 | 55,971 | (7) |
| New York | 216,659 | 228,311 | +5 |
| Palm Beach | 35,058 | 0 | — |
| Port Canavaral | 460,313 | 464,486 | +1 |
| Port Everglades | 372,444 | 401,620 | +8 |
| San Diego | 17,261 | 4,719 | (73) |
| San Juan | 476,459 | 588,918 | +24 |
| San Francisco | 16,410 | 21,493 | +31 |
| Seattle | 8,700 | 1,897 | (78) |
| Seward | 5,700E | 8,495 | +49 |
| Tampa | 121,918 | 168,800 | +38 |
| Vancouver | 259,613 | 297,654 | +15 |
| TOTAL | 4,138,835 | 4,232,151 | +2 |

Source: The Cruise Industry, Cruise Lines International Association, 500 Fifth Avenue, Suite 1407, New York, NY 10110, July 1994, pg. 23.

on the average accommodate some 787 passengers, while small vessels carry fewer than 100 passengers and are sometimes called **mini-cruisers** or **ultra-yachts**.

Until recently, the typical cruise ship was built to hold 850 to 1250 passengers, but today's new ships can accommodate 2000–2500 passengers. Larger cruise ships especially are able to pamper guests with a wide array of services and amenities, most of which are packaged into the cruise. Accommodations onboard vary from sleeping rooms with berths, also called **lowers**, for as many as three or four persons to lavish bedrooms billed as **staterooms**. Food is offered throughout the day in a variety of forms, from seven-course meals to theme event dinners. In terms of recreation, whether the passenger's game is tennis, jogging, aerobics, pumping iron, or perfecting a golf swing, most cruise ships are ready to meet these needs. Many ships now have fully equipped gyms, health spas, and athletic counselors. Cruise lines employ professional onboard **cruise directors** who work full time to plan entertainment and activities for the passengers. These planned activities or entertainment may include full-scale musical productions, individual cabaret performances, discos, bingo, gambling, courses in self-improvement, and so on. For many passengers, the numerous opportunities to socialize on a cruise vacation is one of its major appeals. Passengers seeking to escape stress on a holiday can relax by the pool or on deck and enjoy the warm climate and spectacular sunsets. Cruise enthusiasts frequently refer to this type of vacation as the ultimate getaway—combining fresh air, lots of good food, a variety of activities, and visits to exotic ports.

One reason many vacationers choose a cruise is the opportunity for "**destination sampling**." Passengers can have a brief and safe glimpse of countries, cities, and areas they have not previously visited. 86% of Caribbean Cruises cited destination sampling as a major reason for selecting a cruise. Having sampled a destination, many said they might wish to return for a resort-based holiday.

## Cruise Classification

Cruising is categorized by **Resort**, **Deluxe/Luxury**, **Adventure/Exotic** Cruises.

**Resort cruises** represent the majority with Carnival Cruise Lines, Norwegian Cruise Lines, and Royal Caribbean Cruise Line leading this category. The following characteristics are common to the resort cruise category:

- Ships are large; 1000–2000+ passengers.
- Food and beverage are plentiful, but not necessarily gourmet fare.
- Destinations are normally warm climate places.
- Markets are highly segmented, for instance, families with children and homeowners.
- Shipboard activities such as entertainment, aerobics, and bingo are emphasized.
- Short itineraries—3 to 7 days.

**Deluxe** or **Luxury** Cruises share the following commonalities:

- High level of personal service.
- Capacities vary from 125 to 950 passengers.
- Dining is elegant with crystal tableware and fine china.
- Cabins are usually suites.
- Itineraries are 14 days or longer with some as long as a month.
- Entertainment consists of classical music, shows, and educational lectures.
- A high crew to passenger ratio. For example, Seabourn Cruise Line staffs 140 crew members to serve a maximum of 200 passengers.

**Adventure** or **Exotic** Cruises may be characterized by the following:

- Likely to explore narrow inlets and allow passengers to wade ashore.

- Education is offered as entertainment with experts in various fields giving onboard lectures covering topics of relevance to the trip.

- Ships may be older and smaller having been retired as resort cruise ships.

- Ports of call are out of the ordinary.

- Tourist-type shopping and sightseeing less important than discovering new places and experiences.

- Basic dining services with substantial fare.

- Passengers are older, well-educated; many are professionals and interested in environmental and international topics.

## The Dominance of Foreign Flag Carriers

Except for American Hawaii cruises based in Hawaii, the North American ocean cruise industry is comprised of foreign flag carriers. The **Passenger Services Act of 1886** lies at the heart of this situation. The act was designed to protect the American maritime industry from foreign competition, but unfortunately, it has had the reverse affect.

The Passenger Services Act blocks **foreign flag carriers** from sailing between U.S. ports. It also requires liners flying the American flag to employ U.S. built vessels and American labor, among other regulations. *(4)* An American built cruise ship is generally known to be priced at 50% or more higher than a foreign built ship. American industry observers complain that part of the cost difference is attributed to national subsidies paid to shipyards by such countries as Italy, France, and Germany. The inefficiency of U.S. shipyards, which have not built a cruise liner since 1952, is another factor. Costs of operating a U.S. flagged vessel are 20–25% higher than foreign flag carriers. It has been estimated that U.S. regulations and taxes may account for as much as 80% of the cost difference.

The second negative affect of the Passenger Services Act is to prevent some U.S. cities, Seattle, for instance, from becoming a major cruise port. Foreign cruise liners leaving from San Francisco, Los Angeles, or any other U.S. city are not permitted to serve two U.S. ports; Seattle, consequently, loses to Vancouver, B.C. Canada where 236 cruises docked in 1992, contributing $100 million to that city's economy. The irony is that passengers wishing to leave from the port of Vancouver will fly into SeaTac International Airport at Seattle from where they are bused to Vancouver to board the ship. The same situation occurs further south where Hawaii-bound passengers arrive at San Diego and are bused to Tiajuana, Mexico.

The International Council of Cruise Lines estimated that if the Act were repealed, an additional half million jobs could be created onshore to support vessels that would stop at U.S. ports. The Great Lakes, for example, offer enormous potential for cruising. Indeed, cruising used to occur there. Here again, the Passenger Services Act seems to act as an impediment.

The ocean freight industry faces problems with a similar law called **The Jones Act**, which prevents foreign-flagged vessels from operating between U.S. ports.

## Cruise Ships and Tourist Destinations

### Ports of Call

Cruise liners choose their **ports of call**, or scheduled stop points, for their appeal to passengers. San Juan, Puerto Rico, and Saint Thomas in the Virgin Islands are examples of popular ports-of-call. The cruise ship industry may be viewed by a given port-of-call as either a blessing or a curse. On the one hand, some ports rely heavily on cruise ship passengers as a source of tourist traffic and visitor spending while the ship is in dock; on the other, the visits are short and the spending limited to souvenirs and incidental dining. Additional revenue accrues from dockage and wharfage fees—based on the size of the cruise ship vessel, pilotage fees for directing the ship in and out of port, and supplies such as fresh food and fuel purchased while in port.

### Cross-substitutability of Demand

Cruise lines compete directly with destination resorts. Most offer **all inclusive packages**, covering four to five meals a day plus entertainment and activities, representing a value not easily matched by many resorts. *(5)* Vacationers often find that a holiday onboard a cruise line is as or more satisfying than a destination resort holiday. This is known as

Guests can play volleyball and shuffleboard or use a jogging track aboard a Carnival cruise ship.
Courtesy of Carnival Cruise Lines.

cross-substitutability of demand. From the perspective of the community, however, resort-based tourism is always more profitable than cruise passenger business, because cruise line passengers will only spend a limited amount of time at a port-of-call.

From the mid-1980s to current times, cruise lines averaged a 10% annual growth. Much of this growth came at the expense of destination resorts, hotels, and other travel industry competitors. If a port city also has destination resorts, the owner/manger of the resorts often complain that support for cruise lines means support for their competitors. Some destinations, however, have benefited from traffic generated by cruise and land packages which combine a cruise holiday with a resort stopover at the beginning or end of a cruise.

A survey of vacationers who took both a cruise vacation and a resort vacation in the past five years provided evidence of the potential competitive impact of cruising (see Table 10.3). Owners and managers of destination resorts would do well to study these results and implement competitive strategies.

Despite mixed opinions, many communities recognize the value of the cruise ship industry to the tourism industry and aggressively seek to expand the cruise market. For a small island with a relatively undeveloped tourism industry, such as American Samoa or some of the lesser known islands in the Caribbean, the stopover of cruise ships even for one day may provide the destination with much needed export revenues and market exposure.

## TABLE 10.3
## Vacationer Perceptions of Cruises vs. Resort Vacations

Characteristics that describe cruises versus vacations extrememly well* (among those who took both in past five years, in descending order of net differences).

|  | % Cruises | % Resort Vacations | (+/–) Net Difference |
|---|---|---|---|
| Pampered by staff | 82 | 30 | +32 |
| Well organized | 66 | 34 | +32 |
| Festive | 48 | 16 | +32 |
| Able to have pleasurable dining experiences | 68 | 39 | +29 |
| A good value for the money | 43 | 28 | +15 |
| Able to meet interesting people | 47 | 32 | +15 |
| Hassle free | 54 | 41 | +13 |
| Relaxing | 68 | 57 | +11 |
| Safe | 67 | 56 | +11 |
| Romantic | 40 | 30 | +10 |
| Good way to try out vacation spot | 53 | 46 | +7 |
| Active | 37 | 30 | +7 |

*Top box agreement on a five-point scale.
*Source:* 1994 CLIA Market Profile Study.

## Ports of Embarkation

Miami enjoys a leading position as a **port of embarkation** for cruise traffic, but faces growing competition. Some cruise lines have sought to gain a competitive advantage by offering embarkation away from crowded Miami. Others are seeking ports that offer new itineraries, especially for repeat cruise customers.

Boston aggressively markets itself as both an embarkation port and a port of call. The number of ships calling there doubled from 21 in 1993 to 43 in 1994. Boston was actively supported by the Massachusetts Port Authority (Massport) in securing agreements with cruise lines to create an estimated $17.3 million in new revenue for the city. Promotion did not stop with the agreements. Massport and the New England Chapter of ASTA (American Society of Travel Agents) sponsored a trade show and seminar at Boston's World Trade Center for travel agents and cruise lines. *(6)*

A cruise line may discontinue scheduling stops at a particular port-of-call if it fails to continue attracting passengers, or it may change a port of embarkation if passenger traffic shifts to another embarkation city. This is relatively easy for cruise lines since they do not have substantial capital invested in port facilities. Four reasons are generally cited for dropping a port; these are

* *Economic* The port does not generate a sufficient volume of business to justify using it for embarkation, hence, the reason why Boston aggressively sought the business of travel agents to promote cruise traffic.

* *Passenger interest* Passengers do not have sufficient interest in a port to warrant further calls. The port may have little to offer by the way of duty-free shopping or insufficient attractions of scenic or historic interest for day tours.

* *Political instability/safety risk* Jamaica was dropped as a port of call in the early 1980s, despite high passenger interest, due to political/social unrest on the island. Once the fear diminished, the cruise lines resumed calling on this port. Caracas was also dropped as a port of call by Seawind Cruise Lines in 1993 due to passenger fear of unrest in Venezuela. Seawind substituted a full day at sea for the Caracas port call.

* *Government action* Government actions perceived as negative to a cruise line's interest may also cause a port to be dropped. Royal Caribbean Cruise Lines ceased its twice-weekly visits to San Diego by the Viking Serenade and cut in half the number of calls at Catalina Island because of a California state law banning onboard gambling on ships sailing between California ports. Port authority officials from California ports estimated that California would lose $75.1 million in revenue and jobs as a result of anti-gaming legislation. *(7)*

## Industry Capacity

The cruise industry generated an additional 300,000 to 400,000 new passengers per year in the early 1990s. Such an increase was needed to absorb annual growth of 8,000 to 10,000 new berths. *(8)* Capacity growth in the cruise line industry occurs as a result of larger ships and larger fleets. The following are examples of cruise line investments in larger capacity vessels:

- Royal Caribbean Cruise Lines, with nine ships and a total of 14,228 lower berths, will have four new megaliners in 1995–1996, the Legend of the Seas and the Splendor of the Seas. Each will carry 1,808 passengers. Two additional ships will hold 1,950 passengers each. *(9)*

- Princess Cruise Lines will increase capacity by 70% for 12 vessels in its fleet. The company has ordered a 100,000 ton megaliner capable of carrying 2,600 passengers. This ship will feature the latest technology, including a virtual-reality theatre where passengers can experience different adventures; one, for example, simulates a flight through the Grand Canyon. *(10)*

- Walt Disney will enter the cruise market with two new vessels capable of carrying 2,400 passengers each. Disney will spend $600 million to design and build these ships.

- Carnival Cruise Lines has also ordered a megaliner that can carry 2,600 passengers plus a 900-member crew. Carnival has 17 ships, including its 25% stake in the two ships owned by Seabourn Cruise Line with plans to add at least four more by the mid 1990s.

- With respect to fleet size, cruise lines are planning on adding 28 additional ships to the industry fleet between 1994 and 1998. The expanded fleet and increased capacities of new ships will create 44,000 new berths.

## Vertical and Horizontal Integration

The cruise line industry has experienced **horizontal integration** through mergers with competitors and **vertical integration** with supporting industries. Carnival Cruise Lines offers an example of both vertical and horizontal integration.

### Horizontal Integration

In January 1989, Carnival acquired another cruise line, Holland American Lines, which catered to upscale, mature, experienced cruise passengers. This increased Carnival's market share of the cruise line market and also gave it access to a different market segment than it had been serving.

### Vertical Integration

This form of diversification can occur through the ownership of business enterprises that serve the cruise line, such as a travel agency or a linen supply company. This is called **backward vertical integration**. **Forward vertical integration** occurs when the firm moves closer to serving the total needs of the customer through the acquisition of other travel-related businesses. For example, Holland American Lines owns Westover, which in turns owns or manages 16 hotels in Alaska and the Canadian Yukon along with motor coaches, eight domed railcars, and four luxury day boats. Thus Carnival Cruise Lines through its acquisition of Holland American Lines and its subsidiary Westover, could serve a variety of traveler needs associated with a cruise.

## Threats to the Cruise Industry

Despite dramatic growth and the popularity of cruising, this sector faces numerous risks and problems which must be continuously evaluated and dealt with as individual cruise lines or as an association. These include the following:

### Capacity versus Market

The industry has been highly successful in producing larger annual numbers of customers to meet increased capacity but this can be a dangerous treadmill if incomes fall or customer interest wanes. The industry has traditionally responded with higher advertising and promotional costs and discounting.

### Government Legislation

Governments in many part of the world are beginning to seriously discuss legislation aimed directly at cruise lines. Some Caribbean countries, for example, are responding to complaints from local hoteliers who believe that cruise lines are detrimental to their business; and local government officials are calling for tight controls on cruise ship access and as much as a 200% increase in passenger taxes. They are also demanding that cruise operators contribute more to local economies. *(11)*

As gambling represents a growth industry for many communities in North America and other parts of the world, legislators may view onboard gaming as a threat to local casinos and lottery interests and consider regulations to keep shipboard gaming from overlapping with land-based casinos through taxation, offshore limits, and other legislation.

The U.S. Congress has considered a plethora of cruise line legislation including proposals to impose penalties on ships built with the help of foreign subsidies and the application of U.S. labor standards on foreign-flag ships operating from U.S. ports. *(12)*

### Discounting

Discounting by cruise lines have taught many customers to wait for last minute fire sales. While not unique to cruise lines, this must be viewed as a threat to the financial well-being of the industry. One need look no further than the airline industry to witness the adverse affects of discounting to the "bottom line." In 1991, a price war occurred in the cruise line industry. Almost two-thirds of cruise tickets sold that year were for discounts of 50% or more. *(13)*

### Terrorism

There is always the risk of a dramatic terrorist attack on a cruise ship. The landmark case of the Achille Lauro in October 1985 became a well-publicized event when a faction of the Palestine Liberation Front boarded the Italian ship holding 201 passengers and crew hostage, then murdered an elderly, disabled man in a wheelchair who defied the terrorists.

### At-sea Disasters

Despite safety precautions and modern engineering, shipboard disasters cannot always be avoided. The year 1994 witnessed one of the worst ever ship accidents on a ferry from the Estonian capital, Tallinn, to Stockholm. The ferry capsized in the freezing Baltic Sea. Of the nearly 1,000 people onboard, more than 800 drowned.

In June 1995, Carnival Cruise Lines experienced an onboard fire and demobilization of the ship. The accident was handled in a professional manner by the ships crew and no deaths or serious injuries occurred. Nevertheless, television networks broadcasted scenes of the stranded ship for several days—not the kind of publicity needed or wanted by the cruise industry.

### Non-cruise Line Competition

Destination resorts and hotels are awakening to the fact that cruise lines pose a competitive threat. They will undoubtedly respond with intensified marketing, price competition, and assistance from legislators.

## Market Segmentation

With larger vessels and greater total industry capacity, competition has become intense among cruise lines. Older vessels have had to **reposition** themselves to serve midscale market niches in order to survive, while the entire industry has sought to develop greater marketing sophistication, not only to meet head-on competition, but also to meet competition from resort destinations tapping the same market. Cruise lines aggressively seek market segments with sufficient potential to serve as worthwhile markets, study consumer preferences within these segments, and develop packages/products to meet these needs.

Market segmentation by demographics (age, income, etc.) remains important, but segmentation by psychographics (lifestyle characteristics) is being increasingly used. The following are examples of current market segments developed by cruise lines:

### Families with Children

Disney has targeted the family market for its new cruise line, but is not the only cruise line to aggressively compete for this segment. American Family Cruises converted two Costa Cruise Lines ships into "the American Adventure" and "the American Pioneer." *(14)* These reconditioned ships feature programs and activities for four age groups: Fuzzy Wuzzy's Den for ages 2–4; Rock-O-Saurus Club for ages 5–7, Sea Haunt, ages 8–12, and Club Yes for 13 and older. Each ship features sports, fitness, computer classes, video productions, and environmental issues. Kids are supervised until 1:00 A.M., thus freeing parents to enjoy themselves.

Ski resorts were early pioneers in children's programs. Cruise lines have copied and expanded many programs proven successful at land-based destination resorts. These include kid-sized furniture, special menus such as animal-shaped pancakes, and a professional staff. With the growth of ships devoted to the family market, cruise lines now face the need to market year-round, even though it creates a conflict when parents decide to take a cruise vacation in spring or fall when school is still in session.

### Honeymooners

The honeymoon segment has been a perennial market for cruise lines. Responding to social changes, some cruise lines now feature honeymoon packages for second marriages wherein children will accompany their parents on the honeymoon. *(15)* American Hawaii Cruises discovered that this segment was a large growth market and offered a special third person/child rate.

Carnival Cruise Lines expanded its shipboard wedding program to include ceremonies aboard the Jubilee, which sails each Sunday from Los Angeles. The basic program includes a civil ceremony on embarkation day, marriage certificate, champagne, florals for bride and groom, a cake, and photographic services. *(16)*

### Ethnic Markets

The Fiesta Marina cruise division of Carnival Cruise Lines, offers a cruise specifically designed for the Hispanic market. One of the lines older and smaller ships with 950 passenger capacity was repositioned and reconditioned to serve this market. *(17)* Fiesta concentrated promotions in Central America, South America, Spain, and such U.S. states as Texas, California, and New York with large Hispanic populations. The cruise features menus and schedules written in Spanish, Spanish language movies, and a Spanish-speaking staff.

Similarly, the Star Pisces Cruiseline sailing out of Hong Kong offers a product designed specifically for Chinese families. Meals, entertainment, recreation, and child care services are geared to the preferences and cultural taste of the Cantonese market.

### Health Conscious Segment

Royal Caribbean Cruise Lines hired an in-house dietitian to serve the needs of health conscious travelers. The dietitian works with the ship's chefs to develop low-calorie, low-fat, low-sodium dishes and healthy menus. Another cruise line with a similar name, Royal Cruise Line, plans its menus according to the American Heart Association guidelines to cater to its largely retirement age passengers. *(18)*

### Nostalgia Buff Segment

Cunard Lines offers a nostalgia cruise with such Second World War celebrities onboard as Bob Hope and the Glenn Miller Orchestra. The Queen Elizabeth II also features such nostalgia bands as Larry Elpert and the Manhattan Swing Orchestra.

### Other Segments

Cunard Lines, like many others, offers a variety of theme cruises. Cunard offers more than 60 themes, ranging from jazz to gardening to antique collecting. Lifestyle segmentation is limited only by the creativity of the cruise line, the size of each segment, and the ability to successfully reach and promote the segment.

## Distribution/Sales

Cruise lines rely almost exclusively on travel agents. It is estimated that within CLIA, there are over 20,000 travel agency affiliates. Compared to any other major travel supplier, cruise lines derive the greatest percentage of their revenues through travel agency sales.

| % of Revenue Generated Through Travel Agents | |
|---|---|
| Cruises | 95%+ |
| Airlines | 70–80% |
| Hotels | 10–20% |
| Car rentals | 20–60% |

Travel agents realize that cruises represent good income potential. A single customer can provide a commission of 10–15% on a cruise package costing $1,000 and upwards, providing an income that often exceed the combined commissions earned on an assortment of bookings which include airline, hotel, and rental car. CLIA estimates, for instance, that travel agents earn an average commission per sale of $98 for a land package versus $142 for a cruise. CLIA also estimates that on average a travel agent must spend 1.10 hours to sell a land package and 43 minutes to sell a cruise.

Cruise lines have greatly improved the sophistication of their marketing programs aimed at travel agents. An example is Carnival Cruise Lines with 130 field sales representatives to help travel agents. The company answers calls from agents quickly and mails tickets promptly. Carnival, like other cruise lines, offers free seminars on sales techniques and sponsors "fam trips" for travel agents.

## Cruise Line Advertising/Promotion

The cruise ship industry is young and relies heavily upon people who are taking cruises for the first time. Unlike the purchase of other travel services, most potential buyers have little experience when purchasing a cruise vacation. Likewise, many travel agents may have only limited training or experience regarding cruises.

The need for prepurchase buyer information is probably greatest in this sector of the travel industry. Information on cruises and the cruise ship industry may be found in such publications as *The Complete Handbook to Cruising* by the International Cruise Passenger Association. This books rates cruise ships and makes recommendations for passengers. Other publications include *The Ocean Ferryliners of Europe: The Southern Seas International*, which lists cruises including barges and canal cruises, shiplines, ferry services (passenger and freighters), and ports; *The Worldwide Cruise and Shipline Guide*, published by OAG publications; *Ford's Freighter Travel Guide,* which covers freighter/passenger ships services to all ports worldwide; and *Fielding's Worldwide Guide to Cruises*.

For many years, cruise lines were content to spend more of their advertising budgets to reach travel agents, not the consumer. Today, cruise lines also spend millions of dollars for consumer advertising in television, newspapers, and other selected media. Carnival and Royal Caribbean Cruise lines, for example, had marketing budgets over $50 million each in 1994. Norwegian Cruise Lines spent $25–30 million on advertising in 1993. Despite intensified marketing efforts, many consumers remain confused because of the variety of available cruise products and similarity of names. How does a first time customer who is not familiar with cruise companies, for example, distinguish between Royal Viking Cruise and Royal Cruise or Seabourn Cruise and Seawind Cruise?

## Cruise Line Pricing

Despite occasional bursts of discount wars, the cruise line industry is adopting a more stable approach to pricing. Several now have departments of **yield management** or **revenue management** which have the responsibility of studying pricing trends, booking patterns, competitive strategies, demand elasticity, and yield from an optimal sales mix. These departments are assigned responsibility for improving revenue through prices that are attractive to the market, yet will maximize revenue potential and optimize the use of fleet capacity.

There are two major challenges in cruise line pricing:

1. Establishing a price program and communicating it to travel agents and the general public, and

2. Managing the program on a cruise-by-cruise basis to achieve maximum profitability.

Kloster Cruise Lines has noted that travel agents find fares "cumbersome to use and difficult to remember." Moreover, market research shows that many travel agents are reluctant to recommend some cruises to clients due to a complex pricing structure.

Cruise line prices tend to proliferate in an effort to match competition and to reach a wide range of market segments which, in turn, creates complexity and confusion. Given the critical importance of pricing, the cruise industry will undoubtedly seek more pricing specialists trained in computers, statistics, economics, and operations research as the cruise market grows.

## The Future for Cruising

The future for cruising looks very favorable. Within the U.S., only 6% of the population had taken a cruise as of 1994. Twenty years earlier, 1% had taken a cruise. The growth in the industry shows impressive gains with room for future growth. *(19)* Two factors that contribute to the growth of this industry are high satisfaction levels among cruise passengers, which should create a high percentage of repeat cruisers, and potentially large foreign markets. Western Europe and Japan, for example, offer excellent potential for growth, as do emerging markets in Latin America, notably Venezuela and Brazil.

While the potential for the oversupply of passenger space is ever present, the industry has done a remarkable job of creating new customers to meet its increased capacity. An example of this success is the incentive travel segment which consists of passengers (winners of a sales contest, etc.) who are awarded a cruise as a prize by their employer for exceptional performance. Incentive travel now accounts for approximately 15% of all cruise line bookings. As capacity expands, however, new marketing and management approaches will be required, including

1. *Innovative and improved marketing strategies*   Existing distribution systems must be examined with strategies to not only enhance sales through travel agents, but also employ alternative means of reaching untapped markets.

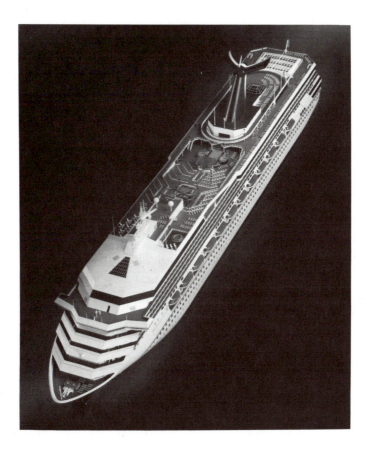

*Carnival Destiny*, a new cruise ship.
Courtesy of Carnival Cruise Lines.

2. *Increased product differentiation*  Niche marketing strategies will be needed to improve brand market share. These can be successful only if there is recognized product differentiation.

3. *Generic product marketing*  The cruise ship industry can benefit by developing exciting ways to promote cruising as an alternative vacation. All members benefit from enlarging the base market.

4. *Mergers*  The industry is likely to experience mergers between competing lines.

5. *Increased management sophistication*  Many of the management practices within this industry were developed in the cargo industry where ships, ports, handling equipment, and unions were the main concerns. These are production-based problems; the cruise industry requires focus on market-based management decisions rather than production. Management practices within the cruise line industry will likely undergo substantial change before the end of this century.

# OTHER SECTORS OF WATER TRANSPORTATION

## Mini-cruisers

The development of the mini-cruiser (sometimes referred to as ultra-yacht) market has been helped by the rehabilitation of U.S. waterfronts and U.S. Coast Guard regulations concerning light marine craft safety. Mini-cruisers operate along the Pacific coast from Alaska to California and Atlantic coastal areas from Maine to the Caribbean. The east coast cruisers use inland coastal waterways as well as the ocean.

A study of the characteristics of passengers onboard mini-cruisers shows the following:

- passengers are predominantly older married couples with fairly high incomes;

- many travel in non-family groups;

- many have previously traveled on larger cruise ships;

- passengers learned of mini-cruisers predominantly through magazine and word-of-mouth advertising;

- mini-cruiser passenger expenditures are relatively high on shore for hotels and food, which benefits other sectors of the travel industry.

## Sail Cruising, Sail Charters, and Charter Yachts

**Sail cruising** is offered by companies such as Windstar Sail Cruises of Miami. This company offers cruising aboard one of two computer-controlled, French-built ships costing $62 million to build. Each has 75 deluxe outside cabins and accommodates 150 passengers. In addition to sails, these ships are equipped with diesel engines.

Clipper Cruise Lines is an example of a smaller niche market player, featuring unusual cruises which are not available through large cruise lines. The 100 passenger Nantucket Clipper offers a series of one or two week cruises around Chesapeake Bay and along the inter coastal waterway. Clipper cruises feature historians and naturalists who discuss such topics as the Civil War and the ecology of Chesapeake Bay. (20)

**Bareboat charters** are available in some parts of the world. These are boats rented without crew or provisions to individuals who make their own arrangements for sailing. Rainbow Pacific, Ltd. of Auckland, New Zealand, for example, maintains a fleet for bareboat charters in the Bay of Islands. Clients sleep and cook aboard and explore the many caves and islands of this part of New Zealand. Rainbow also offers an outdoor fitness program called Challengers which is similar to the Outward Bound program. The Challengers program is popular with corporate groups who wish to emphasize the importance of teamwork and physical conditioning.

Yachting is an activity traditionally associated with the very rich. Today, yacht cruising is available to other income groups by means of **charter yachts**. Owners sometimes find the cost of maintaining a yacht to be exorbitantly high, compelling some to lease their yachts to individuals or to corporations for onboard sales meetings, sightseeing, incentive trips or other purposes. There are a few travel agents who specialize in handling yacht charters.

The 56-foot Wild Harp leaves Nassau Harbor for a 5-hour sailing trip.
Credit: Bahama News Bureau photo by Margareth Guillaume.

Another system of yacht charter, commonly operating in the Caribbean and the Mediterranean, is modeled after the original ownership concept of U-Haul trailers. Under this system, a yacht charter company is formed to operate a fleet of yachts owned by individuals who bought the boats as an investment and not for personal pleasure. The system allows the owners of the yacht charter company to acquire a fleet without borrowing capital, issuing stock, or using their own funds. The company assumes responsibility for managing, marketing, renting and maintaining the yachts. Maintenance is usually outsourced or subcontracted. The yacht charter company is fiscally responsible to the yacht owners. The company's income is derived principally from the revenue produced by bookings. Additional income is sometimes earned on the sale of insurance to charter members. The company and the owners of the yachts share the revenue.

## Cargo Liner, Freighter, and Barge

### Cargo Liners

One of the most enduring, romantic ideas about ocean travel is traveling by **cargo liner** or **freighter**. The term cargo liner and freighter are interchangeable. They have been defined by the International Conventions and Conferences on Marine Safety as a "vessel principally engaged in transporting goods, which is licensed to carry a maximum of 12 passengers." The accommodations on freighters are usually quite comfortable, with many being equivalent to first-class cabins on cruise ships but with generally lower prices. Many modern cargo liners were designed to accommodate a limited number of passengers, as well as freight. The reason for this is simple. The few additional passengers, on the whole, do not impose an unwarranted burden on the officers or the crew, and in fact, tend to make the voyage more enjoyable. But more importantly, the additional revenue from passengers helps to offset the ship's fixed costs. People without time constraints who enjoy the unusual can visit ports throughout the world and see places where cruise ships never stop.

Medical services are not available onboard freighters unless a doctor happens to be a passenger. Although officers are trained in first aid, passengers who are seriously ill must be taken to the nearest port. A disadvantage for some travelers, but perhaps an attraction for others, is that these ships do not have entertainment onboard and must sometimes change itinerary on short notice, depending on weather or the time spent in port unloading or loading freight.

Freighters do very little advertising or sales promotion. They depend primarily on word of mouth, guide books such as *Ford's Freighter Travel Guide*, and on travel agents. Reservations on freighters are handled through travel agents or directly with the shipping company.

## Barges

**Barges** may be flat-bottomed boats used to transport goods on inland waterways or large, roomy boats elegantly furnished and decorated to carry passengers down rivers and canals. River barges move at a snail's pace and usually carry from four to 25 passengers on major rivers in North America and Europe. Although travel by barge has never been thought of as a major means of pleasure sailing, barge cruising on the French canal system has been popular for centuries.

The French canal system began during the reign of Henry IV in the early 17th Century. The canals later evolved into an efficient network, linking the provinces with major trade centers. Early passenger vessels, les Coches d'Eau (water carriages) offered fashionable men and women an alternative to the discomforts of cross-country travel on primitive highways. *(21)* The French Navigation Authority continues to maintain these canals, thus allowing passenger barge travel to continue. The French Country Waterways offers leisurely travel on modern barges decorated with warm wood paneling, handsome provincial furnishings, and oriental carpets. Passengers are served by a bilingual staff. Guest quarters contain private baths, full-size beds, and storage. Suites and double or twin staterooms are available.

Mid-Lakes Navigations of Skaneateles, New York, offers barge travel on canals in New York State. Rideau Lakes Vacation offer tours of Canada's Rideau Canal which stretches 120 miles from Kinston, Ontario to Ottawa. *(22)*

## Ferry Boats

**Ferry boats,** or ferry liners, found in many parts of the world, exist for transporting travelers on fresh and salt water. Many are large oceangoing vessels such as those running from Maine to Nova Scotia, Canada, or between the North and South Island of New Zealand. In the United States, ferry boats have been used to cross Lake Michigan and for transport between Alaska and the state of Washington, as well as in other locations. Modern ferry boats permit travelers to combine the use of a motor vehicle with a trip over

A river barge provides comfortable and leisurely cruising on inland waterways for a limited number of tourists.

large stretches of water by carrying campers and trailers on the boat. For the convenience of passengers, ferry liners may also feature snack bars, restaurants, and staterooms.

### River boats

**River boats**, featuring staterooms, restaurants, and entertainment, provide a popular means of travel in many countries, including England, France, and the former Yugoslavia where boats link the various coastal republics on the Adriatic Sea with Italian and Greek ports. In the United States, river boat transportation has enjoyed a long tradition of operation on the St. Lawrence Seaway and on the Mississippi River.

### Paddle Wheelers

**Paddle Wheelers** sometimes call "**big wheels**" have returned to American rivers. The first paddle wheel steamboats were launched in 1811 to carry passengers and freight on the nation's rivers, particularly the Mississippi, Missouri, and Ohio, and later on the Red River in Texas/Louisiana. By 1892, however, the American writer Mark Twain declared "steamboatings dead." Railroads, diesel powered boats, and an expanding road system had killed them.

The return of the Big Wheel in the 1990s owes its comeback mainly to the advent of gaming legislation. Six U.S. states permit riverboat gambling and five require the use of paddle wheelers. Excursions and dinner cruise paddle wheelers have also appeared on many rivers and lakes offering leisurely travel to nowhere. An estimated 50 paddle boats have been in operation since 1990, with another 50 planned or under consideration. American shipyards in 1994 had over $1 billion in orders. The Delta Queen Steamboat Company commissioned a 418-foot-long paddle wheeler capable of holding 400 passengers on cruises up to 12 days. This boat is powered by two vintage steam engines that had lain sunken in the Mississippi river for years.

# *A* Floating Wedding Cake

"A floating wedding cake" was how a reporter from *USA Today* described the new American Queen paddle wheeler. *(23)* "The American Queen is a wedding cake that invites you to run your fingers through its frosting: iron railing and columns festooned with curlicues and gingerbread trim, 20 flags saluting, elaborate fretwork everywhere. And finally that definitive red paddle wheel pushing its 3,707 ton treasure along."

The Delta Queen Company and The American West Company are betting multi-millions of dollars that travelers 50 years or older will generate sufficient sales to pay back the cost for new paddle wheels and generate a healthy profit. The Delta Queen Company figures that at least 54,000 passengers will be carried by its fleet of paddle wheelers on the Mississippi, Ohio, and Tennessee rivers in 1995. The American West Steamboat Company will offer paddle wheel cruises on the Columbia, Snake, and Willamette rivers.

Delta Queen's research projected a doubling of the market by 2010 as baby boomers near retirement. The owners believe that older cruise clients want the relative coziness and convenience of riverboats and are willing to pay $790 per person double occupancy for a three night cruise in a modest cabin and $2,990 for a seven night cruise in more upscale accommodations.

But will 54,000 middle-aged travelers pay those rates for a riverboat experience, and if so, will the market hold up for several years?

Cruising is obviously a market based on discretionary income and time. What will happen if the U.S. and Canada experience a recession? Older Americans are increasingly concerned about possible reduction in Medicare and Social Security benefits. Many also find themselves caring for grandchildren or fear that older children may lose their economic support in a recession or as a result of a divorce and save for that eventuality.

Then there's the problem with Old Man River. Could national television coverage of spring flooding discourage potential passengers from booking for a summer river cruise?

Delta Queen paddleboat—a "floating wedding cake" offering luxurious riverboat cruises on the Columbia, Snake, and Willamette rivers.

In 1994, gross gambling revenues from riverboats approached $1 billion. Revenue potential of this magnitude has not gone unnoticed by river communities and legislators in need of new sources of economic development and tax revenues. The result will almost certainly be overcapacity, heavy discounting, and bankruptcies before the industry achieves equilibrium.

### Houseboats

**Houseboats** have become increasingly popular in the United States. They can be rented, usually on a weekly basis, on various rivers and large lakes, such as the man-made lakes of the Colorado River. Offering self-contained amenities, houseboats are popular for family vacations. Most houseboats are built on pontoons to assure stability and feature a large cabin with cooking, sleeping, and living quarters.

### Canoes

**Canoes** are very popular in the boundary water areas between Minnesota and Canada, and in parts of Maine. Canoe rental firms also operate on rivers near such metropolitan centers as San Francisco. Firms known as **canoe or wilderness outfitters** supply travelers with guides and all the equipment and provisions needed for these trips. Many of these businesses have passed the point of being small family operations; they rent canoes to thousands of people each year.

### Submarines

**Submarines** are the underwater equivalent of hot-air balloon rides. Neither go very far very fast but both offer an exciting new experience. Since 1985, over two million tourist submarine rides have been taken on forty vessels. The largest submarine operator, Atlantis Submarines has operations in Aruba, Guam, St. Thomas, Cancun, Nassau, Waikiki, Maui, and Kona. A Germany company (Brucker) and a Finnish company build pleasure submarines. Many hotels and cruise lines offer submarine excursions as package deals. Rides normally last about an hour and cost $65 to $86 per passenger. *(24)*

## SUMMARY

Water transportation, once a major element in the plans of every transcontinental traveler, has once again emerged as a major player within the travel industry. The passenger ships of yesteryear, whose decline was signaled by the emergence of mass travel by jet aircraft, have been replaced with modern cruise ships equipped to provide almost every type of service and amenity imaginable. The growth of the cruise industry has been significant over the past two decades, and its future appears assured with a substantial number of potential customers having both time and money for cruise travel. For cruise industry operators, nonetheless, the years ahead will be challenging.

Cruise marketing is becoming more sophisticated, with intensified segmentation, strategic pricing through yield management, greater use of consumer advertising, and closer partnering with travel agents. The cruise line industry can be divided into resort, deluxe/luxury, and adventure/exotic cruises. Mini-cruises or ultra yachts represent yet another segment for niche markets.

Cruise lines are facing dramatic changes as fleet sizes increase, megaliners appear, and horizontal and vertical integration are used for diversification and growth. The threat of over capacity is ever present. However, successful cruise line operators are optimistic that over-capacity will not be a problem since only a small percentage of the population has ever experienced a cruise and demand continues to grow.

In addition to cruise ships, other water transportation options are available to travelers or particular market segments. These include mini-cruisers (or ultra-yachts), sail cruising, freighter travel, and travel by river boat, barge, ferry boats, houseboats, canoes, and paddle wheelers. Despite the large investments required for new ships and boats, members of the water transportation industry are optimistic that the North American customer is sold on cruising and will continue to support this sector of the travel industry.

# DISCUSSION QUESTIONS

1. What are some of the major segments of the cruise market?

2. What are the other types of water transportation offered on a commercial basis?

3. What relation, if any, exists between the Passenger Services Act and the Jones Act?

4. What is the difference between a port-of-embarkation and a port-of-call?

5. What role does destination sampling play in the continuing promotion of travel?

6. Why do cruise lines engage in the practice of repositioning their fleets?

7. Why do foreign flag carriers dominate the cruise line sector?

8. Why do cruise line passengers who wish to visit Hawaii by cruise line first fly into San Diego and then travel by bus to Tijuana, Mexico to begin their voyage?

9. Does cross-substitutability of demand exist for cruise lines? If so, please explain how. If not, why not?

10. Do cruise lines ever engage in horizontal integration? If so, please give an example. If not, why don't they?

11. What is the principal distribution system used to sell cruises to the public in North America?

12. Are cruise lines concerned about product differentiation? Why or why not?

13. What possible disadvantages should travelers consider before booking a voyage on a cargo liner?

14. What is happening to travel by paddle wheelers in the U.S.?

15. Why would anyone consider barge travel? Isn't this a dangerous and inconvenient way to travel?

# SUGGESTED STUDENT EXERCISE

## Short Case Study

Carnival Cruise Lines

Letter to shareholder of Carnival Cruise Lines
From: Mickey Arison, Chairman and CEO

What has enabled us to continue to improve our operating results has been the most aggressive ship building program in cruise industry history. In July of this year, Carnival Cruise Lines introduced its fourth new ship since 1990, the 2,040 passenger Fascination, with a series of sailings from New York. Carnival Cruise Lines and Holland America Line now operate the newest, most modern cruise fleets in the world. And our fleets get younger every year.

We remain very bullish on the future of the cruise industry and this is the primary reason we have been so aggressive with our ship building program. We believe that improvements in our financial performance will continue to be largely driven by capacity additions. In addition to the four new ships which we have scheduled for delivery in 1995 and 1996, we recently announced contracts for the construction of a 1,320 passenger ship to be delivered to Holland America Line at the end of 1997, two more 2,040 passenger SuperLiners to be delivered to Carnival Cruise Lines in 1998 and another 2,640 passenger ship to be delivered to Carnival Cruise Lines at the end of 1998 or early 1999. That puts our existing capital commitments at $2.5 billion, with a total of eight new ships coming into service in the next five years.

We believe that the construction of new, modern ships will become increasingly important as we enter the last half of the 1990s. In addition to the competitive advantages and economies of scale derived from the larger, newer and more efficient vessels, the cruise industry faces more stringent safety standards set by the International Maritime Organization starting in 1997. These new standards, which are not currently met by many of the older vessels in service, are strongly endorsed by your company, which is committed to the highest standards of safety in the cruise industry. The older vessels that do not meet these standards will either be retrofitted at substantial expense to their owners or scrapped. Consequently, these new standards may lead to the retirement of many of the industry's older vessels, but will have very little impact on Carnival Cruise Lines or Holland America Line because of our ship building program.

## Questions

1. Research the 24-year history of Carnival Cruise Lines and analyze the reasons for its success?

2. What do you believe will happen to older ships in fleets such as that of Carnival Cruise Lines? Are there creative new uses that are not currently used by cruise lines?

3. Will Carnival Cruise Lines need to develop new marketing strategies to insure their ships remain filled? If so, what would you suggest?

# REFERENCES

1. *The Cruise Industry: An Overview*, Cruise Lines International Association, 500 Fifth Avenue, Suite 1407, New York, NY 10110.

2. "Cruise Industry Pumping $2.7 Billion Into 7 Cities," *Journal of Commerce*, March 10, 1993, pg. 5b, ISSN 0361-5561.

3. Carnival Corporation 1994 Annual Report, Carnival Place, 3655 N.W. 87 Avenue, Miami, FL 33178-2428, pg. inside cases and pg. 9.

4. Bucholz, Todd G., Carol M. Cropper. "All at Sea," *Forbes*, November 8, 1993, pg. 174–183.

5. "Cruise Industry Making Waves for U.S. Resorts," *Hotel and Motel Management*, March 8, 1993, pg. 13.

6. Major, Brian. "Entry for New Business: Emerging Cruise Embarkation Points Create More Selling Opportunities for Agents," *Travel Agents*, March, 14, 1994, pg. 26, ISSN 1053-9360.

7. "New Law Forces RCCL to Alter Itineraries," *Tour and Travel News*, December 7, 1992, pg. 1, ISSN 0889-3349.

8. "The New Wave: The Ships of '93," *Tour-and-Travel-News*, March 29, 1993, pg. 56, ISSN 0889-3349.

9. "Royal Caribbean Signs $750 Million Credit Deal," *Tour-and-Travel-News*, July 11, 1994, pg. 26, ISSN 0889-3349.

10. Simmons, Jacqueline. *Tracking Travel*, April 26, 1994, Sec. B, pg. 1.

11. Friese, Richard P. "Beating the Recession," *Travel Agent*, December 28, 1992, pg. 56, ISSN 1053-9360.

12. Santo, James. "Congress Strikes Terror in Cruise Industry Hearts," *Tour-and-Travel-News*, March 7, 1994, pg. 6, ISSN 0889-3349.

13. Oliver, Suzanne. "Floating Pleasure Palaces," *Forbes*, December 20, 1993, pg. 182.

14. Myers, Laura L. "Seriously Kidding Around," *Travel-Agent*, February 22, 1993, pg. 27, ISSN 1053-9360.

15. Zabel, Stacey. "Honeymooners Can Bring Their Kids and Still Have an Intimate and Romantic Vacation," *Travel-Agent*, February 15, 1993, pg. 1, ISSN 1053-9360.

16. "Carnival Expands Its Shipboard Wedding Program," *Tour-and-Travel-News*, April 18, 1994, pg. C14, ISSN 0889-3349.

17. "Carnival Cruise Lines Beckons Hispanics," *Advertising Age*, January 25, 1993, pg. 46, ISSN 0001-8899.

18. "Focus on Food: RCCL Hires In-House Dietation," *Tour-and-Travel-News*, April 18, 1994, pg. C12, ISSN 0889-3349.

19. "Industry Insiders Cite Growth as Proof of Recession End," *Journal of Commerce and Commercial*, December 20, 1993, pg. 8A, ISSN 0361-5561.

20. "Clipper's Southern Swing," *Travel Agent*, November 29, 1993, pg. 42, ISSN 1053-9360.

21. Brochure—French Country Waterways, Ltd., P. O. Box 2195, Dubury, MA 02331, 1994, pg. 3.

22. Haines, Cathy. "Riverboats Keep on Rolling, The Luxury of a Cruise Ship, the Intimacy of a Yacht," *USA Today*, February 11, 1993, pg. 6D.

23. Shiver, Jerry. "A Regal New Queen of the Heartland," *USA Today*, Friday, June 9, 1995, pg. 6D.

24. "Submarines Let Tourists Take The Undersea Plunge," *USA Today*, February 25, 1993, pg. D3, ISSN 0734-7456.

# $\mathcal{L}$and Transportation

## LEARNING OBJECTIVES

- To understand the dominant role of personal motor vehicles in North American travel and tourism.

- To be able to explain the growing importance of passenger rail transportation worldwide.

- To be aware of the realignment of the Canadian passenger rail system after NAFTA.

- To understand the importance of motorcoach travel and the problems with intercity commercial bus travel.

- To be able to discuss basic managerial issues facing intercity auto rental.

- To define and use the following terms:

| | |
|---|---|
| American Automobile Association (AAA) | European Passenger Services (EPS) |
| American Orient Express | Eurostar |
| Amtrak | Greenfield airports |
| Bicycle touring | Ground transportation |
| Bullet trains | Intelligent queuing systems |
| Charter and tour service | Intercity bus service |
| Collision damage waiver | Interstate carriers |
| Double tracking | Interstate Commerce Commission (ICC) |

Land transportation

Limousine service

Motorcoach tours

National Railway Historical Society

National Railroad Passenger Corporation

National Railway Labor Act

Orient Express

Passenger miles

Photovoltaics

Railfone

Recreational vehicles (RVs)

Regional carriers

Rental surcharges

Road railer

Rolling stock

RV campgrounds

Seamless transportation services

Shock losses

Solar powered train

Taxi medallions

The Official Domestic Tour Manual

Trains a Grande Vitesse (TGV)

Treno Alta Velocita (TAV)

Tourist trains

Via Rail

X2000 Metroliner

# LAND TRANSPORTATION IN TOURISM

In a technical sense, anything that moves over land—from less conventional horse-drawn carriages and snowmobiles to more conventional cars and limousines—may be considered **land transportation**. From the standpoint of tourism, land transportation in this chapter covers personal cars, motorcoaches (both intercity and charter-tour), for-hire vehicles, taxi service, sightseeing and transfer transportation, and bicycles.

# PRIVATE MOTOR VEHICLES

Compared to every other form of transportation, the automobile remains the most favored mode of transportation between cities in the United States. In terms of total **passenger miles** (a passenger mile is one passenger carried one mile), automobile travel in the United States is well over four times that of all other modes combined. Much of our economy is dependent on private motor vehicles, and the travel industry is no exception. In fact, most of the travel-related recreation market in the United States and Canada, including ski lodges, hunting and fishing resorts, motels, restaurants, amusement parks, and hundreds of other businesses—are almost totally predicated on private passenger vehicle traffic. An entire "subindustry" which caters to the need for food, rest, and fuel has developed along highways to serve private vehicle travelers.

The heavy dependence of the U.S. travel industry on privately-owned vehicles should not be underestimated. In the years following the oil crisis of 1973, market experts and economists made periodic predictions that the travel industry would see dramatic decreases in automobile use. Those who forecast these changes based their opinions on petroleum politics; environmental problems including highway congestion and urban traffic; the rising cost of purchasing, owning, and operating an automobile; the availability of highly competitive packages offered by commercial carriers; and the fact that driving was becoming a less enjoyable activity. They saw the private automobile as being a temporary phase in the long-run growth of travel and tourism, predicting that the industry would again find itself supporting public carriers which use scarce resources more efficiently. But these predictions have yet to materialize, and the automobile continues to dominate the U.S. travel market.

One of the main concerns of automobile travel, however, focuses on the issue of safety. From 1978 to 1991, the average number of annual passenger fatalities for automobiles in the U.S. was 22,834. Scheduled airlines averaged 131 fatalities annually, while buses averaged 37. When these numbers are measured in terms of per 100 million passenger miles traveled, trains, planes, and buses are all about equally safe, putting automobile safety in terms of fatalities at dead last. *(1)*

Besides the automobile, there are other motorized vehicles that play a substantial role in tourism. Motorcycle travel, for instance, has become important in such communities as Daytona Beach, Florida, and Sturgis, South Dakota, where thousands of "bikers" converge for annual social events. Motorcycle travel, once thought to be solely for rebellious youth and "toughs," has become popular with middle age and retired middle- to upper-income individuals who own expensive, large motorcycles. When these individuals go biking, they patronize good quality lodging and restaurant establishments and do as much sightseeing as others do by car.

The **recreational vehicle** or RV market and the camping market have combined to form a strong sector within the travel industry. Except in periods of economic recession or gasoline shortage, about half of the households in the United States can be expected to take a vacation each year by auto, light truck, recreational vehicle, or motorcycle. The U.S. Travel Data Center has reported a steady annual increase in Americans taking camping vacations. Moreover, foreign visitors to the U.S., especially from Canada, Australia, and New Zealand also enjoy the use of rental RVs. Such visitors usually have itineraries that link historical, cultural, and natural attractions. The market of American and foreign visitors using some form of recreational vehicle has helped to spark tourism in rural areas, including farms and ranch lands. *(2)* The popularity of RV's has extended abroad as well. In Japan, for instance, RVs represent 20% of the auto market. *(3)*

The growth in the RV and camping markets has created both problems and opportunities. As public campgrounds today can no longer accommodate all those who wish to use them, rules for using campgrounds have become increasingly stringent. It is not unusual to find campers standing in line for camping permits, and setting up in an area more densely populated per square foot than the urban and suburban areas they left behind.

The RV has increased the popularity of camping vacations and excursion holidays.

Entrepreneurs have been quick to recognize opportunities for establishing private campgrounds to satisfy the growing demands of camping enthusiasts. The result has been the establishment of a system of franchised RV parks throughout North America. These parks started as rather spartan campsites offering only the basic necessities; however, many have since evolved into elaborate parks offering family entertainment such as live music, sport facilities, and mini theme parks. Some offer campers the convenience of shuttle rides into town so they can leave their RVs parked. *(4)*

There are also private membership **RV campgrounds** in North America. The membership system requires a substantial initiation fee to join, plus annual fees that entitle members to enjoy the use of multiple locations. Thousand Trails, Inc., for example, once dominated the private membership RV campground sector in the 1980s, but fell into insolvency when its selling and marketing expenses reached 123% of campground membership sales in 1993. *(5)* Approximately 50% of the company's members were retired people over the age of 65. These older members who had more leisure time wanted to use the campgrounds throughout the year. The company, however, found it too expensive to maintain many campgrounds year round, preferring to open them only on a seasonal basis. Campground usage consequently fell, membership declined, and revenues suffered. Poor economic conditions and inclement weather, especially severe winters which kept members from using campgrounds, added to Thousand Trails' problems.

Publications that offer information on campgrounds and trailer parks include *Woodall Campground Directory, Rand McNally Campground and Trailer Park Guide,* and *RV Campground and Services Directory.*

Another source of information to motorists is the **American Automobile Association** (AAA), the largest of all travel-related clubs with 35 million members. Nearly 22% of the 115.8 million passenger cars registered in the U.S. and Canada belong to AAA members. AAA is a non-profit corporation of 125 affiliated motor clubs with over 1,000 offices in the U.S. and Canada and a workforce of 33,000 employees. *(6)*

Although AAA's emphasis is on automobile travel, the various individual clubs maintain complete travel agency services, which include arranging for air travel, cruise ship, train, and hotel reservations; selling travelers checks and travel insurance; handling car sales and rentals abroad, plus international driver's licenses; and arranging car shipments.

# $\mathscr{R}$AIL TRAVEL

Trains, rather than cars, were the early pioneers of the U.S. domestic travel industry. The railroads were the first to establish resort destinations to stimulate a travel market. Sun Valley, Idaho; White Sulphur Springs, West Virginia; Glenwood Springs, Colorado, and other popular historic resorts owe their existence to the railroads, which needed distant destinations to promote travel by train. The passenger railways, on the other hand, were slow to recognize shifts in social and business travel trends and dynamic market conditions that demanded faster and more convenient modes of transportation. By the end of World War II, passenger trains had lost most of their traffic to the automobile age and the coming of jet aircraft.

Commercial passenger transportation is regulated everywhere by government. In many cases, public carriers, whether government or privately owned, are highly dependent on government support. Local, state, provincial, and federal governments have historically also provided assistance to commercial passenger travel by funding and constructing airports, docks, highways, railroad beds, and other infrastructure needed by commercial carriers to serve the general public. Other assistance has been granted through subsidies, granting of free land and air space rights, tax concessions, mail carrying privileges, and other forms of support. In the U.S., the historic linking of the continent was supported by the direct subsidization by the federal government, plus grants worth millions of dollars in land and mineral rights.

Today, most of the world's private passenger railroads are tourist enterprises designed for sightseeing on day or less than a day trips. Long haul passenger travel primarily occurs on government owned, operated, or subsidized railroads. As travel and tourism continue to grow in economic importance and provide expanded market opportunities, there is renewed interest in rail travel and in developing new relationships between the private and public sectors in underwriting rail enterprises. Much of the renewed interest in rail has been spurred by environmental factors as well as economic ones, including

- *Congestion and pollution*   Virtually all industrialized nations and many third world nations are seriously grappling with the dual problems of congestion and pollution by individual motor vehicles.

- *Cost of motor vehicles*   The cost of owning a personal motor car has outpaced inflation in many countries, including the U.S. and Canada. Lower income population segments must use public transportation or purchase used vehicles; indeed, the current sales of used cars has been soaring in the U.S.

- *Air congestion*   Air congestion has become a global issue. Travel by air may have reached maximum levels in many regions, and there is fear that air safety may be compromised. Over the past several decades, no more than six or seven completely new, otherwise labeled as "**greenfield airports**" have been built around the world as taxpayers are reluctant to underwrite the development of costly new airports.

- *Airline economics*   The world's airline fleets are growing older, profits are ever more elusive, smaller communities are dropped by air carriers, and bankruptcies plague the airline industry.

## European Railways

Dramatic changes are occurring within European railway systems, which may serve as a possible blueprint for restructuring North American railways. *(7)* The Europeans have begun to separate their train systems into two components: (1) the ownership and development of rail systems and (2) the ownership and management of train operations. The construction of a rail line requires huge investments and the condemnation and/or purchase of private land. This is a task best left to government. The management of a railroad includes: pricing, marketing, and other managerial functions. This task is best left to the more efficient private sector. The European Commission responsible for the economic integration of Europe has pressed the governments of the European Union to follow the scheme of separating rail ownership and development from train management. The commission reasoned that the separation would result in a more efficient European railroad system. Such separation has already occurred in countries outside the EU, for example, in New Zealand, Australia, Switzerland, Norway, and Sweden.

### The TGV and Eurostar

High-speed trains known in France as **trains a grande vitesse** (**TGV**) or in Italy as **Treno Alta Velocita** (**TAV**) are important in Europe. Passenger traffic carried by high-speed trains doubled between 1990–1994. One major reason for the European enthusiasm for these trains has been their record of financial success in France.

The French have spent over $25 billion (U.S.) on TGV transportation development since 1970 and claim returns of 9–16% on the investment. Bank loans raised to finance the Paris-Lyons TGV line were completely repaid out of cash flow, as the train captured 90% of the traffic between this city-pair by taking market shares from airlines.

Train à Grande Vitesse (TVG) arrives at Dijon station in the Côte d'Or.
Credit: French Government Tourist Office, N.Y.C.

In November 1994, an important new TGV train service was introduced, connecting London with Paris in three hours and London with Brussels in three hours, fifteen minutes through the English-French Channel tunnel, sometimes referred to as the "chunnel." This service was marketed throughout Europe and North America with full-page ads in select media, including the *Smithsonian* magazine. Prospective passengers were invited to call an 800 number to reach Rail Europe and either make reservations or join "Club Eurostar," which included accompanying travel benefits and a monthly newsletter.

**European Passenger Services** (**EPS**), a state-owned British company which runs Eurostar in conjunction with French railways (SNCF) and Belgian Railways (SNCB), believes it can capture half of the airlines' London-Paris trade. The London-Paris **Eurostar** service was priced cheaper than business class air fares between the two cities and below most economy class air fares.

Eurostar trains are modern and expensive, with costs of $39 million (U.S.) per car. *(8)* Each train is technologically advanced and able to differentiate and deal with three different power and signaling systems (British, French, and Belgian). These trains travel at speeds of 300 kilometers or 186 miles per hour.

Swedish Railways also has a high-speed train, the **X2000 Metroliner** which reaches speeds of 200 kilometers (125 miles) per hour on six routes throughout Sweden. This train now carries one million passengers annually. Unlike other high-speed trains, it does not require special tracks. *(9)*

## Asian Railroads

The Japanese introduced their high-speed **bullet trains** between Tokyo and Osaka over thirty years ago, but the rest of Asia showed little interest until the 1990s. *(10)* Outside Japan, the first high-speed train project is occurring in South Korea. Seoul and Pusan will be linked by a 423 km line, on which 300 kph trains are forecasted to operate by 2001. Estimates call for 80 million passengers a year on this train. Taiwan has plans for a 350 km high-speed train between Taipei and Kaohsiung. Malaysia has plans for a fast train between Kuala Lumpur and Singapore.

The biggest market by far is China where a billion passengers a year crowd into existing trains. China plans to spend $50 billion by the year 2000 to develop modern high-speed trains. Cross-border trains will likely develop, assuming continuing peace and stability within Asia. When this occurs, Asia's airlines could lose millions of passengers a year.

## U.S. Rail Travel and Amtrak

In 1929, U.S. railroads operated some 20,000 passenger trains and carried 77% of intercity passenger traffic—a sharp contrast to present situation. By 1950, with the rapid growth of private automobile ownership and usage, more than half the passenger trains had disappeared, and the railroad's share of intercity passenger traffic declined to 46%. Twenty years later in 1970, railroad passenger traffic further dropped to 7%, and airlines dominated the public carrier market. The country's preponderant mode of travel by private automobile had left the nation with a serious imbalance in its land transportation network.

In 1971, the U.S. Congress authorized the **National Railroad Passenger Corporation (Amtrak)** in an effort to save an alternate form of transportation that possessed priceless assets, including existing tracks and rights of way into the major population centers of the United States. Amtrak is a state-owned enterprise which accounts for all U.S. intercity passenger traffic. With improved efficiencies, Amtrak was able to reduce its level of subsidy from 28% of budget in 1990 to 20% in 1993. However, ridership remained relatively flat, with about 22 million passengers a year. *(11)*

When Amtrak began operations in 1971, most of its equipment was old. Amtrak had inherited passenger trains and locomotives built prior to and during the 1950s. Moreover, ownership of the stations, terminals, and rail yards remained with various private railroads. Train station and yard personnel continued to be employees of the different railroads and had no identification with Amtrak. *(12)* Amtrak has since taken control of yards, stations, and station service staff. In the intervening years, Amtrak has slowly upgraded its fleet and is today exploring the use of high-speed trains. Many improvements have also been made in Amtrak stations located in Washington, DC, and Philadelphia, but more renovation of facilities remains. By 1994, Amtrak revenues covered nearly 95% of the long-term cost of the company's entire national rail system, comprising 220 trains each day. *(13)*

### Transcontinental Train Travel

East-West transcontinental travel by train in the U.S. is possible, but not yet sufficiently convenient or fast enough for many potential passengers. The Sunset Limited from Los

Angeles to Miami has been proposed as the first truly transcontinental train. Proposals call for this high-speed train to run three times per week, requiring 58 hours or nearly 2½ days of travel.

The need for **double tracking** for safety is imperative to the future of passenger rail travel in the U.S. Accidents such as the derailment of a 14-car Amtrak train near Smithfield, North Carolina, in 1994 have compelled railroad planners to focus on the need for double tracking. Double tracking allows trains to proceed in opposite directions on tracks next to each other. Single tracking means that trains proceeding in opposite directions must use the same track. To allow an on-coming train to pass at certain points, one train must pull off onto a side track. *(14)* The Smithfield accident was blamed on having both high-speed passenger and freight operations running on the same right-of-way. The cost and time required to double-track routes comes high, as exemplified by the proposal to build double tracks through the Blue Mountains of Oregon between Meachum and Huntington at an estimated cost/time of $100 million over 10 years. *(15)*

Despite frequent charges that Amtrak is slow to respond to consumer needs, the company has introduced numerous innovations beyond those already discussed.

• *Road railer*  A hybrid rail highway trailer or **road railer**, has been developed and tested for possible use in carrying mail behind Amtrak passenger trains. This is not a new concept as trains formerly carried the mail on their runs. The road railer is expected to provide extra revenue for Amtrak and improve postal service. *(16)*

• *Railfone*  A cellular telephone service known as the **railfone** is available on more than 60% of the Amtrak routes, thus allowing passengers to call anywhere in the world. *(17)*

• *More comfortable seating*  In response to customer surveys that indicated consumer dissatisfaction with seats, Amtrak has developed more comfortable seat cushions. *(18)*

• *Terminal improvements*  As mentioned earlier, the terminals at Washington, DC, and Philadelphia have been greatly improved. Likewise, the amenities at Penn Station in New York City have been upgraded to match the needs of customers accustomed to flying first class. Improvements in other stations are also planned. *(19)*

• *Video entertainment*  Amtrak and Via Rail of Canada have been testing video systems for use onboard trains. *(20)*

• *Seamless transportation*  Midway Airlines and Amtrak offer **seamless transportation service** for rail and air passengers. The service provides single air/rail ticketing and through baggage handling for Midway/Amtrak passengers. *(21)*

In the U.S., railway labor negotiations are governed by the **National Railway Labor Act**, passed in 1967. Under the act, contracts do not expire on a particular date as they do in other industries. *(22)* The act calls for a series of conferences, mandatory mediations and/or arbitrations under the auspices of the National Mediation Board and, if necessary, the appointment of an emergency board panel by the President. Consequently, labor negotiations can be a lengthy and complicated process.

Complicated labor negotiations are not unique to the U.S., but are common to the world's transportation systems. Many nations experience costly strikes or slow downs that adversely affect the reputation of railroad travel.

Passengers traveling on Amtrak's Superliner services can enjoy the diverse landscape and seasons across the U.S.
Courtesy of The National Railroad Passenger Corp.

### American Orient Express

The **American Orient Express** is the only privately owned-and-operated transcontinental train in the U.S. It is an 11-car train with carriages from the period 1940–50. Most of these were built by the Pullman-Standard Company of Chicago and were rebuilt and refurbished in 1989.

The owner, TCS Expeditions of Seattle, offers nine-day spring and fall tours over 4,800 miles. The journey begins in Washington, DC, or Los Angeles and stops in San Antonio, New Orleans, The Grand Canyon, and Charlottesville, Virginia. *(23)*

### Ability to Compete with Airlines

Passenger trains have demonstrated that they can effectively compete with airlines in some markets. This is the case in Europe and in at least one U.S. Amtrak route. The New York–Washington, DC route successfully competes with airlines for four basic reasons:

1. City Center to City Center terminals permit passengers to avoid airport congestion, allowing more time for business.

2. Equipment is well maintained and comfortable.

3. Prices are competitive.

4. The outstanding Washington, DC, terminal, which is modern and efficient, but has managed to retain its traditional charm after renovation.

Other potentially competitive routes may include New Haven–Boston; Boston–New York; Milwaukee–Chicago and Dallas–Houston.

Experiments are being conducted with high-speed trains such as the Swedish X2000 Metroliner tilt train and a high-speed German train. These trains can achieve speeds of 150–160 miles per hour. Amtrak hopes to spend $400-$500 million to build 26 high-speed trains. High-speed trains on the Boston–New York run could reduce travel time to under three hours, making train travel highly competitive with airlines.

Cross substitution of demand between airlines and railroads was demonstrated during airline fare wars of the 90s. When air fares dropped, Amtrak suffered an immediate 4% sales slump. *(24)* However, cooperation between trains and airlines is also possible. A joint project between Amtrak and United Airlines allows passengers to take one leg of the journey by train and the other by air. Passengers can design their itineraries to include stopovers. When the service was introduced in 1991, it generated double-digit passenger increases in excess of gains for conventional modes of travel. Part of the reason for success is price, which was lower than a non-discounted coach airline fare. *(25)*

## The Next Century

Predictions about train travel in the next century always make for interesting reading. The predictions embrace political and technological changes. Technological developments such as high-speed trains are already occurring. Lack of available capital is the primary hindrance to futuristic train travel, but even this problem is gradually being corrected. In 1990, California approved a bond referendum for $3 billion to invest in all projects throughout the state.

The political changes deal with the privatization of the state railroads. A state or federal government may decide to retain ownership and maintenance of road beds and the rail, while selling off the ownership and management rights of the "**rolling stock**" comprised of engines, cars, and other equipment used on the rails to a private for profit company.

The U.S. National Park Service has considered installing a **solar powered train** within Yosemite National Park in an effort to eliminate automobile traffic and pollution. The proposed train would hook up with Amtrak at Merced, California, and would be powered by solar technology known as **photovoltaics**. This train would have photovoltaic skin and photovoltaic stations at ten mile intervals to provide power for all electrical needs, including propulsion. *(26)*

# Via Rail-Canada

The future of passenger rail travel in Canada may be closely linked with the North American Free Trade Agreement (NAFTA). This agreement calls for a common market between Canada, the U.S., and Mexico. As in the case of the U.S., Canada has one passenger train service, **Via Rail**, which is owned and subsidized by its federal government. *(27)* Via had its funding slashed from $600 million in 1989 to $350 million in 1993. Consequently, it cut costs, improved marketing, and announced plans to eliminate such unprofitable routes as the Montreal–Saint John, New Brunswick, run. *(28)* The fate of Via Rail's eastern routes is intertwined with the politics of the region, particularly Quebec. Via Rail also seems more interested in developing north-south routes to capitalize on NAFTA than to improve east-west train travel.

Canadian freight railroads have taken steps to insure that they are participants in the expected growth of trade between Mexico, the U.S., and Canada following the adoption of NAFTA. Canadian National Railway and its three U.S. railroads (Grand Trunk, Western; Duluth, Winnipeg, and Pacific; and Central Vermont) have integrated marketing and operations into a new system known as C.N. North America. This represents a shift from traditional east-west thinking in Canada to north-south. *(29)* After the drop in subsidies for Via Rail, routes were cut from 33 to 19, and the number of trains running each week decreased from 810 to 396. Via has since seen an increase in passengers and revenue due to tighter cost controls and more effective marketing.

The Vancouver–Toronto route has been renamed Canada's Classic Train Experience, with a new service available three times per week. U.S. tourists have traditionally enjoyed this trip through the Canadian Rockies and plains, and the U.S. market has been targeted with an annual marketing budget of approximately $400,000. *(30)*

## Orient Express

Perhaps the most famous of all trains is the fabled Orient Express. This train began over 100 years ago in 1883, running from Paris to Constantinople (now Istanbul) for a distance of 1,900 miles. Kings, spies, movie stars, and presidents have been the patrons of the Orient Express.

Sir Robert Baden-Powell, founder of the Boy Scouts, was a British spy who posed as an entomologist interested in butterflies. As he rode the Orient Express, he carried sketches of imaginary butterflies whose wings contained diagrams of enemy fortifications. Perhaps the most unlucky passenger ever to ride this train was the French President Paul Deschanel. One day in 1920, Mr. Deschanel boarded the train with his staff, but the next morning, he was nowhere on board. Somehow the poor fellow opened the wrong door during the night and fell out. Badly bruised and clad only in pajamas and one slipper, he limped into a railroad hut along the track and announced he was the President of France. "Yes, and I'm the Emperor Napoleon," replied the railroad employee. The political badgering and hints of an onboard scandal that might have caused the mishap finally forced the President's resignation.

The Orient Express was disbanded and sold to the highest bidder in 1977. Then in 1982, an American named James Sherwood reassembled the cars and brought the train back to life. The Orient Express Railroad became part of Orient Express Hotels, but the corporation suffered losses in all years but one between 1989 and 1993. *(31)*

A new train service operating under the name of Eastern and Orient Express now operates between Singapore and Bangkok, Thailand on an old narrow gauge track covering 1,207 miles. *(32)* The Eastern and Orient Express is an exotic luxury rail service consist-

The opulent Eastern and Oriental Express transports passengers 1,200 miles between Singapore and Bangkok, passing breathtaking vistas and beautiful scenery. Courtesy of Eastern and Oriental Express.

ing of 17 modern-looking, dark green carriages with 2 dining cars, 12 sleeping cars, 2 bars, and an observation car. Total passenger capacity is 130 with smartly uniformed attendants to provide service. Compartments have a Victorian look with tasseled tie back drapes, fresh blossoms in a vase, brass table lamps, marble sink, flush toilet, and shower. The train also has a pricey boutique for onboard shopping. Passengers dress for dinner and some may be seen in tuxedos and expensive cocktail dresses. All this inspired one travel writer to describe the experience as the "ultimate theme park ride." *(33)*

Tweetsie—an historic train that continues to serve passengers at a North Carolina theme park.
Courtesy of Tweetsie Railroad.

## Tourist Trains

**Tourist trains** exist everywhere around the world. These trains carry passengers on an excursion basis, rather than providing transportation between two points. They are usually pulled by steam locomotives and may be standard or narrow gauge. In recent years, there has been increased interest in these trains, thanks to nostalgia and the scenic value of many of the areas they travel. Railroad buffs who are members of the **National Railway Historical Society** often sponsor tours, usually selling out all available seats.

The Tweetsie Railroad of Blowing Rock, North Carolina, is an example of a tourist train which has been operating since 1957. It almost vanished from that state as Gene Autry, of movie fame, once desired to purchase and ship it to California. Tweetsie now operates as an attraction within a private amusement park. Other tourist trains such as the Great Smokey Mountains Railroad operate excursions over 114 miles of track. The railroad carried 122,000 passengers during its first year of operation. *(34)*

## COMMERCIAL TRUCK TRAVEL

The transportation of freight via 16-wheeler trucks and other highway freight vehicles might seem to be an odd inclusion in a book dealing with tourism and travel. In reality,

**TABLE 11.1**
**Restaurant Patronage of Truckers at Highway Stop Restaurants**

| Meals Eaten on the Road | % of Truckers Who Eat This Meal at Highway Stop Restaurants |
|---|---|
| Breakfast | 64.2 |
| Lunch | 37.6 |
| Dinner | 71.3 |
| Snacks | 19.9 |
| Coffee breaks | 44.1 |

*Source:*   William A. Coop, Annual Survey XII, 1992, William A. Coop, Inc., 23060 South Cicero, Richton, Park, IL 60471.

this transportation sector is responsible for billions of dollars in travel industry earnings, including revenues from a profitable niche of truck stops, motels for truckers, and highway cafes.

A survey of over 5,000 truckers provides an interesting perspective of the travel expenditure patterns of truckers. *(35)* Note the high percentage of truckers who consume one or more meals, especially breakfast and dinner, at highway stop restaurants (see Table 11.1).

The choice of a stop for truckers is highly influenced by personal factors other than the trucking services available there, quality of the garage or the brand of fuel notwithstanding. Location, quality of the restaurant, availability of clean showers, fast service, and price are stated as the dominant reasons for selecting a stop.

The image of truckers spending the entire night in their trucks is not true, as more than 70% of all truckers will stay in motels while on the road. They not only use motels, but will mostly choose popular brand name properties for their stay (see Table 11.2). The trucker segment is very important to many highway motels, especially during the seasonal slow periods, when there are fewer vacation travelers on the road.

# FOR-HIRE VEHICLES

The auto rental industry provides a critical link service for business and pleasure travelers worldwide. In the U.S., four companies dominate the market, although their market share has shrunk in recent years. Hertz, Avis, National, and Budget experienced a combined market share of 76.6% in 1988 and 61% in 1992. *(36)* Hertz, the world's largest rental car company, had over 5,000 locations in 130 countries in 1994, with revenues of $2.8 billion. *(37)* The growth of smaller companies such as Alamo and market niche companies such as Rent-a-Wreck accounted for the erosion in the market share of the top four.

The economics of the auto rental industry are tied to the general economy for travel and also to the ownership structure of rental firms. American automobile manufacturing companies hold substantial equity in auto rental companies. Hertz is 49% owned by Ford. Ford also has equity ties to Budget. General Motors has equity interest in Avis and

| Table 11.2 Motels At Which Truck Drivers Commonly Stop | |
|---|---|
| Motel 6 | 38.4 |
| Days Inn | 31.4 |
| Super 8 | 28.4 |
| Best Western | 25.2 |
| Comfort Inn | 21.4 |
| Econo Lodge | 17.7 |
| Holiday Inn | 6.6 |
| Red Roof Inn | 6.5 |
| Quality Inn | 6.4 |
| La Quinta | 6.0 |
| Budgetel | 5.7 |
| Knights Inn | 5.0 |
| Travel Lodge | 4.5 |
| Howard Johnson | 4.4 |
| Regal Inn | 4.3 |
| Roadway Inn | 3.4 |
| Ramada Inn | 3.1 |
| Hampton Inn | 1.3 |
| Other | 9.6 |
| Do not use motels | 27.1 |

*Source:* William A. Coop, Inc., Annual Survey XII, 1992, 23060 South Cicero, Park, IL 60471.

National. Chrysler owns Thrifty, Dollar, and Snappy auto rentals. Within Japan, Hertz and Mazda Motor Corporation formed a joint venture. *(38)*

During years when retail automobile sales are slack, automobile manufacturers press auto rental firms to purchase new cars through heavy discounts and attractive buy-back offers. Auto rental companies respond by offering discount prices to the consumer, thus encouraging price wars and low prices. As the retail market for automobiles improves, auto manufacturers eliminate discounts and, in fact, raise prices to auto rental firms. Auto rental firms in turn raise prices to consumers. Price increases of 30–40% are not uncommon when this situation occurs. Additionally, auto rental companies keep their stock longer so that consumers complain they are forced to pay substantially higher prices for older cars.

Yield management is practiced by the big four rental firms. Hertz, in particular has sophisticated pricing programs, allowing the company to remain highly competitive despite swings in the discounts and buy-backs offered by auto manufacturers. Smaller rental car companies generally lack this pricing sophistication.

## Rental Practices

Auto rental companies must continuously reevaluate the way they do business. The following management practices are of importance to the customer and the rental company.

- *No smoking*   There is a trend toward banning smoking from rental vehicles. Hertz, for example, bars smoking in 80% of its fleet. *(39)*

- *Corporate account marketing*   Budget, Dollar, and Alamo have been especially aggressive in using corporate account business to stabilize year-round business. While less profitable than walk-in business, corporate accounts are easily identified and can be reached through a professional salesforce. Corporate accounts limit product/brand selection for many travelers who are informed where they must rent automobiles. In turn, the corporate client receives a favorable discount and the auto rental firm secures a large customer.

- *High-risk driver denial*   Car rental companies have been electronically checking motor vehicle records in such high premium states as New York and Florida to screen out and deny rental to high-risk drivers.

- *Cancellation fees*   Several companies now charge a cancellation fee, for instance, $50 to customers who do not cancel reservations.

- *Rental surcharges*   Hertz initiated a controversial rental surcharge to compensate for shock losses in excess of $45 million incurred by renting to residents in high-risk markets such as some urban markets with high crime or high accident statistics. If the courts allow this practice to stand, it will probably spread to other markets. *(40)*

- *Improved customer service*   Automated check-ins are part of the customer service arsenal used by auto rental companies. These systems allow the customer to quickly return a car. Information is placed into a hand-held computer by a parking lot attendant. This saves customers from standing in a long check-in line and possibly missing their flights.

  Hertz, a recognized leader in customer service, processed more than 10 million reservations worldwide from its call center in Oklahoma City. Call center staff are trained to handle a variety of callers and are supported by an **intelligent queuing system**, the Rockwell GVS3000, that automatically advises callers how long they will be on hold and places them in a waiting line based on the moment they called Hertz.

- *International reservation service*   Rental car companies operate franchises in many parts of the world. International travelers and their travel agents require ease of reservations and booking rental service anywhere they happen to be.

- *Young drivers ban*   Car rental companies regularly ban drivers under the age of 25, regardless of an individual's driving record because actuarial data show young drivers to be high-risk users. Numerous protests have been lodged against this ban, which is believed to be discriminatory against young people and an impediment to promoting travel and tourism. *(41)*

- *Insurance*   Auto rental firms are also in the insurance business, mainly in the sale of **collision damage waiver** coverage to renters. The purchase of insurance by customers at the time of rental is the basis for on-going conflict and concern. Complaints are often heard that such insurance is overpriced and perhaps unnecessary because such insurance may be covered by the customer's credit card company or his/her personal insurance policy. Auto rental companies have also been charged with using high pressure tactics to sell this insurance. Auto rental companies reply that charges need to be high since many who rent autos are careless drivers and expose the autos to theft or damage in ways they would not do with their personal autos. Whatever the truth, auto rental insurance is a good source of income for auto rental companies.

  The rental car insurance problem is by no means confined to the U.S. and is sometimes more pronounced overseas. Auto rental firms in Italy require a $10 per day theft insurance and those in Switzerland require a $33 per day insurance policy euphemistically called the "Superhighway Fee." *(42)*

- *Airport rentals*   Approximately 80% of U.S. auto rentals are made in conjunction with an airline trip, attesting to the importance of airport rental locations. The big four are the dominant companies inside airline terminals and have been exerting pressure on airports to reduce the cost of rental space.

  Second-tier rental companies have found that they can serve the air passenger market by acquiring space near the airport and providing free shuttle bus service. Off-airport sites allow these companies to operate at a lower cost, putting competitive pressure on firms with higher-cost booths in the terminal. The big four have also experimented with off-airport rental space. As a countermeasure, airports have begun to view the possibility of charging a fee to all rental firms that provide back-up and delivery service, but do not rent airport space.

# $\mathcal{G}$ROUND TRANSPORTATION

The term **ground transportation** is generally used to describe buses, jitneys, vans, and limousines that provide transfer service between an airline terminal and hotel or sightseeing service. Although they are public carriers in a sense, it is more common for private companies, rather than the government, to own and operate these businesses in the United States and throughout much of the free world. In some countries—the United Kingdom, the Netherlands, and France, for instance—airport transfer service is provided by buses owned and operated by their respective governments.

Tariff schedules and other information on ground transportation may be found in such publications as *Ground Transportation Services* (published by OAG Publications), *American Sightseeing International World Tariff*, and *Grayline Sales and Tour Guide*.

## Taxi Service

Taxi service is basically intracity in nature, although some will also serve customers between cities of close proximity. The taxi sector is vital to an effective and efficient travel industry, but is often overlooked. When taxi drivers stage an occasional slowdown or strike, their importance becomes immediately apparent.

The taxi industry is subject to licensing and rate regulation by municipal authorities. The rising costs of vehicles, parts, and fuel; shortage of qualified drivers and mechanics; liability insurance availability and cost; robberies and assaults on drivers, and competition are among the many problems confronting taxi operators. Throughout the world, taxis commonly operate in what is regarded as a protected cartel in which a limited number of taxi companies are permitted to compete within a market. **Taxi medallions** in New York City are bought and sold as an investment as they guarantee the right to operate in a fixed supply market. *(43)*

Many cities worldwide are considering deregulating taxis, but the threat of price gouging is often heard. Critics of deregulation contend that deregulation in Phoenix and Seattle led to higher prices. Proponents of deregulation state that when prices increase in a free market, new competitors will enter with better service and a new price equilibrium will be achieved. *(44)* Some free market proponents have proposed establishing taxi stands where cabs would bid to provide convenient, low-priced service. *(45)* In the special case of China, foreign firms may now set up joint venture taxi businesses in some 11 tourist zones as a way to improve taxi service to help build international tourism. *(46)*

Social conditions within the United States have created a new interdependence between the hospitality industry and taxis. A crackdown on drunk drivers and increased liability of restaurants, bars, and hotels for serving alcohol beverages has created a market for cabs to transport intoxicated patrons. Additionally, the large number of elderly shut-ins has created a market for prepared food delivery from restaurants by taxi to the homes of the elderly.

A license to run a taxicab dispatch service has become an entry vehicle into the cellular business. The dispatcher owns the rights to broadcast over certain radio frequencies. Motorola is the largest owner/operator of taxi dispatch frequencies and plans to build on this base. *(47)*

## Limousine Service

**Limousines** serve a unique market niche, competing with both taxis and buses for business. Airlines often contract with limousine companies to provide service for passengers between nearby airports or to transport passengers between airport and lodging when overnight stays become necessary due to inclement weather or delayed flights. Business corporations will contract with limousines to transport their executives and guests between the airport and corporate facilities. Limousine companies have also found market niches other than ordinary travelers—for instance, weddings, proms, and even real estate agents who wish to impress clients. *(48)*

The Internal Revenue Service has taken a special interest in the relationship between limousine companies and hotel employees who may arrange transportation for guests. The IRS believes that millions of unreported dollars pass hands between these parties as commissions. *(49)*

As safety concerns have loomed to the forefront in every walk of life, limousines are increasingly being modified to include the installation of bullet-proof glass to withstand an attack by a baseball bat or to repel small firearms. This reflects a disturbing social problem of civil disruption in cities and the need for security. *(50)*

# *M*OTORCOACH INDUSTRY

The terms bus, coach, and motorcoach are used interchangeably, but the industry is generally referred to as the motorcoach industry and applies to all operators of large passenger buses. This would seem to define a homogenous group of companies; however, such is not the case. The motorcoach industry is actually composed of several subgroups:

- *Interstate carriers*   National motorcoach companies provide service between two or more states within the U.S.

- *Regional carriers*   Regional bus companies usually serve small- to mid-sized communities within a particular area.

- *Tour operators*   Perhaps the most dynamic member of the motorcoach industry, tour operators create and offer tours to meet the price and interest demands of different markets.

- *Charter buses*   Charters specialize in transporting local groups to events and destinations—for example, church groups headed to a revival or a high school band headed to the Cotton Bowl.

- *Public and private buses*   Some municipalities offer charter services using city buses to provide day trips for student groups and tourists. While revenue potential from these groups may be limited, the special bus service brings millions of visitors to zoos, historical sites, and cultural or science exhibits which desire increased public patronage.

Boy Scouts, YMCA, church groups, schools, and other non-profit organizations also own and operate buses. Boy Scout troops frequently travel for campouts, jamborees, and summer camps.

The motorcoach industry is represented by the American Bus Association (ABA), the National Tour Association (NTA), and the United Bus Owners Association. Details concerning rates, schedules, and other useful information are contained in *Russell's Official National Motor Coach Guide*.

## Intercity Bus Service—U.S.A.

**Intercity bus service** in the U.S. is provided primarily by Greyhound Lines, Inc., with a few regional carriers also offering limited service. Increased automobile ownership and airline discounts shrank the bus industry's share of interstate travel from 30% in 1960 to around 6% in 1994. Greyhound is the only transcontinental bus line in the U.S., but the company has experienced severe problems. *(51)* Greyhound Lines suffered through a leveraged buyout from Dial Corporation in 1987, two violent strikes, and reorganization under federal bankruptcy law. Upon emerging from bankruptcy, management ineptitude, lack of attention to customers and employees exacerbated by strong competition from airlines and a poor economy once again forced the company into financial difficulty. When airline fares increased in 1995, Greyhound recaptured many passengers, but it was feared these customers might again return to the airlines should an airline fare war erupt. The future of intercity and transcontinental bus service in the U.S., as well as that of Greyhound Lines, appears to be an unanswered question at this point in time.

## Intercity Bus Service—Mexico

The bus transportation system in Mexico has long been superior to that of the U.S. or Canada. First and second class travel is available by bus in Mexico. In some destinations, as in the case of Guadalajara, separate bus terminals serve these markets. In 1990, government restrictions were lessened, giving Mexican bus companies greater autonomy to set prices and quality of service. The result was an improvement in bus service, maintenance and provision of luxury-type accommodations. Enlaces Terrestries Nacionales offers luxury service to passengers, and first class service has been enhanced on lines operated by Autobuses del Oriente (ADO). (52) The strength of the Mexican bus industry is reflected in the purchase of a major U.S. bus manufacturing company by a Mexican company. (53)

## Regional Carriers

Regional bus companies in the U.S. enjoyed rider increases as Greyhound was experiencing turmoil. The Adirondack Transit Lines, Frank Martz Coach Company, Peter Pan Bus Lines, and Bonanza Bus Lines, among others, provide regional service with bus routes between major cities. Some offer hourly service between city centers.

When airlines discontinue service between cities, regional bus companies usually fill the void. American Airlines discontinued service to and from many outlying cities when it discontinued its Raleigh-Durham, North Carolina, hub. The Carolina Coach Company saw this as an opportunity to expand its service.

Since regional carriers are small, they are often quick to respond to market needs with innovative service and competitive prices. Peter Pan Lines, for example, charged $24.95 one way for its hourly express bus between New York City and Washington, DC, while Amtrak charged $72 and airlines $109 for this service. Peter Pan Lines also offered innovative services such as on-board movies, an executive coach with upholstered swivel chairs and a galley kitchen. To attract college students, it advertised on rock radio stations.

With the passage of NAFTA, some regional carriers have forged ties with Mexican carriers. There has also been talk of developing an interlinking Mexican, U.S., and Canadian bus system by regional bus lines. (54) NAFTA opens interesting opportunities, although the direction and intensity of change are not altogether predictable. Among the speculations are the following:

- Possible development of an international North-South bus system linking major cities of Canada, the United States, and Mexico.

- Interlinked ownership and management of the motorcoach industry among the nationals of any of the three countries.

- Intensified development of international tours via motorcoach.

- Possible boom for manufacturers of motorcoach. This may be a reason why a Mexican company purchased a U.S. bus manufacturing company.

- New career opportunities for international motorcoach industry managers.

## Charter and Tour Service

**Charter and tour service** represents the fastest growing segment of the motorcoach industry. A large variety of tour packages are offered and promoted by tour brokers who charter a motorcoach and arrange all of the other components of a tour, including itinerary, lodging, sightseeing, courier, admission, guides, meals, and other elements of the tour. These packages are then sold through travel agents and directly to sponsoring groups. *The Official Domestic Tour Manual* publishes information on escorted travel by motorcoach and commissionable tour offerings to guide travel agents.

The beginning of the U.S. tour industry is sometimes credited to entrepreneurs in New York City who organized tours of Chinatown and Coney Island. In 1935, the motorcoach tour industry fell under the jurisdiction of the **Interstate Commerce Commission (ICC)** with the passage of the Motor Carrier Act of 1935. In 1982, the Bus Regulatory Reform Act deregulated the motorcoach industry by eliminating the need for brokers to be licensed through the ICC in order to arrange interstate motor transportation. *(55)* The market response was dramatic in terms of growth, marked by a significant increase in memberships within the National Tour Association (NTA). This organization embraces a diverse membership of hotels, cruise lines, and motorcoach companies with an interest in travel and tourism. Membership reached nearly 4,000 in 1994, of which 600 were tour operators.

In 1993, **motorcoach tours** in North America served more than 17 million passengers. *(56)* A 1995 survey of travelers illustrates the daily expenditures of tour travelers (see Table 11-3). The average daily expenditures (ADE) of nearly $156 per motorcoach travelers compares favorably to the ADE of domestic air travelers and better than the much lower ADE of private automobile travelers. Many motorcoach tourists are retired people with substantial income for travel spending on gifts for friends and relatives, personal souvenirs, good meals, snacks, and other products or services on the road.

## The Motorcoach Tour Market

The primary market for motorcoach tours is individuals aged 50 or older. This market segment is sizeable and growing, and has substantial discretionary income and time for travel. By the year 2000, individuals aged 60 and older will account for one out of every six people in the U.S. The senior market controls more than 50% of discretionary income in the U.S. and holds more than 70% of all financial assets—a formidable market segment.

According to the result of a study of tour patrons in the Southeastern states, bus tour customers tend to be economy-minded and averse to risk-taking. They are inclined towards pre-packaged tours over self-planned vacation trips; sociable, enjoying the company of others on a trip; and older, female, and widowed, having less formal education than non-patrons. *(57)* Primary sources of information used by tour patrons are newspapers, travel brochures, and the advice of relatives.

For the market segment under age 50, the motorcoach industry has developed new action tour packages to include white water rafting, hiking, and biking. These fit in with national and international consumer trends for the babyboomer and younger generations. The NTA discovered, however, that action tours are not of interest solely to the young. A third of those over the age of 65 said they preferred floating or hiking to "watching from the bus."

## TABLE 11.3
## Per Day Estimated Average Expenditures of Tour Travelers: 1995
## United States and Canada

| TOTAL TOUR EXPENDITURES (ONE-DAY AND MULTI-DAY) | Per Person/Day Average |
|---|---|
| Tour operator expenditures | $87.42 |
| Passenger expenditure type | |
| Food | $13.64 |
| Shopping | $21.21 |
| Recreation | $17.92 |
| Ground transportation | $2.35 |
| Other | $.59 |
| Total | $143.13 |
| **ONE-DAY TOURS** | **Per Person/Day Average** |
| Tour operator expenditures | $35.00 |
| Passenger expenditure type | |
| Food | $7.37 |
| Shopping | $13.42 |
| Recreation | $11.32 |
| Ground transportation | $0.75 |
| Other | $0.25 |
| Total | $68.11 |
| **MULTI-DAY TOURS** | **Per Person/Day Average** |
| Tour operator expenditure | $100.12 |
| Passenger expenditure type | |
| Food | $13.74 |
| Shopping | $21.67 |
| Recreation | $17.75 |
| Ground transportation | $2.38 |
| Other | $.64 |
| Total | $156.30 |

*Source:*  1995 Economic Impact Study of Leisure Travelers and Group Tour Takers, April 1996, National Tour Association, International Association of Convention and Visitors Bureaus.

## Marketing Tactics

Within the United States and Great Britain, motorcoach companies have introduced imaginative marketing tactics which include:

- *Niche marketing*   Tours have been developed for groups with specialized interests. Gambling tours by motorcoach to casino centers in Las Vegas, Reno, and Atlantic City have proven to be very popular. Over 10,000 buses per week roll into Atlantic City from nearby markets in New York City, Philadelphia, and surrounding areas. The daily motorcoach traffic feeding Atlantic City is important to casinos along the Boardwalk. Casinos in such communities as Laughlin, Nevada or Central City, Colorado depend heavily upon bus tours as well. *(58)*

  Specialized tours are also available for those interested in museums, art galleries, zoological and botanical parks, national parks, specialty shopping at outlet malls, and other attractions. Many motorcoach tours are planned around natural or man-made events. Natural events such as New England's colorful fall foliage have proven popular with motorcoach tours, as have a wide variety of man-made events.

  The success of Branson, Missouri, is in large measure attributed to organized motorcoach tours for country and western music fans. According to American Automobile Association, Branson, with a population of only 3,700 has become the number one tour bus destination and the number two destination by automobile. *(59)*

- *Conventions and meetings*   The American Bus Association and the National Tour Association sponsor annual trade shows for their membership, bringing suppliers and tour operators together to negotiate advance bookings and prices for the next season's tour packages. Appointments between suppliers and buyers are prearranged with tight scheduling at these shows.

- *Assistance by public and quasi-public visitor promotion organizations*   North Carolina, for example, employs a professional staff member whose responsibility is to work with motorcoach companies to bring them into the state. Many convention bureaus, chambers of commerce, tourism promotion boards, and others also employ full-time people to work with the motorcoach industry.

- *Full-time attention by a professional staff person*   Attractions such as Colonial Williamsburg or the Biltmore House employ full-time professionals to work with motorcoach companies.

- *Advertising*   Direct-mail advertising is used to target motorcoach customers while advertising in trade publications aims at travel agents and others who sell motorcoach tours.

- *Special facilities and service for motorcoach drivers and passengers*   These include a special lounge where drivers may relax; greeting service, often performed by costumed employees, for passengers as they arrive and leave; rest room facilities near bus stops at the attraction; special mementos such as photographs for passengers; and discounts on entrance fees, food, or gift items.

- *Commissions for marketing intermediaries*   Commissions for brokers, travel agents, and specialty agents and/or discounts for the bus company are given to build sales.

- *New equipment*   A new generation of buses has been introduced. In addition to more comfortable buses, experiments have been conducted with environmentally compatible fuels, including natural gas and electricity. The Salt Lake City Airport Authority, for example, owns and operates a fleet of 66 vehicles which use natural gas. The H. Power Corporation was the prime contractor in building an electric bus that uses a fuel cell to make electric current by combining oxygen and hydrogen. Although the bus is limited to a 150-mile range, this development shows what may lie ahead for the industry. *(60)*

- *Informality*   Some tour operators have discarded name tags and assigned seating on the bus or at meals. Operators leave seating and tables open on a first-come, first-served basis.

- *New routes and longer tours*   Several companies now offer extensive tours that cover wide geographical areas.

- *Competitive prices*   A range of prices exist for almost every pocketbook.

## Economic Impact of Motorcoach Tours

The economic impact of this sector of the travel industry is significant. In 1995, the total revenues generated by tour travelers in the U.S. and Canada amounted to over $10 billion (see Table 11.4). Motorcoach tours link with many other sectors of the travel industry, as land packages are often combined with other modes of transportation (air, sea, and sail) and involve the sale of food, lodging, sightseeing, entertainment, and merchandise.

## Sightseeing and Transfer Transportation

Some sightseeing and transfer transportation companies operate shuttle buses and limousines between air terminals and central business districts or major resorts on a regular schedule. Popular sightseeing tours may also run on a regularly scheduled basis. Other forms of sightseeing and transfer consist of contract or charter services, sold through wholesalers as part of tour packages. An intermediary, usually a travel agent, may sell a group tour that includes transfer service and a series of sightseeing tours.

Motels and hotels located near air terminals normally offer complimentary shuttle bus service to customers who call from the airport. Factories and retailers of tourist-oriented products sometimes offer free sightseeing tours to bring people to the company's retail showroom after the tour. Travelers are not obligated to buy; however, enough do to make such service worthwhile.

The sightseeing and transfer sector consists of both large and small firms, with the larger firms usually operating fleets of motorcoach buses. Large firms may be independent, divisions of other transportation companies, or owned by tour wholesalers and large ground operators. In both domestic and international markets—Hawaii and Kenya are two examples—companies operate tours on minibus vans, generally directing their services toward the FIT traveler. In Kenya, minivans are employed on safari sightseeing trips. Because these operators often depend on the travel desks of major hotels for their sales, they find it essential to develop good rapport with and provide incentives for tour desk operators to ensure that their services will be promoted.

**TABLE 11.4**
**Total Estimated Direct Revenue Impact of Tour Travelers: 1995**
**United States and Canada**

| TOTAL U.S. AND CANADA ($U.S.) | One Day | Multi-Day | Total |
|---|---|---|---|
| Tour departures by all companies | 319,596 | 235,585 | 555,181 |
| Tour passengers | 12,703,031 | 10,293,414 | 22,996,445 |
| Average departure (# passengers) | 39.75 | 43.69 | 41.42 |
| Passenger days | 12,703,031 | 52,428,150 | 65,131,181 |
| **EXPENDITURES (U.S. $)** | | | |
| By tour operators (includes motorcoach on the road expenses) | $444,561,140 | $5,249,214,021 | $5,693,775,161 |
| By passengers | $420,700,816 | $2,945,171,548 | $3,365,872,363 |
| Total | $865,261,956 | $8,194,385,568 | $9,059,647,524 |
| Per passenger/day | | | $139.10 |
| Transportation | $122,208,414 | $900,878,685 | $1,023,087,099 |
| Motorcoach (off the road) | $122,208,414 | $496,626,568 | $618,834,982 |
| Air, rail, cruise | — | $404,252,117 | $404,252,117 |
| **GRAND TOTAL** | **$987,470,370** | **$9,095,264,253** | **$10,082,734,623** |

*Source:* 1995 Economic Impact Study of Leisure Travelers and Group Tour Takers, April 1996, National Tour Association, International Association of Convention and Visitors Bureaus.

## Specialty Sightseeing

Specialty sightseeing tours, which are popular in many tourist areas, consist of short trips on trackless trolleys, in horse-drawn buggies, or on trackless trains pulled by a jeep or miniature diesel locomotive. Other specialty sightseeing vehicles include bicycles built for two, horseback riding, and bicycle-powered rickshaws. In some communities, entrepreneurs have developed walking tours. These often combine the use of public transportation and guided walks through historic areas.

The specialty sightseeing sector is often the object of complaint by residents or the travel trade because of noise, animal droppings, or the competition posed to traditional sightseeing companies. Despite these objections, specialty sightseeing is growing and may be found in many places, such as, Central Park, New York; Charleston, South Carolina; and Victoria, British Columbia to name a few. Moreover, the specialty sightseeing market offers an opportunity for new entrepreneurs.

Minivans take tourists on safaris in Kenya to hunt animals with cameras instead of rifles.
Courtesy of Abercrombie & Kent.

## Bicycle Travel

In some parts of the world—the Netherlands or China, for example—the bicycle is a means of daily commuting to and from work. However, in the United States, Europe, Nova Scotia and elsewhere, the bicycle is primarily used for recreation and touring. Bicycle touring clubs often sponsor special tours and serve as a basis for camaraderie. The potential market for **bicycle touring** in North America is sizeable. As shown in Table 11.5, over 86 million people own bikes in the U.S. Additional market potential exists among the 140 million bikers in Europe and 63 million in Japan. The lack of sufficient bike trails and roads, however, hampers the growth of this sector of the travel industry.

The greatest handicap to bicycle touring is danger from motorized vehicle traffic. With good reason, bicycles are prohibited from freeways and interstate highways. The bicycle market may be divided into road bikes, mountain bikes, hybrids, and juvenile bikes. Of these, road, mountain, and hybrid bikes are the most important to the travel industry. In the United States, approximately 65% of bicycle sales are hybrids and mountain bikes. The development of the mountain bike created a new form of recreation and a substitute for backpacking for outdoor enthusiasts. Mountain biking also created a clash with hikers and environmentalists who feel that the bikes create erosion and destroy the tranquil-

# *Eureka* Springs

Controversy over tourism growth and bus tours has created hot tempers and discord in Eureka Springs, Arkansas. *(61)* This previously quaint Victorian town of 1900 inhabitants in the Ozarks now hosts over 1 million tourists per year. Many inhabitants feel that tour bus traffic has created a spread of unwelcome T-shirt shops and all-you-can-eat buffets on the edge of town distracting from the town's appearance and creating unwelcome clutter and congestion.

The Great Passion Play and the seven story statue of Jesus, called the Christ of the Ozarks, have caused Eureka Springs to become one of the American Bus Association's top 100 attractions in North America. Downtowners wish to preserve the historic section of town for residents and upscale bed and breakfast travelers. Others known as the "highway crowd" want to expand the attractions on the edge of town and encourage more visitors, particularly bus tours.

The highway people are "overcrowding and destroying stuff" said Shalom Miller, a 61-year old resident. In response, John Cross, the pro-development president of the town bank said, "You wonder why they don't just pack up and go someplace else if they don't like it (the development)."

| TABLE 11.5 Bicycle Market in the United States, Canada, Japan, and Europe | | |
|---|---|---|
| **ESTIMATED NUMBERS (1993)** | **Number of Bikes** | **%** |
| Western Europe | 140,000,000 | 47% |
| United States | 86,500,000 | 29% |
| Japan | 63,242,000 | 21% |
| Canada | 9,000,000 | 3% |
| **ESTIMATED SALES (1993)** | **Number of Sales** | **%** |
| Western Europe | 17,000,000 | 44% |
| United States | 13,000,000 | 34% |
| Japan | 7,313,422 | 19% |
| Canada | 1,400,000 | 3% |

*Source:* National Trade Data Bank, International Trade Commission, Japanese Bicycle Manufacturer's Association, Field Study Report on Transdyn USA, Inc. by George Stoecklein, Patrick Steagall, Tracy Krueger, and Renata Ribeiro, Babcock Graduate School of Management, Wake Forest University, Spring 1995, pg. 9.

ity of the wilderness. Many communities have begun to regulate trails and areas where mountain bikes may travel. Bicycle enthusiasts have called for an increase in roadways and bicycle paths throughout North America. Given the persistent presence of government deficits, it is doubtful that dramatic increases will be seen anytime soon in the development of infrastructure for bicycle travel.

# SUMMARY

One of the most dramatic changes in land transportation is the renewed interest in passenger rail traffic. In North America, Canadian railroads are looking to the south in anticipation of the effects of NAFTA. Europe, Asia, and to some extent, the U.S., are seriously considering or have already implemented high-speed rail. Furthermore, the European Union countries have introduced significant reforms in the ownership and management of their rail and train systems.

Within the U.S., Amtrak, a government owned and subsidized organization, has responsibility for passenger train travel. In Canada, Via Rail has a similar responsibility. Several states have initiated state-owned and run passenger trains in response to perceived customer need and to offset funding decreases for Amtrak. The role of state-run railroads is controversial.

Several technological improvements in addition to high-speed trains have been considered for passenger train travel. Among these is a return to a modern mail car pulled behind a passenger train and the use of solar power to propel trains.

The motorcoach sector, specializing in tours, continues to serve as a dynamic force in the travel industry. Motorcoach tours are increasingly popular and will probably grow in numbers and diversity as the population ages. The personal motor vehicle including autos, RVs, and motorcycles is of primary importance to the North American travel industry. Numerous sectors of travel-related companies are directly dependent on the tourism expenditures of motorists and users of motorcoach services.

Smaller niche players, including sightseeing and transfer bus operators, specialty sightseeing services, bicycle touring, and others also contribute to growth and enjoyment of travel and tourism. Indeed, it is in these niches that new ideas and new entrepreneurs are born to add to the diversity of the land transportation mix for the tourist industry.

# DISCUSSION QUESTIONS

1. Is there any evidence that would lead you to believe that passenger rail travel in North America might someday be competitive with airlines?

2. Explain the role NAFTA has played in the Canadian Rail System.

3. Why have several U.S. states initiated their own state operated railroads?

4. Which form of ground transportation has the worst safety record?

5. What has historically been the role of government with commercial passenger transportation?

6. What influence, if any, is the chunnel likely to have on the European travel market?

7. What is happening in Asia in terms of rail travel? What effect could this have on Asian airline travel?

8. What is Amtrak and why was it formed?

9. Discuss several of the major innovations that are beginning to occur in the U.S. passenger rail sector.

10. What is the significance of commercial truck traffic to the U.S. travel industry?

11. Discuss several of the auto rental practices currently employed by car rental firms. What do you believe is the future for these practices?

12. Is the taxi industry generally regulated or non-regulated? What is the significance?

13. What are the major sub-sectors of the motorcoach industry?

14. What are specialty sightseeing tours?

15. Is the bicycle market large in Europe and North America? Is it large enough to be of importance to the travel industry? In your opinion, what needs to be done to make bicycling a more important part of the industry?

# SUGGESTED STUDENT EXERCISE

## State Run Passenger Trains
Mini Case Analysis

Budgetary problems plaguing Amtrak created a market niche for state-run passenger trains. In 1995, Amtrak cut service by 24% due to a $200 million budget shortfall.

Recognizing the potential importance of train travel to tourism, several states initiated their own railroads. Mount Baker International, owned by the state of Washington, runs between Seattle and Vancouver, BC. Washington state spent $24 million on track repairs and imported sleek new Spanish cars to meet the needs of upscale passenger train enthusiasts.

State-owned trains offer a variety of services, such as food and beverages, not available on Amtrak. Passengers on the Mount Baker line enjoy local ales, smoked salmon, and watch first-run movies. Those traveling on the Piedmont's North Carolina between Raleigh and Charlotte can dine on barbecue pork sandwiches cooked onboard.

In Vermont, bicycle enthusiasts are now encouraged to bring bikes on board. Amtrak previously required that bikes be disassembled and put in a box and thus discouraged bicycle riders. The state train in Vermont features Ben & Jerry's ice cream and offers Vermont teddy bears and maple syrup for sale.

"We can make rail service more desirable because we live here and know our market better," said Merrill Travis, rail-bureau chief of the Illinois Department of Transportation. That might be true, respond critics, but will enough paying passengers use your trains to make them a good investment? North Carolina saw smaller than expected numbers of passengers after initiating the new service. Yet evidence shows that state-owned train travel might work. In Washington state, ridership was up 40% in 1994.

States such as Vermont have several reasons for getting into the train business. State officials say that trains are less damaging to the environment and support ski resort and sightseeing tourism in the rural countryside. Some communities such as Bellingham, Washington, have gotten behind the program. Bellingham built a modern $3.6 million multinational terminal to serve the train, Greyhound bus, and the Alaska Ferry links.

Many small communities suffering from a reduction in airline service have expressed interest in a state-owned train system. The problem is that state legislators are often hard pressed to defend using public funds for a passenger train instead of for social services, schools, or other state-supported activities. *(62)*

## Questions for Study

1. Should U.S. states and Canadian provinces enter the passenger train business? Explain the pros and cons of the passenger train business as demonstrated by historic developments, travel trends and economic changes.

2. What would states and provinces need to do to ensure the financial success of a state run railroad?

3. Do you believe that a state run railroad would increase overall tourism or just take market share away from other modes of transportation such as bus or airline?

# $\mathcal{R}$EFERENCES

1. "Safety Fact Sheet," Amtrak Public Affairs, 60 Mass. Avenue, Washington, DC 20002.

2. Edgell, David L., and Sarah J. Dalton. "Home on the Road: Exploring Rural America is a Commanding Business Asset," *Business America*, Vol 114, November 29, 1993, pg. 18–20.

3. Ono, Yumiko. "Off-Road Vehicles Leave Others in the Dust," *The Wall Street Journal*, September 17, 1993, pg. B1.

4. Pearl, Daniel. *The Wall Street Journal*, June 14, 1994, pg. B1.

5. Thousand Trails, Inc., Disclosure Company No. T474375000

6. "AAA Facts: 1994," American Automobile Association, Public Relations Department, 1000 AAA Drive, Heathrow, FL 32746-5063.

7. "Europe's Railways, Light at the End of the Tunnel," *The Economist*, October 29–November 4, 1994, pg. 23–25.

8. *Ibid.*

9. Foster, Keith. "Getting There is Half the Fun," *International Herald Tribune*, Thursday, July 20, 1995, pg. 18.

10. "Asia's Big New Train Set," *The Economist*, September 17, 1994, pg. 67–68.

11. "Casey Jones Had Better Watch His Speed," *The Economist*, September 17, 1994, pg. 68.

12. Source Book, Amtrak 2000, Amtrak Public Affairs, Washington Union Station, 60 Mass Avenue, NE, Washington, DC 20002, pg. 5–7.

13. Annual Report, National Railroad Passenger Corporation, pg. 15.

14. Burke, Jack. "Latest Amtrak Derailment Renews Questions About Shared Routes with Freight Railroads," *Traffic World*, May 23, 1994, pg. 17–18.

15. "Union Pacific Plans $100 Million Double Tracking in Eastern Oregon," *Traffic World*, March 15, 1993, pg. 33.

16. "Washington Panel Gives Amtrak Preference," *Railway Age*, January 1993, pg. 22.

17. "Phone-y Services Are for Real," *The Cornell Hotel and Restaurant Administration Quarterly*, Vol. 33, No. 3, June 1992, pg. 94.

18. Myers, Nicholas. "The Seating Blues," *Mass Transit*, July-August 1992, pg. 42–44.

19. Roberts, Robert. "New Directions for Amtrak," *Railway Age*, June 1991, pg. 59–60.

20. Kaven, Henry C. "Video on Wheels," *Mass Transit*, March 1991, pg. 40–41.

21. Lewis, Robert G. "Passenger Service Goes Intermodel," *Railway Age*, July 1990, pg. 104.

22. Source Book, Amtrak 2000, Amtrak Public Affairs, Washington Union Station, 60 Mass Avenue, NE., Washington, DC 20002, pg. 24.

23. Wukas, Mark, "American Orient Express," *The Chicago Tribune*, Sunday, August 27, 1995, pg. 8, Section 12.

24. Mallory, Maria, and Greg Bowens. "Oh What a Lovely Fare War," *Business Week*, June 29, 1992, pg. 37.

25. McCarthy, Michael J. "More Taking the Plane and the Train," *The Wall Street Journal*, March 22, 1994, pg. B1.

26. Bowker, Michael. "A Solar Solution for Yosemite," *Technology Review*, November-December 1991, pg. 22–23.

27. "Railways: Red Light, Green Light," *The Economist*, July 17, 1993, pg. 25–26.

28. Gormick, Greg. "Via Rail: Less is More," *Railway Age*, July 1991, pg. 110–111.

29. Bonney, Joseph. "CN & Grand Trunk = C. N. North America," *American Shipper*, February 1992, pg. 48.

30. Green, Carolyn. "Via Acts to Get Back on Track," *Marketing* (McLean-Hunter), April 20, 1992, pg. 4.

31. "Orient Express Hotels Reports Wider Losses for Year and Quarter," *The Wall Street Journal*, April 16, 1993, pg. A9.

32. Astbury, Sid. "ASEAN: Expressly Oriental," *Asian Business*, Vol. 27, October 1991, pg. 20.

33. Barnard, Charles N. "A Moveable Feast: From Singapore to Bangkok by Luxury Train," *Modern Maturity*, Vol. 38, Nol 1, January-February 1995, pg. 53–56.

34. Timblin, Carol. "Traveling the Tourist Trains," *The State*, Snow Publishing Inc., May 1991, pg. 24–29.

35. Coop, William A. Annual Survey XII, 1992, William A. Coop, Inc., 23060 South Cicero, Richton Park, IL 60471.

36. Bowens, Greg. "A Demolition Derby for Hertz, Avis, and the Gang," *Business Week*, October 5, 1992, pg. 85–86.

37. Ramirez, Anthony. "Hertz Appoints a New No. 2 Management Revamping," *New York Times*, August 13, 1993, pg. D3.

38. "Mazda Motor," *Business Japan*, Vol. 20, July 1990, pg. 20.

39. Hirsch, James S. "Smokers Find Travel Industry is Inhospitable," *Wall Street Journal*, February 8, 1994, pg. B1.

40. Gilbert, Evelyn. "Vicarious Liability Law Pits Hertz versus New York City," *National Underwriters*, January 20, 1994, pg. 4.

41. Birenbaum, Steven J. "Auto Rentals: Rough Ride for the Young," *New York Times*, June 5, 1994, pg. 11, Section 3.

42. Pope, Kyle. "Rules of the Road for Car Rentals Abroad," *The Wall Street Journal*, Friday, July 18, 1995, pg. B11.

43. Phalon, Richard. "License to Mint Money," *Forbes*, Vol. 153, June 20, 1994, pg. 255.

44. "Hail to the Taxi," *Fortune*, Vol. 128, December 27, 1993, pg. 142–143.

45. Donald, Thomas G. "Call a Taxi: Cab Drivers in Pursuit of Liberty and Profit," *Barron's*, Vol. 73, July 12, 1993, pg. 10.

46. "China Opens Tourism Industry," *China Business Review*, Vol. 20, January–February 1993 pg. 4.

47. Slutsker, Gray. "The Taxicab as Phone Company," *Forbes*, Vol. 149, January 6, 1992, pg. 41.

48. Mueller, Rose Mary. "Make Deals on Wheels," *Real Estate Today*, Vol. 28, October 1992, pg. 22–23.

49. "The IRS Strikes Again," *The Cornell Hotel and Restaurant Administrative Quarterly*, Vol. 33, December 22, pg. 92.

50. "Civil Violence Sparks Market for Personal Security Vehicles," *Automotive News*, September 28, 1992, pg. 211.

51. Tomsho, Robert. "Real Dog: How Greyhound Lines Re-engineered Itself Right Into a Deep Hole," *The Wall Street Journal*, October 20, 1994, pg. 1 and A6.

52. Blears, James. "Getting Down to Bus-News," *Business Mexico*, Vol. 3, October 1993, pg. 23–24.

53. DePalma, Anthony. "Trade Pact is Spurring Mexican Deals in the U.S.," *New York Times*, March 17, 1994, pg. D1.

54. Tomsho, Robert. "Small Bus Lines Turn Aggressive and Win Riders," *The Wall Street Journal*, Wednesday, December 28, 1994, pg. B1 and B5.

55. "Group Travel: An Idea Becomes an Industry," National Tour Association, Inc., P. O. Box 3071, Lexington, Kentucky, 40596-3071, pg. 2–5.

56. *Ibid.* pg. 7.

57. Cunningham, L.F. and K. Thompson. "The Intercity Bus Tour Market: A Comparison Between Inquiries and Purchasers," *Journal of Travel Research*, XXV, No. 1 (Fall 1966).

58. Wolff, Carlo. "A Different World: Nevada Hiltons Occupy Their Own Special Universe," *Lodging Hospitality*, Vol. 48, November 1992, pg. 36–37.

59. Salomon, Alan. "More Tour Buses Than Residents," *Advertising Age*, Vol. 65, April 25, 1994, pg. 55.

60. Wald, Matthew L. "An Electric Bus Bypasses a Battery Barrier," *New York Times*, May 29, 1994, pg. 8, Section 3.

61. Felsenthal, Edward. "For Fun You Can See a Giant Jesus or File a Lawsuit," *The Wall Street Journal*, Friday, August 11, 1995, pg. A1 and A10.

62. Machalaba, Daniel and Albert R. Karr. "Railroad Crossings: As Amtrak Cuts Back, Some States Revive Passenger Train Lines," The Wall Street Journal, Thursday, June 22, 1995, pg. A1 and A8.

# Chapter 12

# *Air* Transportation

## LEARNING OBJECTIVES

- To gain a historical perspective of the air transportation industry and its place in the travel industry.

- To be aware of the various classifications of commercial airlines in the United States.

- To gain a perspective of international air transportation and the problems facing the airline sector.

- To appreciate management decisions required in the airline industry.

- To understand the forces likely to affect the future of the U.S. air transportation industry.

- To define and use the following terms:

| | |
|---|---|
| Airline Deregulation Act | Federal Aviation Administration (FAA) |
| Cabotage | |
| Capacity-controlled fare | Flag carrier |
| Charter air service | Freedoms of the air |
| Chicago Convention | Hub-spoke routes |
| Civil Aeronautics Board (CAB) | International Air Transportation Act |
| Department of Transportation (DOT) | |
| Federal Aviation Act | International Civil Aviation Organization (ICAO) |

Linear routes

Load factor

Multinational interline traffic agreements

Non-scheduled air service

Overflight charges

Overflight privileges

Route structure

Scheduled air service

# Historical Perspective

*T*he major, singular event that promoted the growth of the commercial airline industry was World War II. The war temporarily disrupted commercial flights, but it brought tremendous long-run gains for the development of the air transportation industry, including:

- the creation of a large body of experienced pilots;
- increased public acquaintance with aviation, as hundreds of thousands of military personnel and civilian employees experienced their first flight during the war;
- increased knowledge of weather;
- improved maps and knowledge of foreign terrain;
- construction of thousands of airfields in wide parts of the world;
- a large assortment of surplus aircraft, which were purchased relatively inexpensively after the war and converted to commercial use;
- increased knowledge of aircraft design, flying techniques, and other knowledge necessary for advancement of the industry; and
- the development of jet aircraft.

The next dramatic step in commercial aviation growth occurred during the 1950s with the introduction and quick adoption of the commercial jetliners, first in the U.S., then soon around the world. The jet aircraft had greatly increased travel speeds and a longer flight distance which enabled planes to fly farther without refueling. It also allowed for smoother flights, and enlarged passenger seating capacity. All of these factors helped to win greater public acceptance of commercial airlines and resulted in formidable competition for slower transportation modes, namely, railroads and passenger ships.

The commercial airline industry again leaped forward in the 1970s with the introduction and widespread use of wide-bodied aircraft such as the Douglas DC-10, Boeing 747, and Lockheed Tristar 1011. These planes further increased passenger comfort and seating and freight capacity. A critical factor behind the success of these aircraft was the improved economics of long-distance air service.

As the airline industry grew, so did the travel industry's dependency on it. Executive business travel and international tourism are almost completely tied to **scheduled air service** which operates on a published schedule of flights, and to a lesser extent, **non-sched-**

Ford Tri-motor with passengers (about 1931).
Courtesy of Trans World Airlines, Inc.

**uled air service** which does not operate on a regular schedule. In the U.S., not only is air transportation important to the contiguous 48 states, but it is especially critical for Alaska and Hawaii, as well as for other American territories, encompassing Guam, American Samoa, Puerto Rico, and the American Virgin Islands. Cruise lines, rental car companies, airport hotels and motels, and ground transportation operators depend on the airline industry to generate the bulk of their business.

The 1980s witnessed still further improvements in aircraft technology with the introduction of such aircraft as the DC-9-80 and Boeing 757 and 767. These are designed for fuel-efficient operation, offering about 30% lower fuel consumption per passenger than the older models. The introduction of the longer-range Boeing 747-400 has dramatically shifted travel patterns with its range of 8,000 miles and seating capacity of 418. New aircraft introduced in the 1990s include the MD 11, Airbus, A-340, and the Boeing 777. The latter was the first twin-engined aircraft certified for long-range, over-water service that did not require a trial period before approval.

The global airline industry, counting both domestic and international carriers, is a giant industry. In 1994, the member airlines of the International Civil Aviation Organization (ICAO) carried an estimated 1.2 billion passengers on international and domestic routes *(1)*—an increase of sixty-fold since the first jetliner flew in 1949. Air transport is also one

Passengers debarking from a DC-3 (about 1943).
Courtesy of Trans World Airlines, Inc.

of the fastest growing sectors of the world economy. The International Air Transport Association (IATA) projects that passenger and freight traffic will increase at an average annual rate of 5% until the year 2000. By the year 2010, aviation's economic impact could exceed $1.5 trillion with over 30 million jobs provided. *(2)*

# U.S. AIRLINE INDUSTRY

The airline industry in the United States is comprised of some of the largest airlines in the world, as well as numerous small airlines serving commuter routes and less populated areas. This section discusses the ownership, regulation, and classification of U.S. airlines.

## Ownership

The U.S. airline industry is based on private enterprise. Airlines are owned by private companies, rather than by the government. This is not the case in many countries where airlines are partially or wholly government-owned and operated, often with subsidies to cover losses. In recent years, a number of large airlines in other countries such as British Airways, Japan Airlines, and Air New Zealand have been privatized in whole or in part.

In the United States, the largest airlines are public stock companies. Ownership is shared by thousands of stockholders who buy and sell stock in airline companies on one of the stock exchanges. Anyone, including foreigners, business corporations, and non-profit organizations, can purchase stock in U.S. airlines. Foreign investment in U.S. airlines, however, is subject to certain restrictions. Federal laws limit foreign stockholders from owning more than 25% of voting common stock and 40% of total investment to prevent their becoming owners of the majority of voting stock or investment.

The ownership of an airline is significant in terms of airline management policy and operating practices. Private ownership means that managers of U.S. airlines are accountable to stockholders. If stockholders become unhappy with the way the company is run, they may vote to replace the board of directors and to make policy and operating changes in the company. With privately-owned companies, the airlines are always under pressure to generate a profit to pay stockholders dividends and to ensure that stock prices do not fall, as well as to make continuous provisions for acquiring new aircraft for replacement and expansion. The air carriers also must remain competitive among themselves and with subsidized foreign air carriers. Domestically, they must also be competitive with alternate modes of transportation. This requires a continuous search for means to decrease costs, increase market share, and diversify into other businesses.

The efficacy of private ownership and management accountability to shareholders for performance is tellingly demonstrated by the fact that six of the top ten airlines, measured in terms of scheduled passenger-kilometers flown, are U.S. airlines (see Table 12.1).

## Regulation

Despite private ownership, airlines have been subject to regulations by all of the federal, state, and local governmental agencies that regulate business enterprise in general. Almost every aspect of the airline business, ranging from labor relations, customer rela-

### TABLE 12.1
### The World's Top Ten Airlines in 1994
### [scheduled passenger-kilometers (millions) flown]

| International | | Domestic | | Total | |
|---|---|---|---|---|---|
| 1. British Airways | 81,053 | 1. American Airlines | 110,357 | 1. United Airlines | 173,834 |
| 2. United Airlines | 67,391 | 2. United Airlines | 106,443 | 2. American Airlines | 159,039 |
| 3. Lufthansa | 51,568 | 3. Delta Airlines | 100,193 | 3. Delta Air Lines | 138,876 |
| 4. Japan Airlines | 49,084 | 4. USAir | 58,198 | 4. Northwest Airlines | 93,135 |
| 5. American Airlines | 48,683 | 5. Northwest Airlines | 53,034 | 5. British Airways | 86,232 |
| 6. Singapore Airlines | 44,947 | 6. Continental Airlines | 51,518 | 6. Continental Airlines | 66,962 |
| 7. Air France | 42,151 | 7. TWA | 28,231 | 7. Japan Airlines | 62,936 |
| 8. KLM | 40,833 | 8. All Nippon Airways | 28,020 | 8. USAir | 61,058 |
| 9. Northwest Airlines | 40,101 | 9. America West | 19,533 | 9. Lufthansa | 56,536 |
| 10. Delta Air Lines | 38,684 | 10. Japan Airlines | 13,853 | 10. Air France | 50,119 |

*Source:*  International Air Transport Association.

tions, accounting practices, and marketing practices to environmental considerations, has been affected by some governmental agency.

Two agencies of the federal government in particular are now responsible for closely monitoring the airlines: the Federal Aviation Administration and the Department of Transportation. Prior to its dissolution in 1985, an agency known as the Civil Aeronautics Board (CAB) also played an important role in regulating competition and air route decisions affecting the airlines.

1. **The Federal Aviation Administration (FAA)**   The FAA was created in 1958 under the enactment of the Federal Aviation Act. The purpose of the FAA is to ensure air safety and to promote the growth of aviation by aiding in the orderly development and use of support facilities and equipment. Despite its critics, the record of air safety in the United States demonstrates that the FAA has been effective in its work.

   The FAA is responsible for:
   - establishing and enforcing safety standards;
   - certifying and monitoring the skills and health of pilots;
   - certifying aircraft;
   - investigating accidents;
   - controlling air traffic;
   - promoting and helping to develop a national system of airports;
   - monitoring aircraft maintenance procedures;
   - ensuring that standards are met in the development, engineering, and construction of new aircraft and equipment.

   The responsibilities of the FAA have placed this agency in daily contact with equipment and aircraft manufacturers, airport managers, pilots, flight attendants, traffic controllers, airline management, and others connected with U.S. aviation.

2. **The Department of Transportation (DOT)**   DOT was formed in 1967 to bring about an integrated U.S. transportation policy and to eliminate having separate agencies for each mode of transportation. Regulatory functions of the DOT enfold carrier entry into domestic routes, consumer protection, and international air routes. These functions, which were formerly under the jurisdiction of the CAB, have been subsequently transferred to the DOT after the phaseout of the CAB. With respect to entry, the DOT has been liberal in allowing U.S. airlines to enter domestic routes of their choice. It has also been pro-free market in allowing more carriers to service international air routes (which will be discussed later in this chapter.) With regard to airline agreements concerning travel agencies, the DOT has the power to grant antitrust immunity, allowing U.S. airlines to collaborate with the agencies. However, the DOT declined to exercise this power, and allowed the formation of the Airline Reporting Corporation (ARC) to foster a procompetitive environment. Consumer protection issues continuously arise in the existing deregulated environment, and the DOT has become involved in the airline default protection plan, airline designation of flights, and consumer complaints about airline services.

U.S. airlines today are still adjusting to meet the changing environment. Despite substantial growth in traffic, the carriers have been experimenting with different strategies on pricing, route, structure, and marketing of services in order to meet increased competition and other challenges posed by rising fuel costs, lagging productivity, and yield. New competition from low cost carriers such as Southwest Airlines—which has fares as much as 50% lower—has made it even more difficult for major airlines to remain profitable.

3. **The Civil Aeronautics Board** The CAB originally was established by law in 1938 to ensure orderly competition and growth within the airline industry. It was the conventional belief that if the U.S. airline industry were permitted to grow without regulations, cutthroat competition might occur, which would lead to the survival of only a few large airlines. It was also feared that a system of open competition might lead to little or no service for some communities, particularly smaller cities.

As a result, the CAB was given power to grant route authorizations for air carriers to engage in interstate and foreign air transportation, to establish a uniform system of the rates and fares that could be charged to the public for air freight and passenger service, to rule on the allowance of mergers and acquisition by carriers, and to rule over unfair competition between air carriers and travel agents.

With a change in the economic and political climate, however, a decision was made by the federal government to deregulate the domestic airline industry. The **Airline Deregulation Act** of 1978 called for the elimination of the CAB and economic regulations over the domestic airline industry. The CAB was terminated on January 1, 1985, with some of its functions transferred to the DOT.

## Classification of U.S. Airlines

Up to 1980, airlines were classified by the CAB under two major groupings, based on type of operations—either **scheduled service** or **charter service**, also known as supplemental service. Scheduled airlines were referred to as certificated route air carriers, authorized to provide service between designated points on a regularly scheduled basis at rates approved by the CAB. Having been issued a Certificate of Public Convenience and Necessity by the CAB, scheduled carriers were permitted to operate in one of the designated classifications: domestic trunk, international, intra-Hawaiian and intra-Alaskan, and domestic regional or local service.

Charter airlines, originally called supplemental airlines, provide nonscheduled airline services in which the flights are chartered, or paid for in full by a tour operator. Most of their business is international, thus placing them in competition with U.S. and foreign airlines for charter business. Charter airlines were not originally permitted to operate regularly scheduled flights for individual passengers; but under a deregulated environment, some charter airlines attempted to offer scheduled services. These attempts were generally unsuccessful due to intensive competition from the major airlines.

Charter flights may be offered by scheduled or charter airlines. Additionally, airlines today can offer seats for both services on the same flight. That is, a block of seats may be sold through a tour wholesaler while other seats are sold on the basis of the regularly

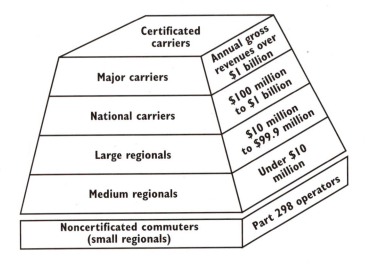

**Figure 12.1**   U.S. airline classifications.

Source:   *Air Transportation: A Management Perspective.*

scheduled service. Regardless of the carrier, charter flights compete with other charter flights as well as with the discount fares offered by scheduled airlines.

In January 1981, new carrier groupings were established. The changing nature of airline operations under deregulation necessitated a reevaluation and restructuring of air carrier groupings for statistical and financial data aggregation and analysis. The board sanctioned the elimination of the historical carrier groupings and adopted newly defined groupings based on size and volume, as measured by total operating revenue. The carrier groupings shown in Figure 12.1 reflect the current classification under the DOT; they are similar to the groupings adopted by the CAB in 1981.

# *I*NTERNATIONAL AIR TRAVEL

International air travel began on a small scale before World War II. Transatlantic flights by dirigibles occurred in 1919, and for a while it appeared as if they might emerge as an alternate system to transoceanic passenger ships. In the summer of 1929, the *Graf Zeppelin* dirigible successfully crossed the North Pole, creating great excitement around the world. The dirigible also flew from Germany to Rio de Janeiro, Brazil, and offered service from Germany to New Jersey for a rate of $2,200. *(3)* Unfortunately, dirigibles were plagued by disasters, and the dream of using dirigibles for commercial passenger transportation disappeared with the disastrous explosion of the German *Hindenburg* at Lakehurst, New Jersey, in 1937.

The history of international aviation in the United States is almost synonymous with the history of Pan American World Airways, which unfortunately went out of business on December 4, 1991 *(4)*—a victim of management miscalculations on the value of the

The *Graf Zeppelin* paused to refuel in Los Angeles for the last lap of her world journey across North America in August 1929.

acquisition of National Airlines to provide a domestic trunk, excessive debt, competition, and changing market economics. The airline began with the efforts of a World War I naval pilot, Juan T. Trippe, who founded Pan Am in 1927 with a fleet of two Fokker F-7 trimotor airplanes, 24 employees, and a contract to fly U.S. mail between Key West, Florida, and Havana, Cuba. In 1928 Pan Am was operating 85 aircraft and carrying more than 100,000 passengers over a network that reached from Alaska to South America. The airline continued to grow, and by 1937 was serving the Pacific and carrying 200,000 passengers. *(5)*

The era of transatlantic passenger flights began in 1939, 12 years after the dramatic inaugural flight from the United States to Lisbon, Portugal, and Marseilles, France, by Charles A. Lindbergh. The famous four-engine *Yankee Clipper*, built by Boeing, carried only mail but was followed the next month by passenger service on another Boeing 314 named the *Dixie Clipper*.

Travel on the *Dixie Clipper* was luxurious. Meals were served in a 14-seat dining room complete with formal table settings. Every passenger had a berth, and there was a private suite in the rear. The fare was $375 one way and $675 round trip. *(5)*

## Regulations

Worldwide tourism would be impossible without a system of international air transportation, but this system requires complex negotiations between nations and carriers in the form of bilateral agreements. **Overflight privileges** must be obtained from all countries that will be crossed on transnational flights. Airlines are, or may be, assessed **overflight charges** for the privilege of flying over other countries, including countries that do not have recognized diplomatic relations with each other, as in the case of Cuba and the United States. Landing rights, fuel purchase agreements, maintenance provisions, and many other considerations require bilateral negotiation.

The world's governments have collectively agreed that a completely free market for international air travel is not feasible, at least not at this point in time. The original concept for a worldwide system of airline regulation occurred in what is known as the **Chicago Convention** of 1944 and the Bermuda Agreement of 1946.

The Chicago Convention marked the beginning of continuous dialogue about the various **freedoms of the air**, but was unsuccessful in establishing a multilateral system of commercial aviation rights. The Bermuda Agreement established the initial worldwide model for future bilateral arrangements concerning the exercise of the different freedoms between countries. Examples of the freedoms of the air are given in Figure 12.2. The eight freedoms of the air are as follows: *(6)*

**First Freedom:** The right of an airline to overfly one country to get to another.

**Second Freedom:** The right of an airline to land in another country for a technical stopover (fuel, maintenance, etc.) but not to pick up or drop off traffic.

**Third Freedom:** The right of an airline, registered in country X, to drop off traffic from country X into country Y.

**Fourth Freedom:** The right of an airline, registered in country X, to carry traffic back to country X from country Y.

**Fifth Freedom:** The right of an airline, registered in country X, to collect traffic in country Y and fly on to country Z, so long as the flight either originates or terminates in country X.

**Sixth Freedom:** The right of an airline, registered in country X, to carry traffic to a gateway—a point in country X—and then abroad to a third country. The traffic has neither its origin nor ultimate destination in country X.

**Seventh Freedom:** The right of an airline, registered in country X, to operate entirely outside of country X in carrying traffic between two other countries.

**Eighth Freedom:** The right of an airline, registered in country X, to carry traffic between any two points of country Y. This right is often referred to as **cabotage**. The 8th freedom is generally viewed as an infringement on the rights of domestic carriers.

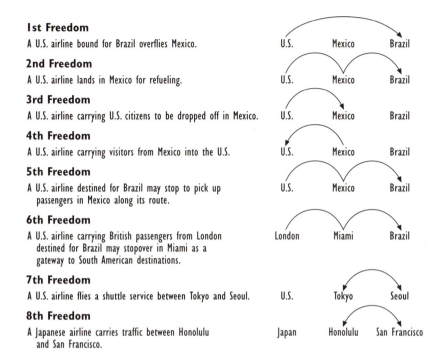

**1st Freedom**

A U.S. airline bound for Brazil overflies Mexico.

**2nd Freedom**

A U.S. airline lands in Mexico for refueling.

**3rd Freedom**

A U.S. airline carrying U.S. citizens to be dropped off in Mexico.

**4th Freedom**

A U.S. airline carrying visitors from Mexico into the U.S.

**5th Freedom**

A U.S. airline destined for Brazil may stop to pick up passengers in Mexico along its route.

**6th Freedom**

A U.S. airline carrying British passengers from London destined for Brazil may stopover in Miami as a gateway to South American destinations.

**7th Freedom**

A U.S. airline flies a shuttle service between Tokyo and Seoul.

**8th Freedom**

A Japanese airline carries traffic between Honolulu and San Francisco.

**Figure 12.2** Examples of "Freedoms of the Air."

Only the first two technical freedoms have gained wide acceptance. The fundamental third and fourth freedoms are also generally granted although nearly always with restrictions on elements such as frequency and points served. The contentious fifth and sixth freedoms remain the subjects of bilateral bargaining. Seventh and eighth freedoms usually are allowed only in special circumstances.

The bilateral air agreement concepts, which emerged from the Chicago meetings, meant that airline service could not be offered between a nation of origin and one of destination unless there was a specific agreement between the two nations as to the details of the service.

Bilateral agreements were established to provide for the orderly development of the international air transportation industry. This meant that three critical areas would be essential parts of bilateral agreements: (1) market participation, (2) capacity and flight frequency, and (3) tariffs.

The purpose of bilateral air agreements was to ensure:

1. Market participation by carriers from each nation. It was thought that airlines might otherwise offer discount fares and extra flights to force competition out of a particular market, which could then lead to international disputes.

2. Economic capacity by preventing duplicate flights and their scheduled frequencies to cover the same territory, which could lead to inefficient use of aircraft by all airlines.

3. A system of tariffs (price controls) to prevent what was regarded as predatory pricing, for example, discount fares in prime markets. *(7)*

The need for bilateral agreements has been intensified by the feeling on the part of small nations that they should have their own national airline or **flag carrier**. A large number of flag carriers are government-owned enterprises. In many cases these airlines are only marginally profitable or are subsidized by the government. They are supported by their governments because of national pride, fear of dependency on foreign airlines, and to ensure air freight for export products. National airlines also provide a means of transporting visitors to support economic growth through tourism development.

As stated previously, U.S. airlines and a few foreign airlines are owned and operated by private enterprises and must operate at a profit. Private carriers are at a disadvantage in competing with government-owned airlines in offering low fares, since government can subsidize the losses of its own carriers.

The use of bilateral air agreements was not sufficient to meet the need for cooperation among international airlines differing in profit orientation. Shortly after the Chicago Conference, a meeting of various scheduled carriers was held in Havana and the International Air Transport Association (IATA) was formed to ensure cooperation among these international carriers. IATA is a voluntary organization, with membership open to any member country of the United Nations. It is supported by dues assessed to 140 active and associate member airlines. This organization also links together with many non-IATA carriers throughout the world in **multinational interline traffic agreements**. These agreements permit passengers to use a single ticket when traveling by two or more carriers throughout the world, as well as facilitate the global movement of air freight.

A primary purpose of IATA has been to establish a system of international rates agreed to by the airlines with the approval of their respective countries. For this reason, many individuals view IATA as a cartel similar to OPEC. IATA also aims to promote worldwide air travel, promote air safety, and act as a clearinghouse for member airlines concerning monies due. The functions of IATA should be distinguished from those of the **International Civil Aviation Organization** (ICAO)—a specialized agency of the United Nations—established to foster cooperation among member nations and to develop and standardize aircraft equipment, training, and planning.

The concept of an orderly market and the controlling forces of bilateral agreements and IATA have come under severe pressure. Many in the industry have called for a revision or dismantling of both. The complaints, which came to a head in the 1970s, led to several carriers dropping out of active IATA membership, causing the organization to lose some of its former impact. *(7)* Five significant forces have been responsible for the mounting criticism of bilateral agreements and IATA; they are

1. *Conflicting national political interests* The nations of the world have become increasingly interdependent; countries actively compete among themselves for the same natural resources and markets, contending with populations and pressures that have often made existing bilateral agreements appear unfair. In some cases, nations have voided these agreements by taking unilateral actions.

2. *Revolutions and wars*  Agreements of any kind between nations have a difficult time surviving when war breaks out or when governments are changed through revolutions. The 1970s and late 1980s was a time of major conflict in many parts of the world; some of these conflicts have continued through present times, disrupting normal air service where conflicts or hostility occur.

3. *Overcapacity*  The introduction of wide-bodied jets meant that the capacity of international airlines to carry passengers and freight worldwide would greatly increase. Load capacity also increased when major airlines began selling used long-range aircraft to developing nations. Through these sales, such long-range aircraft as the Boeing 707, 727, and Douglas DC-8 became available to nations that were previously restricted to relatively short flights by their existing equipment. The increased capacity, however, was not always accompanied by growth in traffic. This resulted in overcapacity in various parts of the world. Under intensely competitive conditions, it was natural for airlines and governments to seek ways to fill as many seats as possible, even if this meant bending or breaking the rules.

4. *Scheduled versus nonscheduled airlines*  The original framework for an orderly international air industry dealt with scheduled airlines. The increasing importance of nonscheduled airlines and charter flights caused considerable confusion and disagreement in the industry. It became difficult to even define these types of air service in a meaningful way. This added to a lessening of the importance of IATA. Bilateral agreements grew more important than multilateral ones.

5. *Sales through wholesalers*  The increasing percentage of business sold in discount package tours by wholesalers has also caused a problem, since these intermediaries are outside the international regulatory framework.

Consequently, IATA's influence in establishing international airfares has diminished, but bilateral agreements between nations are still important aspects of trade negotiations.

## International Air Transportation Competition Act of 1979

In line with deregulation of the domestic airline industry, Congress passed the International Air Transportation Competition Act of 1979. The act was passed in February 1980, encompassing the following ten goals: *(8)*

1. to strengthen the competitive position of U.S. air carriers and to increase profitability;

2. to ensure air carriers the freedom to offer fares and rates that correspond with consumer demand;

3. to reduce restrictions on charter operations;

4. to allow multiple-carrier designations for U.S. airlines, with permissive route authority so that carriers can respond swiftly to shifts in demand;

5. to eliminate operational and marketing restrictions (with respect to capacity and flight frequency);

6. to integrate domestic and international air transportation;

7. to increase the number of nonstop U.S. gateway cities;

International airlines such as Cathay Pacific provide intense competition for U.S. airlines in terms of quality of inflight service and fares.
Courtesy of Cathay Pacific.

8. to provide opportunities for foreign airlines to increase their access to U.S. points if exchanged for benefits of similar magnitude for American carriers with permanent linkage between rights granted and rights given away;

9. to eliminate discrimination and unfair competitive practices against U.S. air carriers in foreign air transportation; and

10. to promote and develop civil aeronautics and a viable, privately-owned U.S. air transport industry.

The passing of this act reaffirmed the U.S. policy of procompetition. Many of the act's policy guidelines have been implemented through liberalized bilateral agreements allowing more U.S. carriers to fly beyond national borders. *(9)* The bilaterals between the U.S. and both Canada and the Netherlands, for instance, are relatively liberal with respect to various provisions of the act.

## Future of International Air Transportation

The direction that international air transportation will take in the future is an important question. The external pressures, which have caused problems with bilateral agreements and IATA, seem to be increasing. Nevertheless, international airlines will remain vital to the continuance of world commerce and tourism. The number of U.S. carriers offering international service, often in competition with one another, has been increasing. Competition across transatlantic routes has always been fierce; and the same is now true for Asia-Pacific routes. Northwest Orient, United Airlines, Continental Airlines, and Delta Airlines have expanded trans-Pacific service from the U.S. mainland to Asian and Pacific destinations. Such Asian/Pacific countries as Japan, Singapore, and Malaysia have been privatizing their national carriers in order to better compete under a deregulated climate. Deregulation has also been adopted by other countries, resulting in more carriers authorized to provide international service. It also should be noted that member countries of the European Union have agreed to a "free market" in aviation.

# AIRLINE MANAGEMENT

The airline business is a tough one, requiring not only decisions made by companies in general, but also some that are peculiar to the airline industry. From 1983–1993, the U.S. scheduled airlines industry incurred losses for six out of the eleven years, and bankruptcies have been occurring. *(10)* The economics of the airline business are not easily understood; there is, first of all, the high capital cost of equipment subject to early physical or technical obsolescence, often before capitalization costs are fully realized. Then there are the problems of regulatory compliance costs, high labor costs not offset by sufficiently high productivity, and the specter of recurring high fuel costs. Not least is the problem of shifting demand on given routes that are affected by seasonality, time of day, day of the week, and competition. Yet, there are few bargains better than an airplane seat today—especially on transatlantic and transpacific long-haul routes, and on U.S. domestic trans-continental routes, where the cost to passengers may be measured in terms of pennies per air mile.

A formula for success in the airline industry lies in achieving a critical balance among four key factors that impact on market demand and profitability. These include route structure, equipment, scheduling, and pricing.

1. *Route structure*   **Route structure** refers to the number, type, and location of markets served by an airline. There are two route structure concepts that are of particular importance in the airline industry: **linear** and **hub-spoke** routes. The concept of linear routes is to schedule the aircraft to fly as great a distance as possible in one direction and then turn around and repeat the flight in the opposite direction. A linear route can have intermediate stops, such as at Denver when flying between Miami and San Francisco. Intermediate stops can allow an airline to generate additional traffic and revenue with limited marginal costs. In many cases, airlines have been forced to adopt a linear route structure because jet aircraft operate most efficiently on long hauls.

   To understand the hub-spoke concept of airline routes, it is necessary to imagine a city as the hub of a wheel. The concept can be viewed on a worldwide basis in which cities are hubs and spokes in a worldwide route system. To illustrate, Lubbock, Texas, serves as a domestic hub city for the small towns and farms that surround it; yet Lubbock serves also as a spoke for the hub city of Dallas. In turn, Dallas serves as a spoke city for Chicago, and Chicago as a spoke for London or Paris. Large airlines are able to combine the concepts of linear and hub-spoke routes.

2. *Equipment*   The high cost of aircraft means that each must be used to the maximum extent permitted. Nor can the cost of ground equipment be ignored in airline management. A rule of thumb in the airline industry is that each jet aircraft requires roughly $1 million in ground support equipment. As the size and complexity of aircraft increase, appropriate ground equipment must be available to match the aircraft. A

decision to service a market with a B-747 or MD 11 will require additional capital outlay for appropriate ground equipment.

Airlines know that the correct type and usage of aircraft is basic to its success. Proper management of aircraft generally necessitates (1) standardizing equipment to permit maximum efficiency in maintenance and repairs; (2) continuous use of equipment with as little downtime as possible for repairs and maintenance, and as little ground time as possible between flights, and (3) proper matching of equipment with markets. An aircraft that is too large or too small to serve a market efficiently leads to real or lost opportunity costs.

3. *Scheduling*    Scheduling refers to the number and hours of flights and the type of equipment assigned to particular routes. This is a complex managerial responsibility that involves the consideration of multiple factors, such as competitive schedules, connecting flights, distances involved, effect on costs, probable air traffic conditions, convenient arrival and departure times, and effect on crew, ground transportation, and other support sectors.

Correct scheduling can mean the difference between profit and loss on a route. It can also mean the difference between happy or unhappy passengers and crews. Improper scheduling can provide a market niche for competitors to exploit. Proper scheduling allows an airline to make maximum use of its existing route structure and equipment and to plan for future routes and equipment, but proper scheduling is not easy even with the assistance of computers.

Scheduling is complicated by the demand for airline space by travelers at certain times of the year. It is often impossible for airlines to supply adequate flights to service markets at such peak travel periods such as Thanksgiving, Christmas, and other holidays or to service resort areas whose business is seasonal. Lack of capacity at peak periods stirs complaints that the airlines are poorly managed or unresponsive to customer needs. The truth is that it is generally impossible for any carrier to handle peak periods without tie-ups and delays. Airlines cannot afford to keep aircraft in reserve or to completely change route schedules to meet peak demands.

4. *Pricing*    Airlines have historically viewed the demand for their services as being relatively inelastic. Deregulation, however, has shown that there are segments of the market that are quite price sensitive. This is especially so with the leisure travel segment where passengers have been known to make travel decisions based heavily on price. The leisure segment is now more than 50% of the domestic U.S. market. Even business travelers are seeking lower fares to minimize their travel costs.

As was the intent, a positive effect of discount pricing is increased utilization of seat capacity. Discount fares led to multiple-tiered pricing, and as many as 100 different fares can exist for a popular route. Discounted fares are also encumbered with such restrictions as advance purchase requirements and penalties for itinerary changes or penalties for cancellations.

Typically, the larger the discount the greater the number of restrictions that apply. The average percentage of seats on airplanes that have been filled with paid (revenue) passengers is referred to as the **load factor.** With discount fares, the load factor increased from about 50% to 62%, but the downside is lower yield. In order to minimize the negative aspect of discount pricing, airlines developed yield management programs to ensure that revenues for each flight would cover its operating costs. This is done by controlling the number of seats which could be sold at discounted fares on each flight. Within the industry, discounted fares are referred to as **capacity-controlled fares**, indicating that only a limited number of seats on each flight are available at the discounted fare.

## Airline Expenses versus Revenues

Management practices within the airline industry are shaped by tight cost and revenue structures, which in turn affect their pricing and marketing policies toward other members of the travel industry and airline passengers.

U.S. airlines receive the majority of their income from passengers; revenue from freight, mail, and other sources is minor by comparison. Personnel cost is the largest expense item. The second largest cost is for fuel. Airlines have little control over fuel costs other than to use fuel conservation techniques and fuel efficient equipment whenever possible. Individual airlines negotiate fuel contracts with suppliers, and some have been able to negotiate somewhat better contracts than others.

Airlines also have only limited control over personnel costs. The industry is heavily unionized, and management must deal with a variety of unions. The entry of many non-union air carriers operating at lower costs has placed added pressure on major carriers to look at labor costs. In recent years, airlines have been able to gain substantial concessions from unions, including two-tiered wage structures which provide lower wages for new employees and changes in work rules. Airlines continue to automate and to reduce labor as much as possible, but this is never an easy task where customers want service and public safety is always a factor. A summary of costs and revenues for U.S. scheduled airlines is shown in Table 12.2. Most recently, airlines have resorted to increasing the number of part-time employees who receive fewer benefits than full-time employees and to contracting out such services as food service and baggage handling.

# ℱORCES AFFECTING THE FUTURE OF THE AIR TRANSPORTATION INDUSTRY

As discussed previously, the airline industry has grown substantially since the end of World War II. The industry is expected to continue to be one of the fastest growing sectors of the world economy. This section discusses the factors that are likely to affect the future of the air transportation industry.

## Deregulation

From 1978 to 1985, the U.S. airline industry has gone through three phases. *(11)* The first was the growth of regional carriers to serve the more profitable medium-haul routes

**TABLE 12.2**

**Operating Revenues and Expenses for U.S. Scheduled Airlines in 1993**

| Operating Revenues | Dollars (thousands) |
|---|---|
| Passenger | 63,950,548 |
| Freight and express | 6,320,531 |
| Mail | 6,242,222 |
| Charter | 3,045,294 |
| Public service revenue | 3,104 |
| Other | 9,230,032 |
| **Total Operating Revenues** | **83,791,731** |
| **Operating Expenses** | **Dollars (thousands)** |
| Flying operations | 23,447,637 |
| Maintenance | 8,945,641 |
| Passenger service | 7,416,358 |
| Aircraft and traffic servicing | 13,106,737 |
| Promotion and sales | 14,697,703 |
| Administrative | 4,211,398 |
| Transport related | 5,849,234 |
| Depreciation and amortization | 4,683,010 |
| **Total Operating Expenses** | **82,357,718** |
| **Operating Income or (Loss)** | **$1,434,013** |
| **Other Expenses** | **Dollars (thousands)** |
| Interest expense | 2,023,596 |
| Income taxes | 181,480 |
| Other | 1,366,659 |
| Net profit or (loss) | $(2,137,659) |

*Source:* Air Transport Association. *(10)*

and major carriers exiting from unprofitable low-traffic, low-yield routes. The second phase saw the entry of new, low-cost, no-frill airlines such as New York Air, People Express, and Midway to tap into high-traffic corridors and regional market segments. In the face of new competition from regional airlines and new entrants, the third phase occurred when the major airlines—American, Delta, and United—developed aggressive competitive strategies, offering lower fares, better service, and more efficient operation to match the lower costs of new entrants, along with frequent flyer programs to increase customer loyalty.

## Travel Industry Offers More Self-serve Options

Many business travelers say it's lonely on the road. Well, it's going to get lonelier.

Those laying the groundwork predict that within a few years, sophisticated travelers will be able to take an entire trip without dealing with travel service employees, except flight attendants.

For instance, United Airlines is installing machines to issue boarding passes and record frequent flier numbers for its shuttle service on the West Coast. Travelers who have already purchased tickets through an on-line service can walk up to one of the machines and insert a credit card. A diagram displays the plane's seating and fliers touch the screen where they want to sit.

Electronic ticketing—or ticketless travel—is already being used by United, ValuJet, and Southwest. Travelers show identification at the airport to get a boarding pass. United plans to make the service available throughout its system on September 18 for those who want ticketless travel.

Delta shuttle fliers on the East Coast can use a Smart Card, similar to a credit card, to buy tickets. The card contains a computer chip with enough information to create a shuttle reservation, credit the passenger's frequent- flier account and charge the flight to the flier's credit card. But a Delta agent has to swipe the card through a Delta machine. So you have to stand in line anyway.

Even travel agencies such as American Express and Carlson Wagonlit Travel are developing software that will let travelers make their own travel plans by computer.

Jim Yasinski, vice president of American Express management Services, says AmEx is rolling out a voice-recognition reservation system. The product, scheduled to hit the market next year, will let travelers make their own airline and eventually car rental and hotel reservations by phone 24 hours a day—without a computer.

"It's time for a new level of service," Yasinski says, "The technology exists and it's moving rapidly."

—Keith L. Alexander

Since 1985, the U.S. airline industry has consolidated and there are only nine major airlines today: American, United, Delta, U.S. Air, Northwest, Continental, America West, Alaska, and Southwest Airlines. The five largest airlines control almost three-fourths of all air traffic. After many successive years of losses, a number of factors have contributed to the airlines' return to profitability in 1995. These factors encompass the completion of restructuring from the airline mergers which took place during the 1990s, cost efficiencies from workforce downsizing and union concessions, successful yield management programs and aggressive off-peak pricing to stimulate air travel, code sharing/joint marketing agreements with international carriers to tap new long haul markets, the capping of commissions to travel agents, and not least, significant growth in air traffic over the past decade.

The total effect of deregulation regarding competition in the pricing, marketing, and distribution of airline services is still evolving and will continue through the 1990s until the industry can fully adjust to all of these changes.

## New Aircraft and Technology

The concept of hypersonic aircraft is being studied by aircraft designers and manufacturers. These airplanes would be designed to cruise at speeds of 4,000 mph, or six times the speed of sound; travel at altitudes of 120,000 feet; and carry some 200 passengers. They would be able to fly from New York to London in under 2 hours or from Los Angeles to Tokyo in 2 hours and 18 minutes. The hypersonic aircraft would be more advanced than the supersonic aircraft, as represented by the Concorde, which cruises at just over 1,450 mph. Although the idea of a hypersonic aircraft is exciting to contemplate, whether there would ever be a commercial market for it is debatable.

## Internationalization of Tourism

The world has become travel and tourism conscious, with many countries having developed new resort destinations to attract the international visitor. The international tourist

## *A* New Era For Aircraft

Good morning, ladies and gentlemen, and welcome aboard the Orient Express, Flight 107 from Los Angeles to Tokyo. Our flying time will be two hours. We regret that the aircraft has no windows, but we hope you will enjoy the panoramic view of earth from 110,000 feet on the TV monitor at the front of the cabin. When we have reached our cruising speed of Mach 5, our cabin staff will be serving you beverages; there will be no time for a meal. During our ascent and descent we do ask that you remain strapped in your reclining chairs. These are specially designed to help your body cope with the G-forces acting on it during acceleration and deceleration. And now, lie back and enjoy your flight...

*Source: Newsweek. (12)*

market is critical to countries that need export exchange for internal development. Pressure will likely be placed on governments to ensure the growth of international air travel to support the health and continuing development of the travel industry. Additionally, expanded air transport is also critical in providing a new and faster mechanism for distributing goods and commodities, as well as passenger services, throughout the world.

## Unsafe Conditions

Additional air traffic means crowded airports and crowded skies. Crowding creates conditions for accidents. Many airports throughout the world are in need of major improvements or relocation. Indeed, the insufficiency of airport and airway capacity has allowed an average of only 1% annual growth in air carrier operations in the last 17 years. Looking toward the future, if the present course continues, some 65 major airports will reach and exceed their designed capacity before the year 2000.

In recent years, hijacking and terrorism have also made air travel less safe, but the number of incidents is very minimal when compared to the total number of flights flown worldwide. Airport checks and more effective airline safety procedures are continually introduced by carriers and airport authorities or imposed by governments to counter the threat of terrorism.

# SUMMARY

The brief history of worldwide air travel has shown remarkable growth. Despite some current problems within the industry, no other viable system of transportation exists for long-haul travel at present. Unless there are major unforeseen world catastrophes—a major war or a worldwide depression—it is certain that the visions of the early commercial aviation pioneers to establish safe, convenient, and affordable air transportation to serve the general public will become a reality for greater numbers of people around the world.

Having now examined all the various modes of transportation—water, land, and air—students can better understand why all of them face future uncertainties, given the variables of high fixed capital and operating costs, price competition between carriers and modes of transport, regulatory changes, and/or changes within the marketing environment. The transportation component of the travel industry is currently in a transition stage from which only the most competitive companies are likely to survive by offering better services at prices that travelers are willing to pay. The competition in price and service quality, in turn, will foster growth in future traffic.

# DISCUSSION QUESTIONS

1. How did World War II promote the growth of the commercial airline industry?

2. What were some of the changes in aircraft technology during the 1980s?

3. Which government agencies regulate the U.S. airline industry? What are the functions of each agency?

4. What are the various classifications of commercial airlines in the United States?

5. What are the eight freedoms of the air? Which ones have been universally accepted?

6. What was the purpose of bilateral air agreements?

7. What are primary problems facing international airlines? How does IATA fit into the picture?

8. What basic managerial problems are common to members of the airline industry?

9. What is the major source of revenues for airlines? What are the largest expense items for airlines?

10. Which forces are likely to affect the future of air transportation?

11. What are some of the new self-serve options offered to air travelers?

# SUGGESTED STUDENT EXERCISE

## JAL Details New Service to the Big Island of Hawaii

Short Case Analysis

Japan Airlines has begun publicizing the thrice-weekly schedule it plans to launch in April between Tokyo's Narita Airport and Keahole Airport on the Big Island. The nonstop flight will take seven hours and 25 minutes. "Many Japanese tourists are now seeking more variety and are visiting Hawaii's neighbor islands as well as Oahu," JAL said in its January newsletter announcing the addition of Kona as its second Hawaii destination.

JAL said it plans to offer executive class and economy class service on Boeing 747-300 aircraft. The flights will leave Tokyo on Mondays, Thursdays and Sundays, and return to Japan via Honolulu on Mondays, Tuesdays and Fridays.

U.S. transportation officials have not given final approval for the service. United Airlines has recommended denial of JAL's application because of United's difficulties getting Japanese government clearance for a flight from Osaka to Seoul.

Additional information

| Visitor Traffic and Room Inventory of Hawaiian Islands | | | |
|---|---|---|---|
| **Islands Visited** | **1994 Islands** | **Available Rooms** | **# of Properties** |
| Oahu | 4,718,940 | 37,032 | 208 |
| Maui | 2,240,600 | 18,443 | 208 |
| Big Island | 1,059,140 | 9,490 | 150 |
| Kauai | 846,070 | 4,631 | 121 |
| Lanai | 78,840 | 367 | 5 |
| Molokai | 78,150 | 579 | 9 |

| Source of Visitors to Hawaii (All Islands) | |
|---|---|
| **Visitor Source** | **1994 Visitors** |
| United States | 3,602,150 |
| Japan | 1,756,340 |
| Canada | 313,760 |
| Australia | 105,070 |
| Korea | 112,440 |
| Germany | 94,040 |
| U.K. | 82,090 |
| Other Foreign | 389,270 |
| *Source:* Hawaii Visitors Bureau, 1994. | |

Questions

1. Keeping in mind the eight air freedoms, is Japan's request for approval of non-stop service to Kona similar or different from United's request to fly from Osaka to Seoul. Why?

2. Which of the eight freedoms would be in effect if JAL was allowed to provide air service between Kona and Honolulu?

3. The Big Island's Kona Airport currently receives no non-stops flights from foreign countries. What airport infrastructure changes will be warranted should JAL's request be approved?

4. List positive and negative effects, including impact on local carriers, of the proposed non-stop service for airline's servicing the Big Island versus the rest of the state if JAL's proposed non-stop flight to Kona is approved.

5. Considering the data on tourist traffic, source of visitors, and room inventory, would the Big Island be able to handle an expanded volume of visitors?

# REFERENCES

1. Waters, S. R. *Travel Industry World Yearbook: The Big Picture 1994–95*. New York: Child & Waters, 1994.

2. *The Economic Benefits of Air Transport*. Prepared for The Air Transport Action Group by International Air Transport Association. Geneva: IATA Centre, ca. 1992.

3. Kane, R. M., and A. D. Vose. *Air Transportation*. 6th ed. Dubuque, Iowa: Kendall/Hunt Publishing Co., 1979.

4. Pan Am; 1927–1991, *Air Transport World*, Feb. 1992, Vol. 29, No. 2.

5. *The First 50 Years of Pan Am, The Story of Pan American World Airways, Inc. from 1927–1977*. New York: Pan American World Airways, Inc., 1977.

6. Gidwitz, B. *The Politics of International Air Transport*. Lexington, Mass.: D. C. Heath and Company, 1980.

7. *Reason in the Air*. International Air Transport Association.

8. *International Air Transportation Competition Act of 1979*. 94 Statute 35, 1980.

9. Toh, R. S. and N. S. Shubat. "The Impact and Effectiveness of the International Air Transportation Competition Act of 1979." *Transportation Journal 25*, No. 2 (1985).

10. Air Transport Association. The Annual Report of the U.S. Scheduled Airline Industry. 1994.

11. Levere, J. "Like Caesar's Gaul, The Changeover's in Three Parts." *Travel Weekly's Focus on Deregulation* (May 31, 1985).

12. "L.A. to Tokyo in Two Hours." *Newsweek* (December 16, 1985).

# Part 6

# *H*ospitality
# and Related Services

# Chapter 13

# *A*ccommodations

## LEARNING OBJECTIVES

- To understand the structure of the accommodations or lodging industry.
- To appreciate the historic development of the hotel industry in the twentieth century.
- To become familiar with the terminology of the lodging industry.
- To be acquainted with the common forms of management practices in the lodging industry.
- To understand the critical factors in the selection of a hotel management company.
- To be aware of alternative forms of lodging and accommodations.
- To define and use the following terms:

| | |
|---|---|
| Advance deposit | Central reservation service |
| All suite hotels | Commercial rate |
| Amenity spas | Confirmed reservation |
| Aparthotel | Convention rate |
| Atrium design | Corporate rate |
| Bed & Breakfast | Crew rate |
| Break-even point | Deeded ownership system |
| Cabana | Deposit waiver |

Double

Double-double

Duplex

Efficiency unit

Elderhostel

Executive floors

Family plan

Fixed cost

Flat rate

Franchise

Franchise rights

Franchisee

Franchisor

Grand luxe hotel

Guarantee of deposit

Guaranteed payment
reservations

Health spa

Holistic learning centers

Homestay

Hospitality suites

Hotel garni

Hotel management contract

Interval ownership

Junior suite

Kitchenette

Lanai

Management contract

No-shows

Overbooking

Owner-operated system

Parador

Parlor

Pension

Penthouse suite

Resort condominium

Revenue management

Right-to-use system

Run of the house rate

Sample room

Schloss

Semivariable costs

Single

Star rating system

Strategic relationships

Studio

Suite

Tiered pricing

Time sharing

Turnkey operations

Twin

Twin double

Variable costs

Voluntary chain

Walking

Weekend rate

Youth hostel

# *T*HE LODGING INDUSTRY

*T*he accommodations or lodging sector is a dominant industry within the travel industry. Besides the revenue directly generated by hotels and motels, these enterprises also support millions of jobs, plus hundreds of thousands of related jobs held by consultants, accountants, architects, and others who provide support services and supplies.

There is no other sector of the travel industry more international in nature than the lodging industry. North American hotel chains are located throughout most of the free world. Likewise, European and Asian hotel chains have expanded beyond their own continents to operate hotels throughout the world.

## Overview of the Development of the Hotel Industry in the 20th Century

The early 1900s until the Great Depression of the 1930s was the era of the **Grand Luxe Hotel**. During this era, the Plaza was built in New York City on what is still today considered the best single-site location in the world. Caesar Ritz created his elegant Ritz Hotel in Paris, which became the prototype for later Ritz-Carltons in London and Madrid, followed by New York and Boston. The Plaza in New York City was called " the greatest hotel in the world" when it opened in 1907. It cost $12 million to build, considered an unprecedented sum for a hotel at that time. Just as the Great Depression started, the plush Waldorf-Astoria on New York's Park Avenue opened in 1931, fulfilling the dream of its creator, Lucius Boomer, and remains today as one of the great hotel properties of the world. Few now remember that this Waldorf-Astoria was not the original, but the second; the original hotel was built at the turn of the century on the present site of the Empire State building. The 1930s were a disastrous time for industry and business. Bankruptcies abounded, claiming the Waldorf as one of the early victims of the depression, as insurance companies and other financial institutions became disillusioned with hotel investments—a disenchantment that was to last until long after World War II.

After World War II, Conrad Hilton perceived that there was a pent-up demand for hotel rooms and leased the 2,000-room Stevens Hotel in Chicago, which had been used by the military. In quick succession, he then acquired the Palmer House in Chicago, the Plaza and the Waldorf in New York, and the Town House in Los Angeles. He soon added other large hotels and brought about a merger between Hilton and Statler in the 50s, the first major chain of modern U.S. hotels. Ernest Henderson did the same with Sheraton. These first modern chains ruled the commercial hotel market until Hyatt and its grand **atrium design** came along in 1967 with the opening of the Atlanta Hyatt Regency, reintroducing the open core architecture of many luxury properties of the late 1800s.

Another major development was the evolution of the standardized roadside motel by Kemmons Wilson, founder of the Holiday Inn chain. Holiday Inns represented the first of the economy-priced accommodations for the ordinary traveler who wanted comfortable and clean rooms without frills. This was the most revolutionary development in the U.S. hotel industry during the 1950s and 1960s, following the burgeoning interstate highway system.

The original Waldorf. The Waldorf opened on March 23, 1893 at Fifth Avenue and 33rd St. On the right, at Fifth Ave. and 34th St., The Astoria was erected on November 1, 1897. The hotel then became The Waldorf-Astoria.
Courtesy of the Waldorf-Astoria.

Overseas postwar hotel development took quite a different course. Along with transatlantic air travel came the beginning of international business and tourism travel. During the era of the grand hotel, air travel was not yet a major factor. People traveled abroad by ship and stayed for long periods of time. With the coming of commercial air travel, the new travelers were a breed apart from the previous generation of class-conscious tourists. They were also more numerous, and developing countries were anxious to attract them. It was not surprising that the first large postwar hotels were government owned or assisted. The first of these, the Caribbean Hilton, was built by a government development company that persuaded a reluctant Conrad Hilton to operate it on a virtually risk-free basis through an instrument known as the **hotel management contract**. The contract separated hotel operations from property ownership, allowing a hotel company to bid for the right to manage a property for a fee plus other considerations. This launched Hilton on a course that led to the first major postwar hotel chain abroad.

The present Waldorf-Astoria is located on Park Avenue occupying one square block between E. 49th and E. 50th Streets.
Courtesy of the Waldorf-Astoria.

Hilton's objectives were to provide a comfortable place for foreign business people to stay and do business and to lure vacationers to Puerto Rico's warm climate and beaches. The Caribbean Hilton was a landmark in hotel engineering, being the first hotel in the world with central air conditioning and automatic elevators. The Inter-Continental hotel chain was developed by Pan American Airways during this same decade but was limited to locations supporting the airline's route structure. The initial purpose of an airline-owned hotel chain was to serve the customers of the carrier and the hotels were mostly viewed as subsidiary operations.

In the 1960s, both tourism and business travel accelerated with the jet age as travel became faster, cheaper, and more available. Big, modern hotels were developed in London, Paris, Rome, Athens, Hong Kong, and Tokyo. It was not until the 1970s that many large full-service hotels were built in the United States. The atrium design in hotels, introduced by architect John Portman, gave a substantial boost to Hyatt, whose dynamic marketing and operational style quickly became popular. Hilton, Sheraton, and Westin

Atlanta's Hyatt Regency: Rebirth of the Roman atruim concept in modern hotels.
Courtesy of the Hyatt Regency Atlanta.

opened new, large, convention hotels. Airport hotels also entered the scene in a big way. Marriott branched out from its industrial catering and restaurant base to become a leader in establishing smaller, comfortable mid-priced hotels in locations away from the city center, such as suburban regional office areas. The wave of new hotel and motel building during the decades of the 1970s and 1980s resulted in over-capacity and depressed occupancies in all but a few key U.S. cities.

## The International Hotel Business

The lodging industry is truly international. Management placement, lodging concepts, financing, and marketing systems are borderless. Hotel and resort managers for major hotel chains, as a rule, may expect multiple transfers to different properties and/or countries over the course of their career. Career opportunities have never been better for truly international managers who speak two or more major languages and have the ability to adapt to foreign environments.

The growth of international travel affects hotels everywhere as lodging generally accounts for 20–30% of total visitor expenditures. Total U.S. receipts from international tourism grew 15% in 1993 to a total of nearly $64 billion. This was the largest increase ever recorded for a single country in a year. *(1)* Data from Tourism Canada shows that the visitor mix of Canadian resorts are 60% Canadian and 40% foreign. By contrast, U.S. resorts had a mix of 91% American and 9% foreign. *(2)* However, the mix of domestic guests to international varies widely by states. Hawaii, for instance, had a mix of resort guests similar to Canada's—54% domestic to 46% foreign in 1995.

The World Travel and Tourism Council estimated that the travel industry generated income of $3.5 trillion in 1993 and forecasted that employment in travel and tourism would increase 50% faster than in any other industry. *(3)* An international industry of this magnitude naturally attracts great interest in cross-border investment and growth.

Well-known international hotel brands such as Hyatt, Omni, Sheraton, Hilton, Holiday Inn, Marriott, Meridien, Forte, Four Seasons, and many others have entered this field. All Nippon Airways, for instance, operates a subsidiary—ANA Hotels—and is determined to make its chain a major player in the international lodging sector. This chain has selected market sites in North America, Europe, Asia, and Australia. *(4)*  Country Lodging by Carlson has become one of the fastest growing hotel brands in the world. *(5)* Chinese investors from Hong Kong, Singapore, and Taiwan have been purchasing U.S. hotels, while investors from many other countries, including the U.S., have entered former communist nations to develop hotels. *(6)* Choice Hotels International received nearly 60% of its growth outside the U.S. in 1993, with a presence in 30 countries and plans to double the number of its international hotels by the year 2000. *(7)*

**Strategic relationships** between partners such as Radisson Hotels International and SAS International Hotels are increasingly being utilized. The Radisson/SAS relationship gives SAS the right to develop and run Radisson Hotels in Europe and gives Radisson the right to market SAS and Radisson hotels throughout the world. *(8)* Strategic relationships between many different partners will probably increase in importance in the international lodging industry.

Training will also assume new importance as international chains work to develop common corporate cultures spanning transnational business interests. Nikko Hotels International, for example, built an executive conference center in its Manhattan headquarters for use in training its management personnel from around the world. The facility provides a high-tech training environment with breakout rooms, videotaping, ergonomic furniture, electronic whiteboards, and remote controlled devices. *(9)*

## Accommodating the Discriminating Travelers

The demand for hotel space by the business traveler has usually been considered to be relatively inelastic. It is the conventional wisdom that the top business executive does not select a hotel on the basis of price, but more for the hotel's location, service, and prestige. As an executive climbs the corporate ladder, the address and status of the hotel accommodating the executive seems to gain in importance. Today, many hotel companies have discovered that old hotels located in prime city areas can be restored or remodeled and turned into prestige hotels for the top-of-the-market segment. These hotels have a certain

Originally built as a luxury apartment on Nob Hill in 1913, the Stanford Court was transformed into an elegant hotel in the early 70s. The spacious lobby features a Tiffany-style stained glass dome and scenic murals depicting old San Francisco.
Courtesy of the Stouffer Renaissance Stanford Court Hotel.

cachet and flavor attributed in part to the architectural taste of an earlier age, and in part to their traditional service reputation. The Copley Plaza in Boston, the Hemsley Palace in New York, and the Stanford Court in San Francisco are three examples of many such restored hotels located in major cities throughout the country. *(10)* The hotel industry has come full circle with the best of the new and restoration of the best of the old—largely done to attract the patronage of the discriminating traveler.

The Kimco Hotel and Restaurant Management Company is an example of a lodging company that refurbishes older properties to serve a niche market. Kimco has 18 hotels and 21 restaurants in U. S. West Coast cities, operating in older buildings that are refurbished as intimate European-style hotels. The company advertises their hotels as offering "affordable elegance." *(11)*

## Lodging Evolution to Meet Changing Traveler's Needs

The variety of rooms offered throughout history were developed in response to customer needs. As social and business needs change, the style of hotel rooms must also change. Astute managers remain ahead of competition by developing and testing new concepts in rooms to meet needs of particular market segments. Hyatt Hotel, for instance, popularized the concept of a "hotel within a hotel;" that is, an **executive floor** with special amenities and "butler service," including a separate check-in/check-out facility for their guests. Executive floors may be found in 20% of the hotels in the United States.

More recently, **all suite hotels** have been developed to meet the needs of travelers seeking a more homelike environment and superior value in terms of space and amenities. Marriott, for example, introduced its new Courtyard concept hotels in 1985, offering travelers the space and amenities of junior suites at moderate rates. In some cases, new room concepts required design and engineering changes. In others, they required little more than the addition or deletion of the furnishings and limited remodeling.

As the traveler composition changes, lodging establishments have recognized changing needs and adapt to meet them. Currently, the industry is building to accommodate the growing needs of the budget and midscale hotel users. There travelers are cost conscious and comfort minded, but less space conscious. The important things are queen-size beds, large six-foot desks, full-size tub and showers, generous closets, and proper outlets for laptops. The special needs of niche markets are also recognized by hotel operators. Travelers from Australia, New Zealand, and the United Kingdom, for example, typically want complimentary coffee and tea amenities in the room; and many hotels will provide this service gratis as part of their mini-bar setup. For Islamic travelers who may have forgotten to pack a prayer rug, some hotels will provide such upon request; and hotels catering to large number of Muslims may even have a special prayer room somewhere on the property.

Technology is becoming an important part of everyday life, and all travelers in the future will expect to find this technology available in their hotel rooms. The following is a list of the technological improvements that corporate travel and meeting planners, for instance, want to see in hotels: *(12)*

- Modular phone jacks
- Modem ports
- Proper wiring for fax transmission
- Proper wiring for quick communications on the Internet or World Wide Web
- Call waiting with custom messages
- Automated message systems
- Capability to use picture phones
- Multimedia video units

While these innovations appear to be skewed towards business travelers, they will eventually be a factor in attracting and serving the next generation of leisure travelers as well.

# Hotel of the Future

Technological advances in information and communications will cause hotels to make dramatic changes in the way they serve and physically accommodate guests. It is a certainty that interactive computing and multimedia devices will be as commonplace in hotel rooms of the future as present-day remote control televisions and touch-tone telephones. Guests will want the option of avoiding interaction with hotel service and clerical personnel by using these devices. To place a room service order, book a restaurant reservation, call for additional towels or personal laundry pickup, or order a shoeshine, all the guest must do is to touch a few icons on his/her television screen.

Technological advancements may alter the physical design and space allocation of hotels in the future. Quite possibly, a computing and multimedia room will be required on every floor of a full-service property. Possibly, the amount and size of meeting rooms and auditoriums will change as guests, wishing to participate in large conferences from the comfort and convenience of their guest rooms, may wish to use interactive video conference devices and remote response terminals to participate.

Direct guest room linkages to a wide variety of online entertainment and informational networks will be a standard requirement in the future. This could mean large access fees for hotels. Rental or usage charges for peripheral devices could also mean big business.

The entire hotel organizational and operational structure may change as a result of technological innovation. Front office functions could be minimized or eliminated. Universal service representatives could tend to virtually every guest need from a single work station. Since guests may initiate many service functions directly through interactive devices, the resources for service staffing could be rechanneled to more productive activities, such as better execution of guest requests. This also holds true for many back office functions. Through better use of technology, many of the clerical functions presently performed in the back offices of hotels may be eliminated.

*Source:* Francis J. Nardozza, Partner, National Hospitality Industry Director, KPMG Peat Marwick, LLP.

The increasing number of professional women who travel has also created change. A study of men and women business travelers revealed that men rated business services and facilities as more important than women. *(13)* Women were concerned about security, personal services, and low price. Fax machines and suites were more important to men than to women. Women rated the importance of in-room hair dryers, irons, ironing boards, room service, and bathrobes more highly than men. Men were more likely than women to use telephones in the bathroom. Both sexes rated sprinkler systems and electronic card keys as being equal in importance. On-going consumer preference studies of this nature are invaluable in helping the industry to keep abreast of changing guest needs and desires.

### Sports and Related Amenities

Motels and hotels have long featured swimming pools as a vital part of their amenities. In recent years, many have begun to emulate resort hotels in providing other sports-related facilities, such as tennis courts, squash courts, ice skating rinks, spas, and fitness centers. The costs of developing and maintaining recreational and sports facilities for hotel guests have become increasingly high. These cost factors are important considerations for hotels in financing development, marketing, and establishing room rates.

### Hotels and Airlines Relationship

Pan American World Airways was the first to realize the importance of linking airplane seats with hotel rooms. In the early years of air travel, adequate hotel facilities did not exist for international airline passengers and crew in many of the foreign nations served by Pan Am. It was from necessity that Pan Am entered the international hotel business, with the opening of the airline's first hotel in Belem, Brazil, in 1949. *(14)* With the subsequent addition of other hotels abroad, the large chain of Inter-Continental Hotels grew and was successfully operated as a subsidiary business until its sale by Pan Am in 1982 to Grand Metropolitan PLC, a British corporation, for $500 million.

Today, the only U.S. airline that owns a hotel is Northwest and that is a single property in Tokyo. Many foreign carriers, however, continue to own hotels. For example, KLM has a 25% share of Golden Tulip Hotels. Air India and Icelandair own and operate hotels. Japan Airlines and All Nippon Airways both own hotels, as does Finnair and SAS. Air France is the majority shareholder in the Meridian Hotel chain. *(15)*

Some airlines owning hotels also offer and promote their own tours, which will include the carrier's hotels in the package. The airline's tour department and the establishment of special reservation services help to promote the hotel division. Despite such apparent advantages, the ownership of hotels by airlines has often shown poor financial results. Although hotels and airlines share some common grounds in marketing, operational logistics and controls—yield management being one such area—there are also many dissimilarities. The skills and knowledge appropriate for managing an airline have not always been compatible with that of running a successful chain of hotels.

## Hotel Definitions, Classifications, and Terms

### Defining a Hotel

Many terms are used to describe lodging facilities in the United States and other countries, but the distinction between them has become blurred. Several of the terms in common usage include "hotel," "motel," "motor hotel," "motor lodge," and "inn." Holiday Inns, Inc., once referred to itself as an innkeeper, yet customers know it as a chain consisting of hotels and motels. It has since dropped the word "inn" from its corporate name and is now known as Holiday Corporation. Motels are sometimes described as not offering bell desk service, yet many motels do offer this service. Originally, one of the distinguishing features of a motel was that it offered convenient, complimentary self-parking for guests. This is still largely true, but some of the larger hotels now have parking lots or garages not unlike those offered by a motel, and parking will be validated at special rates for registered guests. In short, there is probably no single characteristic that serves as a true distinguishing factor for any of the types of lodging.

Members of the lodging industry have recognized that the exact definition of any term is less important than the image it portrays. If a chain feels that the term "inn" connotes a feeling of warmth and friendliness, it may select that nomenclature. If the term "hotel" (originating from the Old French word for hostel, which also means inn), portrays an image of efficiency, service, amenities, and convenient city location, it will be used by chains desiring that image. It is also highly probable that new terms, for example, "airportel" and "condotel," will be coined to complement future developments in travel and tourism.

In other parts of the world, terms used to describe lodging facilities may take on different connotations. In large parts of Latin America the term motel refers to a place patronized by couples who stay for only a few hours, while in Asia and the Far East, motels are virtually unknown.

The term **hotel garni**, also known as **aparthotel** is used to describe smaller commercial European hotels without dining facilities, with the possible exception of a breakfast room for serving continental breakfast—rolls, coffee and fruit juice. Throughout Europe, the terms inn and lodge tend to reflect, to a far greater degree than do their counterparts in the United States, the romantic concepts of these places.

## Hotel Classifications

There are different ways to classify hotels. One way is by location, such as center city, suburb, airport, highway, or destination resort. Another way is by type of property or product; for example, casino hotel, convention hotel, or all suite hotel (see Figure 13.1). For many customers, a more meaningful classification is one based on price, with the presumption that price is related to the quality of facilities and service provided. Price-based classification is more or less the system adopted by the market in the United States, where hotels are categorized as economy or budget, standard or midscale, first class or deluxe.

The classification of hotels is more formal in Europe and other parts of the world, based on a rating system. The **star rating system** seems the best established and its adoption is increasing. The idea for star classification was borrowed from the rating system used for brandy; the higher the number of stars (to a maximum of five), the better the brandy. *(16)* In the case of hotels, stars are assigned according to the quality of restaurants, rooms, amenities, and service. For instance, a five-star hotel is usually a deluxe hotel with top restaurants, fine service, and rooms with private baths. A first-class hotel rating with one or two stars would actually be one of medium range, comfortable with above average service; most rooms will have private baths. A second-class, tourist or

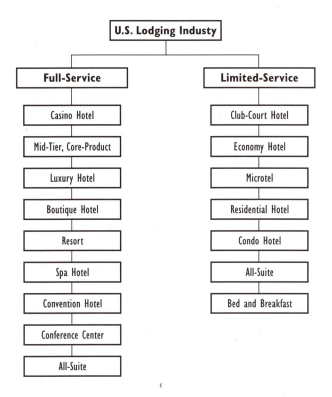

**Figure 13.1**  Hotel products, segmented by facility/service levels.
*Source:*  PKF Consulting.

economy hotel would be a commercial type, often having rooms without private baths. It would be unlikely to merit any stars.

## Accommodations Terms

A number of standard terms are used in the lodging industry to describe types of room accommodations. *(17)* Most of these terms originated in the U.S. and have universal application. The term **single** is used to describe a room for one person. It does not necessarily imply that a single-sized bed will be in the room. In fact, one often finds queen or even king-sized beds in these rooms. A **double room** is a room with one large bed for two persons. Consequently, many single rooms could also serve as a double. The term **twin** is used for a room with two single beds, and a **twin-double** is a room with two double beds. This room may also be referred as a **family room** or a **double-double**.

At one time the word **parlor** was widely used in America to describe a room used in a home for sitting or entertaining guests. This corresponds with the way the word is used today in the hotel business to designate a sitting room adjoining a bedroom. A parlor in a hotel may also be used as a sleeping room by containing a fold-away bed or pull-out couch, in which case it is known as a **studio**.

The **suite** is considered to be the best room in the hotel and is also the most expensive. A suite usually has one or more bedrooms and a parlor. It may also contain a wet bar, more than one bathroom, a small kitchen, and other facilities. A suite that separates into two stories joined by stairs is known as a **duplex**. Some hotels offer a **penthouse suite** opening onto the roof, perhaps with its own rooftop garden, solarium, swimming pool, tennis court, or other amenity. The **junior suite**, which describes a large room divided by an entertainment area and a sleeping space, is becoming increasingly popular in hotels around the world.

In the tropics and in resort hotels the terms **lanai** and **cabana** are often used. A lanai is sometimes thought to mean only an outside sitting area attached to a room, but in hotel terminology it refers to a room with a balcony, a patio, or both, overlooking a landscaped area or a scenic view, for instance, an "ocean lanai." These rooms typically are among the most popular in a resort hotel and also among the most expensive. A cabana typically is a room that faces a swimming pool. Cabanas are often physically separated from the rest of the hotel, but still located on the hotel grounds.

The term **efficiency unit** is sometimes used in the lodging industry to describe a room with limited kitchen facilities, or **kitchenette**.

Certain rooms in a hotel may be designed to serve the needs of commercial travelers. A **sample room**, for example, is used by salespeople to display their merchandise or to set up company exhibits. Such rooms may also be used by recruiters for interviewing purposes. These rooms formerly were quite spartan in terms of furnishings. Many hotels now offer substantially upgraded interview rooms. It is generally considered inappropriate for interviews or other commercial transactions to be conducted in rooms containing a bed since this would detract from a businesslike environment.

Many companies host cocktail hours during conventions and trade shows, creating a demand for **hospitality rooms** or **hospitality suites**. A hospitality room normally has a built-in bar. A hospitality suite is essentially a parlor with a connecting bedroom. In today's "politically correct" environment, many customers request hospitality suites without adjoining bedrooms to avoid any appearances of impropriety.

## Ownership and Management Control

Hotel and motel properties are operated under three basic systems: (1) **owner-operated**, (2) **franchise**, and (3) **management contract**.

### Owner-Operated System

Prior to the advent of the hotel management company—the first being Western Hotels Inc. in 1929 with 17 properties and since renamed as Westin Hotels and Resorts—hotels were operated by their owners. As hotels became more costly to build and more complicated to operate profitably, owners turned their properties over to professional management companies to operate for a fee. In recent years, new generations of owners with sons and daughters or themselves educated in the science and art of hotel management have become interested in managing their own properties. The owner-operators may also be private or publicly-listed companies on the stock exchange that invest in hotels as operating properties, not as real estate holdings. The advantages in the owner-operated system are:

- The owner-operator is independent and may take swift action on day-to-day decisions. Speed of action is especially important when business conditions are dynamic or unstable.

- When ownership and operator are one and the same, the company or individual retains all of the profits earned from operations.

- The owner has full control over management policies, marketing and operating procedures.

There can also be disadvantages in an owner-operated system, and these are:

- If the owner has only one or a few small properties, there is no opportunity to obtain the benefits of a larger referral program and professional marketing program.

- From the viewpoint of the chain, expansion may be slow since it is necessary to acquire ownership of each property, which requires time and capital.

- The owner-manager assumes full risk and liability for all properties.

### Franchise System

There are several variations of franchising, but generally the purpose of a franchise is to offer an owner the advantage of a large chain while leaving ownership and management control in the owner's hands.

Under a franchise system, the owner of a hotel or motel obtains the right to use the name of and to affiliate with a national or international chain, known as a **franchisor**. The owner of the hotel, the **franchisee**, agrees to abide by the management policies of the chain and to remit to the franchisor a fee to purchase the **franchise rights** for an area, plus a percentage of gross sales. The franchisee may acquire the rights to an area as large as a state or an entire nation or as small as an individual location.

As a franchisee, the hotel/motel owner acquires numerous benefits, including:

- The assistance of a national or international reservation and marketing system.

- The right to use a brand name that is known by a large number of travelers.

- Professional managerial assistance, which is especially important for franchisees who have little or no experience in the hotel business.

- Assistance with the establishment of operating standards and training.

- The right to purchase supplies through a central distributor, which may net considerable savings for the franchisee.

- Periodic reviews and inspections to maintain standards.

Some disadvantages of a franchise system to the hotel or motel owner are:

- The franchisee must pay for initial franchise rights and monthly fees based on an established formula.

- The franchise is only as good as the company behind it. If the franchisor is financially weak, fails to provide assistance as it should, or suffers in the marketplace, the franchisee could also suffer.

- The franchisee gives up a certain amount of freedom of management control, particularly in establishing procedures and policy.

The franchising concept is also used in other sectors of the hospitality industry, notably fast food and specialty restaurants.

## Management Contract

Under a **management contract system**, the owner of a hotel or motel contracts with a chain to operate the property for a fee and/or a percentage of gross revenue. Financial terms vary widely from chain to chain. Some concern only a basic fee structure, whereas others include a basic fee plus incentive fee, or a basic fee or incentive fee—whichever is greater. Under a management contract system, the owners are investors who allow someone else to manage their investments. There are numerous reasons why management contracts have appeal for owners and hotel companies alike. In many cases, lenders are reluctant to negotiate long-term mortgages without the assurance of professional management, which in turn reduces the risk of financial loss; thus, owners are compelled to seek the services of reputable hotel companies. For hotel companies, management contracts offer a viable way to expand with minimal or no capital investment. In foreign countries where political instability or foreign ownership laws prevent outside ownership control, a management contract may be the only way that an international hotel chain can establish its presence in those markets.

The management contract system offers the following advantages:

- The chain lends its name to the property, providing the hotel with a recognized brand name plus the chain's national or international reservation system and professional marketing.

- The investor obtains a professional management team.

- The investor does not need to become personally involved in the day-to-day operational problems of the hotel.

- Permanent financing is generally easier to obtain with a well-known operator.

A management contract also has the following disadvantages:

- The owner must pay a guaranteed management fee, which puts all the risk on the owner, not the operator.

- Misunderstandings may occur between management and owners, requiring negotiations to hammer out differences not covered by contractual language.

- Communication gaps are at times unavoidable because of the separation of operation from ownership.

- Although the owner may have no control over operational decisions, the owner is responsible for funding capital improvements which are linked with these decisions.

- Chains work by standard procedures. It is sometimes argued that these are not flexible enough to allow for differences within individual properties or given host cultures.

While all hotel management companies will assume ultimate responsibility for the operation of a property, there is wide variation in the style and quality of their management. A survey of hotel owners who use management companies revealed five critical factors in the evaluation of a hotel management company. *(18)*

1. Past performance as determined by previous contracts with the owner's firm.

2. Past performance as determined by actual management results for other clients.

3. The management company's reputation for integrity.

4. Accessibility of senior management to the owner or owner's representative.

5. The strength of the operator's marketing staff and its track record for the successful marketing and promotion of properties under its management.

It is possible for hotel and motel chains to use a variation of the three systems—owner-operated, franchise, or management contract. An example is the **turnkey operation**, which is one where a hotel management company may design and build a complete hotel, delivering it in a ready-to-operate status. The name turnkey implies that the owner paid for and received a complete hotel for operation without having to become personally involved. In other turnkey situations, the buyer may purchase the franchise and a management contract, or the buyer may purchase only a management contract and not the franchise.

Another variation is the **voluntary chain** or **voluntary franchise** in which the owner acquires only the franchise name and the privileges and responsibilities of the chain but continues to own and operate the property.

## Hotel Economics and Management Practices

The lodging industry throughout the world is surprisingly universal in its economic structure. In general, hotel economics require a two to three years development period for a new property, an ownership period of seven to ten years for a proper return on investment, and a useful life of 30 years for the physical structure. *(19)* In terms of marketing life, however, the time frame is much shorter due to changing needs of lodging consumers. With regard to operations, the primary sources of hotel income are room revenue, food, and beverages, in that order and with few exceptions, labor constitutes the industry's single largest operating cost.

### Break-even Analysis

The **break-even point** is the point at which total costs equal total revenue. In any business, total costs consist of fixed plus variable costs. **Fixed costs** are those that continue regardless of whether the hotel is even open for business. Once a hotel is built, there are fixed expenses such as mortgage payments, property taxes, insurance, interest, depreciation, amortization, and physical plant maintenance. In general, the higher the cost of construction per room, the higher the fixed costs will be. As the name implies, fixed costs remain constant regardless of whether the hotel is empty or full. With the advent of expensive yield management and other electronic information systems, many hoteliers believe that communication/analysis and planning tools have become fixed costs.

**Variable costs** are those that change according to the number of guests in a hotel. As the number of guests in a hotel increases, costs usually considered variables—food and beverage, labor, and operating supplies—will increase.

Hotels also incur **semivariable costs**. These are costs that behave as if they were fixed in the short run. For instance, the salaries of the management team in a hotel are semi-variable. Seasoned management talent is not easy to find, and hotels are reluctant to let skilled supervisors and department heads go, even when occupancy drops. It may be possible to close an entire floor of rooms to save air-conditioning and maintenance costs, but it is not possible to lay off a manager for three months without pay and then expect the person to resume duties at the convenience of the hotel. Obviously, if economic conditions become severe enough, the management team would have to be downsized along with other staff; so the cost of management, unlike mortgage payments, is not fixed but is viewed as semivariable. Operating costs such as telephone, utilities, and administration expenses in a hotel are also considered semivariable since they cannot be reduced below a certain minimum base.

A break-even analysis is an important tool, as it demonstrates the percentage of occupancy at various rates that a hotel must have to cover total costs. The analysis of a break-even point includes all costs and all revenues. If costs increase without a corresponding increase in revenue, the hotel must reach a higher occupancy level to break even. If room rates can be raised without driving away customers and if costs remain static, the hotel will realize higher revenues and a lower occupancy would be needed to achieve the break-even point.

Break-even points will change over time in accordance with shifts between costs and revenues. Hotel managers are well aware of the importance of the break-even point for decision making. They know that if costs such as labor or energy increase, the hotel has the option of raising prices, increasing efficiency, reducing waste, building volume through increased marketing, or other measures.

From the viewpoint of the travel industry, a hotel that understands its cost of production and yield is a better player in the marketplace. The wholesale or retail travel buyers of today are often as sophisticated as hotel operators, and have little patience in dealing with a rooms supplier who cannot negotiate fair rates that will profit both parties.

## Reservation Practices

A high break-even point is one of the reasons why marketing is so important to the successful operation of a hotel. To some extent, it also accounts for the hotel industry's historical practice of overbooking and tiered or multiple pricing.

**Overbooking** refers to the practice of preselling more hotel rooms than the hotel has to offer on a particular date or time period. If a hotel has 1,000 rooms and overbooks by 10% on a given date, it will have made reservations for 1,100 rooms. It is common practice in the industry to overbook by a formula based in part on the historic percentage of **no-shows**, meaning people with reservations who did not show up in prior periods. Unfortunately, overbooking seems to have contributed to the practice by travelers of making multiple reservations during peak periods to protect themselves. These travelers using only one of the reservations then become no-shows at the other hotels. If a guest with a confirmed reservation arrives and no available rooms exist because of overbooking, the hotel has an obligation to help the guest locate another room. The process of turning away guests and sending them to a competitor is called **walking**.

The existence of a high break-even point in the hotel and airline industries is one of the reasons these firms offer **tiered pricing**. Another is that hotel rooms and airline seats are highly perishable. In fact, they are more perishable than bananas or fresh milk. The minute a plane leaves the ground, the chance to fill empty seats with paying customers has been forever lost. Likewise, if a night ends with empty hotel rooms, the manager cannot retroactively fill them. Consequently, the management of hotels and airlines often feel it is better to fill rooms and seats with people who do not pay full fare rather than have the rooms or seats go unoccupied.

Hotels use a variety of methods to reduce the number of no-shows and the need to overbook. One of these is known as the **guaranteed payment reservations** through which the hotel guarantees to reserve a room and the guest guarantees payment even if he or she fails to appear. The only exception to the guaranteed reservation would be when a cancellation is made according to hotel policy. Another method is the **confirmed reservation**. The guest is assured—usually in writing—that he or she has a room confirmed on the basis of an **advance deposit**, which is a prepayment by credit card or check, to cover one or more nights. Without an advance deposit, a **guarantee of deposit** or **deposit waiver** may be required by a hotel to assure a confirmed reservation.

It is also common for hotels to provide preregistration services in which guests are registered before they arrive. With large conventions or tour groups, a separate preregistration desk may be used to avoid long waits at the reception desk and to facilitate check-ins. Preregistration procedures also allow hotels to provide special VIP treatment, such as placing flowers, a fruit basket, or a box of chocolates in the guest's room before arrival.

The correct organizational location of the reservations department is an issue that confronts the management of many hotels. In some hotel companies, reservations is a separate department from sales/marketing. In others, such as Hyatt Hotels, reservations is under sales/marketing. (20)

Hotel reservations are made in a number of ways.

1. *Direct calls*   All hotel properties have reservations departments which encourage direct calls from guests.

2. *Central 800 numbers*   Chains offer **central reservation services** through an 800 number. This service monitors prices and occupancy at member hotels and is equipped to make and cancel reservations for individual properties. A central reservation service typically accounts for 25–30% of the reservations at a property.

3. *Through intermediaries*   Intermediaries, such as travel agents, may soon be able to directly interface with the reservation systems of major hotels without going through a reservation department.

4. *Through hotel salesforce*   Customers may request reservations through the hotel sales staff. When reservations are booked internally, the hotel saves on commissions.

5. *Through the computer*  It will soon be possible for PC owners to make their own reservations with hotels electronically rather than calling a travel agency or a reservations number.

## Pricing and Market Segmentation

The market for hotel rooms is not a generic one, but is based on specific segment needs. Depending on the purpose of travel, whether a trip is for business or pleasure or one that combines business with a holiday, the length of stay, and the characteristics of the travelers themselves—a corporate executive, an airline crew member, a conventioneer, or a vacationing family—the accommodations may be highly price elastic or inelastic. Business travelers, as a rule, are less price sensitive (inelastic) than vacationers who are usually very price sensitive (elastic).

Marketing competition and seasonal lulls in the hotel industry have encouraged tiered pricing to stimulate business from both the commercial and pleasure travel markets. Among the various segments of travelers eligible for special rates—either seasonally or year-long—are the following:

* *Tours and special groups*  The management of the hotel may have sold a block of rooms to a tour wholesaler earlier in the year at a reduced rate to lock in occupancy. This special group rate with a single, flat price applying to any room except suites is known as a **flat rate** or **run of the house rate**. The flat or run of the house rate applies to rooms only on a "best available" basis at the time of arrival.

* *Airline employees*  Employees of airlines with proper identification may receive discounts up to 50% in many hotels. These **crew rates** usually apply only if the hotel has a contract with an airline to provide rooms or on a "space available" basis if a contractual arrangement has not been made.

Airline crews on layovers represent a large market segment for many hotels. Some hotels obtain 30% or more of their revenue from layover business. *(21)* Holiday Inn Worldwide sells 2.8 million crew nights per year. Although airlines contract with the hotels for crew rooms, the crew unions also become involved with hotel committees. Members of these committees accompany airline hotel negotiators. They check out members' complaints and keep databases of good and bad hotels.

Airline crew members can be extremely demanding. Many hotels have provide special services such as rooms with blackout curtains and kitchenettes for the convenience of airline employees. Since the negotiated rates are usually heavily discounted, some hoteliers wonder if airline crews represent a good customer segment. Hotels that serve them argue that although the business is low yield, it is dependable.

* *Family rates*  Many hotels offer a **family plan**, which is a special rate allowing children, usually under 14, to occupy a room with their parents at no additional charge.

* *Travel writers and travel agents*  Special familiarization rates or discounts are available to travel agents and travel writers in many hotels as a means of acquainting them with the property.

- *Convention rates*    Special **convention rates** are often extended to groups attending conferences and conventions, particularly in off-season periods. These rates are often negotiated years in advance.

- *Weekend rates*    Weekends are usually slack periods in hotels that cater to business travelers. Consequently, special **weekend rates** are often available to attract occupancy.

- *Clergy, military, diplomats, and other professionals rates*    Courtesy discounts are often available to members of certain professions, subject to restrictions.

- *Commercial rates*    Special discounts or **commercial rates** are commonly available to business persons. Motels catering to traveling salespeople, truck drivers, and independent business people will usually offer a commercial rate. Whether this is a desirable practice is controversial, as many operators believe that the commercial market is inelastic in demand and would pay the full rates.

- *Corporate rates*    Special **corporate rates** are often available through an arrangement—usually guaranteed occupancy of X number of room nights during the year—between a hotel and a company.

- *Senior citizen rates*    Other special rates, such as for persons over 65, may be offered by motels and hotels. These special rates are usually subject to various restrictions.

- *Association rates*    Discounts of 10% or more are often granted to members of certain associations, notably the American Automobile Association and the American Association of Retired People.

Even though hotels offer a variety of rates for different market segments, they continue to depend heavily on one segment for the majority of their revenues—the business traveler. Some hotels cater almost exclusively to the business traveler; resort hotels also often depend on conventions and meetings attendees as a major segment in addition to vacationers.

The cost of travel for business is considered as an allowable deduction by the Internal Revenue Service (IRS), which means that the hospitality industry is directly affected by any changes in tax law. It is small wonder that the industry is highly conscious of any moves by Congress or the IRS to change allowable tax deductions for business or convention travel purposes.

## Yield Management

One major advancement in hotel pricing is known as **revenue management,** wherein yield management is a critical component. The concept behind revenue management is the planning, implementation, and control of systems and procedures to maximize total revenue. This extends beyond the careful management of the two major components of revenue for the lodging sector: rooms and food and beverage.

Revenue management encourages the development of revenue from other sources such as retail, rentals, and club membership. The position of revenue manager is beginning to be seen throughout the travel industry, but particularly in airlines, hotels, cruise lines, and rental cars firms.

| | Prices | Low Demand | Mid Demand | High Demand |
|---|---|---|---|---|
| A | $100 | 10% | 20% | 50% |
| B | $90 | 25% | 35% | 30% |
| C | $80 | 30% | 25% | 10% |
| D | $70 | 35% | 20% | 10% |

**TABLE 13.1**
**Pricing for Optimal Yield Based on Demand**

Yield management deals with the maximization of income from available room space. The principles behind yield management are not new, but are taken from micro-economics. In a nutshell, yield management recognizes four or five points on the demand curve and assigns different revenue objective percentages to these price points for rooms, depending upon demand. The data in Table 13.1 represent a fictitious pricing program of a hotel under low, medium, and high demand conditions. It may be seen that the percentage distribution of rooms at different prices depends upon the season. Yield managers study the history of booking curves, historical prices, trends, competitive conditions, and other variables. They then assign prices to rooms according to these variables throughout the year. Unlike the simple example shown in the table, a modern yield management system can assign rates for each night based on anticipated and known demand. Yield management assists in determining whether the percentage of rooms in a particular rate/price class should be increased or decreased.

The practice of yield management uses the concept of tiered pricing as previously explained in this chapter. Although the basic process can be performed manually, modern yield management relies on a high-speed, computerized system. Many hotel chains, including Outrigger, Hyatt, Sheraton, Marriott, and Hilton use yield management systems and believe that the practice produces millions of dollars in additional revenue. *(22)*

# ALTERNATIVE FORMS OF LODGING AND ACCOMMODATIONS

Hotels and motels are not the only members of the lodging industry, although they are the predominant group in terms of economic importance. Others include paradors, pensions, resort condominiums, youth hostels, elderhostels, time sharing, health spas, holistic learning centers, and private hotels.

## Paradors

**Paradors** are old convents, monasteries, **schloss**, castles, fortresses, and similar buildings converted into hotels by the government and operated by a national tourism office. Examples of first-class paradors may be found in Spain, Portugal, Ireland, England, France, and Germany where new life has been given to historic buildings that would otherwise be a financial burden. Because they are often priced reasonably with full-meal plans, paradors hold great appeal for tourists who desire the romance and ambiance of the

One of the first-class paradors in Spain, Parador Nacional de Turismo.
Courtesy of Ministry of Information and Tourism, Spain.

past—for example, in a fifteenth-century Augustinian monastery or perhaps a nineteenth-century mansion (see the sidebar *Hotels Fit for a King*).

## Pensions

A **pension** is usually a large home that has been converted into a guest house. Pensions offer food and lodging. Meals are generally served family-style at a set time with a set menu. Many travelers prefer to lodge in pensions, especially in Europe and Latin America, since they portray a more casual family atmosphere. Many offer excellent cuisine and unique decor. Costs of staying in a pension are often, but not always, less expensive than a hotel of comparable quality.

## Resort Condominiums

The concept of **resort condominiums** has been successful in such popular resort areas as Hawaii; Aspen and Vail, Colorado; the Oregon coast; and Florida. A condominium (or condo) is legally an individually-owned residential unit within a multi-unit project, together with an undivided interest in common areas and facilities. Condo owners share a general management and maintenance program for the mutual benefit of all. A successful resort condominium requires planning. *(23)* Among the most important factors in the planning process are

- The condominium must be located and master-planned as an integral part of the resort community.

# *H*otels Fit for a King

Europe has hundreds of castles—complete with battlements, towers, and dungeons—that double as hotels.

Portugal has a network of 36 state-owned "pousadas," or hotels. Some are in historic buildings such as castles, former convents, or monasteries; a few are modern hotels in scenic areas. Portugal also has some privately-owned historic castle hotels, such as the Hotels de Charme.

### Castles on the Rhine

Americans often use "palace" and "castle" as synonyms, but Germans make a distinction between a *schloss*, a palace, and a *burg*, or fortified castle. For example, the 11th-century Auf der Wartburg perches atop a rocky hill in Einsenach, a reminder of a more dangerous age when a good thick stone wall offered the best protection. In contrast, the 14th-century Schloss Diepenbrock is a water-palace, set in a rolling park and protected only by a small moat. Germany's Burgenstrasse, or "Castle Highway," passes more than 40 fortresses, castles, and palaces, with accommodations available in several.

### A Château of One's Own

In most countries, castles tend to be remote from the larger cities. France has hundreds of castle hotels that are splendidly isolated among vineyards, forests, and farms. Most privately run châteaux are available only during a few months a year, and many have fewer than half a dozen rooms. Owners often speak English and may dine with their guests; they can usually arrange for cycling, horseback riding, golf, or other recreational activities in the neighborhood. The 16th-century Mas de la Brune Château, for example, is run by the Comte and Comtesse de Larouzière-Montlosier, and offers its own landscaped park and heated Roman pool.

Some French castle hotels are run like ordinary commercial properties, with all the amenities one would expect from a luxury resort.

### Henry Slept Here

In England, the Landmark Trust has acquired and accurately restored more than 150 historic properties. They include Saddell Castle, built by the Bishop of Argyll in 1508, and Northumberland's Morpeth Castle, which dates back to the 13th century. A few apartments are available on the grounds of Hampton Court Palace, near London—a real royal residence originally built by Henry VIII. With Landmark properties, guests have much of the building, with a kitchen included. There is no staff; guests make their own beds and cook their own meals. Most Landmark properties are available only by the week, although a few allow short stays of three or four days during the off-season.

Castle hotels needn't cost a king's ransom. Although prices vary widely by property, season, and exchange rate, they range from about $100 per night to more than $4,000 per week. However, most cost about the same as an American luxury hotel. And, of course, amenities like moats, battlements, and dungeons are included.

Copyright 1995 by AAA's *Car & Travel* magazine. Reprinted with permission.

- It must be designed for both total single-owner occupancy and flexible division into multiple rental units.

- It must have certain hotel amenities, a reception desk and lobby for example, with front offices for managers and back of house support areas for operating staff. Food and beverage facilities and laundromat are usually optional, but must be considered in terms of vacation renters' needs.

- The condo should have architectural character that creates an appropriate ambiance for vacation living.

A resort condominium is managed by an individual or a management company that takes responsibility for guest services, housekeeping, maintenance, security, and other problems associated with the units. The sale of rental time to others may be handled through travel agents, the condominium management, an airline, a rental or real estate agent, or directly by the owner. A survey conducted in Hawaii showed that over 80% of those who rented the condominium units made arrangements through a travel agent. *(24)* Some travel packages will feature a condominium unit appealing to families rather than a hotel room. In condominium projects with a large number of rental units, extensive guest services may be provided, including organized resort activities and recreation. In fact, in some condos guests may be unable to distinguish the service from that of conventional hotels.

## Time Sharing

One of the most controversial aspects of the lodging industry is a concept called **time sharing**. It may also be called **interval** or **deeded ownership** when the purchaser takes title to the property. The concept of time sharing is to divide ownership and use of a property among several investors, so that all owners share costs and are assured of a certain time to use the property. This is different from a condominium concept, in which an individual owns a complete unit. There are two basic types of time sharing: the interval or deeded ownership system and the **right-to-use system**. The following example explains the concept in practice.

Suppose that a developer or other entrepreneur decides to establish a time-sharing program with an older hotel, an apartment house, or a new development designed especially for time sharing in a popular resort area. The new developer may decide to divide the year into 26 segments of two weeks each and to sell these to 26 different people. In other words, each unit would be sold to 26 different owners, who would each be able to use it for a period of two weeks during the year. Obviously, a scheduling system would have to be developed so that only one owner could use the property at any one time. Under the right-to-use system, the buyers would not hold title to the property, but would instead hold rights to it for two weeks for a guaranteed number of years, while the title would remain with the developer. Buyers frequently acquire use rights for 30 to 40 years, after which the property rights revert to the developer. Under a deeded ownership system, owners would retain title to a proportionate share of the property.

Buyers share the costs of maintenance, taxes, and other costs associated with the units. In return, they receive the following benefits:

- A guaranteed place to stay in a desirable vacation area for many years in the future.

- Shared costs, which may be lower than renting hotel rooms or a vacation house over the period of several years.

- A low initial investment compared to the down payment and monthly payments required to purchase a vacation home or condominium unit.

- A chance to exchange time-sharing units with people who own units in other vacation sites. Some time-sharing companies own properties in such popular vacation areas as Hawaii, Miami Beach, Acapulco, and the coastal areas of Spain. They allow members to exchange their two-week vacation segments with one another.

The time-sharing concept has come under criticism from some people who claim that some time-sharing companies use high-pressure sales tactics. Others claim that time sharing tends to take potential customers away from hotels and restaurants in resort areas. Regardless of the complaints, time sharing now has an established role in the lodging industry. In fact, since 1986 the worldwide time share industry sales have grown at a 14% annual rate compared to the 2% annual rate of the conventional lodging sector, with sales estimated at $4 billion in 1993. During this same period, the number of intervals sold increased from around 240,000 to an estimated 475,000 intervals.

## Youth Hostels

In 1909, an elementary school teacher in Germany conceived a plan to provide low-cost overnight lodging to travelers throughout Europe. Because the plan was directed primarily toward students, it was given the name of **youth hostel**. Today there are approximately 5,000 youth hostels throughout the world under the umbrella of the International Youth Hostel Federation based in Washington, DC. Recently, the organization adopted the new name of Hostelling International.

Youth hostels provide only such basics as a bunk bedroom and a commonly shared washroom. The traveler provides his or her own bedding. Most hostels offer communal living room, cook-it-yourself kitchen, dining area, and sometimes recreational facilities. Requiring hostelers to do a daily chore was once an important aspect of the hostelling philosophy of character building and cost conservation, but many hostels have now dropped the practice. Although hostels are often associated with nonprofit organizations such as the YMCA or YWCA, many in fact are operated as small enterprises under the management of a retired couple or as a service of a national park ministry.

## Elderhostel

**Elderhostel** began in 1975 as a form of hosteling with bunkhouse accommodations, cafeteria food, and budget travel for the senior population segment inured to RV travel or group tours during their retirement years. From the start, however, elderhostel was intended to be more than just an inexpensive holiday option for retirees. Its main purpose was to enlighten, as well as to entertain; these trips were organized to include an element of education, typically linked with a college or university. A university could provide not only dormitory rooms and meals at special rates during term breaks when regular students were off campus, but also faculty members who might be available to give lectures in elderhostel programs.

Over the past two decades, elderhostel, headquartered in Boston, Massachusetts, swelled from a membership of 200 to over 280,000 in 1995. Recognizing that more Americans are retiring earlier, the membership age has been dropped to 55; spouses may be any age but companions must be at least age 50. The Boston office sets a limit on fees to keep the program affordable. As elderhostel gained in popularity, programs have also changed to reflect a shifting perception of travel to suit new retirees, whose ideas of vacation are more active and more upscale in terms of accommodations. Indeed, elderhostelers have participated in such rigorous activities as white water rafting down the Colorado River, bungee jumping in Normandy, to enrollment in Outward Bound programs.

U.S. elderhostel programs operate all over the U.S. and in about 40 countries. They vary in length from one to three weeks, the most common being a one week program with classroom activities during part of five days. Lodging is typically booked in university residence halls on a shared accommodation basis with most meals included. As demand for more upscale accommodations grew, elderhostels in some locations have included the use of off-campus, commercial lodging as well. For example, the elderhostel program in Hawaii—one of the largest in the U.S.—is housed in a resort hotel which includes meals. Classes take place in the hotel, on the road in buses, or through field trips accompanied by instructors.

## Health Spas

There are well over 100 spas, or **health spas**, in operation across the U.S. A health spa, also called health resort, offers programs that are designed to help guests achieve physical or spiritual self-improvement. (25) Many of the early popular spas were built around natural hot springs or mineral water pools, and their programs emphasized sun, fresh air, and exercise under the supervision of trained health personnel. Today's health resort is somewhat more sophisticated, offering anything from weight reduction programs, including supervised diets and tailored exercise regimen, to behavioral modification programs designed to help individuals break smoking habits, control stress, or other desired behavioral change. Some spas even feature "lifestyle centers" to assist guests in developing ways to live longer and healthier lives.

There is also a segment of spas known as the **amenity spa**, which offers a package of special services related to health, fitness, and cosmetic treatment, along with various sports and recreational activities found in the typical resort. The Greenbrier Resort in the Allegheny Mountains of West Virginia, for example, is considered by some as an amenity spa. It contains a state-of-the-art health spa, with a variety of body treatments, including sulfur baths in natural springs, facials, and herbal wraps. *(26)* The Maine Chance spa in Phoenix, Arizona is an example of an amenity spa linked with the promotion of beauty. The spa was developed by Elizabeth Arden of cosmetics fame, and is targeted at high-end customers, charging $2,500 and up per person per week—double occupancy. The Golden Door of Escondido, California, also competes for high-end guests. The market is primarily women, although men or couples are occasionally allowed at a weekly tariff of $3,000 per person, double occupancy. By contrast, the health spa Ashram, located in the hills above Malibu, California, has been compared to a Marine Corps boot camp. For $2,000 per week, guests are forced into a regimen of little food, demanding exercises, and yoga. *(27)*

In Europe, it is estimated that more than 10 million people visit health spas each year. *(28)* The idea of visiting health spas is not a recent phenomenon in Europe. The Romans and Greeks discovered the pleasures of the spas as early as the first century, and the social life of the English, the French, the Germans, and other Europeans often gravitated around the spas from the seventeenth century onward. Today, some health spas of Europe offer such modern techniques as computer determination of the correct amount of sunlight for a patient or medically-supervised rejuvenation programs, including a range of services from customized diets to outclinic cosmetic surgery.

In considering the potential for health spas in North America, one would only need to point to the fact that the American population is aging. Because aging is accompanied by aches and pains, it is possible that this could lead to a boom in health spas in the United States. The senior population also control a high percentage of all household income, and many can afford to purchase the benefits of health tourism.

## Holistic Learning Centers

A variation of health spas called **holistic learning centers** now occupies a small niche in the travel industry. Holistic centers appeal to a market segment that is not content with a passive vacation, and desires to use a holiday to learn a new skill or explore something psychological. The Omega Institute for Holistic Studies, founded in 1977 and located in New York's Hudson Valley, is the largest member of this sector. Attendance at its summer programs reached 10,000 in 1994. Visitors can take a break from everyday life and learn new skills such as the Chinese martial art of Tai Chi, explore art, or improve their emotional and spiritual well-being. Other suppliers in this sector include Esalen Institute in California, Hollybrook Farm in British Columbia (whose attendance doubled between

1990–1995), and the Findhorn Foundation in Scotland. The Walt Disney Company has recently expressed interest in developing holistic centers.

## Private Hotels

The earliest form of overnight lodging for travelers was the private home. This form of lodging is gaining new interests in many countries, including the U.S. and Canada in the form of **bed and breakfasts** (**B&B's**). The concept of bed and breakfast (B&B) has a long history in England and has been developed in other former British territories. In Australia, for example, the firm of Bed and Breakfast International maintains a list of homes and matches them with visitors interested in that type of lodging. *(29)*

The term bed and breakfast is an imprecise term. In the travel industry, a guest room in a private home is simply referred to as a **homestay**. A B&B inn is one with 12 or fewer rooms. A country inn, which can be the center of life in a small community, offers more meals.

A 1994 study of B&B's in the U.S. revealed that the typical B&B is located in a small town under 10,000 population, has 6–7 rooms, 5–6 baths, and 10 parking spaces. Most were owner-occupied homes built before 1920. Typically, these B&B's offered overnight accommodations with breakfast averaging $72 per night with an occupancy rate of 45%. They hired 1–2 full-time and 2 part-time employees. *(30)*

The B&B concept is appreciated by many worldwide travelers who enjoy the hospitality and friendly environment of a private home. Indeed, the availability of B&Bs has become a proven tourism generator in some countries. Government officials from Hokkaido, Japan, for instance, studied B&B operations in Scotland hoping to find a model to stimulate Hokkaido's economic development. The growth of B&B's in Scotland were credited for helping to increase tourism and consequently employment in a country with perennial high unemployment problems. Hokkaido had trailed behind the rest of Japan in economic growth and the introduction of B&Bs was considered as one way of developing alternative tourism. *(31)*

An interesting piece of trivia about B&B's is that twenty of these places in the U.S. have gained reputations for being haunted. Instead of being a negative factor, many reservation agencies report that they receive special requests for lodging at haunted houses, particularly around Halloween. *(32)* Other members of the lodging industry have taken notice of the B&B sector. In 1993, the B&B sector of the U.S. lodging industry was estimated at $1.3 billion in sales. *(33)* This growth has also caught the attention of the Internal Revenue Service which has developed special tax manuals for B&B's. *(34)* At least 65 guidebooks are available in the B&B sector. Lanier Publishing, for one, produces a guide to 9,500 of the estimated 15,000 B&B's in the U.S. and Canada.

## SUMMARY

The accommodations or lodging industry has had a colorful history, replete with numerous periods of boom and bust. In meeting the needs of an increasingly sophisticated and diversified customer base and a growing travel market, the industry has gradually evolved into the large scale and internationalized lodging industry that exists today.

As the needs and tastes of society and business have changed, so too have the style of hotels, hotel rooms, and the products and services provided. The industry of today is highly segmented in terms of the wide variety of lodging options available and the types of markets served. And while the overall function of providing shelter for travelers remains the same, the management of hotels has become increasingly complex.

Automation, changing ownership structures and financing methods, the proliferation of chain hotels, and a heightened awareness of the importance of marketing have all altered the way business is conducted while the overall emphasis on profitability remains. In the next chapter, we will discuss food and beverage operations which are an important source of revenues to hotels, as well as being a key industry sector in its own right within the travel and tourism field.

# $\mathcal{D}$ISCUSSION QUESTIONS

1. In what significant ways has the hotel industry evolved during this century?

2. What differences exist in the rating of hotels in the United States versus that of Europe and other parts of the world?

3. In what ways do the three basic hotel management/operation systems differ?

4. Discuss reasons why you feel the ownership of hotels by airlines has not been successful in the U.S.

5. What are the various classifications of commercial accommodations? How is each type differentiated?

6. What benefits does yield management offer to a hotel?

7. What major factors do you feel are responsible for the growth of the spa sector in North America?

8. What is meant when the hotel industry refers to demand for hotel space by the business traveler as relatively inelastic?

9. Discuss the advantages and disadvantages of a franchise hotel system to the franchisee.

10. Discuss the concept of break-even. Why is it of such extreme concern to the hotel industry?

11. Why is the hotel industry concerned about semivariable costs?

12. Discuss the practice of overbooking from the standpoint of the hotel and from that of the guest.

13. How does the concept of tiered pricing relate to yield management?

14. Name various alternative forms in the lodging industry. In what ways do these alternative forms compete with traditional hotels?

## SUGGESTED STUDENT EXERCISES

Invite an officer of the local convention/tourism bureau and a hotel marketing director of a prominent property to your class to discuss the role of hotels in tourism promotion. You may wish to use some of the following questions in your discussion:

1. Are hotel ratings—Triple-A Diamond, Mobil Star, or other ratings—important in attracting visitors? Discuss ratings with reference to pricing and the setting of room rates.

2. How does a convention bureau work with hotels to bid on a major convention?

3. How do hotels position themselves among competitors in the same class or in the same locality? How about positioning from a national or international perspective?

4. What sort of contractual arrangements do hotels make with their partners in travel— tour operators and air carriers—to fill rooms? What are the benefits to each party?

5. How does the hotel industry track changing trends to accommodate changing visitor needs? Are the information and statistics provided by the convention bureau helpful?

6. How does a hotel work with a convention bureau to promote more tourism to its community?

## REFERENCES

1. Hasek, Glenn. "Inbound Travel Spending Soars," *Hotel and Motel Management*, Vol. 209, February 1, 1994, pg. 1.

2. Owens, Donna J. "To Offset Their Seasonality, Canada's Resorts Should Stretch Their Sessions by Appealing to Multiple Market Segments," *The Cornell Hotel and Restaurant Administration Quarterly*, Vol. 35, No. 5, October 1994, pg. 24.

3. Jesitus, John. "A Brighter Outlook," *Hotel and Motel Management*, Vol. 208, January 11, 1993, pg. 19.

4. Selwitz, Robert. "ANA Seeks International Recognition: Major Expansion Plans Underway," *Hotel and Motel Management*, Vol. 206, June 24, 1991, pg. 2.

5. Hasek, Glenn. "Country Lodging Sees Explosive Growth," *Hotel and Motel Management*, Vol. 209, April 25, 1994, pg. 6.

6. "World Hotels: Thrills Not Frills," *The Economist*, Vol. 330, February 12, 1994, pg. 69–70.

7. Hasek, Glenn. "Choice Hotels Expand Global Network," *Hotel and Motel Management*, Vol. 208, November 1, 1993, pg. 3.

8. McDowell, Edwin. "Radisson and SAS Form Hotel Pact," *The New York Times*, August 12, 1994, pg. D3.

9. "A Hotelier's Conference Center," *The Cornell Hotel and Restaurant Administration Quarterly*, Vol. 33, December 1992, pg. 15.

10. Tremain, A. "Rejuvenating the Obsolete," *Hotel and Motel Management*, October 1978.

11. Garfinkel, Perry. "Bed & Breakfast? No Bed & Dinner," *The New York Times*, January 16, 1994, pg. 7, Section 3.

12. Mandebaum, Robert. "Are We Building the Right Hotels?" *Trends in the Hotel Industry, U.S.A. Edition—1995*. San Francisco: PKF Consulting, p. 4.

13. McCleary, Ken W., Pamela A. Weaver, and Li Lan. "Gender Based Differences in Business Travelers' Lodging Preferences," *The Cornell Hotel and Restaurant Administration Quarterly*, Vol. 35, No. 2, April 1994, pg. 51–58.

14. "As Others View It," *Travel Weekly* XXXVIII (May 14, 1979).

15. Nelms, Douglas W. "Strange Bedfellows," *Air Transport World*, Vol. 30, September 1993, pg. 60–62.

16. Gee, C.Y. *International Hotels Development and Management*, AH&MA Educational Institute, 1994, E. Lansing, pg. 388

17. *Glossary of Hotel/Motel Terms*, New York: Hotel Sales Management Association, 1972.

18. Rainsford, Peter. "Selecting and Monitoring Hotel Management Companies," *The Cornell Hotel and Restaurant Administration Quarterly*, Vol. 35, No. 2, April 1994, pg. 31.

19. Mandelbaum, Robert. "Are We Building the Right Hotels?" *Trends in the Hotel Industry, U.S.A. Edition—1995*. PKF Consulting. pg. 4.

20. Ross, Barbara Jean. "Training: Key to Effective Reservations," *The Cornell Hotel and Restaurant Administration Quarterly*, Vol. 31, No. 3, November 1990, pg. 71–79.

21. Carey, Susan. "Harried Hoteliers Say Flight Crews Demand Perfect Landing Pads," *The Wall Street Journal*, Tuesday, January 3, 1995, pg. 1 and 18.

22. See: Orkin, Eric B, "Boosting Your Bottom Line With Yield Management," *The Cornell Hotel and Restaurant Administration Quarterly*, Vol. 28, No. 4, February 1988, pg. 52–56. Relihan, Walter, Jr. III, "The Yield Management Approach to Hotel-Room Pricing," *The Cornell Hotel and Restaurant Administration Quarterly*, Vol. 30, No. 1, May 1989, pg. 40–46. Lieberman, Warren H., "Debunking the Myths of Yield Management," *The Cornell Hotel and Restaurant Administration Quarterly*, Vol. 34, No. 1., February 1993, pg. 34–41. Kimes, Sheryl E., "Perceived Fairness of Yield Management," *The Cornell Hotel and Restaurant Administration Quarterly*, Vol. 35, No. 1, February 1994, pg. 22–29.

23. Riemer, H. W. "An Architect's Portfolio: The Design of Resort Hotel Condominiums," *Cornell Quarterly*, XIII, No. 3, November 1972.

24. Hopkins, M. and M. Penseyres. "A Study of Resort Condominium Visitor Expenditures," Report prepared for Hawaii Resort Developers Conference by School of Travel Industry Management, University of Hawaii, Honolulu, September 1979.

25. Stein, Timothy, Dev-Chekitan, S., and Tabacchi, Mary H. "Spas: Redefining the Market," *The Cornell Hotel and Restaurant Administration Quarterly*, Vol. 30, No. 4, February 1990, pg. 46–52.

26. Segal, Troy. "The Alleghenies," *Business Week*, May 27, 1991, pg. 125–126.

27. Linden, Dana Wechsler. "Boot Camp by the Sea," *Forbes*, Vol. 149, February 17, 1992, pg. 140–141.

28. "10 Million Europeans Mean Healthy Business for Spas," *Service World International* XI, No. 5 (September–October 1979).

29. "Firm Offering Visitors Rooms in Private Australian Homes," *Pacific Business News* (June 25, 1979).

30. Emerick, Robert E. and Emerick, Carol A. "Profiling Bed & Breakfast Accommodations," *Journal of Travel Research*, Vol. 32, Spring 1994, pg. 20–25.

31. Ram, Jane. "Japan Goes for a Highland Fling," *Asian-Business*, Vol. 30, February 1994, pg. 56.

32. Sullivan, R. Lee. "Spooks Stay Free," *Forbes*, Vol. 152, October 11, 1993, pg. 158–159.

33. Lanier, Pamela, and Berman, Judy. "Bed and Breakfast Inns Come of Age," *The Cornell Hotel and Restaurant Administration Quarterly*, Vol. 34, April 1993, pg. 14–18.

34. Novack, Janet. "The Tax Cheater Handbook," *Forbes*, Vol. 152, November 8, 1993, pg. 202.

# Chapter 14

# Food and Beverage

## LEARNING OBJECTIVES

- To understand the scope and economics of the food and beverage industry.

- To appreciate how "food away from home" serves as a common denominator throughout the travel industry.

- To be aware of trends and changes within the various food and beverage sectors.

- To be able to define and use the following terms:

| | |
|---|---|
| American plan (AP) | Free-standing restaurants |
| Bermuda plan | Full pension |
| Breakfast: Full American, English, and Continental | Modified American plan (MAP) |
| Clustering | Signature dishes |
| Continental plan | Table d'hote |
| Demi-pension | Theme restaurant |
| European plan (EP) | Traditional table service styles: American, English, French, and Russian |
| Fast food | Value pricing |
| Formula restaurants | |
| Franchise foodservice | |

# ℱOOD AWAY FROM HOME

*M*uch of the enjoyment in travel comes from dining out. Travelers consider food away from home not just a convenience, but a necessity. In the U.S., it is estimated that travel-related meals away from home accounted for approximately $100 billion in sales in 1993 *(1)*. Travelers not only patronize lodging and nonlodging restaurants and fast food establishments, they also buy millions of dollars of food and beverages from vending machines and grocery stores on recreational trips. No published figures exist for food and beverage sales generated by travel and tourism on a world-wide basis, but if the 1993 U.S. Bureau of Labor Statistics multiplier for "Food on Out-of-Town Trips" of 21.12% applied, a conservative guess is that restaurant sales (excluding beverages) represented some $720 billion of total world tourism receipts in 1994.

The food and beverage sector may be divided into many different segments, including commercial establishments (restaurants, fast foods, cafeterias, lodging), institutional foodservice (schools, colleges, in-plant, department stores, and hospitals); military foodservice; and private clubs. Aside from commercial establishments, other segments are of little direct importance to the travel industry, yet the traveling public may, for example, have occasionally need for the meals provided by department stores while shopping or in clubs when golfing. Of primary concern to the travel industry are commercial establishments, which include restaurants and lounges, banquet and catering services, transportation foodservice, entertainment foodservice, and hotel and resort foodservice.

As shown in Table 14.1, commercial foodservice establishments in the U.S. account for close to 90% of industry sales. Eating and drinking places, which include restaurants, lunchrooms, limited-menu restaurants, and bars/taverns, provide 69% of the industry's total revenues, whereas lodging provide around 6%.

Non-travel related meals (including beverages) away from home account for approximately 75% of all sales in the U.S. Social changes over the past three decades—including the increasing number of working women, two-income families, single households, and shifts in traditional family structures—have contributed to the phenomenal growth in eating out. These changes have occurred not only in the U.S., but also in many other countries, especially the newly industrialized countries (NICS). Consequently, one of the largest and fastest growing sectors of the industry around the world has been the fast-food and convenience dining business.

## Restaurants

Travelers use public restaurants of all types. Public restaurants can be classified as multiple-unit chain restaurants, **franchises**, and independents. To understand the relationship of restaurants to the travel industry, it is useful to include the category of hotel food and beverage service.

Multiple-unit corporate restaurants operate both as **freestanding** units and as leased spaces within hotels, motels, theme parks, and other locations. Some share the characteristics of franchised restaurants (discussed in the next section), because the parent company may own and operate a group of restaurants and franchise the remainder under the same name. Independent restaurants, on the other hand, are developed variously as fine dining,

**TABLE 14.1**
**U.S. Foodservice Industry**

| Major Segments | Projected 1995 Sales ($ millions) | Percentage of Total |
|---|---|---|
| **Commercial Foodservice** | **258,004** | **89.0** |
| Eating and drinking places: | 201,046 | 69.4 |
| Full-service restaurants | 87,799 | 30.3 |
| Limited-service (fast foods) | 93,352 | 32.2 |
| Commercial cafeterias | 4,862 | 1.7 |
| Social caterers | 3,054 | 1.1 |
| Ice cream, custard | 2,627 | 0.9 |
| Bars/taverns | 9,352 | 3.2 |
| Food contractors | 17,111 | 5.9 |
| Lodging places: | 16,932 | 5.8 |
| Hotel restaurants | 15,638 | 5.4 |
| Motor hotel restaurants | 528 | 0.2 |
| Motel restaurants | 766 | 0.3 |
| Other commercial | 22,915 | 7.9 |
| **Institutional foodservice** | **30,575** | **10.6** |
| **Military foodservice** | **1,098** | **0.4** |
| **Grand total foodservice** | **289,677** | **100** |

Source:  National Restaurant Association.

casual, theme, ethnic restaurants, and so forth. A *small* restaurant is one doing under $1 million in sales, while a *large* restaurant generates $3 million or more in annual volume.

The top 10 restaurant chains in the United States are shown in Table 14.2. **Fast-food** operators—led by McDonald's with sales of $23 billion in 1994—comprise the entire list. McDonald's sales are more than three times that of Burger King, which is the second largest chain. Five of these top ten—McDonald's, Burger King, KFC, Pizza Hut, and Wendy's—have a substantial representation in many parts of the world. As the domestic market becomes saturated and good locations are hard to find, these chains have increasingly looked to the international market for growth and expansion.

## Franchised Restaurants

Chapter 13 discussed the franchising system in the hotel industry. The reasons for the popularity of franchising in the restaurant industry closely correspond to those given for franchising in the hotel industry. Franchises are advantageous to their investors for a

| | TABLE 14.2 Top Ten U.S. Restaurant Chains—1994 | |
|---|---|---|
| **Rank** | **Chain** | **Systemwide Sales (by fiscal year, in $ millions)** |
| 1 | McDonald's | 25,987 |
| 2 | Burger King | 7,500 |
| 3 | KFC | 7,100 |
| 4 | Pizza Hut | 4,797 |
| 5 | Taco Bell | 4,500 |
| 6 | Wendy's | 4,200 |
| 7 | Hardee's | 3,670 |
| 8 | Subway | 2,700 |
| 9 | Domino's Pizza | 2,500 |
| 10 | Dairy Queen | 2,450 |

Source:   *Restaurants and Institutions* magazine. *(2)*

number of reasons. Franchises, as a rule, will provide planning assistance, location assistance, managerial expertise, group purchasing power, operational and training support, and most importantly, the identification of a well-known brand supported by regional, national, and often international advertising and promotion. Financing from lending institutions is usually easier to obtain for franchised restaurants under a proven trademark than for independents.

In the early days of franchising, the usual practice was to sell individual franchise rights for a single restaurant. Although this is still done, the role of a regional franchise has become popular with franchisees and franchisors. A regional franchise allows a franchisee to develop multiple outlets within a specific geographical area.

Franchised chains in the fast food category include such familiar names as McDonald's, KFC (formerly Kentucky Fried Chicken), Pizza Hut, A & W Root Beer, Burger King, Jack-in-the-Box, and Wendy's. They also include limited carry-out establishments, like Orange Julius and Der Wienerschnitzel. Although the fast-food franchise is the most common, table service restaurants, such as Denny's, Steak and Ale, Red Lobster, and buffet-style restaurants, such as Bonanza, are also franchised. These table-service and fast-food restaurants have spread from the United States to many countries throughout the world. American franchise restaurant signs appear with increasing frequency in such faraway cities as Kuala Lumpur, São Paulo, Istanbul, Guatemala City, and Nairobi. McDonald's, for instance, now has more than 4,700 outlets located overseas. In China, it opened 13 outlets in 1993 and plans to open another 15 every year. *(1)*

American fast food suit the busy lifestyles of Asians. In Tokyo, Kentucky Fried Chicken does landslide business, especially during holidays when chicken take-outs require advance reservations.
Courtesy of KFC.

## Fast Foods

Franchised fast-food restaurants have become an industry that has continued to grow despite recessions and inflation. Indeed, hard times have greatly favored fast-food operations over other types of restaurants. From 1980 to 1990, the number of fast-food restaurants increased by 78%; more than any other type of retail store. (1) Fast-food restaurants are projected to have the largest market share of the U.S. foodservice industry.

Fast-food franchising has also promoted the growth of support industries, including the manufacture and distribution of disposable containers. It has been estimated that fast-food franchisors sold more than $300 million of non-food supplies to their franchisees. (3)

The appeal of fast-food franchises to travelers is clearly evidenced by the concentration of these restaurants in resort areas, recreation sites, and theme parks. Fast-food restaurants compete strongly with other types of restaurants and supermarkets for the food dollar of travelers and non-travelers. Supermarkets have responded by introducing their own sit-down restaurants and take-out counters. Nearly half of the supermarkets in the United States now offer some form of carry-out prepared food. The growth in such convenience stores as 7-eleven has meant even more competition for both fast-food restaurants and supermarkets, because convenience stores also offer fast meals, along with gas and groceries.

## Future of Franchising

To retain their market position and market share, franchise food companies will increasingly adopt and reinforce management strategies practiced by successful leaders in the foodservice field. Viable options include the following strategies: expanded menus and **value pricing**, heavy advertising and promotion, upscale facilities, clustering, location in nontraditional sites, and expansion into international markets.

## Expanded Menus and Value Pricing

In the early years of restaurant franchising, the majority of franchised food operations were built around the twin concepts of convenience and limited menus built around one or two product lines. As the market matured and competition entered into the field, it was a virtual certainty that these operations would eventually have to expand their menus to retain old customers and attract new ones. McDonald's is the primary example of a fast-food chain that has adopted a strategy of expanded menus, adding breakfast items to attract an adult market, special children's menus, a variety of salads for the diet- and health-conscious customer, plus the inclusion of specialty products to meet local tastes—for example, saimin (a Japanese noodle soup) and Portuguese sausage and steamed rice in Hawaii, wine in France, or beer in Germany—and value meals. Established fast-food restaurants are not likely to return to a single-product offering, although new chains may enter the field using this strategy.

In addition to menu expansion, value pricing has become an important strategy as competition grows fierce. The concept of value pricing is built around the packaging of food combinations to offer a complete meal at discounted price points to give customers greater value than if they purchased the same items separately. Once viewed as an innovation by the franchised fast-food industry, value pricing is a standard practice in this business.

## Heavy Advertising and Promotion

Fast-food restaurants, in total, spend over $1 billion in advertising each year. One of the prime target markets for fast foods is children, as commercials will attest on Saturday television programs aimed at pre-teenagers. Stimulating sales through contests and coupon promotions has also been widely practiced, although the novelty value of contest games and couponing eventually wears off. As the age distribution changes from country to country, it will probably be necessary for these chains to direct greater efforts to the middle-aged adult and over-55 gray markets. Non-U.S. markets have presented the fast-food franchises with challenging advertising and promotional problems, as some countries either do not allow television advertising or strictly limit the time available for commercials. Also, an ad's content and presentation must be able to penetrate cultural barriers. Advertising messages such as "You deserve a break today" or terms such as "Pepsi Generation" designed for an American audience are often puzzling elsewhere, or may make little sense when translated into other languages.

## A Cultural Faux Pas

McDonald's inadvertently offended thousands of Muslims by printing a Koran scripture on throwaway hamburger bags, then hastily staged a retreat after Islamic leaders complained about desecrating words sacred to Islamic people.

The stir caused by the world's leading purveyor of fast food began with a World Cup promotion that featured flags of 24 competitors in the 1994 summer's soccer championship, including that of Saudi Arabia.

The green and white flag contained the Arabic passage "There is no God but Allah, and Mohammed is his Prophet," sacred words that Muslims said should not be crumpled up and thrown in the trash.

McDonald's printed 2 million of the bags, intended for take-out orders of children's Happy Meals at 520 McDonald's restaurants in Britain. The company acknowledged that the promotion was a mistake and blamed it on advice from an outside consulting agency.

*Source:* Dirk Beveridge, "McDonald's rebuked over Muslim scripture on throw-away bags," *Rocky Mountain News,* 8 June 1994, pg. 42A.

### Expanded Unit Size

During the 1950s and 1960s, fast-food operating units were comparatively small. In many instances, they were no more than simple window- or counter-service units with very limited or no indoor seating. The late 1960s and 1970s saw a trend toward expanded inside seating and more elaborate interior design. By the 1980s, many units built in high-rent shopping and resort areas even bordered on being luxurious, with little resemblance to their predecessors. Today, the investment cost per unit is beginning to approach the higher cost of traditional freestanding restaurants. As investment cost increases, the comparative advantages of fast food over other forms begin to diminish and there is greater risk to be assumed in the investment.

### Clustering

A strategy of clustering involves locating a planned number of units in a certain geographical area or locating one or more units in a group of similar, but competitive, restaurants. *(4)* Restaurant chains may cluster a certain number of restaurants in a specific area in order to (1) receive a better return from advertising and sales promotion, (2) spread distribution costs for company-supplied products over more units, and (3) attain better control of operations through centralized supervision, hiring, and training. For example, when Red Lobster seafood restaurants were first introduced into Dallas, a large number of units were opened almost simultaneously. This strategy not only increased the recognition factor and promotion of that chain within a short period, but also preempted the entry of competitors selling similar products.

Clustering eating places among a group of competitors is done to attract a "critical mass" of traffic to an area or a particular location. Except for special-occasion restaurants, customers do not always plan ahead for eating out, especially if convenience or necessity is the primary motivator. In such instance, people tend to think of going to areas where dining choices and parking will be within convenient reach.

The clustering of restaurants of all types has become a common practice in the United States and in other parts of the world as well. In the Central district of Hong Kong, for example, one would find several square blocks designated as "Food Street" with a cluster of different restaurants featuring various types of Asian or Western cuisines, fast foods and theme restaurants. Patrons, both residents and tourists, can, if they wish, enjoy before-dinner drinks and snacks in a Bavarian setting, move down the street for Szechuan cuisine, and then walk a few doors to an Irish coffee house. Clustering adds spice, variety, excitement with options—elements which are difficult to achieve in a single restaurant standing in isolation.

### Location in Nontraditional and Offshore Sites

As available sites become more difficult to acquire, franchise chains are beginning to look for sites that formerly were overlooked or were considered infeasible because of high overhead. Today, franchise operations are seen in mid-scale hotels and motels, office buildings, schools, colleges and universities, health-care centers, shopping complexes, military bases, tollways, museums, aquariums, and condominiums.

With the maturing of the eating-out market in North America, U.S.-based chains continue to look overseas for new channels of distribution and business expansion. Eating out is a traditional way of life in many countries of Western Europe and Asia, and these markets are less saturated. Fast-food outlets are gaining both in popularity and sales, and compete successfully with classic cuisines, much to the consternation of some governments wanting to preserve the cultural sanctity of their national cuisines.

## Hotel Foodservice

Restaurants within hotels are largely owned and operated by the hotel, but some hotel and motel companies also lease space to independent restaurant operators for a base rent and/or a percentage of gross food and beverage sales. Leasing space to independent restaurant operators has both positive and negative implications. On the one hand, it assures the hotel of guaranteed income; in cases where the lessee is a famous brand name specialty restaurant, the restaurant may also help increase patronage to the hotel as well. On the other hand, the hotel sacrifices potential earnings and has little, if any, control over the lessee's operation. Some hotel chains have recognized the drawing power of brand name restaurants and have attempted to develop their own; Hyatt, for example, developed the name "Hugo" as a brand restaurant in some of its properties.

A large hotel typically offers several types of food and beverage service: coffee shop, grill room, buffet or fine table service restaurant, room service, catering, and banqueting.

In addition to the conventional types of foodservice, some hotels also utilize otherwise nonproductive space, such as lobby areas, foyers fronting meeting rooms, wide hallways overlooking an atrium, hotel sidewalks (zoning permitting), and areas near the swimming pools for serving food and beverages. These spaces are used at selected times of the day with limited menus and seating. Although these areas may not account for a large percentage of the food and beverage sales of a hotel, they help to maximize the use of what is normally considered overhead space and also create activity and diversion for guests.

## Hotel Food Plans

The hotel industry offers a variety of meal plans to the travel and tourism market. Over the years, a list of terms has developed to describe these plans.

Most hotels of the world operate on a **European plan (EP)** system. Under the EP, the rate quoted is for room only and meals are not included. Guests are free to dine as they choose, in or out of the hotel. As guests, they may charge meals purchased in the hotel to their guest folio. To encourage dining in chain-operated hotels, some chains with multiple hotels in the same city or resort area will permit cross-charges to guest folios. For example, a guest staying at the Mirage Hotel in Las Vegas may dine at the Treasure Island Hotel (which is part of the same chain) and charge the meal to his/her room at the Mirage.

The **American plan (AP)** is generally favored by resort hotels, especially in remote resorts where there are few outside restaurants. The AP—also known as **full pension**—includes breakfast, lunch, and dinner. Meals served under the AP are usually **table d'hote**, which offers a set menu with three or more courses at a fixed price. In European hotels, beverages are generally not included in table d'hote menus, and the service staff will offer mineral water, wine, and espresso or other beverages to guests for an additional charge. Tour operators generally favor the AP as it provides additional income margin in the package, and any no-shows at mealtimes are seen as income gains.

**A modified American plan (MAP)**, as a rule, includes breakfast and dinner, but omits lunch, in order to allow guests to spend the full day sightseeing or pursuing other activities without having to return to the hotel for the noonday meal.

The term **demi-pension** or half pension is similar to MAP, and some hotel operators consider it synonymous. A demi-pension includes breakfast and either lunch or dinner.

A **continental plan** includes breakfast with the room and may also be called *bed and breakfast*. The term **Bermuda plan** may be used when the hotel accommodation includes a full American-style breakfast. As explained in Chapter 13, in Europe, the term hotel garni is used to designate hotels offering continental breakfast but no other meals (such a hotel may have a small breakfast room but no restaurants).

It is important to qualify the description of "breakfast." An **American (or full) breakfast** typically includes juice, eggs, grilled breakfast meat, toast, and coffee or tea. It may include other items, as in the southern states of the U.S. where grits or biscuits are also served at breakfast. An **English breakfast** will include a variety of breakfast meats and/or fish, typically kippers, in addition to eggs, hot or cold cereal, fruit, and toast. A **Continental breakfast** usually includes a beverage with rolls or toast, butter and preserves. In Holland and Scandinavian countries, cheese, cold meats, or fish are sometimes included.

All terms should be used with caution and with a note of explanation for the guest, especially since well-travelled guests may have their own expectations about what various plans may mean. There is no government agency or trade association that enforces any kind of standardization when a hotel advertises one of these plans. The quality and quantity of the products within each plan can vary from property to property. Even within a single chain of hotels, the terms may also have various meanings.

## Profit and Cost Trends of Restaurants in Hotels

Although food and beverage operations are important to hotels, the percentage of income from food sales in all hotels declined gradually from 28.5% in 1974 to 20.3% in 1994, while the percentage of income from beverages declined from 11.6 to 5.5%. At the same time, the cost per dollar of sales for both food and beverages also declined from 35.3 cents to 27.4 cents. *(5)*

A number of factors contribute to the decline in food and beverage revenues as a percentage of total sales in hotels. (1) Hotels have undoubtedly done a better job of controlling cost in purchasing and production than they have in generating revenue growth through development of new restaurant concepts and products, marketing, and merchandising. Indeed, some mid-scale and budget hotel operators even regard their restaurants as nuisances to be put up with rather than as profit opportunity centers. The reasons are various—restaurants demand more attention than other aspects of hotel operations and labor problems are constant as is quality assurance. It is therefore not surprising that **formula restaurants** and standardization are the common response. (2) Many hotels fail to provide their guests with the type of food and beverage service they want at the right price. Evidence of what customers really want is all too telling in the rooms of the guests whose wastebaskets are filled with empty pizza cartons and take-out containers from nearby fast-food places. Even as consumers are increasingly turning to fast foods for price and value, many hotels continue to offer only higher-priced coffee shop and traditional tablecloth dining services. A growing segment of consumers are also interested in eating lighter and healthier. Room service, when available, is usually a costly option for guests not on expense accounts, despite the fact that room service is also a money-losing proposition for many hotels. (3) The decrease in the consumption of alcoholic beverages has resulted in lower beverage sales, which in the past had higher margins and could partially help to offset low food profits. (4) Competition for the food dollar is fierce around the world—restaurants are increasingly trendy and the life cycle of some dining concepts may not last longer than 3 to 5 years. At the same time, competition is coming from nontraditional dining sources—supermarkets, convenience stores, and even bookstores with coffee and snack bars. In short, hotels, wherever their location, no longer have a captive audience; neither in-house guests nor local residents in the community can be taken for granted as a source of patronage for hotel restaurants.

Among leading hotel companies that have responded to changes in eating habits is the Sheraton Corporation. In a study of eating habits by *Time* magazine, Sheraton learned that 65% of the food purchased by restaurant customers was not consumed. Based on its own test in Washington, DC, the company reduced the portion sizes and prices by adjusting both to offer better value. *(6)* Sheraton has also responded to the competition from carry-out foods by introducing *L'Express*—an upscale fast-food outlet with carry-out facilities.

Other progressive hotel companies have begun to introduce informal food outlets, including expresso bars, delicatessens, bakeries, restaurants and ice cream parlors. Some hotels are replacing traditional continental menus with seafood or popular ethnic foods such as Japanese, Chinese, Mexican, or Italian fare. New interest in regional American cuisine—particularly Cajun, California, and Southwestern cooking—is also proving to be marketable in hotels.

## Theme Restaurants

In every city throughout the world, restaurants designed around a central theme may be found. Themes run the gamut from converted bank buildings and old firehouses to custom-built windmills. However, the use of a theme in restaurants carries the risk of premature obsolescence. For example, Forte Hotels, one of the world's largest chains, experienced a 5-year life span for its restaurant themes. Although there are some exceptional theme restaurants in this chain that have lasted as long as 10 years, management

Planet Hollywood is an example of a successfully planned mid-priced theme restaurant, capturing customers with the glamour of Hollywood and the magic of movies.
Courtesy of Planet Hollywood, New York.

has generally been unhappy with the results. *(7)* This means that management must anticipate changes at the time of the initial planning so that a theme can be quickly converted to another concept required by dynamic market conditions.

How are themes selected? At present, the process of selecting successful themes is more an art than a science. There are undoubtedly demographic, sociological, and psychographic factors that determine which themes will be successful and which will have longer life spans than others. Market feasibility studies will provide some answers, but restaurant managers must often rely upon intuition, awareness of current events, observance of competition, personal knowledge of the market, as well as their own creativity. The history of many of the best restaurants around the world reflects more the owner's unique ideas, love of good food, and hard work than his or her initial knowledge of business. Indeed, the decade of the 90s have proven to be the era of chef-entrepreneurs—creative individuals who, in many instances, are self-taught chefs with a flair for innovative cookery.

A change in the theme of a restaurant involves far more than simply changing the name and printing new menus. In many cases, it may entail a complete remodeling, new furnishings and fixtures, a change of uniforms, retraining of personnel, and new tabletop settings besides new menus. A change of such magnitude obviously can be very costly. Consequently, a business plan should be prepared long before any theme change is made.

Ramada Inns provides an example of a company that carefully plans theme changes. The company decided it had two distinct market segments to serve—the family market and the upscale dining market. Neither could be successfully served in a traditional coffee shop or a general tableservice restaurant. To meet the needs of the family market, Ramada Inns converted its coffee shops in suburban and roadside inns to informal, reasonably-priced, specialty pancake houses. Concurrently, in its large downtown and airport hotels, which cater to an upscale travel market, the company established several fine dining restaurants under its Summerfields trademark. *(8)* To stay abreast of the market, the company also planned to develop in-house food and wine bars or other bistro-type restaurants appropriate to each hotel's location.

## RESTAURANT MANAGEMENT AND MARKETING

Managing restaurants is a complex task requiring far more than a knowledge of food preparation and serving. Restaurant managers are responsible for product planning, production, marketing, finance, personnel, purchasing, safety and security, and many other operational functions. It is fair to say that being a manager of a high-volume restaurant compares to being the president of a small company, as a single high-volume, moderately-priced restaurant today may account for annual sales exceeding several million dollars.

The major concerns of a restaurant manager may be grouped under the general headings of product development, staffing and service, revenue and cost control, and building customer loyalty. These concerns will be discussed in the following sections.

### Product Development

At the heart of product development is the menu (see Figure 14.1). The menu is not simply a list of offerings with prices attached. It is the central factor in the restaurant planning

## ⚔DELMONICO'S⚔

### RESTAURANT.
### 494·PEARL·STREET.

**BILL OF FARE.**

| | | | | |
|---|---|---|---|---|
| Cup Tea or Coffee, | 1 | Pork Chops, | | 4 |
| Bowl " " | 2 | Pork and Beans, | | 4 |
| Crullers, | 1 | Sausages, | | 4 |
| Soup, | 2 | Puddings, | | 4 |
| Fried or Stewed Liver, | 3 | Liver and Bacon, | | 5 |
| " " Heart, | 3 | Roast Beef or Veal, | | 5 |
| Hash, | 3 | Roast Mutton, | | 5 |
| Pies, | 4 | Veal Cutlet, | | 5 |
| Half Pie, | 2 | Chicken Stew, | | 5 |
| Beef or Mutton Stew, | 4 | Fried Eggs, | | 5 |
| Corn Beef and Cabbage, | 4 | Ham and Eggs, | | 10 |
| Pigs Head " " | 4 | Hamburger Steak, | | 10 |
| Fried Fish, | 4 | Roast Chicken, | | 10 |
| Beef Steak, | 4 | | | |

### Regular Dinner 12 Cents.

Smith & Handford Printers 23 and 25 Dey St N. Y.

**Figure 14.1** In 1834, Delmonico's Restaurant of New York City printed a list of entrees and prices on cards for the convenience of its patrons. These bills of fare were the forerunners of today's menus.

process. The menu reflects the restaurant's theme, and it serves as a primary sales tool. Designed and written well, it creates excitement and helps to establish the restaurant's image. It also determines the kind of production, purchasing, and personnel that will be needed. Consequently, menu planning is a major management responsibility, not simply the chef's. Working together, chefs and managers must also determine what **signature dishes** will be featured, as these are specialty items that help build a restaurant's reputation.

Changes in theme to match changes in consumption habits or customer profiles may require a complete menu revision. Making such revisions requires input from marketing research and from managers familiar with current trends. Makeovers carry high risk but also potential high gain for operators who correctly predict trends. For example, as health-conscious customers began to demand meals with more fresh and less rich ingredients, the restaurant industry responded with *la nouvelle cuisine* and *cuisine minceur* (slimming cuisine). Originating in France during the early 1970s, la nouvelle cuisine offered new methods of preparing traditional dishes, whereas cuisine minceur provided new techniques to eliminate high-calorie butter, cream, and starches found in the rich

## *R*itz Carlton's Macrobiotic Cuisine

Macrobiotic dining is now available at all Ritz-Carlton hotels and resorts. The macrobiotic menu follows the natural food movement developed by the Kushi Institute in the Berkshires of Massachusetts. "Macrobiotic cuisine ensures a nutritious, wholesome dining experience for both road warriors and leisure travelers," said Henri Boubee, director of food and beverages for the Ritz-Carlton. Derived from the Greek words "Macro" and "Bios," meaning Great Life, macrobiotic philosophy teaches that a wholesome, natural diet is the most direct path to good health and vitality. At the Ritz-Carlton in Boston, not only has the famed hotel relaxed its dress rules—jackets and ties are now required only in the Dining Room, allowing a more informal attire for the Cafe, bar, and lounges—it has also come up with a new menu by chef Hans Wiegand for the Dining Room that incorporates traditional favorites and pleasing new dishes.

*Source: The Boston Sunday Globe,* July 30, 1995.

sauces of French *haute cuisine* and in elaborate, classical dishes. Today la nouvelle cuisine is no longer in vogue in trend-setting cities of the world. American-inspired cookery is "in" and some restaurants have embraced *du marché* cookery—improvising menus according to the market availability of fresh ingredients.

Menu expansion involves more than simply adding new items to the listing. A case in point is the children's menu offered by the Denny's chain. This menu was created only after a long period of observing that most children under 12 wasted food for various reasons—too large a portion, dislike of preparation or food combinations, not hungry, etc., indicating an opportunity to make a menu change aimed at this market segment. Denny's marketing research involved examining the menus of 100 competitors, and gathering information from consumer preference panels. Based on their findings, the company decided to expand its menu with a tailored children's line. *(9)*

## Staffing and Service

Except for self-service forms of operations, service—total service from the customer's viewpoint—is key to a restaurant's success. While an occasional bad dish may be forgiven, rude or sloppy service is seldom forgotten. In many types of restaurants—steak and chop houses for example—food products have considerable similarity; it is service that provides the distinguishing difference. Given high turnover and high labor costs (to be discussed in the next section), staffing and training is a constant and universal challenge for restaurant managers.

In French service, food is cooked in front of guests on a small spirit stove. Two servers work together to serve the meal.

Service standards vary not only among types of restaurants, but also from country to country. Staffing ratios in restaurants are highest in Africa and South Asian countries and lowest in North America. While a high staffing ratio is no assurance of impeccable service, it does offer a competitive advantage to the operator who caters to the high-end market. In speaking of their restaurant experiences away from home, travelers, more often than not, think in terms of the total dining experience. Service is as important as the food itself in creating the experience.

There are four styles of services found in foodservice: French, Russian, English, and American. All other forms are variations of these four. Full **French service**—dishes are partially prepared in the kitchen and completed at tableside from a cart—is still to be found in fine dining rooms, mostly in hotels. **Russian service** is primarily employed for banqueting in five-star hotels. This type of service requires trained waitstaff to present the food of each course—arranged on silver platters in the kitchen—to guests before they are served individually. **English service**, sometimes called host service, may be used on special occasions like Thanksgiving, Christmas, or other holidays, but is not considered practical for commercial operation as a rule. **American service**—plate service with minimum staffing is perhaps the most common service around the world today.

The restaurant manager, in dealing with the problem of product development and staffing, needs to think of service as a "delivery system" which is both efficient and gracious—efficiency in transporting the meal to the table and gracious in creating a hospitable dining experience for the customer.

## Revenue and Cost Concerns

The revenues and costs of a restaurant vary according to the type of service and menu offerings. Table 14.3 lists the revenue and costs for different types of restaurants in 1992. The operating statistics clearly indicate two things: first, the greatest percentage of rev-

### TABLE 14.3
### The Restaurant Industry Dollar**

| WHERE IT CAME FROM* | Full-Menu Tableservice | Limited-Menu Tableservice | Limited-Menu No Tableservice | Cafeteria |
|---|---|---|---|---|
| Food sales | 78.4 | 85.8 | 96.7 | 96.0 |
| Beverage sales | 18.6 | 11.4 | 2.8 | 3.1 |
| Other income | 3.0 | 2.8 | 0.5 | 0.9 |
| **WHERE IT WENT*** | | | | |
| Cost of food sold | 26.5 | 30.0 | 31.4 | 33.7 |
| Cost of beverages sold | 5.1 | 3.2 | 0.7 | 1.0 |
| Payroll | 29.2 | 26.6 | 24.1 | 33.1 |
| Employee benefits | 4.6 | 2.9 | 2.3 | 5.1 |
| Direct operating expenses | 6.8 | 5.6 | 5.6 | 7.0 |
| Music and entertainment | 0.6 | 0.5 | 0.1 | 0.1 |
| Marketing | 2.1 | 3.7 | 3.7 | 1.3 |
| Utilities | 2.7 | 2.9 | 2.7 | 2.3 |
| Administrative and general | 3.9 | 4.4 | 5.3 | 3.4 |
| Repairs and maintenance | 1.9 | 1.9 | 1.5 | 1.7 |
| Rent | 4.5 | 5.1 | 6.5 | 3.2 |
| Property taxes | 0.6 | 0.5 | 0.6 | 0.3 |
| Other taxes | 0.5 | 0.7 | 0.4 | 0.4 |
| Property insurance | 0.9 | 1.0 | 0.7 | 0.4 |
| Interest | 0.9 | 0.8 | 0.9 | 0.6 |
| Depreciation | 2.4 | 2.3 | 2.3 | 1.4 |
| Other deductions | 1.0 | 1.0 | 1.4 | 0.3 |
| Corporate overhead | 1.8 | 1.3 | 2.0 | 1.6 |
| Net income before income taxes | 4.0 | 5.6 | 7.8 | 3.1 |

* All figures are weighted averages.
**Based on 1992 data.

*Source:*   Reprinted from *Restaurant Industry's Operations Report '93* published by the National Restaurant Association and Deloitte & Touche.

enue comes from the sale of food; second, the largest cost item aside from the direct cost of the food is labor. Such statistics dispel the myth sometimes heard that restaurants are primarily interested in selling alcoholic beverages rather than food. They also indicate that, despite attempts at automation and self-service, the industry remains labor intensive. Indeed, the largest portion of a restaurant manager's day is devoted to personnel administration, people problems, and controlling labor costs.

## Building Customer Loyalty

Besides financial concerns, an important management responsibility is to ensure customer satisfaction. The restaurant industry is highly competitive, and customers vote with their feet. When customers are bored or unhappy, they take their business elsewhere.

Despite the size and complexity of modern restaurants, it remains important for managers to make special efforts to know their customers. This is not easy in a busy restaurant, but restaurant managers have begun using marketing research to develop a better understanding of their customers. The major chains employ marketing research departments and hire independent marketing research firms to assist them in measuring customer reaction to service, food quality, menu selection, portions, cleanliness, lighting, and other factors. Research is also used to measure strategic problems, such as the product life cycle and advertising effectiveness.

Managers are also responsibile for keeping abreast of the competition and changes in the industry. This is done by personally visiting competitors' restaurants, attending trade shows and seminars, and talking with restaurant supply salespeople and others in the industry.

Customer loyalty depends on providing a consistent quality of food and service and prices to match customer needs. These are basic requirements for any restaurant. Dining out is much more than simply eating. While everyone will at times eat out for convenience, dining well remains an art and a way to acquire new experiences in food and beverages and know about other cultures through the world of cuisine. Indeed, restaurant critics have often likened restaurants to theater—both are forms of entertainment. Customers want an environment that is conducive for celebrating an occasion or for escaping from the drudgery of the workday. They want different environments to match different moods and occasions and to please the people with whom they dine. Seasoned restaurateurs are aware that they are really in show business to entertain and to give pleasure. These managers track industry and consumer trends to stay abreast of competition and always remember that the foodservice marketplace is at once dynamic and fickle.

# OTHER SECTORS OF THE FOOD AND BEVERAGE INDUSTRY

Beside the restaurants, there are other sectors of the food and beverage industry that are important to the travel industry. These include banqueting and catering, grocery stores, vending machines, entertainment foodservice, and transportation foodservice.

## Banquets and Catering

Banquets are most often associated with hotels, but they also are handled by commercial caterers, restaurants, and convention centers. Large hotels typically have a director and staff charged with the responsibility for banquets and catering. Scheduling and managing banquets is very important to large hotels that cater to conventions or incentive groups, and banquet management offers career opportunities. Banqueting revenues are so important in Tokyo hotels, for instance, that the banqueting department is often organized as a separate division of the hotel rather than placed under the food and beverage department.

Catering services are available in the food industry for groups ranging in size from an intimate dinner for two to a catered party for thousands. Hotels and restaurants often provide catering services for outside events. Independent caterers also exist, many of whom will specialize in a particular type of food service, such as Hawaiian luaus, New England clam bakes, or Texas barbecues. These independent caterers sometimes provide only the main items for an event and subcontract beverages or other parts of the meal to other firms.

## Grocery Stores and Vending Machines

Retail establishments selling food and beverages of any kind are in direct competition with restaurants for the food expenditures of travelers. As such, they should be recognized by the travel industry for inclusion when measuring visitor expenditures. Grocery expenditures are particularly important in the case of travelers who go on outdoor vacations or who may stay in condominiums or time-sharing units, but any visitor can have occasional need for grocery stores, if only to buy local food products to take home as gifts.

Hotel guests on holiday will often rent a car and buy food for a picnic lunch in some scenic spot or purchase a bottle of liquor to entertain guests in their room. Travelers from countries with a restricted currency policy sometimes find grocery stores a necessity, not merely a convenience.

Hotel chains have sometimes overlooked this important retail sector. Some have restricted food and beverage stores from acquiring retail sales space on hotel premises. If these stores are well planned and managed, however, they need not detract from nor compete with the hotel but might, in fact, provide additional sales. An exclusive hotel may have reason to reject the idea of a grocery store in its lobby, but many hotels, especially those in resort areas, have successfully operated convenience stores on premises for the benefit of their guests.

The sale of food and beverages to travelers through vending machines is not limited to snack items nor to public spaces in airports or bus terminals. Many hotels offer "minibars," which are small refrigerators containing a variety of alcoholic and nonalcoholic beverages plus snack foods and nonfood items in guest rooms. Control over sales may be remote or manual. Some vending equipment systems automatically record the removal of items from the refrigerator by the guest and then automatically charge the amount to the guest's bill. Other systems require an employee from the hotel to record sales by checking the refrigerator each day. On the whole, hotel operators in the mid and upper scale categories have found guest room vending operations to be profitable with annual volumes often exceeding $1 million without detracting from sales in their public bars or restaurants.

Vending machines offer a plausible solution to the problem of unprofitable 24-hour room service in hotels and motels. Complete lines of chilled lunch and dinner entrees may be sold through cold vending machines, and these meals could be reconstituted in microwave ovens located near the vending machines or in the guest rooms. For such companies as the Marriott Corporation or Stouffers, which own hotels and are also in the business of producing frozen or chilled foods for airlines or grocery stores, this would not be a dramatic step. Recently, Hyatt Hotels, in their reengineering efforts to reduce labor, pursued the concept of experimental "general stores" offering convenience foods to replace unprofitable room service in some properties.

## Recreation Foodservice

Who can imagine going to a ball game, a movie theater, or Disneyland without having something to eat or drink? It is impossible to determine the exact amount of recreation food and beverage dollars that is directly attributable to the travel industry, but it was estimated that Americans spent $8.7 billion in 1995. Among the various segments of the foodservice industry, recreation foodservice, as a whole, has one of the faster growth rates—projected at 4.6% compounded annual growth from 1993–1996. *(10)*

Members of the theme park and amusement industry—Walt Disney World, Knotts Berry Farm, the Six Flags parks, among many others—have departments whose sole responsibility is to manage food and beverage. These operators pay considerable attention to the entertainment value of foodservice and focus on merchandising food and beverages for maximum sales appeal throughout the park. To ensure high quality of products and service, they provide intensive on-the-job training programs for employees.

Other members within the spectator sports segment—baseball and football stadiums and race tracks, for example—contract with companies such as ARA services, which specialize in recreation food and beverage service for this segment of the industry.

## Transportation Foodservice

As any passenger who has ever traveled by train or motorcoach and has spent time waiting at a terminal knows, the availability of food and beverage is important. The transportation foodservice market includes food and beverage sales from airlines, airports, rails, bus terminals, toll roads, and passenger and cargo liners. In 1995, foodservice sales from the transportation market in the U.S. was estimated at $2.8 billion. *(10)*

Airlines serve millions of snacks and meals each year. These meals are prepared in two types of food kitchens: those owned and operated by airlines and those owned and operated by contract caterers. Many airlines own and operate their own food commissaries in the United States and abroad. They prepare onboard meals for their own airline and frequently provide service for other airlines as well.

Airlines are continuously seeking new ideas for improving the cost efficiency as well as the quality of inflight service. Suppliers with new ideas can find a large market opportunity within airlines. Some countries permit commissaries located within their national boundaries to import food products without paying duties as long as the products are exported in the form of meals onboard international flights and are not sold domestically. Food commissaries are generally regarded as desirable enterprises abroad, especially by developing countries, because they employ unskilled or semi-skilled persons and also act as exporters.

Contract caterers, such as Dobbs House, the Marriott Corporation, and Sky Chefs also provide food and beverage service for in-flight use. The Marriott Corporation is one of the

Employee prepares in-flight meal packs at an airline commissary.
Courtesy of LSG Lufthansa Service Sky Chefs.

largest airline caterers, operating some 80 flight kitchens and servicing more than 150 airlines throughout the United States, Mexico, the Caribbean, Africa, and the Middle East.

Travel by train also generates demand for foodservices. Amtrak estimates that 60% of its passengers dine onboard whle traveling, providing the company with tens of millions of dollars in annual sales. *(11)*

Although buses, as a rule, do not feature onboard meal service, the interstate bus system generates demand for millions of meals each year in bus terminals and in restaurants where buses stop. Greyhound Lines, Inc., for instance, has foodservice facilities within terminals. In response to consumer tastes, many of these have been converted into fast-food units and theme restaurants, which has allowed Greyhound to upgrade the appearance of its terminals and to better utilize space. Before the conversion, Greyhound operated foodservice facilities under the name of Post House. The Post House name was generally unfamiliar to people not traveling by bus, and these facilities did not attract many customers from off the street.

Greyhound selected the Philadelphia Post House as a test site for converting its Post House units into fast-food operations. Within 1 year after replacing the Post House with a Burger King at the test site, an operating loss was translated into a healthy profit. As a result of the Philadelphia success story, an additional 28 conversions were made. Greyhound discovered that with a nationally advertised fast-food operator, a much higher percentage of sales came from non-passengers and that more space was made available in terminals for its primary business of bus operations.

## Motorcoach Tours

The $9 billion motorcoach tour industry transports 20 million passengers throughout the country each year. According to the National Tour Association (NTA), a multi-day tour for a typical bus load of 43 tourists generates on average, $6,700 worth of business, of which $630 is spent on food and beverages. *(12)*

Tour operators seek and book various types and qualities of restaurants for different itineraries and price ranges. For instance, tour planners and coordinators may choose a traditional country inn on a New England tour, an Amish farmhouse restaurant in the Pennsylvania Dutch countryside, or a buffet type restaurant or cafeteria where meals can be selected quickly when an itinerary runs tight.

The tour group market offers many benefits to restaurateurs, including the following:

1. *Increased traffic* Motorcoaches can help fill restaurants during slow seasons. Tour groups increase table turnover since passengers are in and out quickly to meet schedule demands. For restaurants located on popular tour routes, the tour group business can be the single most profitable segment.

2. *Less crowded parking* A tour bus displaces four or five regular automobile spaces to fill a restaurant with 40 guests, for example, as compared to the 15 to 20 car spaces that 40 independent diners might use.

3. *Improved planning* Service and food costs can be planned more efficiently because management knows in advance how many guests are arriving at a specific time.

4. *Filling slow periods* Motorcoach operators are usually able to schedule meals either just before or after the normal peak-hour rush, knowing that service is likely to be faster then. Often, additional meal periods can be created to satisfy special needs of a tour bus between regular meal periods.

5. *Packaging and pricing policy* Menus may be preset or packaged at fixed prices, including tax and gratuity. Some restaurants offer the regular menu at one price no matter what the customer orders, whereas others will develop price packages that tie in with differently-priced tours. Price packaging is advantageous not only for the restaurant, but also for the tour operator who needs to know meal charges to build them into the overall tour price.

As the motorcoach and charter market is growing at an annual rate of 10%, the future potential for restaurants, hotels, lodges, and other foodservice operators that cater to tour groups can be very worthwhile despite the special attention required.

# SUMMARY

The food away from home market is enormous, whether measured on a domestic or international level. New trends in dining out, different ways of segmenting the market, innovative styles of cooking and merchandising, and imaginative restaurant design constantly add to the excitement of this dynamic business, and to attracting ever-increasing patronage for food away from home.

Food and beverage operations are a common denominator that cuts across all sectors of the travel industry. This would be expected, not only because eating is a necessity, but because food can also provide an enjoyable experience for travelers. Lacking adequate provision for food and beverage, many sectors of the travel industry—especially transportation and tour operations—would be hampered in terms of scheduling efficiency and service to customers. Others, such as the amusement, entertainment, and attractions sectors, would lose an important revenue center, as well as the ability to enhance the attractivity of their primary product through the entertainment value of dining.

In this chapter we have briefly covered the foodservice element of the recreation and entertainment sector of the travel industry, including some aspects of its marketing and management. Chapter 15 examines other facets of the recreation and entertainment industry as they relate to the travel industry.

# DISCUSSION QUESTIONS

1. What are the major segments of the foodservice industry? Which segment(s) accounted for the majority of all foodservice sales in 1995?

2. Which segments of the foodservice industry are of direct importance to the travel industry? How important are foodservice expenditures by travelers relative to other travel expenditures?

3. How are public restaurants classified?

4. Which companies dominate the foodservice industry in the United States? Which are the top five companies in sales?

5. What are the major trends and changes occurring in franchised restaurants? Fast foods? Hotel foodservice?

6. What are the major types of hotel food plans?

7. What are some of the factors contributing to the decline in food and beverage revenues as a percentage of total sales in hotels?

8. What are the key factors to consider in developing new restaurant concepts and products?

9. What are the different styles of services found in the foodseervice industry?

10. What are the major cost items for restaurants? How do costs vary for different types of restaurants?

11. What are other sectors of the food and beverage industry that are important to the travel industry?

12. How do motorcoach tours benefit restaurants?

13. What are future prospects for the foodservice industry?

# SUGGESTED STUDENT EXERCISE

## Mini Case Study

### Hungry Travelers—No Food

Hungry travelers have become a reality in the late twentieth century. No, these aren't the indigent homeless, but are instead travelers with good incomes and ravinous appetites. Many travel on expense accounts and would be happy to pay for a good meal if such were available.

Airlines and hotels both contribute to the problem. Faced with years of loses, the U.S. air industry was forced to look for cost savings. By cutting food service, airlines were able to recoup $12 billion in losses by 1995. Unlucky passengers who miss the few flights with food service often find they have only minutes to catch a connecting flight at the next terminal so have no time to stop at an airport restaurant. With late flights and bad weather, it's easy to see why travelers often arrive at their hotel late at night having eaten little or nothing all day.

Unfortunately the traveler's plight may not change at the hotel. In 1995, at least 10% of luxury hotels trimmed their room-service hours and close the kitchen at 10:00 P.M. Additionally, many companies restrict their traveling employees to limited-service hotels which often means no food service.

While it's true that travelers could get into their car and search for an all-night diner or fast-food outlet, many are fearful to leave their hotel rooms. Older travelers complain that they don't see well at night and almost everyone is afraid of driving alone on dark streets in the middle of the night in a strange city.

*Source:*  Miller, Lisa, "Airlines and Hotels Say Nuts to Nourishment," *The Wall Street Journal*, Friday, October 6, 1995, pg. B1 and B10.

### Discussion Questions

1. What can hotels/motels do to assist travelers?

2 Does this problem provide an opportunity for creative hotel managers to develop new business opportunities?

3. In your opinion, is the shift away from meal service on U.S. airlines and hotel a temporary phenomena? Explain.

# REFERENCES

1. *The Travel Industry World Yearbook: The Big Picture 1994*. New York: Child and Waters, 1994.

2. R & I 400, *Restaurants & Institutions,* July 1, 1995.

3. *NRA Foodservice Trends, Franchise Restaurants,* 1985. (Occasional Report published by the National Restaurant Association in Washington, D.C.).

4. Sasser, E. W. and I. P. Morgan. *Growth of the Second Tier Food Service Chain: The problems and Potential.* Philadelphia: Laventhol and Horwath, 1977.

5. PKF Consulting. *Trends in the Hotel Industry,* U.S.A. Edition, 1995.

6. *Food Service Chain Executive* VII, No. 3 (March 1979).

7. "Trusthouse Forte: A Giant Is Built." *Services World International* XIII, No. 1 (February 1979).

8. *Ramada Inns Inc., Annual Report*. Phoenix, Arizona, 1978.

9. Packer, L. "Capture New Markets with Menu Expansion." *Food Service Marketing (February 1978).*

10. *Restaurants USA,* Vol. 14, No. 15, December 1995.

11. "Annual Restaurant Growth Index." *Restaurant Business* (September 20, 1986).

12. *1994 Economic Impact of Motorcoach Tours*. National Tour Association.

# Chapter 15

# Amusement, Entertainment, and Sports-related Tourism

## LEARNING OBJECTIVES

- To understand the economics and competitive environment of the amusement, entertainment, and sports-related sector of the travel industry.

- To appreciate the continuing evolution of the amusement segment of the industry, including theme parks and amusement arcades.

- To be aware of the growth of the gaming industry and its economic, political, and social significance.

- To appreciate the relationship between the arts and the travel industry.

- To understand the importance of spectator and participatory sports and recreation in tourism.

- To be able to define and use the following terms:

| | |
|---|---|
| Agri-tours | Amusement playground |
| Amusement arcades | Casino gaming |
| Amusement park | Entertainment agencies |

| | |
|---|---|
| Event marketing | Off-track betting |
| Fishing Lodge/Resort | Pachinko parlor |
| Gaming | Pari mutuel wagering |
| Golf resort | Performing arts |
| Historic attraction | Riverboat gambling |
| Historic site | Ski resort |
| Indian Gaming Regulatory Act | Special events |
| Industrial tour | Special Olympics |
| Junket reps | Theme park |
| Junkets | |

# AMUSEMENT, ENTERTAINMENT, AND SPORTS-RELATED TOURISM

*D*iversions, encompassing amusement, entertainment, sports, and recreation, are a multibillion dollar business that is growing bigger each year in tourism. For millions of people, these activities are the reason for travel. In good times or bad, people seek escape through diversion. Today, more forms of entertainment, amusement, sports, and recreation exist than at any other time in history. Tourism researchers and developers are quick to point out that there are vital links between tourism and the diversion sector beyond the obvious ones in marketing and promotion. These include a shared interest in economic development and capital investments in economic facilities that serve the entertainment business and tourism sectors, environmental concerns, strategic alliances between the arts and tourism, and sports-related tourism, all of which will be discussed in this chapter.

# AMUSEMENT

The amusement sector offers entertainment that is intended to be light, engaging, and providing a diversion away from daily routines. Fun is the common "product" of the amusement business. In this category, we include amusement arcades and parks, theme parks, casinos, and gaming activities.

## Early Amusement Parks

The original **amusement parks** were an outgrowth of private and public picnic grounds. These parks existed on both sides of the Atlantic from at least the eighteenth century. *(1)* Several featured a manually-pushed carousel (usually pushed by three people) as an attraction. In 1878, an American firm perfected a steam-driven carousel that became popularly known as the "merry-go-round," providing a centerpiece to draw people into the parks. A few French parks also experimented with gravity roller coasters in this same time period.

Luna Park, opened in 1903 at Coney Island, was a pleasure garden described by visitor Maxim Gorky as "fabulous beyond conceiving," where ordinary people could enjoy amusements in good society.
Credit: Library of Congress.

The Chicago World's Fair of 1893 featured a midway that included a large rotating wheel designed by George W. Ferris. The midway with its unique "Ferris Wheel" was to serve as the father of amusement parks.

Oceanside amusement parks such as Coney Island in New York City catered to thrill seekers around the turn of the 20th Century. Hair-raising rides, simulated horse races, and games of ringtoss with Kewpie-doll prizes were new "leisure time" activities—the phrase coined in 1907—that beckoned as the workday grew shorter. (2) The crowds reveled in the pseudo-moorish towers and onion-domed pavilions with their necklaces of blazing electric lamps and other architectural fantasies in the park's three main attractions—Dreamland, Steeple Chase, and Luna Park.

Amusement parks spread rapidly to almost every city as adjuncts of urban street railway transportation systems. Their primary purpose was to provide a destination for streetcars. The parks could be judged a success if marginal income from streetcar fares exceeded park operating losses. Street railway amusement parks lived on nickels and dimes and had to appeal to as wide an audience as possible. Admission was free or minimal. Parks advertised throughout the year, targeting special groups—fraternal lodges, schools, trade unions, and the like—as well as the general public. Live entertainment was offered to stimulate repeat visits.

Even in the early days, industry experts advocated the same marketing formula that later proved successful for today's theme parks. "Keep the park sweet and clean, physically and morally" was the advice of one. Another emphasized that "the rule should be to display only that which is proper for any child to see and hear, for where the women and children go, the men will surely follow." *(3)*

A park could be run as a conglomeration of small businesses, coordinated by central management. Concessions within amusement parks were granted to private entrepreneurs who supplied food and rides. The Philadelphia Toboggan Company, for example, agreed to erect a roller coaster at its own expense and charge no more than 10 cents per ride. In return, the park received 25% of receipts and kept out competitors.

The automobile changed the nature of amusement parks. When significant numbers of patrons began to arrive by automobile and not by streetcar, urban railroad companies lost interest, and many parks were sold. After 1930, the amusement park industry fell on hard times, and many closed. But there were also some that continued to operate throughout the 1940s, providing important diversion for Americans during the World War II years when people worked long, odd hours in shipyards and munition factories to help the patriotic war effort. After the war, however, their appeal again faded. Some, such as the fabled Playland at the Beach in San Francisco, permanently closed its doors and its land was used for residential development. In the mid-1950s, the industry experienced a revival with the advent of theme parks.

A few traditional amusement parks still exist, such as Elitchs Gardens and Lakeside Park in Denver, Colorado. These appeal primarily to residents who live within close driving range and only incidentally to visitors who happen to be in the neighborhood.

## Amusement Arcades and Playgrounds

The **amusement arcade** and **playground** sector is an entertainment category which produced revenue of over $5 billion in 1993. *(4)* These arcades may extend from strip shopping center locations with dozens of video and pinball machine arcades in a rental store space, to playgrounds with bumper cars and boats, a waterslide, and other attractions. In Japan, for instance, **pachinko parlors** may be found in the heart of the downtown business districts where young executives can amuse themselves after a stressful day of work by playing Japanese vertical pinball machines for points and non-cash prizes for hours on end.

Today, amusement arcades and playgrounds may be found almost anywhere as auxiliary enterprises of other tourism-related businesses, including hotels, resorts, restaurants, airports and bus terminals, and other locations around the world. In casinos, for example, amusement arcades have proven to be popular with non-gamblers and minors who are not allowed in gaming areas. Some zoos, on the other hand, have found it advantageous to add an amusement playground to generate additional income to help offset the high cost

"Sega City" Interactive Entertainment Center in Irvine, California offers high-tech amusement for customers attuned to the computer age.
Courtesy of Sega of America, Inc.

of maintaining a zoo. The Chessington Zoo in England is one of many to add theme rides alongside its usual animal displays. *(5)*

Sega Enterprises (home video games) plans to build 50 high-tech amusement arcade and parks in the U.S. by the year 2000. The first of these, Joypolis, was built in Japan and features seven interactive virtual reality attractions. Sega predicts that Joypolis will attract 1.2 million visitors per year. *(6)*

Mountasia Entertainment of Atlanta owns 26 mini-parks of 4–5 acres each, which feature video arcades, miniature golf, go-carts, and other attractions. *(7)* Small amusement playgrounds such as this appear to be very profitable, although the market is soon likely to become saturated.

Blockbuster Entertainment Corporation holds a majority interest in Discovery Zone. Based in the Midwest, Discovery Zone is the dominant player of "pay-for-play" playgrounds in the U.S., having recently acquired McDonald's Leaps & Bounds playground concept. *(8)* These playground units, designed for young children, feature complex sliding boards, long and suspended tunnels for crawling, party rooms, video games, physical fitness stations, and snack bars offering hot dogs, granola bars, fresh fruit, fruit juices and pizzas. With the acquisition of Leaps & Bounds, the Discovery Zone had over 300 units in operation around the country in 1994.

Airports around the globe have realized the economic potential of diversion for pre-departure passengers. Amsterdam's Schiphol Airport offers not only extensive duty-free shopping, but also a children's play corner with video games and a jungle gym, a Junior Jet Lounge (a waiting room for unaccompanied children), a golf center offering passengers the opportunity to play a round of simulated golf, and possibly the world's first airport gaming operation—the Holland Casino, with one roulette wheel, three blackjack tables, and 75 slot machines. Singapore's Changi offers sightseeing tours, video tours, movies, science exhibitions, extensive shopping, and even a sauna. Income from these sources covers 20% or more of operating costs at some airports. *(9)*

## Theme Parks

The concept of **theme parks** and the resulting $6 billion industry *(10)* may be attributable to the ingenious late Walt Disney, who developed Disneyland in Anaheim, California, in 1955 , around the theme of Disney characters and America's past, present, and future. Others have followed Disney's lead with varying degrees of success or failure. The Marriott Corporation, for instance, found it was unable to profitably operate the Great America theme park located in Santa Clara, California. The park based on such Americana themes as "Hometown Square," "Yukon Territory," "Yankee Harbor," "County Fair" and "Orleans Place" was sold in 1984 to the city of Santa Clara for $101 million.

Disney remains the industry leader and tends to set standards and trends. The efforts of Disney Productions, therefore, are closely watched by all. When Euro Disney failed to produce the number of forecasted visitors and revenue in its French joint venture, a shockwave was felt through the international community. However, the park now appears to be doing a turnaround since its renaming to Disneyland Paris and financial restructure in 1994. The dismal performance of Euro Disney was followed by the withdrawal of Disney from development of a proposed historical theme park (Disney America) near Manassas Battlefield Park in Virginia. *(11)* Environmentalists, historians, and others viewed the "Disney America" project as vulgar, unnecessary, and a destruction of a historic site. After much public debate, Disney withdrew from the project.

Disney's U.S. theme parks, nonetheless, remain highly popular and are predicted to grow at a rate of 10% until the year 2000. *(12)* Operating income, on the other hand, continues to lag as a cost conscious public has proven highly resistant to price increases in the park. Competition is also becoming more intense as new theme parks are developed around the country, such as the 50-acre "Wonderful World of Oz" park in eastern Kansas and Lego Land in California. *(13)* Analysts warn that the U.S. is saturated with theme parks and that new ones represent risky ventures. *(14)*

The theme park industry is also increasingly international. The case of Euro Disney notwithstanding, Tokyo Disneyland, which attracted 16 million visitors in 1993, proved that theme parks could succeed outside of the United States. *(15)* Besides Tokyo Disneyland, other theme parks have opened in Japan, including the German Happiness Kingdom and Canadian World in Hokkaido, Garasunosato—the "Venice of Japan" near Hiroshima, Holland Village and Huis Ten Bosch in Nagasaki, the Niigata Russian Village, Tobu World, and Shingo-mura, which contains a replica of Christ's tomb. Plans for new Japanese theme parks include a replica of Denmark's Tivoli Park and Cannonball City by Universal Studios. *(16)*

Knott's Berry Farm 6-acre Camp Snoopy Area is the fifth of its theme areas.
The others are Ghost Town, Fiesta Village, Roaring '20s, and Knott's Airfield.
Courtesy of Knott's Berry Farm.

## Gaming

The term **gaming** has generally been substituted as a softer word for gambling. Whatever it is called, the world, and especially the U.S., has experienced a tidal wave of growth in this industry. Legal gambling in the U.S. represents an approximately $300 billion industry. *(17)*

Gambling, or gaming, is a universally controversial topic. In 1976, the Commission on the Review of the National Policy Toward Gambling concluded its three years of research and hearings into the subject of gambling and submitted a report to the President. *(18)* One of the conclusions of the study was that gambling is an issue "so fraught with ingrained moral and philosophical dichotomies and unresolved social questions that no disposition of the subject can ever come close to universal acceptance." Another finding was that states should not expect revenues from legalized casino gambling to significantly ease their financial difficulties. Despite its contentious nature, two facts are indisputable: first, gambling has been a part of the leisure activities of the human race for centuries; and second, gambling in both its legal and illegal forms is big business today. Legal gambling in the United States consists of four basic forms: casinos, parimutuel wagering, lotteries, and gaming activities of non-profit organizations. Lotteries and gambling activities offered by non-profit organizations, with but few exceptions, tend to be more directed toward residents than to visitors.

In the U.S., the modern gaming industry began in Las Vegas in 1946 when Bugsy Siegel opened the Flamingo Hotel and led that city to become a gambling mecca. Decades later in 1978, Atlantic City, New Jersey, became an east coast casino center with the opening of Resorts International on the boardwalk. In 1964, New Hampshire became the first state to offer a state lottery, to be followed by 37 other states. *(19)*

The **Indian Gaming Regulatory Act** of 1988 affirmed that a U.S. Indian reservation had the characteristics of a sovereign nation, and therefore was not governed by state gambling laws. Many tribal councils saw casino gaming as a viable industry and invested in casinos throughout the U.S. According to the National Indian Policy Center in Washington, DC, these tribes grossed between $7.5 and $15 billion in casinos, bingo parlors, and card rooms in 1992, resulting in a profit of nearly $142 million. Approximately 5% of all U.S. gaming receipts are currently generated by Indian-operated facilities. Some 200 of the nation's 280 tribes, spreading from North and South Dakota to Florida, participate in some form of gaming in states where gambling is allowed.

**Riverboat gambling** is now legal in many parts of the U.S. Casinos have developed up and down the Mississippi and Ohio rivers, where Harrahs, for example, has a riverboat casino off Vicksburg, Mississippi.

**Casino gaming** has also become legal in the former mining towns of Central City and Black Hawk in Colorado, drawing the bulk of their patronage from nearby Denver. As more U.S. and Canadian cities seek additional tax revenues and economic growth, gambling is inevitably considered as a possible industry. New Orleans is scheduled to host the world's largest casino and Chicago, Detroit, and Toronto have been touted as possible sites for casinos.

Casino entertainment in the U.S. now outranks total attendance at major league baseball games, arena concerts, and Broadway shows. In 1993, 57 million casino trips were taken, not including the additional 35 million trips to Indian reservation casinos and riverboats. *(20)* The U.S. casino industry was estimated at $10.2 billion in 1992 and forecasted to double by the year 2000. *(21)*

The tremendous increase in casino competition has prompted Las Vegas and Atlantic City to reposition themselves. Atlantic City and the casino industry plan to spend $1.65 billion to reposition the city as a tourist and convention destination with a new $254 million convention center, a convention headquarters hotel, a new rail terminal, development of a three mile central corridor from the Boardwalk to the convention center, plus other capital improvements. *(22)* Atlantic City casinos, hurt by competition from Foxwoods in Connecticut, also convinced the New Jersey Casino Control Commission to allow 24-hour gambling in the city. The impact of the change in regulation was estimated to generate an additional $200,000 per day in revenues. *(23)*

Las Vegas has also undergone dramatic change. By attracting new investments for larger and glitzier themed casino resorts and promoting more entertainment and amusement, including children's programs, Las Vegas has successfully repositioned itself as a family and convention destination, with an increase in visitors from 12.8 million in 1984 to nearly 24 million in 1994. *(24)*

Four new hotels—the MGM Grand, the Luxor, the Mirage-Treasure Island Resorts, and the Excalibur—have developed theme-park-like attractions. The MGM Grand, built

The Oz Casino at the MGM Grand. Slot machines constituting a high percentage of casino revenues are typically located in high traffic areas of the casino. Courtesy of MGM Grand.

at a cost of $1 billion, became the world's largest hotel with over 5,000 guest rooms. *(25)* The Luxor, operated by Circus Circus, is a 30-story pyramid-shaped hotel which cost $375 million to build. Offering a boat ride on the hotel's own river Nile, a museum with the replica of the treasures of Tutankhamen, virtual reality theaters and other imaginative entertainment, it boasts to be "the first casino attraction that is on a par or even better than the best offerings of Disneyland and Universal Studios." *(26)*

Prior to the repositioning of Las Vegas, only 5% of the visitors brought children. The new strategy was designed to allow Las Vegas to participate in the family market while retaining its base as a gaming center. The strategy seems to have succeeded, at least in the short run.

While tourism to Las Vegas increased 7.5% in 1993, it fell by more than 10% in Florida. Numerous other factors, including crime perpetrated against tourists—especially foreign visitors—negatively affected Florida, but freshness of the product was also an issue. Indeed, many in the industry saw Florida's problem as one of a stale destination not keeping up with competition. An Orlando hotelier was quoted as saying he believed, "The mouse had reached the ouch," in reference to Disney World's sagging growth. *(27)*

Gaming growth is not limited to the U.S. as Peru, Greece, and China have announced plans to allow gaming, competing with well-established gambling centers in Macau,

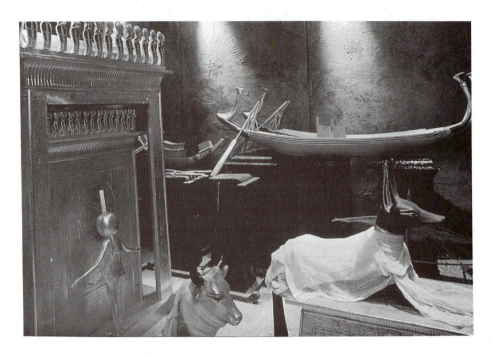

The Luxor's King Tut's Museum and Tomb features replicas of original artifacts exactly as they were found in the burial chamber when Howard Carter first opened Tutankhamen's tomb in 1922.
Courtesy of Luxor Hotel and Casino, Las Vegas.

Panama, the Bahamas, and the Gold Coast of Australia. Competition is changing the face of gaming around the world with respect to patronage. Renowned European casinos in Monte Carlo, Cannes, Baden Baden, and Badgastein, once limited to an elite class in proper attire who paid an admission price, now relax their policies to draw the new breed of middle-class customers. *(28)* While high-stakes table games such as chemin de fer remain popular, the new crowds prefer slot machines and video poker, which constitute 65% of casino revenues. *(29)* In the U.S., a survey of Harrah's Casinos also showed that today's casino players are not the upper class but ordinary people—a high percentage being female, with median household incomes of $38,600. These players are slightly better educated than the general population and about half have white collar jobs. *(30)*

Casinos also operate on cruise ships. The amount of income generated from casinos can run as high as 50% of total onboard cruise revenue; but for most ships, the norm is considerably lower, more like 5–10%. *(31)* Onboard gambling preferences will vary by nationality. In general, North Americans prefer craps, poker, blackjack, and slot machines, while Europeans, Asians, and South Americans prefer roulette, baccarat, and chemin de fer.

## Pari-Mutuel Betting

**Pari-mutuel betting** is defined as "a betting pool in which gamblers who bet on the winners of the first three places—win, place, and show—will share the total amount minus a percentage for the management." In the U.S., this form of gambling includes greyhound dog racing, quarter horse and thoroughbred horse racing, trotter and pacer horse racing, and jai alai.

Until recently, it was illegal in the U.S. to bet on pari-mutuel events except by going to the racetrack and placing one's bet through the windows. This encouraged the illegal use of bookies by gamblers who could not go to the track. The bookie served as a broker between the gambler and the track by taking odds, placing bets, paying off winners and collecting from losers. Today, several states permit **off-track betting**. Off-track betting, while new to the U.S., has been in existence for many years in Australia, Great Britain, and New Zealand.

Legislatures in several states have also considered ways to legalize wagering on professional sports events. Sports associations at state or national levels are generally not supportive as they believe that wagering on sports will threaten the integrity of the games. *(32)*

With other forms of gambling widely available, pari-mutuel wagering has been losing fans in many parts of the world, including the U.S., Canada, and England. In Japan, however, horse racing is enjoying phenomenal success. In 1991, pari-mutuel ticket sales from 40 racetracks operated by the Japan Racing Association and the Japan Regional Horse

The Annual High Hope Steeplechase is contested over the Kentucky Horse Park's 1-mile, 600-foot course each year.
Courtesy of Department of Public Information, Frankfort, Kentucky.

Racing Association totaled some $32.7 billion, and spectators to the tracks increased by nearly 14%. *(33)*

In the U.S., nearly a dozen horse racing tracks have closed. The closures have led to price decline of nearly 50% for thoroughbred horses. *(34)* Still, the sport is far from dead. Total track wagering in 1993 was approximately $10 billion, with approximately 52 million fans visiting horse tracks. Interest in Greyhound racing has also declined, but nevertheless provided $227 million in revenues to some 18 states with tracks in 1991. *(35)*

Reasons for the decline in attendance at pari-mutuel events is generally attributed to the following six factors:

- Off-track betting
- The growth of state lotteries
- The growth of casino resorts
- Riverboat gambling
- Indian reservation gambling
- "Animal Rights" opposition

Pari-mutuel tracks, however, have countered the falling attendance with heavy advertising and by looking into other types of gaming opportunities. Hollywood Park in Inglewood, California, for example, added a $20 million casino to its track site. Many track owners hope to add video poker, slot machines, or other gaming, but have faced strong opposition from small, independent businesses worried about competition for the shrinking consumer dollar.

# ENTERTAINMENT

Hotels, resorts, and cruise shops have always known the importance of entertainment to their business. Today, nearly every organization wishing to attract tourist patronage, including destinations, historic places, and museums, among others, recognize the value of entertainment as a draw. Under the broad umbrella of entertainment, we include live entertainment, events, industrial tours, and the performing and fine arts.

## Live Entertainment

Some time-share management companies, the Marquis Hotel and Resort in Fort Myers, Florida, for example, now employ professional entertainment managers to keep guests happy. Under the direction of a professional manager, Marquis offers planned entertainment programs for all ages, ranging from bingo for senior citizens to hot dog parties for preteens. Although time-share patrons are considered owners of the resort, they must be encouraged to make repeat visits and to continue their time-share payments.

Supervised programs for children are offered at many resorts. Club Med, for instance, offers innovative programs that are as creative and instructive for children as they are fun. These programs include the usual sports and recreation enjoyed by children, as well as the unusual—acrobatics, high-wire walking, trapeze, and other circus acts. At ski resorts located in Steamboat Springs and Vail, there are children's programs run by professionals, including ski instructions, programs for handicapped children, and babysitting services. *(36)* These programs allow parents freedom to enjoy their own vacations at the resort.

Historic restorations, such as Colonial Williamsburg, have also discovered they are involved in the entertainment industry. A tour of old buildings can only hold one's attention for so long. Colonial Williamsburg features hayrides for children, craft demonstrations, battlefield reenactments, and employs costumed employees throughout the colonial village.

Entertainment may even play a role in a ferry service where there is no competition. The Canadian ferry that carries passengers from Maine to Nova Scotia offers live folk music along with slot machines and video games. The ferry decided its business was more than just transportation.

Entertainment, once de rigueur for fashionable hotels, faded with the advent of the television age and the skyrocketing costs of running showrooms. However, times and

A craftsman demonstrates joinery in historical Old Salem in Winston-Salem, North Carolina.
Courtesy of Old Salem.

fashions change, and today certain forms of entertainment are back in vogue at name hotels. The benefits to a hotel brought by popular and well-planned entertainment can be significant. The St. Regis Sheraton in New York City increased dinner business fourfold and hotel occupancy by 2.5% through a carefully planned and executed entertainment program. *(37)* To book talent for its showroom, the St. Regis contracts with a professional entertainment management firm.

Hotel entertainment may be classified as *(38)*

- *Ambient*   Ambient entertainment refers to the use of musicians—a band, a string quartette, a pianist, violinist, or other instrumentalist—to provide background music or create an atmosphere mood in the hotel's restaurants, cocktail lounge, or lobby.

- *Lounge*   Typical lounge entertainment consists of a musical ensemble with backup singers. They often provide both a show and music for dancing.

- *Special events*   Themed events are frequently staged to generate business in empty ballrooms, increase restaurant revenue, or promote occupancy in seasonally-low periods. The publicity and public relations value of special events are also significant considerations for a hotel.

- *Private entertainment*   Hotels generally do not directly enter into negotiations to book private entertainment for a third party. On a commission or fee basis, a hotel may contact a proven entertainment agent on the client's behalf when conventions or incentive groups are booked into the hotel, or it will provide referrals when requested by guests for a wedding party or cocktail reception.

- *Public entertainment*   Hotels sometimes offer public entertainment on a speculative basis. There are three general types of financial arrangements that a hotel may strike with a performer:

  a. The performer accepts a set fee.

  b. The performer will take a lesser guarantee plus a percentage of cover charges.

  c. An outside promoter rents the hotel's entertainment area and is completely responsible for promoting the event (sometimes called a "four-wall deal"). The hotel may assist with advertising in exchange for liquor sales privileges during the event.

## Entertainment Agencies

Hotels, resorts, attractions, convention and meeting planners, among others, generally work with independent **entertainment agencies** to book performances for special occasions. Entertainment agencies are often able to provide quality entertainment at lower prices than the buyer might otherwise obtain. Professional agents handle many acts and entertainers, and can usually provide diversity, as well as last-minute substitutes in emergency situations. These agencies, besides saving management many hours of searching and screening entertainers, can often provide valuable technical advice concerning lighting, sound, and staging.

One disadvantage in working with agents is that they are heavily sales oriented and tend to describe every act as "terrific." As a result, clients seeking entertainment don't always know what they are getting. For this reason, some buyers prefer to work with only one or two agencies they can trust.

Suppliers of entertainment to the travel industry face difficult challenges in the years ahead as present generations, having seen and experienced more than their parents through frequent travel and the magic eye of television, and are easily bored with "sameness." Because of this exposure, they become more discriminating in their choice of passive or active entertainment.

## Grand Spectacle Entertainment

Anyone who has attended a concert by a name rock group like the Rolling Stones, or a country/western group like Alabama, can attest to the tremendous appeal of these events. The size of this industry is portrayed by Irvin Feld and Kenneth Feld Productions, a holding company comprising several giants in the entertainment industry—Ringling Bros. & Barnum & Bailey Circus, Walt Disney World on Ice, Siegfried and Roy at the Mirage in Las Vegas, and George Lucas Super Line Adventure Show. These shows annually take in about $300 million at the gate, plus concessions of about $200 million. *(39)* Ringling Bros. & Barnum & Bailey Circus tours 95 U.S. cities and has created two circus units to tour South America and Asia. *(40)* The desire for live entertainment is truly worldwide and popular entertainers from many nations hold world tours. Mexico, for example, has become a target market for many groups since that nation improved its infrastructure and built large amphitheaters and concert halls. *(41)*

Members of an audience often travel many miles to witness a live event and often remain overnight in local lodging, thus contributing to travel revenues.

## Special Events

R.J. Reynolds, Hiram Walker, Pepsi and United Airlines are a few examples of corporations that sponsor special golf or tennis tournaments, concerts, and other **special events**. Many companies believe that **event marketing** offers a unique and valuable way to build brand awareness, especially in the instance of such products as alcoholic beverages or cigarettes which are subject to certain advertising restrictions.

Thousands of visitors, for example, attend the Great American Beer Festival and the Oregon Brewers Festival (50,000 visitors) who pay an entrance fee as high as $23 to sample from as many as 950 beers from 200 U.S. breweries. *(42)* While the audience outreach will not be as great as media advertising, no one can deny that the personalized nature of an event can often have a great impact in converting customers.

Special events have long served as a reason for travel. Groups or communities throughout the world organize and promote major events ranging from annual festivals— a "Renaissance Faire," for example—to local street fairs. Some winter resorts now sponsor events throughout the year—snowboard contests in the winter and concerts in the summer—to create destination awareness. Even colleges and universities spend considerable time organizing homecoming events to attract thousands of returning alumni, students, and their parents.

Event marketing offers great potential for cooperative work, such as a three-way sponsorship between a university, a commercial line of clothing, and a sports magazine to

# Renaissance Faires

Events that began as "hippie" happenings in the 60s are now joining the ranks of corporate America. Not everyone is pleased. Since their beginnings, Renaissance Faires have given participants a chance to participate in a free-form celebration of the Elizabethan era. Now some feel they are threatened.

The **Renaissance Pleasure Faires** in California depend on part-time participants who serve as actors and street vendors. Workers attend classes where they learn to act Elizabethan, which includes brawling, leeching, and hawking. They also learn about Elizabethan history, language, and culture. Some of the lessons simply don't fit with a society increasingly concerned about issues such as sexual harassment, but that doesn't seem to bother participants or visitors. Instructors warn women participants that when they dress as a wench, they may get grabbed.

A publicly-traded company, Renaissance Entertainment Corporation of Boulder, Colorado, has been acquiring Renaissance Faires and turning them into profit ventures. Miles Silverman, CEO of Renaissance Entertainment, hopes to purchase twenty more faires and build a theme park in Virginia.

Mr. Silverman feels that many people who run faires simply don't know how to manage them very well. When his company acquired the Renaissance Pleasure Fair, it was grossing $8 million per year and losing money. By contrast, a faire in Kenosha, Wisconsin owned by Renaissance Entertainment grossed $2.5 million and made $700,000. This was possible through cost cutting and increasing revenue from gate receipts. Also, instead of company-provided stalls, Kenosha faire vendors build their own stores and then pay Renaissance Entertainment for the right to operate them at the faire.

Experienced faire participants claimed that profit-making companies reduce the excitement and color of a faire in quest of profits. For instance, actors at the California faire grumbled that instead of using 12 bell ringers to lead the queen's parade, Renaissance Entertainment substituted two jugglers. A paying customer complained that the faire is no longer authentic. "Nobody smells. They just talk Elizabethan to sell you stuff."

There has even been talk that participants who now receive a small remuneration would probably pay the admittance fee and continue to participate just to be able to dress and act Elizabethan. Some look at other events that now charge volunteers to participate such as the Vantage Golf Tournament in North Carolina that asks volunteers to pay for the privilege of working at the event. (It should be mentioned that the contributions of these volunteers go to charity—not to the corporation.)

> Responding to criticism, Mr. Silverman reminds people that profitable faires stay in business and continue to offer opportunities each year as opposed to faires that may seem more authentic but go out of business.
>
> *Source:* Adapted from Hardy Quentin, "Ye Olde Bottom Line is a New Attraction at Renaissance Faires," *The Wall Street Journal,* September 28, 1995, pg. A1 and A10.

promote a local ski race. Sports event marketing is so attractive that even non-sports publishers such as *U.S. News & World Report* entered the field through sponsorship of a tour for professional tennis players over age 35. *(43)*

It has been estimated that event marketing will grow 18–20% throughout the 90s and could spur annual tourist expenditures of $4.5 billion. *(44)* As events gain in importance, career positions have developed for event marketing specialists within corporations, convention bureaus, and other travel promotion organizations.

## Industrial Tours

A visit to an industrial plant may not sound exciting, but **industrial tours** are an incredible draw in many communities. The Coors Brewery at Golden, Colorado, for example, is one of the top visitor attractions in that community. Industrial tours once allowed in the Kitchens of Sara Lee in Illinois were so popular that eventually they fell victim to their own success when the plant found the tours disruptive to its heavy production schedule.

When the Saturn Corporation sponsored a homecoming event for Saturn automobile owners at its Spring Hill, Tennessee manufacturing facility, it attracted over 16,000 owners/visitors. *(45)* Despite anti-smoking legislation and sentiment, plant tours of the R.J. Reynolds cigarette factory in North Carolina remain very popular. Visitors come from every state and many countries. To meet the demand, the tour requires the support of a professional tour department operating from 8:15 A.M. to 10:00 P.M. five days a week.

Industrial tours are not the sole province of large companies and associations. The Best Western Dubuque Inn, a 150-room motel, in Dubuque, Iowa, developed daylong **agri-tours** to visit nearby farms, which helped the motel's occupancy. *(46)* In Scottsdale, Arizona, even tours to a sewage treatment plant, hosted by the plant, attract visitors.

Why do visitors participate in industrial tours?

- They are free or rarely charge.

- Samples are sometimes offered.

- People are interested in new technology and the workplace.

- Companies actively promote them through billboards, brochures, and other media.

Communities with interesting plant tours may feature them in visitor promotional literature and at visitor information centers. There is obviously a cost involved in hosting plant tours, so why do so many companies go out of their way to play host? Among the reasons are the following:

- Plant tours are an excellent public relations tool, helping to build community and visitor goodwill, especially for manufacturers of consumer products, whether automobiles, cigarettes, beer, textiles, or other goods.
- Plant tours create customer interest and offer a retail outlet for the company's products, including logo items such as coffee mugs, tee shirts, key chains, etc., which help advertise the company.
- Plant tours assist in the development of a name list used in the direct mail order and catalog business.

An interesting case of what can develop as an outgrowth of industrial tours is the story of the Kentucky Horse Park. The U.S. thoroughbred horse racing industry is centered in Lexington. For many years, visitors were drawn to the horse farms in the area. Mounting visitor interest eventually led to the point where private horse farms could no longer cope with demand. The state of Kentucky subsequently invested $35 million in a thoroughbred horse farm exhibit and visitor showplace, naming it the Kentucky Horse Park. Since its opening in 1978, the park has become the leading visitor attraction in the community.

## Tourism and the Arts

The arts and the visitor industry are often contentious partners, but each needs the other. The term "arts" generally include **performing arts** and fine arts. The former refers to live theater, music, and dance, and the latter to painting, sculpture, and ceramics. Both forms of art are important in tourism, drawing millions of visitors to their host communities.

Attendance and visitors participation have remained fairly constant for arts activities. Overall, about 41% of American adults attend an arts event such as classical music, operas, plays and ballets or attended exhibits at art museums and galleries. This percentage—some 77% of whom are college educated—has remained steady since 1982. *(47)*

There is little doubt that arts-related events or activities can create a reason for travel. The Passion Play at Oberammergau in Bavaria or the Spoleto in Charleston, South Carolina are examples of cultural arts events that lure thousands of visitors every year to their host destinations. Nonetheless, when arts groups request public tourism promotion funds to help market an event, controversy arises. Supporters for the funding may quote the success of arts festivals such as the Montreal International Jazz Festival or Shakespearean festivals that fill hotel rooms with guests. Opponents against the funding will agree that some arts events do have that capability, but contend that the majority are held mainly for the benefit of residents, and therefore, and have little or no effect in promoting or developing tourism. Instead of seeking public tourism funds for promotions, some critics have pointed to the need for arts organizations to become more market driven. Arts organizations are urged to target potential market segments that match their products, applying personal selling to reach key accounts such as hotels, tour operators or retailers, and others with an interest in the arts within the community. *(48)*

The Monet art exhibit, for example, vividly illustrates how the arts can directly benefit tourism. When the Monet exhibit was held in Auckland, New Zealand, it drew visitors

from every part of the country. New Zealanders are known for their love of sports, yet the Monet collection attracted greater numbers than any sporting event, including rugby matches. When the Boston Fine Arts Museum sponsored its "Monet in the 90s" exhibit in cooperation with the Greater Boston Convention and Visitors Bureau and 25 area hotels, all of the hotels sold out their weekend travel packages. *(49)*

In an effort to attract a wider audience, some museums have purchased simulator rides and giant-screen theatres. *(50)* The Denver Museum of Natural History, for example, added an IMAX theater with a 4½-story screen as an additional draw. A time proven method of improving attendance at museum and historical restorations is the staging of commemoration celebrations. In 1994, over one million people participated in the 50th Anniversary of D-Day. Many of these participants found their way to D-Day exhibits at their local museums. *(51)*

The role of museums varies throughout the world. Japanese museums charge admission and are considered to be an institution associated with the elite segment of society. In London, on the other hand, admission is usually free and special programs are periodically organized for the benefit of the general public. Museums there also enjoy the support of the London business community as frequent sponsors of events and exhibits. *(52)*

An interesting trend toward privatization of museums may be happening in cities strapped for money. Philadelphia, for example, privatized its port museums. The implication of privatization is that these institutions must generate enough revenues from public attendance to become self-sufficient. This creates an incentive for museums to work more closely with the travel industry to attract visitors. *(53)*

## Historic Sites and Restorations

Historic sites and restorations are owned and operated by government at all levels and by public trusts, foundations, churches, private individuals, civic or cultural organizations, among others. The National Registry of Historic Places in the United States lists over 36,000 U.S. historic buildings and sites. Some of these historic buildings have been recycled for use as libraries, homes, churches, hotels and inns, theatres, and, in the case of the Teller House in Central City, Colorado, even as a casino. Many also serve as occasional visitor attractions. For example, some "heirloom" communities offer historic home tours once a year when owners graciously open their homes to the public. These historic home tours are organized as fund-raising projects for civic groups, but have the added benefit of attracting thousands of out-of-town visitors.

**Historic attractions** provide a major reason for travel. The Division of Tourism for South Carolina notes that, "Historic attractions play a vital role in South Carolina where tourism is the second largest industry. These attractions draw more visitors than any other single feature during every season but summer when the beaches prove most popular. Also, the revenues from historic attractions can be significant. Colonial Williamsburg, for instance, produced admission revenues of over $22 million in 1993. *(54)* Even young states, Washington and Hawaii, for example, recognize that historic attractions are very important. Washington State maintains an 800 number to call for information about historic sites. 66% of all visitor inquiries to that state relate to historic sites. In Hawaii, top two visitor attractions are monuments of World War II: The National Mem

Cemetery of the Pacific, better known as Punchbowl Cemetery, and the U.S.S. Arizona Memorial. The Alamo in Texas receives over 2.5 million visitors each year. Other historic sites such as Hearst Castle in California, the Biltmore House in North Carolina, and Monticello in Virginia annually host hundreds of thousands of visitors.

**Historic sites** are especially popular with domestic motorcoach visitors, and many historic sites report a small but steadily increasing number of foreign visitors. Visitation to historic sites has long been recognized as a major reason for travel to Europe, Mexico, China, India, and other countries with long histories. Newer countries such as Canada, the United States, Australia, and New Zealand are only beginning to realize the significant economic value of historic sites as visitor attractions.

Historic places often feature special holiday events such as "Thanksgiving at Old Sturbridge Village" in Massachusetts or "Christmas at Mystic Seaport" in Connecticut. These carefully planned events—hosted and served by costumed employees—attract thousands of vacationers. Many of these special events at historic sites are listed among the Top 100 Events in North America by the American Bus Association. *(55)*

It is not essential for a site to be thousands or even hundreds of years old to qualify as an historic site. For example, Graceland, home of Elvis Presley, in Memphis, Tennessee, attracts more visitors than any other building in the U.S., with the exception of the White House. *(56)* Visitors come from virtually every nation of the world. Presley's estate was worth $4.5 million at the time of his passing in 1977; by 1993, it was valued at $100 million, thanks to the promotion of Elvis merchandise, image property rights, and Graceland.

## Scientific Attractions and Tourism

Science, as it relates to tourism, may be as difficult to define as the arts. Many museums, aquariums, zoos, space centers, and similar institutions built with public funds are as much established for scientific and research purposes as they are for public exhibition. Today, the world is preoccupied with science and technology, and attractions based on science have become major visitor attractions. The National Air and Space Museum of the Smithsonian Institute represents history and science, showing advancements made in aerospace technology and science. The Houston Space Center in Texas and Cape Canaveral in Florida are also magnets around which travel decisions are made.

In 1981, Baltimore demonstrated the potential visitor appeal of a well-designed and managed aquarium. Baltimore's National Aquarium attracted 1.5 million visitors per year. Three years later, The Monterey Bay Aquarium (California) opened in Cannery Row, drawing 2.2 million visitors its first year. Since then, aquariums have opened in many other communities, including locations miles from the nearest ocean. Chattanooga, Tennessee, for instance, has an aquarium featuring fresh water fish which annually draws over one million visitors. Some community leaders and tourism planners worry about the overbuilding and market saturation of aquarium attractions. It is estimated that some 30 major aquariums will be built in the U.S. by the year 2000. *(57)* As a modern aquarium would cost an average of $40 million to build, a community must be concerned about sustaining visitor interest and adequate gate revenues. Norwalk, Connecticut; Corpus Christi, Texas, and Camden, New Jersey have all experienced lower than expected visitor attendance at their respective aquaria with resulting cash flow problems. *(58)*

Museums such as the Smithsonian's National Air and Space Museum attract millions of tourists annually and are important providers of services to tourists.
Courtesy of the National Air and Space Museum.

# SPORTS-RELATED TOURISM

As in the case of amusement or entertainment-related tourism, the category of sports-related tourism is broad and inclusive, encompassing attractions, resorts, cruises, tours, and events associated with sports and recreation (see Table 15.1). During the health and fitness conscious decades of the 1980s and 1990s, entrepreneurs have increased the number of sport tours, developed sport-specific resort destinations, established specialized sport cruises, added sports activity facilities and programs to hotel/resort settings, and promoted sporting events as a basis for tourism. In addition, sports attractions (museums, sports stadiums, and sports halls of fame) are looking more and more into tourism for increased visitations. In this section, we will discuss some of the more important sports developments that support tourism and vice versa.

## Spectator Sports

To say that sports are popular throughout the world is an understatement. In the United States, baseball, football, hockey, boxing, and tennis each attract millions of spectators

The *Atlantis* submarine allows tourists to safely experience underwater marine environments.
Courtesy of Atlantis Submarine.

every year. Motorsports, for example, is a sector of professional sports with a highly devoted following. Attendance at North American racing events has been increasing and reached over 13 million fans in 1993. *(59)* Not only are the numbers of spectators impressive, but also the number of active participants. In the past, only the team traveled; spectators remained behind to read about their favorite team or to experience the game through radio and television. Today, it is not unusual for both the team and the spectators to travel to the game, particularly where championship games are involved, as demonstrated by the draw of the Super Bowl, the Rose Bowl, the World Series, and other important games.

Travel by spectators to games represents an important market for carriers, the lodging industry, and the food and beverage industry. Cities bid eagerly for the opportunity to host important games, knowing that such events can bring in millions of dollars in tourist revenues.

Travel by sports spectators and participants is by no means limited to major events. Many smaller communities throughout the world benefit directly from the travel expenditures of those who attend regional sports tournaments. The importance of these events is sometimes overlooked by those involved in tourism planning and promotion.

**TABLE 15.1**
**Categories of Tourism Sport**

| Attractions | Resorts | Cruises | Tours | Events |
|---|---|---|---|---|
| Sports museums Halls of Fame | Fishing/hunting resorts | Sports/celebrity cruises | Golf/tennis tours | Regional/national/ international sport events |
| Sports conferences | Outfitters | Golf cruises | Sports study tours | Championships/ bonspiels/meets/ invitationals/ |
| Demonstrations | Ski resorts | Tennis cruises | Sports adventure tours | Marathons |
| Sports ice sculptures | Sports conferences | Snorkel cruises | Facility/sites event tours | League games/ championships |
| Bungee jumping | Sports camps | Sports cruises | Game safaris | Twinning/ |
| White water rafting | Training camps | Sports attractions visitations | Sports participation tours | Friendships |
| Diving | Volleyball camps | Fishing cruises | Training tours | Games |
| Golf courses | Hockey schools | Yacht charters | Cycle/walking tours | World Cup |
| Ski facilities | Basketball schools | Bareboat chartering | Ski do excursions/ outdoor expeditions | Regattas |
| Water slides | Soccer schools | Card cruises | Adventure tours | Sports festivals |
| Wave tech pools | | | | Super Bowls |
| Stadiums/arenas | | | | Olympic Games |

*Source:*  Adapted from Tourism Sport International Council 1991, Ottawa, Canada.

Even sports that do not ordinarily attract national media attention—soccer, ten-pin bowling, roller skating, bowling on the green, horse shows, softball, rugby, frisbee, swimming, volleyball, and so on—attract thousands of participants and spectators. A YMCA regional swim meet or the state playoffs for softball may draw several hundred visitors who require overnight accommodations. Because many sports events are held on the weekends, local hotels and motels are given an opportunity to fill rooms that would otherwise remain unoccupied.

Certain cities have become centers for regional sports events. For example, Pinehurst, North Carolina; Palm Springs, California; and Myrtle Beach, South Carolina, owe much of their success as visitor destinations to golf. The development of good sports facilities in a community not only provides recreational opportunities for local residents, but may serve as a destination attraction capable of generating millions of dollars in extra revenue.

This does not necessarily imply that cities should spend multimillions for a huge sports arena. Many smaller communities, however, have discovered that expenditures for soft-ball and soccer fields or a swimming pool have reaped economic and social benefits. Capital investments in sports such as ten-pin bowling, skating, or golf, however, are generally private ventures and do not require public investment.

The World Olympics is the biggest of all spectator events. Indeed, countries compete avidly years in advance for the opportunity to host a summer or winter World Olympics. However, the economic cost-benefit of the Olympics to the host community is always uncertain. The state of Colorado, for example, voted not to host the 1980 Winter Olympics after making its initial bid. In subsequent deliberations, it was thought that the cost of building the necessary support facilities and equipment for the event would greatly exceed the return on investment. It was also believed that the extra traffic would interfere with Colorado's traditional ski business and that the potential gains were not sufficient to warrant the expense. On the other hand, Atlanta eagerly sought and successfully won the bid for the 1996 Summer Olympic Games. The problems of hosting differ for each community. They concern such issues as adequacy of travel infrastructure, hotel inventory, housing for athletes, existing sports training and spectator facilities, internal security, local and national support, corporate sponsorships, and hundreds of other details, not least of which involves the expected numbers of visitors and revenues that will be drawn to the community.

Professional sports in North America and in other parts of the world have experienced a virtual explosion in costs. A survey of the top 102 professional sports teams in the U.S. showed that 23 teams lost money in 1991. Costs continue to spiral upwardly. Players and owners clashed over salaries within baseball and hockey in 1994, with resultant strikes and an unsuccessful intervention by the White House in early 1995. The Canadian Football League experienced similar financial problems with every team losing money in 1991. *(60)* Several considered moving to U.S. cities in hopes of drawing larger gates. These financial burdens ultimately mean either bankruptcy for the team or increased prices to spectators—neither of which is encouraging for sports-related tourism.

Television is the primary force that drives the professional sports market. Thanks to the "magic eye," new professional sports are winning fans around the world. A survey by the Sports Marketing Group showed that figure skating and gymnastics—which are widely broadcasted during national regional and international meets as well as during the Olympic Games—are now among the favorite sports in the U.S. *(61)* Without the mass television audience, all sports would undoubtedly suffer dramatic setbacks. In 1991, however, the three major U.S. networks—ABC, CBS, and NBC—all suffered the worst revenue declines in 20 years. *(62)* Much of the decline was attributed to losses on the telecasts of professional sports, serving as a warning to the studios about the realities of keeping the cost of acquiring broadcasting rights in line with media buyer revenues, not simply viewer-market shares.

## Sports Stadiums

In the 1960s, the Kansas City Chiefs football club demanded the first ever U.S. stadium dedicated solely to professional football. *(63)* Since then, sports stadiums have been built in major cities throughout the U.S. and Canada for virtually all major sports. Secondary teams and cities have also spent millions to renovate or build sports stadiums.

City leaders often view a sports stadium as the centerpiece for urban renewal or as a showcase for growth. A modern stadium with sufficient numbers of good seats for spectators is an important tourism resource as it enables a community to host sports competitions and other events, thereby attracting vital tourist expenditures. Financial success from such investment, however, can never be guaranteed. Nashville, Tennessee, for example, built a major sports stadium at a cost of $120 million without first landing a contract with a major sports team. The city and Gaylord Entertainment (owners of Opryland USA theme park) offered $100 million to the Minnesota Timberwolves (NBA) to move to Nashville only to find no interest. Multimillions of dollars have been spent by many smaller cities, including Greenville, South Carolina, and Raleigh, North Carolina, in a gamble to attract better teams, large crowds, and such non-sporting events as rock concerts.

The astrodome in Houston, built in the mid-60s, home of Astroworld, showed that a well-designed stadium could serve as a multiple sports facility and entertainment attraction. Following its example, the owners of the Florida Marlins baseball team, the Miami Dolphins football team and the Florida Panthers hockey team planned to merge the three sports and attract others to a 2500 acre complex north of Miami that would include a stadium and possibly golf courses, a theme park, and a movie studio. *(64)*

New sports stadiums have been built in many countries around the world. At the same time, the world has an overcapacity of convention centers. Since convention centers and sports stadiums often compete for the same non-sporting events, competition becomes intense. Given this scenario and the rising costs of major sports, it would be expected that many communities will experience difficulty issuing bonds to promote the construction of future stadiums. Major labor disputes that draw national or international media attention—the American baseball and hockey players strikes in 1994, for example—do little to assure municipalities or bondholders that debt obligations for a sports stadium would be met.

## Ski Resorts

The $7 billion ski industry in the United States grew at a phenomenal rate during the 1960s and 1970s. Approximately 200,000 new skiers were attracted each year to the activity; but in terms of total number of skiers, the industry peaked in 1988 with 12.3 million skiers. Since then, the industry has lost one million participants, and growth is not anticipated in the near future. *(65)* Many people who took up the sport in their youth are abandoning it largely because it has become too expensive to meet the various costs of travel, lodging, meals, clothing, equipment, and the high chair-lift prices associated with skiing. Skiers who started the sport while single but who now have families are also saddled by the additional cost of child care while at the ski resort.

The ski industry is negatively affected by recessions and weather as well. From the onset of the Persian Gulf War in 1990, over half the **ski resorts** in North America lost money. This resulted in consolidations and closures, with the number of U.S. ski areas shrinking from approximately 1,000 locations in 1975 to 546 in 1994. *(66)* To stay competitive, many of the remaining North American ski destinations have invested heavily in new facilities and equipment. For example, the owners of Blackcomb Mountain,

Aspen is one of the most popular ski resorts in the world. It offers summer events for visitors, as well as skiing in winter.

Canada's top resort, have invested millions into expansion, attracting nearly 800,000 skiers per year with projections of 1 million by the end of the century. *(67)* Some ski resorts are also becoming directly involved with transportation to be competitive. Steamboat Springs in Colorado, for example, guarantees a base income to selected airlines to assure that its ski community will be adequately served by air. Other resorts are involved with light rail and bus systems to bring in skiers.

As a mature industry in North America, skiing faces a number of problems that will affect its future, including:

- *Environmental pressure*   Heavy environmental pressure is being exerted to stop new ski resort development. Sugarbush Ski Resort has done battle with environmentalists over man-made snow from Vermont's Mad River. Environmentalists claim that the drawing of water from the river endangers aquatic life. *(68)* In California, Snow Valley Ski Resort in the San Bernadino Mountains, plans to make artificial snow from treated wastewater, raising environmental health questions. *(69)*

- *Snowboarding*   Nearly 1.5 million individuals have taken up the newer sport of snowboarding. Snowboarders, sometimes referred to as "shredders" or "shred heads," are predominantly young individuals who have never skied. They represent about 11% of ski resort business. One estimate projects 4.8 million snowboarders in the U.S. by the year 2000 and a decrease of 1.9 million, or 1/6 of the skiers. *(70)*

- *Changing market cycles* The baby boomers who made the sport popular during the 60s and 70s are now the "grey market" seeking less hazardous recreation. Their replacement, the young adult market between ages 25 to 35, on the other hand, find that the escalating expenses of a ski trip conflict with other priorities in providing for family needs.

- *Liabilities* Skiing is a dangerous sport. Injuries, including fatal ones, are common to skiing. Many people attribute this to better groomed slopes that permit greater speeds, faster equipment, snowboarders, careless skiers, and poor conditioning and training by some skiers. All of these add to the cost of liability coverage for ski resort operators.

As a result of conditions facing the ski industry, the remaining operators must be ever more professional. SKI, the operator of the Killington and Mt. Snow resorts in Vermont and Bear Mountain Resort in California, has developed a network of information systems to drive every aspect of the business. This includes marketing in which SKI uses a database to send targeted information to potential customers.

The industry itself has also become aggressive in marketing abroad and in targeting niches. About 80% of the skiers in the world live outside the U.S. Foreigners typically spend $250 per day at a ski resort as compared to $150 by U.S. residents. Minority niche markets are also being tapped. For example, groups such as the National Brotherhood of Skiers, a federation of African-American skiers, supply thousands of ski days to the industry. *(71)*

During the 1980s, several large U.S. ski resorts were acquired by Japanese investors. According to experts, a buyer should pay no more than 5–7 times cash flow for a ski resort. *(72)* The Japanese paid considerably more. For instance, the Steamboat Ski and Resort Corporation was reportedly acquired for $110 million by Japan/Camari Kando in 1989. The resort had a cash flow of under $10 million in 1991, which meant valuating the investment at over 11 times cash flow. In other cases, a Tokyo-based sporting goods retailer purchased Breckenridge for $65 million or 13 times cash flow and Vermont's Shatton Mountains in 1989 for about $85 million, or nearly 20 times estimated cash flow. The fact that these resorts are not profitable came as no surprise to industry observers. But current losses notwithstanding, rising prices and further consolidation or closings of ski resorts, as well as recurrent market interest in the sport, may in time make these investments pay off.

## Golf Resorts

**Golf resorts** are an important sector within the travel industry. The number of U.S. golfers is increasing and expected to reach 50 million by the year 2000. *(73)* To serve this growing market, new golf resorts are springing up in many parts of the U.S. The trend today is to design the golf resort as part of a mixed-use development which may include a retirement community, second vacation homes, commercial businesses and professional services.

The golfer's segment is large, affluent and well educated, affording a sizable market for real estate, equipment, and travel. However, as has been the case with the ski and other recreational sectors, the golf industry must also deal with constraints that may limit its full potential for development, including the following:

- *Environment*  Pressures are increasingly mounting against golf resorts from environmentalists for a variety of reasons, including fertilizer and pesticide runoffs, destruction of farm lands and open spaces, destruction of wildlife habitat, extensive land requirements, and heavy water consumption.

- *Prices*  Like skiing, golf enthusiasts have seen dramatic increases in greens fees, cart rentals, and associated travel costs.

- *Costs*  The cost of building and maintaining golf courses is very high. Property taxes represent an additional and seemingly ever-increasing expense. Escalating land prices also affect the development or expansion of golf resorts, particularly in metropolitan or suburban areas.

## Fishing Resorts

The **fishing resort** industry throughout the world remains predominately one of individual proprietorships. Fishing resort operators typically encounter conditions that discourage large investors and chain operators. By their very nature, fishing resorts must be located in remote or semi-remote areas that have limited access. As it is not considered economically feasible to accept guests for only one or two days, many fishing lodge operators have imposed minimum stay policies. This tends to restrict the market to guests who are truly ardent fishing enthusiasts. Fishing lodges are subject to seasonal fluctuations, due to catch limitations and, to some extent, by shifting popularity in fishing locations or by trends in fishing. Many lodges traditionally do not provide adequate financial return beyond the salaries paid to management. In some cases, a husband and wife team owns or is employed to run the lodge, and together their wages do not exceed what they might have made in other jobs. The areas in which the resorts are located often lack the basic infrastructure to support additional capital improvements of a swimming pool, a golf course, a tennis court, or perhaps a larger hotel.

Moreover, fishing lodges in some parts of North America have been adversely affected by environmental pollution, such as water runoff in the Florida Keys, acid rain in the Northeast, or overdevelopment.

A few fishing resorts have attracted international attention through clever use of publicity, with their stories appearing in major media throughout the free world. Solitaire Lodge in New Zealand, for instance, sponsored an event to watch Halley's Comet. This highly unusual event for a fishing lodge attracted wide press coverage.

## Sport Diving

The growing market for sport diving has attracted the attention of national tourism organizations in countries surrounded by ocean with beautiful natural reefs and pristine waters. These organizations seek new opportunities for tourism expansion. While the largest sport diver population is in North America, more than four million divers worldwide have been certified though formal training programs over the past decade; and approximately 500,000 new divers are being trained each year. *(74)* Annual sales in this segment are substantial, as each diver will easily spend from $1,000 to $2,000 on equipment and for travel, accommodations, and meals on dive trips.

## The Disabled Sports Travel Market

The disabled market is small but has been targeted for special attention by various members of the travel industry. A guide book entitled *The Physically Disabled Traveler's Guide* (Resource Directories, Toledo, Ohio) is available for the disabled market segment. Some hotels and resorts cater to these travelers by offering such amenities as pontoon boats or fishing docks able to accommodate wheelchairs. Disabled guests may participate in river rafting, big game hunting, canoeing, and even dog sledding assisted through organizations such as Outward Bound of Minnesota or Wilderness Inquiry II of Minneapolis. Some ski resorts—Winter Park, Colorado, for instance—offer special ski programs for blind and other disabled people.

The **Special Olympics** for the disabled has become an important athletic event, creating a travel market of thousands in the U.S. and abroad. Japan sponsors the International Wheelchair Marathon in which participants from 33 countries compete. *(75)* And Canada sponsors the Canadian Winter Games for the Physically Disabled in which 1,700 disabled athletes from eight countries compete.

## Outdoor Recreation and Tourism

Participation in sports activities are generally bound by the demographic characteristics of a population. This permits travel planners and promoters to target restricted market segments for particular recreational or sports activities. For instance, walking for pleasure or swimming is very popular among older individuals with incomes over $50,000 per year. In a recent National Recreation Survey, 12% of respondents in the survey indicated that they participated in birdwatching or other nature activities. When applied to population figures, this percentage translates into approximately 22 million people nationwide who enjoy birdwatching. A market of this size offers opportunities for specialized enterprises ranging from the sales of tours and lodging to the selling of equipment and literature for birdwatchers.

## Importance of Public Lands

North Americans are fortunate to have a well-developed system of state or provincial and federal land administration for outdoor recreation. The impact of public recreational areas upon the physical and psychological well-being of a nation, as well as its economic system, is staggering. Numerous employment opportunities exist not only within the agencies responsible for the management of recreational parks, forests and natural wilderness preserves, but also with private concessionaires operating on leases or contract arrangement with the government to serve the general public at recreational sites. These concessions may range from small country stores offering groceries and supplies to multimillion dollar investments in lodging and dining.

The very success of the nation's parks, forests, and other outdoor resources has created a multitude of problems. Nearly 300 million people visit national parks each year, and millions more visit national forests, monuments, and areas managed by the Bureau of Land Management.

The popularity of these areas has fomented numerous controversies and problems, including:

- *Helicopter, snowmobile, and airplane access*  Many communities object to hearing or seeing motorized vehicles in or over outdoor public recreation areas. New environmental laws are constantly introduced to restrict the operation of these vehicles, but the economic interest of a community or suggested infringement on individual rights are heard as counter-arguments.

- *Sanitation and law enforcement*  The tidal wave of humanity that visits the outdoors brings with it thousands of tons of garbage and social problems. Federal and state officials are concerned not only with sewage and trash collection, but also with crime that takes place on public lands.

- *Accessibility*  How accessible should public parks and forests be? One sector of society wants more recreational areas closed to vehicular traffic to preserve their natural beauty, while another wants more opened to provide greater convenience for recreationists.

- *Conservation*  Concepts of conservation are changing. While Smokey the Bear epitomized the philosophy of preventing forest and brush fires during the 1970s, a new philosophy says, "let it burn—it's nature's way."

- *Hunting and fishing*  Some people feel that all hunting and fishing should be banned. Others feel it is essential to harvest excess game, to cull overpopulation of certain game, as well as providing recreation and jobs.

These are only a few of the issues that confront the nation and the federal and state departments responsible for the care of public lands. A growing population and increasing social pressures will make public lands even more of a national treasure. A survey by the National Parks and Recreation Association showed that in 1971, 22% of the population felt rushed and stressed in their lives; by 1992, this number had increased to 38%. In 1992, 48% of the population said they had less leisure time than they had five years earlier. *(76)* An increasingly stressed-out population highlights the growing importance of public lands for recreational purposes.

# ʃ UMMARY

People travel for many reasons, not least among them is a human need to acquire new experiences and to find periodic relief from the stress of contemporary living. In tourism, the sectors devoted to recreation, entertainment, and amusement help satisfy these needs.

The amusement, recreation, and entertainment sector of the travel industry is undergoing dramatic change. Gaming has become a megadollar industry and growing ever larger. Many sectors appear to be dangerously close to overcapacity in terms of excess supply to slowing, if steady, markets. In the case of such facilities as sports stadiums and convention centers, the tax payers may be left with large debts. The cost structure of professional sports now threatens to seriously disrupt this sector, while competition poses new challenges within the theme park sector. Also, as new challenges confront these businesses, management must become increasingly professional and essential as competitors vie for market share and profits. Many professional careers exist within the amusement, recreation, and entertainment related businesses, and opportunities will continue to be available as this sector becomes ever more sophisticated with respect to development and technology, marketing and management, and in moving towards consolidation and strategic alliances.

# DISCUSSION QUESTIONS

1. What is the relationship between amusement parks, theme parks, and amusement arcades?

2. What are the major sectors of the gaming industry? Are these sectors gaining or losing in popularity in North America.

3. What are the primary problems/obstacles facing the North American ski industry?

4. Are these risks associated with the growth of sports stadiums and aquariums? If so, identify and discuss them.

5. What is the significance of event marketing to the travel industry?

6. How can tourism and the arts work in partnership?

7. What do you believe are the primary reasons for the growth of urban entertainment centers?

8. Discuss the probable future of pari-mutuel wagering in North America.

9. If Las Vegas continues to grow as a family destination, what should Disney do as a strategic response?

10. What is the possible future for children's programs outside of resorts?

11. Event marketing by cigarette companies has come under criticism by many individuals, including the President of the United States. What is your opinion of event marketing by cigarette and alcoholic beverage companies?

12. What could a hotel or resort do to benefit from the family reunion market?

13. What can a community do to increase its role as a center for regional sports events?

14. What do you believe is the future for hunting and fishing lodges?

15. Discuss the role of public lands. Should these areas serve multiple functions, such as logging, mining, recreation, hunting, fishing, and other uses?

# SUGGESTED STUDENT EXERCISES

1. Make an inventory of the various historic places and cultural events in your community. Analyze them for their importance as tourism draws.

   a. How many visitors come to your community because of those attractions?

b. What are their economic contributions?

c. What, if any, are the environmental or social constraints of these attractions?

d. How might these attractions be better promoted?

2. Check with officials from your nearest sports stadium. What are their opinions about the economic importance of the stadium?

3. Check factories and other industrial or farm organizations in your area to see if they offer industrial tours. Are these viewed as important or unimportant by your community's convention and visitors bureau?

4. Survey the performing and fine arts centers in your community. Do the directors of these centers consider tourism important to the success of their enterprises? What should be done to strengthen the role and relationship of the arts with tourism in your community?

# REFERENCES

1. Shaw, D.V. "Making Leisure Pay: Street Railway Owned Amusement Parks in the U.S. 1900–1925," Department of Urban Studies, University of Akron, paper presented, Avignon, France, May, 12–14, 1986.

2. Strickland, Carol. "The Smiling Aspects of Life," *Civilization*, Vol. 2, No. 3, May/June, 1995, pg. 64.

3. Tingley, C. L. S. "Summer Parks," *Street Railway Journal* 15 (September 15, 1905); "The Management and Equipment of Railway Amusement Resorts," *Street Railway Journal* 27 (March 24, 1908).

4. "Theme Parks: Feeling the Future," *The Economist*, Vol. 330, February 19, 1994, pg. 74.

5. "Zoos: Not Endangered," *The Economist*, Vol. 319, April 13, 1991, pg. 55–56.

6. Hamilton, David P. "Sega Theme Park Touts Thrills Based on High Technology," *Wall Street Journal*, July 19, 1994, pg. B6.

7. Graves, Jacqueline M. "Profit Lessons for Disney," *Fortune*, Vol. 129, June 27, 1994, pg. 13.

8. Sharpe, Anita, and Gibson, Richard. "Blockbuster to Boost Stake in Discovery, Which is Burying a McDonald's Unit," *Wall Street Journal*, July 19, 1994, pg, B6.

9. Rom, Jane. "New Departures in Terminal Contest," *Asian Business*, Vol. 29, April 1993, pg. 66.

10. "Theme Parks: Feeling the Future," *The Economist*, Vol. 330, February 19, 1994, pg. 74.

11. Horwitz, Tony, and Turner, Richard. "Disney and Academics Escalate Battle Over the Entertainment Value of History," *Wall Street Journal*, June 21, 1994, pg. B1–B2.

12. Mahar, Maggie. "Not-so-Magic Kingdom," *Barron's*, Vol. 74, June 20, 1994, pg. 29–33.

13. "Theme Parks: Heart, Brains, Jobs," *The Economist*, Vol. 328, September 4, 1993, pg. 33.

14. Turner, Richard, "New Theme Parks Will Take Owners on a Risky Ride," *Wall Street Journal*, December 2, 1993, pg. B1.

15. Sterngold, James, "Tokyo's Magic Kingdom Outshines It's Role Model," *New York Times*, March 7, 1994, pg. D1.

16. "Jesus and Other Japanese Attractions," *The Economist*, Vol. 330, January 22, 1994, pg. 39.

17. "Gambling in America: King Kirk's Castle," *The Economist*, Vol. 329, December 18, 1993, pg. 61.

18. Commission on the Review of the National Policy Toward Gambling, 1976 Gambling in America. Washington, DC: U.S. Government Printing Office.

19. Shapiro, Harvey, O. "A Full House," *Hemispheres*, October 1994, pg. 78–84.

20. "Survey Shows Gambling's Popularity," *Hotel and Motel-Management*, Vol. 209, March 21, 1994, pg. 3.

21. Grover, Roland, "Will Too Many Players Spoil the Game?" *Business Week*, October 18, 1993, pg. 80.

22. Troy, Timothy N., "Betting Big on Repositioning Plan," *Hotel and Motel Management*, Vol. 208, October 4, 1993, pg. 3.

23. Campbell, Jenny. "Around the Clock Gaming Thrives in Atlantic City," *Hotel and Motel Management*, Vol. 208, July 26, 1993, pg. 3.

24. Rowe, Megan. "Las Vegas Big Gamble," *Lodging-Hospitality*, Vol. 50, February 1994, pg. 26–27.

25. MacDonald, Julie. "Vegas Welcomes New Hotels," *Hotel and Motel Management*, Vol. 208, October 4, 1993, pg. 3.

26. Yoshihashi, Pauline, "Luxor Bets on High-Tech Entertainment," *Wall Street Journal* (Eastern Edition), July 9, 1993, pg. B1.

27. Emory, Thomas, Jr. "Crime Isn't All That's Hurting Florida Tourism," *Wall Street Journal*, Marketplace, Thursday, November 3, 1994, pg. B1.

28. "Rolling The Dice," *The Economist*, Vol. 325, December 26, 1992–January 8, 1993, pg. 89–90.

29. Shapiro, Harvey O. "A Full House," *Hemispheres*, October 1994, pg. 81.

30. "Survey Shows Gambling's Popularity," *Hotel and Motel Management*, Vol. 209, March 21, 1994, pg. 3.

31. Bromberg, Al. "Shipboard Casinos Enjoy a Wave of Popularity with Cruises," *Travel Weekly*, October 6, 1986.

32. Hong, Peter. "Not With our Games You Don't," *Business Week*, July 22, 1991, pg. 24.

33. Pepper, Anne G. "Japan's Horse Racing Mania," *Japan 21st*, Vol. 37, September 1992, pg. 11.

34. Hawkins, Chuck, and Melcher, Richard A. "Horse Sense or Horsefeathers?" *Business Week*, October 23, 1991, pg. 54.

35. "Greyhounds and Grey Hairs," *The Economist*, Vol. 321, October 26, 1991, pg. 35.

36. Makens, James C. "Children at Resorts: Customer Service at Its Best," The Cornell Hotel and Restaurant Administration Quarterly, August 1992, pg. 25–35.

37. Alderson, J.W. "Is Entertainment An Underrated Key to Success?" *Hotel and Resort Industry*, August 1983.

38. *Ibid.*

39. LaFranco, Robert. "The Tightest Man in Show Business?" *Forbes*, Vol. 152, November 8, 1993, pg. 67–68.

40. Collins, Glenn. "Ringling Circus Expanding Its Territory," *New York Times*, July 23, 1994, pg. 37.

41. Blears, James. "Star Crossed Mexico," *Business Mexico*, Vol. 3, December 1993, pg. 31–33.

42. Beaumont, Stephen. "900 Barrels of Beer on the Wall," *Hemisphere*, October 1994, pg. 95–96.

43. Manly, Lorne. "Sports Marketing Draws a Crowd," *Folio: The Magazine for Magazine Management*, Vol. 22, August 15, 1993, pg. 19.

44. Warner, Fara. "Inventive Events Marketers Cutting a Grassroots Edge," *Brandweek*, Vol. 35, January 24, 1994, pg. 18–19.

45. Serafin, Raymond. "Saturn is in Rah Rah Mood for Homecoming," *Advertising Age*, Vol. 65, June 6, 1994, pg. 8.

46. Jacquette, Leslee. "Hotel Set to Harvest Agri-Tour Business," *Hotel and Motel Management*, Vol. 207, September 21, 1992, pg. 4.

47. Robinson, John. "The Arts Hold Steady in Hard Times," *American Demographics*, Vol. 16, February 1994, pg. 9–10.

48. Magrath, Allen. "Give Marketing Performance a Bigger Role in the Arts," *Marketing News,* Vol. 24, October 1, 1990, pg. 16.

49. Barker, Lori, "Artificial Inspiration," *Restaurant Business*, Vol. 89, May 1, 1990, pg. 102.

50. Grover, Ronald. "Imerks: Playpen for the 90's," *Business Week*, March 7, 1994, pg. 73.

51. Flanagan, William G. "D-Day Plus 18,250," *Forbes*, Vol., 153, February 28, 1994, pg. 114–116.

52. Pepper, Anne G. "The Business of Museums," *Japan 21st*, Vol. 38, December 1993, pg. 13.

53. Hass, Nancy. "Philadelphia Freedom," *Financial World*, Vol. 162, August 3, 1993, pg. 36–37.

54. Gatterso, Greg. "Back to the Future," *Direct-Marketing*, Vol. 56, December 1993, pg. 32–35.

55. "The Top 100 Events in North America," Washington, DC, The American Bus Association.

56. "Sellvis," *The Economist*, Vol. 327, April 10, 1993, pg. 66.

57. Underwood, Elaine. "Aquatic Fever: With Government shot for Urban Redevelopment and Tourism: The 1990's Are the Age of Aquariums," *Ad Week's Marketing Week*, Vol. 33, February 10, 1982, pg. 24.

58. Frank, Robert. "Fishing for Business: Cities Hope if They Build an Aquarium, Crowds Will Come," *The Wall Street Journal, Marketplace,* Thursday, October 27, 1994, pg. B1.

59. "NASCAR Leads Attendance Higher at North American Series," *Automotive News*, May 17, 1993, pg. 13.

60. Symonds, William C. "Canadian Football Looks for Daylight," Business Week, December 2, 1991, pg. 106.

61. "Game Plans," The Economist, Vol. 330, March 19, 1994, pg. 108.

62. Foisie, Geoffrey. "Big Three '91 Financial Results Advertise a Bad Year," Broadcasting, Vol. 122, April 13, 1992, pg. 4.

63. Flynn, Michael J., and Linda Kephart Flynn. "Sporting in Style," *Hemispheres*, October 1994, pg. 105–110.

64. Loeb, Marshall. "There's No Business Like Show Business," *Fortune*, Vol. 130, August 8, 1994, pg. 111–112.

65. Warner, Fara. "Economy Class Powder," *Ad Week's Marketing Week*, Vol. 32, December 2, 1991, pg. 18–19.

66. Stern, Richard L. "Downhill Braces," *Forbes*, Vol. 147, May 27, 1991, pg. 55.

67. Koch, George. "Indomitable Snowman," *Canadian Business*, Vol. 67, February 1994, pg. 56–58.

68. Maremont, Mark. "Do Snowy Slopes Mean Dead Fish? It's Angry Environmentalists vs. Slumping Ski Resorts in Vermont," *Business Week*, March 15, 1993, pg. 99.

69. "California Ski Resort to Make Snow from Treated Wastewater," *ENR*, Vol. 230, February 1, 1993, pg. 24.

70. "The Battle of the Piste," *The Economist*, Vol. 327, April 24, 1993, pg. 96.

71. Johnson, Karen L. "Great Skiing," *Black Enterprise*, Vol. 22, June 1992, pg. 85–86.

72. "When Marvin Davis is Selling," *Forbes*, Vol. 147, May 27, 1991, pg. 64.

73. Morse, Sarah, and Pamela Lanier. "Golf Resorts Driving into the 90's," The Cornell Hotel and Restaurant Administration Quarterly, Vol. 33, August 1992, pg. 44–48.

74. Walsh, Don. "Marine Recreation: The Fast-Track Ocean Resource," *Sea Technology*, January 1992, pg. 43.

75. Pepper, Anne G. "Oita's Wheelchair Marathon," *Japan 21st*, Vol. 37, January 1992, pg. 11.

76. Godbey, Geoffrey, and Alan Graefe. "Rapid Growth in Rushin' America," *American Demographics*, Vol. 15, April 1993, pg. 26.

# Chapter 16

# Travel-related Shopping and Financial Services

---

## LEARNING OBJECTIVES

- To appreciate the importance of shopping and traveler financial services to tourism.

- To understand what factors are important to the successful marketing of retail products for travelers.

- To understand how duty-free stores operate.

- To understand changes in the financial services sector.

- To define and use the following terms:

| | |
|---|---|
| Airborne advertising | Duty free stores |
| Briefing | Factory outlet store |
| Cooperative advertising/promotion | Float |
| Cross-selling | General usage cards |
| Custom label | Generic brands |
| Debit cards | Hard currency |
| Delivered merchandise system | Inbound duty-free |
| Direct response/direct mail advertising | In-room shopping |

| | |
|---|---|
| Kiosks | Retail clustering |
| Knock-off merchandise | Shelter advertising |
| Logo merchandise/shops | Signature products |
| Mass display | Smart card |
| Merchandise mix | Special packaging services |
| Multi-media interactive systems | Suitcase tourism |
| Niche farmers | Transit advertising |
| Omiyage | Travel and entertainment card |
| Price points | Travel vouchers |
| Private label brands | Travelers check |
| Product mix management | Upselling |
| Product line extension | |

# TRAVEL-RELATED SHOPPING

Travelers from all parts of the world enjoy shopping. Even the most casual observation of traveler behavior would show that shopping seems to be the first and last thing visitors do upon reaching and leaving a destination. Nor are business travelers any exception. Those who travel for business often squeeze in time to buy gifts for family members or business associates or for themselves before returning home.

For many people, shopping is the main reason for traveling. The term "**suitcase tourism**" is sometimes used to describe this activity. Recent visitors from Japan to Hawaii, for instance, rated shopping as being more important than beaches in their choice of Hawaii as a vacation destination. Travel for the purpose of shopping is especially common in border states or countries where special shopping plazas and other retail amenities are designed and built for visitors from the neighboring country. A study of Mexican visitors to the U.S. showed that 61% of the Mexicans who visited Arizona listed shopping as their primary motivation for the trip. *(1)*

Various countries have developed international reputations as shopping meccas. In Europe, three countries—the United Kingdom, France, and Italy—stand out as places offering a wide range of luxury and specialty goods. English silver, French fashion, and Italian leather products are examples that quickly come to mind when shoppers think of those countries. Within Asia, Hong Kong, and Singapore are popular visitor destinations with a strong shopping image. Indeed, shopping comprises over half of the revenue generated by tourism from these two destinations. Singapore and Hong Kong are similar to other urban destinations with limited visitor attractions where shopping can offer a viable draw for visitors.

## Retailing to Visitors

The importance of shopping to the travel industry is illustrated by the story of the Edmonton Mall—the world's largest and widest indoor shopping complex—in West Edmonton, Alberta, Canada. The mall was developed by the Ghermezian brothers, Iranian émigré entrepreneurs whose financial empire began with the Persian rug business in West Edmonton. The family's original intent had been only to develop a conventional mall with a kiddie train operation as a novelty. *(2)* Eventually, the project expanded into a $792 million mall complete with a church, restaurants, and an amusement park where visitors might surf on 6-foot waves in the indoor waterpark, freefall on a 13-story Daring Drop of Doom in Fantasyland, or shop in a seemingly endless variety of 828 stores. Despite the relative isolation of Edmonton and harsh winters in the area,

Millions of visitors are drawn annually to the West Edmonton Mall for shopping, dining, amusement and complete entertainment offered in five major attractions, including the world's largest indoor wavepool.
Courtesy of West Edmonton Mall, Edmonton, Alberta, Canada.

the mall supports 23,500 jobs and attracts 6 million visitors per year who arrive by auto, charter bus, and plane.

Numerous malls in the U.S. have developed aggressive marketing programs to attract specific groups of tourist shoppers. For instance, wealthy and upper-middle class Mexicans are targeted by malls in Houston, Dallas, San Antonio, Miami, San Diego, Los Angeles, and Scottsdale, Arizona. These visitors find shopping in the U.S. appealing for three main reasons: the wide selection of merchandise available, the relative ease of reaching the U.S., and the excellent tourism support services offered, including good restaurants, comfortable hotels, theatres, and other entertainment amenities.

To promote visitor shopping, some retailers will travel to Mexico each year to participate in Mexico's largest travel show. U.S. shopping malls that cater to Mexicans may offer special shopping discounts in packages available through Mexican travel agencies. Within the Galleria Mall in Houston, some exclusive stores have their own promotional programs for targeting well-to-do Mexican shoppers. Neiman Marcus, for example, sponsors a special invitation-only party for Mexican charge card customers. This store also sponsors fashion shows in Monterey and Mexico City to stimulate buyer interest.

Many sectors of the travel industry benefit from visitor shopping. Year-round Mexican guests represent 14% of the business at Westin Hotels Galleria and Oaks properties in Houston. Over 9,000 Mexican shoppers stay at these hotels between Thanksgiving and Christmas each year. In 1994, Mexico saw a 13% devaluation in the value of the Mexican peso against the U.S. dollar. Nevertheless, hotel bookings by Mexican shoppers increased by 20%, demonstrating the strong lure of shopping to certain markets even under adverse economic conditions.

Airlines also benefit from this shopper influx. Air traffic soars when discount fares are offered between Mexico–U.S. city-pairs, such as Monterey and Houston. Although the trip is short enough to allow relatively easy driving, Mexico shoppers generally find it more advantageous to fly instead of drive. Mexicans returning by auto are limited to tax-exempt goods not exceeding $50, but air travelers are permitted $300 each. *(3)* There are also frequent delays at border crossings.

There is no doubt that shopping can add to travel pleasure. Travelers enjoy purchasing unusual gifts and personal items and are disappointed when they find little selection or nothing to buy at a destination. The role of retail products impacts the travel and tourism in various ways:

- *Products can help advertise the destination.* Certain products such as carpets, food and liquor, hats, handicrafts, and art objects become synonymous with a destination and are recognized even by those who have never visited the area.

- *Products add to the excitement of the destination.* Very few tourists spend all their time on the beach or observing the beauty of the mountains, lakes, or other natural surroundings. Shopping is valued as a leisure activity in its own right.

- *Products support a retail industry.* Retailing is an important source of employment for local residents.

- *Products can create or support a cottage industry for local handicrafts.* This helps to preserve native art forms and culture.

## Products Aimed at Travelers

Not all products are suitable for travelers. Selecting which products to offer requires an understanding of the travelers and their spending habits. Travelers of different nationalities vary greatly in their shopping habits.

Hotels, restaurants, airlines, cruise ships, and others have learned that tremendous profit potential exists in the sale of the right mix of merchandise for visitors. Entertainment restaurants such as Hard Rock Cafe and Planet Hollywood add impressive profit gains through the sale of merchandise. An estimated 40% of Hard Rock's revenue, for example, comes from merchandise sales, mainly to tourists. Similarly, the Harley-Davidson Cafe in New York does an estimated $40,000 to $50,000 per week in merchandise. *(4)*

Cruise lines and airlines both profit from the sale of onboard merchandise. A glimpse of the profit potential available to airlines is provided by SkyMall, a company that sells products through glossy catalogs in the seatbacks of Amtrak, Delta, United, and Continental Airlines. Sales generated through these sources reached $30 million in 1993 compared to $6 million in 1991. *(5)* Passenger boredom in combination with impulse shopping is the greatest asset of this company.

Success in the sale of merchandise to visitors is seldom the result of luck, but instead rests on continuous study and observation of travelers, their shopping habits, and preferences. For example, the Japanese visitor to Hawaii outspends the average visitor by over three times. Examining these expenditures reveals that the Japanese visitor spends less for lodging and food as a percentage of total expenditures than other visitors, and disproportionately more for gifts and souvenirs. Spending for souvenirs and gifts is high among the Japanese due to their custom of **omiyage**, which dictates that travelers return home with gifts for friends and relatives. See Table 16.1.

## Achieving Product Sales Success

To achieve success in retailing to visitors, the travelers' needs must be understood and met. The following marketing and merchandising tactics should be carefully considered and planned, always bearing in mind the psychology of travel spending when visitors are consciously seeking unique gifts and products to take home and subconsciously less inhibited with regard to budgets:

1. Brand names and logos

2. Product and package size

3. Price points

4. Sensory attributes (color, feel, taste, and aroma)

5. Preferred purchase times

6. Location of stores and merchandise

7. Product advertising/promotion

### Brand Names and Logos

Many shoppers within Europe and North America purchase **generic** or **private label brands**. They believe these products give exceptionally good value for the price. Products

| TABLE 16.1 Japanese Tourist Shopping | | |
|---|---|---|
| **TYPES OF STORES PATRONIZED** | **Male (%)** | **Female (%)** |
| Duty free (airport/plane) | 78.6 | 72.6 |
| Gift shop | 44.3 | 56.9 |
| Department store (incl. supermarket) | 43.1 | 57.8 |
| Tax free shop (city/hotel) | 38.4 | 62.5 |
| Specialty shop | 39.5 | 42.8 |
| **FIVE MOST POPULAR ITEMS PURCHASED** | **Male (%)** | **Female (%)** |
| Whiskey | 67.5 | 65.1 |
| Chocolate, candy | 50.9 | 73.9 |
| Tobacco | 56.8 | 57.2 |
| Perfume, cosmetics | 44.8 | 73.1 |
| Clothing | 29.1 | 47.2 |
| **OTHER FACTS** | | |
| • Average expenditures for shopping and omiyage: $984.61 | | |
| • Most popular months of travel: January, March, June, August, December | | |
| • Typical visitor profile: Ages between 20-29, married | | |
| • Packaging of merchandise is as important, if not more, than merchandise itself | | |

*Source:* Chamber of Commerce of Hawaii.

with generic brands are identified only by the product, and not by its brand name. Private labels are normally close copies of manufacturer brands. Large retailers such as Krogers, Eckerds Drug Store, and Kmart carry their own brands of products. These are normally less expensive than manufacturers' brands. Foreign shoppers, however, are not, as a rule, enthusiastic about generic or private label products. Most are highly brand conscious and normally want well-known names associated with class and status.

The sophisticated traveler often views Hermes, Gucci, Crown Royal, and hundreds of other luxury brands as better bargains away from home. Japanese and other Asian visitors will seek out well-known brand name products of all kinds, wherever they travel. Having such products available can be a highly important source of revenue for retailers. For example, top-of-the-line luggage, which carry prices of $1,000 or more, seem to find a receptive market in Japanese visitors who view them as good buys, even though their prices seem breathtaking to most Americans.

A preference for name brand merchandise is not restricted to the Japanese. U.S. retailers indicate that upper-class Mexican shoppers are equally brand-conscious, and not particularly inclined to purchase "**knock-off**" copies or private label merchandise. *(6)* They are also more willing to buy what is available in stock rather than to wait for different colors or styles. Many retailers have learned to capitalize on this need for instant gratification by offering Mexican shoppers such services as on-the-spot alterations or package delivery to their hotels or motels.

## Logos

An interesting phenomena has occurred within the travel industry. Numerous well-known hotels, restaurants, clubs, theme parks, airlines, and cruise ships have established such strong brand names and images that travelers seek out products bearing these identities. Hard Rock Cafe and Disney World are examples of travel industry names that have become valuable properties with respect to their logo images. Which young person would not instantly recognize the distinctive logotype of the Hard Rock Cafe? Would anyone, young or old, anywhere in the world, not know Mickey Mouse or his famous ears?

The sale of **logo merchandise** has become so popular that some upscale hotels have developed **logo shops** within or near their hotels to sell the hotel's own logo products. Singapore's Raffles Hotel has a logo shop in the hotel's shopping mall as does the Peninsula Hotel of Hong Kong and the Sheraton Mirage of Australia's Gold Coast. Many logo shops now cater to non-travelers as well as travelers. The Harley-Davidson Cafe in New York and the Hard Rock Cafe in Hyde Park, London, are among many successful

Model Christy Turington, one of the owners of the Fashion Cafe, signs logo merchandise for a customer in the restaurant's retail shop.
Courtesy of The Fashion Cafe, N.Y.C.

restaurants with merchandise shops that open directly onto the street. The non-restaurant visitor has become an important customer for these shops.

Some logo shops have adopted the strategy of dating to enhance product sales. The Black Dog Tavern in Martha's Vineyard prints dates on their logo T-shirts, making them into collector's items. The tavern annually sells 80,000 articles of clothing. *(7)*

The spa industry has also discovered that the sale of beauty care and accessory products can be one of its more profitable ventures. It is possible to generate a high volume of sales in limited space with low selling costs. Products sold in spa retail outlets fall into three categories: brand name products, private label products, and **custom label** or **signature products**. *(8)* While signature products require some research and planning, they have the advantage of being truly unique to the spa. Thus these items not only produce added revenue, but they also serve as advertising vehicles.

The strategy of **product line extension** is increasingly important in retailing. It is based on developing a line of products as an extension of an already successful brand name. The product line may vary in product attributes such as strength, color, odor, flavor, or size. Thus, successful producers of sun screen products for beachgoers have built line extensions for different demographic segments or to serve different life styles, as in the case of children or skiers and so forth. Sun screen companies have also used different fragrances and different package sizes to extend their lines.

Some hotels have discovered they can use a product line extension strategy to sell the personal care products they provide as amenities in guest rooms. For example, the Randall Products Company, which supplies personal care products to such famous hotels as the Boca Raton Resort and the Waldorf Astoria, also offers larger sizes of the same products which may be purchased for retailing in hotel gift shops. *(9)*

## Product and Package Size

Frequent travelers typically look for quality products that will easily fit into a briefcase or purse. It has been observed that the more a person travels, the less interested they seem to be in carrying large parcels. There are also constraints imposed by airlines and airport security. Airlines have established weight and size limits, as well as limits on the number of items that may be hand carried on board, especially on international flights. Bulky or odd-shaped items that do not fit easily under seats or in overhead racks must be checked in as regular luggage, and this tends to discourage impulse buying.

The success of many traveler-oriented products often depends on how such products are packed and whether **special packaging services** are available. Some retailers solve their customers' problems by featuring airport delivery and special packaging for travel as part of their services. Visitors to Sydney, Australia, for example, may take home boxes of Australian steaks packed in dry ice that will last over the full duration of a long-haul flight. Visitors to Boston often leave with live lobsters packed in special containers. The famous cured hams and bacon of Virginia, Georgia and the other southern states are typically found conveniently packed in muslin bags at the airport of these states for travelers to tote on board. Fresh papayas and pineapples sold at the Honolulu International Airport are prechecked by agricultural inspectors and then packed for ease in carrying onboard the aircraft.

Careful **merchandise mix** decisions made with the traveler in mind contribute greatly to profit improvement and satisfied customers. Sophisticated travelers with space constraints are likely to favor high value, small items such as quality pen sets, silk scarves, jewelry, and perfume. Business travelers like calculators, cameras and electronic items. Attractively packaged food, whether chocolate or cheese, is universally liked by travelers because these items are easy to slip into a tote bag and are suitable as gifts for almost anyone. Travelers who shop for children, on the other hand, are often disappointed to find that most toys are unsuitable or bulky and impossible to fit into hand luggage. There would appear to be a market niche for a toy manufacturer to specialize in quality small gifts for children which can be sold at airports or other tourist shopping stops.

Retailers who cater to foreign visitors arriving by private vehicle often see an opposite product/package size need. These travelers have the space to carry large packages and often look for maximum value in quantity. Also, if these visitors are limited by how much they may bring home because of high custom taxes, then the largest sizes offering maximum value for money is a key selling point.

## Price Points

Retailers offer product lines based on pre-determined **price points**. Brand conscious shoppers of prestige merchandise are prepared to pay higher prices and will seek out costly quality goods. Travelers looking for casual souvenir items, on the other hand, will have lower price points in mind. Retailers recognize that there are appropriate price points for every category of merchandise and class of shopper. Beyond certain price points, sellers also know there will be sales resistance. It is important, therefore, to be able to match products and prices with customer expectations and demands.

Price points for souvenir items will vary by markets, by consumer segments, and by products. If a popular price point is $1.99, vendors should offer a choice of products at that point, rather than at $1.49 or $2.49. The next price point might be $4.99, in which case vendors would offer a selection of goods at that point rather than at $4.49 or $5.49.

Given a limitation of space and the high cost of overhead in many of the stores where travelers shop, price points are especially important in determining the type of merchandise that may be profitably sold to tourists. The use of price points, in a sense, encourages retailers to deal in specialty products for selected market segments. This helps the retailer to reduce his or her investment in inventories by reducing variety and to seek higher turnover in sales, thereby making more efficient use of selling space.

The shopping behavior of travelers has not been studied extensively, but it has been noted that people do buy souvenirs and gifts with categories of recipients in mind. Co-workers and neighbors back home, for example, may merit lower-level price point gifts than close relatives or the boss. Therefore, some understanding of the buyer's intended purpose for the purchase may determine the most appropriate price points.

## Sensory Attributes

Successful retailers to tourists have learned that tastes and preferences are often rooted in cultural and geographic differences. For example, Europeans as a whole tend to buy wines that are full-bodied and dry, while Asians generally prefer wines that are light and less dry. People from the Mediterranean area generally prefer pastels and brighter colors, while those from Scandinavia seem to prefer darker, more subdued colors. There are exceptions, of course, but the point is that when it comes to retailing for visitors, their origins, gender and age are important demographic factors for consideration.

Successful retailers learn by observing their customers and the products they buy. They must remain ever alert to changing traveler demographics and to provide products that correspond with shifting visitor market needs or demands. It is interesting to observe that some airport concessionaires in the U.S. now offer Kosher products to meet the needs of East Coast passengers. And concessionaires and retailers in the Miami Airport offer an array of foods and products geared to Latin taste and style preferences.

## Preferred Purchase Times

Travelers are sometimes disappointed to find that stores are closed when they want to shop because of local customs or laws. One such example is the so-called "blue laws," or Sunday closing laws, which restrict the sale of goods or other activities such as the operation of a movie theater on Sunday. These laws are rooted in the Christian religious tradition dating back to the Middle Ages. The name "blue laws" was coined when the Sunday closing laws of New Haven, Connecticut, were printed on blue paper in 1781. In many communities, however, increased tourism has often served as a catalyst for changing these laws or traditions, making it possible for visitors to patronize tourist stores or to enjoy activities that are restricted or off-limits to residents. New Zealand retailers, for instance, customarily close at noon on Saturday and remain closed until Monday morning. Since short-stay visitors might only have free times for shopping on weekends, stores in tourist areas such as Queenstown, New Zealand, began to stay open, despite a long established tradition of barring commercial activities on weekends.

Late-arriving travelers to hotels often find the gift shop closed, and there is nowhere to purchase forgotten items such as antacids, toothpaste, or headache remedies. A resourceful entrepreneur developed a small display of such frequently purchased items for sale in the hotel's coffee shop or at the front desk after the gift shop closes. The housekeeping departments of some hotels have also stocked personal grooming kits which are available for sale or as complimentary giveaways upon request.

The following are other examples of shopping constraints encountered by visitors:

- Tour groups that leave from the hotel early in the morning and return just before the evening meal. This creates a frantic shopping rush if local stores close at 6:00 or 6:30 P.M.

- Travelers from religious faiths that consider Saturday the Sabbath and cannot shop on this day, even though stores may be closed on Sunday.

- Early departure travelers who find stores closed at their train, bus, boat, or air terminal.

- Travelers who use their lunch hour to shop only to find that it is "siesta" time and stores are closed.

- Travelers who find the store open, but cannot purchase certain items such as liquor because of local laws that restrict the sale of these items to given hours of the day.

- In-transit international passengers who are confined to a special area of the airport whose arrival times and store hours do not mesh or where stores have little to offer in-transit shoppers.

## Location of Stores and Merchandise

As discussed above, tourists and business travelers have time constraints. They may not be familiar with the areas where they are staying, and often do not have access to private automobiles. Consequently, they are unlikely to visit shopping places too far from their hotels. Convenience becomes a major factor for patronage. For this reason, the square footage rental fees for retail space near hotels and tourist areas are generally high and are reflected in the retail prices of the products. Despite the high rental costs of operating in these concentrated traffic centers, merchants find that they are still the best locations for achieving maximum sales.

In Chapter 14, the effectiveness of clustering restaurant facilities was discussed. Similarly, the grouping together of many merchants in a concentrated area (**retail clustering**) provides a positive shopping ambiance. In a real sense, these merchants have become as much colleagues as competitors, attracting more business collectively by working together than by distancing themselves from each other.

One of the earliest European travelers, Marco Polo, discovered the allure and excitement of seeing massive quantities of merchandise piled on docks and in the open markets of Cathay. Upon his return from China, he commented on the use of **mass display**, or **mass merchandising** by eastern merchants and the appeal this had for the buyer. Centuries later, the chronicler for Cortez rediscovered this phenomenon when he saw the marketplace of Mexico City and reported how this created an irresistible buying urge. All the products offered for sale may be similar in price and quality, but the ability to compare prices, sizes, and colors in one place helps to sell more products.

The placement of merchandise within a retail store is also a critical factor in selling goods. Space within most retail stores is limited; therefore, manufacturers of goods for the tourist market should give careful consideration to where their products will be located. New products often have difficulty competing for space in high-traffic, high-volume stores where existing products do well.

Manufacturers often develop special display racks and work closely with retailers to ensure that their products will be placed within eyesight of the consumer. One manufacturer of sunscreen products solved the problem of shelf space in a unique manner. As a young company in the market, the firm had to compete for shelf space with as many as 12 different brands. Someone in the company observed that retailers displayed grass mats for use on the beach in wooden boxes located near the entrance to the store. A decision was made to develop a special beach mat box for retailers that would also include a top shelf for prominent display of the company's sunscreen products; this idea led to better positioning of the product and higher sales.

Another sunscreen products company, Panama Jack of Orlando, Florida, found a market niche by selling its products near the swimming pools of hotels. A Panama Jack employee operating the towel dispensary near the pool would vend these products as a service to guests. Adopting the striking logo of a gentleman in a Panama hat, the company

Mobile vending carts are profitably used to merchandise T-shirts, postcards and other souvenirs bought by visitors at the Opryland Hotel in Nashville.
Courtesy of Opryland.

not only created a persona image for its products, but demand for the logo as well. The popularity of this logo led to a line extension of clothing and accessories by Panama Jack.

Some retailers do well by selling from vending carts or kiosks at poolside, in parking lots of motorcoaches, courtyards, and other locations where there is tourist traffic. **Kiosks** are moveable, individual boutique displays. They may be seen in some airports and occasionally in hotels. Vending carts are fully mobile; although they may carry a limited assortment of merchandise, they can be highly profitable. The Opryland Hotel in Nashville, for example, uses a mobile merchandise cart to sell tee shirts, postcards, and other souvenir items. One such cart annually produces as much as $500,000 gross revenue with a net margin of 40%.

## Product Advertising/Promotion

Although travelers need information about products and services, many dislike being bombarded by "crass commercialization." Operators of hotels, resorts and other guest establishments are usually cautious about inappropriate advertising and sales promotion which may be seen as being counter-productive to the selling of "hospitality services." On the other hand, individual vendors in resort areas providing a service such as windsurfing rentals may show no hesitancy to constantly "get in the face" of tourists through touts, flyers handed to passersby, billboards, signs pulled by airplanes, and other selling tactics.

To control the problem of advertising and promotion proliferation, some visitor destinations—Monterey and Carmel in California are two—will enforce strict signage and advertising codes. Others seem to allow virtually any advertising or promotion as long as it remains within broad legal and moral boundaries.

The need to reach visitors has spawned a large allied advertising and promotion industry at many destinations, including distributed visitor publications; **transit advertising** (subways, buses, airport trams etc.), **shelter advertising** (train depot shelters, bus stop shelters), non-transit mobile advertising (unicycles, boats, etc), **airborne advertising** (blimps, airplanes), hotel in-room or in-house advertising; and briefings at industrial tours.

Target advertising to visitors is not without controversy. Proponents of visitor target advertising and promotion argue that these tactics add excitement and color to a destination. The ads or promotions effectively reach targeted customers and inform visitors who might not otherwise find out about the product or service. They help to generate sales activity and more taxes from visitors, consequently adding to the employment base of the community.

Opponents of such advertising and promotion claim these tactics create

- visually-polluted environments filled with discarded flyers, brochures, and tourist publications;

- noise and distraction—nature's beauty is marred by advertising clutter, especially in the case of billboards;

- visitor stress due to constant pressure to buy or to accept advertising material;

- visitor receptivity to scams and the purchase of inferior merchandise;

- environments that attract exhibitionists, con artists, and other undesirables; and

- distractions that lead to accidents such as pedestrian/vehicle encounters.

Some of the more common forms of advertising and promotion used in the travel industry are discussed in fuller details:

1. *In-room or in-house advertising*   The opportunity to sell to a captive audience is ever present and appreciated by management. Most hotel and restaurant operators understand the concepts of upselling and cross-selling. **Upselling** occurs when a customer buys a higher-priced item than he or she originally intended, as in the case of a suite instead of an ordinary double room. **Cross-selling** occurs when a customer purchases an additional item, such as a glass of wine with the meal. Some restaurants pursue advertising tactics to encourage cross-selling to such an extent that guest tables are literally covered with table tents, suggestive bottles of wine, and other items that little space is left for the meal. Available profit opportunities from upselling and cross-selling can be so great that it may be tempting for operators to go overboard. While many upscale hotels would never dream of allowing advertising flyers or table tents, they seem less averse to in-house promotional TV channels, letters from the general manager

announcing house specials, or putting announcements in closets or bathrooms that the terrycloth bathrobe is available in the gift shop (perhaps also to discourage pilferage).

2. *Briefings*   Tour groups are often invited to a free breakfast the morning following their arrival at the destination. Typically, a bus picks the group up at an appointed time and transports everyone to a restaurant where indeed a free breakfast is waiting. The breakfast may be accompanied by some light entertainment to be followed by a **briefing**, or sales pitch, to promote additional tours and products.

   The complexity and cost of briefings has limited their use to high-traffic visitor destinations. Some critics believe that briefings are high pressure and entrap visitors who were not forewarned the free breakfast would be accompanied by a sales message. Sellers respond that no one is forced to buy anything, that the breakfast was complimentary and that anyone intelligent enough to travel to the destination surely understands that there is no such thing as a "free lunch" or breakfast.

3. *Free tours*   Complimentary tours are often sponsored by merchants or factory outlet stores. Each tour inevitably leads to the factory outlet or gift stores owned by the sponsoring merchants. Disgruntled visitors will complain that most of the tour time is spent at the shopping area and not much in viewing historic or scenic spots. Increasingly, the local visitors' bureau, the chamber of commerce, or other travel organizations, recognizing that these tours give a destination a bad reputation, will pressure such tour operators to fully disclose the nature of their tours and their sponsors.

4. *Quality promotion*   The travel industry within most nations of the world is operated as a free enterprise composed of hundreds of thousands of small, medium, and large businesses serving visitors. In this environment, it is unavoidable that abuses will occur. Nonetheless, the industry individually and collectively (through voluntary trade associations) constantly attempts to reduce travel trade abuses and offer quality products and services to visitors. The example of AIRMALL® is a worthy case for discussion (see sidebar).

When quality advertising and promotion programs are offered to travelers, both the company and the traveler benefit. Vacation travelers in particular are generally in a receptive frame of mind to respond to positive quality promotions. Many products for travelers lend themselves to high quality, exciting promotions. Stern Jewelers of Rio de Janeiro and Hawaiian Holiday Macadamia Nuts of Hawaii are examples of companies with quality promotional techniques for selling products. Although the merchandise of the two companies are vastly different—jewelry versus macadamia nuts—both employ similar promotional techniques, which can serve as guidelines for others. They include:

- Strong emphasis on their product being "local."

- Promotion through local tourist-oriented media, including tourist guide magazines and store window displays in areas with heavy tourist traffic.

- Tours of the store and/or factory. Both companies effectively use their factories and retail stores to maximum advantage by encouraging tourists to visit them for their educational and entertainment value. Tours are well received by visitors and not viewed as entrapment.

# The Case of AIRMALL®

Established at the Pittsburgh International Airport by BAA Pittsburgh, Inc. to ensure quality retailing and quality promotions within the airport, the mission of AIRMALL® is, "to implement a radical new approach to U.S. airport retailing which will ensure that the Pittsburgh International Airport will be the yardstick against which future airport developments will be judged." *(10)*

AIRMALL® guarantees "No Airport Rip-Offs," and provides an 800 number for use by travelers who feel they are treated unfairly by retailers or food concessionaires within the airport. The promotional literature for Airmall® describes the program as follows:

> No doubt, in the course of your travels, you've encountered one too many airport shops selling one too many rip-offs. Fuzzy dice. Tacky bow ties. Unsavory food. At prices so outrageous, you're better off walking the other direction.
>
> Well, how about a departure from the norm?
>
> AIRMALL® at Pittsburgh International.
>
> We don't sell overpriced, useless airport stuff. We opt for down-to-earth prices and tasteful brand names. Like The Nature Company, The Body Shop, The Tie Rack, TGI Friday's and McDonald's, to name a few.
>
> Browse our shops and you'll not only find a wide selection of neat merchandise, you'll get a tax break of sorts: No sales tax on articles of clothing. And don't forget to get a taste of our incredible food. It's first-class all the way.
>
> The ticket to shopping at Airmall® is this. You feel like you're in a mall. You pay prices that are comparable to a mall. And while you're at it, you get to say good-bye to airport rip-offs.
>
> And that's guaranteed.
>
> Everything at AIRMALL® sells at down-to-earth prices. Clothes. Gifts. Food. The works. And that's not just a lot of hot air.

*Continued*

## $\mathcal{T}$he Case of AIRMALL® *(continued)*

You see, we have something called the No Rip-Off Guarantee, and it goes like this:

If you find a product that you bought at AIRMALL® cheaper in a comparable location, call us on it, at 1-800-ITS-FAIR. And we'll refund the difference. And that's guaranteed.

We also guarantee that once you've called, we'll get back to you in writing within five working days. Then, all we ask is that you send us your receipt from the AIRMALL® retailer, along with the location where you saw the comparable product for less. (Please note: The No Rip-Off Guarantee does not apply to promotional or sales items.)

The No Rip-Off Guarantee. It's something we stand by.

The importance of quality retailing and quality promotion within airports can be appreciated by the size of its market. Over a billion passengers fly in and out of the world's airports each year. Research at Pittsburgh showed that passengers had an average layover time of 55 minutes and most had incomes in excess of $60,000. It was decided that these passengers could become loyal customers of stores and restaurants at the airport. This requires: (1) an airport design to facilitate shopping, (2) a good mix of well-known retailers, (3) quality merchandise, (4) prices competitive to off-airport locations, (5) quality promotions, and (6) a customer guarantee.

The results at Pittsburgh was a 250% increase in per passenger retailing in the new airport as compared to the previous one. The TGI Friday's restaurant chain reported that its top franchise was in the Pittsburgh airport and The Sunglass Hut International sells more sunglasses per square foot there than anywhere else in the U.S.

*Source:* BAA's Customer Service Philosophy, BAA Pittsburgh, Inc., P. O. Box 12318, Pittsburgh International Airport, Pittsburgh, PA 15231-0318.

- Maximum use of well-known retailing concepts, including mass display. Neither company simply places products on shelves for sale. They create a buying ambiance in their stores.

- Staffing stores with well-trained and motivated sales people who know how to approach customers.

- Creation of a corporate identity so that consumers know they are not buying just another ruby or package of just any nuts. The products are perceived as being different from the ordinary gem or nut, whether they are or not.

- Developing a hospitable environment for tourists without resorting to hard sell.

- Most of all, standing behind the products they sell.

## Duty-free Stores

Duty-free stores have the distinction of being the first and last places where travelers make purchases during an international trip. **Duty-free stores** are retail stores where merchandise is sold only to travelers leaving the country. The merchandise is sold completely or partially free of the taxes and duties that would otherwise be imposed by the country in which the store is located.

### Characteristics of Duty-free Shops

Travelers do not always understand that the duty-free nature of these stores applies only to the country in which the goods were acquired. The goods are still subject to customs

Duty-free stores at airports provide travelers departing for another country an opportunity to buy luxury merchandise and brand name products free of the customs and taxes normally imposed by the host country.
Courtesy of Duty Free International.

duty and import restrictions in the next destination or home country of the traveler. All countries have some type of import restrictions. These vary by type of product and from country to country.

Duty-free stores are located in airports, at border crossings, in major hotels, at international convention centers, in retail shopping areas frequented by tourists, on cruiseships, and in airplanes. Most carriers sell selected duty-free merchandise, such as tobacco, liquor, perfume, and cosmetics, onboard their international flights.

Duty-free stores are lucrative enterprises, and licenses to operate them are not given out freely. In some countries, the state is the owner. In others, private individuals or corporations own and manage these stores. In a few countries, Guatemala for instance, the stores are operated for the benefit of national charities. Regardless of the form of ownership, duty-free stores are encouraged by governments since they provide numerous benefits:

- They offer the last opportunity to earn revenue from travelers before they leave the country.

- They are a means of producing income from in-transit passengers. International airline passengers who are in-transit between countries often have an hour or more to wait in the terminal before making connections. If in-transit passengers are allowed to visit duty-free stores in the terminal, millions of dollars of revenue can be generated annually by the sale of merchandise to persons who were just passing through.

- They provide direct employment opportunities for sales personnel, clerical workers, and warehouse people.

- They serve as excellent sources for **hard currency**, which is currency from major industrialized, trade nations that have relatively stable economies. Hard currency is in high demand throughout the world. The British pound, the German mark, the Swiss franc, the U.S. dollar, and the Japanese yen are commonly regarded as hard currency. All countries need hard currency for international trade purposes.

Sales in duty-free stores contribute to a positive balance of trade for the nation in which they exist. A single duty-free store can generate sales of many million dollars per year. The leading duty-free store in the United States has been the Waikiki location for Duty-Free Shoppers. This three-story retail complex is located in the heart of the tourist district of Waikiki, and targeted largely at Japanese visitors. Sales in this store have exceeded those in the Honolulu airport by four times and those in Los Angeles by five or six times. *(11)*

The operation of duty-free stores is similar throughout the world. There are three basic models: the delivered merchandise system, the traditional store, and inflight sales. In the **delivered merchandise system**, travelers visit the store and make their selections, pay for purchases with cash or credit cards as in other stores, but do not take the merchandise with them. The customer of the duty-free store must show his or her passport and airticket before the sale can be finalized. He or she signs a sales receipt and is given a copy. The remaining part of the receipt is sent from the sales counter to the warehouse located in or near the terminal, where the merchandise is packed and then hand-delivered to the airline gate before the customer boards the plane. The merchandise is given to the customer upon showing his or her copy of the signed receipt. This system is intentionally complicated to ensure that sales are made only to persons leaving the country.

Duty-free shops at airports are often similar to traditional retail store operations. Customers make their selections, pay for purchases, and take the goods with them. This applies only to duty-free stores in locations that are inaccessible to the domestic traveler, that is, in areas of airports that can be reached only after passing through immigration.

Interesting variations of these merchandising styles are used throughout the world. Many countries now permit and/or operate **inbound duty-free** shops for arriving international passengers where they may purchase duty-free items before passing through immigration check. Duty-free upon arrival offers several advantages: (1) Airlines carry reduced weight since passengers can buy duty-free items after arrival at the port of entry; (2) passengers do not have to be concerned with carrying or storing duty-free items during their flight; and (3) the host destination benefits by obtaining revenue from the sale of items that might otherwise be purchased in another country.

Inflight duty-free exists onboard airplanes and ships crossing international waters. Significant additional revenue may be earned by international carriers from the sales of duty-free merchandise. Airlines generally promote the products in a special seat-pocket brochure and by video on cabin screens. Duty-free merchandise is sold by the flight crew at certain times during the flight. Besides international air carriers, passenger ferries and cruise ships can also sell duty-free merchandise when traversing international waters or crossing international points.

## Types of Merchandise Sold

Duty-free stores have traditionally specialized in the sale of liquor, cigarettes, perfume and cologne, electronic equipment, silver goods, watches, cameras, jewelry, and other items with high import duties. Increasingly, as passengers have become more sophisticated shoppers, many duty-free stores are designed as specialty boutiques offering high fashion merchandise with famous labels. Some are branches of renowned stores, such as Harrod's of London or Takashimaya's of Tokyo, operating in leased space within in duty-free stores.

## Product-mix Management

**Product mix management** is important to all retailers and is a critical aspect in the operation of a successful duty-free store. Not only is store space at airports expensive, but both space and selling time are limited. Duty-free stores are either crowded or empty, depending on the scheduling of international flights. These stores must therefore make maximum use of a period that generally does not exceed one hour before flight time.

Because of space and time constraints, store managers often refuse to include low-priced items in their merchandise mix. They believe that low-priced items encourage crowds of "lookers," but discourage serious shoppers who may be searching for a watch, expensive jewelry, or other high-profit items. The airport in Paris solved this problem in an interesting manner. At the Charles DeGaulle International Airport, there are two duty-free areas: one in the main terminal offering French high-fashion goods and food and beverage products and the other located by the international flight gates. Customers can make purchases through a window, which opens into the international waiting area where travelers are ready to board flights. Lower-priced merchandise is displayed near the windows to take advantage of last-minute impulse buying. The dual setup allows the duty-free stores to carry a broader product mix without the fear of losing serious customers.

Experience has shown that customers of duty-free shops buy only the sizes and brands of merchandise they see on display. Recognizing that customers mostly buy with their eyes, duty-free shops have to carefully plan every inch of display space in their stores. Visible displays are needed for everything that is available for sale. Some duty-free store managers say if they display only one size of a product, a small bottle of liquor for instance, but tell the customer that other sizes are available, customers will, as a rule, opt for the small bottle, not for what they are told is available.

### Direct Mail Promotion of Duty-free Shops

Duty-free shops are today seeking new ways to expand. In 1995, the International Association of Airport Duty-Free Stores conducted an experimental **direct response** (**direct mail advertising**) campaign. A total of 50,000 direct mail pieces were sent to frequent international flyers with minimum annual incomes of $75,000 who travelled on at least three international flights during the previous year. *(12)* The purpose of the campaign was to encourage high-income frequent international flyers to shop at a duty-free store. A reply card and coupons worth $5.00 to $50.00 were enclosed. The campaign produced a 3% response rate, which is considered acceptable. While promotional programs of this nature have long been used by conventional retailers, they are just beginning to be adopted by duty-free stores. Undoubtedly, as competition intensifies, duty-free stores will not only borrow from the lessons of the traditional retailers, but seek other approaches as well.

### European Duty-free Stores

Duty-free stores within Europe sold nearly $8 billion worth of merchandise in 1992, saving consumers an estimated $2 billion in taxes. Nevertheless, their existence is under threat. *(13)* Planners within the new European Union want to abolish duty-free stores. The theory is that when trade barriers among union members disappear, there will be no reason for retaining duty-free stores. Supporters of the existing system, including the British Chancellor of the Exchequer, have argued for allowing these stores to continue until the 21st century. *(14)*

Managers of European airports have been particularly troubled by the proposed dismantling of duty-free stores since they generate major revenues for the airport. Estimates reveal that airline landing fees would need to increase by 40% or more if revenue from duty-free concessions disappeared. *(15)*

### Philippines Duty-free Stores

The Republic of the Philippines offer an unusual example of duty-free shopping that has made this country one of the world's top duty-free merchandisers. *(16)* Four million Philippine citizens temporarily reside abroad as workers to earn export income. Upon their return home, these people usually bring back millions of dollars of goods purchased elsewhere. The government run Duty-Free Philippines agency decided to operate stores within the country for returning citizens with discretionary income earned abroad. These duty-free stores offer non-traditional goods as well as traditional, including brass beds, washing machines, farm equipment, and grocery items, mostly intended for domestic consumption.

By taking the unusual step of establishing an inbound duty-free system for returning citizens, the Philippine government was able to capture additional export dollars into its own economy. The spending by returning expatriates, as well as by international visitors, have helped make Duty-Free Philippines the world's fourth largest retailer behind the DFS Group of San Francisco, Allders International of Britain, and Duty-Free International of Ridgefield, Connecticut.

## Product Selling Linked with Event Marketing

The discussion of event marketing in Chapter 15 stated its importance to the amusement, entertainment, and sports-related tourism sector. Event marketing is also a way for companies to sell their products directly to travel consumers. Niche market product manufacturers like Red Stripe beer, brewed in Jamaica, sold thousands of cases during promotion efforts at U.S. ski resorts and at sporting events. Red Stripe gained considerable notoriety through sponsorship of the Jamaican bobsled team at the 1994 Winter Olympics. *(17)*

Nestea Iced Tea targeted 18–29-year-olds for a sampling program by dispensing products from five 18-wheelers during volleyball matches, baseball games, at theme parks, and at beaches in 60 markets, handing out Nestea cans to 6 million consumers. *(18)* Smartfoods, a Massachusetts-based snack food firm, used stunts such as dressing skiers in giant popcorn bags and distributing free samples. These and other promotional efforts produced a company that was purchased by Frito Lay in 1991 for $14.5 million. *(19)*

## Local Products and Handicrafts

Successful traveler-oriented products, especially souvenirs and gifts, will reflect the best to be found in their country of origin. Thus, Hawaiian pineapples, Mexican tequila, Peruvian llama rugs, Swiss chocolates, German cutlery, French perfumes, Italian leather articles, and Irish crystal are good examples of quality product and country association. Occasionally, there are also a few anomalies. The famous Panama hat, for example, is actually made by Indians in the Sierra Andean region of Ecuador and not in Panama.

The available selection of locally-produced products can have either a negative or positive impact on the image of a destination. An over-concentration of cheap, poorly-made souvenir products can create the impression that the destination is much like its souvenirs—a place for a cheap visit, but not for a quality vacation.

The successful merchandising of quality handicrafts sometimes requires the direct assistance of government. Handicraft producers are generally poorly organized with limited or no resources for marketing and distribution, copyright protection, or professional training. There are also other problems involving the manufacture or sale of local handicrafts, including:

- *Sale of religious or cultural artifacts as souvenirs* Some articles—hand carved or painted sacred icons, for example—have deep religious or cultural significance that

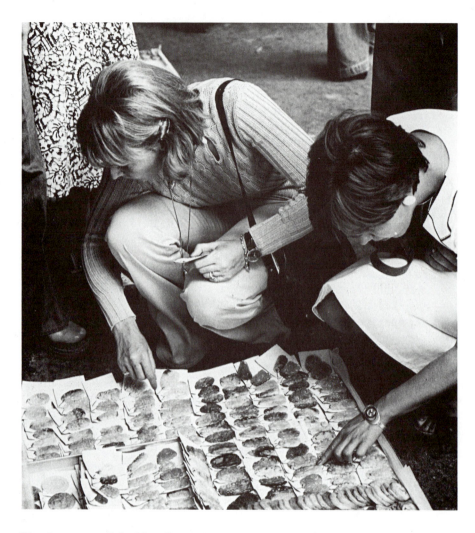

Tourists can still find locally made jewelry and other handicrafts in many
countries.
Courtesy of Hong Kong Tourist Association.

may not be recognized by tourists who value these items as art pieces or souvenirs. A
common complaint heard in many countries, especially in regard to the outflow of
sacred artifacts, is that tourism seems to treat cultural heritage as something that is
"for sale."

- *Lack of quality control*  A successful product inevitably invites competitors, many of
  whom will produce knock-off copies of inferior quality. The traveler is often unfamil-

iar with these items and will be thousands of miles away when defects are discovered. For example, Joaquin Chaverri, whose family of artisans hand manufacture small ox carts in Costa Rica for use as decorative home accessories, complains that competitors use plywood instead of cedar. The quality of these knock-offs is inferior and reflects on all artisans in his trade.

- *Lack of business skills*   The Eskimos of Alaska typify the natives of many developing countries with low literacy rates who have a lack of marketing skills and financing for their craft and little understanding of accounting and finance. Moreover, they encounter serious competition with mass-produced souvenirs from the Orient. *(20)*

On the positive side, the growth of tourism has fostered the emergence of colonies of artists in many parts of the world. Take the case of a colony of talented potters in an area south of Asheboro, North Carolina. These artists have produced such unique and beautiful pottery that visitors are lured from busy highways to buy it.

In an effort to preserve and upgrade the handicraft industry, many countries and states have established programs to assist handicraft development and marketing, including:

- Government-sponsored and managed handicraft centers. Some centers are established in historic villages or in restorations, such as an old church in Mexico City.

- Regional handicraft centers like the Interamerican Center for Handicrafts, funded by the Organization of American States are charged with the mission of developing and promoting authentic handicrafts throughout South America.

- Educational seminars and consulting.

- Purchases of the best pieces of art and crafts by government and private industry for display in public buildings, museums, galleries, hotels and resorts, etc.

- Publicity assistance with placement of stories and photos in trade media and visitor information brochures.

- Mention of handicraft centers in government-supported tourism promotional material.

## Local Agricultural Products

Local product marketing extends well beyond handicrafts. Entrepreneurs throughout the world have recognized tourists' desire to buy unique local agricultural products for themselves or to send as gifts. In wine growing communities, for example, festivals, vineyard tours, and other promotions are held to encourage tourism and product sampling. Vineyards in areas not traditionally associated with wine production, such as Arkansas, Missouri, or southern New Jersey, also offer tours, wine sampling, and product sales. On-site product sales for these products are an important source of revenue for many vineyards. Many have established gift shops and restaurants to serve travelers.

A "back to the land" movement of urban dwellers to the farms starting in the 1960s continues today. Many of these societal "drop outs" were young professionals who grew dissatisfied with government, society, and the stress and depersonalization of life in large cities. Today, many older professionals who have grown weary of the pace of modern society have also decided to become farmers. For most, the journey is not so much a return as an adoption of a slower-paced rural lifestyle. Whether farming is practical as a hobby or as a source of income, a number of these individuals have become boutique wine producers or growers of fresh herbs and organic vegetables, exotic plants, or animals.

Many of these **niche farmers** have discovered that their most reliable markets are hotels, resorts, cruise ships, restaurants, and bed-and-breakfast establishments. These travel industry members have been directly responsible for the success of many agricultural products which were originally considered exotic—snow peas, farm-raised wild game, cultivated herbs, shiitake mushrooms, and free-range chicken, to name a few.

Niche farming for the hospitality trade is not restricted to North America, but can be found in virtually any country with an established or growing visitor industry. One example is an American living outside Shanghai, China, who produces western vegetables—not otherwise available in China—and sells them to international hotels serving a discriminating clientele from both East and West.

## Other Forms of Travel Product Retailing

The travel industry is witnessing the growth of different forms of product and service selling other than traditional retailing at the visitor's destination or enroute. These include mail-order retailing, factory outlet stores, hotel in-room shopping, and inflight interactive shopping.

### Direct Response/Direct Mail

Retail stores that cater to visitors have discovered they can substantially supplement their sales volume through the effective use of direct mail with brochures and catalogues. Tourism, in fact, provides an avenue for establishing a selective interstate (and often an international) mailing list for sending merchandise catalogues. It is possible to sell products nationally and internationally through direct response or direct mail advertising

The International Post Office in Japan, which handles overseas mail, reported that it was receiving approximately 50,000 pounds of mail-order merchandise per day. In 1995, it is estimated that the mail-order business to Japan will contribute three million packages and U.S. companies will make $750 million from mail-order sales to Japan. For resort-based retailers that deal with the Japanese, the mail-order market offers an opportunity to sell merchandise to visitors who have returned to Japan. It also provides the opportunity to develop an ongoing relationship with the customer after they return home by using a customer database. *(21)*

Individuals who first become acquainted with the company's product in the store will often purchase items for themselves or gifts through the mail. The L.L. Bean Company, among many others, has enjoyed tremendous success through its combination of direct mail and company store. The retail store is visited by hundreds of thousands of visitors, but today, even more consumers are reached through direct mail.

### Factory Outlet Stores

A once unique retail concept, the **factory outlet store**, has become important to the tourist trade in many communities. The factory outlet store is a retail store that sells new

**Factory outlet stores have become major attractions for visitors.**
Courtesy of Cannon Village.

merchandise at a discount because of factory overruns, irregular merchandise, discontinued styles, or simply as a retail discount. Factory outlets located in such communities as Reading, Pennsylvania; Burlington, North Carolina; or Williamsburg, Virginia, attract millions of visitors each year. The outlets stores in Reading alone attract over 5 million visitors per year and directly employ 2,500 workers. Their annual sales exceed $300 million. *(22)* The spending multiplier in Reading has been estimated at 1.25, meaning that every dollar spent has yielded an extra 25 cents in sales at other service establishments for an additional $75 million.

The town of Kannapolis, North Carolina, is the home town of Cannon Mills. The entire downtown area has been converted into a factory outlet shopping complex. Visitors can tour the factory and shop at a large selection of stores that feature a wide variety of goods and well-known brands. Regularly scheduled bus tours for shoppers are especially popular among retired people.

### In-room Shopping

Many hotels now offer an in-room TV channel that carries news about local services and products. In the future, it will probably be possible for guests to interactively purchase a variety of products or services including tours, flowers, delivered pizza, ski lessons, gift items, and much more through the TV and to automatically charge these items to their room or credit card. Some hotels also offer catalogs for **in-room shopping** with guaranteed next morning delivery to guests. Thus, a guest who needs a blouse or dress shirt for an unexpected dinner engagement or a gift for a spouse can shop from the convenience of his or her room by fax or an 800 number with prompt service and satisfaction guaranteed.

### In-flight Interactive Purchasing

To maximize the potential selling to airline passengers, **multimedia interactive systems** are being developed and tested on airlines. Revenue estimates as high as $1 million annually per plane have been projected. *(23)* These interactive systems can book hotel rooms, order merchandise, sell in-flight entertainment, and book a passenger's next flight. Virgin Atlantic Airlines was the first airline to implement the system, and found that nine out of ten passengers use the system. British Airways, Singapore Airlines, and UAL Corporation also plan to implement interactive systems.

# 𝒯RAVEL-RELATED FINANCIAL SERVICES

Travel is expensive. No matter what the traveler's mode of transportation, he or she cannot get far without money. Most travelers do not carry large amounts of cash for fear of theft or loss. Also, cash is not always convenient when traveling abroad since it must be converted into the host country's currency. Shopping for the best rate of exchange takes time and effort. The majority of today's travelers, therefore, depend on other financial mediums of exchange, principally credit cards, travelers checks, vouchers, and automatic teller machines (ATMs). Many use a combination of these financial mediums.

## Credit/Debit and Smart Cards

The credit card has become an established substitute for money throughout much of the world. In many instances, it is impossible to cash a check without showing at least one valid credit card. Hotels and car rental agencies usually request all customers to present a credit card upon registration, even though final payment at checkout may be in cash. In recent times, several major lodging companies including Marriott, Sheraton, Hilton, Holiday Inn, Hyatt, Westin, and others have entered into strategic alliances with credit card companies for joint marketing and promotional programs.

Credit cards fall under two categories: general usage and travel and entertainment (T&E). **General usage cards** are issued primarily by financial institutions: Visa, MasterCard, Choice, Discover, and others. **Travel and entertainment cards**, issued by individual credit card companies, are especially important to the travel industry. The major T&E card is American Express. Visa is by far the largest general usage card. A late-

| TABLE 16.2 Major Credit Cards (24) | |
|---|---|
| **T&E** | **General Usage** |
| American Express* | Visa* |
| Charge card introduced 1958 | Introduced 1977 |
| 35.6 million cards worldwide | 375.2 million cards worldwide |
| 89 of Fortune 100 companies provide Amex corporate cards | 197 million cards in the U.S. |
| Accepted at 3.8 million locations worldwide | Accepted at 11.5 million locations worldwide |
| | |
| Diners** | MasterCard** |
| Introduced 1960 | Introduced as Interbank Card in 1966 |
| 6.4 million cards worldwide | 254.4 million cards available |
| 268 Fortune 500 companies have corporate cards | |
| Accepted at 2.5 million locations worldwide | Accepted by 11.5 million merchants |
| | Discover Card* |
| | Introduced 1986 |
| | 41.8 million cards |
| | Accepted at 2.09 million locations |

*1994 figures
**1993 figures

Source: "Credit Card Sweepstakes," *Lodging*, Vol. 20, No. 7, March 1995, pg. 44.

comer to the T&E market segment, Visa has quickly caught up other players and has now exceed them in terms of volume and memberships (see Table 16.2).

It has long been predicted that the United States will eventually enter an era of the "cashless society" where money is no longer used. Credit cards introduced decades earlier became popular in the 1970s, and reduced the need for the ordinary customer to use cash for shopping and travel transactions when dealing with merchants who accepted credit cards. Credit cards provide the cardholder with a pre-determined level of credit which is borrowed against by the cardholder each time the card is used for a purchase. The introduction of **debit cards** by banks and card companies in recent years is an attempt to substitute debt transfers against individual accounts in lieu of cash. Debit cards draw against funds in the cardholder's own bank account.

## Smart Cards

Today, another method of payment is coming on scene: **smart cards**—cards that resemble and work much like credit and debit cards, but in effect are "electronic wallets." Credit and debit cards which store information on a magnetic strip are limited to one type of transaction. A smart card, on the other hand, gets its intelligence from microprocessor chips which can store at least 80 times more data. The memory capacity enables the card to handle complex financial transactions as well as store such information as personal identification and medical records. Prepaid telephone cards are an example of a smart card that contains the stored value of telephone calls. As calls are made, a debit is made against the remaining value of the card until its prepaid credit is used up. Ultimately, a smart card will be used for everything from vending machine purchases to airline ticketing and downloading merchandise coupons through a TV set.

## Advantages of Credit/Debit Cards

The phenomenal growth of credit/debit cards throughout the world may be attributed to the fact they satisfy genuine needs of travelers and the travel industry. These cards provide numerous advantages for the traveler, including:

- *Easy to carry* These cards fit virtually all wallets and purses. In a world where travelers face lack of worldwide uniformity among electronic appliances, VCR's, and even the side of the road on which one must drive, credit/debit cards offer a simplicity and world-wide uniformity of size and appearance. The uniformity of card size means that they will fit imprint machines used by merchants everywhere.

- *Easy to use* Most members of the travel industry throughout the world instantly recognize and accept credit/debit cards. Most merchants from New York and Paris to even remote villages in third world nations will accept major credit/debit cards. Moreover, credit verification is relatively speedy for card transactions today as compared to earlier years.

- *Limited loss provision* When stolen or lost, credit/debit cards are easily replaced and the user is protected by a stop-loss limit if the card is reported lost to the insuring company within a set period of time.

- *Cash conversion privileges* Some cards allow the user to withdraw a pre-set amount of cash per day from an ATM machine.

- *Accounting record* An end-of-month printed statement assists cardholders with their personal financial planning and accounting.

- *Identification and vender acceptance* Hotels, rental car agencies, and other establishments typically require that all customers use a credit card to register. The customer may settle the account with cash, but a card is still required upon registration. Many merchants require two or three items of personal identification plus a credit card before accepting personal checks.

For the vendor, credit/debit cards also offer certain advantages, including reduced risk when accepting cards to settle transactions and improved competitive position over vendors who do not accept such cards. The card receipts are also a means for capturing important customer information, including postal codes and the kind and value of purchases. Unfortunately, few vendors take advantage of this opportunity to learn more about their customers.

Credit card companies sometimes enter into **cooperative advertising/promotion programs** with travel trade members who accept their cards. Visa ran a series of television ads in which it showcased different worldwide members, positioning these members as ones who accepted Visa, but not American Express cards. American Express also offers cooperative promotional programs with its travel trade members. As a leading travel agency, American Express is able to assemble discounted travel packages and offer them to their cardmembers. Working with the Stowe Ski Resort in Vermont, an American Express advertisement for a ski package to Stowe provides an example of the marketing power such integration provides:

> "Vermont's highest mountain comes with momentous savings for American Express cardmembers.

> Let us design a specially-priced package just for you including discounts on airfare, lodging, car rental, lift tickets, and lessons. Package savings range from 30–50% and American Express cardmembers get special bonuses besides.

> Stowe is non-stop excitement on legendary, mile-long trails. Stowe is total relaxation—in a picture-perfect 200-year-old New England village. And for American Express cardmembers, Stowe is the bargain of the year. *(24)*

Despite the positive attributes of credit cards for travel trade vendors, many do complain about the high percentage charge of card issuers and cash flow problems that result from the time lag between sales to the customer and reimbursement from the card company.

## Travelers Checks

**Travelers checks** may be viewed as a form of private company paper currency issued and exchanged for the currency of a nation. They are issued by five major financial institutions: *(25)* Interpayment Inc. (a joint venture of Bank of America and Barclay's Bank), Citicorp, Thomas Cook, VISA, and American Express. Travelers checks generally can be used like cash throughout the world upon endorsement and presenting a passport or other proper identification. If checks are lost or stolen, they will be replaced by the issuing company.

Since private companies issue travelers checks, a profit is expected. Profits are realized in two ways: (1) a small fee, generally 1% is charged to the buyer of travelers checks. In some cases, this fee may be entirely waived. The reason for a low or no fee is that the primary source of profits is earned from the **float**. (2) Float refers to the time lapse between the purchase and cashing of travelers checks. Financial institutions who issue travelers checks receive enormous amounts of funds from the transaction which are used for investments. The greater and longer the float, the more profit potential that exists for issuing companies. Many travelers do not cash all their checks during the trip and may save them for some future trip. This increases the length of float time for the unredeemed travelers checks. In other words, it gives the issuing company extended time to use the purchaser's money without paying interest.

The worldwide market for travelers checks was estimated at $58 billion. *(26)* This represents a huge amount of potential investment capital that is acquired without paying interest to the person who purchases the checks. Financial institutions can and do invest this float capital in a variety of ways that produce profit.

There are four primary reasons why travelers checks are used as a medium of exchange throughout the world. First, they offer a level of security to both the user and the vendor. Personal checks are generally acceptable only within a traveler's own home territory and even cash is sometimes suspect as merchants often have difficulty identifying counterfeit money. Second, the companies which issue and guarantee travelers checks are large, well respected organizations. Third, travelers checks are issued in "hard currency" such as the U.S. dollar, Japanese yen, British pound, Swiss francs, German marks or others. Travelers from developing countries with soft currency usually find it impossible to use such currency outside of their own home country. Fourth, they offer convenience to the user. American Express now offers travelers checks that may be used by two parties—husband and wife, for instance—even though the parties may not be together at the time of use.

### Marketing of Travelers Checks

Travelers checks may be purchased at a bank or other financial institution or through other outlets, including large travel agencies, major hotels, car rental outlets, vending machines located in major air terminals, through ATMs, and by mail. American Express Travelers Checks Group estimates that purchasing travelers checks through an ATM reduces the transaction time from 11 minutes to 70 seconds. (27)

Travelers check companies aggressively market their products to increase the volume of usage. MasterCard obtained the rights to sponsor the 1994 World Cup and to advertise its credit cards and travelers checks at stadiums. To counter the competition from credit cards, ATMs, and other travel check companies, the major issuers of travelers checks have been forced to offer more product features and support advertising and promotional events.

The profile of travelers check users is predominately middle-aged, upscale travelers who purchase them as insurance against loss of currency and as a source of backup funds in case of a problem with credit cards. Companies who insure travelers checks aim much of their advertising and promotion at this market segment, but know they must also create demand among younger travelers. Earlier advertising campaigns were focused on the fear of loss and theft as the dominant message, today's theme is one of convenience aimed at a younger, more diverse market.

## Other Forms of Travel-related Financial Services

### Money Orders

People without credit cards or checking accounts buy and use money orders. Young travelers, in particular, are a market segment for money orders. Money orders can be purchased from several sources, including some retail stores and the postal service. The buyer pays cash plus a small commission for a money order, which is payable only to a designated individual.

Travelers are sometimes sent a money order by family members or friends when they run out of funds. Aliens who do not trust the banking system or do not wish to leave a "paper trail" of their financial transactions often send money orders to family members in their home country.

### Wired Transfers

Wired money is often the avenue of last resort for travelers in trouble. These travelers will call family members or friends to ask them to "wire" money. The individual who wires the money must take cash to a company handling such transactions, for instance, a Western Union office. After receiving the money plus a commission charge, the company sends an electronic message to a branch near the troubled traveler. The branch office is instructed to pay out the agreed amount of cash to the traveler upon presentation of proper identification.

### Travel Vouchers

**Travel vouchers** are prepaid (or promissory) authorization issued by airlines, tour operators, travel agencies, and other travel intermediaries to travelers such as airline crews, passengers who are delayed and require overnight accommodations, or members of tours for lodging, transfers, meals, or other services.

Vouchers are generally not redeemable for cash and may be used only with preselected travel industry members such as specified restaurants or hotels. These factors greatly limit the use and growth of vouchers.

### Automatic Teller Machines

The dollar volume of ATM transactions has been growing at a rate of 14% per year. By contrast, the market for travelers checks has been stable, except for developing markets in Latin America and Asia. *(28)*

ATM networks such as CIRRUS, PLUS, and others offer travelers the ability to withdraw cash away from home with a debit against their bank accounts. This provides convenience for the travelers and saves them from conversion charges reaching as high as 13% in some retail stores and restaurants. *(29)*

Although ATMs may provide convenience, there are the usual problems of occasional "window" shutdowns and lack of machine availability in some destinations as well as charges associated with each transaction and the question of safety at night in some locations. Many travelers, therefore, use a combination of ATMs, credit cards, and travelers checks as a hedge against all possible exigencies.

## SUMMARY

Travelers are inveterate shoppers. A casual observation of the volume of retail business conducted in airport stores gives evidence of the size of this travel industry sector. Duty-free stores, handicrafts, and specialty agriculture products represent only a few of the retailing opportunities that complement the travel industry. Non-retail sectors of the travel industry, including hospitality service providers, have also discovered that the sale of merchandise offers significant profit potential.

The sales success of traveler-oriented products depends upon understanding the ever-changing needs and profiles of travelers. In planning for the tourist market, retailers must consider seven critical aspects: brand names and logos, product and package size, price points, sensory attributes, preferred purchase times, location of stores and product merchandising, and advertising and promotion.

Duty-free stores are unique to international travel. Duty-free stores may be found in airports, in shopping areas, and on-board cruise lines, international airlines, and some passenger rail trains. Dramatic changes within the new European Union may threaten to change or even eliminate duty-free stores, but new forms of product retailing will undoubtedly spring up to replace them.

Many individuals who may not view themselves as part of the travel industry are, in fact, highly dependent upon its continuing growth and success. The attorney who decides to leave a law office in Chicago and grow organic vegetables in Iowa or artists who display paintings on the sidewalk of Picadilly are dependent on the customers generated by the travel industry. The travel industry has a long history of spawning entrepreneurial growth. The tremendous potential for providing new products and financial services to the travel industry will surely continue to serve as a catalyst for entrepreneurial growth throughout the world.

Financial services for travelers encompass credit/debit cards, smart cards, travelers checks, vouchers, money orders, wire transfers, and ATMs. Many travelers use two or more of those services when they travel, especially credit cards, travelers checks, and ATMs. All of these financial services are vital to travelers with respect to convenience, access, safety, and conversion of currency. Travel-related financial services are also vital to the tourist industry in numerous ways. Without credit cards, for example, doing business by distance would be nearly impossible. Already, the Internet is being used to book and pay for travel services through the secured coding of credit cards.

The promise of a "cashless society" in which financial transactions are made through electronic means has only begun. Future travelers may have choices of financial mediums that can scarcely be imagined today.

# ⅅISCUSSION QUESTIONS

1. What are the various types of duty-free stores, and how do they differ from one another?

2. What are some of the factors that are key to boosting the sale of products for travelers?

3. What are some considerations regarding product mix that a shop manager must consider to ensure success of retail sales to the traveler market?

4. What are some problems faced by the handicraft section throughout the world?

5. If you were offered two locations for your souvenir shop, would you rather be placed in a relatively busy area where you are the only store of your kind or would you like to be placed in a shopping center where you are with many of your competitors as well as many other shops? Please explain why.

6. In your opinion, what should a local visitor's bureau do to promote the retail products sector of their visitor industry?

7. Discuss the importance of brand name merchandise to the travel industry.

8. Discuss the need to carefully consider product package sizes when offering products to travelers.

9. What are price points? How are price points used in the sale of retail products?

10. Discuss three of the major reasons how credit/debit cards effectively serve the travel industry.

11. What is the significance of co-operative advertising by credit card and travelers check companies to an individual travel service provider?

12. How might credit card receipts serve as an important source of marketing information to a restaurant or hotel?

13. Could a company that issues travelers checks give them free of charge to travelers and still earn a profit? Please explain.

14. What is hard currency? How might hard currency relate to the expanding market for travelers checks in a developing country with soft currency?

15. Does the use of an ATM overseas offer the user any advantages in foreign exchange conversion? Please explain.

## SUGGESTED STUDENT EXERCISE

### Short Case Analysis

#### Shop Till They Drop

Forget Waikiki Beach or the other beautiful sights of Hawaii, let's go shopping at Kmart. In June of 1994 that seemed to be the sentiment of large numbers of Japanese visitors. *(30)* "You would think people would come here to see Hawaii," grumbled a manager of one of Honolulu's visitor attractions, "but Kmart. People are strange nowadays."

That strangeness could be attributed to record lows for the U.S. dollar against the Japanese yen, making U.S. products considerably less expensive. The dollar/yen imbalance caused Kmart, Home Outlet, and Eagle Hardware to become top tourist attractions in Honolulu. Japanese shoppers were so intent on visiting the Waikele shopping mall, home of Kmart and other stores, that many paid $40 a head to be taken there by van or bus.

A tour bus pulled up in front of Waikele's Saks Fifth Avenue discount outlet called "Off 5th" and 44 Japanese tourists dislodged, wearing yellow stickers that said, "save-save." And indeed they do save, with prices such as $40 for a white dress shirt compared to $100 in Japan, or designer shoes by Salvatore Ferragamo for $120 compared to $165 in Waikiki or $350 in Japan. Although the Japanese traditionally buy well-known brand names, in the market of 1994, a shark-like feeding frenzy developed among Japanese shoppers who seemed intent on buying everything. A Japanese wife complained of her husband, "He buys things that are not useful." Indeed, the husband had his arms full of camping lanterns and running shoes.

| Waikele Outlets | | |
|---|---|---|
| Anne Klein | Famous Footwear | Nordic Track |
| Bass Company Store | Fragrance Outlet | Oasis Cafe |
| B.C.B.G. | Genuine Kids | Ocean Pacific Factory Outlet |
| Big Dogs | Geoffrey Beene | Off 5th Saks Fifth Ave Outlet |
| Blue Wave | Guess? | Olga/Warner's |
| Bose | Izod | Oshkosh B'Gosh |
| Bugle Boy | Levi's Outlet | Paris Fashions |
| California Luggage | Local Fever | Rocky Mt. Chocolate Factory |
| Carter's for Kids | Local Motion | Sgt. Leisure |
| Colours & Scents | Mascetti Collection | Sunglass Hut |
| Converse | Max Studio | Van Heusen |
| Corning Revere | McInerny Designer Outlet | Vans Shoes |
| Donna Karan New York | Mikasa | Villeroy & Boch |
| Eagle's Eye Ladies' & Kids | Nine West | Welcome Home |
| Ever Blue | Ninth Month Maternity | |

In fact, the shopping frenzy sometimes led to disappointment as some shoppers seemed frozen into inaction. A 23-year-old Japanese shopper sadly proclaimed this fact as he reboarded the bus for his hotel. "I saw something better in every store so I bought nothing."

## Discussion Questions

1. If you were advising merchants in Waikiki or other traditional shopping areas, what would you suggest they do to meet competition from lower cost retailers away from the tourist center?

2. What would you suggest that traditional visitor attractions in Honolulu do to regain the Japanese market?

3. Have you personally witnessed a shopper frenzy such as the one described in the case? Describe how shoppers react.

# REFERENCES

1. de Gennaro, N., and R. J. Ritchey. "Mexican Visitors to Arizona Identified as Valued Market," *Arizona Review*, 27 Nos. 8–9 (August-September 1978).

2. "Canadian Mega Mall Has it All," *Winston-Salem Journal*, December 15, 1986.

3. Ortega, Bob. "Wealthy Mexicans Head Stateside to Shop," *The Wall Street Journal*, Marketplace, Thursday, December 22, 1994, pg. B1 and B10.

4. Ossorio, Sonia. "Check Out This Hoot of a Mass Market," *Tampa Bay Business Journal*, Vol. 13 (3), Section 1, January 15, 1993, pg. 11.

5. Banerjee-Neela. "They Don't, However Shop Until They Drop," *The Wall Street Journal*, November 10, 1994, pg. B1.

6. Ortega, Bob. "Wealthy Mexicans Head Stateside to Shop," *The Wall Street Journal*, Marketplace, Thursday, December 22, 1994, pg. B10.

7. Brellis, Matthew. "Dogfight Over Vineyard T-Shirts Goes to U.S. Court," *The Boston Globe*, August 7, 1992, Metro/Region Section, pg. 17.

8. Monteson, Patricia A., and Judith Singer. "Turn Your Spa Into a Winner*,*" *The Cornell Hotel and Restaurant Administration Quarterly*, Vol. 33, No. 3, June 1992, pg. 44.

9. "Little Amenities Spawn Big Bottles," Randall Products International Packaging Digest, Vol. 31 (10), September 1994, pg. 64.

10. "BAA 21st Century Airports Detail Strategies for the Next Millennium," Airmall, P.O. Box 12318, Pittsburgh International Airport, Pittsburgh, PA 15231-0318.

11. "Duty-Free Incorporated," Duty-Free Concession Honolulu Reports, Documents and Articles, Vol. 1, March 1982.

12. Tersy, Miguel E. "Duty-Free Shops Use DM to Lure Shoppers," *DM News*, February 27, 1995, pg. 4.

13. Marcom, John, Sr. "Scotch at $850 a Bottle," *Forbes*, Vol. 148, November 25, 1991, pg. 190.

14. "Beyond the Call of Duty Free," *The Economist*, Vol. 321, November 2, 1991, pg. 50.

15. Paylor, Anne. "Goodbye Duty Free," *Interravia*, Vol. 46, March 1991, pg. 17–18.

16. Lambert, Bruce. "International Business: In Philippines, Duty-Free With a Difference (or two)," *The New York Times*, Saturday, June 24, 1995, pg. 18.

17. Khermouch, Gerry. "Promotion: Labott's Keeps Red Stripe Running with Cool Promos," *Brandweek*, Vol. 35, February 7, 1994, pg. 11.

18. Khermouch, Gerry. "Nestea Iced Tea," *Brandweek*, Vol. 35, March 21, 1994, pg. 16.

19. "Marketer of the Month: Kernels of Wisdom from Ken Meyers," *Sales and Marketing Management*, Vol. 143, March1991, pg. 24–25.

20. Green, H., and W. Greene. "Alaska Native Arts and Crafts Cooperative Inc.," Case Study, University of Alaska and University of North Dakota.

21. "Japan's Mail-Order Catalog Boom Surged in '95," "*Round the Rim*," PacRim Marketing Group Inc., Winter 1996.

22. Patton, S. G. "Factory Outlets and Travel Industry Developments: The Case of Reading, Pennsylvania," *The Journal of Travel Research*, XXV, No. 1, Summer 1986.

23. Coleman, Brian. "It's a Plane! It's an Interactive Arcade," *The Wall Street Journal*, November 10, 1994, pg. B1.

24. Advertisement, "From Jet to Gondola, American Express, American Express Cardholders Pay Less to Ski," *The Winston-Salem Journal*, December 4, 1994.

25. Sims, John. "How You Can Get the Most Out of Your Travelers Checks," *Money*, Vol. 20, December 1991, pg. 165.

26. *Ibid.*

27. Fisher, Lawrence, M. "ATM's to Dispense American Express Travelers Check," *New York Times*, May 31, 1994, pg. D6.

28. Radigan, Joseph. "People Do Leave Home Without Them," *United States Banker*, Vol. 103, June 1993, pg. 35+.

29. Sokolov, Raymond. "Attention Tourists: Forget Travelers Checks, Think ATM," *Wall Street Journal*, March 17, 1994, pg. A14.

30. Carlton, Jim. "Japanese Skip Waikiki, Head for Kmart," *The Wall Street Journal*, The Marketplace, Thursday, June 24, 1995, pg. B1.

# Appendix

## Abbreviations and Acronyms of Travel-related Organizations

| | |
|---|---|
| AAA | American Automobile Association |
| AAR | Association of American Railroads |
| ABA | American Bus Association |
| ACTOA | Air Charter Tour Operators of America |
| AGTE | Association of Group Travel Executives |
| AH&MA | American Hotel and Motel Association |
| AITO | Association of Incentive Travel Operators |
| AMHA | American Motor Hotel Association |
| AOCI | Airport Operators Council International, Inc. |
| ARC | Airlines Reporting Corporation |
| ARTA | Association of Retail Travel Agents |
| ASTA | American Society of Travel Agents |
| ATA | Airport Transport Association |
| ATC | Air Traffic Conference |
| AYH | American Youth Hostels |
| CAAA | Commuter Airline Association of America |
| CHART | Council of Hotel and Restaurant Trainers |
| CHRIE | Council on Hotel Restaurant and Institutional Education |
| CAB | Civil Aeronautics Board |
| CLIA | Cruise Lines International Association |
| CMAA | Club Managers Association of America |
| CMTA | Common Market Travel Association |
| COTAL | Confederation of Latin American Tourist Organization |
| DATO | Discover America Travel Organization |
| ETC | European Travel Commission |
| FAA | Federal Aviation Administration |
| FERC | Federal Energy Regulatory Commission |
| FMC | Federal Maritime Commission |
| GIANTS | Greater Independent Association of National Travel Service |
| HREBIU | Hotel and Restaurant Employee and Bartenders International Union |
| HSMA | Hotel Sales and Marketing Association |
| IAAPA | International Association of Amusement Parks and Attractions |
| IACA | International Air Charter Association |

| | |
|---|---|
| IACVB | International Association of Conventions and Visitor Bureaus |
| IAFE | International Association of Fairs and Expositions |
| IAMAT | International Association of Medical Assistance to Travelers |
| IATA | International Air Transport Association |
| IATC | Inter-American Travel Congress |
| IATM | International Association of Tour Managers |
| ICAO | International Civil Aviation Organization |
| ICC | Interstate Commerce Commission |
| ICCA | International Congress and Convention Association |
| ICTA | Institute of Certified Travel Agents |
| IFSEA | International Food Service Executives Association |
| IHA | International Hotel Association |
| IPSA | International Passenger Ship Association |
| ISHAE | International Society of Hotel Association Executives |
| ISTA | International Sightseeing and Tours Association |
| MAA | Motel Association of America |
| MPI | Meeting Planners International |
| NACA | National Air Carrier Association |
| NAMBO | National Association of Motor Bus Owners |
| NATA | National Air Transport Association |
| NATO | National Association of Travel Organization |
| NIFI | National Institute for the Foodservice Industry |
| NPTA | National Passenger Traffic Association |
| NRPA | National Recreation Parks Association |
| NRA | National Restaurant Association |
| NTA | National Tour Association |
| NTSB | National Transportation Safety Board |
| PATA | Pacific Asia Travel Association |
| PATCO | Professional Air Traffic Controllers Organization |
| RVIA | Recreational Vehicle Industry Association |
| SATH | Society for Advancement of Travel for the Handicapped |
| SATW | Society of American Travel Writers |
| SITE | Society of Incentive Travel Executives |
| TIA | Travel Industry Association of America |
| TTRA | Travel and Tourism Research Association |
| UFTAA | Universal Federation of Travel Agents Association |
| UTC | International Union of Railways |
| USTOA | United States Tour Operators Association |
| USTDC | United States Travel Data Center |
| USTDS | United States Travel Data Service |
| USTTA | United States Travel and Tourism Administration |
| WATA | World Association of Travel Agents |
| WTO | World Tourism Organization |
| WTTC | World Travel and Tourism Council |

# Glossary

**Accreditation**—Approval by conferences or associations for allowing the sale of tickets and other travel services.

**Affinity group**—Members of an organization, club, or association that was formed for purposes other than travel but which also would qualify for certain group travel privileges.

**Agent**—A person authorized to sell the products or services of a supplier.

**Airbus (aerial bus)**—A jumbo jet carrying twice as many passengers as a 707 and specializing in short- and medium-haul trips.

**Airline codes**—The system of abbreviations for airlines, airports, class of fares, and other items adopted by airlines and travel agents throughout the world.

**Air mile**—International air mile; a measure of distance equaling about 6,076 feet.

**Airport entertainment**—Entertainment of various kinds, including video arcades, shopping, exhibits, and other diversions located in an airport for passengers.

**Air taxi**—Aircraft carrying up to 19 passengers, operating usually within a limited radius of 250 miles.

**Air traffic control**—A service operated by appropriate authority to promote the safe, orderly, and expeditious flow of air traffic.

**Air transport services agreements**—Bilateral accords with respect to scheduled (and sometimes nonscheduled) air transportation services between nations.

**All-expense tour**—An inclusive tour that offers many included services for the stated price. It probably includes most, if not all, meals, sightseeing, taxes, tips, and extras.

**Allocentrics**—Individuals with a strong need for variety and new experiences; when traveling they seek destinations that offer an opportunity to experience different cultures and environments.

**Amenity spas**—Health spas that permit guests to participate in recreational and social activities similar to those at destination resorts.

**American Orient Express**—A private tour train of 11 remodeled and rebuilt carriages from the 1940s–1950s that operates two transcontinental U.S. tours per year.

**American plan (AP)**—Meal plan that includes three meals daily with the price of accommodations.

**Amtrak**—The name used by the National Railway Passenger Corporation, a quasi-public corporation established by Congress in 1971.

**Amusement arcades**—A range of entertainment centers. Some contain video machines only, while others contain bumper boats/cars and other amusement park-type rides.

**Astrodome**—A multi-purpose recreation complex in Houston that includes the Astroworld.

**ATMs**—Automated teller machines which dispense currency and can also serve as a vendor for travelers checks.

**Automated sales systems**—A variety of systems including an 800 number, computerized sales, and any new technology in which face-to-face sales contacts are not present.

**Average room rate**—Total revenues from room sales in a hotel, or collective room revenues of a destination, divided by the total number of available rooms. Average room rates may be computed on a daily basis for an individual property or on an annual or seasonal basis for a destination.

**Balance of trade**—A practical definition of an economic concept. Each nation is assumed to be one business entity dealing with other nations/business entities. When a business (country) sells (exports) more than it buys (imports), it has a positive balance of trade. When it buys (imports) more than it sells (exports) it has a negative balance of trade. Tourism is a part of the balance of trade.

**Barge travel**—A form of river travel, especially popular in Europe but also available in North America. These barges do not carry freight. Limited barge travel is sometimes available on cargo-carrying river barges.

**Base boat charters**—Sail charters which offer renters the chance to skipper their own boats without a professional crew.

**Bed and breakfasts (B & Bs)**—A home with several bedrooms converted for use by transient guests who generally receive breakfast along with lodging.

**Bermuda plan (BP)**—Hotel accommodations with a full, American-style breakfast included in the price of the room.

**Bias**—Giving preference, as in listing a certain airline's schedules first in a computerized reservation system.

**Bicycle touring**—Cross-country touring by bicycle; may be organized by niche tour operators or pursued as an unorganized form of tourism.

**Big wheel**—A term synonymous with *paddle wheelers*.

**Bilateral air agreement**—A treaty, or negotiated agreement, between two nations for reciprocal air services covering details of equipment, scheduling, specific air freedoms, taxation, landing privileges, and other factors of importance to each party in the agreement.

**Break-even analysis**—A method to determine the percentage of occupancy at various rates that a hotel must have to cover total costs.

**Break-even point**—The point at which total costs equal total revenue.

**Briefings**—A promotional practice wherein visitors are usually given an enticement to attend an event and are then exposed to a sales pitch for visitor services and products.

**Bulk fare**—Fare available only to tour organizers or operators who purchase a specified block of seats from a carrier at a low, noncommissionable price and then have the responsibility for selling the seats, including a commission in their marked-up seat price.

**Bus Regulatory Reform Act**—A U.S. act enacted in 1982 that deregulated the motor-coach industry and eliminated the need for tour brokers to be licensed by the ICC.

**Cabotage**—Nautical and air transport term. Restriction of the right to transport between two points within a country. An air use of the term applies to cabotage fares, which are special reduced fares restricted to residents traveling within the boundaries of that country and to which IATA rates do not apply.

**Cancellation fees**—Fees charged to customers who fail to cancel an unused reservation for a rental car or hotel room; also a penalty imposed by an airline for cancelling a booked flight.

**Canoe outfitter**—A private company or individual who rents canoes and furnishes them with supplies for a canoe trip.

**Cargo liner**—Vessel principally engaged in transporting goods, licensed to carry a maximum number of passengers, usually 12; also called *cargo freighter*.

**Central 800 number**—A toll-free call number that allows guests to call for information concerning hotels within a chain and to book reservations throughout the chain.

**Certified air carrier**—One of a class of air carriers holding certificates of public convenience and necessity, authorizing the holder to engage in air transportation. This group consists of certified route carriers authorized to provide scheduled service and limited nonscheduled service, and supplemental carriers authorized to engage in nonscheduled service.

**Certified meeting planner**—A professional designation for convention/meeting planners who have fulfilled certain requirements.

**Certified travel counselor (CTC)**—Professional certification awarded to travel agents who have successfully completed a study program developed and administered by the Institute of Certified Travel Agents.

**Charter service**—Nonscheduled air transport services whereby the party or parties receiving transportation obtains exclusive use of an aircraft at published tariff rates and the remuneration paid by the party receiving transportation accrues directly to, and the responsibility for providing transportation is that of, the accounting air carrier. This term also has general application to any other mode of transport; such as motorcoach, ship, and train, where the entire capacity or a minimum number of seats are hired by contract for exclusive use.

**Child**—Variably defined. Airlines normally classify a child as 2 through 11, but other travel suppliers classify the range to 14, 16, or even 18 years of age.

**Circle trip**—A trip involving different outbound and inbound destinations in departing and returning to the origin city. Example: Tampa to Atlanta to New Orleans to Las Vegas to Tampa.

**City pairs**—The terminal pair communities in an air trip, that is, the origin and destination cities of a flight on a one-way basis.

**Commercial rate**—Special discounted rate offered by a hotel or other supplier to a company, group, or individual traveler on a qualified basis.

**Commercial traveler rates**—Discounted rates available to guests from businesses who have a contract with the hotel/motel.

**Commission**—Payment received by travel agents for the sale of air transportation, hotel accommodation, tours, rental cars, and other products and services, usually computed as a percentage of sale made by the agent.

**Common carrier**—Any commercial carrier that is in the business of transporting goods or passengers for hire as a public utility.

**Commuter airline**—An airline that offers frequent roundtrip service to/from smaller communities and some larger airport hubs with a published flight schedule of such services principally to serve business commuters.

**Computerized reservation system (CRS)**—An electronic information system connecting individual travel agencies to a central computer, making immediate inquiries and reservations possible with an airline, hotel, car rental, and other travel services.

**Concession**—A part of an operator's (hotel, cruise ship, amusement park, public park) premise or operation that is leased out to a second party for retailing or other business purposes; concessions may be granted on a fixed rental basis or more commonly on a rent plus revenue-volume basis.

**Concierge**—An individual who is professionally trained to handle special requests or services for guests, usually in a luxury-class hotel.

**Conference**—An association of air carriers established to provide a set of operational rules that are fair to operators and to prevent cutthroat competition among them. A conference may establish and enforce agreed upon rules, ethical practices, safety standards, and documents, and serve as a clearinghouse for information. It may also establish travel agency rules and regulations.

**Conference center**—A self-contained facility usually located in a secluded area, designed and staffed to handle conferences and business meetings as its primary function, often providing limited accommodations and meals.

**Consolidator**—A person or company that combines individual bookings from travel agencies to qualify for group fares on scheduled or chartered flights, earn override commissions, or reduce the possibility of tour cancellations, passing on part of the savings to the originator.

**Consortiums**—Groups of persons or travel agency companies that pool together their resources to obtain some travel benefit such as higher commissions, advertising, 24-hour call-in service, or other services.

**Continental plan (CP)**—Bed and breakfast, meaning hotel accommodations as specified and breakfast according to the custom of the country.

**Convention**—Business or professional meeting, usually attended by large numbers of people. In Europe the more prevalent term for convention is *congress*.

**Convention rates**—Discounted rates extended to individuals who attend a convention or conference.

**Cooperative**—An association of travel agencies who band together to acquire savings on travel packages and sometimes other benefits like the purchase of group health plans.

**Cooperative advertising and promotion**—Joint advertising/promotion programs between a principal and cooperating businesses, for instance, between a visitors' bureau and hotels, airlines, attractions, and other travel suppliers.

**Corporate accounts**—Sales with organizations such as companies, trade associations, and universities rather than with individual travelers.

**Courier**—European term for a professional travel escort. Related terms include tour escort, tour director, tour leader, and tour manager; also an individual who accompanies important documents or packages to their destination in return for a discounted or free-of-charge airplane seat

**Cover charge**—A fee, usually a flat amount per person, charged to patrons to cover the cost of music and entertainment.

**Cross selling**—The tactic of selling additional products to complement other purchases made by a customer, thus creating multiple sales at the same time and place.

**Cruise counselor**—A travel agent who is professionally trained and qualified to advise clients about cruise products and services.

**Cruise director**—Paid onboard professional who is entrusted with assisting passengers, helping to organize events, and, in general, helping to insure that passengers have a pleasant and safe cruise.

**Cultural tourism**—Tourism that focuses upon the heritage and culture of a country and its people, monuments, historic sites, traditional architecture, artifacts, events, and cultural attainments in the arts.

**Culture shock**—When a person becomes shocked and disoriented at a place because of the severe contrast to their own familiar lifestyle and customs; also, disorientation of residents when encountering foreign visitors for the first time.

**Currency restrictions**—Limitations established by a country to control the amount of money taken in, out, or exchanged within a country.

**Customs**—Formal procedure whereby all persons entering a country must declare their possession of specific kinds or amounts of items purchased in another country under the jurisdiction of a government agency that has the right to inspect, restrict, seize, and/or impose taxes on goods brought into a country. Also refers to the normal manners or behavioral procedures of a society.

**Customs duty**—Tax on certain goods being imported.

**Day rate**—A special rate for a room used by a guest only during the day up to a specific hour, such as 4:00, 5:00, or 6:00 P.M.

**Deadhead**—Rail, bus, or airline terms for an empty cargo/passenger trip segment.

**Deeded ownership system**—A form of time sharing in which owners hold title to the property.

**Delivered merchandise system**—Duty-free merchandise is delivered to the plane, train, or vessel by the duty-free store and given to the customer upon boarding to ensure that the merchandise will leave the country of purchase.

**Demi-pension**—Same as *modified American plan*.

**Deregulation**—By the federal law enacted in 1978, the elimination of the CAB and government regulation of the airlines and other suppliers with regard to routes, fares, and other specifics.

**Destination development**—The general planning, developing, and marketing of a destination to attract visitors.

**Destination planner**—An independent professional who provides or contracts destination services such as ground transportation and entertainment for clients.

**Destination resort**—A full-service resort offering a wide variety of recreation, entertainment, shopping, dining, meeting facilities, and other amenities, satisfying all needs of the guest within the resort.

**Direct response marketing**—Another term for fulfillment marketing; direct selling to a customer through a media such as television, radio, print or direct mail in which the customer purchases something or asks for free information about a travel service.

**Domestic independent tour (DIT)**—Same as *FIT*, but more commonly used in the North American context of an independent, prepaid trip within the country.

**Domestic trunks**—Domestic operations of the domestic trunk carriers. This group of carriers operates primarily within the geographic limits of the 48 contiguous states of the United States (and the District of Columbia) over routes serving primarily the larger communities.

**Double tracking**—Two sets of parallel train tracks allowing trains to operate in opposite directions at the same time.

**Duty-free**—Exemption from locally-imposed taxes.

**Duty-free imports**—Government-specified list of item categories and their quantities that may be brought into the country free of tax or duty charges.

**Duty-free stores**—Retail stores in which merchandise is sold only to travelers who are leaving the country. Merchandise is sold completely or partially free of the taxes and duties that would otherwise be imposed by the country in which the store is located. Travelers must normally show a passport and an outbound ticket before purchases are allowed.

**Eastern and Orient Express**—An exotic, luxury passenger train service from Singapore to Bangkok, Thailand.

**Ecotourism**—A segment of the travel industry in which participants visit and study natural attractions such as national parks without damaging the environment.

**Economy hotel**—Hotel with limited facilities and services targeted at budget travelers. Also referred to as *second class* or *tourist hotel*.

**Elderhostel**—An alternative holiday option combining learning and adventure for people 55 years of age and older; it is associated with a college or university where guests are typically housed in dormitory facilities.

**English breakfast**—Usually includes juice, hot or cold cereal, bacon or ham, eggs, kippers or sausages, toast, butter, and jam or marmalade.

**Entertainment agency**—A firm that plans and contracts for professional entertainment for clients such as clubs; also referred to as *entertainment management firms*.

**Entry requirements**—The official documents required to enter a country, including a passport, visa, or document showing inoculations.

**Escorted tour**—A tour that includes the services of a professional escort to handle ground details and problems. Also called a *conducted tour*.

**Escrow accounts**—Funds placed in the custody of licensed financial institutions for safekeeping. Many contracts in travel require that agents and tour operators maintain customers' deposits and prepayments in escrow accounts.

**Ethnocentrism**—A tendency to judge all others by one's own standards and to concentrate on that local sphere or environment.

**Eurostar**—The high-speed passenger train linking London and Paris.

**Event marketing**—A form of product promotion involving the sponsorship of events such as golf tournaments that use the name of the sponsoring company or product.

**Excursion**—Usually a side trip out of a destination city; may be used interchangeably with tour or sightseeing.

**Excursion fare**—Usually a round-trip fare with restrictions such as minimum and maximum stay and advance purchase requirements.

**Excursionist**—Temporary visitor staying less than 24 hours in the destination visited and not making an overnight stay (including travelers on cruises).

**Exit restrictions**—Restrictions enforced by a country to curb outbound travel.

**Familiarization trips/tours**—A trip or tour offered to travel agents or travel writers to acquaint them with new product or destination and the services of the suppliers for promotional purposes, usually at a discount price or FOC (free of charge). Also called a *fam trip*.

**Family rate**—Hotel rates for families that normally permit children under 14 to occupy a room with their parents at no additional charge.

**Ferry boats**—Large vessels designed to carry passengers and their vehicles across wide bodies of water either on lakes or oceans.

**First-class hotel**—Hotel offering a high standard and variety of services. In Europe, a first-class hotel ranks below a luxury or grand luxe hotel. In Asia, first class may mean a four-star property where five stars denotes the top classification.

**Fishing lodge**—A lodging establishment that specializes in accommodations, meals, and guide service for fishing enthusiasts; may also be called fishing resort.

**Fixed average rate**—A rate that is the same for all rooms. It may be derived by taking an average price for all the rooms such as suites, junior suites, doubles, and singles.

**Fixed costs**—Costs such as mortgage payments, interest payments, and insurance which will continue regardless of whether a hotel is open or not.

**Flag carrier**—Term usually referring to the national airline of a country.

**Flat rate**—Special room rates for a group negotiated in advance where all rooms in the property, which may or may not be subject to certain restrictions, are priced at the same rate.

**Float**—The amount of money represented by travelers checks that are ouitstanding or are in process of redemption.

**Food cover**—A unit of foodservice provided to a customer. This term is not synonymous with "meal" because a food cover may comprise only a cup of coffee or a bowl of soup.

**Foreign exchange earnings**—Revenues earned from foreign currency spent by foreign tourist. *Net foreign exchange earnings* refer to the amount remaining after the costs of imported goods, services, and expertise necessary to provide and maintain tourist facilities are subtracted from the monies generated by visiting foreign tourists.

**Foreign flag carriers**—Ships registered in and flying the flag of a nation other than the U.S.

**Foreign independent tour (FIT)**—An international trip with the itinerary prepared to the individual traveler's specifications. Some suppliers refer to FIT as free and independent travelers to denote travelers who have made independent arrangements.

**Franchise**—The right to market a service and/or product, often exclusive for a specified area, as granted by the manufacturer, developer, or distributor in return for a fee; prevalent in the fast-food service industry.

**Freedoms of the air**—The eight basic traffic rights, as bilaterally arranged between nations or established by treaty.

**Frequent flyer program (FFP)**—A program whereby bonus miles are offered by the airlines to passengers who accumulate travel mileage premiums which are exchanged for free travel.

**Fulfillment marketing**—Refers to the process of advertising a product or service to a prospective customer and fulfilling the customer's request for additional information about the product or service; also called *direct response marketing*.

**Gateway city**—A city that functions as the first destination for visitors to the area, due to location and transportation patterns.

**Grand luxe hotel**—Classic luxury hotels built and operated from the early 1890's until the Great Depression of the 1930's; the term is sometimes used to denote a contemporary luxury hotel offering amenities and service in the grand traditions of the past.

**Grand spectacle entertainment**—Rock concerts and other live events that attract large crowds of paid viewers.

**Greyhound dog racing**—A form of pari mutuel wagering in which adult greyhound dogs race around a track, trying to catch a mechanical rabbit.

**Ground operators**—A supplier that provides local transportation, transfer service, sightseeing, and other services.

**Ground transportation**—A catch-all term generally used to describe buses, jitneys, vans, limousines, and other vehicles that provide transfer service between an airline terminal and a hotel or sightseeing service.

**Group inclusive tour (GIT)**—Prepaid tour, including transportation, accommodations, sightseeing arrangements, and other services. Special air fares are provided to the group, requiring that all members must travel on the same flight round-trip and must travel together during their entire time abroad.

**Guarantee of deposit**—A deposit by the guest in form of cash, or more commonly a credit card number, to assure a confirmed reservation.

**Guaranteed rate**—A rate which is guaranteed to the guest, even if a higher-priced room must be assigned upon arrival.

**Guaranteed reservation**—The hotel guarantees to hold the room for the guest; the traveler must pay for the room whether or not it is actually used.

**Guest house**—A home converted for use as lodging for transient guests. The owners may offer one or more meals with the lodging.

**Handle**—With respect to gambling, this refers to the total amount wagered or the volume of business.

**Hard currency**—The currency of established, industrial nations that is generally accepted internationally for trade, commerce and tourism.

**Harness racing**—A term covering both trotter and pacer racing.

**Health spas**—A destination resort that offers programs for guests that are intended for physical or spiritual self-improvement.

**Health tourism**—Tourism associated with travel to health spas or resort destinations where the primary purpose is to improve the traveler's physical well-being through a regimen of physical exercise and therapy, dietary control, and medical services relevant to health maintenance.

**Historic attractions**—Battlefields, homes, military forts, or any physical structures and sites with special historic significance that will draw visitors.

**Historic restorations**—Restorations of historic buildings, such as homes, churches, and government buildings.

**Historic sites**—Sites, like battlegrounds, which have historic significance and have been deemed historic sites by a government agency or a non-profit group such as the National Trust or an historic society.

**Host community**—The residents of a town, area, or nation who serve officially or accidentally as hosts by sharing their community resources and culture with tourists.

**Hostel**—A French word from which the word hotel originated. Today, the word refers primarily to inexpensive, no-service lodging used heavily by youthful backpackers.

**Hotel garni**—A term used to designate European hotels that do not have a restaurant.

**Houseboat**—A boat used on inland lakes and rivers normally built on pontoons and designed to resemble a small house.

**Hub-spoke concept**—A concept involving the establishment of a particular city as a central point to which longer-haul flights are scheduled and which serves as a connecting point where other flights are deployed or made to smaller cities. The routing of schedules through a central connecting city ensures heavier passenger loads.

**Import restrictions**—Government regulations regarding the type and quantity of goods returning residents are allowed to bring home after a trip abroad.

**In-flight interactive purchasing**—New technology using interactive computers at the passenger's seat which allows passengers on airlines to order videos, onboard merchandise, make reservations for future flights, and reserve rental cars and hotels.

**In-room shopping**—A system that allows hotel guests to purchase products or services directly from their rooms. Interactive television will permit guests to order products/services displayed on the television through an interactive medium and have them billed directly to a credit card or to their room.

**Inbound agents**—Ground operators who specialize in services for incoming visitors, particularly tourists from foreign countries.

**Incentive company/firms/houses**—A professional firm assisting clients with designing, promoting, and executing incentive travel programs or acting as an intermediary for both buyers and suppliers.

**Incentive travel**—Sometimes called motivation travel, this refers to the use of travel as a reward for meeting or exceeding objectives such as sales goals.

**Inclusive tour (IT)**—An advertised package or tour that includes the accommodations and other components such as transfers and sightseeing.

**Independent tours**—Tours without an escort.

**Indian Gaming Regulatory Act (1987)**—A U.S. federal act affirming that an Indian reservation had the characteristics of a sovereign nation and was not governed by state gambling laws.

**Infrastructure**—In a general sense, infrastructure applies to the physical support system of a destination, including roads, electricity, water, telephone, airports, and other necessities.

**Intelligent queuing systems**—Software-driven systems that automatically place phone customers in a waiting line based on the time they placed a call.

**Interline agreements**—Agreements involving two or more air carriers to cooperate on specific actions, such as interline travel rights and privileges or to share airport facilities or other resources.

**Intermodal**—Using different types of transportation, as in a tour using a combination of rail, air, and motorcoach services.

**International tourist receipts**—Statistical computation of the total amount of money spent by international visitors in each receiving country.

**Interstate Commerce Commission**—A U.S. federal commission responsible for overseeing commercial interstate transportation/commerce.

**Jai alai**—A fast-paced gambling game played primarily by Latin Americans in which a small rubber ball is hurled against a wall by players and caught in a hand-held basket on a handle.

**Jitney**—Car, van, or small bus to carry a small number of passengers.

**Joint fare**—A fare agreed upon by two or more carriers to provide service from origin to destination, or a fare for an off-line connection (within a country).

**Jones Act (1920)**—A law established by the Merchant Marine Act of 1920, also known as the Jones Act, provides that merchandise transported between points in the United States must be transported in vessels built and registered in the United States and owned by citizens of the United States.

**Junior suite**—A room not as large as a traditional suite but larger than a normal room. The room will usually have a sitting area and good-sized desk.

**Junket**—A subsidized trip offered by a casino to attract high rollers and potential gamblers; also a pleasure trip taken by an official at public expense.

**Junket reps**—Independent reps paid by commission to bring players, particularly premium players, to a casino.

**Key account management**—The management of special accounts that provide the majority of sales. Sometimes called national accounts management.

**Kiosks**—Small retail shops located in courtyards, beaches, or many other locations convenient to travelers. These are generally not permanent retail stores. Also, free-standing information booths in tourist areas.

**Lanai**—A room that overlooks a landscaped area or a scenic view and contains a balcony, a patio, or both.

**Land arrangements**—Land services such as transfers, sightseeing tours, and so on; services provided by a ground operator which may include airport transfers, lodging, sightseeing, and entertainment.

**Limited service hotel**—A hotel selling rooms only, without restaurants or other guest services.

**Load factor**—Percentage of seats filled from the total number of seats available in an airplane.

**Lounge entertainment**—Professional entertainment such as a piano player and a vocalist in the lounge and bar area of hotels and resorts; also refers to a secondary act as opposed to the headliner in the main showroom of a casino.

**Management contract**—An agreement between the owner(s) of a property such as a hotel, restaurant, convention center, or resort complex and a professional management company to develop and/or operate such property for a consideration, typically a fee plus percentage of the gross operating profit.

**Meeting and convention planner**—A professional consultant who specializes in the planning and execution of conventions and business meetings for corporate clients, professional or trade associations, and other groups.

**Megaliner**—Extremely large cruise ship capable of carrying as many as 2,600 passengers with a 900 member crew.

**Midcentrics**—Individuals who are in the midrange between allocentrics (those wanting to experience new destinations and cultures) and psychocentrics (those wanting to travel only to familiar, "tried and true" destinations). Midcentrics are willing to try new experiences as long as they are not too challenging.

**Mini cruise**—This term is used interchangeably with ultra yachts. This is a niche cruise that generally operates along both North American coasts and may also use inland waterways.

**Minimum connecting time**—The amount of time required to change planes established by regulation.

**Modified American plan (MAP)**—Meal plan that includes two meals daily (usually breakfast and dinner) with the price of accommodations.

**Motivation travel**—Another term for incentive travel.

**Motorcoach**—A general term for buses; a bus designed to carry passengers for touring, frequently equipped with toilet facilities.

**Motorcoach broker**—One who charters the motorcoach, prepares any or all of the other components of the tour, including the itinerary, lodging, sightseeing, courier, admission, guides, meals, and other items. The broker assumes complete responsibility for the trip or tours; also another term for motorcoach tour operator.

**Multiplier**—With respect to the travel industry, the multiplier typically encompasses and measures the direct and secondary effects of visitor expenditures on an economy.

**National Railway Labor Act (1967)**—A U.S. law calling for a series of conferences and mandatory mediations between labor and management in the railway industry in lieu of dealing with labor contract expiration on pre-determined dates.

**National Tourism Organization (NTO)**—Also known as national tourism administration (NTA). The primary government agency charged with the implementation of national goals and public policy with respect to tourism.

**Net rate**—A wholesaler rate to be marked up for eventual resale to the consumer.

**Net wholesaler rate**—A rate is marked up by wholesale sellers of tours to cover distribution, promotion, and so on.

**Nonscheduled air services**—Revenue flights that are not operated in regular scheduled service, such as charter flights and all nonrevenue flights incident to such flights.

**North American Free Trade Agreement (NAFTA)**—A broad trade agreement between Canada, the U.S., and Mexico that calls for the elimination of trade tariffs and other barriers to a common trade market.

**Off-track betting**—Betting on horse races and other legal gambling events away from the place where the event is being held.

**Official Airline Guide (OAG)**—Publication that provides current data on available airline services between city pairs. There is also an electronic edition of the OAG.

**Official Domestic Tour Manual**—A publication with information on motorcoach tours as well as commissions available to travel agents.

**Omiyage**—A Japanese custom that dictates that travelers return with gifts for friends and relatives.

**On-time performance**—The number and percentage of aircraft, flights arriving on time or within 15 minutes of the carrier's published scheduled arrival time for any specified flight or group of flights during any specified period.

**Open jaw**—An arrangement, route, or fare, authorized in a tariff, permitting the traveler to purchase round-trip transportation in which the departure point will not be from the same arrival point upon return; for example, a round trip from San Francisco to Denver returning from Salt Lake City to San Francisco.

**Orient Express**—An historic passenger train from Paris to Istanbul disbanded in 1977, but restarted in 1982.

**Overflight**—A scheduled flight that does not stop at an intermediate point in its scheduled route because (1) the point is certified as a flag stop, and there is not traffic to be deplaned or enplaned; (2) the carrier has received authority to temporarily suspend service to that point; (3) weather conditions or other safety and technical reasons do not permit landing; or (4) for any other reason. The aircraft need not fly directly over the point.

**Overflight charge**—Fee assessed to air carriers for the privilege of flying over another nation.

**Overflight privilege**—Permission granted by one country for an air carrier to another country to fly over its land.

**Override commission**—Extra commission paid to travel agents by suppliers based on incremental quantity or volume of sales.

**Package**—Prearranged elements included in a trip, such as hotel accommodations, meals, sightseeing, and transfers. A package is less inclusive than a tour.

**Paddle wheeler**—A steam-propelled river boat that used to travel on U.S. rivers such as the Mississippi and Ohio. Contemporary paddle wheelers carry hundreds of passengers, offer berths, food and beverages, entertainment, and, in some cases, gambling.

**Parador**—A Spanish word referring to a castles, abbeys, or other historic buildings that have been restored for use as lodging accommodations, commonly operated by a government department.

**Pari-mutuel betting**—A betting pool in which those who bet on the winners of the first three places share the total amount minus a percentage for management; a form of gambling that includes thoroughbred and quarter horse racing, harness racing, and jai alai.

**Passenger miles**—One passenger carried one mile; this is calculated by multiplying the number of miles traveled times the number of passengers.

**Passenger Services Act**—A U.S. law enacted in 1886 that prohibits foreign flag carriers from sailing between U.S. ports.

**Passenger ship**—A ship whose primary purpose is to transport people from one country to another as opposed to pleasure cruising.

**Peak period**—Hotels and tourism-related businesses normally experience three seasonal cycles—peak, shoulder, and trough. The peak season has the highest occupancy.

**Pension**—A French word commonly used in Europe meaning *guest house* or *boarding house*.

**Pilgrimage**—A trip taken for religious or spiritual reasons.

**Port-of-call**—A port visited by cruise lines for purposes of allowing passengers to disembark for shopping, sightseeing, or other leisure activities.

**Port-of-embarkation**—A port from which cruise lines leave and return.

**Preferred purchase times**—Specific days and times of the day when travelers want to shop.

**Price points**—Pre-selected price levels at which retailers price a line of merchandise that is roughly equal to the value a customer is willing to pay for. If customers feel that certain types of souvenirs are worth around $10, then retailers aim for that price point instead of $11 or higher.

**Primary supplier**—The supplier who produces the goods or services offered to the customer or through the travel distribution system.

**Private label merchandise**—Products which are sold under the retailer's or the distributor's own label (brands) instead of the producer's or manufacturer's brand.

**Product dating**—The practice of placing a date on merchandise to create obsolescence or sometimes to create a collector's market.

**Product line extension**—The practice of extending a product line by developing different attributes such as sizes, colors, or fragrances.

**Product positioning**—The strategy of positioning a product or service in the customer's mind in terms of ranking among competing products or services.

**Professional congress organizer**—Same as *certified meeting/convention planner*.

**Psychocentrics**—Individual with a strong need for consistency and the familiar or tried and true in their lives; when traveling they prefer to visit "safe" destinations, avoiding unknown accommodations, food, or entertainment.

**Public land usage**—Use of federal and state public land for recreation and other public purposes.

**Quarter horse racing**—A form of pari mutuel wagering (horse racing) popular in the U.S. West in which horses known as cowboy horses or quarter horses race against each other.

**R.V. campgrounds**—Campgrounds established for use by recreational vehicles. Such campgrounds typically have utility hookups including water and sewage, offering common showers/bathrooms for male and female campers as well as a playground for children and other amenities.

**Rack rate**—The regular published rates of a hotel. When special rates are quoted, they represent a discount from the rack rate.

**Re-entry permit**—Document allowing alien residents to return from trips outside the country.

**Rebate**—The practice of charging or taking less than the rates, fares, or charges specified in the air carrier's currently effective tariffs to induce a sale or purchase.

**Receiving agent**—Another name for an inbound agent.

**Recreational vehicle (RV)**—A motorized self-contained camping trailer or a truck or van used for traveling. Also an off-the-road vehicle such as a dirt bike or dune buggy.

**Regional carrier**—A carrier serving a particular area only; a bus company that serve small- to mid-sized communities within a particular geographic area.

**Rental surcharges**—Additional rental charges assessed to individuals who are deemed to be high-risk.

**Repositioning**—Changing the position of the product among its competitors in the marketplace. For example, an older cruise ship is used to serve the adventure/exotic market instead of the deluxe market the ship was originally designed to serve.

**Resort condominium**—Individually-owned property at a resort area that is commonly rented out to short-term guests by a resort condominium management company.

**Retail clustering**—The placement of several retailers within an area that encourages shopper comparisons of competitive products and increases the breadth and depth of available merchandise assortment.

**Retail travel agent**—A travel agent who sells travel products on a retail basis on behalf of his/her principals—airlines, cruise lines, hotels, car rentals, etc.—for a commission to the general public; another name for a *travel agent*.

**Revenue management**—This term is sometimes used synonymously with *yield management* but is often viewed as more encompassing than yield management as it addresses the maximization of total revenues from all sources.

**Revenue passenger mile**—One paid passenger transported one mile. Revenue passenger miles are computed by summation of the products of the revenue aircraft miles flown on each interairport hop multiplied by the number of revenue passengers carried on that hop.

**Right to use system**—A form of time sharing in which owners do not hold title to the property, but instead hold rights to it for a given number of days each year for a guaranteed number of years.

**River boat**—Any type of multi-passenger boat that plies inland waterways, including barges and paddle wheels.

**Road railer**—A hybrid rail-highway trailer tested for possible use as a mail car behind Amtrak passenger trains.

**Rolling stock**—The equipment used on top of rails such as the engine and passenger cars.

**Run-of-the-house**—All available rooms in a hotel such as suites, junior suites, doubles, and singles offered to a group at the same rate per room, regardless of type of room.

**Sailing permit**—Document required of U.S. residents having resident alien status who are traveling abroad, attesting that they are not delinquent in the payment of any income tax liability.

**Sales distribution system**—The method by which a travel industry supplier sells its products/services to customers.

**Satellite ticket offices**—Travel industry supplier sales offices that are not the primary sales office but are intended to supplement the sales work of a central sales office, often located in secondary locations.

**Satellite ticket printer (STP)**—A printer at a location other than the main premises. For travel agencies these printers can dispense tickets for travel products.

**Scheduled air carrier**—Airline or carrier that publishes its transportation services timetable.

**Scheduled service**—Transport service operated over an air carrier's certificated routes pursuant to published flight schedules, including extra section and related nonrevenue flights.

**Seamless connectivity**—An electronic system that allows a customer to access reservation systems of travel suppliers from a PC and directly make reservations without the aid of a third party such as a travel agent.

**Seamless transportation**—Single ticketing for passengers that allows them to purchase one ticket and travel by interconnecting modes of transportation, including rail, bus, ship, or airplane.

**Seasonality**—High and low seasonal fluctuations in market demand due to the time of year specifics of the area's attractions and its ability to attract visitors.

**Secondary suppliers**—Those who provide travel services to the customer through primary suppliers.

**Semivariable costs**—Costs such as salaries that behave as if they were fixed in the short run.

**Short takeoff and landing aircraft (STOL)**—An airplane capable of taking off and landing within a relatively short horizontal distance.

**Shredders**—A name given to *snowboarders*.

**Side trip**—An optional trip offered to participants of a tour.

**Sightseeing company**—A company providing guided sightseeing in a city or town area.

**Sightseeing tour**—A tour within the city limits showing the main places of interest—avenues, churches, museums, monuments, and so on.

**Signature product**—Another term for a logo product; in restaurants, these products are specialty dishes for which the restaurant is known.

**Ski resort**—A winter resort devoted primarily to snow skiing but which may offer other activities such as swimming and skating.

**Snowboarding**—A downhill snow sport on which the participant places both feet on a single board.

**Social tourism**—A subsidized system of travel through government, employer, or labor union intervention to achieve social goals and purposes.

**Solar-powered trains**—Trains that are propelled by solar power supplied through a photovoltaic covering (skin) on the train as well as by photovoltaic stations along the way.

**Special fare**—Other than normal fares, special fares have various restrictions, such as advance purchase, specified length of stay, limited or no schedule charge privileges, and limited or no cancellation rights.

**Special interest tours**—Prearranged, packaged itinerary designed to appeal to or respond to a request by a group of persons who have a particular interest area of study or activity; for example, culture and the arts, sports, nature study, or shopping.

**Specialty channeler**—An intermediary who may represent either buyer or seller in the design, development, or marketing of specific interest travel. Specialty channelers include incentive travel firms, meeting and convention planners, hotel representatives, interline representatives, association executives, corporate travel offices, and travel consultants, among others. Another name for *specialty intermediaries*.

**Specialty intermediaries**—Travel intermediaries who specialize in a niche of the travel industry.

**Strategic alliance**—An agreement between two companies wherein each party agrees to assist the other in order to achieve greater results for the mutual benefit of both parties.

**Structured fare**—The particular fare charged for trips of varying distances and the relationship between coach fares and fares for the other classes of service. The manner in which the fare level should be distributed to, and recouped from, the passenger transport services operated by the air carriers. Used most often in rate-making.

**Supplier**—One who offers the products or services sold through the travel retailers or in some cases directly to the public.

**Supporting documents**—Those additional papers necessary to verify a transaction: birth certificate, health certificate, passport, visa, voter registration card, and so on.

**Table d'hote**—A set menu of several courses offered at a fixed price; sometimes called a *prix-fixe menu*.

**Taxi medallion**—A license normally granted by a city to operate a commercial taxi within a defined geographical area.

**TGV**—"Trains a grande viterse;" high-speed passenger trains used in several European nations.

**Theme park**—As the name implies, a park which is developed around a theme such as cartoon characters, or fantasy, adventure, historic events, science and technology, or other concepts.

**Themed events**—Events held within hotels and resorts that are developed around a particular theme, such as Saint Patrick's Day.

**Thoroughbred horse racing**—A form of pari mutuel wagering (horse racing) in which thoroughbred horses race around a track. One well-known race involving thoroughbreds is the Kentucky Derby.

**Through fare**—A total fare from point of origin to destination, which may be a local fare, a joint fare, or a combination of separately established fares.

**Ticket stock**—Refers to the supply of tickets an agency keeps on hand and for which the agency has legal responsibility.

**Ticketless travel**—A program whereby airline passengers are not given a ticket in advance of their flight, but receive only a confirmation number and are issued their boarding pass upon proof of identity at the gate.

**Tie-in selling**—The strategy of two non-competing organizations supporting each others' sales by using the name of the other party in advertising and promotion.

**Tiered pricing**—Various rates for the same hotel rooms. Several different rates may be offered due to perceived elasticities of demand for various customer segments.

**Time sharing**—Concept dividing the ownership and use of a lodging property among several investors; generally each time-sharing purchaser is able to use the unit for a specified interval (e.g., 2 weeks) each year for a specified period of time. The multiple owners share the prorata costs of maintenance, management, and taxes.

**Tour breakage**—Lodging, meals, transfers, admissions, etc., which are costed into the package, but not used by the purchaser, providing extra profit for the tour operator.

To price tours competitively, operators often put an estimated percentage return of breakage in their costing elements.

**Tour broker**—A person or company that organizes and markets tour products.

**Tour desk**—The desk at a hotel or airline that is used specifically for selling tours and packages.

**Tour escort**—A person designated as the leader of the group, usually for the entire travel experience, although he/she may be assisted by other guides.

**Tour operator**—A company that is responsible for the delivery and/or operation of all facets of the tour, usually providing an escort; other similar terms include *tour wholesaler*, *wholesale tour operator*, *tour packager*, used interchangeably.

**Tour package**—A joint service that gives a traveler a significantly lower price for a combination of services than could be obtained if each had to be purchased separately by the traveler. Thus, the total price of a package tour might include a round-trip plane ticket, hotel accommodations, meals, sightseeing bus tours, and theatre tickets.

**Tour program**—A season of tour packages represents a tour program.

**Tour wholesaler**—A person who contracts with hotels, sightseeing, and other ground components to provide ground packages for sale to individuals through travel agents and direct air carriers to be used in conjunction with scheduled air transportation. (see *tour operator*)

**Tour-basing fare**—A reduced-rate excursion fare available only to those who buy pre-paid tours or packages. Inclusive tour, group inclusive tour, incentive group, contract bulk inclusive tour, tour basing, and group round-trip inclusive tour-basing fares are all tour-basing fares.

**Tourism policies**—Generally refers to public policies designed to achieve specific objectives relevant to tourism established at the municipal, state, or federal level.

**Tourist**—Temporary visitors staying at least 24 hours in the country visited and the purpose of whose journey can be classified as leisure, i.e. recreation, holiday, healthy, study, religion, or sport; or business; family; mission; or meeting.

**Tourist trains**—Retired steam engine driven trains that formerly carried passengers on regular routes but now serve as a tourist attraction covering a limited area.

**Trade fair**—An organized event to bring people to a specific location to view a display of products and services, to exchange information, and/or to buy and sell the products or services that are specific to a particular trade, business, or industry.

**Transfer**—Transportation service from an airport, railway station, or other terminals to the hotels of clients.

**Transit advertising**—Advertising on commercial transit vehicles such as buses or taxis.

**Travel advisory**—Caution issued by an authoritative body such as the state department, regarding the safety, changing conditions, or risky practices of a specific travel destination.

**Travel agency**—A private for-profit company that assists and makes travel arrangements for clients and receives a commission from travel providers such as airlines and resorts.

**Travel agent**—An individual who works for a travel agency and assists clients with travel needs.

**Travel agent commission**—The payment by airlines and other travel suppliers to a travel agent of specified amounts of money (usually a percentage) in return for the agent's sales of travel products.

**Travel allowance**—Restrictions on the amount of foreign exchange that residents of a country may purchase before departing on a trip; and/or the amount of national currency residents of a country may take out of the country and convert into foreign currency.

**Travel and entertainment card**—A credit card issued by companies such as American Express and Diners Club primarily for use in travel. The distinction between T&E cards and general usage cards is lessening.

**Travel clubs**—Organizations that arrange travel tours for members often at highly discounted rates.

**Travel consolidators**—Private for-profit companies or individuals who acquire discounted unsold travel services such as airline seats and sell them at a discount to the public.

**Travel industry**—The composite of organizations, both public and private, that are involved in the development, production, distribution, and marketing of products and services to serve the needs of travelers.

**Travel industry distribution**—The process of moving travel products and services from suppliers to ultimate consumers.

**Travel insurance**—Regular insurance tailored to cover travelers and their personal effects. May be sold by a regular broker; however, most travel agents and tour carrier personnel are specially licensed insurance agents with the power to issue such policies and immediately bind the insurance company.

**Travel intermediaries**—Individuals who provide sales services between the travel supplier and the customer.

**Travel night**—A promotional event normally co-sponsored by a visitor destination or a supplier such as a cruise line, along with travel intermediaries featuring entertainment and information about the particular travel service.

**Travel oriented products**—Products that are specifically designed or selected to be purchased by travelers.

**Travel vouchers**—An exchange authorization for prepaid (or promissory payment) lodging, transportation, or other travel services which is not redeemable for cash, issued by a travel agent, an airline or other travel operator. Also called *coupon and exchange order.*

**Traveler profile**—Characteristics used to describe various travel market segments.

**Travelers checks**—Paper currency issued and backed by private financial institutions which can be exchange for national currency.

**Treno Alta Velocita (TAV)**—The Italian high-speed passenger train.

**Turnkey operation**—A program in which a hotel management company designs and develops a complete operating hotel for an independent owner/franchisee.

**Ultra yacht**—Another word for a *mini-cruiser.*

**Up-selling**—The practice of convincing customers to purchase an upgraded or more expensive item or service than they originally intended to buy.

**Variable costs**—Costs that will fluctuate up or down in accordance with the volume of occupancy.

**Vertical integration**—Expansion of a company by acquiring full or partial ownership of other businesses that can feed into or directly relate to the total service or core product of the acquiring company.

**VFR**—Classification of travelers whose purpose in traveling is visiting friends and relatives.

**Via Rail**—The Canadian passenger train service owned and subsidized by the Canadian government.

**Video flight information**—In-flight information displayed on a screen accessible from a passenger's seat.

**Video shopping**—In-flight purchasing of products through interactive computers from a passenger's seat.

**Visa**—An endorsement on a passport or document used in lieu of a passport by a consular official indicating that the bearer may gain entry into the country of issue.

**Voluntary chain**—A program in which a hotel owner acquires a franchise name, privileges, and responsibilities but continues to own and operate the property; also called voluntary franchise.

**Wagon-Lits**—European pullmans. Sleeping cars on European railroad, consisting of a private bedroom with a lavatory and accommodations for one or two people.

**Walking**—The process of turning away guests due to lack of rooms and sending them to another hotel with available rooms.

**Weekend rates**—Discounted rates given to guests who stay at a hotel during the weekend (normally considered Friday and Saturday nights).

**Wholesale travel agent**—One who does not sell on a commission basis (as opposed to a retail travel agent) but contracts for large blocks of advanced reservations on airlines and other services such as hotels and tour packages at volume-based prices for resale. The wholesale travel agent assumes his or her own financial risk for all unsold products.

**Wholesaler**—An intermediary who specializes in organizing tour packages and selling them through travel agents. (see *tour operator*).

**Wilderness outfitter**—Another term for a *canoe outfitter*.

**X2000**—The Swedish high-speed passenger train.

**Yield**—Air transport revenue earned per unit of air traffic carried. May be calculated and presented several ways, for instance, passenger revenue per passenger-mile, per aircraft-mile, per passenger ton-mile, and per passenger.

**Yield management**—A tiered pricing system to enhance company profits by providing a mix of customers who pay different prices based on different demand conditions.

**Young drivers ban**—A practice by many auto rental companies to refuse rental service to drivers under the age of 25 regardless of their driving record.

**Youth hostels**—Inexpensive lodging popular in many parts of the world, particularly Europe. Guests normally sleep in their own sleeping bags and share in the housekeeping and cooking.

# Index

# About the Authors

## Chuck Y. Gee

Chuck Y. Gee has been Dean of the School of Travel Industry Management at the University of Hawaii since 1976. He has also served as an advisor to the tourism industry in the People's Republic of China and holds honorary professorships at several Universities in China. Gee is a technical advisor the U.S. State Department and the Department of Commerce at the World Tourism Organization General Assembly, and he has been appointed to the 15-member Travel and Tourism Advisory Boards of the U.S. Department of Commerce under the Carter, Reagan, and Bush administrations. He has won many professional honors for his contributions to the industry, both in the U.S. and internationally. He has served as author or co-author on three additional textbooks, including *Resort Development and Management, Professional Travel Agency Management*, and *International Hotels: Development and Management*.

## James C. Makens

Dr. Makens is currently a faculty member at the Babcock Graduate School of Management at Wake Forest University. Previously he served as Associate Dean in the School of Travel Industry Management at the University of Hawaii, and with an affiliate of the Harvard Business School in Central America. He has served as a consultant to airlines, hotels, restaurant chains, tourism ministries, and historic restorations, as well as fifty corporations, including Quaker Oats, R.J. Reynolds, and Sara Lee. He has authored a dozen articles published in the *Cornell Hotel and Restaurant Quarterly*, and a book entitled, *The Hotel Sales and Marketing Planbook*. Additionally he has co-authored three other books, including *The Travel Industry, Professional Travel Agency Management*, and *Hospitality and Tourism Marketing*.

## Dexter J. L. Choy

Dexter Choy is a Professor in the School of Travel Industry Management where he teaches courses in travel research, travel marketing, travel agency management, tourism development, and tourism policy. He also serves as an industry consultant to various Asian and Pacific countries, as well as private corporations. Over the years, Dr. Choy has lectured in numerous international seminars, including the Executive Development Institute for Tourism, the Strategic Management Program for the Travel Industry, and the Hong Kong Hotel Association Summer Program.